William Chappell

The Roxburghe Ballads

William Chappell

The Roxburghe Ballads

ISBN/EAN: 9783744775007

Printed in Europe, USA, Canada, Australia, Japan

Cover: Foto ©Thomas Meinert / pixelio.de

More available books at **www.hansebooks.com**

The Roxburghe Ballads.

EDITED,

WITH SPECIAL INTRODUCTIONS AND NOTES,

BY

J. WOODFALL EBSWORTH, M.A., CANTAB., F.S.A.

EDITOR OF FOUR REPRINTED "'DROLLERIES' OF THE RESTORATION," "THE BAGFORD BALLADS" WITH THEIR "AMANDA GROUP OF POEMS," "THE TWO EARLIEST QUARTOS OF A MIDSUMMER NIGHT'S DREAM, 1600:" AUTHOR OF "KARL'S LEGACY; OR, OUR OLD COLLEGE AT NIRGENDS," AND "CAVALIER LYRICS, FOR CHURCH AND CROWN."

WITH COPIES OF THE ORIGINAL WOODCUTS.

Vol. VI.—Part 3.

HERTFORD:

Printed for the Ballad Society,

BY STEPHEN AUSTIN AND SONS.

1888.

HERTFORD:
PRINTED BY STEPHEN AUSTIN AND SONS.

No. 29.

[Very good 'Contents'; despite the Suffragan Critic *en derrière*.]

CONTENTS OF PART XVIII.

*** *Important Notice.*—Owing to the necessity of our breaking up the four-hundred pages of new matter into two separate issues, *viz.* Part XVIII. and Part XIX., completing the *penultimate* Volume Sixth, this *Temporary Table of Contents* is here given, showing the entire continuation as now ready for issue, in the *Two Parts*: except that the Part XIX. contains additionally the *Prologue*, *Preface*, *Camarades Deux*, with full *Tables of Contents*, and of *Errata* to Vol. VI.

Although separated, for financial reasons, both portions are completed ready for simultaneous issue to subscribers, who pay up arrears for 1888 and 1889. Progress is already being made on Vol. VII., in conclusion of the Roxburghe Ballads, for the following years' issue. Members are careless of the risk they run through their own delay of payments to keep the printing maintained in its present efficiency.—THE EDITOR.

PAGE

Editorial Prelude: A New Stave to an Old Tune . . 449

Hallo, my Fancy! 450

Percy Folio earliest version 451

Bedlam School-men (with Wm. Cleland's interpolations) . 452

Alas! poor Scholar, whither wilt thou go? By Dr. R. Wild 456

The Young Man's Labour Lost 458

Phillida flouts me! or, The Country Lover's Complaint . 461

The Answer, Barnaby doubts me! By A. Bradley . . 463

Editorial Intermezzo: From the Priory to the Abbey . . 464

Second Group of Good-Fellows' Ballads.

In Praise of the Black Jack 466

"Merry Knaves are we three-a." By John Lyly, 1584 . 467

Song in Praise of the Leather Bottel. By John Wade . 470

Jack Had-Land's Lamentation. Probably by John Wade . 475

Wit bought at a Dear Rate . . . 478

PAGE

A Groat's-worth of Good Counsel for a Penny; or, The Bad Husband's Repentance 480
Two-Penny-worth of Wit for a Penny; or, The Bad Husband turn'd Thrifty 483
Nick and Froth; or, The Good-Fellow's Complaint, etc. . 486
The Noble Prodigal; or, The Young Heir newly come to his Estate. Probably by Thomas Jordan . . . 490
The Bad-Husband's Folly; or, Poverty made known. . 493
News from Hyde-Park; or, A very merry Passage, etc. . 496
The Good-Fellow's Counsel; The Bad Husband's Recantation 499
The King of Good-Fellows; or, The Merry Toper's Advice . 502
The Old Man's Wish. By Dr. Walter Pope. . . 507
Mark Noble's Frolic. 510
The Jolly Gentleman's Frolic; or, The City Ramble. . 513
A Jest; or, Master Constable 515
Editorial Finale: How the Frolic Ended . . . 518

End of The Groups of Good-Fellows.

God Speed the Plow, and bless the Corn-mow . . 523
The Ploughman's Art in Wooing 526
The Milk Maid's Resolution. 529
True-Blue the Ploughman; or, A Character of several Callings 532
The Rich Farmer's Ruine, who murmur'd at the Plenty of the Seasons, because he could not sell Corn so dear . 535

A Group of Legendary and Romantic Ballads.

PAGE

Editorial Dedication to Miss Julia De Vaynes . . 539

Sonnet on the Odyssey, by Andrew Lang . . . 540

The Greeks' and Trojans' Wars 543

The Wandering Prince of Troy; or, Queen Dido . . 548

The Sonnet of Dido and Æneas. Probably by Humphrey Crouch 552

A Looking Glass for Ladies; or, (Penelope) A Mirror for Married Women 553

The Tragedy of Hero and Leander; or, The Two Unfortunate Lovers 558

An Excellent Sonnet of the Unfortunate Loves of Hero and Leander. By Humphrey Crouch 560

The Love-sick Maid; or, Cordelia's Lamentation for the absence of her Gerhard (=Gerhard's Mistress) . . 563

The Famous Flower of Serving-Men; or, The Lady turn'd Serving Man. By Laurence Price . . . 567

Constance of Cleveland, and her Disloyal Knight . . 572

The Northern Lass's *Ballow*: "Peace, wayward bairn!" . 575

The New Balow; or, A Wench's Lamentation, etc. . . 577

A Sweet Lullabie. By Nicholas Breton, 159¾ . . 580

Montrose's Lines; or, A Proper New Ballad . . . 581

Original First Part (here given as Second: now new Third) . 582

A Proper New Ballad; being the Regret of a True Lover for his Mistress's Unkindness 584

Diaphantas' Words to Charidora, upon a Disaster. (Probably by Sir Robert Aytoun, *see Appendix*, p. 774) . . 585

PAGE
The Forlorn Lover's Lament. (*Ibid.*) . 586
The Gallant Grahams [Walter Scott's Minstrelsy version] 588
The Gallant Grahams of Scotland 590
The Life and Death of Sir Hugh of the Græme . . 595
Sir Hugh in the Græme's Downfall: hanged for stealing the Bishop's Mare 598
Thomas Armstrong's Last Good Night, 1600 . . 600
Johnny Armstrong's last Good-night. By T.R. . . 604
A Delectable New Ballad entitled Leader Haughs and Yarrow. By Nichol Burn, the Violer 607
The Words of Burn, the Violer 608
Lord Gregory. By Dr. John Walcot, 1787 . . . 609
The Lass of Ocram 613
The memorable Battle fought at Killiecrankie, by Chief Clavers and his Highland men, 1689 616
Three Ballads on the Earl of Mar 617
"Now, now comes on the Glorious Year." By T. D'Urfey, 1707 *Ibid.*
A Dialogue between the Duke of Argyle and the Earl of Mar 620
An Excellent New Ballad, Mar's Lament for his Rebellion . 621
The Clans' Lamentation against Mar & their own Folly, 1715 622
Jacobite Song, 1746: "Let mournful Britons." . . 623
A New Song called the Duke of Cumberland's Victory over the Scotch Rebels at Culloden-Moor, near Inverness, 1746 634
England's Glory; or, Duke William's Triumph over the Rebels in Scotland, 1746 626
"The Hunt is up! the Hunt is up!" . . . 627
Percy Folio. Fragments of Lord Barnett and Little Musgrove. 629
The Old Ballad of Little Musgrove and the Lady Barnard . 631
Lamentable Ballad of the Little Musgrove & the Lady Barnet 633
The West-Country Damosels Complaint; or, The Faithful Lovers' Last Farewell 635
Sir William of the West; or, The entire Love and Courtship between a Noble Knight and Beautiful Mary, a Minister's Daughter in Dorsetshire 638
Fair Margaret's Misfortunes; or, Sweet William's Dream on his Wedding Night, etc. 641
Two Ballads on Lord Thomas and Fair Eleanor . . 643
The Unfortunate Forester; or, Fair Eleanor's Tragedy . 645
A Tragical Ballad on the Unfortunate Love of Lord Thomas and Fair Eleanor; together with the Downfall of the Brown Girl 647
The Lady Isabella's Tragedy; or, The Step-Mother's Cruelty 651
The Spanish Lady's Love 655

(*Ending Part XVIII.*)

PAGE

A Dialogue between an Englishman and a Spaniard . 657
The Beggar-Maid and King Cophetua. By Tennyson . 658
A Song of a King and a Beggar. By Richard Johnson, 1631 . 659
Cupid's Revenge; or, An Account of a King (Cophetua) who slighted all Women, and was forced to marry a Beggar. 661
The Wandering Prince & Princess; or, Musidorus & Amadine 664
The Complaint of Fair Rosamond (*Extracts*). By S. Daniel, 1591 668
The Life and Death of Fair Rosamond, King Henry the Second's Concubine. By Thomas Deloney . . 673
The Unfortunate Concubine; or, Rosamond's Overthrow . 676
Queen Eleanor's Confession: showing how King Henry, etc. 680
The Noble Lord's Cruelty; or, A Pattern of True Love . 682
A proper new ballad entitled Jephtha, Judge of Israel . 685
The Legend of the Wandering Jew . . . 688
Complainte du Juif Errant 691
The Wandering Jew; or, The Shoe-maker of Jerusalem. (Attributed doubtfully to T. Deloney, but probably later.) 693
The Wandering Jew's Chronicle, 1662 . . . 695
Later Additions, 1727 698
"Ich bin der alte Ahasver" (for Leland's translation, see p. 779) 699
The Judgment of God shewed upon one John Faustus, D.D. . 703
Witchcraft discovered and punished; or, the Trials and Condemnation of three Notorious Witches at Exeter, 1682 . 706
King Leir (Extracts from 'A Mirour for Magistrates,' 1574) . 709
Of King Leir and his three Daughters. (By Wm. Warner, 1589) 712
A Lamentable Song of the Death of King Leare and his Three Daughters. By Richard Johnson, before 1620 . 714
Tragical History of King Lear, and his Three Daughters . 717
On the Ign. Don.'s 'Great Cryptogram' fiasco . . 720
Lancelot du Lac: From Malory's Morte d'Arthur . . 721
The Noble Acts, newly found, of Arthur of the Table Round. By Thomas Deloney 722
An excellent Ballad of St. George and the Dragon . . 727
An Heroical Song on the worthy and valiant Exploits of our noble Lord General, George, Duke of Albemarle, etc. . 730
Percy Folio MS. fragment of Guy and Phillis . . 733
A Pleasant Song of the Valiant Deeds of Chivalry, achieved by that noble Knight, Sir Guy of Warwick, etc. . 734
The Heroic History of Guy, Earl of Warwick. By H. Crouch. 737
How it became impossible to exclude the Chevy-Chase ballad . 738
A Memorable Song on the Unhappy Hunting in Chevy Chase, between Earl Piercy of England and Earl Douglas . 740
King Henry V., his Conquest of France, in revenge for the Affront offered by the French King, etc. . . 744
A New Ballad of King John and the Abbot of Canterbury . 747
The King and the Bishop; or, Unlearned Men hard, etc. . 751

PAGE

The Old Abbot and King Olfrey 753
Moderation and Alteration. By George Colman, junior, 1789 . 755
The Old Courtier of the Queen, & New Courtier of the King 756
An Old Song of the Old Courtier of the King's, with a New Song of a new Courtier of the King's. By T. Howard . 758
Editorial Epilogue 760

End of the Group of Legendary and Romantic Ballads.

Mock-Beggar's Hall, with its situation in the spacious Country called Anywhere 762
A Lamentable Ballad of the Ladie's Fall . . . 764
The Fair Maid of Dunsmore's Lamentation, occasioned by Lord Wigmore, once Governor of Warwick-Castle . 767
The Lamentable Song of Lord Wigmore, Governor of Warwick Castle, and the Fair Maid of Dunsmoore, as a Warning, etc., with the Complaint of Fair Isabell, for the Loss of her Honour. By Richard Johnson, 1612 . . 771
Manuscript version of Dainty, come thou to me . . 773
Love in a Calm, 1659 774
On Diaphantus and Charidora. By Sir Robert Aytoun . 775
The Lord's Lamentation; or, The Whittington Defeat, 1747 . 777
An earlier 'Complainte du Juif Errant.' . . . 778
Ahasuerus: Song of the Wandering Jew. Trans. by C. G. Leland 779
Pepysian broadside version of St. George and the Dragon . 780
The Birds' Harmony (Bodleian and Pepysian earlier version). 782
The Sea-man's Song of Captain Ward, the famous Pirate of the World, and an Englishman born 784
A Pleasant Ditty of the King and the Soldier ("Our noble King in his Progress") 786
An Elegy on Captain Thomas Blood, 30 August, 1680 . 787
The 'Nell and Harry' Group, long dissevered, but re-united.
"Fair Nelly and her dearest dear" = Nelly's sorrow at parting with Henry. 789
"Their sails were spread" = Henry setting forth . . 790
"I loved you dearly, I loved you well" = Nelly's Constancy . 791
"Fair maid, you say you loved me well." Seaman's Answer . 792
The Faithful Mariner on board the Britannia to fair Isabel in London 793
The Unchangeable Lovers, with The Maiden's Answer . 795
Saylors for my Money: A new Ditty in Praise of Sailors and Sea Affairs. By Martin Parker. 797
List of Accredited Authors of Ballads in this Sixth Volume . 799
Editorial Finale to Vol. VI.: Phantasmagoria . . 800
Index of First-Lines, Burdens, Tunes, Titles, and Sub-titles 801

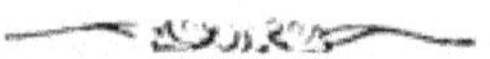

A New Stave to an Old Tune.

WHEN we all grow so rigidly moral
That we cannot afford to be shock'd,
But, like dear little Babes sucking coral,
Are in Cradle-Delusions well rock'd,
There may then be no call for Old Ballads,
French-novels, cayenne, or game-pie:
We shall all mope on cold tea and sallads,
In the pale wash'd-out time, By and Bye!

When we've Peace-Arbitrators to rule us,
No nation allow'd to make war,
Future Bismarcks *or* Ferrys *may fool us,*
And Court-plaister with Treaties each scar;
Woolwich-*Infants, torpedoes,* Greek-*fire,*
Iron-clads, rifle-bores, folks decry:
Let us hope they'll of quarrels grow shyer,
With nought to defend, By and Bye.

When we grow most heart-rendingly pious,
Salvationists *being upheld,*
Although they outrageously try us
In temper, while 'War-Cries' are yell'd;
We may yield our Cathedrals and Abbeys,
Our old Minsters that soar to the sky,
To be white-wash'd for ranters and tabbies—
But not yet, till we reach By and Bye.

When they heave down each monarch and bishop,
As 'expensive, luxurious, effete,'
They a substitute brand-new must fish-up,
To make their millennium complete.
Vegetarians may croak things unpleasant,
Local Option keep ev'ry one dry;
For my part, still content with The Present,
I won't stay till their sweet By and Bye.

J. WOODFALL EBSWORTH.

NOVEMBER 19, 1884.

Hallo, my Fancy!

"And near me on the grass lies Glanvil's book—
Come, let me read the oft-read tale again,
The story of that Oxford scholar poor
Of pregnant parts and quick inventive brain,
Who, tired of knocking at Preferment's door
One summer morn forsook
His friends, and went to learn the Gipsy lore,
And roam'd the world with that wild brotherhood,
And came, as most men deem'd, to little good,
But came to Oxford and his friends no more."

—Matthew Arnold's *Scholar Gipsy.*

WE possess in the *Roxburghe Collection* the original ballad of "Hallo, my Fancy! whither wilt thou go?" and the clever imitation of it, written by Dr. Robert Wild, beginning "In a melancholy study, none but my self." Additional verses of the former were attributed as early work to William Cleland, a Lieut.-colonel among the Covenanters in the North, but he is said to have been born in 1661, and there are extant printed copies of Wild's imitation, dated 1656, in *Wit and Drollery*, p. 143; and 1661, p. 223.

Dr. Wild's "The Shiftless Student" (p. 456) was certainly written before the close of 1641, *circâ* February, 164½; the original six stanzas *were entered in the Stationers' Registers* to Richard Harper, 30 Dec., 1639, as '*Ha, ha, my fancy!*' We attach little weight to the claim advanced posthumously in 1697 for Cleland's authorship. At that date, in "*A Collection of several Poems and Verses composed upon various Occasions*," it appears as the opening piece, "Hollow, my fancie?" It was afterwards reprinted by James Watson in "*A Choice Collection of Comic and Serious Scots Songs*," 1706; but Scotch publishers and critics enjoy an unenviable notoriety for annexing unblushingly the works of English writers, declaring them to be indisputably of Caledonian birth. They *falsely* claim for him the final stanza.

As to Cleland, if we were to admit the claim made for him as author of eight of the ten supplementary stanzas, we defy any person to regard these additions as worthy companions of the rich and fanciful original six stanzas belonging to a much earlier date. In them are visible alike poetic imagination and constructive talent. To mark the distinction clearly, and for all time, we degrade into brevier type the somewhat incongruous Clelandisms, while printing the original stock in long-primer type. Moreover, we give on p. 451 the authentic transcript of the unextended poem, as copied into the Percy Folio MS., certainly before 1650. To this we owe the important correction "Through the *welkin* dance I;" instead of the corrupt reading "*Vulcan* dansy," in third line: and "fiery elf," *i.e.* Will-of-the-Wisp, instead of 'Fairy elf,' in the fourth line.

[Percy Folio MS., British Museum Add. MS., 27,879, fol. 194, 195.]

Hollowe me Fancye.

IN a Melancholly fancy, out of my selfe,
thorrow the welkin dance I,
all the world survayinge, noe where stayinge ;
like vnto the fierye elfe, [= Will o' th' Wisp.
Ouer the topps of hyest mountaines skipping,
Ouer the plaines, the woods, the valleys, tripping,
Ouer the seas without oare of shipping,
hollow, me fancy ! wither wilt thou goe ?

Amydst the cloudy vapors, faine wold I see
what are those burning tapors
wch benight vs and affright vs,
& what the Meetors bee.
Faine wold I know what is the roaring thunder, [fo. 195.
& the bright Lightning wch cleeues the clouds in sunder,
& what the cometts are att wch men gaze & wonder,
Hollow, me, &c.

Looke but downe below me where you may be bold,
where none can see or know mee,
all the world of gadding, running of madding,
none can their stations hold :
One, he sitts drooping all in a dumpish passion,
another, hee is for mirth, and recreation ;
the 3d. he hangs his head because hees out of fassion,
Hollow, &c.

See, See, See, what a bustling !
Now I descry one another Iustlynge !
how they are turmoyling, one another foyling,
& how I past them bye !
hee y^{ts} aboue, him [tha]ts below despiseth ; [blotted.
hee y^{ts} below, doth enuye him that ryseth ;
eu[er]ye man his plot & counter plott deviseth.
Hollow[, etc].

Shipps, Shipps, Shipps, I descry now !
crossing on the maine, I'le goe too, and try now,
what they are p[ro]iecting & p[ro]tecting ;
& when thé turne againe.
One, hees to keepe his country from inuadinge ;
another, he is for Merchandise & tradinge ;
the other Lyes att home like summers cattle shadding.
Hollow[, etc].

Hollow, me fancy, hollow !
I pray thee come vnto mee, I can noe longer follow !
I pray thee come & try [me] ; doe not flye me !
Sithe itt will noe better bee,
Come, come away ! Leave of thy Lofty soringe,
Come stay att home, & on this booke be poring !
For he y^t gads abroad, he hath the lesse in storinge.
Welcome, my fancye ! welcome home to mee !

Finis.

[Roxburghe Collection, III. 537. Also, with differences, Douce, II. 269.]

Bedlam Schoolman.

Or, some Lines made by an *English* Noble Man, that was in *Bedlam*.

To its own proper Tune, *Holow my Fancie, whither wilt thou go?*

INto a Melancholick *Fancie*,
Out of my self;
Into the [Welkin dance I], ["*Vulcan* dancie."
All the World surveying, No where staying,
Just like a *Fairie Elff*: [*Cf.* p. 450.
Out o're the tops of highest mountains skipping,
Out o're the hills, the trees, and valleys tripping,
Out o're the ocean Seas, without an oare or shipping:
Holow, my Fancie! wither wilt thou go?

Amidst the misty vapours,
fain would I know
What doth cause the tapers? ["Tapours."
Why the Clouds benight us, and affright us;
while we travel here below?
Fain would I know what makes the roaring Thunder?
And what these lightnings be, that rent the clouds asunder?
And what these Comets are, on which we gaze and wonder?
Holow, my Fancie! [*whither wilt thou go?*]

Fain would I know the reason,
why the little Ant, [misprinted "Aunt.'
All the Summer season,
Layeth up provision, upon condition,
to know no Winter's want?
And how these Huse-wives, that are so good and painful,
Do unto their Husbands prove so good and gainful?
And why these lazy *Drones*, to them do prove disdainful?
Holow, [*my Fancie! whither wilt thou go?*]

Ships! Ships! I will discrie you,
amidst the main;
I will come and try you,
What you are protecting, and projecting,
What's your end and aim?
One goes abroad for Merchandise and Trading,
Another stayes to keep his Countrey from invading,
A third is coming home with rich and wealth of loading.
Holow, [*my Fancie! whither wilt thou go?*]

When I look be[low] me, ["before me"]
there I do behold,
There's none that sees or knows me;
All the World's a-gadding, Running and madding,
none doth his station hold:
He that is below envieth him that riseth,
And he that is above, him that's below despiseth,
So every man his plot and counter-plot deviseth.
Holow, [*my Fancie! whither wilt thou go?*]

Look! Look! what a bustling, [*Al. lect.*, "See, see."
Here I do espy!
Each one another justling,
Every one turmoiling, One another spoiling,
As I did pass them by:
One sitteth musing in a dumpish Passion,
Another hangs his head, because he's out of fashion,
A third is fully bent on sport and recreation:
Holow, [*my Fancie! whither wilt thou go?*] [1]

Fain would I be resolved,
how things are done?
And where the Bull was calved,
Of bloody *Phalaris*, And where [the] Taylor is, [" *Falaris.*"
that works to the Man-in-the Moon?
Fain would I know how *Cupid* aims so rightly?
And how these little *Fairies* do dance and leap so lightly?
And where fair *Cynthia* makes her ambles nightly?
Holow, [*my Fancie! whither wilt thou go?*]

In conceit like *Phaeton*, [Attrib. to *Cleland.*
I'll mount *Phœbus'* chaire!
Having ne're a hat on,
All my hair's a-burning, in my journeying,
Hurrying through the Air!
Fain would I hear his fiery Horses neighing!
And see how they on foamy bitts are playing!
All the Stars and Planets I will be surveying!
Holow, [*my Fancie! whither wilt thou go?*]

---

[1] Here intervenes a stanza (but not by William Cleland) in later copies:—

Amidst the foamie Ocean,
Fain would I know
What doth cause the motion,
And returning, in its journeying,
And doth so seldom swerve?
And how these little Fishes, that swim beneath salt water,
Do never blind their eye, methinks, it is a matter
An inch above the reach of old *Erra Pater!*
Holow, my Fancie! whither wilt thou go?

[" *Erra Pater:*" see introduction and notes to the "Wandering Jew," *post.*]

O, from what ground of Nature, [*Cleland's.*
Doth the *Pelican*,
That self-devouring creature,
Prove so froward, and untoward,
Her Vitals for to strain!
And why the subtile *Fox*, while in death's wounds is lying,
Doth not lament his pangs, by howling and by crying?
And why the milk-white Swan doth sing when she's a dying.
Holow, [*my Fancie! whither wilt thou go?*]

Fain would I conclude this, [*Cleland's.*
at least make an essay,
What similitude is;
Why Fowls of a feather Do flock and fly together?
and *Lambs* know Beasts of prey?
How Nature's Alchymists, these small laborious creatures,
Acknowledge still a Prince in ordering their matters,
And suffers none to live, who slothing lose their features?
Holow, [*my Fancie! whither wilt thou go?*]

I'm rapt with admiration, [*Cleland's.*
when I do ruminate,
Men of one Occupation,
How each one calls him 'Brother!' Yet each envieth other,
and yet still intimate!
Yea, I admire to see, some Native's farther sund'red
Than *Antipodes* to us. Is it not to be wond'red,
In Myriads ye'll find of one mind scarce an hundred!
Holow, [*my Fancie! whither wilt thou go?*]

What multitude of notions [*Cleland's.*
doth perturb my Pate,
Considering the motions,
How [th'] Heavens they are preserved! and this World served,
in moisture, light, and heat!
If one Spirit sits the outmost Circle turning,
Or if one turns another continuing in journeying;
It rapid circles' motion be that which they call burning,
Holow, [*my Fancie! whither wilt thou go?*]

Fain also would I prove this, [*Cleland's.*
by considering,
What that which you call Love is?
Whether it be a Folly, or a Melancholy,
or some Heroick thing!
Fain would I have it proved, by one whom Love hath wounded,
And fully upon one [his own] desire hath founded, [" their."
That nothing els could please them, tho' the World were rounded?
Holow, [*my Fancie! whither wilt thou go?*]

To know this World's Center, [*Cleland's.*
Height, depth, breadth, and length,
Fain would I adventure,
To search the hid attractions of Magnetick actions,
and Adamantick strength! [Adamantine.
Fain would I know, if in some lofty mountain,
Where the Moon sojourns, if there be trees or fountain?
If there be beasts of prey? or yet be fields to hunt in?
Holow, [*my Fancie! whither wilt thou go?*]

Fain would I have it tried, [*Cleland's.*
by Experiments,
By none can be denied;
If in this bulk of Nature there be voids less or greater,
Or all remains compleat?
Fain would I know if Beasts have any Reason?
If *Falcons* killing *Eagles*, do commit a Treason?
If fear of Winter's want makes Swallowes fly the season?
Holow, [*my Fancie! whither wilt thou go?*]

Holow! my *Fancie*, holow! [*Original*, resumed.
Stay thou at home with me,
I can thee no longer follow,
Thou hast betray'd me, and bewray'd me;
It is too much for thee.
Stay, stay at home with me! leave off thy lofty soaring;
Stay at home with me, and on thy books be poring:
For he that goes abroad, layes little up in storing:
Thou[*'rt*] *welcome home, my Fancie, welcome home to me!*

Finis.

[No publisher's imprint or woodcut. In white-letter, a comparatively modern Reprint. Date of earliest composition—without additions—certainly before 1641. The original is virtually preserved for us in its integrity, without later admixture, in the *six stanzas version* of the invaluable PERCY FOLIO MANUSCRIPT, now in the British Museum, Addit. MS. 27,879, which we print, for comparison, in our introduction on p. 451. Its first and second stanza correspond with ours; its third with our fifth; its fourth with our sixth; its fifth with our fourth; and, finally, its sixth with our sixteenth, or seventeenth if we include the stanza in note, p. 453. So there are eleven stanzas not of original manufacture. It is reprinted, similarly, in *Wit and Mirth*, 1684, p. 73.]

⁂ The gallant Cavalier is anonymous who gave us this 'Bedlam Schoolman,' with its burden of "*Hallo, my Fancy! whither wilt thou go!*" He found a worthy imitator, and speedily, *not later than* 1641, in Dr. Robert Wild, whose "*Alas, poor Scholar! whither wilt thou go?*" follows, to the same tune, on our p. 456:—the prototype of Matthew Arnold's "Scholar Gipsy," with all his associations of Oxford loveliness clinging around him for ever. It is a vigorous and lively satire, worthy of John Cleveland, displaying the college student of troubled times; far beyond anything that *in later days* young Cleland could have written at St. Andrews or Edinburgh. It was printed among Dr. Robert Wild's poems, in earliest collected editions, but this is not certain evidence though plausible. Wild was ultimately a non-conformist, but not disloyal. He wrote the "Iter Boreale," beginning "The day is broke, *Melpomene* be gone!" in honour of Lord General George Monk's march from Scotland to London, 1660. Also, a comedy, called "The Benefice," printed in 4to. 1689. This was founded on the long-earlier "*Return from Parnassus; or, The Scourge of Simony,*" acted at Cambridge in 1602, and reprinted at Oxford (with the long-lost preceding 'two parts,' from Thomas Hearne's MSS., at the Bodleian) in 1886.

From Arnold's poem of 'The Scholar Gipsy,' mentioned above, we have taken the fourth stanza as our motto, on p. 450. In exquisitely melodious verse, it tells anew the story from Glanvil's *Vanity of Dogmatizing*, 1661, and embodies the dissatisfied weariness of our later day; even as James Thomson did, appallingly, in his *City of Dreadful Night*, 1880. Robert Wild's 'Poor Scholar' or 'Shiftlesse Student,' is sadder than Glanvil's, despite the vein of mockery.

[Roxburghe Collection, III. 633.]

Alas, poore Scholler! Whither wilt thou go? or,

Strange Alterations which at this time be,
There's many did think they never should see.

To the Tune of, *Halloo, my Fancy, etc.*

IN a Melancholy Study,
None but my self,
Methought my Muse grew muddy
After seven years Reading, and costly breeding,
I felt, but could find no pelf:
Into learned rags I've rent my Plush and Satten
And now am fit to beg in *Hebrew, Greek*, and *Latin*;
Instead of *Aristotle*, would I had got a Patten. [monopoly, patent.
Alas, poor Scholar! whither wilt thou go?

Cambridge, now I must leave thee,
And follow Fate,
College hopes do deceive me;
I oft expected to have been elected,
But Desert is reprobate.
Masters of Colleges have no common Graces,
And they that have Fellowships have but common places,
And those that Scholars are, they must have handsome faces:
Alas, poor Scholar! whither wilt thou go?

I have bow'd, I have bended,
And all in hope
One day to be befriended:
I have preach'd, I have printed, what e'er I hinted,
To please our English Pope. [*i.e.* Archbp. *Laud.*
I worship'd towards the East, but the sun doth now forsake me;
I find that I am falling, the Northern winds do shake me: [1641.
Would I had been upright, for Bowing now will break me:
Alas, poor Scholar! whither wilt thou go?

At great preferment I aimed,
Witness my Silk;
But now my hopes are maimed:
I looked lately to live most stately
And have a Dairy of Bell-ropes'-Milk; [*i.e.* Benefice.
But now, alas! my self I must not flatter,
Bigamy of Steeples is no laughing matter: [Pluralities.
Each man must have but one, and Curates will grow fatter.
Alas, poor Scholar! whither wilt thou go?

Into some Country Village
Now I must go,
Where neither Tythe nor Tillage
The greedy Patron and parched Matron
Swear to the Church they owe:
Yet if I can preach, and pray too on a sudden, [i.e. extempore.
And confute the *Pope*, at adventure, without studying,
Then ten pounds a year, besides a Sunday Pudding!
[*Alas, poor Scholar! whither wilt thou go?*]

All the Arts I have skill in,
Divine and Humane,
Yet all's not worth a shilling;
When the women hear me, they do but jeer me,
And say I am profane:
Once, I remember, I preached with a Weaver,
I quoted *Au'stin*, He quoted *Dod* and *Cle[a]ver*.
I nothing got; He got a Cloak and Beaver:
Alas, poor Scholar! whither wilt thou go?

Ships, ships, ships, I discover,
Crossing the Main:
Shall I in, and go over,
Turn Jew or Atheist, Turk or Papist,
To *Geneva* or *Amsterdam*?
Bishopricks are void in *Scotland*, shall I thither?
Or follow *Windebank* and *Finch*, to see if either
Do want a Priest to shrive them? O no, 'tis blust'ring weather.
Alas, poor Scholar! whither wilt thou go?

Ho! ho! ho! I have hit it,
Peace, good-man Fool!
Thou hast a Trade will fit it;
Draw thy Indenture, Be bound at adventure
An Apprentice at a Free-School.
There thou may'st command by *William Lillye's* Charter;
There thou may'st whip, strip, and hang, and draw, and quarter,
And commit to the Red Rod both *Will* and *Tom* and *Arthur*.
Aye, aye, 'tis thither, thither will I go. [Orig., I, I, 'tis.

[Written by **Robert Wild**, D.D.]

[No imprint. Three woodcuts. Printed for the Booksellers in *London* before 1668. Date of composition 1641: time of Secretary Windebank and Finch's flight from England to France, January 164½. The cuts are not yet re-engraved. They are, 1st, a studious man, enrobed, sitting disconsolately, gazing on the hearth where damp twigs are smouldering; a tortoise at his feet. 2nd, a Pilgrim, with cockle-shell of St. Iago in flap-hat, and staff in hand. 3rd, picture of a ship, within an ornamental frame.]

[Roxburghe Collection, IV. 81: Pepys Coll., III. 329.]

The Young-Man's Labour lost.

He with a fair Maid was in love,
But she to him unkind did prove:
As by this ditty you shall hear,
If young men they will but draw near;
And Maidens too it doth advise,
To learn henceforth to be wise.

TO THE TUNE OF, *The Jearing Young Man.* [See p. 459.]

AS I past by a green-wood side, a pritty couple I espy'd,
A young-man and a dainty lass, but mark what after came to pass:
He thought her humours for to fit, but yet she was too ripe a wit;
She would not yield to his desire, as by this story you shall hear.

To complement he did begin, the maid's affection for to win,
With speeches fair he did intreat, and often said his heart would break;
Quoth he, "I am my father's heir, and have threescore pound a year,
I will maintain you gallantly, if thou wilt yield my bride to be.

"Therefore I pray you be not coy, for thou shalt be my only joy;
If thou deny'st thou wilt break my heart, for did'st thou know the deadly smart
Which I sustain both day and night, for thee which art my heart's delight,
Therefore my dearest pitty me, or I shall dye for love of thee."

The Maid.

"Good Sir, I thank you for your love, of your discourse I don't approve;
For many now-a-days I see, do bring themselves to poverty,
By marrying whilst they are so young, but I'le not do my self such wrong:
Therefore forbear, thy suit's in vain, I will not marry I tell thee plain.

"You say you have threescore pound a year, what if thou hast? I do not care,
I knew those who had three times more, and spent it all upon a whore:
And so may thou for ought I know, for all you make so fair a show:
Then be content, and do not prate, for fear that I should break thy pate."

The Young-Man.

The young-man standing in amaze, and on the maid did strangely gaze;
At last he made her this reply, and unto her these words did say:
"What ails thee for to be so cross, in troth I like thee worse and worse:
Of all the maids that e're I see, I never heard the like of thee.

"Sweet-heart, believe me, or else chuse, I'de have thee know I am none of those,
That spend my means upon a whore, or run upon the ale-wives score:
No, I will better be advis'd, It's good to be merry and wise:
For friends I see are very scant, if that a man do come to want."

Maid.

"My friend," quoth she, "what you have said, is not half true I am afraid;
I cannot think you're so precise, one may see plainly by your eyes:
Your hair is of the colour right, to couzen maids is your delight:
But thou shalt ne'r prove false to me, or I will ne'r prove true to thee.

"Therefore forbear my company, and henceforth come not [to] me nigh,
For I am not resolv'd to wed, nor yet to lose my maiden-head:
A single life is void of care, for marry'd wives must pinch and spare
Their charge for to maintain, I see: therefore a single life for me."

The Man.

" Seeing thou provest so unkind, I am resolv'd to change my mind :
A hundred pound I have in store, and threescore pound a year and more :
If I can find an honest girl, I'le prize her more than gold or pearl,
And she shall live a Ladie's life, after she's made my wedded wife.

" And so farewel, thou scornful dame, in time thou may'st repent the same,
That thou to me didst prove untrue, in time thou mayst have cause to rue :
Before that I will marry thee, I will be hang'd upon a tree :
Rather I will give my wealth and store to one that begs from door to door."

Maid.

" Farewel, be gone, thou sawey Jack, with thy wealth and money prithee pack !
My portion is an hundred pound, in silver and good gold so round :
Besides my mother she doth cry, I shall have all when she doth dye ;
Then what need I care for thy wealth, even as thou said'st, go hang thy self !

" For I am resolved as I begun, to end and so conclude my song,
A single life I hold it best, and thereon still my mind is prest.
For marriage brings sorrow and care, so in it I'le not have a share :
Since young-men are so fickle grown, I am resolv'd to hold my own."

So maids of you I'le take my leave, let no false young-man you deceive ;
For many they are hard to trust, scarce one in twenty proveth just :
I for my own part will advise, all maids henceforth for to be wise :
And have a care who you do wed, for fear you bring a knave to bed.

Finis.

Printed for *F. Coles*, *T. Vere*, *J. Wright*, *J. Clarke*, *W. Thackeray*, and *T. Passinger*.

[Black-letter. Two woodcuts : as below. Date, *circâ* 1676. "The Jeering Young Man" (not yet found) was entered on the Registers in 1674 ; as a transfer.]

J. W. E.

Phillida Flouts me.

"My Phyllida, my Phyllida, is all the world to me!"
—Austin Dobson: *At the Sign of the Lyre.*

THIS is the delightful complaint of a befooled Inamorato; not many degrees removed above Master Slender, whose disappointed passion for "Sweet Anne Page" brought him to an untimely end, if we are to believe Jem White's *Falstaffe Letters.* That 'Phillida flouts me' belongs to the closing days of Queen Besse is proved by it being styled 'a new Northern tune,' when cited for "A short and sweet sonnet made by one of the Maides of Honor upon the Death of Queene Elizabeth," 1602, beginning, "Gone is Elizabeth," and printed in the 1612 edition of *The Crowne Garland of Golden Roses.* It was probably the same tune as *I am so deep in love* (see p. 252).

"Phillida flouts me" was one of the fair milkmaid's three songs mentioned in Izaak Walton's *Compleat Angler*, 1653, along with "Come, Shepherds, deck your heads," and "As at noon Dulcina rested," already given on p. 166. The music is reprinted in Mr. William Chappell's *Popular Music*, p. 183, with the words from *The Theatre of Compliments; or, New Academy*, 1689; as previously adopted by Joseph Ritson in his *Ancient Songs*, p. 235, 1792.

Its highest grace and honour came in recent days, when the witcheries of the old flirtation and perplexity were made pictorial, by the dainty sportiveness of Edwin A. Abbey (*cf.* pp. 463, 464).

[*Other readings*: —1st stanza, Oh, what a pain . . I cannot bear it . . She so torments . . . heart faileth, And wavers . . . may, She loves still to gainsay, etc. 2nd stanza, *Will* had her to the *Vine* . . . lookt askance, etc. 4th stanza,

I often heard her say, that she loved posies; [our 7th stanza.
In the last month of *May* I gave her roses,
Cowslips and gilly-flowers, etc.

Our fourth stanza comes next,—Swig whey until you burst, eat bramble-berries [doubtful reading, as '*whig*' meant sour whey, the supposed origin of the nick-name applied to the *sour-douk* butter-milk drinking Scotch disloyalists]: *wether's* skin [the right word, not 'weaver's,' *al. lect.*, unless that were a cant-word for silk]. Instead of our ninth stanza, beginning "I cannot work," some run thus—

Which way soe'er I go, she still torments me;
And, what soe'er I do, nothing contents me.
I fade and pine away,
. . . . all because my dear, etc.

Lastly, "She hath a cloth of mine," instead of "if she frown," this reading,

But if she flinch on me, she shall ne'er wear it;
To *Tibb* my t'other wench I mean to bear it.
And yet it grieves my heart,
So soon from her to part.
Death stings me with his dart:
Phillida flouts me! [See also *Marginalia.*

With music it was reprinted by John Watts in *The Musical Miscellany*, vol. ii. p. 132, 1729, and on p. 136 there followed "The Answer" (see our p. 463, *post*).

[Roxburghe Collection, III. 142, apparently unique, as broad-side.]

Phillida flouts me;

Or, [The] Country Lover's Complaint.

Who seeks by all means for to win his Love,
But she doth scorn him, and disdainful prove;
Which makes him for to sigh, lament and cry,
He fears for *Phillida* that he shall dye.

To a Pleasant Tune, Or, *Phillida flouts me.*

OH! what a plague is Love! How shall I bear it?
She will unconstant prove, I greatly fear it:
It so torments my mind, that my strength faileth,
She wavers with the wind, as the ship saileth.
Please her the best you may,
She looks another way,
Alas and well-a-day!
Phillida flouts me.

At the Fair yesterday, she did pass by me;
She lookt another way, and would not spy me.
I woo'd her for to dine, I could not get her;
Dick had her to the wine: he might intreat her!
With *Daniel* she did dance,
On me she would not glance,
Oh thrice unhappy chance!
Phillida flouts me.

Fair Maid, be not so coy, do not disdaine me;
I am my mother's joy: Sweet, entertain me!
Shee'l give me, when she dyes, all things that's fitting,
Her Poultry and her Bees, and her Geese sitting;
A paire of *Mallerds* beds, [Eider-down; *al. l.* mattress.
And barrel full of shreds.
And yet, for all these goods,
Phillida flouts me!

Thou shalt eat curds and cream, all the year lasting,
And drink the chrystal stream, pleasant in tasting;
Wig and whey till thou burst, and Bramble Berries;
Pye-lid and pasty-crust, Pears, Plums, and Cherries.
Thy raiment shall be thin,
Made of a weather's skin;
All is not worth a Pin:
Phillida flouts me!

Cupid hath shot his Dart, and hath me wounded,
It prickt my tender heart, and ne'er rebounded:
I was a fool to scorn his Bow and Quiver,
I am like one forlorn, sick of a Feaver:
Now I may weep and mourn,
Whilst with Love's flames I burn,
Nothing will serve my turn,
Phillida flouts me.

I am a lively Lad, howe'er she take me,
I am not half so bad as she would make me.
Whether she smile or frown, she may deceive me;
Ne'r a girl in the Town but fain would have me.
Since she doth from me flye,
Now I may sigh and dye,
And never cease to cry
Phillida flouts me!

In the last moneth of *May*, I made her posies,
I heard her often say that she loved Roses;
Cowslips and Jilli-flowers, and the white Lilly,
I brought to deck the bowers, for my sweet *Philly*,
But she did all disdain,
And threw them back again,
Therefore it's flat and plain,
Phillida flouts me.

Fair Maiden, have a care, and in time take me;
I can have those as fair, if you forsake me,
For *Doll* the dairy-maide laught at me lately,
And wanton *Winifred* favours me greatly.
One cast milk on my clothes,
T'other plaid with my nose;
What wanton toys are those?
Phillida flouts me.

I cannot work and sleep, all at a season;
[Love] wounds my heart so deep, without all reason.
I fade and pine away, with grief and sorrow, ["Grief," orig.
I fall quite to decay, like any shadow. [*a. l.* "I 'gin to."
I shall be dead, I fear,
Within a thousand year,
All is for grief and care:
Phillida flouts me.

She hath a cloute of mine, wrought with good *Coventry*,
Which she keeps for a sign of my Fidelity.
But in faith, if she frown, she shall not weare it :
I'll give it *Doll* my maid, and she shall tear it.
Since 'twill no better be,
I'le bear it patiently,
Yet all the world may see
Phillida flouts me!

London, Printed for *F. Coles*, in *Wine-street*, near *Hatton-Garden*.

[In Black-letter. Two woodcuts (to be re-engraved), oval busto of a young Cavalier; ditto of a Cavalier Lady. Date of original issue, *circâ* 1600.]

⁂ On p. 460, *ante*, we mentioned the modern reply, printed by and for *John Watts*, at *Wild's Court*, near Lincoln's-Inn Fields, 1729. The imitation shows Bradley's inability to understand the true character of the Swain or of the Jilt :—

The Answer.

(By Mr. A. Bradley.)

OH ! where's the plague in Love, that you can't bear it ?
If men would constant prove, they need not fear it.
Young Maidens, soft and kind, are most in danger ;
Men waver with the wind, each man's a Ranger.
Their falsehood makes us know
That two Strings to our Bow
Is best, I find it so :
Barnaby doubts me!

Of the eight stanzas we give the fourth, and the eighth, *finale* as :—

What tho', when I did say that I lov'd Posies,
You, in the month of *May*, brought me sweet Roses?
You never shew'd the thing that most wou'd please me ;
A gay gold Wedding-Ring wou'd soon have eas'd me.
I should not with disdain
Have thrown it back again ;
I think 'tis flat, and plain,
Barnaby doubts me!

. . . .

The Cloth I have of thine, wrought with blue *Coventry*,
Which thou gav'st as a sign of thy Fidelity,
I'll give it back again, to thee, as Token
That by a perjur'd Swain, my sad heart's broken.
Oh ! *Barnaby* unkind,
Thou'lt quite distract my mind :
Too late, alas ! I find
Barnaby doubts me!

⁂ We on p. 460 told of the charming illustrations to "*Phillida Flouts me,*" furnished by Mr. Edwin A. Abbey to *Harper's Monthly Magazine* in 1887, lxxv. 188. He deserves a better tribute of thanks than our poor payment on p. 464.

From the Priory to the Abbey.

THE world had grown sordid and shabby ;
"Is it worth while to live?" men could ask :
Their biceps once firm now felt flabby,
They were tired of frolic or task.
Had this gone on much longer, the nation
Would have found itself forced to conjoin
In one grand Suicide operation :
Cut adrift from love, freedom, and coin.

The world had grown sordid and shabby :
But there came here across the Big main,
To comfort worn hearts, Edwin Abbey,
Who fills life with enjoyment again.
His the fancies, brisk, varied and loving,
His the pencil, with lightness and grace,
To bring back what old Time was removing—
Pluck the veil from each long-hidden face.

The world had grown sordid and shabby
To eyes that were blinded or dim,
School'd to death by each epicœne Tabby,
But it always held bright gleams for him.
Guiding back to the lost Happy Valley,
Where Herrick *or* Goldie *could dream,*
He recalls to bloom Carey's *nymph* 'Sally,'
With her Islington *strawb'ries and cream.*

The world has grown sordid and shabby,
But it knows its best friends, even now ;
It welcomes with praise Edwin Abbey—
'Twines English rose-wreaths for his brow ;
Lists to ballades from Dobson *and* Lang *too,*
"At Sign of the Ship" or "of Lyre ;"
Grown happy, by true poets sang to :
Their Lays, like his brush, all admire.

J. W. EBSWORTH.

JANUARY 20, 1887.

A Second Group of Ballads on Good-Fellows, from the Roxburghe Collection.

"Too long have I been a drunken Sot,
And spent my means on the Black Pot,
Both jugs and flaggons I loved dear,
For all my delight was in strong Beer.
Once I had Gold, though now I've none,
Whilst I had money they'd wait me upon,
But now 'tis turn'd to Farthings three,
And 'tis Old Ale has undone me!
—*Wade's Reformation* (See p. 469)."

In Praise of the Black Jack.

(1671. *To the Tune of The Leather Bottel.*)

" Be your liquor small, or as thick as mudd,
The cheating bottle cryes 'Good, good, good!'
Whereat the master begins to storm,
'Cause it said more than he could perform,
And I wish that his heirs may never want Sack,
That first devis'd the bonny Black Jack.

" No Tankard, Flaggon, Bottle nor Jugg,
Are halfe so good, or so well hold Tugg. [Stiff drink.
For when they are broke, or full of cracks,
Then we must fly to the brave Black Jacks.
And I wish that his heirs may never want Sack, etc.

" When the Bottle and Jack stand together, O fie on't!
The Bottle looks just like a dwarfe to a gyant;
Then had we not reason [such] Jacks to chuse,
For this 'l make Boots, when the Bottle mends shooes.
And I wish that his heirs, etc.

" And as for the bottle, you never can fill it
Without a Tunnell, but you must spill it; [i.e. Funnel.
'Tis as hard to get in, as 'tis to get out:
'Tis not so with a Jack for it runs like a spout.
And I wish that his heirs, etc.

" And when we have drank out all our store,
The Jack goes for barme to brew us some more;
And when our stomacks with hunger have bled,
Then it marches for more to make us some bread.
And I wish that his heirs, etc.

" I now will cease to speak of the Jack,
But hope his assistance I never shall lack,
And I hope that now every honest man
Instead of *Jack* will y'clip him *John*:
And I wish that his heirs may never want Sack,
That first devis'd the bonny Black Jack."

*** The Black Jack was often a converted Jack-Boot, that had given up warfare or foreign travel, and settled down into assisting conviviality. See the fine specimens preserved respectively at the British Museum (marked C. R. 1646, formerly at Kensington Palace); at the Cambridge Antiquarian Society; and in Edinburgh at the Society of Scottish Antiquaries. (See p. 469, *post.*)

A Second Group of Good Fellows.

Crytieus.—"Merry knaves are we three-a.
Molus.—"When our songs do agree-a.
Calypho.—"O now I well see-a,
What anon we shall be-a.
Crytieus.—"If we ply thus our singing,
Molus.—Pots then must be flinging,
Calypho.—If the drinke be but stinging.
Molus.—I shall forget the rules of grammar,
Calypho.—And I the pit-pat of my hammer.
Chorus.—"To the Tap-house then let's gang and rore,
Call hard, 'tis rare to vamp a score,
Draw dry the tub, be it old or new,
And part not till the ground looke blew."

—John Lyly's *Sapho and Phao*, ii. 3, 1584.

HETHER Dullness has not slain more souls than Drink has engulphed, is an enquiry debated with useful result, if we arrive at an affirmative conclusion. Dullness drives men and women to dissipation, or else they stagnate into imbecility. Temperance is herself so beautiful, while purity and cheerfulness are the graces that adorn her, that one might expect her professed worshippers to be eloquent in hymning her praise. Yet how dreary are the platitudes in which they indulge! how repellingly and not alluringly they paint her portrait, until it becomes vulgar and ugly as their own hypocritical faces. Affecting to be religiously abstemious and self-denying, how is it that their bleared eyes, and the unsightly feature which stands sentry betwixt them, always serve as beacons to warn us back from a treacherous shore? No wonder that an indignant poet raised his howl of reprobation, mistaking the false prophets as the accredited agents of an obnoxious creed. Hence came delirious prayers to be freed from the thraldom of sanctimonious pretences, as when he wildly sang,

'What ailed us, O gods, to desert you
For creeds that refuse and restrain?
Come down and redeem us from virtue,
Our Lady of Pain!'

He seemed longing, in sheer perversity, to exchange in a trice

'The lilies and languors of virtue
For the raptures and roses of vice.'

This was paying a tribute of deference to the Tartuffes, Maw-worms, and Stigginses of the hour, such as no sensible men of the world need offer. We should *use* the good gifts of Bacchus, Ceres, Momus and Thespis, without abusing them. Why leave the cakes and ale to be enjoyed by the fools alone, or to be pilfered on the sly by the unco-guid and rigidly-righteous when nobody is looking? We know their tricks and their manners. Let us take our lawful share, being wise in our generation, and laugh good-humouredly at the "little fools who drink too much," but still louder at the "greater fools" who refuse to drink at all.

The broadside-ballad writers usually knew their way about town; in at the ale-house door, without blushing; walked out sober after a tolerable interval; and got home betimes. If not always thus discreetly, they at least paid their score, by giving their unconverted companions or ingenuous youth the benefit of their own experience. They had "learnt in suffering what they taught in song." So we accept another Group of their instructive Bacchanalian ditties. They were liberal-hearted, and bestowed 'A Groat's-worth of Good-counsel for a Penny' (the invariable price of a ballad-sheet). 'Wit is bought at a Dear Rate' is, on the contrary, the theme of another. 'Jack Had-land's Lamentation' agrees in principle with 'The Bad Husband's Folly.' 'A Jest' is the song about "Master Constable," a precursor of "Mark Noble's Frolick." For its rollicking praise of a convenient drinking-cup commend we "The Leather Bottél." Good wine needs no bush, and most people care not what it is held in, so long as it comes to hand or mouth. 'Glasses, glasses is the only drinking!' said Falstaff; but he had a bias when bowling over Dame Quickly's silver goblets.

The genuine *Leather Bottél* resembled what we should now-a-days call a "pocket-pistol" while out deer-stalking or peppering the grouse. It seldom erred by being too small (an unpardonable fault, whenever the liquor is good, since even at the change-house, in Tam O'Shanter's time, "the ale was growing better"). One good leather-bottél ought to hold enough drink for two, because "company is aye the best, crossing o'er the heather." Well ribbed, of stout leather, the bottél defied breakage or leakage. Specimens were figured in the late Llewellyn Jewitt's '*Reliquary*,' vol. xxv. They became scarce articles of jewellery, owing to their having been 'loved not wisely but too well' of old, and country squires are charitably supposed to have taken them to the grave, 'loath to depart' without them. Whether this was on the same principle of prevision and provision for the "Happy Hunting-Grounds" as our American cousins, Indians of the wild West; or wisely to remove temptation from a later and degenerate race whose heads appear weak in comparison, this Deponent sayeth not.

As to the tune, it is surely found on p. 514, in that treasury of all such good melodies, William Chappell's *Popular Music of the Olden Time* (whereon, even now, we ourselves are working at his desire to prepare a *Second Edition*). It was also in his *Collection of National English Airs*, 1858, i. 21; ii. 53. Probably, the name of "*The Bottel-maker's Delight*" refers to an earlier version.

As to the authorship, it has hitherto been considered anonymous, but we are the first to publicly acknowledge (from evidence in the Bodleian Library) its parent to have been JOHN WADE. He has been mentioned already on pp. 331, 336, where two of his ballads appear. To the same tune as "Wade's Reformation," viz. *It is Old Ale hath undone me*, was appointed to be sung "Jack Had-Land's Lamentation" (pp. 465, 475): perhaps Wade's.

In Wm. Chappell's *Old English Ditties*, p. 192, "The Leather Bottél" begins, "When I survey the world around;" but it is modernised. Some variations begin, "Now God above," etc.; a Somersetshire version is "God above who rules all things" (Bell's *Ballads and Songs of the Peasantry*, n d. p. 203, founded on James Henry Dixon's Percy Society compilation, 1846, p. 208), and the number of stanzas differs in the numerous editions. "That God above," etc., is another variation. Two copies are in the Roxburghe Collection (II. 257; III. 432); Bagford, I. 49; Pepys, IV. 237; Wood, E. 25, art. 56; Douce, I. 119 *verso*, and a British Museum 4to. p. 14. It is also, there beginning "Now God above," found in the *New Academy of Compliments*, 1671, p. 310; *Wit and Drollery*, 1682, p. 96; several editions of *Pills to Purge Melancholy*, in that of 1719, iii. 246; and on the first page of *Wit and Mirth*, 1684. As "Now God alone," etc., it is on p. 75 of the 4to. Collection of *Diverting Songs*, 1738, so it has had a long lease of well deserved popularity. A companion ditty soon followed, in praise of the Black Jack (from one splendid specimen of which we made a drawing, a quarter of a century ago, at the Scottish Society of Antiquaries in Edinburgh). We have no doubt that the original song "In Praise of the Black Jack" is the short version given on our p. 466 (from *Westminster-Drollery*, part ii. 1672, p. 94), and that the eleven-stanza version (which we added complete in *Appendix*, p. lxv to our reprint of the same work in 1875), had been 'spun out.' It thus began:—

'Tis a pitiful thing that now a days, Sirs,
Our Poets turn *Leather-bottel* praisers;
But if a Leather theame they did lack,
They might better haue chosen the bonny Black Jack:
For when they are both now well worn and decay'd,
For the Jack than the Bottle much more may be said;
And I wish his soul much good may partake
That first devis'd the bonny Black Jack.

[Roxburghe Collection, II. 257; Bagford, I. 49; II. 111; Pepys, IV. 228; Wood, E. 25, art. 56; Douce, II. 257; III. 432.]

A Song
in Praise of the Leather Bottel;
Shewing

How Glasses and Pots are laid aside,
And Flaggons and Noggins they cannot abide;
And let all Wives do what they can,
'Tis for the Praise and Use of Man;
And this you may very well be sure,
The Leather Bottel will longest endure:
And I wish in Heaven his Soul may dwell,
That first devised the Leather Bottel.

To the Tune of, *The Bottel-maker's Delight*, etc.

GOD above, that made all things,
The Heavens, the Earth, and all therein,
The Ships that on the Sea do swim,
To keep th' Enemies out that none comes in;
And let them all do what they can,
'Tis for the Use and Praise of Man:
And I wish in Heaven his Soul may dwell,
That first devised the Leather Bottel.

Then what do you say to those Cans of Wood?
In faith they are, and cannot be good;
For when a Man he doth them send
To be filled with ale, as he doth intend;
The Bearer falleth down by the way
And on the ground the Liquor doth lay;
And then the Bearer begins to ban,
And swears it is 'long of the Wooden Can;
But had it been in a Leather Bottel,
Although he had fallen, yet all had been well;
And I wish [in Heaven his Soul may dwell,] etc.

Then what do you say to those Glasses fine?
Yes, they shall have no Praise of mine; [qu. Yet?
For when a company they are set
For to be merry, as we are met;
Then if you chance to touch the Brim,
Down falls the Liquor and all therein;
If your Table-Cloath be never so fine,
There lies your Beer, Ale or Wine:
It may be for [such] a small Abuse
A young Man may his Service lose:
But had it been in a Leather Bottel,
And the Stopple in, then all had been well:
And I wish [in Heaven his Soul may dwell,] etc.

Then what do you say to these black Pots three?
True, they shall have no Praise of me,
For when a Man and his Wife falls at Strife,
As many have done, I know, in their Life;
Thay lay their Hands on the Pot both,
And loath they are to lose their Broath;
The one doth tug, the other doth ill,
Betwixt them both the Liquor doth spill;
But they shall answer another Day,
For casting their Liquor so vainly away:
But had it been in the Leather Bottel,
[The one may have tugg'd, the other have held;]
And they might have tugg'd, till their Hearts did ake,
And yet their Liquor no harm could take:
Then I wish [in Heaven his Soul may dwell], etc.

What do you say to the Silver Flaggons fine? ['Then'
True, they shall have no Praise of mine;
For when a Lord he doth them send
To be filled with Wine as he doth intend;

The Man with the Flaggon doth run away, ['he doth'
Because it is Silver most gallant and gay:
O then the Lord he begins to ban,
And swears he hath lost both Flaggon and Man;
There is never a Lord's Serving-Man, or Groom,
But with his Leather Bottel may come:
Then I wish [in Heaven his Soul may dwell], etc.

A Leather Bottel we know is good,
Far better than Glasses or Cans of Wood,
For when a Man is at work in the Field,
Your Glasses and Pots no comfort will yield;
Then a good Leather Bottle standing him by,
He may drink always when he is a dry;
It will revive the Spirits and comfort the Brain,
Wherefore let none this Bottle refrain:
For I wish [in Heaven his Soul may dwell], etc.

Also the honest Sith-man too, [Scythe-man.
He knew not very well what to do,
But for his Bottle standing him near,
That is filled with good Household-beer:
At Dinner he sits him down to eat,
With good hard Cheese, and Bread or Meat,
Then this Bottle he takes up amain,
And drinks and sets him down again;
Saying, "Good Bottle, stand my Friend,
And hold out till this Day doth end:
For I wish [in Heaven his Soul may dwell]," etc.

And likewise the Hay-makers they,
When as they are turning and making their Hay,
In Summer-weather, when as it is warm,
A good Bottel full then will do them no harm;
And at Noon-time they sit them down,
To drink in their Bottles of Ale nut-brown;
Then the Lads and Lasses begins to tattle,
"What should we do but for this Bottle?"
They could not work if this Bottle were done,
For the Day's so hot with heat of the Sun:
Then I wish [in Heaven his Soul may dwell], etc.

Also the Leader, Lader, and the Pitcher, [Corn-stackers.
The Reaper, Hedger, and the Ditcher,
The Binder, and the Raker, and all
About the Bottel's Ears doth fall;
And if his Liquor be almost gone,
His Bottel he will part with to none,

But says, "My Bottel is but small,
One Drop I will not part withal:
You must go drink at some Spring or Well,
For I will keep my Leather Bottel:"
Then I wish [in Heaven his Soul may dwell], etc.

Thus you may hear of a Leather Bottel,
When it is filled with Liquor full well,
Though the Substance of it be but small,
Yet the Name of the thing is all.
There's never a Lord, Earl, or Knight,
But in a Bottel doth take Delight,
For when he is hunting of the Deer,
He often doth wish for a Bottle of Beer:
Likewise the Man that works at the Wood,
A Bottel of Beer doth oft do him good:
Then I wish [in Heaven his Soul may dwell], etc.

Then when this Bottel doth grow old,
And will good liquor no longer hold,
Out of the side you may take a Clout,
Will mend your Shooes when they'r worn out;
Else take it and hang it upon a Pin,
It will serve to put many odd Trifles in,
As Hinges, Awls, and Candle-ends,
For young Beginners must have such things:
Then I wish in Heaven his Soul may dwell,
That first devised the Leather Bottel.

[Written by **John Wade**.]

London: Printed by and for *W. O.* and sold by *I. Walter*, at the *Hand and Pen* in *High Holbourn.*

[In White-letter. One woodcut, as on p. 470. Date of composition *circâ* 1662. In only one early, and rare copy, have we found the authorship assigned, as above, viz. in Anthony à Wood's, E. 25, (56), where it is described as "a pleasant new Song in Praise of the Leather Bottell by JOHN WADE. *London*, Printed for *R. Burton*." The Pepysian was printed for F. Coles, Vere, Wright, Clarke, Thackeray and Passinger. Both of Bagford's in white-letter for W. Onley, the first sold by B. Deacon. Douce's first is like our own, for W. O., Sold by I. Walter; Douce's second is merely an Aldermary Church-yard, Bow-Lane, modern reprint. Such is Roxb. Coll., III. 132, with its two rude woodcuts, 1st, a bewigged *bon-vivant* sitting at a table, smoking a long pipe; 2nd, a Silenus-like naked Bacchus, holding a huge drinking-cup in one hand and a bottle in the other. The popularity of 'The Leather-Bottel' is proved by these numerous editions. Line 16 is from *Deacon's*.]

*** That delightful artist, Edwin A. Abbey, who has caught the spirit of our old ballads, promises speedily to illustrate "The Leather Bottél" in *Harper's Monthly*, as he has already done "Phillida flouts me!" "Sally in our Alley." George Wither's "I loved a Lass, a fair one," and, earlier, Herrick's love-songs.

Jack Had-land's Lamentation.

WE have already (on p. 469) mentioned the tune of *It is Old Ale that has undone me*, one appointed for the following ballad, and taking its name from the burden of "Wade's Reformation," in our *Bagford Ballads*, p. 6 (1st stanza is on p. 465). Another name of the same tune is *The Maid is best who lies alone*. (See ballad with this burden given in the *Appendix* to *Bagford Ballads*, p. 1020. Another is extant, in the Pepys Collection.)

That John Had-land, or Jack Had-land, was a proverbial expression for one who, like the melancholy Jacques, had spent the profits of his own land in seeing the lands of other people, appears the more probable when we remember that Frances Coules had about 1628 printed a ballad written and signed initially by Richard Climsell *alias* Crimsell, entitled "John Had-land's Advice," beginning "To all men now I'le plainely show how I have spent my time." It was sung to the tune of *The bonny bonny Broome*, and has been reprinted by Mr. William Chappell (*viz.* on p. 268 of Vol. III. among these *Roxburghe Ballads*, from Roxb. Coll., I. 522). The burden is sufficiently lugubrious:—

But now I may with sorrow sadly say, My heart is filled with woes,
Had it not beene for the good Ale-tap, I had gone in better cloathes.

Climsell is a dreary long-winded complainer, by habit and repute. His thirteen twelve-line stanzas are a heavy infliction. To have eaten one's cake and thereafter bemoan or grumble because the coin that paid for it is no longer kept in hand or laid out at usury, is to our mind the silliest of unmanly maundering. Horace knew better, wise old heathen that he was. A puling race has succeeded; cheap sensualists, sneaking 'Dead-heads,' who evade payment of entrance fees or garnish, and are discontented with the entertainment to which they contributed neither profit nor applause. Shame it is:

Ah, miserable race! too weak to bear,
Too sad for mirth, too sceptical for prayer!
Surely on you the Scripture is fulfilled,
To bid the mountains cover your despair!

Whatever whim possessed hearty John Wade to enter into competition with Crimsell, and beat him unmistakeably, by adopting name and subject about forty years later, can only be learnt satisfactorily some midnight hour when his ghost revisits this upper sphere and discloses the secrets of the prison-house. We wait patiently till then. It is a fact not generally known, except by Swedenborgian *illuminati*, that the lemures and eidola of people retain their former characteristics in the Elysian fields—and elsewhere. Hence it is that Wade is still a pleasant companion, inspiring convivial ditties, while Climsell afflicts our righteous soul with unimprovable sermonizing, in sæcula sæculorum.

[Roxburghe Collection, II. 228; Bagford Coll., II. 59; Pepys, II. 23; Huth, I. 136; Douce, I. 99; Jersey, II. 27.]

Jack Had-Land's Lamentation,

That sold and made away his 'State,
And spent his money early and late;
And let his Wife and Children want,
Now he makes great moan and does repent;
And desires all good-fellows where e're they be
To take warning of his poverty.
He was cast in prison, at that bout,
His poor Wife she helpt him out:
She had small reason to do that thing,
But true love is a gallant thing;
There is scarce a Tap-house in *London* town
Will help a Man when he is cast down.

To the Tune of, *It is Old Ale that has undone me* [see p. 474].

This may be Printed. **R[ichard] P[ocock]**.

TO all Good-fellows I'le declare,
To take Example and have a care,
And do not spend your means in waste,
For you will repent it at the last:
For I my self was blindly led,
And made all away, I was so bad;
Let all I say be warn'd by me,
Of drinking and bad company.

I had Land and Living of my own,
And a fine Estate, it was well known;
It was worth threescore pound a year,
And I spent it all in Ale and Beer,
My Hostess was all my delight,
And I sat up swilling day and night.
Let all, I say, [be warn'd by me,] &c.

I never took no care at all,
God knows I had a sudden fall;
I sold my 'State then all away,
To maintain the Ale-house night and day.
My Wife and Children was so poor,
Neighbours cry'd shame at me therefore:
Let all, I say, [be warn'd by me,] &c.

I would come home drunk unto my Wife,
And lead her such a weary life,
And she would speak me then so fair,
And intreat me with a lovely care,
And say, 'Good Husband, be content,
Alas! you will these things repent;"
Let all, I say, be warn'd by me,
Of drinking and bad company.

My little naked Children, they
Were almost pin'd, as neighbours say, [=emaciated.
And starv'd so sore for want of close, [=cloathes.
I had no care of them, God knows;
Now all is gone, and nothing left,
I may say, 'Farewell Dagger with dudgeon and Haft:'
Let all, I say, [be warn'd by me,] &c.

I cast myself into some Debt,
And was arrested then for it;
Because that I could get no Bail,
They cast me in a nasty Gaile;
And there I lay from my poor Wife,
She reliev'd me or I had lost my life:
Let all, I say, [be warn'd by me,] &c.

When I was in that misery,
Ne'r an Ale-wife that would come to me;
For all I had spent my 'state away,
I had no help of them, I say:
But my poor wife was my best friend,
And succoured me unto the end:
Let all, I say, [be warn'd by me,] &c.

Then my poor wife she sought about,
And she made a friend and got me out;
She sold her Wedding-Ring away,
To pay my Fees without delay;
And did so rejoyce at my release,
And brought me home agen in peace:
Let all, I say, [be warn'd by me,] &c.

Now all is spent I plainly see
There is no help nor no remedy,
But labour hard and work full sore,
That money will be better than all before;
And bring it home unto my Wife,
And love her as I love my life:
Let all, I say, [be warn'd by me,] &c.

A man that has a state or has good means [= estate.
Ne'r use so much these tippling Queans;
They drown your money so very sore,
And make you at the last be poor;
I am sure that I may say the same,
But alas, alas, I was to blame:
Let all, I say, [be warn'd by me,] &c.

Let every one that goes along,
Take notice of this new-made Song,
And take example now by me,
That am fallen into this Poverty;
I wish that I might be the last,
But alack-aday, I am not the first:
Let all, I say, [be warn'd by me,] &c.

So to conclude, to end the strife,
Let every man love his own Wife;
And save his money, and keep his store,
Drink not too much to make you poor,
A man that has Grace will then repent
To see his Wife and Children live in want.
Let all, I say, be warn'd by me,
Of Drinking and lewd Company.

[Probably by **John Wade**: and to his Tune.]

Printed for *P. Brooksby*, at the *Golden-Ball* in *Pye-Corner.*

[In Black-letter. Three woodcuts, 1st, the Hostess (belonging also to "The Bad Husband's Folly," *post*, p. 493), given on p. 475; 2nd and 3rd are on p. 486. Date, between August, 1685, and December, 1688, being licensed by R. Pocock.]

[Roxburghe Collection, II. 520; Pepys, IV. 259; Jersey, I. 365.]

Wit bought at a Dear Rate.

Being a Relation of the Misery one suffers by being too kind-hearted. Wishing all people to beware of that undoing quality, and to be frugal and saving, that in aged years their life may be as comfortable as in youth it was pleasant and jolly.

To the Tune of, *Turn, Love, I prethee, love, turn to me.*[1]

If all the World my mind did know, I would not care a pin,
If I were young, I would take heed, my life how to begin;
I would not be kind-hearted, but money keep in store,
Which if that I in youth had done, *I should not now be poor.*

When in prosperity I was, I then of friends had plenty,
But now adversity is come, I find not one in twenty;
Then was I treated well of all, and had of gifts good store,
If wise I had been in my youth, *I should not now be poor.*

This World I liken to the tide, which oft doth ebbe and flow,
Some are to great riches brought, and some do fall full low;
The joys and pleasures of this life, like flowers fade, therefore
We in our youth must frugal be, *or in age must be poor.*

Some for an honest livelihood do use endeavours great,
And though they work both day and night, they scarce get bread to eat;
There's some again, with little pains, have riches in great store;
To me blind Fortune is unkind, *therefore I must be poor.*

Yet I a little comfort find, that I am not alone;
Thousands there be as good as I, do daily make their moan:
If yet I could some money get, I would it keep in store,
Too kind I have been in my youth, *and now I must be poor.*

Some with extravagant expence make their estates to fly,
And some who little had before, are made when friends do dye:
So various are our fortunes here, some need, and some have store,
But if in youth we be not wise, *we must in age be poor.*

[1] The tune here mentioned belongs to a ballad reprinted on p. 277, "Come turn to me, thou pretty little one, and I will turn to thee." The line above might have read, "pleasant and jolly." See *Popular Music*, p. 528, for the air.

This age is grown to such a pass, that they who go but mean,
And to their friends for kindness go, they give them no esteem:
So cruel and hard-hearted are people now, therefore,
Youth must be wise, and careful be, *or else in age be poor.*

When plenty in my purse I had, I then relieved many,
But now I come to need myself, not pittied am by any:
I toil and weary out my days, yet still am troubled sore,
For charity is waxed cold, *and quite turn'd out of door.*

Love from me long time since is gone, but patience tarries still,
Poverty comes oft to my door, and vows to have his will:
If Providence doth not step in, as he hath done before,
I always shall in sorrow sit, *and in my age be poor.*

Good people all be warn'd by me, do not too freely live,
Slight not my Council nor Advice, which here to you I give:
Make use of it at present time, lest you for evermore,
Hereafter dearly do repent, *and in your age be poor.*

Youth for most part is prodigal, age bears a frugal mind,
More families are not undone, than those who are too kind:
If that in time my words you mark, you may still more and more
Live in esteem, continue rich, *(if not) live to be poor.*

While that you live in good estate, you shall have company,
But when that you have need of some, you then alone shall be:
While you do feast and give good gifts, keep for your self some store,
For if that you do part with all, *you then must needs be poor.*

Despise not now what I here say, but take it in good part,
What here you read you well may think is spoken from the heart:
It comes from one who troubled is, each day, in mind full sore,
Who in their youth have been too kind, *therefore must now be poor.*

Farewel, my friends, I wish you all may warning by me take,
And in your youth while you are strong, your future fortunes make:
Be courteous, kind, to every one, yet as I said before,
Be careful in your youthful time, *or else in age be poor.*

With Allowance.

Finis.

London, Printed for *F. Coles*, in *Vine-Street*, near *Hatton-Garden.*

[Black-letter. Two cuts, 1st, the long-robed man given in Vol. II. p. 349: 2nd, as on p. 478. Date, *circa* 1616-72.]

*** The ballad of "A GROAT'S-WORTH OF GOOD COUNSEL FOR A PENNY" appealed to customers by a double temptation, it offered a bargain below cost price, a fourfold gain, and, while practically recommending outlay for purchase, it theoretically encouraged thrift, as the 'bad Husband's' Repentance had nothing to do with matrimony; he was merely a man who failed to '*husband*' his resources frugally. The same consideration applies to "Two Penny-worth of Wit for a Penny; or, the Bad Husband turned Thrifty" (on p. 483).

[Roxburghe Collection, II. 204; Pepys, IV. 78; Rawlinson, 566, fol. 19; Huth, I. 127; Jersey, II. 93.]

A Groatsworth of Good Counsel for a Penny; or, The Bad Husband's Repentance.

Bad Husbands all, come hear what I have pen'd,
I hope this song to you will be a friend,
And let no man now spend his means in waste,
It brings him into poverty and disgrace,
And now bad Husbands hear what I say,
And save a groat against a rainy day.

To the Tune of *Packington's Pound*; or, *Digby's Farewel.* [*Cf.* pp. 331, 346, 483.] With Allowance.

COme hither, good fellows, and hear what I say,
A new song I will sing if you please for to stay,
And if you will be [all] warned by me,
To be careful in time and save your mon[e]y:
Foul Winters are long, and cold weather is hard,
And a man without money no one will regard,
Let your wife and your children be your chief care,
For wring-spiggots care not, how hard they do fare.

There's some are so cunning they'l hold you in play,
For to get your money, they'l cause you to stay:
With so many fine words, and may chance a fine bit,
While your money doth last, she will cause you to sit
Until their strong liquor doth fire in your face,
You are apt all your money then to part with apace;
Then the ale-wives market is got to a head,
While your wife and children may chance to want bread.

If you sell house or Lands, or put goods into sale,
If they see you have money you shall not want ale;
For as long as my money did hold out and run,
I was bravely respected by every man:
But now I do know and I plainly do see,
It was more for the love of my money than me;
As long as a man has a coat on his back,
To fill in their liquor they will not be slack.

This by experience I find to be true,
Which makes both my back and my belly to rue;
For when I had gold and silver good store,
There would be such bussings to set me ashore:

But I have spent and wasted my store,
I may knock twenty times e're they open the door,
And if I say, 'I want money, will you trust me a quart?'
Then they say, 'Honest friend, we're not trusted malt.'

If a man can be wise and consider this Song,
It may chance do him good for to guide him along,
For spending and wasting consumes a man's state,
Then he falls into misery and repents when too late.
But that's not the way, as I told you to-day,
It 's the ale-wives' delight to make them their prey.
The best thing that I know is for a man to take care,
Then his wife and his children the better will fare.

What is a man better to have store of means [won],
And waste it away like butter in the sun,
Then [is] he, like a cow that doth fill a great pale, [=pail.
And after to cast it all down with her heel,
But be careful to labour in an honest way,
Then God he will bless you by night and by day,
That man is bewitcht that hath a good state of his own,
And not be content till 'tis gone down the red lane. [*i.e.* gullet.

If you drink the very shirt and coat from your back, [2nd Part.]
If some get your money they care not who lack,
And they sit in their chair in pomp and in state,
As long as you have a penny they'l hold you in prate;
But if they see that your pockets are bare,
They say, 'Honest friend, we will fill no more beer:
Pray pay your reckoning and go home to your wife,
If she chance to [o'er] look you, she'l lead you a bad life'

I told you before in a Song I did sing,
That winter is long[1] and much hunger doth bring,
And many a family comes unto want,
Where husbands are given to drink and to rant:
Therefore it is good to keep something in store,
And learn to pass by [their] ale-houses' door,
And think of cold winter, for be sure it will come,
If means then be wanting then all are undone.

Let old Age and Sickness be a man's chiefest care,
Be sure it will come, we must all have a share,
Then bad husbands will think what they spent in vain pots
When they have gone home and made themselves sots;

[1] This cannot refer to "Drive the cold winter away!" which is by Martin Parker, and of much earlier date ("All hail to the days," in *Roxb. Ballads*, i. 84). It more probably alludes to the opening portion of the present song (*Cf.* lines 5 and 6), while the final half-sheet counts as a Second Part. *Digby's Farewell* was not of earlier date than 1672, the action at Sole Bay, on May 28.

Is it not then folly for a man to do so?
He knows not his friend then, I say, from his foe;
He wasteth his wit and consumes his estate,
And repenteth his folly when it is too late. 72

Now in spending your money be not too free,
But trust to yourselves when you do not see me,
And be sure to save something against a rainy day,
Then your own pot at home the better will play;
And to your own Wife and Children be kind,
And that will be the part of an honest man's mind,
And not spend your money in a drunken crew,
Lest they want it at home, then the fault is in you. 80

Now in the Conclusion I have a word more to say,
Take every one one [ballad], and make no delay,
The price is but a penny, and that is not dear,
The best penny worth of wit that you bought this 2 year;
And be sure to observe it when you have it at home,
It may chance do you good when I am dead and gone,
It may save you a groat when you would cast it away,
For to do you good in a cold winter's day. 88

[Publisher's name cut off from Roxburghe copy. Huth's and Rawlinson's were printed for *P. Brooksby* and Licensed by *Roger L'Estrange*. In Black-letter. One woodcut, the same as on p. 490. Date between 1672 and September, 1685.]

*** An Answer to this is extant (in the Jersey Collection, I. 20, now Earl Crawford's Bibliotheca Lindesiana, and), in C. 22. e. fol. 150:—

The Merry Gossip's Vindication
To the Groatsworth of Good Councel Declaration.

To the [same] Tune of *Digbie's Farewell*. Eleven stanzas in all. It begins,

"A company of gossips that love good bub [*i.e.* Drink.]
They met at an Alehouse, where they did Club,
They call'd for the Short Pot, and likewise for the long,
'Come, Tapster, be quick, for we soon must begon.'
They cupt it about, and they made such great hast[e],
Till their nose and their face were all in a blaze;
A man he may work all the days of his life,
But he must ask his wife's leave if he intends for to thrive."

Printed, like our original, for *Philip Brooksby*, at the *Golden-Ball* in *Pye-Corner*. With the same woodcut to both, as on our p. 227, and 462. Martin Parker had written "A Pennyworth of Good Counsell," beginning, "Of late it was my chance to walk, for recreation in the Spring." Reprinted in *Roxburghe Ballads*, vol. ii. 295, to the tune of *Dulcina*: a ballad in this vol., p. 166.

Two Penny-Worth of Wit.

Another self-pitying complaint for having been "too kind" to fellow-revellers and hostesses. Compare *Note* on p. 479. Bankrupt revellers expected to enjoy unlimited credit: it seemed reasonable to the thirsty.

[Roxburghe Collection, II. 482; IV. 66; Douce, II. 231vo.; Jersey, I. 60.]

Two-penny-worth of Wit for a Penny; or, The bad Husband turn'd Thrifty.

This Man that wrought his own decay,
And spent his money night and day;
Is turn'd to saving, I do swear,
There's few with him that can compare:
And lives so civil in his ways,
That all his neighbours give him praise,
And does repent his wicked crime,
And desires good Fellows to turn in time;
There's many a man runs himself clear out,
When Ale's in his head, then Wit is out.

To the Tune of, *Packington's Pound.* [See p. 331.]

ALl Company-Keepers come hear what I say,
Here's a notable Song if you please for to stay,
It will learn you good councel, be rul'd by a friend,
If you go to an alehouse your money to spend:
For four-pence or sixpence, you may spend I do say,
If you call any higher it's all thrown away;
Then *Barnaby* will begin to work in your head,
There's many does forget that their Children want Bread.

Observe a good hour, and loose not your time,
If you meet with a friend that you needs must go drink,
I desire you to take this councel of mine,
Keep wit in your noddle, and your pockets some chink:
Then your wife will [be] pleased, your children glad,
And a great deal of comfort there will to be had:
But if you spend all your money and make your self poor,
Then your rent will be wanting, you'l be turn'd out of door.

To see some men when they are full of drink,
What a beastly condition it is we may think,
That they hardly can know one man from another,
They abuse their best friend if it be their own brother.
They'l tumble i' th' dirt, and they'l stagger i' th' street,
And affront e'ry man and woman they meet,
That when they are sober will scorn to do so,
For they hardly can know their friend from their foe.

For I my own self have been in the same way,
And wasted my money by night and by day,
And never did think how my Children was serv'd,
Till neighbours did say that they almost were starv'd.
If my wife chance to say that any thing she did lack,
I would call her base whore and be sure pay her back;
That was the best comfort I could her afford,
Then I out to the Ale-house, and spent like a Lord.

I sold all my goods, and I wasted my store,
And at the long run I was grown very poor,
A hundred and fifty good pounds I have spent,
As long as any was left I could not be content;
My hostess she would be so merry with me,
When I call'd for liquor and paid for 't too free;
And with slabering and kissing she pleasd me to th' life,
Thus I like a villain did wrong my poor wife.

At last I consider'd, and did think in my mind,
How to my own family I had been too unkind;
Which troubles my conscience to think on the same,
That with drinking and swilling I was much to blame;
My Children was bare, and hard they did fare,
And I of their misery never took care,
But now I'le begin for to live a new life,
And take pains to maintain both my Children and wife.

For I to the Ale-house have been too kind,
Which to my undoing I plainly do find;
My poor little Children are fallen into want,
Which grieves me to see them, full sore I repent,
That I had such fortune for to be so led,
With Drunken companions which caus'd me be bad,
But he runs a long race, that ne'r has an end, [Cf. 191.
I make much of my money that God does me send.

I'le be careful of my children and make much of my wife,
And provide meat and drink for to preserve their life,
That little that's left I hope to make it more,
With taking of pains, and with working full sore:

And ale-wives go hang themselves with what they have got,
No more of my money shall fall to their lot;
I have sow'd my wild Oats and I will have a care, [See p. 49[illegible].
Of drunken companions that made me so bare.

It is a brave thing when a Winter comes cold,
To have something in store, with that a man may be bold,
Either land-men or sea-men what ever they be,
All young-men consider, be ruled by me,
For hostesses [of] tap houses will fill you no beer, [" and."
No longer than your money holds out, you may swear,
For I my own self now do find it too true,
Which makes me to speak, for what I spent I do rue.

Since I took a good course and forsaken the bad,
With my wife and my Children there is enough to be had,
But while I kept drinking and losing my time,
All my whole household was ready to pine:
But it is a long day that ne'r has an end,
Therefore all good-fellows be rul'd by a Friend,
Keep money in your pockets and good cloaths to your back,
Drink to do your selves good, but take heed of a Crack.[1]

Now in the conclusion that man is well blest,
That lives sober, and quietly, and forgoes Drunkenness,
He never will be out of reason with his wife,
If God give him a blessing he's free from all strife.
It is a brave thing if a man do take pains,
If he work ne'r so hard if he bring home the gains;
Therefore take this councel I pray you of mine,
It's a penny well bestow'd, he that takes up in time.

Finis.

Printed for *J. Deacon*, at the *Angel* in *Guiltspur Street*.

[In Black-letter, with three woodcuts, first, the Old Cavalier, on p. 137, or p. 186; second, a table and cups, being fragment of Tinker-ballad cut, Vol. V. 161; third, for a small new cut of revellers at table with musicians in gallery, we have *substituted* a small cut on p. 483. Date of the ballad, *circa* 1680.]

Note.—A Crack was a loose bona roba, such as Justice Shallow had known.

*** With the ensuing ballad entitled "Nick and Froth," denouncing the tricks of tapsters and hostesses in giving false measure, may be associated Humphrey Crouch's ballad "The Industrious Smith" (reprinted in vol. i. pp. 469—471), he remonstrating against objectional practices, was answered:—

"But," quoth the good wife, "Sweet heart, do not rayl,
These things must be, if we sell Ale!"

Tune and burden of *We'll drink this Old Ale no more, no more!* not identified.

[Roxburghe Collection, II. 376; Huth, II. 42; Jersey, II. 162.]

Nick and Froth;

Or,

The Good-fellow's Complaint for want of full Measure.

Discovering the Deceits, and Abuses of Victuallers, Tapsters, Ale Drapers; and all the rest of the Society of Drunkard-makers: By filling their Drink in False Flaggons, Pimping Tankerds, Cans, call'd Ticklers; Rabbits, Jugs, and short Quarterns, to the grand abuse of the Society of Good-fellowship.

Good Fellows Drinks their Liquor without flinching,
Then why should Knavish Tapsters use such pinching.

Tune of, *We'l Drink this Old Ale no more, no more.*

[These cuts belong to p. 477.]

ALl you that are Free-men of Ale-Drapers hall
And Tapsters where ever you be,
Be sure you be ready to come at my call,
And your knavery here you shall see.

A knot of Good-fellows we are here inclin'd,
To challenge you out if you dare,
A very sharp Tryal you're like to find,
Although it be at your own Bar.

Your cheats and abuses, we long did abide,
But times are so wondrous hard,
That Losers may speak, it cannot be deny'd,
Of our Measure we have been debar'd.

But now we'll show you a trick (you knaves),
And lay you all open to view,
It's all for your Froth and your Nick (you slaves),
And tell you no more than is true.

If in a cold morning we chance to come,
And bid a good morrow my Host,
And call for some Ale, you will bring us black Pots,
Yet scarce will afford us a Toast.

For those that drink Beer, 'tis true as I'me here
Your counterfeit flaggons you have,
Which holds not a quart, scarce by a third part,
And that makes my Hostis go brave.

But now pimping tankerds are all in use,
Which drains a man's pocket in brief:
For he that sits close, and takes of his dose,
Will find that the Tankerd's a thief.

Bee't tankerd or flaggon, which of them you brag on,
We'l trust you to Nick and to Froth;
Before we can drink, be sure it will shrink,
Far worser than *North* Country cloth.

When Summer is coming, then hey, brave boys,
The tickling Cans they run round,
Pray tak't in good part, for a *Winchester* Quart
Will fill six, I dare lay you a Pound.

Your Rabbits and jugs and coffee-house Mugs
Are ready when e're you do call,
A P—— take his trade, such measures that made,
I wish that Old *Nick* had them all.

When we have a fancy our noses to steel,
And call for some *Nance* of the best, = Nantz.
Be sure the short Pot must fall to our lot,
For now they are all in request.

Scarce one house in twenty, where measure is plenty,
But still they are all for the Pinch;
Thus every day, they drive custome away,
And force us good Fellows to flinch.

Sometimes a man may leave something to pay,
  Though seldom he did it before ;
With *Marlborough* Cholke, you his patience provoke
  When ever he clears off his score. [*vide*, Note.

The women likewise, which are not precise,
  But will take a Cup of the best,
Tho' they drink for pleasure, they'l have their measure,
  Or else you shall have little rest.

There's *Billings-gate Nan*, and all her whole gang
  Complaining for want of their due :
True Topers they are, as e're scor'd at Bar,
  For they'l drink till their noses look blew.

A Pot and a Toast will make them to boast
  Of things that are out of their reach :
So long as a groat remains in the coat,
  They over good Liquor will preach.

In *Shoo-makers Row* there's true hearts you know,
  But give them their measure and weight,
They'l scorn for to stir, but stick like a Bur,
  And tope it from morning till night.

Then there's honest *Smug*, that with a full jug
  Will set all his brains on a float :
But you are such Sots to fill him small Pots,
  Will scarce quench the spark in his throat.

With many such Blades, of several trades,
  Which freely their money will spend ;
But fill them good drink, they value not chink
  Where ever they meet with a friend.

Most Trades in the Nation give their approbation
  How that you are much for to blame :
Then make no excuses, but cease your abuses,
  And fill up your measure for shame.

[Colophon lost, but the Huth copy was printed for *R. Burton*, in *West-Smithfield*. In Black-letter. Four woodcuts: 1st, the smokers on p. 490 ; 2nd, the girl (fragment) on p. 329 ; 3rd, the man, vol. iii. p. 613 ; 4th, mutilated, of man, vol. i. p. 210. We insert cuts belonging to p. 477. Date *circâ* 1665.]

*** '*Marlborough chalk*' had a slit in it, so that each downward stroke left a *double-score* for the reckoning. This kind of second-sight was limited to tapsters. Tipplers had the gift of double-vision in a different way ; like the Westminster Home-un-Ruler, who, looking at the full moon alongside the illuminated Clock-Tower (at an angle), said, "I must be very far gone. I've often seen *two* moons ; but to-night I see *six* !" Charles Keene immortalized the speaker, in *Punch*.

The Noble Prodigal.

THIS jovial ditty belongs to the date immediately preceding the Restoration, 29 May, 1660. The reference to George Monck, afterwards the Duke of Albemarle, is in second portion. As "A Medley" it reappeared in the rare first edition of *Merry Drollery*, p. 130, 1661; p. 138 of the edition 1670 (and reissue in 1691). It was also in the *Loyal Garland* of 1686 (reprint p. 69), and probably earlier in five lost editions. That it was composed for some city banquet appears certain, and it may not improbably have been one of Thomas Jordan's numerous successes. It was sung to six consecutive dance-tunes:—First, *the Jew's Coranto*; second, *the Princess Royal*; third, *Come hither, my own Sweet Duck* (from a lively ballad "The Insatiate Lover," which we reprinted in our 1876 edition of *Choice Drollery*, p. 247, from *Merry Drollery*, ii. 106, 1661 edit.); fourth and fifth, *French Tricatees*, and sixth, *A new Country dance*. Thus the jig was kept up throughout. The variations in book versions are not important. Line 10, 'He was, Sir Reverence, a Parliament man.' Line 14, 'Then Royalists, since you are undone.' Lines 17, 18, 'We'll tipple . . . and drink our woes,' etc. Line 30, 'Sackific.' Lines 35, 36, we may read 'belfry' if we choose, preferring the fry, 'and a snatch.' Line 37, 'Wee's be bonny and jolly.' Line 43, 'Till *Mauris ap Shenkim*,' etc. Line 50, '*Intrent*, Monsieur.' Line 54, *caret*. *Nota Bene*. The two other portions to end are absent from *Merry Drollery*, but are valuable as indicating the hopes cherished of a return to monarchy. Royalists did not forget the baseness of the Scots selling their own native-born King Charles I. to the Parliament in 1642; therefore they marked the strangeness of Scotland to begin to be true. It certainly had not recently proved itself the Land of the Leal. There was still half-heartedness in the Presbyterian acceptance of Charles II. In next lines is one of the stale allusions to Cromwell as a brewer's drayman of Huntingdon; another to the short-cloaked Independent as a Jesuit in spirit; and a third to the ballad-singers having been severely persecuted whenever they dared to turn the Rump Parliament into ridicule, by simply telling to what depths of degradation it had fallen. Here is the first stanza of "The Insatiate Lover."

Come hither, my own sweet Duck, and sit upon my knee,
And thou and I will truck for thy commodity,
If thou wilt be my honey, then I will be thine own;
Thou shalt not want for money, if thou wilt make it known.
With hey ho, my honey! My heart shall never rue,
For I have been spending money, and among the jovial crew.

[16 stanzas.]

Music is in Playford's *Dancing Master*, 1665 and 1686 editions.

Roxburghe Collection, II. 372; Huth, II. 44; Jersey (Lindesiana, I. 383.)

The Noble Prodigal;

or,

The Young Heir newly come to his Estate.

Who very kindly doth invite you all,
To feast upon his Father's funerall.

A NEW MEDLY OF SIX AYRES.

First Ayr. The Jew's Coran[to].

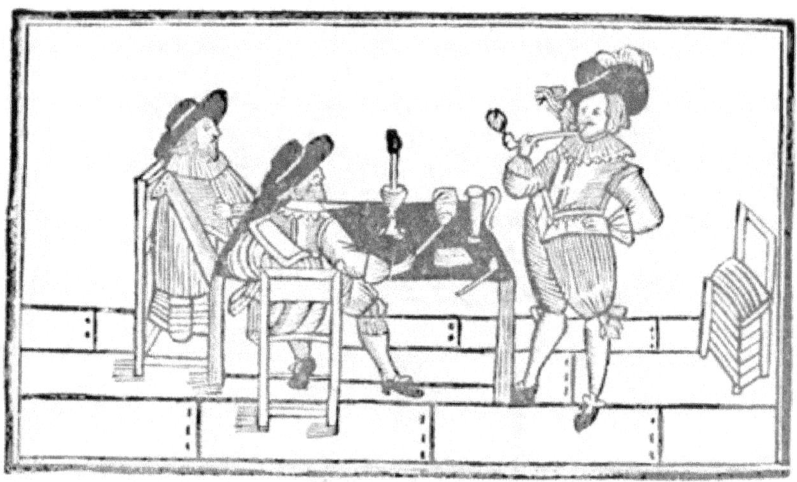

LEt's call, and drink the Cellar dry,
There's nothing sober underneath the sky,
The greatest Kingdoms in confusion lye,
Since all the world grow mad, why may not I?

My Father's dead, and I am free;
He left no children in the world but me.
The Divel drank him down with usury,
And Ile repine in liberality.

When first the *English* war began,
He was precisely a politick man,
That gain'd his state by Sequestration,
till *Oliver* began
To come with sword in hand, and put him to the run.

Then, jovial Lads, who are undone
So by the Father, come home to the Son,
Whom wine and musick now do wait upon,
he'l tipple up a tun,
And drink your woes away, jolly hearts, come on, come on.

Second Ayr. Princess Royal.

Here's a health to him that may [*i.e.* to *George Monk*.
Do a trick that shall
advance you all,
And beget a very jovial day. [*al. lect.* a merry.
Fill another bowl to hee
Who hath drank by stealth
his Landlord's health, *i.e.* the absent Charles II.
If his spirit and his tongue agree
The land shall celebrate his fame,
All the world enbalm his name,
Not a right good fellow
But will satisfie the same. [*al. lect.* Sackifie.
The bells full merrily shall ring.
All the town shall dance and sing,
More delights than I can tell ye
When we see this noble Spring,
Wee'l have Ladies by the belfry,
And a snatch at t'other thing.

The Third Ayer. Come hither, my own sweet Duck.[1]

Wee's aw be merry and jolly,
Quaff, carouse and reel;
Wee's play with *Peggy* and *Molly*,
Dance, and kiss, and feell;
Wee's put up the Bag-pipe and Organ,
And make the *Welch* Harper to play,
Till *Mauris* ap *Shon* ap *Morgan* [*al. l.* ap *Shenkin* ap.
Frisk as on St. *Taffie's* day. [misprint, Fisk.
Hold up, *Jinny*.
Piper, come play us a Spring,
All you that have musick in ye,
Tipple, dance, and sing.

[1] Page 489 holds first stanza of original (*c.* 1656); here is the second:—

I prethee leave thy scorning, which our true love beguiles,
Thy eyes are bright as morning, the sun shines in thy smiles;
Thy gesture is so prudent, thy language is so free,
That he is the best Student which can study thee.
With hey ho, my honey! my heart shall never rue, etc.

Fourth Ayer. French Tricatees.

Let de *French Mounseiur* come and swear,
 Begar, Mounseiur!
Dis is de ting vee long to hear
 So many a year,
Dancing vill be lookt upon,
Now de man of Yron is gone, [*i.e.* Old *Noll.*
Me glad his dancing day be done.
When de flower de luces grows
With de *Enlish* Crown and Rose,
Dat's very good as we suppose,
De *French* can live without de nose. [*Morbo gallica.*

Fifth Ayr. French Tricatees.

Spain and *England* then,
 like men,
Shall love and make a League agen,
Holland Boors shall quaff,
 end laugh,
Poor *Irish* swim in *Usquebaugh*,
James and *Jinnikin* = *Jenkin.*
touch the *Minnikin*,
Drink till all the sky look blew;
 by this sweet change
Wonders shall ensue,
 almost as strange
As *Scotland to be true.*

Sixth Ayr. A new Country-dance.

No Drayman shall with his dul feet [u]prear,
 Lord in the Common-weal;
Or Jesuite in the Pulpit appear,
 Under a Cloak of zeal:
Musician[s] never be noted
 For wandring men of ease, [*i.e.* cited as vagabonds.
But they shall be finely coated,
 And permitted to sing what they please.
If all things do but hit well, as
 Who knows but so't may be,
Though now you be very jealous,
 Then you'l laugh and be merry as we.

[In Black-letter. Roxburghe and Huth, no imprint. Three woodcuts: one on p. 490; the second, a man, on p. 163: the third, a woman, on p. 166. Date, the eve of the Restoration, early in May, 1660.]

[Roxburghe Collection, IV. 31; Pepys, IV. 77; C. 22. e. 82.]

The Bad-Husband's Folly;

Or,

Poverty made known.

A Man may waste and spend away his store,
But if misery comes he has no help therefore;
This man, that brought himself into decay,
Shews other Good Fellows that they go not astray.

To the Tune of, *Come hither, my own Sweet Duck.* [See p. 489.]

TO all Good-Fellows now I mean to sing a Song,
I have wrought my own decay, and have done myself great wrong;
In following the Ale-house I have spent away my store,
Bad Company did me undo, but I'le do so no more.

That man that haunts the Ale-house, and likewise the Drunken Crew,
Is in danger to dye a Beggar without any more ado;
Would I might be an Example to all Good-Fellows sure;
Bad Company [*did me undo, but I'le do so no more*].

I had a fair Estate of Land, was worth forty pounds a year,
I sold and mortgaged all that, and spent it in strong Beer;
My wife and friends could not rule me, until I did wax poor:
Bad Company [*did me undo, but I'le do so no more*].

I came unto my Hostis[s], and called for Liquor apace,
She saw my money was plenty, and she smiled in my face;
If I said "Fill a Flaggon!" they set two upon the score,
Bad Company [*did me undoe, but I'le do so no more*].

I ranted night and day, and I let my Money flye,
While my wife was almost dead with grief, to hear her children cry;
For they were almost starv'd and pin'd, they wanted food so sore:
Bad Company [*did me undo, but I'le do so no more*].

At two a clock i' th' morn I would come Drunken home,
And if my wife spoke but a word, I'd kick her about the room;
And domineer and swear, and call her [foul names a sc]ore,
Bad Company [*did me undo, but I'le do so no more*].

Then I fell sick upon the same, and lay three months and more,
But never an Ale-wife in the Town would come within my door;
But my poor wife was my best friend, and stuck to me therefore:
Bad Company [*did me undo, but I'le do so more*].

My wife she sold her Petticoat, and pawn'd her Wedding-Ring,
To relieve me in my misery, in any kind of thing;
O was not I a woful man, to waste and spend my store,
And let my wife and children want at home, but I'le do so no more.

When I began to mend a little, I walkt to take the air,
And as I went along the Town I came by my Hostise's door;
I askt her for to trust me two-pence, she denyed me [and swore]:
The Money that I have spent with her! but I'le do so no more.

As soon as I get strength agen I'le fall to work apace,
To maintain my wife and children, for my Hostises are base:
I see who is a man's best friend, if he be sick or poor,
Bad Company [*did me undo, but I'le do so no more*].

And when I do get money agen, I'le learn for to be wise,
And not believe the Drunken Crew, that filled my ears with lyes;
And carry it home unto my wife, and of my Children take more care;
Bad Company [*did me undo, but I'le do so no more*].

He runs a very long Race that never turns again, [*Cf.* 481.
And brings himself unto disgrace, and poverty for his pain;
But now I will be careful sure, and forgo the Ale-house door;
Bad Company [*did me undo, but I'le do so no more*].

Now to conclude and make an end what I have put in Rhime,
That all Good-fellows they may see to amend their lives in time;
And learn for to be Thrifty, to save something by in store:
Bad Company [*did me undo, but I'le do so no more*].

Printed for *J. Deacon* at *Angel* in *Guilt-spur-street* without *Newgate*.

[In Black-letter. One woodcut, as on p. 475. Date *circâ* 1680. We have taken the liberty of making two small alterations of the text which we generally reproduce in its integrity. Line 23 is "call her b—h and w—;" and line 35 was "denyed me the more." We substitute another cut on p. 493.]

Newes from Hyde-Park.

"You have known better days, dear? So have I—
And worse too, for they brought no such bud-mouth
As yours to lisp 'You wish you knew me!' Well,
Wise men, 'tis said, have sometimes wished the same."
—*Robt. Browning.*

EVERY sensible person must feel contempt for such weak-kneed hypocrites and prurient prudes as those who raise an outcry if by chance they surreptitiously catch sight of this really harmless ballad. Cattle of that sort are easily shocked. They have so keen a scent for impropriety that they have been heard to denounce "The Vicar of Wakefield" because of a seduction in it; and they refuse to go up the Thames beyond Twickenham, or to visit the Peak of Derbyshire, because there are objectionable names of localities in the neighbourhood. They are for ever finding bodkins at the World's-end, and other inopportune places, like Mrs. Foresight in Congreve's "Love for Love," or losing them, like Mrs. Frail; so it is whispered. Wolves-in-sheep's-clothing, "Thomas Maitland" and Co., may denounce the "Hyde-Park Frollic!"

The fact is, the Roxburghe-Ballad of "Newes from Hyde-Park," is all "square fun." Its mirthful warning against the gaudy "Peacocks" who are dangerous whited-sepulchres is quite as potent as any Puritan sermon, and couched in decent language. The baffled Gallant may behave better in the country than he threatens. It is all idle talk. He will again escape out of mischief, and discreetly enter into the torpedoed harbourage of matrimony (poor fellow!); perhaps as happily as Jerry Hawthorn in Pierce Egan's book, "The Finish," after Bob Logic had painfully died on a sick-bed, Corinthian Kate swallowed poison, and Corinthian Tom broken his neck at a steeple-chase. Wild oats that have to be sown are an ill-favoured crop, we admit, but worse if they are scattered late in life, when the corrupt harvest is more abundant. Our gallant nearly burnt his fingers, but we have it on good authority, that he "left sack, and lived cleanly, as a nobleman should do." In the reign of the Merry Monarch were a few naughty damsels, beside cakes and ale. "The pity of it, Iago! the pity of it!"

The tune took its name of "The Crost Couple" from the title of a ballad beginning "I'le tell you a tale no stranger than true" (Roxb. Coll., II. 94, reprinted in these *Roxburghe Ballads*, vol. iii. p. 648). Other names were adopted from the present ballad, one being *Hide Park*, and another from the burden, *Tantara rara tantivee.* Music is given in *Pills to Purge Melancholy*, iv. 138, and in Mr. Chappell's *Popular Music of the Olden Time*, p. 326. It was "a New Northern Tune, much in fashion;" compare *Sir Eglamour* and *The Friar in the Well*, as similar tunes, *Ibid.*, 274, 276.

[Roxburghe Collection, II. 379; Pepys, III. 257; Wood's, E. 25, fol. 92; Euing, 250; Douce II. 166, III. 67; Jersey, II. 220; Ouvry, I. 47.]

News from Hide-Park;

Or,

A very merry Passage which hapned betwixt a North-Country Gentleman and a very Gaudy Gallant Lady of Pleasure, whom he took up in the Parke, and conducted her (in her own Coach) home to her Lodgings, and what chanced there, if you'll venter Attention the Song will declare.

To the Tune of, *The Crost Couple.* [See 495, and vol. iii. p. 648.]

ONe evening, a little before it was dark,
 Sing *Tantara rara tan-tivee,*
I call'd for my Gelding and rid to *Hide*-Parke,
 On tantara rara tan-tivee.
It was in the merry month of *May,*
When meadows and fields were gaudy and gay,
And flowers apparrell'd as bright as the day,
 I got upon my tan-tivee.

The Park shone brighter than the skyes,
 Sing *Tantara rara tan-tivee,*
With jewels and gold and Ladies' eyes,
 That sparkled and cry'd, "Come, see me!"

Of all parts of *England*, *Hide*-Park hath the name
For coaches and horses, and persons of fame;
It look'd, at first sight, like a field full of flame,
Which made me ride up tan-tivee.

There hath not been seen such a sight since *Adam's*,
For perriwig, ribbon, and feather.
Hide-Park may be term'd the market of Madams,
Or Lady-Fair, chuse you whether;
Their gowns were a yard too long for their legs,
They shew'd like the Rainbow cut into rags,
A Garden of flowers, or a Navy of flags,
When they all did mingle together.

Among all these Ladies I singled out one,
To prattle of Love and Folly;
I found her not coy, but jovial as *Joan*,
Or *Betty*, or *Margret*, or *Molly*;
With honours and Love, and stories of chances
My spirits did move, and my blood she advances,
With twenty quonundrums and fifty-five fancies, [q. Conundrums?]
I'd [soon] have been at her, tan-tivee.

We talk't away time until it grew dark,
The place did begin to grow privee;
For Gallants began to draw out of the Park,
Till their Horses did gallop, *Tan-tivee*:
But finding my courage a little to come,
I sent my Bay-Gelding away by my Groom,
And proffer'd my service to wait on her home,
In her coach we went both, tan-tivee.

I offer'd and proffer'd, but found her straight-laced,
She cry'd, "I shall never believe ye;"
This arm-full of Sattin I bravely embraced,
And fain would have been at *tan-tivee*:
Her lodging was pleasant for scent and for sight,
She seem'd like an Angel by Candle-light,
And like a bold Archer I aim'd at the white,
Tan-tivee, tan-tivee, tan-tivee!

With many denials, she yielded at last,
Her Chamber being wondrous privee,
That I all the night there might have my repast,
To run at the Ring *tan-tivee.*
I put off my cloathes, and I tumbled to Bed;
She went to her Closet to dress up her head,
But I peep'd in the key-hole to see what she did,
Which put me quite beside my Tan-tivee.

She took off her head-tire, and show'd her bald pate,
  Her cunning did very much grieve me,
Thought I to myself, " If it were not so late,
  I would home to my lodgings, believe me ! "
Her hair being gone, she seem'd like a Hagg,
Her bald-pate did look like an *Estritche's* Egg,
" This Lady " (thought I) " is as right as my leg,
  She hath been too much at Tan-tivee."

The more I did peep, the more I did spy,
  Which did to amazement drive me ;
She put up her finger, and out dropt her Eye,
  I pray'd that some Power would relieve me :
But now my resolve was never to trouble her,
Or venture my carkis with such a blind hobbler,
She look'd with One Eye just like *Hewson* the Cobler,
  When he us'd to ride tan-tivee.

I peept, and was still more perplexed therewith :
  Thought I, " Tho't be Mid-night I'le leave thee ;
She fetcht a yawn, and out fell her Teeth,
  This Quean had intents to deceive me :
She drew out her handkerchief, as I suppose,
To wipe her high fore-head, and off dropt her Nose,
Which made me run quickly and put on my hose,
  " *The Devil is in my Tan-tivee !* "

She washt all the Paint from her visage, and then
  She look'd just (if you will believe me)
Like a *Lancashire Witch* of four-score and ten,
  And as [if] the Devil did drive me
I put on my cloathes and cry'd 'Witches' and w[orse],
I tumbl'd down stairs, broke open the doors,
And down to my Country again to my Boors
  Next morning I rid Tan-tivee.

You North-country Gallants that live pleasant lives,
  Let not curiosity drive ye
To leave the fresh air and your own Tenants' wives,
  For Sattin will sadly deceive you :
For my part I will no more be such a Meacock
To deal with the plumes of a *Hide-park Peacock*,
But find out a russet-coat wench and a haycock,
  And there I will ride tan-tivee.

London, Printed for *F. Coles*, *T. Vere*, and *J. Wright*.

[In Black-letter. Three woodcuts; 1st, on p. 496; 2nd, new, but similar to one on p. 89, with Venus drawn by doves in a car, above little figures; 3rd, the couple toying, as in vol. iii. p. 400. Date, soon after Restoration, 1660.]

[Roxburghe Collection, II. 196; Jersey, II. 55; Huth Coll. I. 121; Rawlinson, 149; Wood, E. 25, fol. 19.]

The Good-Fellow's Counsel:

Or, The Bad Husband's Recantation.

Proving by Arguments, both just and fit,
That he which spends least money has most wit.

To the Tune of, *Tan Tirye.* [See p. 495.]

I Had no more wit, but was trod under feet,
And all was for want of money;
I dayly did walk in the fear of a Writ,
And all [was for want of money;]
But now I'm resolved to be more wise,
And early each morning I mean for to rise,
There's none for a sluggard that shall me dispise,
When I have no want of money.

I was such a drudge, that it made me to grudge,
Because I had got no money,
On each man's occasions I forced was to trudge, ["for'st."
Because I had got no money.
But now I'm resolved I'le do so no more,
I'le drink no strong Ale upon the old score, [*Cf.* p. 486.
And then I do hope I shall never be poor,
When I have no want of money.

I was such a[n un]thrift, that I could not make shift,
And all was [for want of money.]
I was ready to hide my head in a clift,
And all [was for want of money;]
But now I'm resolved my trade for to mend,
I'le work and get money to keep and to spend,
And then I am sure my foes will me befriend,
When I have no [want of money].

I was like a Fool, that's sent unto school,
And all [was for want of money];
And every vile fellow my actions did rule,
And all [was for want of money;]
But now I'm resolved, I will mend my trade,
I'le get as good cloath[e]s, as I can get made,
And then I shall be a bonny bonny Blade,
When I have no want of money.

The Second Part, TO THE SAME TUNE.

For when I was poor and had not a store,
Of that which we use to call money,
Then all my proud Neighbours would pass by my door,
Because they knew I had no money.
I'le warrant you, they'd never ask me to go
To drink a strong pot, because they did know
My purse and my credit was grown very low,
For want of this raskally money.

Then all my acquaintance my person did slight,
And all was for want of this money,
And some with-held from me that which was my right,
Because they knew I had no money.
Let me go, let me come, there was no man would heed,
When I try'd to be trusted I never could speed,
But all my friends fail'd at the time of my need,
Because they [knew I had no money]. 18

Now, all my dear friends, be advised by me,
All you that have wanted this money,
Observe but rich people, they are not so free,
Because they do love to get money.
Though present you be, all the whilst that they dine,
You'l find them as free 'as a hungry swine,'
Then I'le not be lavish of that which is mine,
And I shall have plenty of money.

For a nig[g]ardly gallant I'le not be a slave,
That is not the way to get money;
Their cloath[e]s are so gay, they are forced to crave,
And to pinch the poor Labourer's money.
These needy young Gallants they are not for me,
Your ordinary people are always most free,
And 'tis better to work for a Farmer than he,
For then a man's sure of his money. Is he??

From a paunch-belly'd Hostiss I am to refrain,
If ever I mean to get money,
For she both my purse and my credit will stain,
In making me spend all my money.
She'l ask me to eat when she thinks I have din'd,
Or of some salt bit she will put me in mind,
That will make me to drink, and be spending my coin,
That she might be taking my money.

With a Pick-pocket longer I am not to deal,
If ever I mean to get money ;
For they have broke more than ever they'l heal,
In cheating poor men of their money.
I never will give to a counsel a Fee,
An A[t]torny shall ne'r take a penny of me,
For I with my neighbours so well will agree,
When I have got plenty of money.

All roystering blades I do mean to forsake,
If e're I intend to get money ;
They'l tempt me to wrestle and cudgels at wake,
And cause me to spend all my money.
We sing, and we dance, and we fuddle about,
And when we are in we can never get out,
Until we have given our pockets the rout,
But that's not the way to get money.

But here comes a danger, that's worse than the rest,
That will tempt a young man to spend money,
A beautiful whore when she's handsomely drest,
Will quickly consume a man's money.
But all such decoys I intend for to shun,
And honester ways I do mean for to run,
My credit shall raise in the face of the Sun,
When I have got plenty of money.

I'le buy me a house, and I'le buy me some Land,
When I have got plenty of money ;
And I will keep servants shall be at command,
When I have got [plenty of money :]
And after all this, I will get a rich Wife,
For I shall be free from care and from strife,
And I shall live richly all [th'] days of my life,
When I have got plenty of money.

Finis.

Printed for *P. Brooksby*, next the *Golden Ball* by the *Hospital-Gate* in *West-Smithfield.*

[In Black-letter. Two woodcuts, an Ale-wife with jug and spittoon (to be given hereafter), and the youth, p. 75 n. Date of issue, *circa* 1672, or earlier.]

*** See *Tantivee note*, p. 505, on "Tom Tell-Troth," to the same tune. Also for *King of Good-Fellows* note, instead of an *Introduction* to the ballad.

[Roxburghe Collection, IV. 52.]

The King of Good Fellows;

Or,

The Merry Toper's Advice.

Being a Pleasant New Song much in Request.

This is the Man whose Company once had
Will make men cheerful, though of late but sad:
He hates curmudgeons, but does court the blade,
That will spend free, for Drinking is a Trade;
By it long Nights flye swift, and seem but short,
No pastime's like unto true Tipling sport.

To a Pleasant New Tune. [See p. 505.]

I Am the King and Prince of Drunkards,
Hectoring roaring tipling Boys:
I always use to drink whole Bumpers,
And the Ale-house fill with noise.
In the Tavern I do rant and roar,
I drink more Wine then any can;
Therefore am I, both far and nigh,
Call'd a Hogshead, not a Man.

I rant and roar, and I call for more,
I practice drinking night and day:
I always boast that I drink most,
Yet never a farthing do I pay.
But if any falls asleep, to their pockets I do creep,
And out their Purses I do draw,
The Reckoning I do pay, and so go my way,
And I leave them a sighing, Ye, ho!

Some says, Drinking does disguise men,
And their wits turns out of doors:
Fools they are, and I am sure no wise men,
For they lye like sons of w . . . es.
For when a man's in drink, he speaks what he [doth] think,
He's not drunk, but frank and free.
It is not with them so [when] they'r a cup too low,
For they are disguiz'd with modesty.

The Second Part, to the same Tune.

All the night I do tipple good Wine,
   Which resists both heat and cold :
And pay devotion at *Bacchus* his shrine,
   Whilst the Hogshead it does hold.
For the meanest slave, by drinking grows brave,
   And all cares they are lay'd aside :
The Prisoner is free, if drunk he be,
   And no longer does grief abide.

'Twas I that lately drank a Pi[nt] pot,
   Fill'd with Sack unto the brim,
And to my Friend, and he drank his Pot,
   So merrily went about the Whim :
Two gaspins at a draught I pour'd down my throat, [*Al. lect.* Gallons.
   But hang such trifling things as these !
I laid me all along, put my nose unto the Bung,
   And drank out a Hogshead-full with ease.

I heard of a man that drank whole Tankards,
  Called himself "The Prince of Sots:"
Dam such idle puny Drunkards,
  Melt their tankards, break their pots.
A friend and I did joyn for a cellar full of Wine,
  And we drank the Vintner out of door,
We drunk it all up, in a morning at a sup,
  And greedily stared about for more:

With that my friend he made a motion,
  Said, "Let's not part with such dry Lips!"
And straight we went unto the Ocean,
  Where we met with a fleet of Ships;
They were laden all with Wine, and they swore 'twas superfine,
  And they said they had ten thousand Tun:
We drank it all at sea, not a drop suckt the key, [quay.
  And the Vintners swore they were undone.

For a man that can stoutly tipple
  Need not fear, the World goes well:
It will make [one] caper, though a cripple,
  And bid sorrows all farewel.
Then "t' other round!" is still the sound,
  "Come fill us more wine, boys, with speed!
We ne'er ought shall lack, whilst we hand [round] Sack,
  'Tis that which our spirits does feed."

Come bring in twenty Gallons more,
  Let us drink till the world it runs round;
And twenty to that we'l set o' th' score,
  We can but be put in the Pound. [*Absit omen!*
But catch me if they can, for I will be gone,
  And find out fresh quarters next night:
I'le drink the Town dry, and what care I?
  I'le do 't if it be but for spight.

Come, wash the glass, fill a bumper,
  Here's a health to each honest Lad:
And a confusion to each Rumper,
  Let's drink while 'tis to be had:
Whilst the Stars they look blew, and day again we view,
  For there's nothing that's sober found:
The sun sucks the Ocean, the stars in their motion
  All do carrouse it round. [*Cf.* p. 505, on Cowley.

Finis.

Printed for *J. Jordan*, at the sign of the *Angel*, in *Guiltspur-street*, without *Norgate*.

[In Black-letter. Two woodcuts; on p. 475 and p. 503. Date, *circa* 1665.]

Of this same ditty a mutilated version, entitled "Bacchus Overcome," and beginning "My friend and I, we drank whole pi. pots," is extant in J. Roberts's *Collection of Old Ballads*, 1725, vol. iii. p. 145. A different adaptation of our Roxburghe Ballad, beginning "I am the jolly Prince of Drunkards," *with the music-notes of the tune*, is in *Vocal Music*, 1775, vol. iii. p. 70, London, printed by Baker and Galabin in Cullum-street, for Robert Horsfield, No. 5, in Stationers-Court, Ludgate-street. Only four stanzas, the second begins "I've heard that a fop, who could toss a full tankard" (in *Old Ballads* this is "I heard of a Fop that drank whole Tankards"); the third commences "My friend to me did make a motion:" the fourth deserves reproduction:—

"Then we went unto the *Canaries*,
Thinking to light on a better touch;
There did we meet with the *Portugueze*,
Likewise the *Spaniards* and the *Dutch*.
'Twas in the river *Rhine*
We drank up all the wine,
Thinking to drain the ocean dry.
Bacchus swore he never found,
In the Universe all round,
Two such thirsty souls as my friend and I."

This is supplemented, finally, in the *Old Ballads*, p. 147, with another stanza:

"'Out!' cries one, 'what a Beast he makes himself;
He can neither stand nor go.'
Out! you Beast, that's a grand mistake, Sir,
When e'er knew you a Beast drink so! [*N.B.*
'Tis when we drink the least
That we drink the most like a Beast,
But when we carouse it Six in a hand,
'Tis then, and only then,
That we drink the most like Men,
When we drink till we can neither go nor stand.

We need do no more than refer to Cowley's verse-paraphrases of Anacreon, allusions to the thirstiness of the sun, and the unsteady motion of the planets. Sack says, "What are all these tipplings worth, if thou sip not me?" Ritson gave our ballad in his *English Songs*, 1783, vol. ii. 44, music in vol. iii.

⁂ *Note to* p. 501. Another ballad, Roxburghe Coll., IV. 79, to the same tune of *Tantara ra ra Tan-tivee*, is entitled "Tom Tell-Troth;" printed for *J. Wright, J. Clarke, W. Thackeray*, and *T. Passinger*; excessively silly thus begins:

"I kill'd a Man, and he was dead, *fa la la la la la*,
I kill'd a Man, and he was dead, *fa la, etc.*
I kill'd a Man, and he was dead,
And run to St. *Albans* without a head,
With a fa la, fa la la la, fa la la la la la la." [Twelve stanzas.]

Of Dr. Walter Pope's "Old Man's Wish," there are two parodies, recorded on next page, 506 (contained in *One Hundred and Eighty Loyal Songs*, 1685, pp. 235 to 238). Another is entitled "*Jack Presbyter's Wish*," already reprinted (*vide* iv. 648). "If the Whigs," etc. To a different tune is "A Young Man's Wish," beginning, "What strange affections;" and a second, in triplets, beginning:—

"If I could but attain my Wish,
I'd have each day one wholesome dish,
Of plain meat, or fowl, or fish."—*Bell's Peasantry*, p. 22.

The Old Man's Wish.

"As life itself becomes disease,
Seek the chimney-nook of ease."
—*Burns: Friar's-Carse Hermitage*, 1788.

AMONG our *Roxburghe Ballads* have already appeared several composed by Walter Pope, M.A., M.D., and an original F.R.S., whose celebrated "Old Man's Wish" adorns the next page: in 1684 it set a fashion in song-writing. His "Catholick Ballad," 1674, is in vol. i. pp. 89-93; a Continuation, supposed to be his also, was added in our vol. iv. pp. 105-109, entitled "Room for a Ballad, or a Ballad for Rome," 1674. His "Miser" and his "Salisbury Ballad" were named in the *Bagford Ballads*, pp. 647-648, 770, 1878; this "Geneva Ballad" is in *Roxb. Bds.*, iv. pp. 649-652, with its "Answer."

Walter Pope was born at Faulsey, North Hants, and became first Scholar of Wadham College, Oxford; submitting to the intolerant Parliamentary visitation, he was admitted probationary Fellow on 9th of July, 1651. In 1658 he became one of the University Proctors; avowed himself as a loyalist at the Restoration in 1660, and retained his Fellowship; became Gresham Astronomy-Professor in 1661; was made Registrar of Chester by his uterine brother John Wilkins, the bishop of that diocese, and resided often at Salisbury. His life was considered heathenish or pagan, even for that not excessively strict age. He cherished a grievance against Claude Duval the handsome Normandaise (who had an unfortunate fall from a cart, with a rope round his neck to avoid injury by reaching the ground prematurely: see our forthcoming *Cavalier Lyrics, Second Series*; one entitled "A Romance of the Road, Anno Domini 1669," being devoted to the memory of the gallant highwayman); a contemporary broadside on whom was reprinted among our *Bagford Ballads*, pp. 14-16, 1876, "Devol's Last Farewell." Duval's superior attractions had withdrawn from Dr. Walter Pope's 'protection' a certain "Miss," and the turncoat Fellow avenged himself on his successful rival by lampooning him after death, in a fictitious *Memoir of Duval*, and forging a Testamentary Letter, supposititiously addressed to the ladies who bewailed the gallant malefactor. Walter Pope had been intimate with Seth Ward, Bishop of Salisbury, and quarrelled with him for the same cause, the abduction of another "Miss," which loss he similarly avenged by lampooning his rival. Surely Pope's temper or miserliness must have told against him, since so many Light-skirts proved fickle. Still, not everybody can boast of having been twice jilted, for the sake of a bishop and a highwayman. These are his chief claims to distinction, mentioned by Anthony à Wood (in *Athenæ Oxonienses*, vol. iv. p. 725, Bliss's edition), who gives an additional verse of "The Old Man's Wish," "which went about the great city in manuscript," dispersed through London in November, 1685:

May I live far from *Tories* and *Whigs* of ill nature,
But farthest of all from a sly *Observator*;
May I ne'er live so long as to write for my bread,
And never write longer than wise men will read.

The Observator, viz., Sir Roger L'Estrange (see our vol. iv. pp. 243, 257), gave a biting reply. That Walter Pope was a time-server and turn-coat, of loose morals, and irreverent, is beyond dispute. His fourth line shows resemblance to Doll Tearsheet's fondling of Falstaff's white head in *Henry IV., Part Second*, act ii. scene 4: "Look whether the withered Elder hath not his poll clawed like a Parrot!" Walter Pope had liking for Dolls, Hits and Misses.

Music and words of "The Old Man's Wish" are found in *Pills to Purge Melancholy*, 1719, iii. 17; with two parodies, each entitled "The Old Woman's Wish," beginning, "When my hairs they grow hoary," and "If I live to be Old, which I never will own." They are not *too* moral in tone. Compare p. 505.

[Roxburghe Collection, II. 386; Pepys, IV. 370; Douce, II. 171 *verso*.]

The Old Man's Wish:

The Old Man he doth wish for Wealth in vain,
But he doth not the Treasure gain;
For if with Wishes he the same could have,
He would not mind nor think upon the Grave.

To a pleasant new Play-house Tune.

IF I live to grow old (for I find I go down),
Let this be my fate in a Country Town;
Let me have a warm house, with a stone at the gate,
And a cleanly young Girl to rub my bald pate:
May I govern my passion with an absolute sway,
And grow wiser and better, as my strength wears away,
Without gout or stone, by a gentle decay.

In a Country Town, by a murmuring brook,
The ocean at distance, on which I may look;
With a spacious plain, without hedge or stile,
And an easy pad-nagg to ride out a mile:
May I govern my passion with an absolute sway,
To grow wiser and better, as my strength wears away;
Without gout or stone, by a gentle decay.

With a pudding on *Sunday*, and stout humming liquor,
And remnants of *Latine* to puzzle the Vicar;
With a hidden reserve of *Burgundy*-wine,
To drink the King's Health as oft as I dine:
May I govern my passion with an absolute sway,
And grow wiser and better, as my strength wears away;
Without gout or stone, by a gentle decay.

With *Plutarch*, and *Horace*, and one or two more [1]
Of the best Wits that liv'd in the ages before;
With a dish of roast mutton, not venison nor teal,
And clean (tho' coarse) linnen at every meal;
May I govern my passion, etc.

And if I should have Guests, I must add to my wish,
On *Frydays* a mess of good buttered fish;
For full well I do know, and the truth I reveal,
I had better do so, than come short of a meal:
May I govern my passion, etc.

With breeches and jerkin of good country gray,
And live without working, now my strength doth decay:
With a hog's-head of Sherry, for to drink when I please,
With Friends to be merry, and to live at my ease;
May I govern my passion, etc.

Without molestation may I spend my last days,
In sweet Recreation, and sound forth the praise
Of all those that are true to the King and his Laws,
Since it be their due, they shall have my applause:
May I govern my passion, etc.

With a country Scribe for to write my last Will,
But not of the tribe that in chousing have skill:
For my easie pad-nagg I'll bequeath to *Don John*, [2]
For he's an arch wag, and a jolly old man:
May I govern my passion, etc. [3]

With courage undaunted may I face my last Day;
And when I am dead, may the better sort say,
"In the morning when sober, in the evening when mellow,
He is gone, and has left not behind him his Fellow:
For he govern'd his passion with an absolute sway,
And grew wiser and better as his strength wore away,
Without gout or stone, by a gentle decay.

[By Dr. **Walter Pope.**]

Printed by *W. O.* for *B. Deacon*, at the *Angel* in *Guilt-spur street.*

[In Black-letter. Two woodcuts, as on p. 507. Date of publication, 1684.]

---

[1] *Alter lection*, "With *Horace* and *Petrarch*," etc.

[2] Nickname, from "Don John" of Spain, concerning whom Charles II. cross-examined that atrocious perjurer Titus Oates? Compare *Loyal Songs*, 1685, p. 66.

[3] In other prints we find this penultimate stanza:—

When the days are grown short, and it freezes and snows,
May I have a Coal-fire as high as my nose;
A fire, which (once stirr'd up with a prong)
Will keep the Room temperate all the night long, *May I govern, etc.*

Mark Noble's Frolic.

Flute.—"Must I speak now?"
Quince.—"Aye, marry, must you; for you must understand he goes but to see a noise that he heard, and to come again."
—*A Midsummer Night's Dream*, iii. 1.

We have already (in *Bagford Ballads*, pp. 202-208) printed an unique version of this pleasant story, the Bagford, entitled "The Ranting Rambler," to the tune of *The Rant, Dal derra rara*, and beginning, "I pray now attend to this ditty." We also (*ibid.* p. 203) gave extracts from "The Jolly Gentleman's Frollick; or, the City Ramble," of date before 1686, beginning, "Give ear to a frolliesome ditty." Yet another version is preserved in the Pepysian Collection, V. 199, in white-letter, beginning, "Behold, what noise is this I hear!" Sung to the tune of *Logan Water* (see iii. 476), it bore title of "The Frolliesome Wager;" or, The Ranting Gallant's Ramble through the City, where being stepp'd by the Watch and Constable [he] was sent to the Counter, brought before the Mayor, whose Daughter begg'd his Pardon." Printed for *Charles Bates*, or *Jonah Deacon*. They are all on a similar foundation.

It is altogether unprecedented this five-fold telling of the same tale in a set of ballads *not* founded on a theatre-song. Or let us say four-fold, since there is little beyond general resemblance in the rare original, "A Jest, or, Master Constable" (see our p. 515), of date *circâ* 1650. Although here the point of the jest is that the Dogberry of the Watch is being perpetually worried or bantered as "Master Constable," we already find the quibble about "twenty shillings" as equivalent to a name, it being *Mark Noble*; also his play on the local title of Little-Britain. The tune and the swing of verse were then changed, with more liveliness and brevity to recommend the ditty. Of the three ballads to the dance tune of *The Rant* (="How happy could I be with either!") our unique Bagford "Ranting Rambler" appears the best; but "Mark Noble's Frollic" is little behind it. We have only a poor modern Bow Church-yard exemplar, corrupted from the editions *circâ* 1665 of "The Jolly Gentleman's Frollic." The unique Pepysian "Frollicksome Wager" adopts a different tune, dissimilar in metre. Where five authors have already laboured, none except a churl begrudges the small additional cost of catgut in celebrating the Sequel, and we give it on p. 518, as *Finale* to the Second Group of Good-Fellows.

The Rant tune is in Mr. Chappell's *Popular Music*, p. 554.

[Roxburghe Collection, II. 359; Pepys, IV. 324; Huth, II. 21; Jersey, I. 98.]

Mark Noble's Frollick;

Who being

Stopp'd by the Constable near the Tower, was examin'd where he had been; whither he was going; and his Name and Place where he dwelt: to which he answered, 'where the Constable would have been glad to have been'; and where he was going 'he dare not go for his Ears'; as likewise his Name, which he called Twenty Shillings; with an Account of what followed, and how he came off.

To the Tune of, *The New Rant.* Licensed according to Order.

ONe night, at a very late hour,
A Watch-maker home did repair;
Who, coming along by the Tower, ["When"
Was stopp'd by the Constable there.

"Friend, come before Mr. Constable,
To see what his Worship will say!"
"You'd have me do more than I'm able,
I fear I shall fall by the way." 8

"Sir, tell me, and do not deceive me,
Where have you been playing your part?"
"Kind Mr. Constable, believe me,
Where you'd have been with al[l] your Heart.

"Sweet *Bacchus* in Bumpers w[as] flowing, ['were.'
Which Liquor all mortal Men chears,
And now after all I am going,
Where you dare not come for your Ears."

"Your Words they are sawey and evil,
This may be a Charge to your Purse:
For why? you are something uncivil,
To answer a Constable thus.

"Oh, where do you dwell, with a whennion? [*i.e.* curse.
Cross Humours we will not allow."
"Sir, out of the King's own Dominion,
Pray, what can you say to me now?"

"Pray, what is your Name? you cross Villain,
Be sure that you answer me true."
"Why, Sir, it is just *Twenty Shilling*,
I think I have satisfyed you."

"What Trade are you, Brewer or Baker?
Or do you a Waterman ply?"
"No, Sir, I'm an honest Watch-maker,
My Trade I will never deny."

"Have you e'er a Watch you can show, Sir?
We'll see how it suites with our Clocks."
"Yes, Faith, and a Constable too, Sir, [*i.e.* watch-key.
I wish you were all in the Stocks." [wheels-rack.

"You Sawey impertinent Fellow,
Because you have answer'd me so,
Although your mad Brains they be mellow,
This Night to a Prison you go."

Therefore without any more dodging,
The Lanthorns were lighted streightway; [" was."
They guarded him to his strong Lodging,
To lye there while Nine the next day. [while = until.

Next Morning the Constable brought him
Before a Justice to appear,
And earnestly then he besought him,
A Sorrowful Story to hear.

[So] all the Transactions he told him, [mutilated.
To which the good Justice reply'd,
From Liberty he would withhold him,
Till the Naked Truth should be try'd.

The Tradesman returned this answer,
"The Truth I will never deny;
If I may speak without offence, Sir,
I scorn'd to be catch'd in a lye.

"I said nothing which was unfitting,
As solemnly here I profess;
The King he is King of *Great Britain*,
And I live in *Britain the less*.

"The next thing that causes the Trouble,
My Name he would have me to show,
The which is right honest *Mark-Noble*,
And that's Twenty Shillings, you know.

"Then asking me where I was going,
And I being void of all fears,
Right readily made him this Answer,
Where he dare not go for his ears.

"I rambl'd all day, yet the centre,
At night was to lye by my wife;
Instead of his ears, should he venture,
I' faith, it might cost him his life."

Now when he had given this relation,
Of all that had past in the night,
It yielded most pleasant diversion,
The Justice he laughed outright.

"It seems that a glass of Canary
Conducted the Gallant along;
I find that he's nothing but merry,
Intending no manner of wrong.

"Therefore I will free him from Prison,
Without any charges or f[ee]s,
It being no more than right [reason],
You watch not for such m[en as these]."

Printed for *B. Deacon at the Angel* in *Gilt-spur-street.*

[In Black-letter, slightly mutilated near the end. Three woodcuts: 1st, the cupola tower, a fragment of the Rupert cut, vol. v. p. 380; 2nd, the man, of this vol. p. 59; 3rd, the young man, p. 510. Date of issue before 1668.]

Henry Huth's copy was printed for *Brooksby*, *Deacon*, *Blare*, and *Back*.

[Roxburghe Collection, III. 430; Ouvry Coll., I. 70; Huth, I. 112; Pepys, IV. 336; Jersey, I. 43; Douce, I. 106 *verso*.]

The Jolly Gentleman's Frollick; or, the City Ramble.

Being an Account of a Gentleman who wager'd to pass by the Watch, and give no Answer, but was stop'd by a Constable, and sent to the Counter, and next Day clear'd before my Lord Mayor, by the Intercession of his Daughter.

TO A PLEASANT NEW TUNE OF, *The Rant, Dal dera Rara*, etc.

GIve ear to a Frolicksome Ditty, of one that a Wager would lay,
He'd pass e'ery Watch in the City, and never a word he would say,
But, *Dal dera rara, del dara*, etc. ["*Doll-ra-roll*," *passim.*

The Constable spoke to his Watch-men, "Brave Boys, it is my delight,
And orders I have, to catch men, who ramble too late in the Night,
The Humour [*of Dal dera rara*], etc.

"The streets do ecchoe, we hear, Boys, with Mad-men coming along,
My staff is ready, ne'er fear, Boys, we'll make them alter their song,
The Humour [*of Dal dera rara*]," etc.

"Stand, stand!" said the Watch-man, "the Constable now come before,
And if a just story you'll [hatch], man, I'll light you home to your own door."
The Humour [*of Dal dera rara*], etc. ["tell"

"This is a very late season, which surely no honest men keep,
And therefore it is but just reason that you in the Counter should sleep."
The Humour [*of Dal dera rara*], etc.

"Take away this same Fellow, and him to the Counter convey,
Although his Frolick is mellow, he something To-morrow will say.
The Humour [*of Dal dera rara*], etc.

"Open the gate, make no scorning, take charge of the Prisoner there,
And we will soon in the morning appear before my Lord-Mayor."
The Humour [*of Dal dera rara*], etc.

"A Bottle of Claret I'll fill, Sir, some pipes of tobacco beside,
And if that it now be your will, Sir, a Bed for you soon we'll provide."
The Humour [*of Dal dera rara*], etc.

The Frolick soon eccho'd the Prison, the Debtors his Garnish would have;
Without demanding the reason, whate'er they requir'd he gave.
The Humour [*of Dal dera rara*], etc.

The Constable soon the next day, Sir, this comical matter to clear,
The Gentleman hurries straightway, Sir, before my Lord-Mayor to appear.

"My Lord, give ear to my story, while I the truth do relate,
The Gentleman who stands before ye, was seiz'd by me at *Cripplegate*.
The Humour [*of Dal dera rara*], etc.

"I nothing could hear but his singing; wherefore in the Counter he lay,
And therefore this morning I bring him, to hear what y'r Lordship would say."

"Come, Friend, the case does appear now, that you was in a mad fit;
I hope that you may be clear now, since sleep has restored your wit."
The Humour [*of Dal dera rara*], etc.

"This Gentleman sure is distracted, he has over-heated his brain ;
Since he in this manner has acted, to the Counter I'll send him again.
The Humour [of Dal dera rara], etc.

"A Prison sure it will tame him, and bring him soon to his sense ;
There's nothing else can reclaim him, from this his notorious offence."

O then bespoke my Lord's Daughter, and thus for him did intercede :
"Dear Father, you'll hear that hereafter this was but a Wager indeed.
The Humour [of Dal dera rara], etc.

"Therefore be pleased, kind Father, to hear one word more of me,
And show to me so much favour, this Gentleman may be set free."

"Well, Daughter, I grant the petition, the Gentleman home may repair ;
But then 'tis upon this condition, of paying my Officers there.

"Come, Sir, your Fees we require, you now are freed by the Court,
And all that we do desire, you'll find out some other new sport."

Thus seeing he might be released, if he his Fees did but pay ;
He then was very well pleased, and so he went singing away.
'*The Humour [of Dal dera rara]*,' etc.

Printed in *Bow-Church-Yard, London*, where may be had all sorts of Old and New Ballads.

[In white-letter, with one rude woodcut, not worth copying, of a man holding a quarter-staff or oar, a tree behind him on one side, a house on the other. The late J. P. Collier's copy, afterwards the late Frederick Ouvry's, and now the Earl Crawford's, is a much earlier edition. It was printed for *Charles Bates*, at the Sun and Bible, in Guilt-spur Street, before 1685. The Huth exemplar for *Bates*, at White Hart in West Smithfield. Douce's for J. Cluer and J. Cobb.]

*** The *Bagford Ballads* version (pp. 202-208 of our 1877 reprint) ends more gallantly, although it gives not in detail the speeches of the Lord-Mayor and his daughter, the youth with courtly grace recognizing the service of the lady :—

To pay which the Gallant was ready, yet never a Word did he say,
But made a Bow to the Young Lady, and then he went singing away,
The Kant, dal derra rara, etc.

There is no wife in this version. Of course not. The wife was not *in posse*, only *in esse*. We know all about it and have already told the sequel of the story, condensed in prose narrative in our *Bagford Ballads*, p. 204, whereunto Ballad-Society members can return, and much good may it do them.

We give on p. 518 additional verses, hitherto unprinted, from the unique MS. preserved in the Muniment chest at Nirgends College (where are gathered uncatalogued treasures, most of the waifs and strays that have been vainly sought for centuries, and which form a sort of spectral library, absolutely priceless and occasionally undecipherable, for perusal of which "No Irish need apply").

On p. 515 we for the first time reprint, from the Roxburghe Collection (III. 208), what appears to be the original version of the whole series, "A Jest ; or, Master Constable." It is of no literary merit, all the charm of the narrative being reserved for "Mark Noble's Frollick" and "The Ranting Rambler." It is long-winded in the extreme, the ballad-writer's Pegasus being a steed, like *Pyramus*, "as true as truest horse that yet would never tire,"—except the unhappy outside spectators and auditory. No other copy is known, both "A Jest" (*circâ* 1650) and "The Ranting Rambler" (date certainly *before* 1668) being unique.

[Roxburghe Collection, III. 208.]

A Jest; or, Master Constable.

To the Tune of, *The Three Pilgrims.*[1]

A Pretty Jest I shall declare, which I not long agoe did hear,
Of one who did intend to jeere, *Master Constable.*

I hope there's none wil matter make Of that that I intend to speake,
Of a busy man who the place did take, *Of a Constable.*

For I hope each wise man wiser is Than to think he is touch'd in this,
For thinking so, he thinks amiss, *'Twas a busy Constable.*

For this is but a merry Jest, Which will, I hope, no man molest,
For I no grudge beare, I protest, *To any Constable.*

Then pray you let this poor man pass, for he for money sings, alas!
Let none then show himselfe an asse, *Like this Constable.*

He, as his Office did direct, to set his watch was circumspect,
And nothing therein did neglect, *Like a Constable.*

Also when any passed by, he did examine them strictly,
Observing with discretion's eye; *A wise Constable.*

At length it chanc'd that one came neer, And he demanded "Who goes there?"
"You know not," (said he, without fear) "*Master Constable.*"

"Come hither, that I may you see, and now what are you? show to me."
"No Man nor Woman," replyed he, "*Master Constable.*"

"Where have you been?" then asked he, "That you thus crossly answer me:
Know you not the authority *Of a Constable?*"

"Yes, I know your authority, and I have been for certainty
Where you would have been glad to be, *Master Constable!*"

Then said the Constable, "Some end will come hereof, but say, my friend,
Whither to goe doe you intend?" "*Why, Master Constable*:

---

[1] Any ballad of *The Three Pilgrims* we have not yet found, but the tune agrees with that of "The Essex Ballad," beginning "In *Essex* long renown'd for Calves" (*Bagford Ballads*, p. 752), and is probably the same tune early known as *With a fading*; next as *A Pudding*, but in Revolutionary times revived as *An Orange.*

"I am going thither where —— you dare not goe for your right eare."
"What, you are set upon the jeere!" *said the Constable.*

"What is your name? pray tell me that, who dare so boldly to me prate,
Be briefe, and truth to me relate," *said the Constable.*

"Twenty shillings I am nam'd, I thereof need not be asham'd,
Although by you I may be blam'd, *Master Constable.*"

"Sir, that hereafter we shall see. But in the meantime tell to me
Where your dwelling place may be," *Quoth the Constable.*

"Out of the King's dominion, I doe dwell," said he, "assuredly,
As my Neighbours can testifie, *Master Constable.*

"But in the King's dominion you are now, my friend, and you shall rue
That still cross-language you renew *To a Constable.*"

"I am at your dispose," said he, "But pray you hear this word from me,
You shew your selfe herein to be *A wise Constable!*"

To prison then incontinent the Constable this good man sent,
Although the same he did repent, *Like a Constable.*

Before a Justice, the next day, the Constable bore him away,
And to his Worship thus did say, *like a Constable:*

"Sir, in my Watch the last night I this fellow tooke, who saucily
Jeer'd me and my authority," *said the Constable.*

Then quoth the Justice, "What said he, that might to you distasteful be?
And I'le between you judge fairly, *Master Constable.*"

"First 'who goes there?' was ask'd by me; 'you cannot tell,' replyed he:
And thus he did begin crossly," *said the Constable.*

"'Come before my authority, and now what are you, tell to me:'
'No Man nor Woman,' replyed he," *said the Constable.*

"'Where have you been, then?' I enquir'd, 'Where you to be would have desir'd.'
Thus I againe by him was jeer'd," *said the Constable.*

"'Whither goe you?' then said I, and he still crossly did reply,
Where for my ears I durst not be," *said the Constable.*

"'What is your name, Sir, tell to me:' 'Twenty shillings,' replyed he,
['Deem you] these answers fit to be *give[n to] a Constable!*'

"I askt his dwelling place also, and he this answer did bestow,
'Out of the King's dominion know,'" *Quoth the Constable.*

"But when he saw I'de him convey to prison untill the next day,
'You are,' quoth he, 'I needs must say, *A wise Constable!*'

"You my complaint have heard," said he, "Now pray you judge 'twixt him and me,
That I may satisfied be, *being a Constable.*"

Then said the Justice, "Was not he in drink that he thus answer'd thee?
If so, that might the reason be, *Master Constable!*"

"No, to your Worship I doe vow, he was as sober as we are now;
And therefore doe no favour show," *said the Constable.*

Then said the Justice, "What say you. Is this that he alledges true?
If? how durst you such carriage shew *Toward a Constable?*"

"Sir, I speake truth, first he ask'd 'Who goes there?' I said he did not know,
If he had he would let me goe, *Like a Constable.*

"And I am a Taylor by my Trade, 'who are no men' by your proverb made;
Nor am I a Woman, I'le perswade *Master Constable.*

"Then next he asked of me where I had been? which was at good cheer,
And you'd as gladly have been there, *Master Constable.*

"And I was going, thus I said, where you durst not go for your head;
For it was with my wife to bed, *Master Constable.*

"And, Sir, *Marke Noble* is my name, and in your ears I dare proclaime
That twenty shilling is the same, *Master Constable.*

"The King of Great *Brittain* is King, as fame throughout the world doth ring,
But in little *Brittain* is my dwelling, *Master Constable.*

"And I pray your worship further, here, If I in any thing did erre,
It was that I did him prefer *For a wise Constable.*

"And Sir, he ought [to] give me content, both for my wrong imprisonment,
And loss of time with money spent *Through the Constable.*"

Then said the Justice, "Good Sir, heare! this man makes all his words appear
To be the truth, and not a feere, *Master Constable.* [*i.e.* tricksy sprite.

"And you have been too much to blame, to take away thus his good name,
And 'tis fit you pay [him] for the same, *Master Constable.*

"You said that he was not in drinke, and therefore come lay down your chink,
It is in vaine backward to shrink, *Master Constable.*

"To pay his charges I you enjoyne, and a French crown for loss of time,
And friendly drink a pint of Wine: *So farwell, Constable.*"

Which done, the man went merrily home, his wife rejoyc'd to see him come,
Where he to her told the whole summ, *of the Constable.*

Thus of this Constable I end, desiring favour of each Friend,
For what in mirth by me is pen'd *of this Constable.*

But if there's any fault doth find, such men they have a guilty mind,
Or too too busy are inclin'd, *Like this Constable.*

Finis.

London, Printed for *Francis Grove* on *Snow-hill*. Entered according to Order.

[In Black-letter. Four woodcuts, of which the first is a black-hatted Cavalier in cloak, trunk-hose, and riding boots; second the man with staff as on p. 329; third, on p. 515, but without Watchman's dog; fourth, here. Date, *circâ* 1650.]

Finale to Second Group of Good-Fellows.

How the Frollic Ended.

Being a Sequel to the Bagford Ballad called "The Ranting Rambler," and to the same Tune of the Rant, dal derra rara.

(See p. 503.)

YOU have heard of the frollicsome Wager
Our young 'Ranting Rambler' did win:
When he saw the fair maid, to engage her
Affection he fain would begin,
With a Rant, dal derra rara, etc. [*Repeat*, passim.

If he talk'd of a Wife, it was fibbing;
No wife, trade, or business had he:
He loved wagers and mirth, not wine-bibbing,
His heart was still open and free.

Altho' lock'd up for jesting and singing,
Where rogues may atone sin or crime,
No discomfort could daunt him from springing
Brisk as lark in the next morning's prime.

The Lord Mayor's only daughter that morning
Thought well of this handsome young spark;
She who look'd on all tipplers with scorning,
And roysters who brawl in the dark.

"*It were pity so handsome a fellow*
By revels imperill'd his health!
He once on a turn has been mellow:—
Ah me! I have youth and I've wealth.

"*His ruffles lack neat-handed mending,*
I'm sure that he has not a wife;
There's no pleasure in ranting or spending,
He is wasting good looks and good life."

He had seen she was fair, sweet, and modest,
Her blue eyes shone brightly he knew;
Their first meeting had been of the oddest,
Better chances next time might ensue.

So they each stray'd across Temple-gardens,
(Fortune favours young Lovers like these,)
They met without tutors or wardens,
To talk or touch hands at their ease.

Did she blush when she saw him, and smile too?
Did he stammer, feel somewhat ashamed?
"*She thinks I was foolish, and vile too!*"
But she frown'd not, she never once blamed.

She turn'd not aside with aversion,
But found courage to give him hope soon :
They took boat on the Thames *for diversion,*
And came back by the light of the moon.

With Scriveners' and Usurers' charges
His estate had been burthen'd full sore ;
Since she sighs for his past, he enlarges
On his love, now his folly's no more.

Let him win back his Home, she will share it !
Such a wife would yield heavenly bliss !
Her father may threaten. . . . To dare it
He needeth no bribe save her kiss.

Was it wrong that she kept on believing
The words of so gallant a youth ?
In such fervour could be no deceiving :
His eyes—and his lips—told of truth !

How it ended needs no tame narration,
Her father she coax'd to be kind ;
Content with his daughter's new station,
Wish'd them joy, tho' he growl'd "Love is blind!"

He bought-up all Mark's *debts and mortgages ;*
He punished the sharpers and cheats,
In the pillory dealt them just wages,
Cart-tail'd them well-whipt, in the streets.

It is said that from Trade he retired,
The wealthiest Mayor of his day,
So soon as he thrice was grand-sired,
And sang to her babes in their play,
The Rant, dal derra rara, etc.

"Old Rowley" *himself once invited*
The Bride and her Rambler to Court ;
But they still kept aloof, more delighted
With safe rural virtues and sport.

Should you pass near their mansion in Surrey,
You will find I have told you no lie ;
None leaves it in dudgeon or hurry,
But would gladly stop there till he die.
The Rant, dal derra rara, etc.

J. W. EBSWORTH.

November 2, 1887.

End of the Groups of Good-Fellows.

Additional Note on 'God speed the Plough.'

*** Our next ensuing ballad, "God Speed the Plough," has been reprinted by Mr. John Payne Collier in his *Book of Roxburghe Ballads*, 1847, p. 312. Modern variations occur in the Suffolk version, J. H. Dixon's *Ancient Poems and Songs of the Peasantry*, printed for the Percy Society, 1846, p. 42, and the Rev. Mr. Broadwood's *Old English Songs as now sung by the Peasantry of the Weald of Surrey and Sussex*, 1843. The earliest known dated copy is one beginning "Well met, my friend, upon the high-way walking on," in *The Loyal Garland*, 1686 edition (reprint, for Percy Society, No. lxxxix. 1850, p. 66), but it is probable that it had appeared long before, this being the fifth edition. Whether the Plough song appeared in early copies of 1665 is not certain. There are many differences in the versions. The woodcut, on p. 523, with its quaintly introduced labels, like pennons, had been seen in Civil-War tracts of 1641. The very old tune, "*I am the Duke of Norfolk*," was mentioned in vol. iv. p. 355.

For two other songs, "The Painful Plough," beginning, "Come all you jolly Plough-men, of courage stout and bold;" and "The Useful Plough," beginning "A Country life is sweet, in moderate cold and heat, To walk in the air;" also "The Farmer's Song," beginning "Sweet *Nelly*, my heart's delight," see James Henry Dixon's *Ancient Poems, Ballads and Songs of the Peasantry of England*, 1846, Percy Society, No. lxii. vol. xvii. pp. 167 to 173.

The Woodcut here given belongs to "True Blue the Plough-Man," of our pp. 532–534; apparently introduced into that ballad because of its reference to Millers and Windmills. For a similar reason the other woodcut of the same ballad, viz., "*Tom Taylor* and his wife *Joan*," serves the purpose, for the sixth stanza, but originally belonged to "*Tom* the *Taylor* near the *Strand*," Roxburghe Collection, II. 263; IV. 27.

[See p. 534.]

God Speed the Plough.

"Let not Ambition mock their useful toil,
Their homely joys and destiny obscure;
Nor Grandeur hear, with a disdainful smile,
The short and simple annals of the poor."
—Gray's *Elegy in a Country Churchyard.*

THE title of this ballad was chosen to secure popular acceptance. The early condition of our agricultural labourers in England has scarcely been examined with the attention and impartiality it may deserve. Even now, when politicians, as well as local democrats, are working as agitators to secure their own ends, we are nationally indifferent to the welfare of a large decreasing class of ill-educated workers, hitherto industrious, patient, and simple-minded, who have been indispensable to the welfare of our country in times past; who have only recently begun to think for themselves on the great social problems, and coöperate for attainment of what they believe to be their just rights; but whose future, unless they resort to Emigration, is one of the most inscrutable of mysteries, such as no Parliamentary sphynx can answer, "staring right on, with calm eternal eyes."

In regard to physical comfort, perhaps also in social morality and individual intelligence, the improvement among our ploughmen is indisputable. Despite the increasing difficulties met by our farmers, exposed to the ruinous competition of foreign producers, in grain and cattle, the hired labourers of the present race secure a better habitation, more abundant and wholesome food, with unbroken rest, than what rewarded the toil of their forefathers: that is, so long as children come not too fast, and sickness does not break down the bread-winner, the two evils destroying independence. Records are far from ample, but such as are attainable seem to indicate that "the hewers of wood and drawers of water," the lower orders of countrymen in days of old, had a hard lot to bear. The changeful seasons regulate labour with succession of variety, like the crops produced, so that no monotony of toil is felt long enough to be unbearably wearisome. Yet the mechanical routine from day to day superinduces a certain amount of deadness or dullness in the mind, which enables the ploughman to endure without a murmur such hours of little altered employment as might appear slavery to the more irritable and insubordinate town-dweller. Like the horses that he guides, the sheep that he tends, the very poultry and cattle that he feeds, his pleasures are centred in the due acceptance of food and drink and slumber, with that half-recognized sense of freedom and robustness which help to balance the discomforts of inclement wind and weather. "The rest of the labouring man is sweet." His enjoyments are few, but are keenly welcomed.

His children are happier, their mother is more easily contented, and he himself is less fearful of the future, than are those persons whose lives are devoted to commerce and manufactures. If it be difficult to awaken him to higher thoughts than his mill-horse round of daily routine, he at least enjoys the freedom from imaginary cares, or far-reaching speculations.

There is a great gulf, of more than three centuries, between the ploughman, as described in the Vision of William Langley, about 1377, and the following ballad. But, as we know, it was only as a mask of disguise that "Piers the Ploughman's" character was assumed. Chaucer's Canterbury Pilgrim is a safer portrait for our guidance, and the honest simplicity of that weather-beaten conscript-father, whose toilsome lot was cheerfully borne, cannot fail to touch the heart of all who are not spoilt by luxury and selfishness. Chaucer (to whom is attributed wrongly "The Plowman's Tale") makes him own-brother of the poor parson of a town:—

With hym ther was a Plowman that was his brother,
That hadde ylad of donge ful many a fother,
A trewe swynkere and a good was he,
Lyuynge in pees and parfit charitee.
God loued he best with al hese hoole herte,
At alle tymes thogh he gamed or smerte,
And thanne his nyghe-bour rigt as hym selue.
He wolde thresshe and þerto dyke and delue,
For Cristis sake for euery pore wight,
With-outyn hyre, gif it laye in his mygt.
His tythes payde he ful faire and wel,
Bothe of his propre swynk and his catel.
In a Tabbard he rood vpon a mere.

—*Cf. Ellesmere* MS., 529—541.

Following our Roxburghe Ballad, as text, our notes or marginalia show variations of *The Loyal Garland.* To adapt any poem for popular acceptance in the broadside-ballad-form, more was necessary than adding a few incongruous or appropriate woodcuts. Theatre-songs were too short, and book-poems too long, to suit the penny market. Moreover, some spicery might be required for the mild lentils; while over-proof liquors were watered down to the bar-standard of easy tipple. There being no real newspapers, and the modern novel newly at its birth, our street ballads were the people's library; the travelling Chapman was the priest of their secular literature—the Orpheus who moved stocks and stones with music. As Wordsworth sang,

"An Orpheus! an Orpheus! he works on the crowd,
He sways them with harmony merry and loud,
He fills with his power all their hearts to the brim—
Was aught ever heard like his fiddle and him?

For an *Additional Note* on the ballad, see p. 520.

[Roxburghe Collection, II. 188; Pepys, IV. 272; Euing, 127.]

God speed the Plow, and bless the Corn-Mow.

A Dialogue between the Husband-man and Serving-man.

The Serving-man, the Plow-man would invite
To leave his calling, and to take delight;
But to that by no means [he] will agree,
Lest he thereby should come to beggary.
He makes it plain appear a country life
Doth far excell; and so they end the strife.

The Tune is, *I am the Duke of Norfolk.* [See vol. iv. p. 355.]

J.W.E.

My noble Friends, give ear, if mirth you love to hear,
I'l tell you as fast as I can,
A story very true, then mark what doth ensue,
Concerning of a Husband-man.

Serving-Man.

A Serving-man did meet a Husband-man in the street,
And thus unto him he began:
"I pray you tell to me of what Calling you be;
Or if you be a Serving-man."

Husband-man.

Quoth he, "My brother dear, the coast I mean to clear,
And the truth you shall understand.
I do no one disdain, but this I tell you plain,
I am an honest Husband-man."

Serving-Man.

" If a Husband-man you be, then come along with me,
I'le help you as soon as I can,
Unto a gallant place, where in a little space,
You shall be a Serving-man."

Husband-Man.

" Sir, for your diligence, I give you many thanks,"
Then answered the Plowman again,
" I pray you to me show, whereby that I might know,
What pleasures hath a Serving-man."

Serving-Man.

" A Serving-man hath pleasure, which passeth time and measure,
When the Hauk on his fist doth stand,
His hood and his verril's brave, and other things we have,
Which yeelds joy to a Serving-man."

Husband-Man.

" My pleasure's more than that, to see my Oxen fat,
And to prosper well under my hand.
And therefore I do mean, with my horse and team,
To keep my self a Husband-man."

Serving-Man.

" O 'tis a gallant thing, in the prime time of the Spring,
To hear the hunts-men now and then.
His Beaugle for to blow and the hounds run all a row, [bugle.
This is pleasure for a Serving-man :

"To hear the Beagle cry, and to see the Faulcon fly,
And the hare trip over the plain,
And the hunts-men and the hound, makes hill and dale resound,
This is pleasure for a Serving-man." ["rebound."

Husband-Man.

" 'Tis pleasure you know to see the Corn to grow,
And to grow so well on the land ;
The plowing and the sowing, the reaping and the mowing,
Yeelds pleasure to the Husband-man."

Serving-Man.

" At our table you may eat all sorts of dainty meat ;
Pig, cony, goose, capon, and swan ;
And with lords and ladies fine, you may drink beer, ale, and wine,
This is pleasure for a Serving-man."

Husband-Man.

" While you eat goose and capon, I'le feed on beefe and bacon,
And piece of hard cheese now and then ;
We pudding have, and souse,[1] always ready in the house,
Which contents the honest Husband-man."

Serving-Man.

" At the Court you may have your garments fine and brave,
And Cloak with gold lace layd upon,
A shirt as white as milk, and wrought with finest silk,
That's pleasure for a Serving-man."

Husband-Man.

" Such proud and costly gear is not for us to wear,
Amongst the bryers and brambles many on[e ;]
A good strong russet Coat, and at your need a groat,
Will suffice the Husband-man.

" A Proverb hear I tell, which likes my humour well, [q. hear?
And remember it well I can ;
If a Courtier be to[o] bold, he'l want when he is old,
Then farewel the Serving-man."

Serving-Man

" It needs must be confest that your Calling is the best, ;
No longer discourse with you I can,
But henceforth I will pray by night and by day,
Heavens bless the honest Husband-man."

Finis.

["Finis."]

[Publisher's name cut off. Euing copy, printed for *W. Gilbertson*, at the sign of the *Bible*, in *Gilt-spur-street*. One woodcut, on p. 523. Date, *circâ* 1665]

[1] Souse is meat (pork chiefly) laid in brine-pickle, ready for boiling.

The Ploughman's Art of Wooing, and The Milk-Maid's Resolution.

HITHERTO we have heard the Ploughman's praise, chanted by himself without any pretence of modest diffidence. We now give two ballads to the favourite tune of *Cupid's Trappan*. (See *Popular Music*, pp. 555-557 for the notes of this tune, with mention of the various names it bore, chiefly, from the original, "*Cupid's Trappan* ; or, *Up the Green Forest*," beginning, "Once did I love a bonny, bonny Bird," found in Euing Collection, 35 ; Pepys, III. 107 ; and Douce, I. 39 *verso*.) It was originally described as A New Northern Tune. First, comes the Damsel's complaint, "Once did I love." Second, "The Young-man put to his Shifts." Third, the Ploughman proclaims his irresistible attraction, as a conqueror of hearts. Fourth, the Milk-maid indignantly rebukes his boastfulness. Second and fourth begin similarly, but come from different publishers. They are all four sung to the same tune. We delay "A Young Man put to his Shifts ; or, The Ranting Young Man's Resolution," which begins "Of late did I hear a young damsel complain" (see *Note* on p. 528).

[Roxburghe Collection, II. 260; Huth, II. 54; Jersey, III. 85.]

The Plowman's Art in Wooing.

The brisk young Plowman doth believe
  If he were put to tryal,
There's not a maid in all the Shire
  Could give him the denyal.

Tune of, *Cupid's Trappan.* [See p. 528.]

I AM a young man that do follow the Plow,
  But of late I have found out an art,
And can when I please with abundance of ease
Deprive any maid of her heart, brave boys,
    Deprive [any maid of her heart].

To think how they'l yield, as I walk in the field,
Mythinks is se pleasant to me,
I long to be nigh her who'l burn like a fire,
If she but my favour doth see, brave boys!
    If she [but my favour doth see].

Such wenches, I think, must be certainly mad,
Whose hearts are betray'd with a smile,
But they quickly find such a change in my mind,
That will them of all pleasure beguile, brave [boys!
    That [will them of all pleasure beguile].

[It] will make them look pale, like maidens so stale, ['And'
That for a good Husband doth long,
And this unto me such pleasure will be,
That I shall thereof make a song, brave [boys!
    That [I shall thereof make a song].

For who can delight in a thing that is fond? [*i.e.* foolish.
'Tis a thing that I never could do;
My passion is gone when she doates upon *John*,
Then another Girl I must go wooe, brave [boys!
    That [another girl I must wooe].

And in a month's space, it will be her case,
If she can be easily wonn,
To mourn and bewail beneath the *Milk-pale*, [*pail*,
And to cry she's forsook and undone, brave [boys!
    And to cry [she's forsook and undone].

I could ne'r understand there's a man in the land
Could delight in what's easily gain'd,
But if it be so, that Love they long show,
Then their passion must surely be feign'd, brave [boys!
Then [their passion must surely be feign'd].

Then give me the wench that has so much sence
When a Youngster doth come upon tryal,
Will so cunningly deal that his heart she may steal,
And seemingly give the denyall, brave [boys!
And [seemingly give the denyal].

She surely will find young men be more kind,
If she be but strange and untoward;
For men like the fire do burn with desire,
If they meet with a maid that is froward, brave [boys!
If [they meet with a maid that is froward].

But it is the fashion throughout all the nation,
And chiefly in Country Townes,
Men maidens beguile who are won with a smile,
And then they'r destroy'd with their frowns, brave [boys!
And [then they're destroy'd with their frowns].

And it may be said, there's not a Milk-maid,
Although she be never so fair,
But if once I begin, her heart I would win,
And by my fair words would betray her, brave [boys!
And by [my fair words would betray her].

It is a rare thing to hear the Girls sing
"Oh! my love hath forsaken me quite,
And for his dear sake, my heart it doth ake,
I languish by day and by night, brave boys:
I languish [by day and by night]."

As I follow the Plow, my thinks I see how
They look pale, and their lips they do tremble;
'Cause they were mistaken, and are forsaken,
By youngsters that much did dissemble, brave [boys!
By youngsters [that much did dissemble.]

I will have t'other bout, and without any doubt
I'le compass the thing I desire;
For I cannot well pass, if I meet with a Lass,
Till her heart it be set on a fire, brave [boys!
Till her [heart it be set on a fire].

There's *Margret* and *Jone* who still lye all alone,
But I'le venture to lay twenty shilling,
If a motion I make to cure their heart ake,
To lye with me both will be willing, brave [boys!
  To lye [*with me both will be willing*].

There's *Susan* and *Kate* that long for to ha't,
And are vigorous in their desire,
But before they are mad, let some lusty young lad
Make haste and extinguish their fire, brave [boys!
  Make [*haste and extinguish their fire*].

Printed for *P. Brooksby*, at the *Golden Ball* in *West-Smith-field.*

[In Black-letter. Two woodcuts, *viz.* the Prince Rupert of p. 246, and the Spotted Girl, in oval, of p. 40, Left. Date, *circâ* 1672.]

*** The tune of *Cupid's Trappan*, mentioned on our pp. 526 and 529, was known also as *I've left the world as the world found me*, and *The Twitcher*, or properly *The Maid's Twitcher*, with its first line, "*A Damsel I'm told*," of late date, *circâ* 1751. Four of its earlier names were borrowed from a single ballad in Pepys Coll., Douce, III. 107, and Euing. 35, *viz. Cupid's Trappan*, or, The Scorner Scorn'd; or, The Willow turn'd into Carnation;" this was then "A New Northern tune now all in fashion." From its first line of first verse, of second verse, and the burden, it was entitled *Bonny, bonny Bird; Up the green Forest;* and *Brave Boys.* (See Chappell's *Popular Music of the Olden Time*, pp. 555-557; music given from *Flora*, ballad-opera.) The original tune begins:

Once did I love a *bonny bonny Bird*,
  And thought he had been my own;
But he loved another far better than me,
  And has taken his flight, and is flown, *Brave Boys!*
  And has taken his flight and is flown.

Up the Green Forest, and down the green Forest,
  Like one much distressed in mind,
I whoop'd and I whoop'd, and I flung up my Hood,
  But my Bonny Bird I could not find, *Brave Boys!*
  But my Bonny Bird I could not find. Etc.

It is barely possible that the reserved ballad "A Young Man put to his Shifts," beginning "Of late did I hear a young Damsel Complain" (Roxburghe Coll., ii. 548—see *Appendix*), may, as Mr. Chappell believed, have preceded those of the Plowman and Milk-maid, our pp. 526 and 529. But these two were certainly in sequence: the other held less connection with "Once did I love," than did "The Batchelor's Forecast; or, *Cupid* Unblest," printed by P. L. for R. Burton, and beginning "Once did I love and a very pretty girl." This was the true "*Answer to Cupid's Trappan*, or *Up the Green Forrest*," as it claims to be:—

Of late did I hear a young damsel complain,
  And rail much against a young man;
His cause and his state I'le now vindicate,
  And hold battle with *Cupid's* trappan, brave boys,
  And hold battle with Cupid's *trappan.* Etc. (*Cf.* p. 525.)

[Roxburghe Collection, II. 347; Jersey, III. 78.]

The Milkmaid's Resolution.

Let young men prate of what they please,
Cause young men have been kind,
They'l find no more such Fooles as these
To please each apish mind.

TUNE, *Cupid's Trappan.* [See p. 528.]

OF late I did hear a young man domineer,
And vapour of what he could do;
But I think he knew how for to manage the Plow,
Far better than maidens to woo, brave boys!
Far better [than maidens to woo].

And he surely doth think that we maidens are mad,
For to mind ev'ry clown we do see;
Should his love be exprest with a vow and protest,
I'de believe no such boobies as he, brave [boys!
I'de [believe no such boobies as he].

Though his bottles of Ale, and other fine things,
He bestows on me ev'ry day,
It is my intent, when his money is spent,
To bid him begone and away, brave boys!
To bid [him be gone and away].

I'le give him good words while his money doth last,
And tell him I dearly do love him;
When his cash is all gone, I'le tell him, my man *John*,
There's others I fancy above him, brave [boys!
There's others, I fancy above him.]

And that which is worse, when once they do find
A maiden's poor heart it is won,
They'l laugh and they'l jeer, they'l giggle and sneer,
That they this poor maid hath undone, brave [boys!
That [they this poor maid have undone].

Some men they [make] love for what they can get,
And 'tis certain there's many a Lubbard;
Will sigh and will pant, seeming ready to faint,
And all for the love of the cubbard, brave boys!
And all [for the love of the Cup-board].

And others, so long as they think a poor maid
Has been careful and saved some money,
This maiden will find he will prove very kind,
And call her his joy and his honey, brave boys!
And [call her his joy and his honey].

Yea, if this poor soul will be such a foole
To hearken to this fellow's tale,
Shee'l to poverty fall, he'l beguile her of all
She hath got by the merry milk-pail, brave boys!
[She hath got by the merry milk-pail].

And she that doth carry the merry milk-pail,
And delights for to milk the brown Cow,
May sure be as good, be it well understood,
As the Looby that follows the Plow, brave [boys!
As the [Looby that follows the Plow].

Yet each pittiful clown will boast up and down
Of the maidens that he hath betray'd;
If all were like me, such things should not be,
Nor ever hereafter be said, brave boys!
Nor [ever hereafter be said].

Keep but at a distance, and then they will be,
Like men quite bereaved of sence;
Then the best of them all into passion will fall,
And be ready to dye for a wench, brave boys!
And [be ready to dye for a Wench].

Tho' some of them now, do say they know how
To make any maiden to yield,
But I would defie any man that should try
In the midst of the merry Broom field, brave [boys!
In [the midst of the merry Broom-field].

For my modesty shall defend me from all
That say 'tis so easy to win
The poor virgin's fort, of which they make sport,
And delight in this treacherous sin, brave boys!
And [delight in this treacherous sin].

Then maidens beware, of such villains take care,
Whose delight is your absolute ruine;
If they conquer with ease, and gain what they please,
They'l soon be a-weary of wooing, brave boys,
[They'll soon be a-weary of wooing].

But if you stand off, and at them do scoff,
You'l find they will burn like a fire,
When you make them to bow, let your reason know how
To grant them the thing they desire, brave [boys,
To grant [them the thing they desire].

Then take my advice, you maids that are wise, ['free'
I'le assure you I speak not in jest,
Ne'r play with the dart till you poyson your heart,
For a single life it is the best, brave [boys!
For [a single life it is the best].

There's some that are married before they had wit,
That with sorrows are sorely opprest,
Then think it not strange, I am not for a change,
For a single life it is the best, brave boys.
For [a single life it is the best].

Printed for *P. Brooksby* at the *Golden-Ball*.

[In Black-letter. Two woodcuts, *both reserved:* 1st, a Young Cavalier, with love-locks and plumed hat; full-length of Milk-maid in flowered gown, with milk-pail on her head (it belongs also to the "Deptford Frolic," *Cf.* our vol. iv. p. 31). Date, *circâ* 1665.]

True-Blue, the Ploughman.

"True-Blue will never stain."—*Old Ballad truism.*

BALLADS on a succession of Trades and Callings were always popular of old. They afforded the sort of Saturnalia that bestows more than customary license; even when the Lord of Misrule held his Court at Yule, or when a mock Tilt was held within the lists, and the Hobby-Horse riders plunged and reared their "fiery and untamed steeds"; flapping meanwhile at everybody in turn with bladders full of peas, a saucy weapon at the end of a Fool's bauble. There were many, no doubt, who felt equally afflicting the smart and sting of a festive singer in the market-place; with such a strain as "True Blue, the Ploughman," for example, they were compelled to repress publicly their indignant anger. To 'grin and bear it' was the only safe response.

The tune is named *The Country Farmer*, from a *Roxburghe Ballad*, reprinted in vol. iii. p. 363, followed by a Sequel, p. 366, and second Sequel in vol. iv. on p. 17. Tune in *Popular Music*, p. 562. Begins, "There was a brisk Lass."

Thomas Pearson's bookbinders committed manifold offences in shearing off lines from broadsides, to force the future *Roxburghe Ballads* within their type-ornament environment. They robbed us of lines 33, 34 of "*True-Blue* the Ploughman;" also its colophon with *Philip Brooksby's* name. Thanks to our knowledge of an unmutilated duplicate, and the unfailing courtesy of the Earl of Crawford, our reprint is correct.

[Roxburghe Collection, II. 471; Jersey, II. 26.]

True Blew the Plowman;

Or,

A character of several callings which he could not freely fancy, when he found their grand Deceit.

He never yet would change his Note,
He'd rather be a slave,
Nay, wear a poor and thread-bare Coat,
Than be counted as a Knave.

To the Tune of, *The Country Farmer* [See p. 531].

This may be Printed R[ichard] P[ocock].

NOw Trading is dead, I resolve to contrive,
And study some calling in order to thrive,
But I will be just in whatever I do,
My name I must tell you is honest *True Blew*:
Though Fortune does oftentimes smile on a Knave,
By their unjust dealings they do get and save,
But honest *Plain-dealing* does live like a slave,
While Ranting brave *Hectors* goes gallant and brave.

At first I considered what Trade I might be,
To live with *Plain-Dealing* without Knavery,
I would be a Brewer at first I did think,
And then to be sure I shall never want drink:
But straightways I thought of the Brewers' old fault
Who put in the *Water* and left out the *Mault*;
If I should do so, and make pittiful Beer,
I should have the curse of the *Tinkers* I fear.

As I was a walking along very sad,
I met a fine Hostess that wanted a Lad,
Her words were so winning, I could do no less,
But go along with her to tend on the Guests.
She said, "When you wait on a jolly boon crew,
Each Pot as you draw, then be sure you score two,"
I told her "False-dealing now never would do,"
'Twas better be "ragged and torn and true." [1]

[1] These words recall the burden and title of an excellent ballad by Martin Parker, reprinted in vol. ii. p. 409, beginning, "I am a poor man, God knows."

" If this be your dealings I never will stay,"
Thought I then, " I'le pack up my awls and away,"
I finding by this how the current did run,
Poor men by those Ale-wives are often undone:
No wonder it is now that they are so great,
To flourish in Silks at so gallant a rate,
'Tis folly that makes men to sell their Estate,
While Ale-wives can flourish and drink in their plate.

[Then home to my Father I went again,
And of my hard fortune I did complain.][1]
He told me no trouble nor cost he'd spare,
Of me he would take a particular care:
I would have a calling without all deceit,
But with such a one, I as yet could not meet;
My Father was willing my joys to compleat,
And now of a *Taylor* I mean for to treat.

I went upon liking a *Taylor* to be,
And now I will tell you a passage I see,
One brought [to] my Master some cloath for a cloak, ['in.'
And he at his cabbaging had a good stroak:
For taking his Sheers he whipt off an ell, ['Shiers.'
And straight he condemn'd it, and sent it to Hell,[2]
Down under his shop-board, which when I did see,
Thought I then " I'le ne'r be Prentice to thee."

A lusty brave *Miller* came up to the Town,
And I as a Prentice with him must go down,
Thought I, " With an honest man now I am blest,"
But soon I did find him as bad as the rest:
For if you'l believe me, I think in my soul,
He had a great Dish was as big as a bowl,
And there was old taking and taking of Toul,[3]
Thus he would be fishing against all controul.

Beside he was counted a slippery blade,
And fain would be toying with every Maid;
There was a young Lass, and her name it was *Kate*,
With whom he would fain have bin playing the mate:
One day as she came with her grist to the mill,
My master the *Miller* was tempting her still,
The maiden with courage catch'd hold of his ham,
And tumbled him headlong into the Mill-dam.

---

[1] Two lines lost, fifth stanza: we recover them from Earl Crawford. *Cf.* p. 531.
[2] No profanity: he indicates the *receptacle under the shop-board* wherein odd pieces of cloth accumulate for future use. 'Hell' is always full, of cabbage.
[3] Taking toll like Chaucer's Miller of Trumpington. '*Old*' = continuous.

It hap'ned to be the lower-side of the Mill, [down-stream.
But yet he lay crying and calling out still;
I could not tell well what the matter might be,
And therefore to him I did run hastily.
But when in the River I did him find,
Thought I, in my heart, "Thou art serv'd in thy kind,"
And thus by the maiden the *Miller* was fool'd,
For then in the river his courage was cool'd.

Thought I, "I will ne'r be a slave to this elf,
For fear he should make me as bad as himself,
With some honest Farmer I'le get me a place, [*v. infra.*
Where I may live happy, and free from disgrace."
And thus I did leave the old *Miller*, I'le vow,
Then taking my self to the *Harrow* and *Plow*,
'Tis free from deceiving, all men will allow,
I labour and live by the sweat of my brow.

[Printed for *P. Brooksby.* Two woodcuts: one below, the other on p. 520: see *Note* there. Date, as licensed by R.P., 1685-88.]

, Alas! for this conscientious inspector of moral nuisances. If he took service, likely enough, with the 'Rich Farmer' whose 'Ruine' is chronicled in the next ballad (Rox. Coll., II. 396), the scrupulous lad would find that calling exposed to temptation like the tailor's and miller's. Another ballad is "A Warning to all Corn-Hoarders," the fate of Inglebred, a miserly farmer, "Good people all."

[Roxburghe Collection, II. 396; Huth, II. 66; Douce, II. 186 *verso*; Euing, 398.]

The Rich Farmer's Ruine;

Who murmured at the Plenty of the Seasons, because he could not sell Corn so dear as his covetous heart desired.

To the Tune of, *Why are my Eyes still flowing*, As it is play'd on the Violin.

[See p. 536 for *Note*.] This may be printed **R**[**ichard**] **P**[**ocock**].

A Wealthy man, a Farmer, who had of Corn great store,
Yet he was cruel always to the poor;
And as the truth of him does very well appear,
He thought he ne[ve]r sold his Corn too dear;
As to the Market one day he did go,
Finding the prices of corn to be low, [orig. Prizes.
Said he, "Before I will sell ought of mine,
I'le carry it home for to fatten my Swine.

"In former days, as I can make it well appear,
By my own Farm I got a hundred a year;
I sold for ten the corn that will not now fetch five,
Is this the way for a Farmer to thrive?
Yet I will now sell no more at this price,
But am resolved to stay for a Rise."
Thus he resolved to hoard up his store,
That he might then make a prey of the poor.

Another Farmer likewise then was standing by,
Who, when he heard him, he thus did reply;
"You have a Farm, and likewise Land, which is your own,
What cause have you then to make this sad moan?
I that have nothing but what I do Rent,
With years of plenty, rejoyce in content:
Give Him the praise who such plenty does send,
Lest when you murmur you highly offend."

Said the Miser, "What tho' I have got house and land?
Yet I would have you now well understand,
I am not free to see the wasting of it all,
And after that into poverty fall:
Have we not reason, alas! to complain,
To see the Cheapness of all sorts of Grain?
If it continue, as sure as the Sun,
I shall be ruin'd and clearly undone."

"Aye! but neighbour, pray tell me wherefore do you grieve?
Does not a plenty the poor men relieve?
Here do I find, had you your will in selling Grain,
Then might the poor soon have cause to complain:
For you are cruel, most harsh and severe,
And think you can never sell it too dear."
"Why," says the other, "what's poor men to me?
I'le keep my corn till one peck will fetch three."

Then home he went, and bitterly he did repine,
And in his substance he soon did decline;
For he was soon as poor as any man alive,
For after this he by no means could thrive;
As he was walking one day round his ground,
His House was robb'd of five hundred pound;
Yet this was but the beginning of woe,
For in two years he was brought very low.

His Corn did waste, and many of his Cattle dy'd,
Also great losses and crosses beside;
Both house and land through perfect need at length he sold,
Nothing but Ruine he then could behold:
Tho' all was blasted and clearly decay'd,
Yet none would pitty him, but thus they said:
"Seeing the poor he did thus circumvent,
This is no more than a just Punishment."

Like one forlorn and desolate, he then did roam,
Having no dyet, apparel, or Home,
But his poor life he ended, lodging in a barn;
From whence all covetous Farmers may learn
How to give thanks for a Plentiful Year,
And not to murmur that Corn is not dear:
For those that shall do it most highly offend:
Think of this *Farmer's* Unprosperous End.

Finis.

Printed for *I. Back*, at the *Black Boy* on *London-Bridge*, near the *Draw Bridge*.

[In Black-letter. Two woodcuts: 1st, resembling the Shepherd on p. 166, Left; but with cottages, and no crook at the end of his staff; 2nd, a group of figures, men, women, children, on the ground. Date, 1685-88.]

The tune of "The Rich Farmer's Ruine" is named from a ballad beginning "Why are my eyes still flowing?" reprinted in *Bagford Ballads*, p. 89, 1877.

A Group of

Legendary and Romantic Ballads

From the Roxburghe Collection.

EDITED AND ANNOTATED

BY

JOSEPH WOODFALL EBSWORTH, M.A., F.S.A.

"To them was Life a simple art
  Of duties to be done,
A game where each man took his part,
  A race where all must run;
A battle whose great scheme and scope
  They little cared to know,
Content, as men-at-arms, to cope
  Each with his fronting foe.

"Man now his virtue's diadem
  Puts on, and proudly wears—
Great thoughts, great feelings, came to them
  Like instincts, unawares:
Blending their souls' sublimest needs
  With tasks of every day,
They went about their gravest deeds
  As noble boys at play."
—*R. M. Milnes*, [illegible]

HERTFORD:

Printed for the Ballad Society,

BY STEPHEN AUSTIN AND SONS.

1888.

THIS GROUP OF

Legendary and Romantic Ballads,

(Several not hitherto Reprinted.)

IS DEDICATED

TO A TRUE FRIEND, STUDENT OF HISTORY AND LOVER OF BALLAD LITERATURE,

J. H. L. DE VAYNES,

OF UPDOWN, THANET,

EDITOR OF 'THE KENTISH GARLAND,' 1881–2:

With thanks from Fellow-Members of the Ballad Society.

1888.

Y Friend, *whose thirst for Ballad-lore*
Has been approved this many a year,
Accept from me one Tribute more,
You, who my 'Lyrics' *hail'd of yore:*
Tribute no less sincere.

They were of modern growth, to fade,
Like wild-flowers the hot hand soon kills:
Pluck'd haply where few feet had stray'd,
'Mid moss-boled trees in woodland glade,
Water'd by tinkling rills.

Whatever charm of freshen'd hue
Or graceful shape they hoped to bear,
They gain from praise bestow'd by you:
Loyal to Church and Crown, and true
To those who Oak-leaves wear.

But now I bring no Songs of mine,
Save this, to greet your willing eye:
From Bards of a far earlier line
These ballad-histories I entwine:
You will not cast them by.

Legends and Love-tales fanciful,
That cheer'd the ingle nooks of old;
When wintry skies were grey and dull,
And ghostly memories would pull
The trailing garment's fold.

Stories that oft drew smile or tear,
To harm no listening maid or youth;
Of warnings breath'd by mystic Seer,
Slain lovers borne on rustic bier,
Or scorn that turn'd to ruth.

When Barons' halls were gay with song
Of Minstrels plying harp and voice,
Men gladly heard—nor deem'd too long—
These tales of crush'd oppressors'-wrong,
That made their hearts rejoice.

For wholesome faith in HIM *Who rules*
Guided the teaching of their day ;
They had not learnt in hopeless schools
The doctrine of our knaves and fools,
Who neither love nor pray :

They welcomed sunshine on their path,
They bravely faced the chilliest blast ;
Staunch upright men, whom England *hath*
Found prompt to curb th' Invaders' wrath,
In many a peril past.

We, also, in our later times,
Unconquer'd yet by gloom or cold,
Find pleasure in these ancient rhymes ;
Such as give joy in other climes :
More loved because they're old,

Where e'er our Empire fronts her fate :
Whether beyond the Atlantic *wave,*
Or where that loyal burst of late
Spoke Australasia's *heart elate,*
Ready and firm and brave ;

Wherever English speech may sound,
Even though our little Isle be dumb,
There, doubt not, in the Earth's wide round,
These Ballads old shall long be found :
Welcome to them must come.

So let me link with them your name,
For sweeter then may seem their strains ;
They wear no vulgar smirch of shame,
Though rough and crude : sufficient fame
If prized by thee, De Vaynes.

J. WOODFALL EBSWORTH.

16, xi. 1887.

A Group of

Legendary and Romantic Ballads.

The Greeks' and Trojans' Wars.

"As one that for a weary space has lain
Lull'd by the song of *Circe* and her wine
In gardens near the pale of *Proserpine*,
Where that Ææan isle forgets the main,
And only the low lutes of love complain,
And only shadows of wan lovers pine,
As such an one were glad to know the brine
Salt on his lips, and the large air again,—
So gladly, from the songs of modern speech
Men turn, and see the stars, and feel the free
Shrill wind beyond the close of heavy flowers,
And through the music of the languid hours,
They hear like ocean on a western beach
The surge and thunder of the Odyssey."

—*Andrew Lang.*

F THE ENSUING BALLAD, AS OF SOME others in this Group, "*Legendary and Romantic*," the rarity is great: we know only three exemplars, the Roxburghe, the Douce, and the Rawlinson. It appears to have never hitherto been reprinted, and therefore it is the more fitting to open our Group, with its striking chief woodcut, originally from some untraced book. The cut fell into the hands of Thomas Symcocke, and perished in the Great Fire of 1666.

It is unnecessary and inexpedient, in our limited space, to enter fully into the subject of the Ten Years' War and Siege of Troy; on which also are several other consecutive ballads, celebrating the "Wandering Prince of Troy," the so-called "Pious Æneas," Dido Queen of Carthage's fickle lover; with separate Praise of Penelope, the lady of the web, whose cupboard-lovers found *un mauvais quart d'heure*, when the husband Odysseus returned home unexpectedly to his Ionian isle; as Lambro the sea-solicitor did to his daughter Haydee on her island of the Cyclades. The lovers of the Hellespont have two ballads devoted to their woes, their meetings and their hapless fate. These are the only Grecian legends in our Group, which holds the "Roman Wife," but is otherwise confined to early and apocryphal British history or more modern romance.

To Humphrey Crouch, author of this ballad (probably the father of John Crouch, an almost contemporary elegiac poet, who survived to write in May, 1681), we are indebted for several other ballads, already reprinted from the Roxburghe Collection (Vol. I. 158; I. 264; and II. 362), *viz.* 'The Industrious Smith,'="There was a poor Smith," *circâ* 1635 (*Roxb. Ballads*, i. pp. 469-471); and 'The Mad-Man's Morrice'="Heard you not lately of a man" (*Ibid.*, ii. pp. 154-158), which is also in *Merry Drollery*, 1661, i. 169, and *Merry Drollery Compleat*, 1670 and 1694, p. 178. On a subsequent page of the present volume we reprint his ballad of "Hero and Leander," beginning "How fares my fair *Leander?*" (Roxb. Coll., III. 150 and 478), and a fragment of his prose account of "Guy, Earl of Warwick," 1655 (*Ibid.*, III. 218), accompanying the ballad on that warrior, 159½ (*Ibid.*, III. 50 and 708). That Crouch was popular among the prentices and humbler citizens (if any citizens could be considered humble during the contentious intolerance of Civil-War times when our Humphrey flourished) is certified by the great sale of his cheap writings, many a time re-issued. He had a certain rough and ready manner, suited for Chap-book literature, in which his *Love's Court of Conscience*, 1637, *The Distressed Welshman, Welch Traveller, Tom Tram, England's Jests Refined* were esteemed 'hugely.' He is believed to have been 'the moderniser of *The History of Tom Thumb*,' according to W. C. Hazlitt, who reprinted the original *Tom Thumbe, His Life and Death*, 1630, in John Russell Smith's Library of Old Authors, the second vol. of *Remains of the Early Popular Poetry of England*, p. 175 (as Joseph Ritson had done in his *Pieces of Ancient Popular Poetry*, 1791, pp. 93-113); and added, on pp. 192-250, *The History of Tom Thumb*, in three parts, the extended version attributed to Humphrey Crouch. To him is also assigned, on credit simply of initials (which might as well refer to Hugh Crompton, whose portrait is in *Pierides*, 1658), "An Elegie sacred to the Memory of Sir Edmundbury Godfrey," 1678: unlikely to be his.

The tune of Crouch's "Greeks and Trojan Wars" is marked as *The Conscionable Caveat.* We have met with no ballad of this name: the one entitled "A Conscionable Couple," beginning "This doth make the world to wonder" (reprinted in *Roxb. Ballads*, vol. iii. p. 561, from Roxb. Coll., II. 66), is in different metre, and to the tune of *The Faithful Friend.* But we venture to assert our belief, that the missing "Conscionable Caveat" ballad began with the line "Young man, remember delights are but vain;" the same tune being used for his "Industrious Smith," already mentioned above as reprinted, ii. 469

The ensuing ballad is on the subject of Achilles and his faulty relations with Deidamia. (Compare *Note* on p. 541.)

[Roxburghe Collection, III. 158; Rawlinson, 181; Douce, III. 27 *verso.*]

The Greeks' and Trojans' Wars.

Cursed by that wanton Knight, Sir *Paris*,
Who ravishes *Hellen* and her to *Troy* carries;
The *Greeks* in revenge (and to fetch her again)
A mighty great army do quickly ordain:
Imagine you see them besieging old *Troy*,
Which after ten years they at th' last destroy.

Tune is, *A Conscionable Caviat* [*sic*, see p. 542].

OF *Greece* and *Troy* I shall you tell,
What cruel wars betwixt them fell,
Paris he was Author of the same,
For plundering of the *Grecian* Dame,
He ravish'd her and he brought her unto *Troy*:
this you know,
But that short measure of fond pleasure
Caus'd great *Ilium's* overthrow.

For when the *Grecians* heard the same,
Their hearts with ire began to flame,
They counsel took and did decree
To raise an Army speedily,
To fetch that piece, fair *Hellen* of *Greece*,
back again,
Or else the gallant *Grecians* valiant
By the *Trojans* must be slain.

Achilles he was in disguise,
When first he heard of this enterprize,
He Lady-like with a Lady lay,[1]
Until her [passion] did them both bewray:
"Away, fond Lass, for I from hence must pass
unto *Troy*!"
But her note still is, "Dear *Achilles*,
Stay with me, my only Joy!

"Wilt thou be gone and leave me so,
Unto the *Trojans'* wars to go?
If thou with me wilt stay behind,
Here thou shalt entertainment finde."
"Fond fool, avoid, for I must be imploy'd,
out of hand;
For the inraged *Greeks* ingaged
All march under my command."

"My dear *Achilles*," then said she,
"Alas! what shall become of me?
My heart thy love 't hath set on fire,
I gave to thee what thou didst desire."

---

[1] Deidamia was the lady in question. Thetis, to keep her own son Achilles from going to Troy, where she foresaw he would be slain, had concealed him disguised in feminine attire among the women at the court of Lycomedes. He debauched Deidamia, and the fruit of this dishonourable imprudence was her disgrace and the birth of Pyrrhus, who became king of Epirus. Homer avoids this scandal. (See Pausanias, and John Gay's Opera of *Achilles*, 1733.)

"'Vaunt, foolish girle! bright honour is the pearl
I must seek:
Wanton courting, idle sporting,
Fits not now a valiant *Greek.*"

"Thou knowest, sweet-heart, I am with child,
Thy flattering tongue hath me beguil'd;
Why then from me wilt thou depart,
And leave my breast without a heart?"
"Cease complement, for now my mind is bent
other waies;
Such injoyment is imployment,
Fit for idle peaceful daies.

The Second Part, TO THE SAME TUNE.

"*Ulisses* would seem mad 'cause he
Would stay with his *Penelope;*
But no illusions must take place,
Though millions dye for one fair face,[1]
It shall be seen their *Lacedemon's* Queen,
whom that Boy
Violated, shall be rated
At the price of *Greece* or *Troy.*"

"If Sir," saith she, "one face hath force
To raise so many foot and horse,
Why may not mine, prais'd oft by you,
Have power to keep what is my due?"
"Plead not thy face, there's difference in the case,
very great:
Our monar'chal light were dark all
Should we wink at this defeat."

[1] Compare the Clown's mocking song, on Helen of Greece, in *All's Well that Ends Well*, Act i. sc. 3:—

"Was this fair face the cause, quoth she,
Why the *Grecians* sacked *Troy!*
Fond done, done fond! [*bis*]
Was this king *Priam's* joy?

"With that she sighed as she stood [*bis*]
And gave this sentence then;
Among nine bad if one be good [*bis*]
There's yet one good in ten."

See also scene fourteen of Marlow's *Dr. Faustus*, before 1593:—

"Was this the face that launch'd a thousand ships
And burnt the topless towers of *Ilium?*
Sweet *Helen*, make me immortal with a kiss!
Her lips suck forth my soul," etc. [*Compare Note*, p. 556.]

Let noble *Britains* notice take
Of this allusion which I'le make;
Imagine all the power of *Greece*,
To fetch great *Agamemnon's* Niece,
Are sacking *Troy*, which they at last destroy
utterly;
They will fetch her, from her Letcher,
By all this extremity.

Ireland is our *Hellen* fair,
Ravish'd from us through want of care
The *Paris* that hath done this rape
Is fond security (that ape!)
As now you hear, *Achilles* with his Dear
Will not stay;
If *Mars* summon, no fond woman
Can a Souldier's soul betray.

So let brave *English* Souldiers seek
For president that gallant *Greek*: [i.e. precedent.
Let's leave our toies, which slaves retard,
And to our honour have regard:
Ireland doth shake our honour at the stake,
lies ingaged.
'Tis our *Hellen*, stoln by villain:
Fall on him like *Greeks* inraged.

Let all home-bred strife alone,
And as the *Greeks* all joyn'd in one
Their loss and honour to repair,
Let their example be our care,
And never leave, until that we receive
for our pains
Death or honour: when w' have won her,
We shall find sufficient gains.

Finis. **H[umfrey] C[rouch].**

London, Printed for *F. Grove.*

[In Black-letter. Four woodcuts: 1st, the armed warrior of p. 566; 2nd, the Lady of p. 171, R.; 3rd is on p. 513. Date, *circâ* 1640.]

The Rawlinson copy was Printed for *F. Coles, T[homas] Ve* [*sic*, for *Vere*, *John*] *Wright*, and *J. Clarke*. Douce, Book III. 27 *verso*, has *London*, but n.p.n., "New Tune," and the title of this modern copy runs "An excellent new Ballad of fair *Hellen* of *Greece*, and *Paris*, Prince of *Troy*," etc. Date, *c.* 1641.]

*** Our final three or four stanzas form political landmarks in Charles I.'s reign. Crouch perverted his theme, in order to secure attention by referring to that always-discontented Ireland, alike the Jonah and the evil-genius of Britain.

The Wandering Prince of Troy, or Queen Dido.

"When *Dido* found that *Æneas* would not come,
She mourn'd in silence, and was *di do* dum."
—*Porson: Facetiæ cantat.*

BY both these names was the ballad popularly known, "Æneas, the wandering Prince of Troy" (as in the seventh line), and "Queen Dido;" while *Troy Town* was an additional title for the tune. Although we find entered in the Stationers' Registers, on 8th June, 1603, our 'ballade,' to Edward Aldee, "The Wandringe Prince of Troy," Book C., fol. 96 verso (*Transcript*, iii. p. 236), there is no earlier copy known to be extant than John Wright's, *circâ* 1620, and a later one of *Clarke, Thackeray*, and *Passinger*, after the Restoration of 1660 (Pepys Coll., I. 84 and 48).

Probably this ballad-tune is the same as that of "*Diana and her Darlings dear*" (a ballad already reprinted in vol. ii. p. 520: *vide post* and index). The music is given in Mr. Wm. Chappell's *Popular Music*, p. 372, with the whole of our ballad, quotations from *The Penniless Parliament of thread-bare Poets*, 1608; from James Fletcher's *The Captain*, act iii. 3, and *Bonduca*, i. 2; with Sir Robert Howard's *Poems and Essays*, 1673. Also an incomplete list of ballads sung to the tune, including *The Roxburghe Ballads*, "When God had taken for our sins," and "You that have lost your former joys" (respectively reprinted in vol. i. p. 288, "The Duchess of Suffolk's Calamity," and ii. 454, "The Spanish Tragedy" of 'haplesse Hieronimo,' the subject of Kyd's drama). We print two other ballads to the same tune, "A Looking-Glass for Ladies," *Penelope* (on p. 553), and "Lord *Wigmore*," *post*.

In the Additional MS. No. 27,879, page 515 (=iii. 502 of 1868, *i.e.* the *Bishop Percy's Folio Manuscript*), is a print of "Queene Dido," agreeing with that on our pages. We cannot claim poetic grace or pathos for the ballad. But it was a favourite with the populace in the 17th, 18th and 19th centuries. It had 'a story.'

Most of the ballads in this "Legendary and Romantic Group" have a fullness of incident, in contrast to the commonplace sentiment and emotionalism characterising the ordinary ephemeral broadsides—at least, those which are not coarse and broad in humour, dear to the lower-class readers. It was unkind and irreverent of Charles Cotton to make Dido kill herself *sus per col.* (*Scarronides*, Book iv.)

"With what natural and affecting simplicity our ancient ballad-maker has engrafted a Gothic conclusion on the Classic story of Virgil, from whom, however, it is probable he had it not. Nor can it be denied, but he has dealt out his poetical justice with a more impartial hand than that celebrated poet."—Dr. Percy, *Reliques of Ancient English Poetry*, 2nd edition, iii. 193, 1767.

Ovid's *Fasti*, Book 3, tells of Dido's Ghost appearing to her sister Anna:

"Nox erat: ante torum visa est adstare sororis
Squalenti *Dido* sanguinolenta comâ,
Et 'Fuge ne dubita, mœstum fuge,' dicere, 'tectum.'"

[Roxburghe Collection, III. 43, 730; C. 20, f. 14, art. 21; Bagford, II. 10; Euing, 87, 88; Jersey, II. 311; Pepys, I. 84, 518; Douce, III. 102 *verso*, IV. 35.]

A proper new Ballad, intituled

The Wandering Prince of Troy.

THE TUNE IS, *Queen Dido.* [See p. 447.]

WHen *Troy* Town for ten years' warrs
Withstood the *Greeks* in manfull wise,
Then did their foes increase so fast,
That to resist none could suffice;
Waste lye those walls that were so good,
And Corn now grows where *Troy* Town stood.

Æneas, wand'ring Prince of *Troy*,
When he for land long time had sought,
At length, arrived with great joy,
To mighty *Carthage* walls was brought,
Where *Dido* 's Queen, with sumptuous Feast,
Did entertain this wand'ring guest.

And as in hall at meat they sate,
The Queen desirous news to hear,
"Of thy unhappy ten years' warrs
Declare to me, thou *Trojan* dear,
The heavy hap and chance so bad
That thou, poore wand'ring Prince, hast had."

And then anon this worthy Knight [*al. lect.*, comely
With words demure, as he could well,
Of his unhappy ten years' warrs
So true a tale began to tell,
With words so sweet, and sighs so deep,
That oft he made them all to weep.

And then a thousand sighs he fetcht,
And every sigh brought tears amain,
That where he sate the place was wet,
As if he had seen those wars again.
So that the Queen with ruth therefore,
Said, "Worthy Prince, enough! no more."

The darksome night apace grew on, [*a. l.*, drew on.
And twinkling stars i' th' skys were spread, [in skyes.
And he his dolefull Tale had told,
As every one lay in his bed:
Where they full sweetly took their rest,
Save only *Dido's* boylling brest.

This silly woman never slept,
  But in her chamber all alone
As one unhappy always kept, [a.l. wept.
  Unto the walls she made her moan : [And to.
    That she should still desire in vaine
    The thing that she could not obtain.

And thus in grief she spent the night,
  Till twinkling stars from skys were fled ;
And *Phœbus* with his glist'ring beams
  Through misty clouds appeared red.
    Then tydings came to her anon
    That all the *Trojan* ships were gone :

And then the Queen, with bloody knife,
  Did arm : her heart as hard as stone :
Yet some-what loath to loose her life,
  In wofull case she made her moan, [a.l. woeful wise.
    And rowling on her care-full bed,
    With sighs and sobs, these words she said.

"O wretched *Dido*, Queen !" quoth she,
  I see thy end approaching neer, [a.l. approacheth.
For he is gone away from thee,
  Whom thou did'st love and hold so dear :
    Is he then gone, and passed by ?
    O heart, prepare thy selfe to dye !

"Though reason would thou should'st forbear,
  To stop thy hand from bloody stroke,
Yet fancy said thou should'st not fear, sayes.
  Who fettered thee in *Cupid's* yoke :
    Come, Death," quoth she, "and end the smart !"
    And with those words she pierc'd her heart.

[The Second Part, TO THE SAME TUNE.]

When Death had pierc'd the tender heart
  Of *Dido, Carthagenian* Queen,
And bloody knife did end the smart
  Which she sustain'd in wofull teene,
    Æneas being shipt and gone,
    Whose flattery caused all her moan :

Her Funerall most costly made,
  And all things finisht mournfully,
Her body fine in mould was laid,
  Where it consumed speedily.
    Her Sister's tears her Tomb bestrew'd,
    Her subjects' grief their kindnesse shew'd.

Then was *Æneas* in an Isle,
  In *Grecia*, where he liv'd long space,
Whereas her Sister in short while
  Wrote to him to his foule disgrace: [*al. lect.* vile.
    In phrase of letters to her mind,
    She told him plain he was unkind.

"False-hearted wretch," quoth she, "thou art,
  And trayterously thou hast betray'd [*a.l.* treacherously.
Unto thy lure a gentle heart,
  Which unto thee such welcome made;
    My Sister dear, and *Carthage* joy,
    Whose folly wrought her dire annoy.

"Yet on her death-bed when she lay
  She pray'd for thy prosperity,
Beseeching God that every day
  Might breed the[e] great felicity:
    Thus by thy meanes I lost a friend;
    Heaven send thee such untimely end!"

When he these lines, full fraught with gall,
  Perused had, and weigh'd them right,
His lofty courage then did fall,
  And streight appeared in his sight
    Queen *Dido's* Ghost, both grim and pale,
    Which made this valiant Souldier quail.

"*Æneas*," quoth this grisly Ghost, [*a.l.* ghastly.
  "My whole delight while I did live;
Thee of all men I loved most,
  My fancy and my will did give:
    For entertainment I thee gave,
    Unthankfully thou digg'dst my Grave,

"Wherefore prepare thy fleeting Soule
  To wander with me in the ayre,
Where deadly grief shall make it howle,
  Because of me thou took'st no care.
    Delay no time! thy glass is run,
    Thy date is past, and Death is come."

"O stay awhile, thou lovely spright! [*Æneas* replies.
  Be not so hasty to convey
My soul into eternall night,
  Where it shall nere behold bright day:
    O do not frown! thy angry look
    Hath made my breath my life forsooke.

"But woe is me, it is in vain, [*al. lect.*, all is in vain.
 And bootlesse is my dismall cry;
Time will not be recal'd again,
 Nor thou surcease before I dye:
  O let me live, to make amends
  Unto some of thy dearest friends! [text, "my."

"But feeling thou obdurate art,
 And wilt no pity to me show,
Because from thee I did depart,
 And left unpaid what I did owe,
  I must content my selfe to take
  What lot thou wilt with me partake." 132

And like one being in a Trance,
 A multitude of ugly fiends
About this wofull Prince did dance,
 No help he had of any friends:
  His body then they tooke away,
  And no man knew his dying day.

Printed for *F. Coles*, *T. Vere*, and *W. Gilbertson*.

[The Bagford copy was licensed and entred according to Order: *London*, printed by and for *W*[*m*]. *O*[*nley*], and sold by the Booksellers of *Pye-corner* and *London-Bridge*. Ewing, 87, for *Coles*, *Vere*, and *J. Wright*; *Ibid.*, 88, by and for *A. Milbourne*, in white-letter. 2nd Roxb., is of Aldermary Church-yard; Pepys, I. 84, for *John Wright*; *Ibid.*, I. 548, for *Clark*, *Thackeray*, and *Passinger* (*Cf.* p. 547). In Black-letter. Three woodcuts: 1st, a small fragment of procession at opening of Parliament, 1640, King Charles I. on horseback; 2nd, the Turkish ship (like one below), also belonging to *Captain Ward* pamphlet, mentioned on p. 410 *ante*; 3rd, new cut of the burning city, meant to represent destruction of Troy, with a Knight and Lady. 2nd Roxburghe has only one woodcut, across both columns: of Dido meeting Æneas on the sea-shore. Date of re-moulding, May, 1603. An original issue, 1564-5, of "A ballett intituled *The Wanderynge Pryncе*," entered to T. Colwell, in Stationers' Registers (*Transcript* I. 270), was probably distinct from ours.]

[This cut belonged to John Taylor's *Praise of Hempseed*, 1620.]

Constant Penelope: A Looking-Glass for Ladies.

"From night to morn I take my glass,
In hope to forget my Chloe."—*Old Song.*

EXEMPLARY people, of unassailable moral propriety, are unfortunately addicted to make their possession of all the cardinal virtues a public and private nuisance, by pharasaical self-proclamation and obtrusiveness. It need not be wondered at that good-tempered, easy-going sinners give them a wide berth; not having Bensonian ethics laid to heart as regulating their choice and affections. To find "Constant Penelope" held aloft throughout the ages, as a model for imitation, "A Looking Glass for Ladies," when addicted to taking a glass at odd moments, must be as trying an ordeal to the bewitching but worryingly incomprehensible sex, as it was for the proverbial ostracizer in Athens, whose sole objection to his guide, philosopher and friend, at voting-time with the shard, was that he was weary of hearing him called "Aristides the Just."

Readers who have lost confidence in "pious Æneas," as we have in most demonstratively pious hypocrites from the Puritans upward (there is no going downward to a deeper deep than those gentry), will be glad to resume acquaintance with the much nobler "wandering Prince" Odysseus, "he the wise and good Ulysses, kept from Ithaca so long." We see his impress on his Penny (unknown to numismatical classic-coin collectors), the girl he left behind him, and whom he found still desirable but somewhat the worse for un-wear at his return. "Match'd with an aged wife," Tennyson showed him, when the old insatiable longing had recaptured him, and tempted him "to sail beyond the sunset, and the baths, of all the western stars until he die." Although there are extant three copies, distinct publications of our ballad, which is above the average of merit, it is remarkable that it appears to have been never reprinted in modern time, except in Percy's *Reliques*, Book iii. of third vol., 1765, etc.

We must not quit *Troy Town* memories, or 'Dido Dumb,' or 'Pious Æneas'! (so named from his filial attention to Anchises, beside his supposed obedience to the Gods: paying his own expenses and taking his pleasure by the way,) without giving a ballad that was sung so early as 1618; and quoted by Humfrey Crouch, 1637, in his *Love's Court of Conscience* (*cf.* p. 513); music in *Pills*, vi. 192:—

The Sonet of Dido and Aeneas.

"*Dido* was a *Carthage* Queen, and loved a *Troian* Knight, [*a.l.* When *D.*
Which wand'ring many a coast had seen, and many a dreadful fight;
As they a hunting rode, a showre drove them in a lucklesse hour
Into a darksome Cave,
Where *Æneas*, with his charms, lockt Queene *Dido* in his arms,
And had what he would crave.

"*Dido Hymen's* rites forgot, her love was wing'd with haste;
Her honour she regarded not, but in her brest him plac't.
And when her love was new begun, *Jove* sent down his winged sonne
To fright *Æneas'* sleeping.
Who bade him by [the] break of day from Queen *Dido* steale away,
Which made her fall a weeping.

Dido wept, but what of this? the Gods would have it so:
Æneas nothing did amisse, for he was forc't to go.
Learn, Lordlings, then no vows to keep with false loves, but let them weep;
'Tis folly to be true.
Let this lesson serve your turn, and let twenty *Didoes* mourn,
So you get daily new."

[Roxburghe Collection, II. p. 284; Rawlinson, 83; Jersey, I. 241; Pepys, IV. 81.]

A Looking Glass for Ladies;

Or,

A Mirrour for Married Women.

Lively setting forth the rare Constancy, Chastity, Patience, and Purity of *Penelope*, the Wife of *Ulisses*, one of the *Grecian* Generals, who during the Ten Years' absence of her Husband at the siege of *Troy*, was solicited, and importun'd, by numbers of Emminent Suitors; who attempted her Chastity, and endeavoured to violate her Honour; but never could prevail. She addicted her self wholly to Charity, and good Housewifery, until her Husband's return. Which may serve as a Pattern for all Ladies, Gentlewomen, and others to imitate her virtuous Example.

With Allowance.

Tune of *Queen Dido; or, Troy Town*. [See p. 547.]

WHen *Greeks* and *Trojans*, fell at strife,
And Lords in armour bright were seen,
When many a Gallant lost his life,
About fair *Hellen*, beautie's queen:
Ulisses, General so free,
Did leave his dear *Penelope*.

When she this woful news did hear,
That he would to the Warrs of *Troy*,
For grief she shed full many a tear,
At parting from her onely joy;
Her Ladies all about her came,
To comfort up this *Grecian* Dame.

Ulisses, with a heavy heart,
Unto her then did mildly say,
"The time is come that we must part,
My honour calls me hence away;
Yet in my absence, dearest, be
My constant Wife, *Penelope*."

"Let me no longer live," she said,
"Than to my Lord I true remain;
My honour shall not be betraid,
Until I see my love again:
For ever I will constant prove,
As is the harmless Turtle-Dove."

Thus did they part with heavy cheer,
And to the Ships his way he took;
Her tender eyes dropt many a tear,
Still casting many a longing look:
She saw him on the surges glide,
And unto *Neptune* thus she cry'd:

"Thou God, whose power is in the Deep,
And rulest in the Ocean Main;
My loving Lord in safety keep,
Till he return to me again:
That I his person may behold,
Which I esteem far more than gold."

Then straight the ships with nimble sayls,
Were all convey'd out of her sight,
Her cruel fate she then bewails,
Since she had lost her heart's delight:
"Now shall my practice be," quoth she,
"True vertue and humility."

"My patience I will put in ure, [i.e. practice.
And charity I will extend,
Since for my woe there is no cure,
The helpless now I will befriend:
The Widdow and the Fatherless,
I will relieve, when in distress."

Thus she continued, year by year,
In doing good to every one;
Her fame was noised everywhere,
To young and old the same was known:
No company that she would mind,
Who were to vanity inclin'd.

Meanwhile *Ulisses* fought for Fame,
'Mongst *Trojans* hazarding his life,
Young Gallants hearing of her name,
Came flocking for to tempt his wife:
For she was lovely, young and fair,
No lady might with her compare.

With costly gifts, and jewels fine
They did endeavour her to win,
With banquets, and the choicest wine,
For to allure her unto Sin:
Most persons were of high degree,
Who courted fair *Penelope*.

With modesty and comely grace,
Their wanton suits she did deny;
No tempting charms could ere deface
Her dearest Husband's memory;
But constant she did still remain,
Hopeing to see him once again.

Her Book her daily practice was,
And that she often did peruse;
She seldom looked in her glass,
Powder and paint she did not use;
I wish all ladies were as free
From Pride, as was *Penelope.*

She in her Needle took delight,
And likewise in her Spinning-wheel,
Her maids about her, all, she taught,
To use the Distaff, and the Reel:
The Spiders that on rafters twine,
Scarce spins a thread more pure and fine.

Sometimes she would bewail the loss
And absence of her dearest love;
Sometimes she thought the Seas to cross,
Her fortune on the waves to prove:
"I fear my lord is slain," quoth she,
"He stays so from *Penelope.*"

At length the Ten years' Siege of *Troy*
Did end, the flames the City burn'd;
Which to the *Grecians* was great joy,
To see the Towers to ashes turn'd:
Then came *Ulisses* home to see
His constant Dear, *Penelope.*

Then blame her not if she was glad,
When she her Lord again had seen:
"O welcome home, my dear," she said,
"A long time absent you have been:
The wars shall never me deprive,
Of thee again, whilst I'me alive."

Young ladies may example take,
And by this lesson they may learn,
And keep this pattern for her sake,
'Twixt vice and virtue to discern:
And let all women strive to be
As constant as *Penelope.*

Printed for *F. Coles*, *T. Vere*, *J. Wright*, and *J. Clarke.*

[Black-letter. Five cuts: 1st and 3rd on p. 552; 2nd, the ship, p. iv; 4th, ditto, repeated; 5th, the couple on p. 419, right, of vol. iii.]

The Tragedy of Hero and Leander.

" On *Hellespont*, guilty of true love's blood,
In view and opposite two cities stood,
Sea-borderers, disjoin'd by *Neptune's* might:
The one *Abydos*, the other *Sestos* hight.
At *Sestos Hero* dwelt; *Hero* the fair,
Whom young *Apollo* courted for her hair,
And offer'd as a dower his burning throne, [N.B.
Where she should sit, for men to gaze upon. . . . . .
It lies not in our power to love or hate,
For Will is over-rul'd by Fate. . .
Where both deliberate, the love is slight:
Who ever lov'd, that lov'd not at first sight." [N.B.

—*Hero and Leander*, by Christopher Marlow.

NOT printed until 1598, five years after the untimely death of Marlow (followed by a second edition with completion by George Chapman), the unfinished poem, *Hero and Leander*, by nobility of style, the rich sonorous music, the tender pathos and beauty of the Sestiads, deserved the high honour received from Shakespeare a few months later, by being in so unexampled a manner quoted, and the silent singer with his 'mighty line' affectionately addressed,

Phœbe.—" Dead Shepherd, now I find thy saw of might,
'Who ever loved, that loved not at first sight!'"

—*As You Like It*, act iii. sc. 5.

Seeing that this clearly refers to Marlow (to be recognized by every contemporary), we may feel certain that the playful allusion to the same theme, in the self-same comedy, resulted from the dead shepherd's bequest of his theme:—

Rosalind.—" Leander, he would have lived many a fair year though Hero had turned nun, if it had not been for a hot Midsummer-night; for, good youth, he went but forth to wash him in the Hellespont, and being taken with the cramp, was drowned: and the foolish coroners of that age found it was 'Hero of Sestos.' But these are all lies."

—*As You Like It*, Act iv. sc. 1.

Moreover (parathentically we note), Marlow's words on Helen's beauty, "Was this the face that launched a thousand ships" (*cf.* p. 545) were remembered *and quoted*, when Shakespeare had anew to describe Helen in *Troilus and Cressida*, Act ii. sc. 2, " She is a pearl, whose price hath *launch'd above a thousand ships.*"

Even, the Duke's speech in *Measure for Measure*, v. 1, " Be sometimes honour'd for *his burning throne*" was an additional token of Shakespeare's remembrance of Marlow. (*See our motto above.*) Others were the playful quotations of " By shallow rivers," etc., in *The Merry Wives*, from Marlow's pastoral song, "Come live with me"; and Pistol's " Holloa! you pamper'd jades of Asia," from *2nd Henry IV.*, from *Tamburlaine*, Part II. iv. 4.

The tune used for our "Tragedy of *Hero* and *Leander*" is known from the burden of the original, *I'le never love thee more!* a ballad *temp. Jacob. I.*, beginning, " My dear and only love, take heed." On our p. 581, we here give (from Roxb. Coll., III. 579) the song written by the brave Montrose (after he had awakened from being misled by the rebellious Covenanters in the north), loyally fighting to make reparation for his first error: he kept the same burden, and began similarly with "My dear and only love, I pray." Ours is the only known broadside copy of early date. It is reprinted by James Watson, in his *Choice Collection of Comic and Serious Scots Poems*, part iii. p. 107, 1711. The tune is given in Chappell's *Popular Music*, p. 380, from Gamble's MS., 1659, and it is also in *The Dancing Master* of 1686. It is the same tune as *O no, no, no! not yet*, a tune cited already in these *Roxburghe Ballads* (reprinted in vols. i. p. 282, "Death's Dance;" ii. 198, "A Pleasant Ditty of a Maiden's Vow;" iii. 179, "The Pensive Prisoner's Apology," alternated with the tune of Lovelace's *When Love with unconfined wings*). The original ballad appears to be "The Night Encounter," of *Merry Drollery*, p. 69, 1661, and *Merry Drollery Compleat*, p. 250, 1670, 1691; it was reprinted under the present Editor in 1875, by Robert Roberts of Boston, beginning thus,

> When *Phœbus* had drest his course to the West, [= addrest.
> To take up his rest below,
> And *Cynthia* agreed in her glittering weed
> Her light in his stead to bestow;
> I walking alone, attended by none,
> I suddenly heard one cry,
> "*O do not, do not kill me yet,*
> *For I am not prepared to die.*"

In our *Bagford Ballads*, p. 142, 1877, we reprinted "The Swimming Lady," beginning "The Four and Twenty day of June," to the same tune. To this tune was sung "I wish I was those gloves, dear heart!" which is a proper new ballad on the Regret of a true Lover for his Mistress's Unkindness (Roxb. Coll., II. 574). Others are in Douce Coll., III. 86 verso and 87 verso; also the Pepysian Coll., Vol. I. pp. 256, 280, 278, and 394, all to the same tune.

Our ensuing ballad was included by our well-loved friend the late John Payne Collier in his *Book of Roxburghe Ballads*, p. 227, 1847. He also indicates the translation from Martial's Epigram at the close of our third stanza. A Pepysian ballad by William Meash, "*Leander's* Love for Loyal *Hero*," to the tune of *Shackley Hay* (*v. Popular Music*, 367), beginning, "Two famous lovers once there was" (*Percy Folio MS.* iii. 296), was printed at London by J. W., *i.e.* John Wright. There is a modernization of our ballad in Allan Ramsay's *Tea-Table Miscellany*, part iv., 1740, "Hero and Leander: an old Ballad," beginning with our second stanza, "*Leander* on the Bay of *Hellespont* all naked stood." Also in Herd's *Scottish Songs*, 1791 reprint, vol. i. 258. Martial's line is:—

Parcite, dum propero; mergite, dum redeo.—*Spect. Liber*, xxv.

[Roxburghe Collection, III. 152; Euing, No. 347; Douce, II. 221 *verso*.]

The Tragedy of Hero and Leander;

Or, The Two Unfortunate Lovers.

Famous *Leander* for his love renown'd,
In crossing of the *Hellespont* was drown'd;
And *Hero* when his corps she once espy'd,
She leapt into the waves, and with him dy'd.

To a pleasant new Tune; or, *I will never love thee more.* [See pp. 556, 583.]

COme, mournful Muse, assist my quill, whilst I with grief relate,
A story of two Lovers true, cut off by cruel fate:
Death onely parts united hearts, and brings them to their graves,
Whilst others sleep within the deep, or perish in the waves.

Leander on the bay of bliss, *Pontus*, he naked stood;
In passion of delay he sprang into the fatal flood.
The rageing seas, none can appease, his fortune ebbs and flows,
The heaven down showres, and rain down pours, and the wind aloft it blows.

The Lad forsook the land, and did unto the Gods complain,
"You rocks, you rugged waves, you elements of hail and rain!
What 'tis to miss true Lovers' bliss, alas! you do not know;
Make me a wrack as I come back, but spare me as I go."

"Behold on yonder tower, see, where my fair beloved lyes!
This th' appointed hour, hark how she on *Leander* crys!"
The Gods were mute, unto his sute, the billows answered, "No;"
The surges rise up to the skyes, but he sank down below.

Sweet *Hero*, like dame *Venus* fair, all in her Turrit stood,
Expecting of her Lover dear, who crossing was the flood:
A feeble light, through darksome night, she set her Love to guide:
With waveing arms, and love's alarms, with a voice full loud she cry'd.

"You cruel waves, some pitty show unto my dearest friend;
And you, tempestuous winds that blow, at this time prove more kind:
O waft my love secure to shore, that I his face may see;
With tears your help I do implore, your pitty lend to me."

"Let each kind Dolphin now befriend, and help my love along;
And bring him to his journey's end, before his breath is gone;
Let not a wave become his grave, and part us both for ever;
Pitty my grief, send him relief, and help him now or never."

The fierce and cruel tempest did most violently rage;
Not her laments nor discontents its fury could asswage;
The winds were high, and he must dye, the Fates did so ordain:
It was design'd, he ne'r should find his dearest Love again.

She spread her silken vail for-to secure the blazing light,
To guide her Love, lest on the rocks his wearied limbs should smite:
But cruel Fate, it prov'd his date, and caused him to sleep;
She from above, beheld her love lye drowned in the deep.

Her show'ry eyes with tears brought in the tide before its time;
Her sad lamenting groans likewise unto the skys did climb:
"O Heavens! (quoth she) against poor me, do you your forces bend?"
Then from the Walls in haste she falls, to meet her dying friend.

Her new bedewed arms about his senceless corps she clipps, ["new."
And many kisses spent in vain upon his dying lipps:
Then wav'd her hands unto the lands, singing with dying pride,
"Go, tell the world, in billows strong, I with my Love have dy'd."

Thus did they both their breath resign unto the will of Fate;
And in the deep, imbrace and twine, when Death did end their date.
Let Lovers all example take, and evermore prove true,
For *Hero* and *Leander's* sake, who bids you all adieu. 48

Printed for *R. Burton*, at the *Horse-shooe* in *West Smithfield*, neer the *Hospital-gate*.

[Black-letter. Three cuts: 1st, half-lengths of a hatted Cavalier and Lady; 2nd, Ships, on p. 413; 3rd, a Lady, *busto*. Date, *circá* 1649. *Cf.* pp. 541-542.]

An Excellent Sonnet of the Two Unfortunate Lovers, Hero and Leander.

"Priscian a little scratched. 'Twill serve."—*Love's Labour Lost*, Act v. sc. 1.

WE entertain a faint suspicion that Humfrey Crouch (who avowedly wrote the "Excellent Sonnet of the Unfortunate Loves of Hero and Leander)" was the unnamed author of our earlier written *Roxburghe Ballad*, p. 564, entitled, "*Gerhard's Mistress*," beginning, "Be gone, thou fatal Fiery Fever." Crouch met us in "The Greeks and Trojan Warres," on p. 544; and comes once more into this volume with a poem, not ballad, on "Guy, Earl of Warwick," *post*. It is permissible to express wonder at the glaring oversight whereby he misrepresents the respective sex of the two hapless lovers. To interchange them thus, when unable to defend themselves, was "adding a fresh terror to death": like having one's Obituary celebration written by Walter Maitland, and sung to a 'hanging tune.' Humfrey Crouch's classical knowledge cannot have been profound or expansive, for he thought the Hellespont was a river, though no doubt his readers were content: since the water drowned the young people, whether it were salt or fresh. But to name the lady of Sestos 'Leander,' and the swimming youth of Abydos a 'Hero' (a less unnatural blunder, suggestive in its way), was inexcusable. If in the manner of Sterne's Obadiah, when sorely badgered, concerning the mishap caused by the other Jackass, Crouch similarly tried to shirk the responsibility, saying that it was not *his* fault, we are apt to be incredulous, like Father Shandy, who replied, "How, do I know that?"

The five-line *Argument* on next page is from second copy (Roxb. Coll., III. 478, reprinted by *J. White* of *Newcastle-on-Tyne*, with two cuts, *circá* 1755).

[Roxb. Coll., III. 150, 178; Pepys, III. 322; Douce, 195 *verso*; Euing, 89.]

An Excellent Sonnet of the Unfortunate Loves of

Hero and Leander.

Tune of *Gerard's Mistris.* [See *note* on pp 566.]

[Giving an Account how *Leander* fell in love with the famous *Hero*; but being disappointed by her cruel Father, who confined her in a Tower, *Leander* resolving to swim over the *Hellespont* to fetch her away, a mighty Storm arose, and he was drowned near her window; for sorrow of which, she leaped into the Sea to him.]

Hero. [For *Hero* read *Leander* and *vice versa, passim.*

"HOW fares my fair *Leander?* [= *Hero*, see p. 559.
O vouchsafe to speak, lest my heart break,
I banisht am from thy sweet company;
'Tis not thy Father's anger can abate my love, [*al. lect.*, 'abase.'
I still will prove
Thy faithful friend until such time I dye; though Fate
And Fortune doth conspire to interrupt our love:
In spight of Fate and Fortune's hate,
I still will constant prove,
And though
Our angry friends in malice now our bodies part,
Nor friends nor foes, nor fears nor blows,
Shall separate our hearts." [Line 18 in original.

Leander. [*i.e. Hero.*

"What voice is this that calls *Leander*
From her bower? from yonder Tower,
The eccho of this voice doth sure proceed."

Hero. [*i.e. Leander.*

"*Leander*, 'tis thy *Hero*, fain
Would come to thee, if it might be,
Thy absence makes my tender heart to bleed, but oh!
This pleasant river *Hellespont*, which is the people's wonder,
These waves so high do injury, by parting us asunder,
And though there's Ferry-men good store,
Yet none will stand my friend,
To waft me o'er to that fair shore,
Where all my grief shall end."

Leander. [Hero.

"*Hero*, though I [,*Leander*,]
Am thy constant Lover still, and ever will,
My angry Father is thy Enemy; He still
Doth strive to keep 's asunder;
Now and then, Poor Ferry men!
They dare not waft thee over, lest they dye.
Nor yet, dare they convey me, unto my dear *Hero* now; [=Leander.
My father's rage will not assuage, nor will the same allow.
Be patient
Then, dear *Hero*, now, as I am true to thee; [=Leander.
Even so I trust thou art as just, and faithful unto me."

Hero. [=Leander.

"Is there no way to stay
An angry Father's wrath, whose fury hath
Bereav'd his child of comfort and content?"

Leander. [=Hero.

"O no! Dear *Hero*, there's no way Leander.
That I do know, to ease my Woe;
My days of joy and comfort now are spent.
You may,
As well go tame a lyon in the wilderness,
As to persuade my Father's aid, to help me in distress.
His anger, and this River, hath kept us asunder long;
He hath his will, his humour still,
And we have all the wrong."

Hero. [Leander.

"'Tis not thy Father's anger
Nor this River deep, the which shall keep,
Me from the imbracements of my dearest friend;
For through this silver Stream my way I mean to take,
Even for thy sake.
For thy dear sake my dearest life I'le spend,
Though waves and winds should both conspire
Mine enemies to be;
My love's so strong, I fear no wrong can happen unto me:
O meet me in thy garden
Where this pleasant river glides,
Lend me thy hand, draw me to land,
What ever me betides.

"Now must I make my tender
Slender arms my oars! Help! watry powers,
Yea, little fishes, teach me how to swim!
And all the sea-nimphs guard me, unto yonder banks!
I'le give you thanks;
Bear up my body, strengthen every limb!
I come, *Leander*, now prepare thy lovely arms for me! [*Hero.*
I come, dear love! assist me, *Jove*, I may so happy be!"
But oh! a mighty tempest rose, and he was drown'd that tide,
In her fair sight, his heart's delight,
And so with grief she dy'd.

But when her aged Father
These things understands, he wrings his hands,
And tears his hoary hair from off his head;
Society he shuns and doth forsake his meat,
His grief's so great:
And oft doth make the lowly ground his bed.
"O, my *Leander!* would that I had dyed to save thy life;
Or that I had, when I was sad,
Made thee brave *Hero's* wife! [Read *Leander's.*
It was my trespass, and I do confess
I wronged thee;
Posterity shall know hereby,
The fault lay all in me.

"But since the waves have cast
His body on the land, upon the sand,
His corps[e] shall buried be in solemn wise;
One grave shall serve them both, and one most stately Tomb:
She'l make him room,
Although her corps[e] be breathless where she lies.
Ye Fathers, have a special care now, whatsoe'er you do!
For those that parts true loyal hearts,
Themselves were never true.
Though Fate and Fortune crosse poor Lovers,
Sometimes, as we know,
Pray understand, have *you* no hand
Even in their overthrow!"

Finis. [Written by] **H[umfrey] Crouch.**

Printed for *F. Coles*, *T. Vere*, and *J. Wright*.

[In Black-letter, duplicate of Euing's exemplar at Glasgow, formerly J. O. Halliwell's. Douce's, by and for *W. O.* Four woodcuts: 1st, the youth on p. 585, left, of vol. iii.; 2nd, the woman in *this* vol. p. 166, right; 3rd and 4th, man and woman, on p. 168. Date, *circâ* 1661.]

[Roxburghe Coll., II. 300; III. 901; Bagford, II. 120; Jersey, II. 174; Pepys, III. 321, 311; Douce, I. 133, 136; III. 39; Euing, 171; Huth, I. 162.]

The Love-Sick Maid;
Or,
Cordelia's Lamentation for the absence of her Gerhard.

TO A PLEASANT NEW [PLAYHOUSE] TUNE.

"BEgone!
Thou fatal fiery feaver, now be gone!
Let Love alone,
Let his etherial flames possess my breast,
His fires
From thy consuming heat no aid requires,
For swift desires
Transports my passion to a throne of rest;
Where I,
Who, in the pride of health,
Did never feel such warmth to move,
By sickness tam'd am so inflam'd,
I know no joys but love:
And he,
That trifled many tedious hours
Away, my love to try,
In little space hath gain'd the grace,
To have more power than I. 18

"Depart!
Thou scorching fury, quick from me depart!
Think not my heart
To thy dull flame shall be a sacrifice;
A Maid,
Dread *Cupid*, now is on thy Altar laid,
By thee betray'd;
A rich oblation to restore thine eyes:
But yet,
My fair acknowledgment
Will prove thou hadst no craft
To bend thy Bow against thy foe,
That aim'd to catch the shaft:
For if
That at my breast thy arrows [See *Note*, p. 564.
Thou all at once let flie,
She that receives a thousand sheaves,
Can do no more but dye. 36

[*Note.*—Thus far we print with the wasteful expenditure of space, in broken lines, following the text, to show the system. *We compress the 18-line stanzas.*]

"No more!
You learn'd physitians, tire your brains no more,
Pray give me o're!
Mine is a cure in Physick never read;
Although you skilful Doctors all the world doth know,
Pray let me go! [*a.l.* In Learning flow.
You may as well make practice on the Dead;
But if
My *Gerrard* dai[g]n to view me, with the glory of his looks,
I make no doubt to live without Physitians and their books.
'Tis he
That with his balmed kisses can restore my latest breath;
What bliss is this, to gain a Kiss, ["That."
Can save a maid from death? 54

"To you,
That tell me of another World, I bow,
and will allow
Your Sacred Precepts, if you'll grant me this,
That he
Whom I esteem of next the Deity
May go with me,
Without whose presence there can be no bliss:
Go, teach
Your Tenets of Eternity to those that aged be!
And not perswade a Love-sick Maid
There's any heaven but he.
But stay!
Methinks an icy slumber hath possest my frenzy'[d] brain;
Pray bid him dye, if you see I shall never wake again." 72

Note.—Instead of our broadside reading at end of the second stanza,

"For if that at my breast thy arrows thou all at once let flie,
She that receives a thousand sheaves can do no more but dye."

The following is the version used by Henry Bold for his translation in 1664:—

Nor did I fear, though at my Bosom, all at once,
Such Darts did move;
She that receives a thousand sheaves,
She can no more but love.

Henry Bold published this ballad, "An excellent new Song called *Gerhard* and his Mistress," in his *Poems Lyrique*, etc., p. 105, with his parodies of it, beginning, "Away, you grievous things call'd Mistresses!" as "A Mock to 'Be gone, thou fatal fiery fever!'" followed by "Away you fool! wilt thou love less?" and Henry Bold's own Answer, "Now thou knowest, I love more." The 1664 version ends without "The Answer," of our pp. 565, 566. The phrase '*playhouse* tune' suggests that the first two stanzas were the entire original song, at some theatre, in a lost drama. All that follow are mere ballad-monger's work. Was it by *Humphrey Crouch*? He copied both rhythm and tune, on p. 560.

The Young-Man's Answer; or, his Dying Breath, Lamenting for his fair *Cordelia's* Death.

To a Delightful New Tune.

"Come on! thou fatal messenger from her that's gone;
Lest I alone
Within that quenchless flame for ever fry;
The Lake of love being kindled, wherein none can take
rest, but [to] wake
Where slumber hath no power to close the eye;
Whilst I,
That by my fair *Cordelia* desire to take a sleep,
With lids wide-spread upon my bed, am forc'd a watch to keep:
And she,
That waited many tedious hours, my constancy to try,
Is now at rest, while I, opprest, fain would but cannot dye.

"Dispatch, thou scorching Fury, quickly now dispatch!
By Death I watch
To be releast from this tormenting flame;
The Dart, sent from dread *Cupid*, sticks fast in my heart,
I, wanting art,
Had not the power for to resist the same; though she,
Who, by her late acknowledgement,
Profest thou had'st no craft, [the shaft:
Yet from thy bow thou mad'st her know what power lay in
But then
Thou sent'st another arrow, which me of hopes bereft;
Most like a foe, to wound me so, for whom no cure is left.

"Wherefore did you Physitians give my Mistress o're?
Had you no more
Experience, but what you in books have read?
Or why (you learned Doctors) did you cease to try
Your skills, when I
Might have reviv'd her, if she'd not been dead?
And yet
Suppose that I in person had present been to view her;
Is there such grace in any face to work so great a cure?
But now
I'm come too late to kiss her, which were it not in vain,
After her death, I'd spend my breath to fetch her back again.

"Unto the fair *Elizium*, thither will I go,
Whereas I know
She is amongst those Sacred ones prefer'd. When I
Shall be admitted for to come so nigh,
"Pardon!" I'll cry,

"For my long absence, wherein I have err'd:
And since
By her I was esteem'd, so much on Earth, being here,
Hence, for her sake, no rest I'll take,
Till I have found her there:
No more,
But only I desire to hear my Passing-Bell;
That Virgins may lament the day
Of *Gerhard's* last Farewell." 144

[Printed for *Wm. Onley*. 2nd copy, printed for *Wm. Thackeray*, *Will. Whitwood*, and *Tho. Passinger*.]

[In Black-letter. Three woodcuts: 1st and 2nd, together, as in vol. iii. p. 664; 3rd, p. 84 right, of present vol. Some copies, with our woodcut of p. 104, were printed by and for *A.M.*, *i.e.* *Andrew Milbourne*; Douce 2nd is for *W. Thackeray*. Date, certainly a few months or years before 1664. (*Cf.* p. 564.) Probable date of *Gerhard's Mistress* is 1660. This woodcut belongs to p. 546.]

[Roxburghe Collection, III. 762; Pepys, III. 142; Wood, E. 25, fol. 75; Douce, I. 83 *verso*, III. 30 *vo.*, 110 *vo.*, IV. 26; Euing, 111.]

The Famous Flower of Serving-Men;

Or, the Lady turned Serving-Man.

[Her Lord being slain, her Father dead,
Her Bower robb'd, her Servants fled,
She drest her self in Man's attire,
She trimm'd her Locks, she cut her Hair.
And therewithal she chang'd her name,
From fair *Elise* to *Sweet William*. *Euing copy.*]

[To A DELICATE NEW TUNE, or *Flora's Farewell* (*cf.* p. 105); or *Summer Time*; or *Love's Tale*. See *Note*, p. 570.]

"You beautous Ladies great and small,
I write unto you, one and all;
Whereby that you may understand
What I have suffered in this land.

"I was by birth a Lady fair,
My father's chief and only heir;
But when my good old father dy'd,
Then I was made a young Knight's bride.

"And then my love built me a bower
Bedeck'd with many a fragrant flower;
A braver bower you ne'er did see,
Than my true-love did build for me. [" what m.l."

"But there came thieves late in the night,
Who rob'd my bower and slew my Knight;
And after that my Knight was slain,
I could no longer there remain.

"My servants all did from me fly
In the midst of my extremity,
And left me by myself alone,
With a heart more cold than any stone.

"Yet tho' my heart was full of care,
Heaven would not suffer me to despair;
When in haste I chang'd my name
From fair '*Elise*' to sweet *William*. [" *Elize*."

"And hereupon I curl'd my hair,
And drest my self in man's attire, [*a.l.* therewithal.
My doublet, hose, and beaver hat,
And a golden band about my neck.

"With a silver rapier by my side,
Much like a Gallant I did ride;
The thing that I delighted in,
It was to be a Serving-man.

"Thus cloath'd in sumptuous man's array,
I nobly rid along the highway;
And at [the] last it chanced so
That I to the King's Court did go.

"Then to the King I bow'd most low,
My love and duty for to show;
And so much favour I did crave
That I a Serving-man's place might have.

"'Stand up, brave youth!' the King reply'd,
Thy service shall not be deny'd:
But tell me first what thou can'st do?
Thou shalt be fitted thereunto.

"'Wilt thou be usher of my hall,
To wait upon my Nobles all,
Or wilt thou be tapster of my wine, [*a.l.* Taster.
To wait on me when I do dine?

"'Or wilt thou be my Chamberlain,
To make my bed so soft and fine?
Or wilt thou be one of my Guard,
And I'll give thee a great reward?'"

Sweet *William* with a smiling face,
Said to the King, "May it please your Grace
To shew such favor unto me,
Your Chamberlain I fain would be."

The King did then his Nobles call,
For to ask council of them all,
Who gave consent Sweet *William* he
The King's own Chamberlain should be.

[The Second Part, to the same Tune.]

Now mark what strange thing came to pass,
As the King one day a-hunting was,
With [all] his Lords and noble train,
Sweet *William* did at home remain.

Sweet *William* had no company then,
With him at home but an old Man;
And when he found the house was clear,
He took a Lute that he had near. [*orig.* "flute."

Upon the Lute *Sweet William* play'd, [*Ibid.*
And to the same he sung and said,
With a sweet melodious voice,
Which made the old man to rejoice:—

"My father was as brave a Lord
As ever *England* did afford, [*a.l.* *Europe*.
My mother was a Lady bright,
My husband was a valiant Knight: [*a.l.* gorgeous.

"And I my self a Lady gay,
Bedeck'd in glorious rich array,
The bravest Lady in the Land,
Had no more pleasure at command.

"I had my musick every day,
Harmonious lessons for to play;
I had my virgins fair and free,
Continually to wait on me.

"But now, alas! my husband's dead,
And all my friends are from me fled;
My former joys are past and gone,
For now I am a Serving-man."

At last the King from hunting came,
And presently upon the same,
He called for his good old man, [Original *G.o.M.*
And thus to speak the King began:

"What news, what news, old man?" said he, [=quoth
"What news hast thou to tell to me?"
"Brave news," the old man he did say,
"Sweet *William* is a Lady gay."

"If this be true thou tell'st to me,
I'll make thee a Lord of high dégree;
But if thy words do prove a lie,
Thou shalt be hang'd up presently."

But when the King the truth h[ad] found, ["he found."
His joys did more and more abound;
According as the old man did say,
"Sweet *William* was a Lady gay."

Therefore the King, without delay,
Put on her gallant rich array, [*a.l.* glorious.
And on her head a crown of gold,
Which was most famous to behold.

And then for fear of farther strife,
He took '*Sweet-William*' for his wife:
The like before was never seen,
A Serving-Man to become a Queen! 112

[By **Laurence Price.**]

Printed and Sold in *Aldermary Church-Yard, Bow Lane, London.*

[In White-letter. Two modern woodcuts, not important: 1st, a Lady sumptuously dressed; 2nd, a poor copy of the female conclave cut, given already in vol. iii. p 532. Douce copy printed for *Elizabeth Andrews;* Wood's "for *J. Hose.*" In the Euing copy the authorship is marked "By L. P.," for Laurence Price, concerning whom see pp. 64 to 66, and 105 *note.* Also the list of alternative tunes and the argument motto-verse between title and ballad, here restored to place. With three cuts and in Black-letter. *London,* Printed for *John Andrews,* at the *White Lion* near *Pye-Corner.*" Date *circa* 1657. Pepys copy printed for *W. T.* and *T. P.*, to a dainty Tune, etc.]

*** Doubting the ability of any Lady or Serving-man to sing an autobiographical ditty while playing on the flute, except in symphony or between the stanzas, we follow an older version which renders it 'Lute,' instead of our broadside's 'flute.' Thus 'the faire *Elise*' could sing intelligibly. Bishop Percy's modernizer was probably himself, "I think we do know the sweet Roman hand!" He ignores the *g.o.m.* of line 91, and makes the king overhear the lady's song. Like Othello, "Upon this hint he spake." It is wholly autobiographical and sweetly imbecile. Moreover, the enamoured king makes dishonourable proposals to her, which are rejected, before he advances his bid to an offer of marriage:—

"The richest gifts he proffer'd me, His mistress if that I would be!"

These are the Episcopal "improvements!" (*sic, sic,* "and very sick!")

Note.—We here first identify the authorship as by *LAURENCE PRICE,* but have no space or inclination to trace the foreign imitations, analogues, or possible precursors in Swedish and Danish collections; or the garbled traditional "Sweet Willie" of Kinloch's *Ancient Scottish Ballads,* p. 96. This is one of those genuine story-ballads that gave pleasure of old, and secured popularity, attested by numerous editions. Like most of its class, while failing to stir the emotions by pathetic language, it employs the dramatic style of autobiographic monologue in part, and then reverts to ordinary narrative. It was a bold expedient to make the romantic adventures of this widowed lady effect as great a conquest over the bewildered King as though the 'fair Elise' had been a maiden pure, hitherto unawakened to love. We are incapable of deeming her bold and forward. One might as soon think of censuring Viola, who captivates the Count Orsino; but in *Twelfth Night* it is the man who is fickle, not the girl who admits a second love.

We have here abundant choice of tunes. For the first tune, *Flora's Farewell* (*by the same Laurence Price*) and our introduction, on pp. 105-107, *ante;* for the second tune, of the numerous ballads (chiefly of the Robin Hood series), beginning "*In Summer-time,* when leaves grow green," the tune befitting our "Famous Flower," is given in *Popular Music,* p. 393, belonging to "King Edward the Fourth and the Tanner of Tamworth," also to "Robin Hood and the Curtal Friar." The third tune is of "*Love's Tide;* or, A Farewell to Folly," a ballad in the Douce Collection, I. 134, beginning, "How cool and temperate am I grown!" Printed for *F. Coles,* etc. To the Tune of, *Wert thou more fairer than thou art,* or *Lusty Bacchus.* Of the original song, "Love in a Calme," printed in Playford's *Select Ayres,* p. 42, 1659, the music was by Henry Lawes.

Constance of Cleveland.

WE have here a romantic ballad belonging to the first year of James I.'s reign, incontestably entered to William White, on 13th June, 1603 (*vide* Stationers' Company Registers, Book C., fol. 97=vol. iii. p. 237, of Edward Arber's *Transcript*, 1876): again registered as a *Transfer*, 14th Dec., 1624). The already-ancient tune was printed, with the opening line, "'Twas a youthful Knight, which loved a gallant Lady," in the Jan Jans Starter's collection of music, *Friesche Lust-Hof*, printed at Amsterdam in 1634, and probably also in earlier editions. The tune had been used in "bloody Mary's" reign for a ballad beginning "*Mary* doth complain, Ladies, be you moved, With my lamentations and my bitter groans." It is in the *Crown Garland of Golden Roses.* Another ballad to the tune of *Crimson Velvet*, beginning "In the days of old, when fair *France* did flourish," was written by Thomas Deloney, entitled "An excellent Ballad of a Prince of England's courtship of the King of France's Daughter;" reprinted by Mr. William Chappell, from Roxb. Coll., I. 102, in these *Roxburghe Ballads*, i. 309; he has also given the tune and the words of our ensuing ballad in his *Popular Music of the Olden Time*, p. 179. The words alone had been reprinted previously by the late John Payne Collier in his *Book of Roxburghe Ballads*, p. 163, in 1847, with remarks that deserve to be quoted completely. It shows how accurately he had guessed the date (the registration is 13 June, 1603 as noted above); he may have remembered having consulted the Registers, when beginning his admirable *Extracts* from them for the genuine Shakespeare Society, that issued so much good unpretentious work deserving of respect and gratitude:—

"This romantic ballad, in a somewhat plain and unpretending style, relates incidents that may remind the reader of the old story of *Titus and Gisippus*, as told in English verse by Edw. Lewicke, as early as 1562: the ballad is not so ancient by, perhaps, thirty or forty years; and the printed copy that has come down to our day is at least fifty years more recent than the date when we believe the ballad to have been first published. The title the broadside ('Printed for F. Coles, J. W., T. Vere, W. Gilbertson,') bears is, 'Constance of Cleveland: a very excellent Sonnet of the most fair Lady Constance of Cleveland and her disloyal Knight.' We conclude that the incidents are mere invention, but 'Constance of Rome' is the name of a play, by Drayton, Munday and Hathway, mentioned in Henslow's Diary under the year 1600 (p. 171). The tune of '*Crimson Velvet*' was highly popular in the reigns of Elizabeth and her successor."

*** None need doubt that the name of the tune is derived from the 185th half-line in Thomas Deloney's 'King of France's Daughter,' mentioned above:—

The Children [they did bring] as their father willed,
Where the Royal King must of force come by,
Their mother, richly clad in fair *Crimson Velvet*, [N.B.
Their father all in gray, comely to the eye. Etc.

[Roxburghe Collection, III. 94 ; Pepys Coll., I. 138, 476 ; Jersey, II. 322.]

Constance of Cleveland:

A very excellent Sonnet of the most Fair Lady, Constance of Cleveland, and her disloyall Knight.

To the tune of, *Crimson Velvet.* [See p. 571.]

IT was a youthfull Knight lov'd a gallant Lady,
 Fair she was and bright, and of vertues rare,
Herself she did behave so courteously as may be,
 Wedded they were brave, joy without compare.
Here began the grief, pain without relief,
 Her husband soon her love forsook ;
To women lewd of mind, being bad inclin'd,
 He only lent a pleasant look.
The Lady she sate weeping while that he was keeping,
 Company with others moe.
" *Her words, my Love, beleeve not ! come to me, and grieve not !*
 Wantons will thee overthrow."

His fair Ladie's words nothing he regarded ;
 Wantonnesse affords such delightfull sport.
While they dance and sing, with great mirth prepared,
 She her hands did wring in most grievous sort.
" O what hap had I, thus to wail and cry ?
 Unrespected every day.
Living in disdain, while that others gain
 All the right I should enjoy.
I am left forsaken, others they are taken,
 Ah, my love, why dost thou so ?
Her flatteries beleeve not, come to me and grieve not !
 Wantons will thee overthrow."

The Knight with his fair piece at length the Lady spied,
 (Who did him daily fleece of his wealth and store),
Secretly she stood, while *she* her fashions tryed,
 With a patient mind, while deep the strumpet swore :
" O Sir Knight," quoth she, " so dearly I love thee,
 My life doth rest at thy dispose.
By day and eke by night, for thy sweet delight,
 Thou shalt me in thy arms inclose.
I am thine for ever, still I will persever
 True to thee, where ere I go."
Her flatteries beleeve not ; come to me, and grieve not !
 Wantons will thee overthrow.

The vertuous Lady mild enters then among them,
  Being big with child as ever she might be.
With distilling tears, she looked then upon them,
  Filled full of fears, thus replyed she:
"Ah! my love, and dear, wherefore stay you here?
  Refusing me your loving wife;
For an harlot's sake, which each one will take,
  Whose vile deeds provoke much strife:
Many can accuse her, O my love, refuse her,
  With thy lady home return!
Her flatteries beleeve not, come to me, and grieve not!
  Wantons will thee overthrow."

All in a fury then, the angry Knight up-started:
  Very furious when he heard his Ladie's speech.
With many bitter terms his wife he ever thwarted,
  Using hard extreams while she did him beseech.
From her neck so white he took away in spite
  Her curious chain of purest gold,
Her jewells and her rings, and all such costly things,
  As he about her did behold.
The harlot in her presence, he did gentle reverence,
  And to her he gave them all.
He sent away his Lady, full of wo as may be,
  Who in a swound with grief did fall.

[The Second Part, TO THE SAME TUNE.]

At the Ladye's wrong the Harlot fleer'd and laughed:
  Enticements are so strong, they overcome the wise;
The Knight nothing regarded to see the Lady scoffed,
  Thus was she rewarded for her enterprize.
The Harlot all this space did him oft imbrace,
  She flatters him, and thus doth say:—
"For thee I'le dye and live, for thee my Faith I'le give,
  No wo shall work my love's decay,
Thou shalt be my treasure, thou shalt be my pleasure,
  Thou shalt be my heart's delight.
I will be thy darling, I will be thy worldling,
  In despight of Fortune's spight."

Thus he did remain in wastfull great expences,
  Till it bred his pain, and consum'd him quite.
When his lands were spent, troubled in his sences,
  Then he did repent of his late lewd life.

For relief he hyes, for relief he flyes,
  To them on whom he [had] spent his gold;
They do him deny, they do him defie,
  They will not once his face behold.
Being thus distressed, being thus oppressed,
  In the fields that night he lay,
Which the harlot knowing, through her malice growing,
  Sought to take his life away.

A young and proper lad they had slain in secret,
  For the gold he had, whom they did convey,
By a Ruffian lewd, to that place directly,
  Where the youthfull Knight fast a-sleeping lay.
The bloody dagger then, wherewith they kill'd the man,
  Hard by the knight he likewise laid,
Sprinkling him with blood, as he thought it good,
  And then no longer there he stayd.
The Knight being so abused was forthwith accused,
  For this murder which was done;
And he was condemned, that had not offended:
  Shamefull death he might not shun.

When the Lady bright understood the matter,
  That her wedded Knight was condemn'd to dye,
To the King she went with all the speed that might be:
  Where she did lament her hard destiny.
"Noble King" (quoth she) "pitty take on me,
  And pardon my poor husband's life:
Else I am undone, with my little son:
  Let mercy mitigate this grief."
"Lady fair, content thee, soon thou would'st repent thee,
  If he should be saved so.
Sore he hath abus'd thee, sore he hath misus'd thee,
  Therefore, Lady, let him go."

"O my liege," quoth she, "grant your gracious favour,
  Dear he is to me, though he did me wrong."
The King reply'd again, with a stern behaviour,
  "A Subject he hath slain, dye he shall e're long,
Except [that] thou canst find any one so kind
  That will dye and let him free."
"Noble King," she said, "glad am I apaid,
  That same person will I be.
I will suffer duly, I will suffer truly,
  For my Love and husband's sake."
The King thereat amazed, though he her beauty praised,
  He bad[e] from thence they should her take.

It was the King's command, on the morrow after,
  She should out of hand to the Scaffold go:
Her husband was to bear meanwhile the sword before her,
  He must eke, alas! give the deadly blow.
He refus'd the deed, she bid him proceed,
  With a thousand kisses sweet.
In this wofull case, they did both imbrace,
  Which mov'd the Ruffians in the place
Straight for to discover this concealed murder,
  Whereby the Lady saved was.
The harlot then was [starved], as she well deserved: ["hanged."
  This did virtue bring to passe. 132

Printed for *F. Coles, J. W[right], T. Vere, W. Gilbertson.*

[In Black-letter. Three woodcuts: 1st, the woman and man on p. 209; 2nd, the black-hatted figure of p. 281, Left; 3rd, the Woman in hoop with feather-fan, of vol. i. 253. Date of original issue, as registered, 15th June, 1603. Our exemplar was printed later, after the Pepysian (for Coles, Vere, Wright, and Clarke), *c.* 1655. The penultimate line "might have rhymed," says Horatio.]

The New Baloo.

"Peace, wayward bairn! O cease thy mone!
Thy far more wayward Daddy's gone,
And never will recalled be
By cryes of either thee or me:
For should we cry until we dye,
We could not scant his cruelty. *Ballow, Ballow,* etc.

"He needs might in himself foresee
What thou successively might'st be;
And could he then (though me forego)
His Infant leave 'ere he did know
How like the Dad would be the Lad,
In time to make fond maidens glad? *Ballow, Ballow,*" etc.

—Brome's *Northern Lasse,* Act. iv. Sc. 1, 1632.

THERE have been acrimonious controversies carried on, without dignity or knowledge, in recent years, concerning one or other of the versions extant of a song known as "*Baloo*" or "*Balow* my Babe!" We can first settle the authorship of the original *Balloo* "Lullaby"—the writer of which was neither Scotchman nor Scotchwoman, Lady Anne Bothwell or 'Lady' Wardlaw (Robert Chambers's Mrs. Harris, supposed to have written everything Scotch, and much more, in ballad literature, at beginning of 18th century); but an Englishman whose date was *circâ* 1545–1626, *viz.* Nicholas Breton; who had printed the original 'Sweet Lullabie' in his '*Arbor of Amorous Deuices,*' 159⅞. It is strange that this poem, (so popular when reprinted as a street-song that we are able to record five exemplars) was not recognised as his, although little changed on the broadsides. There is only one copy of the book, and that imperfect; preserved at Trinity College, Cambridge. The Rev. Dr. A. B. Grosart reprinted it in the *Works of Nicholas Breton* (see his excellent *Chertsey Worthies' Library*, 1879, Part 80).

We add here "A Sweet Lullabie," on p. 580, for comparison with our "New Balow," because there are corruptions of text in *Roxburghe Ballads*, vol. ii. p. 525. The poem deserves to be seen in its integrity. It is the fountain-head of all the Balloo rivulets.

It is indeed a "*Sweet Lullaby.*" As a broadside ballad, with corruptions and variations of text, it is in Roxb. Coll., I. 387; Bagford Coll., I. 56; II. 151 (no p. n.); Pepys, I. 480; Douce, II. 206. The Roxb. was 'Printed by and for A.M. (that is, Andrew Milbourne), and Sold by the Booksellers of London.'

The next in date appears to be the version (*vide* Percy Folio MS., iii. 516), in Elizabeth Rogers's MS. Virginal Book (Addit. MS., 10,337), beginning "Baloo, my boy, lye still and weep!" In John Gamble's MS., *with the music*, of date 1649, the first line is "Ballowe, my babe, lye still and sleepe." Pinkerton's MS., 4to., 46, 'The Ballow (Allane's),' begins, "Balow, my babe, frowne not on me; who still," etc. This has seven stanzas. In Palmer's MS., six stanzas, the commencement is "Balow, my babe, ly still and sleepe! It grieves," etc. Percy Folio MS., iii. 522, followed by Dr. Thomas Percy, has "Balow, my babe, lye still and sleepe! It greeues me sore to see thee weepe;" etc. We now reprint "The New Balow; or, A Wenche's Lamentation," etc., 1626-27, beginning "Balow, my babe, weep not for me." (We need scarcely mention the composite and 'popular' versions, in Whitelaw's *Scottish Ballads*, 196; whence comes the copy in *Illustrated Book of Scottish Songs*, p. 340; or one in *Watson's Choice Collection of Scots Poems*, iii. p. 79, 1711, claimed as Scottish and there first entitled "Lady *Anne Bothwell's* Lament;" followed similarly in Allan Ramsay's *Tea-Table Miscellany*, 1725, vol. ii. Some modern issues are in S. C. Hall's *Book of British Ballads*, p. 411, and in Robert Chambers's *Scottish Ballads*; W. E. Aytoun's *Ballads of Scotland*, ii. 44, 1858.

Our Roxburghe Ballad on next page is a probably unique broadside and has been reprinted once only to our knowledge, *viz.* in R. H. Evans's *Old Ballads*, vol. i. p. 259, 1810. As "Baloe my Babe," it was early entered to Margaret Trundle in Stationers' Registers, under date of 1626-27, among the *Ballades*, Book *D*, fol. 145 = *Transcript*, iv. p. 181.

In our *Amanda Group of Bagford Poems*, 1880 (No. 20 of Ballad Society Publications), p. *177, we reprinted a rare imitation, four stanzas, entitled "The Forsaken Maid. To the tune of '*Balloo.*'" From the Drollery *Mock Songs and Joking Poems*, 1675, p. 126. It begins, "My dearest Baby, prethee sleep, it grieves me sore to see thee weep." We need not repeat it here.

*** The supposed Scottish origin, a hundred years too late, and all the senseless chatter about Lady Anne Bothwell, may be consigned to Mr. Donnelly and his 'Hang-Hog is the Latin for Bacon' crypto-grammarification.

By the way: of all the idiotic '*fads*,' or fraudulent misrepresentations, utterly unworthy of acceptance by any person outside of Earlswood Asylum, Hanwell, Colney-Hatch, or Morningside, the Delia-Bacon craze or Bacon-dethronement-of-Shakespeare pretence, re-issued by Donnelly and Co., Limited (illegitimately shooting leaden pellets, across the stalking-horses of the *Nineteenth Century* and *Daily Telegraph*, long before the still-unrealized production of distinct evidence or proofs. Feb. '88), was the most audacious and culpable slander of the greatest Englishman ever born. It came, as immoral dynamite, from an Irish-American. Shakespeare answered him anticipatively in *Twelfth Night*, ii. 5:—

Malvolio.—"What should that alphabetical position portend?"

Fabian.—"Did not I say he would work it out? *the cur is excellent at faults?*"

[Roxburghe Collection, II. 573. Probably unique.]

The New Balow;

Or, a Wenche's Lamentation for the loss of her Sweet-heart, he having left her with a Babe to play her, being the Fruits of her Folly.

The tune is, *Balow*. [See previous page.]

BAlow, my Babe, weep not for me,
Whose greatest grief's for wronging thee;
But pity her deserving smart,
Who can but blame her own kind heart,
For trusting to a flattering friend;
The fairest tongue, the falsest mind.
Balow, my babe, [*weep not for me*], etc.

Balow, my Babe, ly still and sleep,
It grieves me sore to hear thee weep:
If thou be still I will be glad,
Thy weeping makes thy mother sad;
Balow, my boy, thy mother's joy,
Thy father wrought me great annoy.
Balow, balow [*weep not for me*], etc.

First when he came to court my love,
With sugred words he did me move:
His flattering and fained chear
To me that time did not appear.
But now, I see that cruel he
Cares neither for my babe nor me.
Balow, balow, [*weep not for me*], etc.

I cannot choose but love him still,
Altho' that he hath done me ill;
For he hath stolen away my heart,
And from him it cannot depart:
In weal or woe, where ere he go,
I'le love him, though he be my foe.
Balow, balow, [*weep not for me*], etc.

But peace, my comfort! curse not him,
Who now in seas of grief doth swim,
Perhaps of Death: for who can tell
Whether the Judge of heaven or hell,
By some predestinated death,
Revenging me, hath stopt his breath,
Balow, balow, [*weep not for me*], etc.

If I were near those fatal bounds,
Where he ly[es] groaning in his wounds,
Repeating as he pants for breath,
Her name that wounds more deep than death,
O then what woman's heart so strong
Would not forget the greatest wrong?
Balow, balow, [weep not for me], etc.

If linen lack, for my love's sake,
Whom I once loved, then would I take
My smock even from my body meet,
And wrap him in that winding sheet;
Ay me! how happy had I bin,
If he had nere been wrapt therein.
Balow, balow, [weep not for me], etc.

Balow, my babe, spare thou thy tears,
Until thou come to wit and years;
Thy griefs are gathering to a sum,
Heaven grant thee patience till they come:
A mother's fault, a father's shame,
A hapless state, a bastard's name.
Balow, balow, [weep not for me], etc.

Be still, my babe, and sleep awhile,
And when thou wakes then sweetly smile!
But smile not as thy father did
To c[o]usen maids: O heaven, forbid!
And yet into thy face I see
Thy father dear, which tempted me.
Balow, balow, [weep not for me], etc.

Balow, my babe! O follow not
His faithless steps who thee begot,
Nor glory in a maid's disgrace,
For thou art his too much, alace!
And in thy looking eyes I read
Who overthrew my maiden-head.
Balow, balow, [weep not for me], etc.

O! if I were a maid again,
All young men's flatteries I'd refrain:
Because unto my grief I find
That they are faithless and unkind;
Their tempting terms hath bred my harm,
Bear witness, babe, lyes in my arm.
Balow, balow, [weep not for me], etc.

Balow my babe, spare yet thy tears,
Until thou come to wit and years;
Perhaps yet thou may['st] come to be
A courteour by disdaining me:
Poor me, poor me! alas, poor me!
My own two eyes have blinded me.
Balow, balow, [*weep not for me*], etc.

On Love and fortune I complain,
On them, and on my self also:
But most of all mine own two eyes
The chiefest workers of my wo;
For they have caused so my smart,
That I must die without a heart.
Balow, balow, [*weep not for me*], etc.

Balow, my babe, thy father's dead—
To me the Prodigal hath plaid:
Of heaven and earth regardless, he
Prefer'd the wars to me and thee.
I doubt that now his cursing mind
Make him eat accorns with the swine.
Balow, balow, [*weep not for me*], etc.

Farewel, farewel, most faithless youth
That ever kist a woman's mouth!
Let never a woman after me
Submit unto the curtesie;
For if she do, O cruel thou,
Would wrong them: O who can tell how?
Balow, balow, [*weep not for me*], etc.

Finis.

[No publisher's name or woodcut. Black-letter. Original issue, 1626-7.]

A Sweet Lullabie. [See p. 576.

COme, little babe, come silly soule,
  Thy father's shame, thy mother's griefe,
Borne as I doubt to all our dole,
  And to thy selfe vnhappie chiefe:
    Sing Lullabie and lap it warme,
    Poore soule that thinkes no creature harme.

Thou little think'st, and lesse doost knowe,
  The cause of this thy mother's moane;
Thou want'st the wit to waile her woe,
  And I my selfe am all alone:
    Why doost thou weepe? why doost thou waile?
    And knowest not yet what thou doost ayle.

Come, little wretch, ah silly heart!
  Mine onely ioy, what can I more?
If there be any wrong thy smart,
  That may the destinies implore:
    'Twas I, I say, against my will,
    I wayle the time, but be thou still.

And doest thou smile, oh thy sweete face,
  Would God himselfe he might thee see,
No doubt thou would'st soon purchace grace,
  I know right well, for thee and mee;
    But come to mother, babe, and play,
    For father false is fled away.

Sweet boy, if it by fortune chance,
  Thy father home againe to send,
If death do strike me with his launce,
  Yet may'st thou me to him cōmend:
    If any aske thy mother's name,
    Tell how by loue she purchast blame.

Then will his gentle heart soone yeeld,
  I know him of a noble minde,
Although a Lyon in the field,
  A Lamb in towne thou shalt him finde:
    Aske blessing babe, be not afrayde,
    His sugred words hath me betrayde.

Then may'st thou ioy and be right glad,
  Although in woe I seeme to moane,
Thy father is no Rascall lad,
  A noble youth of blood and boane:
    His glancing lookes, if he once smile,
    Right honest women may beguile.

Come, little boy, and rocke a sleepe,
  Sing lullabie, and be thou still;
I that can doe nought else but weepe,
  Wil sit by thee and waile my fill:
    God blesse my babe, and lullabie,
    From this thy father's qualitie.

Finis. [By **Nicholas Breton.**]

[Printed by R.I. (Richard Jones), in *The Arbor of Amorous Deuices*, 159¾.]

[Roxburghe Collection, III. 579.]

[Montrose's Lynes; Or,]

A Proper New Ballad.

To the Tune of, *I'le never Love thee more.*[1]

MY dear and only love, I pray
  That little World of thee
Be govern'd by no other sway
  But purest Monarchie;
For if Confusion have a part,
  Which vertuous souls abhore,
I'le call a Synod in my heart, A.D. 1645.
  And never love thee more.

As *Alexander* I will reign,
  And I will reign alone;
My thoughts did ever yet disdain
  A Rival on my Throne.
He either fears his fate too much,
  Or his deserts are small,
That dares not put it to the touch,
  To gain or lose it all. [misp., 'at all.'

But I will reign and govern still,
  And alwayes give the Law,
And have each Subject at my will,
  And all to stand in aw[e]:
But 'gainst my Batteries if I find
  Thou kick, or vex me sore, [a. l., 'storm.'
As that thou set me up a blind, As if, me as a.
  I'le never love thee more.

And in the Empire of thy heart,
  Where I should solely be,
If others do pretend a part,
  Or dare to share with me: [" dares."
Or Committees if thou erect, [pr. a. Committees.
  And go on such a score:
I'le laugh and smile at thy neglect, [a.l. smiling mock.
  And never love thee more.

[1] On p. 557 we mentioned this tune of *I'll never love thee more*, which takes its name from the burden of the original anonymous song beginning "My dear and only Love, take heed," of date *circa* 1625, antecedent to the spirited lines of Montrose by nearly a score of years. Although thus written earlier, the original here appears as a *Second Part*, on p. 582; having been dragged at the chariot-wheels of the Conqueror, to swell his triumph.

But if thou will prove faithful then,
And constant in thy word,
I'le make thee glorious by my Pen,
And famous by my Sword :
I'le serve thee in such noble [ways], ["sort."
Was never heard before :
I'le crown and deck thy head with bays,
And love thee more and more.

[By James Grahame, Marquis of Montrose.

[*Note.*—Other versions " But if no faithless action stain thy love and constant word, I'll make thee famous by my pen, and glorious by my sword." Here end 'Montrose's lines,' as they are styled in MS., early written on the broadside.]

The Second Part [not by Montrose.]

MY dear and only love, take heed, how thou thy self expose,
Let not a[ll] longing lovers feed upon such looks as those :
I'le marble-wall thee round about, my self shall be the door,
And if thy heart chance to slide out, *I'le never love thee more.*

Let not th[eir] oaths, like volies shot, make any breach at all, ['thy.'
Nor smoothness of their language plot which way to scale the wall ;
Nor balls of wild-fire love consume the Shrine which I adore,
For if such smoak about thee fume, *I'le never love thee more.* ['foam.'

I know thy vertues be too strong to suffer by surprise ;
If that thou slight'st their love so long, their siege at last will rise,
And leave thee conqueror in thy health and state thou was[t] before,
[Yet] if thou prove a common wealth, *I'le never love thee more.*

But if by fraud, or by deceit, thy heart to mine come,
I'le sound no trumpet as I wont, nor march by tuck of drum :
But hold my arms as Ensigns up, thy falsehood to deplore ;
And after sigh, and bitter weep, *that e're I lov'd so sore.*[1]

I'le do with thee as *Nero* did, when *Rome* he set on fire :
Not only all relief forbid, but to an hill retire :
And scorn to shed a tear to save thy spirit grown so poor, ['smile.'
But laugh and [sing] thee to thy grave, *and never love thee more.*

[Here ends the original song, as in *Wit and Drollery*, p. 33, 1656. This unauthorized portion is virtually a *Third Part*, of less merit, anonymous.]

THen shall my heart be set by thine, but in far different case,
For mine was true ; so was not thine, but lookt like *Janus* face.
Thy beauty shin'd at first so bright, and woe is me therefore !
That e're I found the love so bright, *that I could love no more.*

My heart shall with the Sun be fixt, for constancie most strange ;
And thine shall with the Moon be mixt, delighting still in change :
For as thou waves with everie wind, and sails through everie shore,
And leaves my constant heart behind, *how can I love thee more ?*

[1] *Al. lect.*, preferable :—And after such a bitter cup, *I'le never love thee more.*

Yet for the love I bare thee once, lest that thy name should die,
  A monument of marble stone, the truth shall testifie ;
That every Pilgrim passing by may pity and deplore,
  And sighing read the reason why *I cannot love thee more.*

The golden Laws of Love shall be upon these pillars hung,
  A single heart, a simple eye, a true and constant tongue :
Let no man for more loves pretend, than he hath hearts in store :
  True love begun will never end, *love one and love no more.*

And when all gallants, led about, this monument to view, — ["lead."
  It's written both within and out, thou'rt treacherous, I true :
Then in a passion they shall pause, and thus [cry,] sighing sore,
  "Alas! he had too just a cause, *never to love thee more.*"

And when the 'tressing gods do face, from East to West doth flee,
  They shall record it, to thy shame, how thou hast loved me :
And how in odds our love's been such as few hath been before,
  Thou lov'd too many, I too much : *that I can love no more.*

The misty mounts, the smoking lakes, the rocks' resounding echo,
  The whistling winds, the woods that shake, shall all with me sing hey ho :
The tossing seas, the tumbling boats, tears dropping from each oar,
  Shall tune with me their turtle notes, *I'le never love thee more.*

Yet as the turtle chast[e] and true her fellow so regrates,
  And daily sighs for her adieu, that ne're renews her notes :
But though thy faith was never fast, which grieves me wondrous sore,
  Yet I shall live in love so chast[e], *that I shall love no more.*

Finis.

[No publisher's name, or woodcut. White-letter. Early part called in MS. "Montrose's Lynes." Date of his portion soon after 1643. In the Douce Collection, I. 101 *verso*, to the same tune, is a ballad beginning, "My dear and only joy, take heed," entitled, "I'll never love thee more ; being the Forsaken Lover's Farewell to his Fickle Mistress." In Rawlinson Coll., 190 *verso*, is "My dear and only love, take heed," similar to our second part ; also Pepys Coll., III. 266, the *original* ballad (eight stanzas, similar to our Second Part, p. 582) ; it is entitled "I'le never Love thee more ; being a true Love-Song between a young Man and a Maid. To a new Tune, called, *O no, no, no, not yet !*" It has the same beginning, etc., as ours, "My dear and only Love, take heed." *London*, printed for *F. Coles, T. Vere, J. Wright*, and *J. Clarke.* Douce's broadside is a distinct issue, printed for *Wm. Whitwood*, at the *Golden Lyon*, in *Duck-lane.*]

*** Although of little merit intrinsically, three Roxburghe Ballads are here for the first time reprinted, one of them appointed to be sung to the same tune ; and the other two (themselves connected together by names and subject) probably taking it as an alternative tune, instead of *The Bonny Broom.* Both the latter ballads treat of *Diaphantus* and *Caridora.* All three were printed in sequence, on one side of a sheet (unique), and are in the same measure. We cannot affirm that they were distinguishedly 'beautiful in their lives,' but 'in their death they were not divided.' (For the tune of *The Bonny Broom* see Wm. Chappell's *Popular Music*, p. 461.) Until we find proof to the contrary, we shall regard the three songs as portions of one story. See the *Trois étoiles Note* on p. 586.

[Roxburghe Collection, II. 571. Probably unique.]

A Proper New Ballad;

Being the Regrate of a true Lover for his Mistriss' Unkindnesse.

To a new Tune, *I'le ever love thee more.*

I Wish I were those gloves, dear heart, which could thy hands inshrine;
Then should no sorrow, grief, nor smart, molest this heart of mine:
But since the Fates doth this deny, which leaves me to deplore,
My dribling eyes shall never dry, *until thou love me more.*

But O! that I might shrouded be within these arms of thine,
And that my soul might say of thee, that thou were freely mine:
Then prostrate at thy feet I would thee, doubtlesse, still adore,
And so in spight of Fate I should *essay to love thee more.*

I shall defy that mortal Wight, enjoy thee who so will,
Than I to soar an higher flight in love, or mount me till: [till = *Until.*
But since to one I must resigne thee quite, and give thee o're,
I'le love him for that face of thine, *which made me love thee more.*

Nay, sure, some sacred Angel haunts within that heart of thine,
Whose secret power my soul enchants, which from thy eyes do shine:
But O! that I could thee inflame, as I did him implore,
That so by reason of the same, *thou yet might love me more.*

But happie is thy servant sure, that such a love enjoies,
Whose smiles does all disasters cure, whose frowns breeds all annoies:
As *Phœbus*, breaking through the cloud, gives heat and light in store,
So when thou doth thine eyes unshroude, *they make me love thee more.*

I wish I were a Hauk, to soar within the skie of love,
And that thou metamorphos'd were into a Turtle Dove:
There would I catch thee with delight, with pleasure plum[e] thee o're,
And so should none beneath our flight *attempt to love thee more.*

Thy face is as a heaven which holds two shining suns of love,
The which thine eye-lids clouds infold, in ivorie orbs they move:
Their absence makes me like to die, their presence burns me sore;
So still in these extreams I lie, *and yet must love thee more.*

To lodge betwixt those ivorie hills, which in thy bosom dwells,
From whence the sugred nectar trills, in sweetness that excells;
There would I surfeit with delight, my self, and ne're give o're,
Till love should so our souls unite, *as ay to love thee more.*

I like the Salamander am, that in the fire remains,
And not consumed with the flame, I live in pleasant pains:
O! that these bodies were to act, as free as minds to soare,
Then surely I at length would make *my Lasse to love me more.*

Since of the days desires our dreams the true ideas are,
I wish that of mine eyes the beams in sleep inclosed were:
That slumbring I might thee possess, whom daylie I adore,
For waking I dare scarce transgress, *and yet must love thee more.*

But yet if thou would condescend unto my dear request,
And suffer me my health to spend, upon thy candid breast: [= candida.
Then surelie I, or ever let, imperiously would soare, [*let* = hindered.
As praising thee at highest rate, *and so would love thee more.*

Some comfort unto those belong, who common lovers be,
Since they upon surmise of wrong, can set their fancie free:
But should I die by thy disdain, which others would abhore,
My pure affection shall, unstain'd, *aspire to love thee more.*

Then let not black ingratitude so dear a Saint disgrace,
For it would taint the finest blood, and stain the fairest face:
Since thou mayest love, and yet be chast, and still behind have store,
Then slight not him who doth attest *the gods, he'l love thee more.*

Finis.

Diaphantas' Words to Caridora, upon a Disaster.

THe sweetest saint incenc'd may be, and for a moment mov'd
To wrath by some disaster hie, against her best belov'd:
But let it be, I were thy foe, as first I'le lose this breath,
Thou should'st not suffer down to go the sun upon thy wrath.

"I'le only curse the sullen star, reveal'd th' unhappie hour,
Which did me from thy presence bar by his malignant power:
That planet I shall still allow, while as I here remain,
Whose bless'd aspect shall bring me to my first estate again.

"But yet these strains which I to thee in favour did impart,
Thou slighted them, which threw on me a deadlie wounding dart:
And yet I shall be loath to grieve thee in the least degree,
For thou shalt *Charidora* live, I *Diaphantas* die. [*sic.*

"In holie writs heavens pardons such, [who] true as infants be, ['as.']
But I could wish to weep as much for sin's I mourn for thee:
Resemble then these heavenlie powers, and grant him thy good will,
Who wishes all to you and yours, that heaven can bring you till. [=to.

"How like am I unto a [K]night, that dwells beneath the Pole!
Who entertains a six months' night before their sun doth role:
Since in thy absence night doth lie, thy presence shineth clear,
Lend but the twilight of thine eye, to make my day appear.

"So shall my leaden spirits rise from out this bed of care,
To welcome thee into our skies, which now in darkness are:
But if my suit thou shalt denie, and render frowns for love,
Then shall that stain upon thee lie, while I shall constant prove.

"The ship that cuts the aisure tide, and from her course is driven [=azure.
By tempest, the magnettick guide yet brings her to the haven:
So we, in midst of Nature's main, when passion's storms do blow,
Are driven averse, yet back again by love are led also.

"Since grace and nature doth agree, things striving to restore,
Shall such a stain be found in thee? the saint whom I adore,
As to denie for to be led by grace, and stop thine ears,
O do not! lest for thee I shed my sanguine drops in tears."

Finis.

[In Black-letter. No woodcut. What follows, in a continuation, may be a reply to a Pepysian ballad, being marked to the same tune as it is, *viz. The bonny bonny Broom*, yet it evidently is connected with our two preceding ballads, and could be sung to the tune of "Montrose's Lines," My dear and only love, I pray" = *I'll never love thee more. Note* the Scotticism *till* = to, in them both.

[Roxburghe Collection, II. 575. Probably unique.]

The Forlorn Lover's Lament.

To the tune of, *The bon[n]y Broom.* [See *Note*, below.]

SIr, do not think these lines have flow'd from youthful hearts or hands,
  But from a friend, who's thrice conjoin'd in *Hymen's* holy bands:
Nor *Charidora* did not prove, by half so much unkind
To *Diaphantes*, since his love could never match my mind.

" Nor *Coradon*, who turn'd his song, and sorrows to the Broom, [N.B.
Could never match with me in wrong, which shows me to consume:
Poor Lovers in this lovelesse age are left to mourn alone,
And wondred at by such as rage my love to look upon.

" Even as the Lillie in the hedge is prick'd on either side,
So I'm tormented by the rage of those who swell with pride:
The surges of the swelling tide, and the walls broad that be,
As yet they never could divide my heart from loving thee.

" I live in anguish grief, and smart, for thou enjoyest mine,
And I must live without an heart, until thou send me thine:
Which if thou could incline to do, it should such comfort send,
To me, who comfortlesse am now, and like my life to end.

" For I should take it as a pledge, since thou hast mine from me,
Least I should die without an heart, let me have thine from thee:
Then might we both together live, as one by hearts exchang'd,
But keeping both, if thou survive, just heavens will be aveng'd.

" But I will rest in hope that thou will send me answer kind,
To me who live in torment now, until I know thy mind. ['lives.'
I do expect no frowns from thee, because I did presume
To send these lines, when minding me to sing them as the Broom.

Finis.

[Black-letter. No Publisher's name (*Scottish*), or woodcut. Date, *circâ* 1675.]

*** Pepys Collection, I. 40, is a Black-letter ballad of seven stanzas, entitled, "The new Broome." *London*, printed for *F. Coles.* Begins thus:—

Poore *Coridon* did sometime sit hard by the broome alone,
And secretly complaind to it against his only one,
He bids the broome, that blooms him by, beare witness to his wrong,
And, thinking that none else was nie, he thus began his Song:
The bonny broome, the well-favour'd broome, the broome blooms faire on hill,
What ail'd my love to lightly mee, and I working her will? Etc.

See second stanza of our ballad, "The Forlorn Lover's Lament," and *Appendix*.

We need not here pursue the enquiry how far or how little this "New Broome" sweeps onward in imitation of the old "*Broome, broome on Hill, broome,*" mentioned in Wager's "The Longer thou livest the more fool thou art," *circâ* 1567. Still earlier named in *The Complaint of Scotland*, 1549: "*Brume, brume on hil*" (*Early English Text Society, Extra Series*, No. xvii. p. 64, 1872.)

The Gallant Grahams of Scotland.

"Presbyteriani ligaverunt, Independantes trucidaverunt."—*Salmasius.*

TO the best of our belief, the broadside ballad of "The Gallant Grahams," contained in the Roxburghe and Douce Collections and therein alone, has not been hitherto reprinted. It was probably little known, except to Joseph Ritson, at the beginning of this century, and (through his sending a transcript) to "Mr. Walter Scott, Advocate, of Edinburgh," who was even then preparing his delightful work *The Minstrelsy of the Scottish Border.* In vol. iii. pp. 171-187, the first edition, 1803, appears the ballad "from tradition, enlarged and corrected by an ancient printed edition, entitled 'The Gallant Grahams of Scotland,' to the tune of *I will away, and I will not tarry*, of which Mr. Ritson favoured the editor with an accurate copy." *The Tune is not yet identified*; but the words seem to refer to the second line of the Scottish version: "*I maun away, and I may not stay.*"

Had we been able to see in its integrity, or its absolute corruption (such being the more probable condition), the ballad as first taken down from oral tradition, always inaccurate, mis-remembered and mis-transmitted, before it reached Walter Scott in fragments, we should find little in common with our broadside beyond the general idea, with here or there some local designation. But Ritson soon enabled Scott to use the connected although corrupted printed copy. He was fated to work more restorative-wonders with the *Border Ballads* than the duller-witted, heavy-styled, and injudiciously 'emendatory' Bishop Percy had done when he produced the *Reliques* in 1765. Scott well knew how to bridge over gulfs, and make dry bones to live. That he himself was the remodeller or re-constructor of many intelligible glowing ballads, persistently, throughout *The Minstrelsy*, from the suggestive but self-contradictory fragments which his ready instinct showed him to have been formerly connected, is demonstrable. He gave us marvellous treasures in these Border-Ballads. But he was the Arachne who spun the threads from within. Many of them, by their superiority to rival manufactures, approve the Master's hand. Some were as thoroughly his own entire creation (beside "The Eve of St. John,") as were his soon-following "Novels by the Author of *Waverley*." Scott thus ends his introductory remarks on the Gallant Grahams:

"There seems an attempt to trace Montrose's career, from his first raising the royal standard, to his second expedition and death; but it is interrupted and imperfect. From the concluding stanza, I presume the song was composed upon the arrival of Charles [the Second] in Scotland, which so speedily followed the execution of Montrose, that the King entered the city, while the head of his most faithful and most successful adherent was still blackening in the sun." (*Cf.* p. 589.)

The Gallant Grahams.

[Scott's *Minstrelsy* version.]

"NOW, fare thee weel, sweet *Ennerdale*![1] baith kith and countrie I bid adieu;
For I maun away, and I may not stay, to some uncouth land which I never knew.

"To wear the blue I think it best, of all the colours that I see;
And I'll wear it for the gallant *Grahams*, that are banished from their countrie.

"I have no gold, I have no land, I have no pearl, nor precious stane,
But I wald sell my silken snood, to see the gallant *Grahams* come hame.

"In *Wallace* days when they began, Sir *John* the *Graham*[2] did bear the gree,
Through all the lands of *Scotland* wide; he was a lord of the south countrie.

"And so was seen full many a time: for the summer flowers did never spring,
But every *Graham*, in armour bright, would then appear before the King.

"They all were dressed in armour sheen, upon the pleasant banks of *Tay*;
Before a King they might be seen, these gallant *Grahams* in their array.

"At the *Goukhead* our camp we set, our leaguer down there for to lay;
And in the bonnie summer light, we rode our white horse and our gray.

"Our false commander sold our king unto his deadly enemie,
Who was the traitor *Cromwell*,[3] then; so I care not what they do with me.

"They have betrayed our noble prince, and banish'd him from his royal crown;
But the gallant *Grahams* have ta'en in hand for to command those traitors down.

"In *Glen-Prosen*[4] we rendezvoused, marched to *Glenshie* by night and day,
And took the town of *Aberdeen*, and met the *Campbells* in their array.

"Five thousand men, in armour strong, did meet the gallant *Grahams* that day,
At *Inverlochie* where war began, and scarce two thousand men were they.

"Gallant *Montrose*, that chieftain bold, courageous in the best degree,
Did for the King fight well that day; the Lord preserve his Majestie!

"*Nathaniel Gordon*,[5] stout and bold, did for King *Charles* wear the blue;
But the Cavaliers, they all were sold, and brave *Harthill*,[6] a Cavalier too.

"And *Newton Gordon*,[7] burd-alone, and *Dalgatie*,[8] both stout and keen,
And gallant *Veitch*,[9] upon the field a braver face was never seen.

"Now, fare ye weel, sweet *Ennerdale!* countrie and kin, I quit ye free;
Cheer up your hearts, brave Cavaliers, for the *Grahams* are gone to high *Germany*.

"Now brave *Montrose* he went to *France*, and to *Germany* to gather fame,
And bold *Aboyne*[10] is to the sea, young *Huntly* is his noble name.

"*Montrose* again, that chieftain bold, back unto *Scotland* fair he came,
For to redeem fair *Scotland's* land, the pleasant, gallant, worthy *Graham!*

"At the water of *Carron* he did begin, and fought the battle to the end;
Where there were killed, for our noble king, two thousand of our *Danish*[11] men.

"*Gilbert Menzies*,[12] of high degree, by whom the king's banner was borne,
For a brave Cavalier was he, but now to glory he is gone.

"Then woe to *Strachan* and *Hacket*[13] baith! and, *Lesley*, ill death may thou die,
For ye have betrayed the gallant *Grahams*, who aye were true to majestie.

"And the laird of *Assint* has seized *Montrose*, and had him into *Edinburgh* town;
And frae his body taken the head, and quartered him upon a trone.

"And *Huntley's* gone,[14] the self-same way, and our noble king is also gone;
He suffered death for our nation, our mourning tears can ne'er be done.

"But our brave young King is now come home, King *Charles* the Second in degree;
The Lord send peace into his time, and God preserve his Majesty!"[15]

*** Sir Walter Scott gives no less than seven pages of small-type *Notes* to his version in the *Minstrelsy*, which owes so much to his having inspected Ritson's copy of our broadside. Than his *Minstrelsy Notes* no man ever wrote better, few equal: in them the future 'Wizard of the North' fleshed his maiden sword in unconscious preparation for the Waverley Novels of later years. To them, in their entirety, readers must turn. We condense the chief explanations.

1 "*Ennerdale*, a corruption of *Endrickdale*. The principal and most ancient possessions of the Montrose family lie along the water of Endrick, in Dumbartonshire." (Walter Scott, *Minstrelsy S. B.*, iii. 181.)

2 "Sir *John* the *Graham*, the faithful friend and adherent of the immortal Wallace, slain at the battle of Falkirk."—*Ibid.* A.D. 1298.

3 *Cromwell.* "This extraordinary character . . was no favourite in Scotland." It was a Scotchman (though only an Ecclefechanite, soured and dyspeptical) who was to come forward as an enthusiastic white-washer of faulty but brave 'Old Noll.' In more recent years Midlothianites lost their senses, crofters took to rebellion and deer-stealing, or greedy for plunder began to hunger anew for disestablishment.

4 *Glen-prosen*, in Angus-shire.

5 *Nathaniel Gordon* was one of the Gordons of Gight. He pillaged Elgin of 14,000 marks in silver on 24 July, 1645. He was taken prisoner at Philiphaugh. Owing to the bloodthirsty cravings of the Presbyterian clergy, perverting the Scripture which told of Samuel demanding the slaughter of Agag, Nathaniel Gordon was brought first of the prisoners to the block, on 6th January, 164$\frac{5}{6}$.

6 *Harthill.* Leith of Harthill, a determined loyalist, and hater of the Covenanters. In most of Montrose's engagements, and comrade of Nat. Gordon.

7 *Newton Gordon*, burd alone (*i.e.* surviving son), that is, Gordon of Newton.

8 *Dalgatie.* Sir Francis Hay of Dalgatie. Condemned to death along with Montrose, he was deprived of spiritual attendance and comfort as a Catholic, refusing on principle the service of bigotted Calvinists, he died gallantly, first kissing the axe while devoid of a crucifix, and avowing his fidelity to his Sovereign. What could they do with our brave Cavaliers except butcher them in cold blood, whenever they won the chance? Shall there be forgetfulness of such things, and men be allowed to drift anew into rebellion, separatism, and anarchy, to be inevitably followed by worse tyranny?

9 Gallant *Veitch*, presumably David Veitch, brother to Veitch of Dawick, who with others of Peebleshire gentry was taken at Philiphaugh, 13 Sept., 1645.

10 *Aboyne* and *Huntly.* James Earl of Aboyne, who fled to France, and died there, broken-hearted, on hearing of King Charles's execution in 164$\frac{8}{9}$. He became representative of the Gordons, as 'Young Huntly,' on the death of his brother George at the battle of Alford, 2 July, 1645.

11 *Danish* men. Montrose's foreign auxiliaries, not exceeding 600 in all.

12 *Gilbert Menzies*, younger of Pitfoddells, who bore the royal banner in Montrose's last battle, refused to accept quarter, and died in defence of his charge.

13 *Strachan* and *Hacket.* Sir Charles Hacket and Colonel *Strachan*, victor at Corbiesdale, May, 1650: officers in the service of the so-called Estates.

14 "And *Huntly's* gone, the self-same way" of martyrdom. This was "George Gordon, second Marquis of Huntley, one of the very few nobles in Scotland who had uniformly adhered to the King from the beginning of the troubles; was beheaded by the sentence of the parliament of Scotland (so calling themselves) upon the 22 March, 164$\frac{8}{9}$, one month and twenty-two days after the martyrdom of his master." (Scott's whole note is excellent, on Huntley's natural distrust for Montrose, whose early disloyalty he could not forget.)

15 This final stanza appears incongruous with the beginning, and added later. Or was the first stanza prefixed afterwards to localize the ballad to Ennerdale or Endrickdale? The farewell to the place, "to kith and kin," was quite unnecessary after the Restoration. Was it only the coronation, June, 1651.

[Roxburghe Collection, III. 380; Douce Coll., III. 39 *verso*.]

An excellent New Ballad, entituled,

The gallant Grahams of Scotland.

Tune of, *I will away, and I will not tarry*, etc. [*Cf.* line 87.]

"BEtrayed me! how can this be?
When by day-light upon a Day,
I met Prince *Charles* our Royal King,
And all the *Grahams* in their array.

"They were all dress'd in armour keen,
Upon the pleasant Banks of *Tay*:
Before a King they might be seen,
Those gallant *Grahams* in their array.

"I have no gold, I have no land,
Nor have I pearl nor precious stones;
But I would sell my silken snood,
To see these *Grahams* but well come home.

"To speak of these *Grahams*, I think it best,
They're Men amongst good company;
Into the lands where we did walk,
They're Lords into the South Country.

"They won the praise in *Wallace's* days,
For the summer flowers did never spring
But the gallant *Grahams*, in armour clear,
Did then appear before the King.

"At the *Goukhead* we set our Camp,
Our Rigour down there for to stay, [*q. misp.* Leaguer?
Upon a dainty summer's day,
We rode our white horse and our grey.

"For they were then in armour seen,
As gold shines on a summer's day,
The gallant *Grahams* were assembled there,
Before King *Charles*, his Majesty.

"I'll crown them night, I'll crown them day,
And above great Lords of high degree,
For all the Lords that I have seen,
The *Grahams* are the bravest company."

As I came by the *Bunche's* Park,
I heard my true love's sister's [sing]; ["son."
"We loos'd our cannon on every side,
Even for the honour of our King.

"Our false Commander has betray'd our King
And sold him to his enemy, [1646.
By a nobleman, to *Cromwel* then;
So I care not what they do with me.

"For he strives to subdue the land,
And over *England* to be King,
Fair *Scotland* by him to be govern'd,
And over the nations for to reign.

"They have betray'd our Noble Prince,
And banish'd him from his Royal Crown;
But the gallant *Grahams* have ta'en in hand,
For to command that Traytor-Lown.

"Now *Dalgitie* was stout and bold,
Courageous in high degree;
[But] the Cavaliers they were all sold, [" At."
And young *Harthil*, a Cavalier too.

"*Nathaniel Gordon*, both stout and keen,
Newton Gordon, Burd alone; [*i.e.* last-left son.
Upon the Green he might be seen;
For a bolder face was never known.

"A braver man was never seen,
Neither in *Kent* or *Christendom*:
To fight now for his Royal King,
Lord give his enemies their doom!

"At *Bogle haugh*, where we did advance,
Our Parliament there for to stay,
But our Nobles they were banish'd off,
At *Goln-Yla* where we advance. [q. *Glen Isla?*

"*Glemproson*, where we randezvous'd
To *Glenshie* we march'd both night and day,
And of *Bredainlie* we took the town, [*a.l. Aberdeen.*
And met the *Campbells* in their Deray.

"Ten thousand men in armour strong [*a.l.* five t.
Did meet the gallant *Grahams* to play,
At *Inverlochie* where they began,
And about two thousand men were they. [*a.l.* scarce.

"And tho' their number did far exceed
The gallant *Grahams* upon that day,
Yet their hearts were true, they did not fear,
To meet the *Campbells* in their Deray.

" For the *Gordons* then did give a while, [*i.e.* hesitate.
To face the *Campbells* upon that day;
Who from their friends fell far aback;
Unto their enemies for ever and ay.

" Gallant *Montrose*, then that chieftain bold,
Couragious in high degree:
Did for the King fight valiantly,
The Lord preserve his Majesty.

" Now fare you well, you *Innerdale*,
Lord *Keeth* and kindred I bid adieu;
And I shall away, and I shall not stay,
To some uncouth land that I never knew.

" To wear the Blue I think it best, [*qu.* colour ?
By any Colonel that I see;
[Cheer up your hearts, brave Cavaliers,
For the *Grahams* are gone to *Germany*.

" To *France* and *Flanders*, where they advanc'd,
And *Germany*, who gave [them] fame;
For my Lord *Alboin* is to the sea, [*James*, E. of *Aboyne*.
Young *Huntly* is his noble name.

" He went to *France* for his Royal King,
King *Charles* then, and above degree
I'll give the honour to the gallant *Grahams*,
For they are a brave company.

" *Montrose* then, our chieftain bold,
To *Scotland* free is come again;
For to redeem fair *Scotland's* land,
The pleasant, worthy, gallant *Grahams*.

" At the Water of *Ensdale* they did begin,
And fought a battle to an end;
Where there were kill'd for our noble King,
Two thousand of our *Danish* men. [" *Donish*."

" *Gilbert Menzies*, and of high degree,
The King's Baron bold was born,
For a brave Cavalier was he,
But now into glory he's gone.

" The King's banner in hand he bore,
For he was a brave valiant man;
Betrayed was he a night before,
By Colonel *Hacket* and *Strachen* then.

To the[e] Colonel *Hacket* now,
  And *Strachen*, ill death may thou die!
For ye have betrayed our gallant *Grahams*,
  Who were true to his Majesty.

The Laird of *Ashen* has catch'd *Montrose* [*a.l.*, Assint.
  And had him into *Edinburgh* town;
And from his body ta'en his head,
  And quarter'd him upon a Trone. [= weighing-scaffold.

Now *Huntley's* gone that same way,
  Prince *Charles* also, our Royal King,
Hath suffer'd death for our Nation,
  Our mourning tears can ne'er be done.

Our gallant young King is now come home, [*qu.* 1651?
  Prince *Charles* the Second, and above degree:
The Lord send Peace in his time
  And God preserve his Majesty!

Now fare you well, you *Innerdale*, [*Endrickdale.*
  Kith and kin that you may well ken;
For I will sell my silken snood
  To the gallant *Grahams* came home. [To = so that.

Since *Wallace's* days that we began,
  Sir *John* the *Graham* did bear the gree; [prize, misp. 'Green.'
For the honour of our Royal King,
  The Lord preserve his Majesty!

'For[e] all the lords in fair *Scotland*,
  From the highest to the lowest degree;
The noble *Grahams* are to be preferr'd,
  So God preserve *Charles* his Majesty.

[No printer's or publisher's name, or date. One woodcut. Douce copy is duplicate of Roxburghe. Date doubtful, as to composition, but this broadside must have been printed about the middle of 18th century—probably a reprint or modernization of an earlier suppressed edition. That it had been rigorously hunted down by Government is betokened by its extreme rarity. It has not hitherto been reprinted thus direct from the broadside, to the best of our knowledge. Probably the Restoration stanza, the 33rd, was a late addition; the original belonging to the Interregnum, *circa* 1651. The traditional version of Walter Scott begins with our line 33, "Now fare thee weel, sweet *Ennerdale!*" (p. 588). The woodcut, coarse in execution, is a portrait of Charles I., in an oval frame, with two winged Cupids for angels above. Compare *Notes*, p. 589, *passim.*]

Sir Hugh of the Graeme.

"The man shall have his *Mare* again, and all shall be well."
—*Midsummer Night's Dream*, iii. 2.

SEEING how often, for the sake of 'the penny siller' or 'the gude red goud,' King Jamie the First of England sold what had hitherto been considered the honours of knighthood to a crowd of disreputable adventurers, we need not begrudge the privilege to the ballad-writer who conferred the title of '*Sir* Hugh of the Grime' on the moss-trooper Hughie Græme or Graham, as he is rightly styled on p. 597. We have here the English original of the ballad; long antecedent to any authoritative record of the Scottish traditional version, used by Walter Scott, from materials gathered by William Laidlaw, in Blackhouse, Selkirkshire. We on p. 600 add one of these later Scotch versions. Their final stanza forms a prelude to "Johnny Armstrong's Good-Night" (p. 604).

The dense dull stupidity of our English populace during the eighteenth century, and to a less degree in the closing quarter of the preceding century, is well proved by the prosaic tenor of their street ballads. All that is brightest and best in the "popular ballads of England and Scotland" belongs to the northern land, where poetry found a worthy reception in the mind of the lads and lasses whose own lovely mountains and lakes, wild moorlands, and romantic streams, appeared to be the native home of legendary lore. The witcheries of old time there lingered, with music and tenderness, that the outer world still receives with wonder and delight. Into the consideration of the Scottish traditional ballads, the separation of the borrowed or adulterated materials from the genuine foundation, we dare not enter here. The subject has been one of our favourite studies since we early roved through the 'land of the mountain and the flood,' and some day we may be able to succinctly relate the result of our investigations. Meantime, let us declare unhesitatingly that to Sir Walter Scott (*facile princeps* among collectors, compilers, and re-arrangers in dramatic form of fragments and corrupt versions that fell in their way,) is owing the highest credit for giving us such an unequalled body of ballad-literature, text and annotations, as he furnished in his *Minstrelsy of the Scottish Border.* He was at heart too true a poet, too skilful a romantic novelist, to be content with such antiquarian exactitude and drudgery as satisfied the worthy but atrabilious Joseph Ritson. Fortunately we hold both of them: each foremost in his own way. But, seeing how perishable was traditionary ballad-lore, it is well for us that Scott arose at the right time to save much that had survived; with the creative art to weld into completeness what he found in scraps, self-contradictory, garbled, and inconclusive.

[Roxburghe Collection, II. 291; III. 344; Pepys, II. 148; Jersey, I. 173; Rawlinson, 566, fol. 9; Douce, II. 204, *verso*.]

The Life and Death of
Sir Hugh of the Grime.

[No tune mentioned.]

AS it befell upon one time,
About Mid-summer of the year,
Every man was taxt of his crime,
For stealing the good Lord Bishop's mare.

The good Lord *Scr*[*oop*] he sadled a horse, ["*Screw*."
And rid after this same scrime,
Before he did get over the Moss,
There was he aware of Sir *Hugh of the Grime*.

" Turn, O turn, thou false traytor,
Turn and yield thy self unto me;
Thou hast stolen the Lord Bishop's mare,
And now thou thinkest away to flee."

" No, soft, Lord *Screw*, that may not be,
Here is a broad-sword by my side,
And if that thou can'st conquer me,
The victory will soon be try'd."

" I ne'r was afraid of a traytor bold,
Although thy name be *Hugh in the Grime*,
I'le make thee repent thy speeches foul,
If day and life but give me time."

" Then do thy worst, good Lord *Screw*,
And deal your blows as fast as you can:
It will be try'd between me and you,
Which of us two shall be the best man."

Thus as they dealt their blows so free,
And both so bloody at that time,
Over the Moss ten yeomen they see,
Come for to take Sir *Hugh in the Grime*.

Sir *Hugh* set his back against a tree,
And then the men encompast him round,
His mickle sword from his hand did flee,
And then they brought Sir *Hugh* to the ground.

Sir *Hugh* of the *Grime* now taken is,
And brought back to *Garland* town, [*Carlisle*.
The good wives all [cry'd] in *Garland* town,
" Sir *Hugh* in the *Grime*, thou'st ne'r gang down."

The good Lord Bishop is come to the town,
And on the Bench is set so high,
And every man was taxt to his crime,
At length he called Sir *Hugh* in the *Grime.*

"Here am I, thou false Bishop,
Thy humours all [for] to fulfil,
I do not think my fact so great,
But thou may'st put it into thy own will."

The Quest of Jury-men was call'd,
The best that was in *Garland* town,
Eleven of them spoke all in a breast,
"Sir *Hugh* in the *Grime*, thou'st ne'r gang down."

Then other Questry-men was call'd,
The best that was in *Rumary*,
Twelve of them spoke all in a breast,
"Sir *Hugh* in the *Grime*, thou'st now guilty."

Then came down my good Lord *Boles*, [? Sir *Geo. Bowes*.
Falling down upon his knee,
"Five hundred pieces of gold would I give
To grant Sir *Hugh* in the *Grime* to me."

"Peace, peace, my good Lord *Boles*,
And of your speeches set them by;
If there be eleven *Grimes* all of a name,
Then by my own honour they all should dye."

Then came down my good Lady *Ward*, [? Lady *Gray*, of *Wark*.
Falling low upon her knee,
"Five hundred measures of gold I'le give
To grant Sir *Hugh* of the *Grime* to me."

"Peace, peace, my good Lady *Ward*,
None of your proffers shall him buy;
For if there be twelve *Grimes* all of a name,
By my own honour they all should dye."

Sir *Hugh* of the *Grime's* condemn'd to dye,
And of his friends he had no lack,
Fourteen foot he leapt in his ward,
His hands bound fast upon his back.

Then he lookt over his left shoulder,
To see whom he could see or spy,
There was he aware of his Father dear,
Came tearing his hair most pittifully.

"Peace, peace, my Father dear,
And of your speeches set them by;
Though they have bereav'd me of my life,
They cannot bereave me of heaven so high."

He lookt over his right shoulder,
To see whom he could see or spy,
There was he aware of his Mother dear,
Came tearing her hair most pittifully.

"Pray have me remembred to *Peggy* my wife,
As she and I walkt over the Moor,
She was the causer of my life,
And with the old Bishop she plaid the whore.

"Here *Johnny Armstrong*, take thou my sword, [*Cf.* p. 595.
That is made of the mettle so fine:
And when thou com'st to the border side,
Remember the death of Sir *Hugh* of the *Grime*."

Finis.

Printed for *P. Brooksby*, at the *Golden-Ball*, in *West-Smith-field*, neer the *Hospital-gate*.

[In Black-letter. One woodcut. Some other copies begin "As it befell upon a time." Compare the Scottish Border ballad, or "Hughie the Græme," beginning "Gude Lord Scroope's to the hunting gane," and the later ditty, "Hughie Graham," beginning "Our Lords are to the mountains gane." Variations noted. Date of Brooksby's issue, 1672-92. 2nd is of Bow Churchyard.]

*** The woodcut seems to have originally belonged to a Robin Hood ballad, and is to follow in the group of seven or more in the concluding volume. A severed portion, to right, is the figure of a Friar (see Vol. IV. p. 253); two Archers stand facing him, with bows, and a Lady sits on the ground betwixt them.

The Bishop of Carlisle, whose mare Hughie Graham '*conveyed*,' is supposed to have been Robert Aldridge, consecrated in 1537, holding the see until his death on March 5, 155$\frac{5}{6}$. Previously he had been Canon of Windsor, May, 1534, and Provost of Eton College, June, 1536. The attack on his moral character *in re fœminæ*, is possibly a grace of the balladist. But *it mought ha' bin.* That it was a shady episcopate in his time may be taken for granted, seeing that Bernard Gilpin, 'the Apostle of the North,' shied at it, for substantial reasons, when offered to him: "In that diocese I have so many acquaintances and friends, *of whom I have not the best opinion*, that I must either connive at many irregularities, or draw upon myself so much hatred that I should be less able to do good there than anywhere else." Bishop Aldrich had earned by subserviency most of his temporal 'good things' from Henry VIII., etc., favouring the divorce, and being a Boleynite, until he became Almoner to Jane Seymour. Yet Erasmus wrote of him as '*juvenis blandæ cujusdam eloquentiæ*' (*Peregrinatio Religionis ergo*); this was early, before intercourse with Cranmer taught Aldrich the worse ways. He was an Episcopal Vicar of Bray. Leland wrote an Encomium on him In 1555 bills of complaint were exhibited before him, against 400 borderers, among whom may have been Hughie Graham. The man's Mare (whichever way we take it) secured his condemnation.

[Roxburghe Collection, III. 456.]

Sir Hugh in the Grime's Downfall;

Or, a New Song made on Sir Hugh in the Grime, who was hang'd for stealing the Bishop's Mare. [Note, p. 597.

GOOD Lord *John* is a hunting gone,
  Over the hills and dales so far,
For to take Sir *Hugh in the Grime*.
For stealing of the Bishop's mare. *He derry derry down.*

Hugh in the Grime was taken then,
And carried to *Carlisle* town;
The merry women came out amain,
Saying the name of *Grime* shall never go down. *He derry derry down.*

O then a jury of Women was brought,
Of the best that could be found:
Eleven of them spoke all at once,
Saying the name of *Grime* shall never go down. *He derry derry down.*

And then a jury of Men was brought,
More the pity for to be!
Eleven of them spoke all at once,
Saying "*Hugh* in the *Grime*, you are guilty," etc.

Hugh in the *Grime* was cast to be hang'd,
Many of his friends did for him leet, [leet=attend.
For 15 foot in the prisin he did jump,
With his hands tyed fast behind his back, etc.

Then bespoke our good lady *Ward*,
As she set on the bench so high,
"A peck of white pennys I'll give to my lord,
If he'll grant *Hugh Grime* to me. *He, etc.*

"And if it be not full enough,
I'll stroke it up with my Silver Fan;
And if it be not full enough,
I'll heap it up with my own hand," etc.

"Hold your tongue now, lady *Ward*,
And of your talkitive let it be;
There is never a *Grime* came in this Court
That at thy bidding shall saved be," [etc.]

Then bespoke our good Lady *Moor*,
As she sat on the Bench so high,
"A yoke of fat oxen I'll give to my lord,
If he'll grant *Hugh Grime* to me," etc.

"Hold your tongue now, good Lady *Moor*,
And of your talkitive let it be,
There is never a *Grime* came to this Court,
That at thy biding shall saved be," etc.

Sir *Hugh* in the *Grime* look'd out of the door,
With his hand out of the Bar,
There he spy'd his father dear,
Tearing of his golden hair. *He derry, etc.*

"Hold your tongue, good Father dear,
And of your weeping let it be:
For if they bereave me of my life,
They cannot bereave me of the Heavens so high.

Sir *Hugh* in the *Grime* look'd out at the door,
Oh! what a sorry heart had he!
There spy'd [he] his Mother dear,
Weeping and wailing, "Oh! woe is me!" etc.

"Hold your tong[u]e now, Mother dear!
And of your weeping let it be;
For if they bereave me of my life,
They cannot bereave me of Heaven's fee. etc.

"I'll leave my sword to *Johnny Armstrong*, [*Cf.* pp. 591, 604.
That is made of mettal so fine:
That when he comes to the Border side,
He may think of *Hugh* in the Grime." *He derry, etc.*

London: Printed and sold by *L. How.*

[In White-letter. Two rude woodcuts: a horseman, and gibbet with its usual adornment. Date of print, *circâ* 1770?]

[This woodcut belongs to "*Johnnie Armstrong's Last Good-Night*," on p. 604.]

Johnny Armstrong's Last Good Night.

"The night is my departing night,
 For here nae longer must I stay;
There's no a friend or fae of mine
 But wishes that I were awa'.

"What I hae done for lack o' wit
 I never, never can reca';
I trust ye're a' my friends as yet:
 Gude night, and joy be wi' you a'!"

—[*Thomas*] *Armstrong's Good Night*, 1600.

AMONG our "Romantic Ballads" we are glad to have the right to include a few from the Roxburghe Collection that form connecting links with the Scottish ballads. We admit unhesitatingly the woful inferiority of our English street-ditties, the reprints of penny broadsides, the literature of our lower and middle classes two hundred years ago, and a century earlier, as compared to those spirit-stirring and pathetic Border-Ballads for the chief part genuinely and intensely Scottish, that have floated down to us traditionally, and been snatched by such men as David Herd, Sir Walter Scott, Robert Jamieson, William Motherwell, and a few others (disregarding the mere rubbish and forgeries produced in emulation of the industry and good fortune of these true searchers and recorders). The baldness of narrative, devoid of all gleams of brilliant poetry, "the light that never was on land or sea, The consecration and the Poet's Dream," in our prosaic hum-drum dreary "Tragedies" and "Laments," leaves much to be desired. We remember "The Clerk's Two Sons of Owsenford," which, with other of those loveliest Scottish ballads, may nevertheless have had an originally English foundation; but, if so, they have passed through an alchemist's alembic in the North Countrie, and all that might otherwise have been dull and commonplace has "suffered a sea-change, Into something rich and strange." We remember a score, many a score, of beautiful ditties which belong to the Scottish people exclusively beyond dispute, and which any nation ought to be proud of possessing. It is the fashion of the day, harmless enough, but seldom pursued with either taste or discriminating learning (mere pedantry and laborious idleness instead thereof, that affect the bulk of material and self-display for professorship, with coöperation of multitudinous nobodies in our "Daylight of the Dwarfs"), to announce the close connection of poems, ballads and myths, with their transmutation during dispersal. Every tale or fancy must, according to these stupendous Pundits, have been originally a Solar Myth or a Nature Cryptogram. Nothing could have been meant to be what it appears! Nobody ever was able to enjoy a romance for its own sake, but must perpetually have been 'sat upon' by his Magi, the teachers of occultism: *i.e.* that the seasons succeed one another; that the sun disappears when it goes below the horizon; that the wind is forcible, and takes liberties unwarrantably with an octogenarian's unshorn beard; that buried grain may possibly, under favourable circumstances, reappear in a new crop, "brought to me like Alcestis from the grave," etc., etc., etc. One might imagine that a School-Board regulated the dream-language of the civilized world since the Deluge. But the stupidity is in the interpreters, not in the ancient Greeks, poets or sculptors We have to endure the vivisectionists of literature and art, who "murder to dissect." They are not of genius, like Paganini, although they fiddle continually on one string. He lifted up our souls in rapture with his wondrous skill, his "Witch's Dance under the Walnut Tree;" but they—send their listeners to sleep, or drive them frantic. Surely they might leave unrack'd, undismember'd, unbranded into ugliness, our *Romantic and Legendary Ballads.*

Unhappily for ourselves we are here limited to such as belong to the Roxburghe Collection. Let us at least avail ourselves of our legal rights, in "Sir Hugh of the Græme, "Johnny Armstrong," the "New Balow," and "The Gallant Grahams."

Our earliest English version of "Johnnie Armstrong's Last Good Night," there entitled "A Northern Ballet," resolves itself, so far as we have evidence, into the appearance of that pleasant Drollery of the Interregnum, "*Wit Restored*, 1658, in several Select Poems not formerly published," p. 123. The book owes its birth to the friendship of two gallant and loyal Cavaliers (the terms were synonymous, and naturally so), Sir John Menzies, or Mennis, and Dr. James Smith. Hence, we are of opinion that to Sir John Menzies we are indebted for the introduction of such northern ditties as "The Old Ballet of Shepherd Tom," "Little Musgrave and the Lady Barnard" (see our p. 631), "The Miller and the King's Daughter," and the present ballad. In fact, it is by no means improbable that Menzies and Smith themselves might have been the authors of considerably more than they are accredited with, in *Musarum Deliciæ*, 1656, *Wit Restored*, 1658, and even possibly in *Wit's Recreation* of 1640.

It is unlikely that any extant ballad on Johnny Armstrong's death, or of his men, appeared until 1600. But the lines quoted as motto on our previous page are believed traditionally to have been composed by Thomas of the gang, when about to be executed for having, in the way of business, slain Sir John Carmichael, Warden of the Middle Marches. The death of Armstrong had mischanced in March, 1525, under James V.; but the ballad account applies clearly to King James VI. of Scotland, before he crawled south, there to become a mischievous James I., unhappily for England.

He drove the Catholics by his severe penal laws to the abortive Powder Plot. Johnnie Armstrong sadly declares the truth :—

> I have ask'd grace from a graceless face,
> No pardon there is for you or me.

The description is life-like, but it is of James VI., not of James V. Instead of the 'waeful Woodie,' it were better to think of Johnnie dying on a well-fought field; although stabbed treacherously in the back by 'a cowardly Scot,' the reiver fell not in flight from his foes. That Edinburgh had risen, like the later Porteous mob, to wreak the vengeance of petty traders on the eight-score men and their leader, in sheer spite, not loyalty, is exactly what might have been expected. Much of the gorgeous finery could not have been previously purchased honestly with money, 'chalk' was out of the question, and since the spoiling of the Egyptians there have been few concessions to borrowers. Dare we hint that the night's minions, St. Nicholas's Clerks, and agents of Mercury, had employed another process of transfer?

In earliest boyhood we rambled frequently, making many sketches, amid the border keeps and other localities of legendary and ballad lore. We retain a few of these sketches, unpublished, one being the so-called "Johnny Armstrong's Gilnockie Tower," with its bare walls frowning across the meadows and corn-fields, and a small cottage farm peacefully nestling beside what was formerly a threatening haunt of men, who held cheap the lives of others and themselves, and in their mis-governed country as often righted abuses of the feudal tyranny and Calvinistic fanaticism as they inflicted wrongs on those who opposed their 'conveyancing.'

On the prowess, fortune and fate, of our Johnnie Armstrong we need not dwell, seeing that he found already his chronicler in the best of all ballad-editors, that great and good Walter Scott to whom we owe so much, in the *Minstrelsy of the Scottish Border.* That his death took place *circâ* 1529, and at the hands of James V. of Scotland, not at Edinburgh, but when the King, leading an army of ten thousand men, marched through Ettrick Forest and Ewsdale, appears certain. And that the brave Armstrong died on the gallows-tree, and not fighting with sword in hand as our English broadside misrepresents, is a fact we cannot gainsay, awkward though it sound. Yet how many heroes, before and since, have gone "up a long ladder and down a wee tow," without more than physical damage. Remembering that John Brown was hanged, and that thousands of scoundrels still remain without a rope-cravat round their thrapple, it almost appears an honourable distinction to have been suspended. Better are the hanged than the unhanged in the world's history. Have not poets loved to celebrate their deeds and chant their requiem? Have not romancers and dramatists bent their genius to extend such renown, while tears on ladies' cheeks attested their sorrow? Imitation being the sincerest flattery, a weaker race try to emulate their lawlessness, and attain their reward.

The old ballad first printed, from the Bannatyne MS., by Allan Ramsay, in his Collection entitled *The Evergreen*, 1724, keeps more closely to the historical fact than does ours, which he styles "the common one." The original "*Johnie Armstrong*" begins thus:—

Sum speiks of lords, sum spekis of lairds,
  And sic lyke men of hie degrie;
Of a Gentleman I sing a sang,
  Sum tyme call'd Laird of *Gilnockie.*
The King he wrytes a luving letter,
  With his ain hand sae tenderly,
And he hath sent it to *Johny Armstrang*,
  To cum and speik with him speedily.
The *Eliots* and *Armstrangs* did convene;
  They were a gallant company—
"We'll welcome Hame our Royal King;
  I hope he'll dine at *Gilnockie*."

The fatal locality is indicated in the penultimate or 32nd stanza:

"Fareweil! my bonny *Gilnock* hall,
  Quhair on *Eske* syde thou standest stout!
Gif I had lived but seven yeirs mair,
  I wad haife gilt thee round about."
John murder'd was at *Carlinrigg*,
  And all his gallant companie;
But *Scotland*'s heart was never sae wae,
  To see sae mony brave men die—
Because they saved their country deir
  Frae *Englishmen!* Nane were sae bauld,
Quhyle *Johnie* liv'd on the Border syde,
  Nane of them durst cum neir his hauld.

On pp. 343-348, vol. i., of the *Appendix* to an excellent Collection of '*Scotish Ballads and Songs, Historical and Traditionary*' (edited, with thorough mastery of the subject, by the late James Maidment, and published by William Paterson, Edinburgh, 1868), is given an abstract of a book called "The pleasant and delightful History of *Johnny Armstrong*, showing his many noble deeds in his youth, in divers countries," etc.; an apocryphal narrative, printed and sold by C. Randall of Stirling in 1803; no doubt "an abridgement of an earlier edition of a popular story on the subject of Armstrong." Herein he appears as a 'brave jolly man,' living at his own castle in Westmoreland. A brief memoir of Johnnie Armstrong is furnished to *The Dictionary of National Biography*, vol. ii. pp. 93, 94, 1885 by Arthur Henry Bullen. The Thomas Armstrong (nephew of '*Kinmont Willie*' Armstrong), who is credited with having written the "Good Night" which forms our motto on p. 600, was executed in November, 1600; his slaughter of the Warden of the Middle or West-Marches, Sir John Carmichael, having taken place near Lochmaben, on the previous 16th of June, 1600.

[Roxburghe Coll., III. 513; Bagford, I. 61; II. 94; Pepys, II. 133; Euing, 151; Wood, 401, p. 93; 102, p. 59; Douce, I. 103; III. 45; Huth, I. 141.]

Johnny Armstrong's last Good-night. Declaring how he and his Eight-score Men fought a bloody Battle with the *Scottish* King at *Edinburgh.*

[To a pretty Northern Tune, *Fare you well, Gilltnock-hall.* (Wood's)]
Licensed and Entered according to Order.

"IS there never a man in all *Scotland*, [*The King asks of one :*
From the highest estate to the lowest degree,
That can shew himself now before the King?
Scotland is so full of treachery!"

"Yes, there is a man in *Westmoreland*, [*The Reply.*
Johnny Armstrong they do him call;
He hath no lands, nor rent coming in,
Yet he keeps eightscore men within his hall.

"He has horse and harness for them all,
With goodly steeds that are milk white,
With their goodly belts about their necks,
With hats and feathers all alike."

The King he writes a loving letter,
And with his own hand so tenderly,
And hath sent it unto *Johnny Armstrong*,
To come and speak with him speedily;

When *Johnny* look'd [on] this letter, Good faith! [*Transposed.*
He look'd as blith as a bird on a tree;
"I was never before a King in my life,
My father, grandfather, nor none of us three.

"But seeing we must go before the King,
Lord! we will go most gallantly;
Ye shall every one have a velvet coat,
Laid down with golden laces three.

"And ye shall every one have a scarlet cloak,
Laid down with silver laces fine, [*a.l.* 'five.'
With your golden belts about your necks,
With hats and feathers all alike."

But when *Johnny* went from *Gilltnock-Hall*, [*i.e.* Gilnockie Tower.
The wind blew hard, and full fast it did rain;
"Now fare thee well, thou *Gilltnock*-Hall,
I fear I shall never see thee again."

Now *Johnny* is to *Edenborough* gone,
  With his eight-score men so gallant to see,
And every one of them on a milk-white steed,
  With their bucklers and swords hanging to their knee.

But when *John* came the King before,
  With his eight-score men so gallant to see,
The King he mov'd his bonnet to him,
  He thought he had been a king as well as he.

"O! pardon, O! pardon, my sovereign Liege,
  Pardon for my eight-score men and me;
For my name it is *Johnny Armstrong*,
  A subject of yours, my Liege," said he.

"Away with thee, thou false traitor,
  No pardon I will grant to thee;
But to-morrow morning by eight of the clock,
  I will hang up thy eight-score men and thee."

Then *Johnny* look'd over his left shoulder,
  And to his merry men thus said he,
"I have asked grace of a graceless face,
  No pardon there is for you or me."

Then *John* pull'd out his nut-brown sword,
  And it was made of metal so free;
Had not the King mov'd his foot as he did,
  John had taken his head from his fair body.

"Come follow me, my merry men all,
  We will scorn one foot for to flye;
It shall ne'er be said we were hung like dogs,
  We will fight it out so manfully."

Then they fought on like champions bold,
  For their hearts were sturdy, stout, and free,
'Till they had kill'd all the king's good guards;
  There were none left alive, but two or three.

But then rose up all *Edenborough*,
  They rose up by thousands three;
A cowardly Scot came *Johnny* behind,
  And run him thorow the fair body.

Said *John*, "Fight on, my merry men all,
  I am a little wounded, but am not slain,
I will lay me down for to bleed a while,
  Then I'll rise and fight with you again."

Then they fought on like mad men all,
'Till many a man lay dead on the plain;
For they were resolv'd before they would yield,
That every man should there be slain.

So there they fought couragiously,
'Till most of them lay dead there, and slain;
But little *Musgrove*, that was his foot-page,
With his bonny *Grizzle* got away unta'en. [grey-steed.

But when he came to *Giltknock* hall,
The Lady spied him presently,
"What news? what news? thou little foot-page,
What news from thy Master and his company?"

"My news [it] is bad, Lady!" he said,
Which I do bring, as you may see:
My master, *Johnny Armstrong*, is slain,
And all his gallant company."

"Yet thou art welcome home, my bonny *Grizzle*,
Full oft thou hast been fed with corn and hay,
But now thou shalt be fed with bread [and] wine;
Thy sides shall be spurr'd no more, I say."

O then bespake his little son,
As he sat on his Nurse's knee,
"If ever I live to be a man,
My father's death reveng'd shall be."

[By **T. R.**]

[No Publisher's name on Roxburghe copy, which is in white-letter, but Anthony à Wood's couple, black-letter, were printed for *Francis Grove*, and bear the initials of T.R. as author. Can these be for Thomas Robins? Pepys copy for *W. Thackeray*, and *T. Passenger*. The Bagford couple and Euing's copy are marked '*London*, Printed for and by *W*[*illiam*] *O*[*nley*] and sold by the Booksellers of *Pye-corner* and *London-Bridge*. 1st Douce, *London*, by *T. Norris*, to Northern Tune, '*Fare thou well, Giltnock Hall*. 2nd Douce, n.p.n. to North-country Tune. Title, "The last Good Night of the valiant *Johnny Armstrong*, showing how," etc. W.O.'s issue has "Licensed and entered according to Order," and "To a pretty Northern tune." Our Roxburghe woodcut (p. 599) is in *Bagford Ballads*, p. 365, "The Couragious Soldiers of the North," 1690; nearly the same date of issue as this Roxburghe print.]

*** It is possible, and not improbable, that this "*little Musgrove*," who was Johnnie Armstrong's foot-page, and escaped on his leader's "bonnie *Grizzle*" (lines 79, 80), was identical with the "*Little Musgrave*," a Northern Borderer (*Cf.* our ballad on pp. 631 to 634), who became entangled with the Lady Barnard or Barnet: perhaps of Barnard-Castle, Yorkshire.

[Roxburghe Collection, II. 572; III. 725.]

A Delectable New Ballad, intituled

Leader-Haughs and Yarow.

To its own Proper Tune.

WHen *Phœbus* bright the azure skies with golden rayes enlightneth,
These things Sublunar he espies; herbs, trees, and plants he quick'neth;
Among all those he makes his choise, and gladly goes he thorow,
With radiant beams, and silver streams, through *Leader Haughs* and *Yarow*.[1]

When *Aries* the day and night in equal length divideth,
Old frosty *Saturn* takes the flight, no longer he abideth;
Then *Flora* Queen, with mantle green, casts off her former sorrow,
And vows to dwell with *Ceres* fell in *Leader Haughs* and *Yarow*.

Pan playing on his Oaten reed, with Sheepherds him attending,
Doth here resort their flocks to feed, the Hill and Haughs commending;
With bottle, bag, and staff with knag, and all singing good morrow,
They swear no fields more pleasure yields, than *Leader Haugh* and *Yarow*.

One house there stands on *Leader* side, surmounting my descrybing, [*Thirlestane*.
With ease-rooms rare, and windows fair, like *Dædalus'* contriving;
Men passing by do often say in [th'] South it has no marrow; [*i.e.* peer.
It stands as fair on *Leader* side, as *New-wark* does on *Yarow*.

A mile below, who list to ride, they'll hear the Mavis singing,
Into St. *Leonard's* bank she'l bide, sweet Birks her head o'er-hinging;
The Lint-white loud, and *Progne* proud, with tender throats and narrow,
Into St. *Leonard's* banks do sing as sweetly as in *Yarow*.

---

[1] *Note.*—The broadsides read '*Yarow*' instead of *Yarrow*, *passim.*

On Nichol Burn (as he calls himself, not Burne) is a brief note in Robert Chambers' *Songs of Scotland*, 1829, p. 305, "This song is little better than a string of names of places [!]. Yet there is something so pleasing in it, especially to the ear of a 'south-country man,' that it has long maintained its place in our [Scottish] collections. We all know what impressive verse Milton makes out of mere catalogues of localities.

"The author, *Nicol Burne*, is supposed to have been one of the last of the old race of minstrels. In an old collection of songs, in their original state of *ballants*, I have seen his name printed as '*Burne the Violer*,' which seems to indicate the instrument upon which he was in the practice of accompanying his recitations. I was told by an aged person at Earlston that there used to be a portrait of him [*i.e.* of *Burne*] in Thirlestane Castle representing him as a douce old man, leading a cow by a straw-rope. Thirlestane Castle, the seat of the Earl of Lauderdale, near Lauder, is the castle of which the poet speaks in such terms of admiration. It derives the massive beauties of its architecture from [Jn. Maitland] the Duke of Lauderdale, who built it, as the date above the doorway testifies, in the year 1674. The song must therefore have been composed since that era. It was printed in *The Tea-Table Miscellany*," 1725. Robert Chambers did not reprint the three final stanzas of our broadside.

Our minstrel '*Nicol Burn* the Violer' must not be confounded with another Nicol Burn, Burne, or Brown, controversialist and Scotchman, who, in 1581, had published in Paris a "Disputation concerning the Controversit Headdis of Religion haldin in the Realm of *Scotland*." He was a right-minded Professor of Philosophy at St. Andrews; where Professors were, and are, scholars.

The lap-wing lilteth o'er the Lea, with nimble wings she sporteth,
But vowes she'l not come near the tree where *Philomel* resorteth;
By break of day, the Lark can say, I'le bid you all good morrow,
I'le yout and yell, for I may dwell in *Leader Haughs* and *Yarow.*

Parke, Wanton-Walls, and *Wooden-cleugh*, the *East* and *Wester Mainses*,
The Forrest of *Lauder's* fair enough, the corns are good in *Blanshies*;
Where Oats are fine and sold by kind, that if ye search all thorow,
Mearns, Buchan, Marr, none better are, than *Leader Haughs* and *Yarow.*

In *Burn-Milne-boge* and *Whitslead-Shawes*, the fearful Hare she haunteth,
Bridge-haugh and *Broad-wood-shiel* she knawes, to the *Chapel-wood* frequenteth;
Yet, when she irks, to *Kaidslie-Birks* she runs, and sighs for sorrow,
That she should leave sweet *Leader Haughs*, and cannot win to *Yarow.*

What sweeter Musick would ye hear, than Hounds and Beigles crying?
The Hare waits not, but flees for fear, their hard pursuite defying;
But yet her strength, it failes at length, no bielding can she borrow,
At *Haggs, Cleckmae*, nor *Sorr[ow]lesfield*,[1] but longs to be at *Yarow.*

For *Rockwood, Ringwood, Rival, Aymer*, still thinking for to view her,[2]
But O! to fail her strength begins, no cunning can rescue her;
O'er dubb and dike, o'er s[h]eugh and syke, she'l run the fields all thorow,
Yet ends her dayes in *Leader Haughs*, and bids farewell to *Yarow.*

Thou *Erslington*[3] and *Colden-knowes*,[4] where *Humes* had once commanding,
And *Dry-Grange* w th thy milk-white Ewes, 'twixt *Tweed* and *Leader* standing;
The birds that flees through *Rid-path* trees, and *Gledswood* banks all thorow,
May chant and sing, sweet *Leader-Haughs*, and the bony Banks of *Yarow.*

But *BURN* cannot his grief asswage, whileas his dayes endureth,
To see the Changes of this Age, which day and time procureth;
For many a place stands in hard case, where *Burns* were blyth beforrow,
With *Humes* that dwelt on *Leader-side*, and *Scots* that dwelt in *Yarow.*

The words of Burn the Violer.

WHat? shall my Viol silent be, or leave her wonted Scriding?
But choose some sadder Elegie, not Sports and Mirds deriding;
It must be faine with lower strain, than it was wont beforrow,
To sound the praise of *Leader Haughs*, and the bon[n]y Banks of *Yarow.*

But floods has overflown the Banks, the greenish Haughs disgracing,
And trees in Woods grows thin in ranks, about the Fields defacing;
For Waters waxes, Woods do waind; more, if I could for sorrow,
In rural verse, I would rehearse, ot *Leader Haughs* and *Yarow*;

But sighs and sobs o'rsets my breath, sore saltish tears forth sending,
All things sublunar here on Earth are subject to an ending;
So must my Song, though some what long, yet late at even and Morrow,
I'le sigh and sing, sweet *Leader Haughs*, and the bon[n]y Banks of *YAROW.*

Hic terminus hæret.

Finis.

[Black-letter, 2nd copy in White-letter. No p.n. Date, *circâ* 1690.]

Notes.—[1] *al. lect.*, "In Sorrowless Fields."
[2] *al. lect.*, "With sight and scent pursue her."
[3] = *Earlston*, formerly *Ercildoun*. [4] *Cowden-knowes*, with its *Broom.*

The Lass of Ocram.

> "Ah, ope, Lord *Gregory*, thy door! a midnight wanderer sighs,
> Hard rush the rains, the tempests roar, and lightnings cleave the skies."
>
> "Who comes with woe at this dread night—a pilgrim of the gloom?
> If she whose love did once delight, my cot shall yield her room."
>
> "Alas! thou heard'st a pilgrim mourn, that once was prized by thee:
> Think of the ring, by yonder burn, thou gav'st to Love and me!
>
> "But should'st thou not poor *Marian* know, I'll turn my feet and part;
> And think the storms that round me blow, far kinder than thy heart."
>
> —*Lord Gregory*, by Dr. John Walcot, *c.* 1787.

WE are happy to be the first (so far as we know) to reprint "The Lass of Ocram," which probably affords the earliest extant text of this truly interesting and pathetic love-tale. On it Dr. Walcot at his best (see above; also p. 212, where a fragmentary song of 1787 is given), and Sir Walter Scott still later, tried their powers. There are various corrupt and fraudulent versions afloat, and even our Roxburghe Ballad is somewhat flawed, a modernized reprint of *one that may have belonged to the days of Mary Queen of Scots*. It is the authentic fountain-head of all the others.

Rude as it is, and evidently damaged in transmission to us (notably in the opening stanza, with its three-fold "sure," and its reiterations concerning the building of the "ship of Northern fame"), it has a touching simplicity and directness. The girl, whose honour had been basely wounded in the past by her sordidly-trafficing lover, makes a last appeal to him, in the darkness of the night, amid inclemency of wind and rain. She finds the castle-door closed against her prayers for shelter; with disguised voice the hateful mother of the wronger, Lord Gregory, questions her thrice from the grating, until she gains the knowledge that her prurient malice had desired, when she reviles and drives hence the poor despairing victim to perish with her unfathered baby in the storm. A stanza or more may have been lost, but the leaving unbridged such abrupt transitions was far from unusual of old. The awakening of the tardy lover, too late to save the girl from insult and destruction, is followed by the malediction on his own mother who had acted so remorselessly.

In a fragment from *The Scots' Musical Museum* (see p. 212 *ante*), the cold brutality of the lover is unredeemed by kindness:—

> "If you are the lass *that I lov'd once*, as I trow you are not she,
> Come, give me some of the tokens that past between you and me!"

Such a demand, urged at so inauspicious a time, would be amazing, if we did not gain the clue from our "Lass of Ocram" ballad, that it is the feigned voice of the mother speaking, instead of the lover, while he sleeps unconscious of her cruel treachery.

The curse is left to speed home to its mark, not "coming home to roost," but poetical justice demands that the woman who has unsexed herself to torture a lost girl may wither away in heart and soul, dreading to die, yet shuddering at each return of dawn.

In his *Minstrelsy of the Scottish Border* (vol. ii. p. 58), Sir Walter Scott gave 39 stanzas; "The Lass of Lochroyan: now first published in a perfect state;" beginning with our lines 61-76, p. 614:—

"O wha will shoe my bonny foot, and wha will glove my hand?
And wha will lace my middle jimp wi' a lang lang linen band? [*cf.* p. 611.
"O wha will kame my yellow hair, with a new made silver kame?
And wha will father my young son, till Lord *Gregory* come hame?"
"Thy father will shoe thy bonny foot, thy mother will glove thy hand,
Thy sister will lace thy middle jimp, till Lord *Gregory* come to land.
"Thy brother will kame thy yellow hair, with a new made silver kame,
And God will be thy bairn's father, till Lord *Gregory* come hame."
"But I will get a bonny boat, and I will sail the sea;
And I will gang to Lord *Gregory*, since he canna come hame to me." etc.

Scott's version was compounded from "three manuscript copies and two from recitation. Two of the copies are in Herd's MSS.; the third is that of Mrs. Brown of Falkland."—*Minstrelsy S.B.*, iii. 56, 1803. By the way, "Love Gregory," or Gregor (perhaps MacGregor), not Lord Gregory, appears to have been the true title. Lochroyan is in Wigtonshire, near Stranraer.

David Herd and George Paton had earlier printed in their *Ancient and Modern Songs, Heroic Ballads*, etc. (vol. i. p. 149, 1776: not in the single vol. edition, 1769), "The Bonny Lass of *Lochroyan*," twenty-eight and a half four-line stanzas, beginning, "O, wha will shoe my bonny feet? Or wha will glove my hand?" Our "proud merchant-man" (Scott's "rank robber," and Herd's "rude rover,") then directs her where to find her "love Gregory." The "bonny ship" is described as "cover'd o'er with pearl: and at every needle-tack was in't there hang a siller-bell." This is more fanciful than our Roxburghe-ballad prototype of an armour-clad, with its "sides of the beaten gold, and doors were of *block-tin*." The Rover is dazzled by her beauty, and asks:—

"O whether art thou the Queen hersell? or ane of her *Maries* three? [*N.B.*
Or art thou the Lass of *Lochroyan* seeking love *Gregory*?"

"O I am not the Queen hersell, nor ane of her *Maries* three;
But I am the Lass of *Lochroyan*, seeking love *Gregory*."

"O sees na thou yon bonny bower, it's a' cover'd o'er wi' tin:
When thou hast sail'd it round about, love *Gregory* is within."

When she had sail'd it round about, she tirl'd at the pin,
"O open, open, love *Gregory*, open and let me in!

"For I am the Lass of *Lochroyan*, banisht frae a' my kin."
[Then his mother heard, and spak till her, while *Gregory* sleepit within.]

Next follow the demands to tell the love-tokens: the exchanged rings come first (no word of the changed linen); then the confession of dishonour is obtained; yet surely unnecessarily (except on the supposition of it being misplaced) is a later inquiry made for "mair o' the tokens, past between me and thee"[1]:—

> Then she turn'd her round about, "Well since it will be sae,
> Let never woman who has born a son hae a heart sae full of wae.
>
> "Take down, take down that mast of gould, set up a mast of tree,
> For it disna become a forsaken lady to sail sae royallie." [See Note 2.

Then comes, abruptly, Gregory's awakening, with his telling the dream which had been caused either by half-hearing her voice, or by that true mystic sympathy, which materialists reject and despise.

> "I dreamt a dream this night, mother, I wish it may prove true,
> That the bonny Lass of *Lochroyan* was at the yate just now."
>
> "Lie still, lie still, my only son, and sound sleep may'st thou get;
> For it's but an hour or little mair since she was at the yate."
>
> "Awa, awa, ye wicked woman! and an ill death may you die;
> Ye might have either letten her in, or else have waken'd me.
>
> "Gar saddle to me the black," he said, "Gar saddle to me the brown,
> Gar saddle to me the swiftest steed that is in a' the town."
>
> Now the first town he came to, the bells were ringing there;
> And the neist town he came to, her corpse was coming there.
>
> "Set down, set down that comely corpse, set down and let me see,
> Gin that be the Lass of *Lochroyan*, that died for love o' me."
>
> And he took out his little pen-knife, that hang down by his gar'e;
> And he's ripp'd up her winding-sheet, a long cloth-yard or mair.
>
> And first he kist her cherry-cheek, and syne he kist her chin,
> And neist he kist her rosy lips; there was nae breath within.
>
> And he has ta'en his little pen-knife, with a heart that was fou sair;
> He has given himself a deadly wound, and word spoke never mair.

Thus ends Herd's version, printed in 1776, saved from earlier years. Where he found fragments he honestly gave them as such. He was the best of our Early-Ballads editors, rival seekers for *Reliques*. Jamieson and Motherwell (himself a true poet) were able men, but could not resist the temptation to manufacture and add connecting links or "improvements." Allan Cunningham was fraudulence

---

[1] Here, if anywhere, comes in a doubtful 38th stanza given by Maurice Ogle in 1871 (*Ballad Minstrelsy of Scotland*, p. 7), *Fair Annie of Lochryan*:—

> "Oh! ha'e ye gotten anither fair love, for all the oaths ye sware?
> Then fare ye weel, fause *Gregory*, for me ye's ne'er see mair!"

[2] Robert Jamieson's remembered 23rd stanza (1805) might follow Herd's on the 'mast of gold' being unsuitable for a forsaken lady:—

> "Tak down, tak down the sails o' silk, set up the sails o' skin;
> Ill sets [=suits] the outside to be gay, whan there's sic grief within."

He reads, "lace my middle jimp wi' a new-made *London* band:" Scott, '*linen*.'

personified, and thus well suited Cromek. We entertain respect and liking for Robert Kinloch, an assiduous hunter of waifs and strays, late in the day, when the game had become scarce. Charles Kirkpatrick Sharpe was a genuine Last of the Mohicans, shrewd, skilful, and honest, to whom we owe lasting gratitude: we often saw him in our young days, and twice was this small editorial head patted by his hand, while we gazed at his spotless gaiters with awe. Wm. Edmondstoune Aytoun stood among the best of workers at interweaving the most telling stanzas of differentiated versions into one harmonious narrative. He neither falsified nor mutilated causelessly: he simply re-cast or soldered them into mosaic-work.

As for the untrustworthy recitations, the so-called "traditionary" variations, pretended to be carried down from hoar antiquity by garrulous old women, half-blundering and half-fraudulent, they need not detain us here. Elizabeth Cochrane's song-book version begins, "Fair *Isabell* of *Rockroyall* she dreamed where she lay," and by aid of idle repetitions it is inflated to thirty-five stanzas. Nor care we more for Widow Stevenson's nearly-worthless version, (in Pitcairn's MSS., iii. p. 1), which, lacking the beginning, starts with "She sailed west, she sailed east, she sailed mony a mile; Until she cam to Lord *Gregor's* yett, and she tirled at the pin." Here the seeker is called "the bonny Lass of Ruchlaw Hill." In Peter Buchan's MSS. ii. 149, his *Ballads of the North of Scotland*, ii. 198, 1828, and J. H. Dixon's *Scottish Traditional Versions of Ancient Ballads* (Percy Society, vol. xvii. 1845), one beginning, "It fell on a Wodensday, Love *Gregory's* ta'en the sea," she is "Lady Janet," but in Robert Jamieson's she is "Annie of Lochroyan." Some few genuine relics are in "The Lass of Aughrim" (transferring the scene to *Aughrim*, Roscommon, Ireland, and with curious similarity of name to our Roxburghe "*Ocram*"), preserved by Mr. G. C. Mahon of Ann Arbor, Michigan, as it had been sung by a labourer at Tyrrelspass, West Meath, Ireland, about 1830. It begins, "Oh! who'll comb my yellow locks, with the brown berry comb?" Charles Kirkpatrick Sharpe's fragment, from Galloway and Dumfriesshire, holds no more than one valuable stanza:—

"O open the door, Love *Gregory*, O open and let me in;
The wind blows through my yellow hair, and the dew draps o'er my chin."

In Herd's version we note the absurdity of Gregory ordering his horses and riding after his mistress, who had gone off from his castle, even as she had come to it, in a ship by sea. The ring, the ship, and the castle (Rock Royal) are persistently described as of "block tin!" Was the author a Cornish miner? Dervaux says, perhaps it was all on account of Love Gregory being on an island, blockt in by the waves, and over-wearied by his "witch-mother."

[Roxburghe Collection, III. 488.]

The Lass of Ocram.

I Built my Love a gallant ship,
And a ship of Northern fame,
And such a ship as I did build,
Sure there never was seen;
For the sides were of the beaten gold,
And the doors were of block tin,
And sure such a ship as I built,
There never [before] was seen. [Text, "There sure."

And as she was a sailing
By herself all alone,
She spied a proud merchant-man
Come plowing o'er the main.
"Thou fairest of all creatures,
Under the heavens," said she,
"I am the Lass of *Ocram*,
Seeking for Lord *Gregory*."

"If you are the Lass of *Ocram*,
As I take you for to be,
You must go to yonder island,
There Lord *Gregory* you'll see."

"It rains upon my yellow locks, [She lands.
And the dew falls on my skin;
Open the gates, Lord *Gregory*,
And let your true love in!"

"If you're the Lass of *Ocram*,
As I take you not to be,
You must mention the three tokens
Which pass'd between you and me."

"Don't you remember, Lord *Gregory*,
One night on my father's hill,
With you I swaft my linen fine,
It was sore against my will;
For mine was of the *Holland* fine,
And yours but *Scotch* cloth;
For mine cost a guinea a yard,
And yours but five groats."

"If you are the Lass of *Ocram*,
As I think you not to be,
You must mention the second token.
That pass'd between you and me."

"Don't you remember, Lord *Gregory*,
  One night in my father's park,
We swaffed our two rings,
  It was all in the dark ;
For mine was of the beaten gold,
  And yours was of block tin ;
And mine was true-love without,
  And yours all false within."

"If you are the Lass of *Ocram*,
  As I take you not to be,
You must mention the third token,
  Which past between you and me."

"Don't you remember, Lord *Gregory*,
  One night in my father's hall,
Where you stole my maidenhead,
  Which was the worst of all."

"Begone, you base creature !
  Begone from out of the hall !
Or else in the deep seas
  You and your babe shall fall."

"Then who will shoe my bonny feet,
  And who will close my hands,
And who will lace my waste so small,
[*cf.* p. cii.] Into a landen span ?

"And who will comb my yellow locks,
  With a brown berry comb ?
And who's to be father to my child,
  If Lord *Gregory* is none ?"

"Let your brother shoe your bonny feet,
  Let your sister close your hands,
Let your mother lace your waist so small,
  Into a landen span.
Let your father comb your yellow locks,
  With a brown berry comb,
And let God be father of your child,
  For Lord *Gregory* is none."

"I dreamt a dream, dear mother, [*Lord Gregory speaks.*
  I could wish to have it read,
I saw the Lass of *Ocram*
  A floating on the flood."
"Lie still, my dearest son,
  And take thy sweet rest ;
It is not half an hour ago,
  The maid pass'd this place."

"Ah! cursed be you, mother!
And cursed may you be,
That you did not awake me,
When the maid pass'd this way!
I will go down into some silent grove,
My sad moan for to make;
It is for the Lass of *Ocram*,
My poor heart now will break."

[White-letter. No printer's name. Woodcut of ship. Date of issue, *circâ* 1765.
See the introduction for variations, especially the conclusion given by Herd.]

*** If we are enabled to see the seventh volume of these *Roxburghe Ballads* to its conclusion, the legitimate FINALE of the whole series, whereof we are unwilling to despair, there will be a small group devoted to the ballads illustrating the stormy reign or usurpation of William and Mary. For this group might have been kept waiting "THE MEMORABLE BATTLE FOUGHT AT KILLIECRANKIE," July 17, 1689, wherein the usurper's forces were routed under General Mackay by the gallant Claverhouse, John Graham, Viscount Dundee. But amid the uncertainties of this slippery world, wherein many an *oubliette* opens suddenly and our comrades unexpectedly sink to disappear for ever, our only safety lies in making sure of the present. Therefore, availing ourselves of the pretext that surely the glorious death of Claverhouse was an event alike romantic and tragical, we introduce it without delay, in sequence to others of "The Gallant Grahams." The noblest of the race were Montrose and Claverhouse, both loyal and chivalrous, both giving their lives cheerfully for their respective kings of the Stuart line.

[Roxburghe Collection, III. 104; Douce Coll., III. 51.]

The Memorable Battle fought at Killycrankie, by Chief Clavers and his Highland Men.

To the Tune call'd, *Killy Cranky.*

CLavers and his *Highland* men came down upon the raw then,
Who being stout gave many a clout, the Lads began to claw then:
With sword and targets in their hands, wherewith they were not slaw then,
And clinkin clankin on their crowns, the Lads began to claw then.

O'er brink and brank, o'er ditch and stank, he staik amang them a' then,
The *Butter-box* got many knocks, the riggans pay'd for a' then. [*riggan*=backbone.
They got their Paiks with sudden Straiks, which to their grief they saw then,
And double dunts upon their rumps, the lads began to fa' then.

Her skip'd about, and leap'd about, her flang among them a' then,
The *English* blades got broken heads, their crowns her clave in twa then,
The *Durk* and *Door* made their last hour, such was their final fa' then, [*Skene dhu.*
They thought the D——l had been there, that gave them such a paw then.

Jack Presbyter an's Covenant came whigging up [th'] hill then,
Though *Highland Trews* would not refuse for to subscribe the Bill then;
In *William's* name he thought na shame, would stop the deed at a' then;
But her nane sell *Stock*, with many a knock, cry'd *furich Whigs awa' then.*

Sir *Hugh Macdow* with his men true, came skiping o'er the brink then;
The *Hogan Dutch*, that feared such, they bred a horrid stink then:
The true *Maclain* his gate has gone, and come upon a raw then;
None could withstand his heavy hand, he strake with such a paw then.

[White-letter, one cut: a hand-to-hand battle of footmen. Here ends the broadside, without colophon. A printed copy in the Editor's possession, dated 1778, gives various readings and two additional stanzas. These stanzas, late additions, were adopted by Joseph Ritson, in his *Scottish Songs*, 1794:—

"*Oh' on a ri! Oh' on a ri!* why should she love King *Shames*, man?
'*Oh' rig in di! Oh' rig in di!*' she shall break a' her banes then;
With 'Furichinish,' and stay a while, and speak a word or twa, man,
She's gi' a straike, out o'er the neck, before ye win awa' then.

O fy for shame, ye're three for ane, her nainsell's won the day, man.
King *Shames'* red coats shou'd be hung up, because they ran awa' then:
Had bent their brows, like Highland trews, and made as lang a stay, man,
They'd saved their King, that sacred thing, and *Willie* ran awa' then.

Variations, line 4.—Wi' mony a fearful heavy sigh (weak and inadmissible); line 5, O'er bush, o'er bank, o'er ditch o'er stank (a stank is a pool of stagnant water, broader than a ditch); the *Butter-box* was a time-honoured nick-name for the Dutch common-people and soldiers, even as *Hogen-Mogens* applied to their High-Mightinesses who ruled them; *paiks* are pokes, and *dunts* are knocks, very-often double-knocks, in this case well administered; line 16, *Furich-Figs* awa' man (corrupt version; the meaning is, 'Aggressive Whigs, be off!'; line 17, Sir Evan Du, *i.e.* Evan Dhu, or the black Evan; Maclean = our Maclain; penultimate stanza, *Och on a rie!* a highland lament, *Och!* = Alas! as is *Oh' rig in di! Furichinish* is not (as John Jasper said) "unintelligible;" probably from *furich*, otherwise *fooroch*, or *foorich*, signifies bustle, confusion caused by haste. We repeat, the battle was fought on July 17, 1689.]

Three Ballads on the Earl of Mar.

"There's some say that we wan, some say that they wan,
Some say that nane wan at a', man;
But one thing I'm sure, that at *Sheriffmuir*
A battle there was which I saw, man:
And we ran, and they ran, and they ran, and we ran,
And we ran: and they ran awa, man!"
—*Sheriffmuir*, by the Rev. Murdoch McLennan of Crathie.

THE solution of the difficulty as to who deserves to be held the triumphant victor in any sharply contested game, or one played without skill and determinate courage on either side, may be safely left to occupy our attention during the coming glacial period, when the sun gives up business, the earth has exhausted her coal-mines and cooled her inside, as thoroughly as she has unbaked her crust. The indecision is not alone for 'the Race of the Sherriemuir' on 13 November, 1715, or as it is sometimes styled "The Bob of Dumblane." "Gin it were na weel bobbit, weel bobbit, weel bobbit, an it were na well bobbit we'el bob it again!" sang John Campbell, second and best Duke of Argyle, who appears in our ensuing ballads. They deserve preservation here, although they are somewhat intrusive among our less-historical Romantic Ballads. We afford them shelter and annotation; being unwilling to leave them to the tender mercies of Chance, awaiting a seventh volume of *Roxburghe Ballads*.

The tune cited for use in "*Mar's Lament*," in 1715, had been composed for Tom D'Urfey's opera of "The Modern Prophets," 1707, a song full of national ardour, not to say boastfulness (some folks, like Dame Quickly, "cannot abide swaggerers," but then they keep disorderly houses themselves): Boasting, *with deeds*, not being a bad thing while the country is endangered by foreign foes and internal divisions, although anti-Jingoists and pro-Separatists may affect to be shocked. We give the song complete, but need not annotate the interpolation. The music is in *Pills to Purge Melancholy*, i. 25, and in *The Merry Musician*, i. 239, 1716.

A Song by Tom D'Urfey.

NOw, now comes on the Glorious Year! *Britain* has hope, and *France* has fear;
Lewis the war has cost so dear, he slyly peace does tender:
But our two Heroes so well know the breach of his word, some years ago,
They resolve they will give him another blow, unless he *Spain* surrender.

Health to the Queen, then straight begin! to *Marlborough* great, and to brave *Eugene*.
With them let valiant *Webb* come in, who late perform'd a wonder:
Then to the ocean an offering make, and boldly carouze to brave Sir *John Leak*,
Who with mortar and cannon *Mahon* did take, and make the Pope knock under.

Beat up the Drum a new Alarm, the foe is cold, and we are warm;
The *Mounsieur's* troops can do no harm, tho' they abound in numbers:
Push then once more, and the War is done, old men and boys will surely run;
And we know we can beat 'em if four to one: which he too well remembers.

Seven years later Tom D'Urfey again wrote words to the same tune, on what he chose to call "The happy Accession to the Crown and coming-in of our Gracious Sovereign, King George" the First. It also has three stanzas, of which this is the opening:—

Britains, now let joys increase, revel all in happy days,
Royal *George* has crost the seas: ye natives, homage tender.
Fate to save us made him haste, *Britain's* Genius doubly blest,
And renown'd as was e'er in Ages past the Saint our Isles defender. Etc.

Tom won nothing by his attempts to propitiate the pigmy Georgius of Hanover! who "hated arts and despised literature, but liked train oil in his salads, and gave an unlimited patronage to bad oysters." Did he not publicly declare, "I hate all Boets and Bainters," and did not his precious son, George II., threaten our Hogarth with a flogging at the halberts, because he lampooned the silliness of the Grenadiers' March to Finchley?

As to the tune of *Bonny Katharine Ogie*, named for the ballad on p. 622, "The Clans' Lamentation against *Mar* and their own Folly:" The music is in Playford's *Dancing Master* of 1686, the Appendix, entitled "*The Lady Catharine Ogle*, a new Dance."

The earliest known words sung to the tune were written by Tom D'Urfey, one of the Anglo-Scotch indecorous absurdities wherein Londoners delighted, and which were often adopted with favour in the North Countrie, even in sapient Auld Reekie (conceiting itself later with being 'Modern Athens' and *arbiter elegantiarum*). He called it "Bonny *Kathern Loggy*: A Scotch Song." Its seven stanzas are unworthy of type-reprint, but this is the first of them, for identification (music and words in *Pills to Purge Melancholy*, vi. 274-276, 1720):

As I came down the hey-land [*vel* Highland] Town, there were Lasses many
Sat in a rank on either bank, and ene more gay than any;
Ise leekt about for ene kind face, and I spy'd *Willy Scroggy*,
Ise spir'd of him what was her name, and he caw'd her *Kathern Loggy*.

The date of this was certainly as early as 1715, or earlier, because it is not only named for the tune of the "Clans' Lamentation," 1715, but also for a discreet "New Song to the tune of *Katherine Loggy*, in *The Merry Musician*, i. 224 (dated 1716), beginning, "As I walk'd forth to view the plain, upon a morning early, with a sweet scent to cheer my brain." The burden was *Katherine Ogee*: eight stanzas. By some unknown hand, altered and adopted as Scotch, it was reprinted in Allan Ramsay's *Tea Table Miscellany* (vol. i. p. 133, first edition, song lxix.), as *Catherine Ogie*, commencing, "As walking forth to view the Plain, upon a morning early, While May's sweet scent," etc.

Stalwart Cavaliers entertain a sovereign contempt for the weak-minded, unfilial, and fulsomely belauded "Good Queen Anne;" they never forgive her omission of the often-projected but unperformed act of reparation to her family. She had enjoyed selfishly all that life enabled her to grasp or retain. Conscience pricked her, but she hesitated. The intrigues woven around her death-bed having led to the Elector of Hanover's accession to the English throne, for which he was unfitted by anything save the courage of a military adventurer, the Chevalier de St. George's hand was soon forced by John Erskine, Earl of Mar, raising the flag of insurrection (we cannot call it rebellion, since it was in behalf of the rightful heir, although unseasonably). There remained nothing but to fling away the scabbard, and use the sword and target, as many brave Highlanders were ready to do, at Braemar in Aberdeenshire, on that memorable 26th of August, 1715. Huntly, Tullibardine, Seaforth, Linlithgow, with the Viscounts of Kilsythe, Kenmure, and more, swore allegiance to King James III., "the Old Pretender."

"God bless the King, God save the State's defender!
God bless (no harm in blessing) the Pretender!—
But who Pretender is, and who is King,
God bless us all! is quite another thing."

By the 6th September the noblemen and chieftains of clans, with their respective feudal retainers, gathered at Aboyne, where Mar raised the Standard and proclaimed James King of England, Scotland, and Ireland. How the inaction and divided councils depressed their hopes, to ruin the few chances of success, among the gallant gentlemen who threw away their lives for the lost cause (as others equally impetuous and noble were to do thirty years later, when they "went out in the 'Forty-five"), is a tale that can never become wearisome or forgotten.

Unfortunately for their fortunes and lives, Mar was not a skilful commander, being wholly destitute of the military judgment and overwhelming power that had been shown successively by Montrose and by Claverhouse. Otherwise he might certainly have gained all Scotland for James, and it is not improbable that England would have followed soon after. As mismanaged, however, it became inevitable failure, and the defeat in 1715 was the real cause of ruin in 1746, when the old gentry hung back from Derby.

On the 10th November Mar consented to move his forces southward from Perth. Then followed "The Bob of Dumblane" with Argyle, in which the advantages remained with the Whigs. With only half of his forces retained on the morning of the 14th, Mar retreated to Perth, and our three ballads tell some portion of the saddening story of the Stuart loyalists.

The Old Chevalier, James Frederick Edward Stuart, arrived 22 Dec. His flight on Feb. 4th, 171⅚, with Mar, Meltort, Drummond, and others, was a sorry exchange for death on a well-fought field.

These rude ballads are all on the side of the government. Though they exaggerate the excesses of the Highlanders, they are not so rancorous or foul as the London political squibs of the same date. The tune, *The Hart* (*sic*, for *Hare*) *Merchants Rant*, is not found.

Notes to p. 620.—[1] John Campbell, second Duke of Argyle, Commander-in-Chief of the Georgian forces. He survived until 1743.

[2] John Erskine, Earl of Mar, went abroad with James III., died in 1733.

[3] The headstrong river Allan, rushing past the ruined Abbey of Dumblane.

[Roxburghe Collection, III. 329.]

A Dialogue between his Grace the Duke of Argyle, and the Earl of Mar:

Or, an Excellent New Song, to the Tune of *the Hart Merchant's Rant*, etc.

ARGYLE and *Mar* are gone to war, which hath bred great confusion,
For Church and State they do debate, through difference and division.
And yet, for what I know not that, I hope I speak no treason,
Some say it's Self, some say it's Pelf, and some say it's Religion,
Which e'er it be, I tell to thee, and that I will not spare, Sir,
The Blades come from the Braes of *Mar*, they brave us every where, Sir.

Argyle.[1] [See *Notes*, p. 619.

Says great *Argyle* within a while, "I'le make *Mar* for to rue, Sir,
That such great Folly in his brain did happen for to brew, Sir,
Tho' *Mar's* men now do ramble throw the *North*, both here and there, Sir,
I'le make them to draw up their Trew, and whipe their buttocks bare, Sir.

Mar.[2]

Says good Lord *Mar*, "Do you so dare both me and all my men, Sir,
While I have might, I will you fight, from *Stirling* flit your Den, Sir."

"The last time that I flited it, you had no cause to boast, Sir, *Argyle.*
For any thing that then you wan, it was unto your Coast, Sir, [=cost.
When at *Dumblain*, unto your pain, we fought it very fair, Sir,
When that *Mar's* men were forc'd and fain to run like any Hare, Sir; [*cf.* tune.
Some to the hills, some to the haughs, and some to *Allan* Watter,[3]
And unto some it was no more, their sculls were made to clatter.
And those that did escape the sword, did we not them surround, Sir,
When the four-score of Highland Men were in the water drown'd, Sir?"

Mar.

"Though my men do ramble thorough the *North* both here and there, Sir,
The half of what's said is not true: the Truth I do declare, Sir,
It's said they pillage and plunder all, in places where they come, Sir,
But by this they soon would catch a fall, and unto ruin run, Sir,
And as for that was at *Dumblain*, we lost so many men, Sir,
Perhaps we may recruit again, and that we'll let you ken, Sir.
If that once more we shall engage, we shall know how it goes, Sir,
Whiskie shall put our brains in rage, and Snuff shall prime our nose, Sir.
With Swords and Guns into our hands, we'll stoutly venture on, Sir,
Yea, Durks and Targets at command, of these we shall want none, Sir."

Argyle.

"Do what you can to prove the Man, your attempts shall prove in vain, Sir,
For sure *Argyle* shall lead the Van, and the victory shall gain, Sir.
Tho', like a Cock, *Mar*, in the North, abroad hath sent his crow, Sir,
Clapping his wings now beyond *Forth*, perhaps he'll get a blow, Sir.
Argyle, like to a Lyon bold, will grip him in his paws, Sir,
And that perhaps e're it be long, he'll make him stand in awe, Sir.
For lo! a conjunct company, both of *Scots* and *Dutch* men,
They're at a call on *Mar* to fall; they're almost all none-such Men:
Besides great numbers of Gentlemen, whom they call Volunteers, Sir,
The most and best whereof consist of valiant *Scotish* Peers, Sir."

Finis.

[In White-letter. Two rude chap-book woodcuts, 1st, a man shooting with bow-and-arrow; 2nd, a kilted Scot riding in woman-fashion on a nag, and playing a Scotch fiddle, symbolically. *Notes* are on p. 619. No colophon. Date, 1715.]

[Roxburghe Collection, III. 585.]

An Excellent New Ballad, entituled,

Mar's Lament for his Rebellion.

To the Tune of, *Now comes on the Glorious Year.* [See p. 617.]

Noble *Argyle* when he went on, while drums did rattle and trumpet sound,
"Come, brave Boys, we'l stand our ground, for three to one we'l fight them."

As soon as *Mar* did see the same, he cryed aloud with grief and woe,
"We are not able to fight our Foe, let us turn back with mourning.

"Yonder's *Argyle*, that champion great, who to our King hath no respect;
With bombs and cannons he'l make us quake, let us for Peace implore him."

These men with courage bold went on, like lyons to the prey each one,
"For if to the King this thing be known, he'l nobly reward us!"

Each man unto the spoyl he gat, some got plaids and snuff-mills in their pack,
Some had Targets, and some had none, to keep them from the volleys.

Saith *Mar*, "I will to *London* go, perhaps the King will favour show,
But mercy, I fear, there will be none to such a rebel as I am.

"I have wrought folly in this land, both sword and gun I did command,
Out of every place I fetcht a Clan, for to revenge this quarrel.

"With fear and terror I may dread, what shall be the Exent of this Head, [*sic.*
Our Land's become a Field of Blood, it's all through my occasion."

He hath brought us from our native place, here to suffer much disgrace;
His heavy Curse come on his face, for he hath wroght our Ruine.

"All for our King we did appear, our cries and groans we thought he'd hear,
And for our Laws he would appear, yet he doth not regard us.

"Two thousand men from me are gone, to pull the King out of his Throne;
But now they are taken every one, they are made to beg for pardon.

"Here in *St. Johnstown* I do ly, with sighs and groans and tears I cry; [= *Perth*
I know that many of us shall dye, like dogs we must be hanged.

"Here I am surrounded about, no place nor corner [I] can get out;
For if to the fields I should go out, they're at my heels pursuing.

"For if to the Highlands I should flee, there will be no Refuge for me,
No cove, no grove, no rock I see, to keep me from their Fury.

"*Argyle* he is so valiant still, that many of my men he'l kill,
Upon me he advances still, at length he will undo me.

"He with his mighty cannon-balls, he'l batter down both Towns and Walls,
And many of my Captains falls, they bleeding ly before him.

"Certainly we have all been mad, first when that bargain we had made;
He'l send us neither help nor aid, to keep us from their fury.

"My rebellious weapons I'll lay down, and will be Subject to the Crown,
To all generations its be-known, that I shall still be Loyal.

"Our horrid plots we did contrive, thinking the King for to deprive,
But none of our designs did thrive, they were so ill contrived.

"We were forty thousand in this Land, all bound by Association Band,
We thought we would get help at hand, but *France* has us deceived.

"A bold Attempt indeed we did make, when the Castle we design'd to take,
But all did prove to no effect, our plots were all discover'd. [*Edinburgh*, 1715.

"We know not which way now to turn, for our Magazine's all destroy'd and burn'd;
For all our projects are backward turn'd, we've wrought our own Confusion."

Finis.

[White-letter. Two cuts; man smoking, and ship. No colophon. Date, Oct. 1715.]

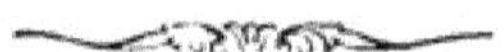

[Roxburghe Collection, III. 336. No duplicate known, or recorded.]

The Clans' Lamentation against Mar and their own Folly.

To the Tune of, *Bonny Katharine Ogie*. [See p. 618.]

As I did travel in the *North*, I in discourse took pleasure,
To talk with those that were our Foes, when that we could get leasure:
That they rose in Rebellion, I did ask, what was the reason? [*Text transp.*
And what great madness moved them, for to work such great Treason?—

Against both King and Parliament, and Government all over,
And would not join to *George* our King, the great Prince of *Hanover*.
They answer'd me with one accord, "We may think shame to tell you,
That we such simple fools have been to join with such a fellow.

"He did send letters unto us, and falsly did us flatter,
Desiring us for to arise, and *Hanoverians* scatter;
And that he would bring o're our King, and would put off *Hanover*;
And that our King he should possess both *North* and *South* all over.

"But now, alas! we suffer for our Folly in this matter,
For now we risen are, and we shall never be the better;
For we did once encounter with that mighty man of valour,
Who's like a Lyon in his strength, but comely in his feature.

"Even great *Argyle* your General will make us to repent it,
That we so foolishly should have even unto *Mar* consented:
And tho' many of us fell, ev'n at the same engagement,
Yet we did go along with him, by his false To[ol's e]nticement. [*mutilated.*

"He told us we should see our King, e're we were two months older,
But now we see it is a lye which makes our hearts the colder:
For he did bring a man to us, that might have been his father,
Who said, he would not [want] *Pop'ry* quite, but want our kindness rather.

"It had been better for us all, that *Mar* had ne're been born,
For now, alas! we are become all the whole Nation's scorn:
For now we have left all our lands, likewise our life's in danger;
Alas! that e're we did agree for to fetch in a Stranger.

"But now we're forc'd to take [our] flight before King *George's* army,
Of soldiers brisk, and volunteers, like them there are not many,
That made us from Saint *Johnstoun* run, and likewise from *Dundee*, Sir,
And also thorow all the towns, into the *North*-country, Sir.

"Alas! alas! we are undone, for now and evermore then:
We know not where to hide our selves, neither in hole nor bore then:
For like a *Partridge* they do hunt us, both o're Hills and Glens, Sir,
Which makes us for to rue the day, that we were named *Clans*, Sir.

"But now, alas! we cannot help what we have done amiss, Sir,
But now we're like to end our days, in grief and heaviness, Sir,
Oh, and alas! we leave our lands, with Lamentation, Sir,
Likewise our wives and children all: have pity them upon, Sir.

Finis.

[No publisher's name or woodcut. White-letter. Date, Nov. 1715. "A weak invention of the enemy!" fabricated by a Scotch non-combatant: the rhyme in penultimate line, Lamen-ta-shee-on, is decisive. The tune belongs to Tom D'Urfey's song, in *Pills to P. M.*, vi. 275; the music is given in the admirable new edition, 1887, of Mr. John Muir Wood's *Songs of Scotland*, p. 60.]

Note on Line 31.—'*St. Johnstoun*' is, of course *Perth*, the fair city on the Tay, the beauty of which is measured by more than its Inches.

Culloden, and 'the butcher' Cumberland.

"Let mournful *Britons* now deplore the horrors of *Drummossie* Day!
Our hopes of Freedom all are o'er: the Clans are all away, away!
The clemency so late enjoyed, converted to tyrannic sway,
Our laws and friends it once destroy'd, and forced the Clans away, away.

"This fate thus doom'd, the *Scottish* race to Tyrants' last power a prey,
Shall all those troubles never cease? Why went the Clans away, away?
Brave sons of Mar, no longer mourn! Your Prince abroad will make no stay;
You'll bless the hour of his return, and soon revenge *Drummossie* Day."

—*Jacobite Song*, to the tune of *The Clans are coming*, 1746.

SUCH was the rose-coloured prospect beheld by a sentimentalist who stayed safely at home during the final struggle for the Stuarts in 1746; if indeed the song were not written at a later date by one of those true-hearted Jacobite Ladies who sang all the most touching Laments for the lost cause, keeping alive the love, although devoid of hope. We ourselves possess a large private collection of genuine *Jacobite Relics* (James Hogg's were untrustworthy, catchpenny, and garbled, some absolutely fraudulent); but few of them have poetic merit. We restrict ourselves here to the rare Roxburghe Collection originals, all of them, unhappily, *on the wrong side*.

The tune here assigned to the "New Song, on the Duke of *Cumberland's* Victory at *Culloden*-Moor" is marked as *The Earl of Essex*. But it is neither, 1st, the one known as *Essex's Last Good Night*, or *Well-a-day!* so called from ballads, beginning, respectively, "All you that cry, 'O hone! O hone!'" and "Sweet *England's* prize is gone! Well-a-day!" Nor does it agree with the rhythm of, 2nd, *Essex's Lamentation*, or "*What if a day!*" *i.e.* "What if a day, or a month, or an hour, crown thy delights with a thousand sweet contendings." (Both these tunes are given in *Popular Music*, pp. 176 and 311.)

[Roxburghe Collection, III. 789.]

A New Song.

Call'd the Duke of *Cumberland's* Victory over the *Scotch* Rebels at *Cullodon-Moor* near *Inverness*. Made by a Soldier who was in the Engagement.

To the Tune of, *The Earl of Essex*. [See p. 623.]

YOu Subjects of *Britton*, now you may rejoice,
And pray for King *George* with heart and voice.
The Popish Pretender has now run away,
Just like his old Daddy no longer could stay.

The brave Duke of *Cumberland* he did command,
And happy was we that had such a Hand,
He greatly encouraged his Soldiers that Day,
And it was our care his Command to obey.

We followed the Rebels thro' dirt and thro' mire,
And for to come up with them was our desire;
At length we did wade through the fresh River *Spey*,
And when we came over they still run away.

We still advanc'd after them [during] four days,
Over mountains, thro' rivers, and many rough ways;
At length we came up with them near *Inverness*,
And there we quickly put them to distress.

They had thirteen Pieces of Cannon that Day,
Which quickly upon us began for to play;
Our cannon we turned it, and levell'd it so true,
We made all the Rebels begin to look blue.

They thought to come in upon Us sword in hand,
But as we was ordered, we firmly did stand;
We poured in our small Shot so, when they drew nigh,
That many fell dead, and the rest they did fly.

They was in such hast[e] they their Cannon did leave,
And then the *Pretender* did weep and did grieve; [Fact!
They left all their Baggage their hast[e] it was such,
And their Amunition, which grieved them much.

Our Light-horse and Dragoons they did closely pursue,
With Broad Swords and Pistols great numbers they slew,
The ground it was covered with wounded and slain;
So, *Popish* Pretender, thy hopes are in vain!

Three thousand that Day we la[id] dead on the ground, ["lay"
Besides many skulking in Cabbins we found;
And many deserted, their kale-yards to set,
Which put the *Pretender* into a great fret.

Altho' they had got an Assistance from *France*,
The brave Duke of *Cumberland* made them to dance,
He took many Prisoners, and blasted their hope,
For he was not commanded by General *Cope*. [See *Note*.

To hang all the Rebels you have my consent,
Because with a good King they are not content;
The World it is come to a very bad Pass,
For they want to have *Britton* be ruled by an Ass.

Let each Loyal Subject then fill up a Glass,
And drink to King *George* and about let it pass;
And when your hand's in, let your Liquor not stand,
But fill up another to brave *CUMBERLAND.*

For He's a Commander couragious and bold,
In following the Rebels he will not be controul'd;
I wish he may always have Health and Success,
For such a Commander is a great Happiness.

Note.—Line 40 is a well-deserved gird against sleepy-headed Sir John Cope ('Hey! *Johnnie Cope*, are ye waukin' yet?'), who was caught napping, as Morse found his mare, by Charles Edward Stuart before the Battle of Prestonpans, near Tranent, 21st Sept. 1745. *Johnnie Cope* was unanimously absolved from blame by a council of officers, and died 28 May, 1760.

[The Colophon is at the end of the companion ditty, "England's Glory," p. 626.]

⁂ Printed on the same sheet with the other ballad, William, Duke of Cumberland, and the victory at Culloden, but by an inferior hand. The author of this "New Song" possessed far more of the spirit of olden bard and warrior than did any of the common herd, the political hacks who wrote their Grub-street rhymes to order of the Walpole clique pay-masters in town. Remembering the cruel butchery which followed so speedily on the defeat of the brave Highlanders, the slaughter of their wives and children by the troopers of Cumberland William, eternally remembered as "the Butcher," not to mention the ruthless execution of many gallant gentlemen and noblemen on scaffolds reeking with the best Scottish blood, it is noteworthy that these two ditties were appropriately issued, along with other Sheffield cutlery, "*Near the Shambles.*"

There is one small woodcut of a Grenadier at top of "A New Song," on the same sheet. For this we here substitute our own reduced copy of another Royal Grenadier of the same date, from Hogarth's Foundling-Hospital picture, "*The March to Finchley*" (mentioned on p. 618).

[Roxburghe Collection III. 789, on same leaf.]

England's Glory;

Or, Duke William's Triumph over the Rebels in Scotland.

BRITTONS all your voices raise,
Huzza! the *British* Hero;
And sound the brave Duke *William's* Praise,
And make the Vallies echo:
For now me Boys we've got the Day, [sic. *Hibernicè.*
For which we long did wish and Pray,
Let every Churchman with me say,
God save the brave Duke *William.*

When our Champion orders gave,
To march and give them Battle,
Our Soldiers gave three loud Huzzas,
Whilst Cannon loud did Rattle;
When to the river *Spey* they came,
So eager was they for the game,
They all leaped in and through it swam,
Lead on by brave Duke *William.* [=led.

The Rebels look'd like Men amaz'd,
To see the *Brittons* coming;
They 'spyed the Duke and on him gazed,
But soon they all were running:
On *Cullodon*-Moor they made a stand,
Eight thousand Men with sword in Hand;
But all the World must needs commend
The conduct of brave Duke *William.*

Our Soldiers bravely stood their ground
And briskly they did Fire,
The vain Pretender quickly found
'Twas time for to retire.
Three thousand slain they left behind, [text, "Sousand,"
A thousand more that's now confined;
And *Monsieur* you shall quickly find
A Champion in Duke *William.*

Pray God preserve great *George* our King,
The Glory of our Nation;
Let every Popish Rebel swing
At *TYBURN*, their old Station:
But loyal subjects soon will see,
The sweet effects of Liberty,
Preserved from Popish Tyranny,
By *GOD* and brave Duke *William.*

Sheffield: Printed by *Francis Lister*, near the *Shambles*, 1746.

[In White-letter. One woodcut of a Grenadier: *Cf.* p. 625. Date, April, 1746.]

*** With this sub-section of Jacobite, or *Anti-Jacobite Roxburghe Ballads*, we quit for the present the Scottish portion of our group. But there is good reason for believing that "Little Musgrave" was of the Armstrong Borderers, and Lady Barnard of the Barnard-Castle Yorkshire family (*cf.* pp. 606, 627).

Little Musgrave and Lady Barnard.

"The Hunt is up! the Hunt is up! and now it is almost day,
And he that's in bed with another man's wife,
It's time to get him away."
—Wedderburne's *Gude and Godly Ballatts*, 1621.

ALTHOUGH there have been, as usual, many claims urged from the North for the Scottish authorship of this grand old ballad, grounded on the existence of numerous and widely varying 'traditionary' mis-recollections thereof, collected zealously with more or less inaccuracy (especially less), no tittle of trustworthy evidence has ever been produced in support of such claims. On the contrary, we possess proofs manifold and convincing, more than a century older than any Scottish versions or garbled reminiscences of the English broadsides, that it belonged solely to us. Little Musgrave himself may have been a Westmoreland Borderer. Names of towns or other special localities were often modern interpolations to suit particular markets and auditories, changeable at will; but as far as they go, the references to Oxfordshire and Bucklesfieldbury point clearly to the home of the story: though modern Scotch recitations introduce "Dundee" recklessly.

That every existing copy is partially corrupt may be granted, since the progress of deterioration was rapid in the transmission of ballads orally, and little less so in the reprinting from an early edition. Not alone sheer blundering, but wanton interpolation by incompetent hands, were always to be feared and expected. As an example of this, take the original final stanza, which assigned the higher place within the grave to Lady Barnard, because she "came of the nobler kin," being corrupted in both of the distinct Roxburghe modern exemplars into the absurdity of misprints, "for she's of the better *skin*."

It was, evidently, already an old-established favourite ballad before it was quoted or intentionally misquoted by James Fletcher, after his merry use and wont, in *The Knight of the Burning Pestle*, act v. sc. 3, printed in 1613, but of date 1610 (our 14th stanza):—

And some they whistled, and some they sung,
Hey down, down!
And some did loudly say,
Ever as the Lord *Barnet's* horn blew
"Away, *Musgrave*, away!"

In his *Bonduca* (act v. sc. 2, before March, 1619), he shows a loose remembrance (or recovery) of one stanza in the *Drolleries'* version:—

[*He*] set the sword unto her breast, [Misquoted, "she."
Great pity it was to see
That three drops of her life-warm blood
Ran trickling down her knee.

Fletcher's *Monsieur Thomas*, act iv., holds the unmistakeable parody of Lord Barnard's conditional promise and threat:—

"If this be true, thou little tiny page,
This tale that thou tellest me,
Then on thy back will I presently hang
A handsome new livery.

"But if this be false, thou little tiny page,
As false it well may be [so],
Then with a cudgel of four feet long
I'll beat thee from head to toe."

There is a virtual completeness in the version given in *Wit Restored*, 1658 (twice reprinted, Park, 1817; Hotten, 1873, but never rightly edited, as it well deserved to be), and again in *Wit and Drollery*, third extant edition, 1682, p. 81. Much earlier than any of these had been transcribed the Percy Folio MS., p. 53, but it is unfortunately woefully mutilated, lacking nine and a half of the opening stanzas, and seven and two halves nearer the end of our *Wit Restored* print. Of broadside versions now remaining, the earliest in date of issue is Henry Gosson's (Pepys Coll., I. 364); another (Pepys, III. 314) was printed for J. Clark, W. Thackeray, and T. Passenger; one of our Roxburghes (III. 146) was for Coles, Vere, Wright, and Clarke; the Bagford (I. 36), for W. Onley.

We need write no more on the Scottish so-called traditional versions, than record on p. 630 their first lines, titles, and position. They have no authority whatever, being self-evidently imitations.

We depend on the three distinct embodiments, 1st, the Drolleries; 2nd, Henry Gosson's broadside; and 3rd, the Percy Folio fragments, copied on next page. The Roxburghe copy has a sorry ending, with its methodistical moralization, clumsily expressed (p. 634).

Amid all imperfections of its gradual deterioration, there is visible to any true espial the tragic beauty of the story. Except in one hideous stanza (26th of *Wit Restored*, where the Lady is treated similarly to Sta. Agatha: the stanza being clearly condemned on the authority of the *Bonduca* quotation), the injured husband stands forward as a noble figure, a man who disdains to take any unfair advantage of an unarmed foe; who lets him win the first stroke, but who, when he himself deals the second stroke, leaves no third blow to be needed. Goaded to desperation by his Lady, who desires not to live, he slays her in one fierce moment of uncontrollable rage. But pity for the ill-starred pair comes to him, and he yields them the grace of re-union in the grave; all the more willingly (if we are to accept the Percy Folio reading and some others) because of his discovery that her folly or crime had been caused by the delirium of impending child-birth, a mere craze to bring Little Musgrave close beside her—and that he has slain his own true child, his son and heir indisputably, in slaying her.

It is almost as with Haidee (that exquisite episode in the *Don Juan* of Byron, whom the paltriest scribblers now traduce and disparage):

She died, but not alone; she bore within
A second principle of life, which might
Have dawned a fair and sinless child of sin,
But closed its little being without light,
And went down to the grave unborn, wherein
Blossom and bough lay withered with one blight:
In vain the dews of heaven descend above
The bleeding flower and blasted fruit of love.

This ill-omened secret meeting of the lady and Musgrave was their first as well as their last: this fact the husband himself is prompt to recognize. No question could arise as to her former sinlessness: none as to the lawful paternity of the unborn son. This consideration mitigates the horror and loathing that might otherwise attend our judgement of her shameless avowal of passion. It is like a glimpse into Nature's dreadful secrets.

[Percy Folio Manuscript, Brit. Mus. Add. MS. 27,879, fol. 53.]

[A Fragm^t of ye Ballad of Lord Barnard & the Little Musgrave.]

[*The beginning half-page is lost.*]

For this same night att B[. . . .]/ litle Musgreue is in bed wth thy wife:

If it be trew, thou litle foote page/ this tale thou hast told to mee,
then all my lands in Bucklefeildberry/ Ile freely giue to thee.

But if this be a lye, thou litle foot page,/ this tale thou hast told to mee,
then on the highest tree in Bucklesfeild-berry/ all hanged that thou shalt bee.

Saies Vpp & rise my merrymen all/ & saddle me my good steede,
for I must ride to Bucklesfeildberry/ god wott I had neuer more need.

But some they whistled, and some thé sunge/ & some they thus cold say,
"When euer as Lo: Barnetts horne blowes/ away Musgreue, away!"

"Mie thinkes I heare the throstlecocke,/ me thinkes I heare the Jay,
Me thinkes I heare Lo: Barnetts horne:/ away, Musgreue, away.

"But lie still, lie still, litle Musgreue/ & huddle me from the cold,
for it is but some sheaperds boy/ is whistling sheepe ore the Mold.

"Is not thy hauke vpon a pearch/ thy horsse eating corne & hay,
& thou, a gay lady in thine armes/ & yett thou wold goe awaw.

By this time Lo: Barnett was come to the dore/ & light vpon a stone,
and he pulled out 3 silver kayes/ & opened the dores euery one.

And first he puld the coucering doune/ & then puld doune the sheete,
Saies, "how now, how now, litle Musgreue/ dost find my gay lady sweet?"

"I find her sweete," saies litle Musgreue/ the more is my greefe and paine:

[. . . *Lower half of the page is lost: having broken away.*]

Soe haue I done the fairest Lady/ y^t euer wore womans weede, [fol. 54.

Soe haue I done a heathen child/ wch ffull sore grieueth mee,
for wch Ile repent all the dayes of my life,/ and god be with them all 3.

Fin[i]s.

["Heathen child" was so misinterpreted as to be glossed "? wild, loose knight:" although the reference is clearly to an *unbaptised* because *unborn infant.*]

It must have been a direct recognition of the slain child: judging by Lord Barnard's final prayer "and God be with all three." The Scotch MSS. generally agree in this particular incident, amid their divarications. Thus the Campbell MS., II. 43, which indulges in wholesale slaughter (making Musgrave a married man, brutally and unnecessarily), ends thus idiotically:—

He's ta'en out a rappier then, he's struck it in the strae, [=stroked.
And thro' and thro' his lady's sides he gar'd the cauld steel gae.

'I am not sae wae for Little *Musgrave*, as he lys cauld and dead,
But I'm right wae for his lady, for she'll gae witless wud. [*id est*, mad.

'I'm not sae wae for my lady, for she lies cauld and dead;
But *I am right wae for my young son*, lies sprawling in her bluid.'

First crew the black cock, and next crew the sparrow:
And what the better was Lord *Barnaby*? He was hanged on the morrow.

Robert Jamieson (a sensible editor, worth a dozen Peter Buchan mosaicists and mud-pie reconstructors) adds a final stanza, after the "A grave, a grave":—

But oh, how sorry was that good lord,
For a' his angry mood,
When he beheld his ain young son,
All weltring in his blood!

Motherwell's MS. p. 643 (from recitation of Mrs. McConechie, Kilmarnock), accounts for the three deaths by making Lord Barnard kill himself:—

He lean'd the halbert on the ground,
The point o't to his breast,
Saying, 'Here are three souls gaun to heaven,
I hope they'll a' get rest.' [*Cf.* p. 649.

A silly drivelling version recovered by Dr. Joseph Robertson at Leochel, in Aberdeenshire, Feb. 12, 1829, begins, "It s four and twenty bonny boys;" ends,

There was nae main made for that Ladie,
In bower whar she lay dead!
But a' was for her bonny young son,
Lay blobberin amang the bluid.

Instead of the calm deep anguish of the husband, so reticent, in his penance, Peter Buchan's tiresome tediousness ravels out the threads (192 lines!!) thus:—

'Ye'll darken my windows up secure, wi' stanchions round about,
And there is not a living man shall e'er see me walk out.

'Nae mair fine clothes my body deck, nor kame gang in my hair,
Nor burning coal nor candle light shine in my bower mair.

In Robert Jamieson's *Popular Ballads and Songs*, 1806, i. 170, "Lord Barnaby," begins "I have a tower in Dalisberie." Motherwell's *Minstrelsy* fragment in his Appendix, 1829, p. xx, "It fell upon a Martinmas time." (For Motherwell's MSS. pp. 120, 305, 371, 643, see *English and Scotch Popular Ballads*, 4to., July, 1885, vol. ii. p. 242, *et seq.*, viz. "Little Musgrave is to the Church gone;" Little Sir Grove = "'It's gold shall be your hire,' she says;" Lord Barnabas's Lady = "Four-and-twenty Ladies fair;" and Wee Messgrove = "Lord Barnard's awa.") Kinloch's MS. has "There were four-and-twenty gentlemen a playing at the ba'." Peter Buchan's untrustworthy MS., I. 27, and James Henry Dixon's *Scottish Traditional Versions of Ancient Ballads* (Percy Society, vol. xvii. p. 21), begin, "Four-and-twenty handsome youths."

*** The earliest printed copy, extant, the *Wit Restored* version, of 1658, being a less corrupted text than our comparative late broadsides, we give it also.

[Wit Restor'd, 1658, p. 171: *Ibid.* 1873, p. 388.]

The old Ballad of Little Musgrave and the Lady Barnard.

AS it fell one holy-day, *hay downe*, as many there be in the yeare,
When young men and maids together did goe, their Mattins and Masse to heare,

Little *Musgrave* came to the church-dore, the Preist was at private Masse,
But he had more minde of the faire women, than he had of our Lady['s] grace.

The one of them was clad in green, another was clad in pale,
And then came in my Lord *Barnard's* wife, the fairest amongst them all;

She cast an eye on little *Musgrave*, as bright as the summer sun,
And then bethought this little *Musgrave*, 'This lady's heart have I woonn.'

Quoth she 'I have loved thee, little *Musgrave*, full long and many a day.'
'So have I loved you, fair Lady, yet never word durst I say.'
'I have a bower at *Buckelsfordbery*, full daintyly it is geight, [*dight.*
If thou wilt we[n]d thither, thou little *Musgrave*, thou's lig in mine armes all night.'

Quoth he, 'I thank yee, faire lady, this kindnes thou showest to me;
But whether it be to my weal or woe, this night I will lig with thee.'

With that he heard a little tyne page, by his ladyes coach as he ran,
'All though I am my ladye's foot-page, yet I am lord *Barnard's* man.
My lord *Barnard* shall knowe of this, whether I sink or sinn;'
And ever where the bridges were broake, he laid him downe to swimme.

'A sleepe or wake! thou Lord *Barnard*, as thou art a man of life,
For little *Musgrave* is at *Bucklesfordbery*: abed with thy own wedded wife.'

'If this be true, thou little tinny Page, this thing thou tellest to mee,
Then all the land in *Bucklesfordbery* I freely will give to thee.
But if it be a ly, thou little tinny Page, this thing thou tellest to me,
On the hyest tree in *Bucklesfordbery* then hanged shall thou be.'

He called up his merry men all, 'Come, sadle me my steed!
This night must I to *Buckellsfordbery*, for I never had greater need.'

And some of them whistl'd and some of them sung, and some these words did say,
And ever when my lord *Barnard's* horn blew, 'A-way, *Musgrave*, a-way!'

'Me-thinks I hear the Thresel-cock, me-thinks I hear the Jaye,
Me-thinks I hear my Lord *Barnard*, and would I were away.'

'Lye still, lye still, thou little *Musgrave*, and huggell me from the cold;
'Tis nothing but a shephard's boy, a driving his sheep to the fold.
Is not thy hawke upon a perch? thy steed eats oats and hay;
And thou [a] fair Lady in thine armes, and would'st thou be away?'

With that my lord *Barnard* came to the dore, and lit a stone upon,
He plucked out three silver keys, and he open'd the dores each one.
He lifted up the coverlett, he lifted up the sheet,
'How now, how now, thou litell *Musgrave*, doest thou find my lady sweet?'

'I find her sweet,' quoth little *Musgrave*, 'The more 'tis to my paine;
I would gladly give three hundred pounds that I were on yonder plaine.'

'Arise, arise, thou littell *Musgrave*, and put thy cloth-es on,
It shall ne'er be said in my country I have killed a naked man.
I have two Swords in one scabberd, full dere they cost my purse;
And thou shalt have the best of them, and I will have the worse.'

The first stroke that little *Musgrave* stroke, he hurt lord *Barnard* sore;
The next stroke that Lord *Barnard* stroke, Little *Musgrave* ne're struck more.

With that bespake this faire lady, in bed whereas she lay,
'Although thou'rt dead, thou little *Musgrave*, yet I for thee will pray,
'And wish well to thy soule will I, so long as I have life:
So will I not for thee, *Barnard*, although I am thy wedded wife.

He cut her paps from off her brest, great pitty it was to see,
That some drops of this ladie's heart's blood ran trickling downe her knee. [*Cf.* pp. 627, 628.
'Woe worth you, woe worth, my merry men all! you were ne'er borne for my good:
Why did you not offer to stay my hand, when you see me wax so wood? [*i.e.* wud = mad.
'For I have slaine the bravest Sir Knight that ever rode on steed,
So have I done the fairest lady that ever did woman's deed.
'A grave, a grave,' Lord *Barnard* cry'd, 'to put these lovers in:
But lay my lady on upper hand, for she came of the better kin.'

[Roxburghe Collection, III. 146, 340; Bagford, I. 36; II. 65; Pepys, I. 364; III. 314; Wood, 401, fol. 91; Douce, I. 151 *verso*; Jersey, II. 185.]

A Lamentable Ballad of the Little Musgrove, and the Lady Barnet.

To an excellent New Tune. [See *Popular Music*, p. 170.]

AS it fell out on a [high] Holly-day, as many more be in the Year,
Little *Musgrove* would to the Church and pray, to see the fair Ladies there:
Gallants they were of good degree, for beauty exceeding fair, [" there"
Most wondrous lovely to the eye, which did to the Church repair.

Some came down in red velvet, and some came down in Pale: [*a.l.* Pall.
The next came down the Lady *Barnet*, the fairest among them all:
She cast a look on Little *Musgrove*, as bright as the Summer's Sun,
Full well then perceived Little *Musgrove*, Lady *Barnet's* Love he had won.

The Lady *Barnet* meek and mild saluted this Little *Musgrove*,
Who did repay her kind courtesie, with favour and gentle love:
"I have a Bower in merry *Barnet*, bestrewed with Cowslips sweet,
If that you please, [my] Little *Musgrove*, in Love me there to meet.

"Within mine arms one night to sleep, for you my love have won; [*a.l* to lie.
You need not fear my suspitious Lord, for he from home is gone."
"Betide me life, betide me death, this night I will lye with thee;
And for thy sake I'll hazard my breath, so dear is my love to thee."

"What shall we do with our little Foot-page, our counsel for to keep,
And watch for fear Lord *Barnet* come, while we together sleep?" *a.l.* meet.
"Red Gold shall be his hire," quoth he, and silver shall be his fee;
So he our counsel safely keep, that I may sleep with thee." [If . . he but keep.

"I will have none of your gold," he said, "nor none of your silver fee:
If I should keep your counsel, Sir, 'twere great disloyalty. [*a.l.* Madam.
I will not be false unto my Lord, for house, nor yet for Land,
But if my Lady prove untrue, Lord *Barnet* shall understand."

Then swiftly ran this little Foot-page unto his Lord with speed,
Who then was feasting with his own friends, not dreaming of this ill deed:
Most speedily the Page did hast[e], most swiftly he did run,
And when he came to the broken bridge, he bent his breast and swam.

The Page did make no stay at all, but went to [his] Lord with speed, [" to the."
That he the truth may say to him, concerning this wicked deed: [might tell.
He found his Lord at Supper then, great merriment they did make,
"My Lord," quoth he, "this night upon my word, *Musgrove* with your Lady doth sleep."

"If this be true, my little Foot-page, and true that thou tellest to me,
My eldest Daughter I'le give thee, and wedded thou shalt be:
If this be a lye, my little Foot-page, and a lye thou tellest to me,
A new pair of Gallows shall be set up, and hanged thou shalt be."

"If this be a lye, my Lord," (he said), "and a lye that thou hearest of me,
Never stay a pair of gallows to make, but hang me on the next tree.
Lord *Barnet* call'd his merry men all, away with speed he would go,
His heart was so perplex'd with grief, the truth of this he must know. [*a.l.* sore.

"Saddle your horses with speed," he said, "and saddle me my white Steed;
If this be true, as the Page hath said, *Musgrove* shall repent this deed."
He charged his men to make no noise, as they rode along the way,
"Wind no horn" (quoth he) "on your Life, lest our coming it should betray."

But one of them that *Musgrove* did love, and respected his friendship most dear,
To give him notice Lord *Barnet* was come, did wind the Bugle most clear;
And evermore as he did sound, "Away, *Musgrove*, and away!
For if he take thee with my Lady, then slain thou shalt be this day."

"O hark! fair Lady, your Lord is near, I hear his little horn blow,
And if he find me in your arms thus, then slain I shall be, I know.
"O lye still, lye still, little *Musgrove*, and keep my back from the cold,
I know it is my father's Shepherd, driving sheep unto the Pinfold.

Musgrove did turn him round about, sweet slumber his eyes did greet,
When he did awake, he then did espy Lord *Barnet* at the bed's-feet.
"Rise up, rise up, little *Musgrove*, and put thy clothing on; ["O rise."
It never shall be said in *England* fair, that I slew a naked man.

"Here are two good swords," Lord *Barnet* said, "the choice *Musgrove* shall make,
The best of them thy self shall have, and I the worst will take;
The first blow [that] *Musgrove* did strike, he wounded Lord *Barnet* sore;
The second blow Lord *Barnet* gave, *Musgrove* could strike no more.

He took his Lady by the white hand, all love to rage convert,
And with his sword, in most furious wise, he pierc'd her tender heart;
"A grave, a grave!" Lord *Barnet* cry'd, "prepare to lay us in.
My Lady shall lye on the upper side, because she is the better kin." ["Skin."
Then suddenly he slew himself, which griev'd his friends full sore,
The death of these [three] worthy wights with tears they did deplore. [*a.l.* lovely w.
This sad mischief by lust was wrought, then let us call for Grace,
That we may shun this wicked vice, and fly from sin apace. [*a.l.* such w. deeds.

London, Printed for *F. Coles*, *T. Vere*, *J. Wright*, and *J. Clarke*.

[Black-letter. Two woodcuts, on p. 137, one here. The modern edition (Roxb. C., III. 340), was "printed and sold in *Aldermary* Church-yard, Bow Lane, *London*," with the stanzas sub-divided like (Bagford's) W. Onlen's, beginning "As it fell out on a *high* holiday." Wood's exemplar = 1st Roxb.]

[Roxburghe Collection, II. 499; Euing, 381; Jersey, II. 48; Douce, II. 245 *vo.*, 254 *vo.*]

The West-Country Damosel's Complaint.

Or,

The Faithful Lovers' last Farewel. Being the Relation of a Young Maid who pined herself to death, for the Love of a Young-man, who, after he had notice of it, dyed likewise for grief.

Careless young-men, by this a warning take,
How you kind Virgins (when they Love) forsake:
Least the same fate o're-take you, and you dye
For breach of Vows, and Infidelity.
Be kind, but swear not more than what you mean,
Least Comick Jests become a Trajeck Seean.

To the Tune of, *Johnny Armstrong.* [See p. 604, and *Note.*]

"WHen will you marry me, *William*,
And make me your wedded wife?
Or take you your keen bright Sword,
And rid me out of my life."

Will. "Say no more so then, Lady,
Say you no more then so;
For you shall into the wild forrest,
And amongst the buck and doe. 8

"Where thou shalt eat of the hips and haws,
And the roots that are so sweet,
And thou shalt drink of the cold water,
That runs underneath [thy] feet."

Now she had not been in the wild forrest
Passing three months and a day,
But with hunger and cold she had her fill,
Till she was quite worn away. 16

At last she saw a fair tyl'd house,
And there she swore by the Rood,
That she would to that fair tyl'd house,
There for to get her some food.

Note.—Although no early exemplar of this ballad is known, it is probable that it had first appeared long before *Philip Brooksby's* reprint. The subject and the treatment show it to be antique, of similar date with *Constance of Cleveland*, certified by Stationers' Registers as June 11th (not 13th, on our p. 575), 1603.

But when she came unto the gates,
Aloud, aloud she cry'd,
"An alms, an alms, my own Sister,
I ask you for no pride."

Her Sister call'd up her merry men all,
By one, by two, and by three,
And bid them hunt away that wild Doe,
As far as e're they could see.

They hunted her o're hill and dale,
And they hunted her so sore,
That they hunted her into the forrest,
Where her sorrows grew more and more.

She laid a stone all at her head,
And another all at her feet,
And down she lay between these two,
Till Death had lull'd her asleep.

When sweet *Will* came and stood at her head,
And likewise stood at her feet,
A thousand times he kist her cold lips,
Her body being fast asleep.

Yea, seaven times he stood at her feet,
And seaven times at her head,
A thousand times he shook her hand,
Although her body was dead.

"Ah, wretched me!" he loudly cry'd,
"What is it that I have done?
O wou'd to the powers above I'de dy'd,
When thus I left her alone.

"Come, come, you gentle red-breast now,
And prepare for us a tomb,
Whilst unto cruel Death I bow,
And sing like a swan my doom.

"Why! could I ever cruel be
Unto so fair a creature?
Alas, she dy'd for love of me,
The loveliest she in nature!

"For me she left her home so fair,
To wander in this wild grove;
And there with sighs and pensive care,
She ended her life for Love.

"O, Constancy! in her thou'rt lost,
Now let women boast no more;
She's fled to the *Elizium* coast,
And with her carry'd the store.

"O break my heart, with sorrow fill'd,
  Come, swell, you strong tides of grief,
You that my dear love have kill'd,
  Come yield in death to me relief.

"Cruel her sister, was 't for me
  That to her she was unkind?
Her husband I will never be,
  But with this my love be joyn'd.

"Grim Death shall tie the marriage bands
  Which jealousie shan't divide,
Together shall tye our cold hands,
  Whilst here we lye side by side.

"Witness, ye groves, and chrystial streams,
  How faithless I late have been,
But do repent with dying leaves,
  Of that my ungrateful sin.

"And wish a thousand times that I
  Had been but to her more kind,
And not have let a virgin dye,
  Whose equal there's none can find.

"Now heaps of sorrow press my soul,
  Now, now 'tis she takes her way,
I come, my love, without controule,
  Nor from thee will longer stay."

With that he fetch'd a heavy groan,
  Which rent his tender breast,
And then by her he laid him down,
  When as Death did give him rest.

Whilst mournful birds, with leavy boughs
  To them a kind burial gave,
And warbled out their love-sick vows
  Whilst they both slept in their grave.

Finis.

Printed for *P. Brooksby*, at the *Golden-Ball* in *West-Smithfield*, neer the *Hospital-gate*.

[Black-letter. Three woodcuts: 1st and 2nd, the lady and young man of p. 666; 3rd, Cupid shooting at a girl under a tree, given on p. 189. Date, *circâ* 1673.]

*** Another *William* appears in the following lively ballad, also of the West-country. It is a happier and more prosaic love-tale than the present lugubrious ditty, which is nevertheless not without its own charm and pathos. "It dallies with the innocence of Love, like the Old Age." Sir William of the West belongs conclusively to the last reigns of the Stuarts, *circâ* 1685.

[Roxburghe Collection, II. 518; Pepys, III. 283; Jersey, I. 335.]

Sir William of the West;

Or,

The Entire Love and Courtship between a Noble Knight and Beautiful Mary; a Minister's Daughter in Dorsetshire.

TUNE OF, *The Ring of Gold.* [See p. 639.] Licensed according to Order.

YOung *William* met his love, taking her pleasure,
Whom he did prize above all wordly treasure;
When she appear'd in sight, said he, "Sweet jewel,
Thou art my heart's delight, O! be not cruel.

"Let me one smile injoy, thy heart surrender;
Love, be no longer coy to thy Pretender;
My fading joys restore, why should'st thou grieve me?
Thy charms I do adore, dearest, believe me!

"*Mary*, my only joy, pity thy Lover!
Do not my life destroy, while I discover,
How I am here inflam'd by thy fair beauty:
Sure I cannot be blam'd to own my duty.

"I am commanded so by *Cupid's* power;
Darts from whose fatal bow soon will devour
My life, if I deny to fall before thee,
Therefore, Love, live or dye, I will adore thee.

"Five hundred pounds a year I am possessing,
And if thou wilt, my dear, grant me the blessing,
Thou shalt be Dame of all, I can't deny thee;
If now in love I shall, dearest, lye by thee.

"Here take both heart and hand, I dearly love thee,
No Lady in the land shall shine above thee;
The same shall ever hold, no friend shall check thee,
In robes of shining gold and pearl I'll deck thee.

"Love, had I now this day the gold of *Crœsus*,
I'd not be drawn away; kind Heaven bless us:
Still will I dote on thee, this is no story,
Thou should'st a partner be of all my glory."

The Damsel then reply'd, "If you are loyal,
I yield to be your Bride without denyal:
Gain but my friends' good will, father and mother,
Whom I have honour'd still, above all other.

"When you have their consent that we should marry,
Then I am well content, long we'll not tarry;
At their discretion I still will be guided,
Who from my infancy for me provided."

"I hope," said he, "my Love, they'll not deny me,
If my sweet tender Dove will but stand by me."
With that he streight did go, in hopes to have her;
They never answer'd no, but freely gave her.

She was a fair young dame, a Parson's daughter;
He from a Baron came, of whom hereafter
A large account I'll give when I have leisure,
How they in triumph live, joy, peace, and pleasure.

Printed for *P. Brooksby, J. Deacon, J. Blare*, and *J. Back*.

[In Black-letter. Three woodcuts, 1st.—The Lady with mask and small ridiculous dog, of vol. iv. p. 409, left; 2nd.—The Young Man of our p. 510; and 3rd.—The zig-zag and tears ornament, given below. The tune of *The Ring of Gold* is not identified, but it is cited in ballads, beginning respectively thus:

1.—"A wealthy Yeoman's Son;" title, "The *Kentish* Yeoman and *Susan* of *Ashford*."
2.—"All joy I bid adieu;" = Answer to The Lady's Tragedy.
3.—"My youthful charming fair;" = Answer to the Covetous-minded Parents.
4.—"Ranging the silent shades;" = Bleeding Lover's Lamentation.
5.—"Stout Seamen, come away!" = The Boatswain's Call.
6.—"*Susan*, my heart's delight;" = The Couragious Cornel.
7.—"*Thomas*, why come you not?" = The Bashful Bachelor.
8.—"Why is my Love unkind?" = The Lady's Tragedy.
9.—"Young *William* met his Love;" = Sir *William* of the West.

Of these, Nos. 4, 5, and 9 are reprinted among *Roxburghe Ballads*, the former two in vol. iii. pp. 456, 463; the last is here given. Others elsewhere.

*** A promise is given, in the final stanza, which was probably left unfulfilled, for we know not of any Sequel or so-styled Answer to the present Ballad. Happy is the land that has no annals, was said of old. Lucky is the marriage devoid of all tragic sequel beyond that which quiet decay and death must bring. And these have more of blessing than of suffering.

Fair Margaret's Misfortunes.

"You are no love for me, *Margaret*,
I am no love for you."
—*The Knight of the Burning Pestle*, iii. 3.

"When it was grown to dark midnight
And all were fast asleep,
In came *Margaret's* grimly ghost
And stood at *William's* feet."
—*Ibid.*, ii. 8 (*Beaumont and Fletcher*, 1610).

THAT there is a close relation existing between the two ballads (reprinted on pp. 645 to 649) devoted to the tragedy of Lord Thomas the Forester with Fair Eleanor, and the present ballad of "Fair Margaret and Sweet William" (on p. 641)—better known as "Margaret's Ghost," cannot fail to impress every thoughtful reader, and suggest the suspicion that they are all three variations of one tale. In two of them the "Brown Girl," *alias* "Brown Bride," whose wealth is her chief or only charm, holds little prominence of character and position; but in the one beginning "Lord Thomas he was a bold Forester" she is the malignant and uncontrollable fury whose sudden outburst of (not altogether unreasonable) jealousy impels her to murder her beautiful rival. She cannot brook Eleanor's quietly contemptuous criticism, "Methinks she looks wondrous brown!" and by her savage resentment she draws down on her own head the punishment which her intended husband is not unwilling to inflict. In the other *Roxburghe* version (p. 645), "The Unfortunate Forester," the deserted Eleanor stabs herself, and is not stabbed by the Brown Girl; who, for anything asserted to the contrary, might survive them all. This guiltlessness and final safety of the Brown Girl combine to set a wide division between the two versions.

After all, the resemblances and coincidences with "Lord Thomas" in "Fair Margaret's Misfortunes" are little beyond what may be called the common stock-in-trade of a ballad-monger's art. Chief are, the friendship that had well-nigh blossomed into love, and the reckless manner in which the girl, who knows herself to have been secretly beloved, publicly avows her affection and despair.

*** The incidents of the growth and intertwining of a Rose and a Briar above the graves of lovers occur also in "Lord Lovel," and other ballads of similar date. These were "stock properties," transferable like the woodcuts.

At the close of his labours in Editing these *Roxburghe Ballads* (on pp. 666-676 of vol. iii.), our revered friend Mr. William Chappell, F.S.A., mentioned this broadside, and hoped for the discovery of an earlier issue than those which remain alone accessible. We partially follow his suggestion of adopting [but square-bracketted], as true text, the quotations from *The Knight of the Burning Pestle*, written in 1610. Against his decision *in re* David Malloch, *alias* Mallet, the Supreme Court refuses to sanction any appeal. Dismissed with costs.

[Roxburghe Collection, III. 338; Douce, III. 27.]

Fair Margaret's Misfortunes;

Or,

Sweet *William's* Dream on his Wedding Night, with the sudden Death and Burial of those noble Lovers.

[ITS OWN TUNE, *Fair Margaret and Sweet William*; *Popular Music*, p. 383.]

AS it fell out upon a day,
  Two lovers they sat on a hill; ["set," *bis*.
They sat together a long summer's day,
  And could not take their fill. [*al. lect.* talk.

"I [am] no [love for] you, *Margaret*, ["I see no harm by you."
  And you [are no love for] me; ["see none by me."
Before to-morrow at eight o'[the]clock
  A rich wedding you shall see."

Fair *Margaret* sat in her bower-window,
  A combing of her hair;
And there she espy'd sweet *William* and [his] bride,
  As they were a riding near.

Down she laid her ivory comb,
  And up she bound her hair;
She went away forth from the bower,
  But never more came there.

When day was gone, and night was come,
  And all men fast asleep,
There came the spirit of fair *Margaret*,
  And stood at *William's* bed-feet.

"God give you Joy, you true lovers,
In bride-bed fast asleep;
Lo! I am going to my green-grass grave, 'text, "Grove."
And I am in my winding-sheet."

When day was come, and night was gone,
And all men wak'd from sleep,
Sweet *William* to his Lady said,
"My-dear, I've cause to weep.

"I dream'd a dream, my dear Lady,
Such dreams are never good;
I dream'd thy bower was full of red swine,
And my bride-bed full of blood."

"Such dreams, such dreams, my honoured Sir,
They never do prove good;
To dream thy bower was full of swine,
And thy bride-bed full of blood."

He called [up] his merry men all,
By one, by two, and by three;
Saying, "I'll away to Fair *Margaret's* Bower,
By the leave of my Lady."

And when he came to Fair *Margaret's* Bower,
He knocked at the ring;
So ready were her seven Brethren
To let Sweet *William* in.

The[n] he turn'd up the covering sheet,
"Pray let me see the dead!
Methinks she looks both pale and wan,
She has lost her cherry red.

"I'll do no more for thee, *Margaret*,
Than any of thy kin,
For I will kiss thy pale wan lips,
Tho' a smile I cannot win."

With that bespoke the seven brethren,
Making most piteous moan,
"You may go kiss your jolly brown dame,
And let our sister alone."

"If I do kiss my jolly brown dame,
I do but what is right;
For I made no vow to your sister dear,
By day nor yet by night.

"Pray tell me then how much you'll deal,
Of white bread and your wine?—
So much as is dealt at her Funeral to-day,
To-morrow shall be dealt at mine."

Fair *Margaret* dy'd to-day, to-day,
  Sweet *William* he dy'd [on] the morrow ;
Fair *Margaret* dy'd for pure true-love,
  Sweet *William* he dy'd for sorrow.

Margaret was buried in the lower chancel,
  And *William* in the higher ;
Out of her breast there sprang a rose, [*Note*, on p. 640.
  And out of his a briar.

They grew as high as the church top,
  'Till they could grow no higher ;
And there they grew in a True Lover's Knot,
  That made all people admire.

Then came the clerk of the parish,
  As you this truth shall hear,
And by misfortune cut them down,
  Or they had now been there.

Printed and Sold in *Aldermary* Church-Yard, *Bow-Lane*, *London*.

[White-letter, with two woodcuts, one on p. 641 ; the other of a funeral.]

Two Ballads on Lord Thomas and Fair Eleanor.

"Beauty and Anguish walking hand in hand
  The downward slope to death."
—Tennyson's *A Dream of Fair Women.*

OF our two distinct versions, one, "The Unfortunate Forester," has not been previously included among Collections of Reprints. It is appointed to be sung to the tune of the well-known ballad, *Chevy Chase* (see p. 740), viz. "God prosper long our noble King, our lives and safeties all, A woful hunting once there did in *Chevy Chase* befall." Music of this ballad is given in Mr. W. Chappell's *Popular Music of the Olden Time*, p. 199. In the same priceless collection, p. 145, is given the tune of *Lord Thomas*, which is shown to be an adaptation of *Who list to lead a soldier's life?* to which tune was sung "The Lord of Hosts hath blest our Land." Ritson mentioned in 1790 a minstrel who "was within these two years to be seen in the streets of London ; [where] he played on an instrument of the rudest construction, which he, properly enough, called a *hum strum*, and chanted (among others) the old ballad of *Lord Thomas and Fair Elinor*, which, by the way, has every appearance of having been a minstrel song."—*Ancient Songs.* (We give on our next page a woodcut, illustrating this rude musical instrument.)

All the extant copies of this antique ballad are indisputably corrupt; and we cannot expect to benefit largely by turning to the so-called traditional versions, which are usually still less trustworthy. (Compare Note on p. 649.) Among the curious variations one most interesting is the long-winded "Lord Thomas and fair Annie," which shows the interweaving (early or late) with "Fair Margaret and Sweet William," the ghost appearing to the bridegroom on his wedding-night, summoning him from his Brown Bride.

"Lord *Thomas* and fair *Annet* sat a' day on a hill,
When night was cum and the sun was set,
They had not talkd their Fill."—(41 stanzas.)

Dr. Percy printed this in his *Reliques* (iii. 240, 1767, second edition), with some corrections, from a MS. copy transmitted from Scotland; probably sent by G. Paton. In *Scottish Traditional Ballads* (Percy Society, xvii. 94, 1845), is a version of "Lord Thomas" beginning, "I'm here at thy Gate," from *The Cigar* of 1825; of no importance.

Our p. 647 Roxburghe version of "Lord Thomas" is nearly identical with that of J. Roberts's *Collection of Old Ballads*, 1723, i. 249; *Coll. Diverting Songs*, 1738, p. 453; Percy's *Reliques*, 1767, iii. 78 (there said to be from the Pepysian black-letter broadside); Joseph Ritson's *English Songs*, ii. 185, 1783, and his *Ancient Songs* of 1790, p. 89. Allied to this, in Robert Jamieson's *Popular Ballads*, i. 22, 1806 (from Mrs. W. Arnot of Aberbrothick's recitation), is a version beginning "Sweet *Willie* and fair *Annie* sat a' day on a hill."

The moralization at close of "The Unfortunate Forester" would of itself suggest it to be the later version. Objectivity belongs to a healthy youth-time of poetry; subjectivity is generally a sign of mental decrepitude and poetical disease or decadence. Sometimes a song stops flowering, runs to seed, and be-pods into a sermon.

[*"Singing Sam" of Derbyshire's "Hum-Strum,"* 1760. See p. 643.]

[Roxburghe Collection, II. 553; Pepys, IV. 48; Jersey, I. 362.]

The Unfortunate Forrester;

Or, Fair Elener's Tragedy.

Shewing how Lord Thomas, once a bold Forrester, fell in love with the fair Lady Elener, but his Mother would not suffer him to marry her, but told him of another that was far Richer: then the Lord Thomas, not willing to be undutiful to his Mother, appoints his Wedding-Day, and invites fair Elener to come to his Wedding: who contrary to her Mother's knowledge came, and having seen his Bride she stabb'd herself, which Lord Thomas seeing, took the same Dagger, and kill'd himself.

Tune is, *Chevy Chase* [pp. 643, 740]. With Allowance.

AMongst the Forresters of old, one *Thomas* of great fame;
A Champion great, both stout and bold, Lord *Thomas* was his name.
In shooting too his name was good, the King's deer he did slay,
He did excel bold *Robin Hood*, and often won the day.

Lord *Thomas*, as they did him call, with beauteous *Elener*,
So deep in love did chance to fall, he could love none but her.
She also loved him as well, and no love there was lost;
But mark what afterwards befell, both in their loves were crost.

This *Elener* that was so fair, no portion had at all;
Lord *Thomas* if he come but near, would always on her call.
Lord *Thomas* had a mother who his love did understand,
She made him swear he would nothing do unless she did command.

He promis'd her he would obey, and hearken to her voyce;
Therefore desir'd her to say, where he should make his choice. [for.
"Oh! Son," quoth she, "this *Elener* is fair enough, 'tis true;
And thou may'st chance to beg with her! Such matches fit not you.

"I know a pritty black-brow'd Lass, though not so handsome quite;
She her in wealth doth far surpass, which will give thee delight."
"Well, Mother, since it is your will," Lord *Thomas* humbly said,
"I straight way will the same fulfill, & marry the Black-brow'd Maid."

This thing did much his mother please, and so she went away;
But Lord *Thomas* he could find no ease, by night, nor yet by day.
He on the morrow mounts his steed, and to *Elener* did ride,
His love-sick heart with grief did bleed, to think what would betide.

When to fair *Elener* he was come, he knockt hard at the gate;
The fearful Virgin being at home, ask'd who 'twas knock'd so late?
"'Tis I, fair *Elener*, my dear!" his voice she streight-way knew:
And as soon as e're she heard him there, the gates streight open flew.

Lord *Thomas* uttered then his mind, and with great grief he cry'd,
"My mother to me is unkind, and hath gotten me a new Bride.
"You to my Wedding I invite, and I must not be deny'd;"
They crying kist, then bid good night, and Lord *Thomas* away did ride.

Fair *Elener* with grief and woe was stricken almost dead,
She to her mother streight did go, and told her what he said.
She ask'd her mother leave to ride, to see if he had got,
Instead of her, another bride, for she believ'd him not.

Her mother would not give her leave, that she should go to see,
But she her mother did deceive, and slipt out privately.
She cloath'd her servants all in green, and with her they all did ride,
She did excel Beautie's fair Queen in all her glorious pride.

When to Lord *Thomas* she was come, she ask'd to see his Bride;
He took her into a private room, where they together cry'd.
He bid her look at that window, for there she might be seen:
"Methinks," quoth she, "good Sir, you know, I am to her a Queen."

Herself to murder she was bent, and turning to a bed,
A dagger to her heart she sent, and streight-way fell down dead.
Lord *Thomas*, seeing she was slain, the self-same dagger took;
He vow'd in Heaven her to obtain, then to his heart he strook.

Let Parents therefore have a care, how that they do deny
Their children's choice, lest that they share those Lovers' destiny.

London, Printed for *W. Thackeray*, *T. Passenger*, and *W. Whitwood*.

[In Black-letter. Three woodcuts: woman and man (without the *Cantabridgian* centre-piece) on p. 258, and ornament with vase. Date, *circâ* 1676.]

[Roxburghe Collection, III. 554; Bagford, II. 127; Pepys, III. 316; Douce, I. 120 *vo.*; III. 58 *vo.*; IV. 36; Ouvry, II. 38; Jersey, III. 88.]

A Tragical Ballad on the Unfortunate Love of Lord Thomas and Fair Eleanor: Together with the downfal of the Brown Girl.

To a pleasant tune, call'd, *Lord Thomas, etc.* [See p. 643.]

LORD *Thomas* he was a bold Forester,
And a Chaser of the King's Deer;
Fair *Eleanor* was a fine Woman,
And Lord *Thomas* he lov'd her dear.

"*Come, riddle my Riddle, dear Mother,*" he said.
And riddle us both as one,
Whether I shall marry with fair Eleanor,
And let the Brown Girl *alone?*"

"*The* Brown Girl *she has got Houses and lands,*
And fair Eleanor *she has got none;*
Therefore I charge you on my Blessing,
Bring me the Brown Girl *Home.*"

And as it befell on a high Holiday, Cf. p. [illegible]
As many did more beside,
Lord *Thomas* he went to fair *Eleanor*,
That should have been his Bride.

But when he came to fair *Eleanor's* Bower
He knocked there at the Ring;
But who was so ready as fair *Eleanor*,
For to let Lord *Thomas* in?

"What news, what news, Lord *Thomas?*" she said,
"What news hast thou brought to me?"
"I am come to bid thee to my Wedding,
And that is bad news for thee."

"O God forbid! Lord *Thomas,*" she said,
"That such a thing should be done:
I thought to have been thy Bride my own self,
And you to have been the Bridegroom."

"Come, riddle my Riddle, dear Mother!" she said,
"And riddle it all in one,
Whether I shall go to Lord *Thomas'* Wedding,
Or whether I shall tarry at Home?"

"There's many that are your Friends, Daughter,
  And many that are your Foe.
Therefore I charge you, on my Blessing,
  To Lord *Thomas'* Wedding don't go!"

"There's many that are my Friends, Mother,
  If a thousand more were my Foe:
Betide my life, betide my death,
  To Lord *Thomas'* Wedding I'll go."

She cloathed herself in gallant attire,
  And her merry Men all in Green;
And as they rid thorough every Town,
  They took her to have been a Queen.

But when she came to Lord *Thomas's* Gate,
  She knocked there at the Ring;
But who was so ready as Lord *Thomas*
  To let fair *Eleanor* in?

"Is this your Bride?" fair *Eleanor* said, [" she said."
  "Methinks she looks wonderous brown:
Thou might'st have had as fair a Woman,
  As ever trod on the ground."

"Despise her not, fair *Eleanor*," he said, [*al. l.* '*Ellin.*'
  "Despise her not unto me:
For better I love thy little finger,
  Than all her whole Body."

This brown Bride had a little Pen-knife,
  That was both long and sharp;
And betwixt the short ribs and the long,
  Prick'd fair *Eleanor* to the Heart.

"Oh! Christ now save thee!" Lord *Thomas* he said,
  "Methinks thou looks wonderous wan:
Thou us'd for to look with as fresh a Colour
  As ever the Sun shined on."

"Ah! art thou blind? Lord *Thomas*!" she said,
  "Or can'st thou not very well see?
Oh! dost thou not see my own Heart's Blood
  Run trickling down my knee?"

Lord *Thomas* he had a sword by his side,
  As he walked about the Hall;
He cut off his Bride's head from her shoulders,
  And he threw it against the wall.

He set the hilt against the Ground,
  And the point against his Heart.
There was never three Lovers that ever met,
  Did e'er so soon depart. 76

Licensed according to Order.

Finis.

Newcastle-upon-Tyne: Printed and sold by *Thomas Saint.*

[In white-letter, duplicate of Douce, III. 58. The Douce I. 120 *verso* is dated 1677, Printed for *F. Coles*; but Douce IV. 36 is modern, *J. Pitts*, of *Seven Dials*. Two woodcuts, Bagford, for *W. Onley*, and the booksellers. The earliest reprint was printed for *Thomas Lambert* (*circa* 1636-41), but not accessible, and perhaps a mistake for *Thomas Saint*. The Pepys exemplar (III. 316) has "This may be Printed, *Ro. L'Estrange*. Printed for *J. C.*, *W. T.*, and *T. P.*;" *i.e. J. Clarke*, *Thackeray* and *Passinger*, before 1685, with five woodcuts. Our Roxburghe cuts are the Youth of p. 33, left, and the Lady of iii. 402 right]

*** In Graham R. Tomson's (*Canterbury Poets*) edition of *Border Ballads*, 1888, there is given on p. 41, as though it were a rich discovery, a garbled copy of our present broadside, but reported as "from a MS.," telling that "this poem was, with the tune to which it is sung, learnt by my grandmother from an old woman named Becky Duck, who was my great-grandmother's nurse." It is simply a slightly disguised copy of our broadside version, stupidly entitled "Lord Thomas*ine* and Fair Ellin*n*or." We suppose the peculiar feminine spelling was adopted as a cheap trick to give it an antique *ærugo*. Where it differs from the *Roxburghe Ballads*, vi. 647 649, it differs for the worse. Thus two additional Stanzas are given following our final line, "There was never three Lovers that ever met, Did e'er so soon depart,"—which is rendered, nonsensically, "And never three lovers so soon did meet, Nor sooner did they part." (Onley's print reads, "More sooner they did depart.") The heart-stricken dead man is made to deliver an exordium, including the Brown girl in his posthumous arrangements:—

"'A grave, a grave let there be made,
  And let it be wide and deep;
And fair *Ellinnor* shall rest by my side,
  And the brown girl at my feet.'

"A grave, a grave there then was made,
  And it was both wide and deep;
And fair *Ellinnor* was laid by his side,
  And the brown girl at his feet."

This is merely an unwarrantably-borrowed and inappropriate '*conveyance*' from the end of "Little Musgrave." (Compare our pp. 632, 634, 640, and 641.) We admit that the old ballad minstrels had a certain stock-in-trade of phrases and stanzas, such as the coming to a yett and tirling at the pin (or knocking at the Ring, if Southron); the description of a foot-page hastening by road, and breasting the water when he swam; the rose and briar intertwining; the stroking a sword-blade on the straw, to cleanse it of blood, or, like stropping a razor, to give it an edge. We need not accept fresh transmutation of stock.

The Lady Isabella's Tragedy.

Isbrand.—"A fragment, quite unfinished,
Of a new ballad, called 'The Median Supper.'
It is about *Astyages*: and I
Differ in somewhat from *Herodotus*:—

'*Harpagus*, hast thou salt enough? hast thou broth enough to thy kid?
And hath the Cook put right good stuff under the pasty lid?'
'I've salt enough, *Astyages*, and broth enough, in sooth;
And the Cook hath mixed the meat and grease most tickling to my tooth.'"

—*Death's Jest Book*, iv. 4.

OF impious and inhuman banquets the seekers after sensation could generally find exemplary narratives at all periods of the world's history. In classic story we have Thyestes and the ill-starred Itys, slain by revengeful Progne to punish Tereus for the wrong done to her and Philomela. Dante has shown to us the grim satisfaction of Ugolino when gnawing eternally the skull of his mortal foe. The horrible depravities of Sawney Bean Lean and his gang of cannibals in their cave afforded an attractive chap-book, sure to be purchased at Falkirk Tryst and when Leith carters held their annual 'ploy,' even as the lowest rabble of Seven-Dials and Whitechapel to this hour revel in the still more disgusting serial issues of 'Sweenie Todd, the Demon Barber,' and his neighbour Cook who baked the savoury meat-pies. There were people to revel in such literature, ever since nursery romances diverted childhood with Blunderbores and other bone-pickers, whom Jack the Giant-killer slew. If you incline to listen to such legends as may "make your flesh creep," nobody need object now to "The Lady Isabella's Tragedy." It had a long term of favour, and the requital of the meritorious Scullion-boy was popularly appreciated, also the execution of the cruel Cook, who was boiled in lead (like Lord Soulis, of later ballad-date): this became pictorially a Decapitation grant.

The tune (sometimes marked *Agincourt*) is entitled *The Lady's Fall* (p. 765, delayed), ballad begins, "Mark well my heavy doleful tale, you loyal Lovers all; and heedfully bear in your breasts a gallant Lady's Fall." Before it was thus named the tune was known as *In pescod time*: *Popular Music*, p. 196:—

In Peas-cod time when hound to horn gives ear till Buck be kill'd,
And little lads, with pipes of corn, sat keeping feasts a-field, etc.

(See, for the words, Arthur Hy. Bullen's handsome 1887 reprint of *England's Helicon*, of date 1600, "The Shepherd's Slumber," p. 222.) The tune was also known as *The Hunt is up*, and was one of those used for the ballad of *Chevy Chace*. Several other *Roxburghe Ballads* were sung to the same tune, *viz.* "The Bride's Burial;" "The Cruel Black;" "The Gentleman in Thracia;" "A Warning to Maidens," or, "Young Bateman;" "Belgick Boar;" "Bloudy News from Germany;" A Warning for Married Women:" and "John True." (*Roxb. Bds.*, vol. i. 186; ii. 49; iii. 194; ii. 262; iii. 437, 467, 200; and ii. 641). Also, another ballad (given on p. 695), "The Wandering Jew."

[Roxburghe Collection, II. 278; III. 682; Bagford, I. 35; II. 66; Euing, 182; Pepys, II. 149; Wood, E. 25, fol. 51; Jersey, II. 117; Douce, I. 111; II. 142 vo.; III. 60; Ouvry, II. 36.]

The Lady Isabella's Tragedy;
Or,
The Step-Mother's Cruelty.

Being a Relation of a most lamentable and cruel Murder, committed on the Body of the Lady Isabella, the only Daughter of a Noble Duke, occasioned by the means of a Step-Mother and [acted by] the Master-Cook, who were both adjudged to suffer a cruel death for committing the said Horrid Act.

To the Tune of, *The Ladie's Fall.* [See pp. 650, 761, 765.]

THere was a Lord of worthy fame, and a-Hunting he would ride,
Attended by a noble Train of Gentry by his side.
And whilst he did in chase remain, to see both sport and play,
His Lady went, as she did feign, unto the Church to pray.

This Lord he had a Daughter fair, whose beauty shin'd so bright:
She was belov'd both far and near of many a Lord and Knight.
Fair *Isabella* was she call'd, a Creature fair was she,
She was her father's only joy, as you shall after see.

But yet her cruel step-mother did envy her so much,
That day by day she sought her life, her Malice it was such.
She bargain'd with the Master-Cook to take her life away,
And, taking of her Daughter's book, she thus to her did say:

"Go home, sweet daughter, I thee pray, go hasten presently,
And tell unto the Master-Cook these words that I tell thee.
And bid him dress to dinner straight that fair and milk-white Doe
That in the Park doth shine so bright, there's none so fair to show."

This Lady, fearing of no harm, obey'd her Mother's will,
And presently she hasted home, her mind for to fulfill.
She streight into the Kitchin went her message for to tell;
And there the Master-Cook she spy'd, who did with malice swell.

"You Master-Cook, it must be so, do that which I thee tell,
You needs must dress the milk-white Doe, which you do know full well."
Then streight his cruel bloody hands he on the Lady laid,
Who quivering and shaking stands, whilst thus to her he said:

"Thou art the Doe that I must dress; see here, behold my knife!
For it is pointed presently to rid thee of thy life."
O then cry'd out the Scullion-boy as loud as loud might be,
"O save her life, good Master-cook, and make your pies of me:

"For pity sake, do not destroy my Lady with your knife;
You know she is her Father's joy, for Christ's sake save her life."
"I will not save her life," he said, "nor make my pies of thee;
But if thou dost this deed bewray, thy butcher I will be."

[Now] when this Lord he did come home, for to sit down and eat,
He called for his Daughter dear to come and carve his meat.
"Now sit you down," his Lady said, "O sit you down to meat,
Into some Nunnery she is gone, your Daughter dear forget."

Then solemnly he made a vow before the company,
That he would neither eat nor drink untill he did her see.
O then bespake the Scullion-boy, with a loud voice so high,
"If that you will your Daughter see, my Lord, cut up that Pye;

"Wherein her flesh is minced small and parched with the fire:
All caused by her Step-mother, who did her death desire:
And cursed be the Master-cook, O cursed may he be!
I proffer'd him my own heart's blood, from death to set her free."

Then all in black this Lord did mourn, and for his Daughter's sake,
He judged for her Step-Mother to be burnt at a stake.
Likewise he judg'd the Master-cook in boyling lead to stand;
And made the simple Scullion-boy the Heir to all his Land.

[London:] Printed for *P. Brooksby* at the *Golden Ball* in *Pye-corner*.

[In Black-letter. Inappropriate woodcut, a Decapitation. We follow Bagford's first copy (2nd is in White-letter), printed for *W. O.*, with same cut. Date, *c.* 1672.]

[Roxburghe Collection, III. 682; John White's Newcastle Reprint.]

Their Lamentation.

[*Cf.* p. 683.

NOw when the wicked Master-Cook beheld his Death draw near,
And that by friends he was forsook, he pour'd forth many a Tear,
Saying, "The Lady whom I serv'd prompt me to do this Deed,
And as a Death I have deserv'd, 'tis coming on with speed.

"I must confess these hands of mine destroy'd the Innocent,
When her dear breath she did resign, my heart did not relent."
This said, into the boiling Oil he presently was cast;
And then, within a little while, the Lady went at last

From Prison to the burning Stake, and as she pass'd along,
She did sad Lamentation make unto the numerous Throng:
These were the very words she spoke, "The Daughter of my Lord
I doom'd to death, the Laws I broke, and shall have my Reward."

Then to the burning Stake they ty'd the worst of all Step-Dames,
Where by the Laws she fairly dy'd, in smoak and burning flames.
Now let their Deaths a Warning be to all that hear this Song:
And thus I end this Tragedy, the Duke he mourned long.

Finis.

[*Newcastle-upon-Tyne*: Printed and sold by *John White*.]

The Spanish Lady's Love.

Phraxanor.—"Thou art not form'd to love, but ever to be loved."
Joseph (Aside).—"This fascinating danger walls me round,
Leaving no door that's open to escape.
She's gone too far for one who ne'er recedes,
And her blind passion, as a torch illum'd,
Will ne'er recoil before explosion.
A single hope remains invisible,
A silken thread to carry all this weight.
Could I allume a virtuous fire in time,
We were all saved."
—*Joseph and his Brethren*, by Charles Wells, Act ii. sc. 3.

SEEING that we know the date of this ballad issue to have been early in June, 1603 (it having been entered to William White along with eight others, including "The Ladye's Fall," "The Bryde's Buryall," and "Ye fayre Lady *Constance* of *Cleveland* and of her Disloyall Knight," on '11th Junij, 1603:'), we are freed from many vague conjectures, indulged in heretofore. We safely regard the descent of the English seamen-warriors on Cadiz to have taken place a few years earlier, *viz.* in 1596. If we feel inclined to examine the conflicting claims of various families to be the lineal descendants of this gallant Englishman, and (every one of them) the indisputable possessors of the identical necklace of brilliants which the generous 'Spanish Lady' bestowed, both in the ballad and its woodcut, even as Rebecca gave her noble gift to Rowena, why it is free for us to choose or to reject whomsoever we may.

Of course, it was virtuous in the extreme for the Englishman to remain "always true to Poll," and we laudably extol the continence of Scipio as we do that of patriarchal Joseph, or any other exemplary character. But, as Robert Nichol sang, "Wisdom's aye sae cauld! I wad rather ha'e the ither ane than *this* Bessie Lee!" We hanker after that impassioned Spanish Lady, and we might have yielded to her virtuous attraction. "One is not loved every day," in that self-sacrificing fashion. She deserved a happier fate than abandonment to the nunnery or the Inquisition. It would be too much to hope that the Englishman went back again to Spain, after his English wife died (she *did* die, we suppose, some time or other—they certainly buried her—or else she must now be a mature ter-centenarian). People get double chances occasionally, though Sir John did not. It is almost certain that Potiphar's wife (with due propriety, and after a discreet interval) became the lawful wife of Joseph in Egypt and the mother of Ephraim and Manasses. Nothing stands against the theory, except the Masoretic points; but they count for nothing with modern interpreters and commentators, or with catechetical Zulus and Coxian laudators of the Hymnologist who erased the Lord's Prayer, and substituted the Multiplication Table for the Ten Commandments at Natal.

Our ballad continued to be popular, and was transferred with many others, on 14 Dec., 1624, to John Wright, Cuthbert and Edward, with Pavier, Grismond, and Henry Gosson. On it a correspondence took place in 1846, in the *Times* (April 30, May 1). *The Edinburgh Review* devoted a paper (No. 168, vol. lxxxiii., April, 1846), also *The Quarterly Review* (No. 156, vol. lxxviii., Sept. 1846), to reviewing Lady Dalmeny's pictorial illustrations of "The Spanish Lady's Love."

The conflicting claimants number among them Sir John Bolle of Thorpe Hall, Lincolnshire, Sir Richard Levison of Trentham, Staffordshire, Sir John Popham of Littlecot, Wilts, Sir Urias Legh of Adlington, Cheshire, and, for anything known to the contrary, the Tichborne *vel* Orton himself. "On Sir John Bolle's departure from Cadiz the Spanish Lady sent as presents to his wife a profusion of jewels and other valuables, among which was her portrait drawn in green ['green is forsaken']: plate, money, and other treasures." There is also a portrait of Sir John Bolle, taken in 1596, *ætatis* 36, "with a gold chain round his neck," as Celia tells Rosalind: of course, the very identical chain given to him by his Spanish lady-love. Is, not this convincing? But so many chains and jewels were brought away, so many hearts broken or made tender by our irresistible Lady-killers, that some people remain incredulous.

The portrait of Sir John Bolle was engraved by Basire. In 1846 it was at Ravensfield Park, Yorkshire, Mr. Bopville being owner. It had been painted by Zuccaro, and "represents a true soldier, with a quiet determined look. His hair is scanty and closely cut, his brow both broad and lofty, the face long, glance mild and thoughtful, nose aquiline, beard thick and square; he is dressed in a tight surtout, embroidered at the cuff and collar: and he grasps his toledo as a man who knows the use thereof" (*Quarterly Review*, lxxviii. 340). Born in 1560, he had married Elizabeth Waters, about 1595, before the Cadiz expedition, his son and heir Charles Bolle coming of age in 1616, the year of Shakespeare's death. (*Vide* Archdeacon Cayley Illingworth's *Topographical Account of the Parish of Scampton*, 1808, 4to.) He seems to have never returned to Cadiz (Elizabeth had knighted him for his exploits there under Essex, who made him Governor of Kinsale), since he died so early as 1606, and was buried in Haugh Church; with three sons and four daughters, lawful issue, grouped in funereal effigies on the tomb, behind his kneeling self, and his wife. It is interesting to know that the portrait of "the Green Lady" (as the Spanish Virgin was called, from her then-fashionable but suggestive costume) was preserved at Thorpe Hall until 1760; "where to this day there is a traditionary superstition among the vulgar [why vulgar?], that Thorpe Hall was haunted by the green lady, who used nightly to take her seat in a particular tree ['all among the leaves so green, O!'] near the mansion; and that during the life of his son, Sir Charles Bolle, a knife and fork [not a spoon?] were always laid for her, if she chose to make her appearance." Thackeray, who made a Titmarshian attack on the post-nuptial character of Ivanhoe's Saxon wife, in his *Rebecca and Rowena*, would have chuckled over the probable discomfort of Lady Elizabeth Bolle, *née* Waters, under this visitation and ceremonial. But we, who are accustomed to entertain any number of Cavalier ghosts and fair ghostesses, and who devoutly believe in a certain "African Princess" with a few other articles of faith, not admissible into Horatio's philosophy, can fully sympathise with Sir John's remembrances—although he returned home to his *première amour*: leaving the girl behind him.

[Roxb. Coll., II. 406; Bagford, I. 48; II. 36; Jersey, III. 86; Ewing, 340; Pepys, III. 148; Wood, E. 25, fol. 11; Douce, II. 210, 211 *vo.*; III. 84 *vo.*]

The Spanish Ladie's Love.

To a pleasant new Tune.

WILL you hear a *Spanish* Lady, how she woo'd an *English* man?
Garments gay, as rich as may be, bedeckt with jewels, had she on:
Of a comely countenance and grace was she;
Both by birth and parentage of high degree.

As his prisoner there he kept her, in his hands her life did lye;
Cupid's bands did tye them faster, by the liking of an eye:
In his courteous company was all her joy;
To favour him in any thing she was not coy.

But at last there came commandment for to set all ladies free,
With their jewels still adorned: none to do them injury:
O then said this Lady gay, "Full woe is me!
O let me still sustain this kind Captivity!

"Gallant captain, take some pitty on a woman in distress;
Leave me not within this City, for to dye in heaviness:
Thou hast set, this present day, my body free;
But my heart in prison still remains with thee."

"How should'st thou, fair Lady, love me whom thou knowst thy country['s foe?] [text "hate."
Thy fair words make me suspect thee: serpents lye where flowers grow."
"All the harm I think on thee, most courteous Knight,
God grant upon my head the same may fully light!

"Blessed be the time and season that thou came on *Spanish* ground,
If you may our foes be termed, gentle foes we have you found:
With our City, you have won our hearts each one,
Then to your country bear away that is your own."

The Second Part, to the same Tune.

"Rest you still, most gallant Lady, rest you still, and weep no more,
Of fair flowers you have plenty, *Spain* doth yield you wonderous store.
Spaniards f[r]aught with jealousie we oft do find,
But *English-men* throughout the world are counted kind."

"Leave me not unto a *Spaniard*, thou alone enjoy'st my heart,
I am lovely, young and tender, love is likewise my desert:
Still to save thee, day and night my mind is prest;
The wife of every *English-man* is counted blest."

"It would be a shame, fair Lady, for to bear a Woman hence,
English Souldiers never carry any such without offence."
"I will quickly change my self if it be so,
And like a page will follow thee where e're thou go."

"I have neither gold nor silver to maintain thee in this case,
And to travel is great charges, as you know, in every place."
"My chains and jewels every one shall be thy own,
And eke a[n] hundred pound in gold that lies unknown."

"On the seas are many dangers, many storms do there arise,
Which will be to ladies dreadful, and force tears from wat'ry eyes."
"Well in worth I shall endure extremity:
For I could find [it] in [my] heart to lose my life for thee."

"Courteous Lady, leave this folly! here comes all that breeds the strife,
I in *England* have already a sweet woman to my wife;
I will not falsifie my vow for gold nor gain;
Nor yet for all the fairest dames that live in *Spain*."

"O how happy is that woman that enjoys so true a friend!
Many happy days God send her! and of my suit I'll make an end:
On my knees I pardon crave for my offence,
Which love and true affection did first commence:

"Commend me to that gallant Lady, bear to her this chain of gold;
With these bracelets for a token, grieving that I was so bold;
All my jewels in like sort take thou with thee,
For they are fitting for thy wife, but not for me.

"I will spend my days in prayer, love and all her laws defie;
In a Nunnery I will shrowd me, far from any company;
But e're my prayer have an end, be sure of this,
To pray for thee and for thy love, I will not miss.

"Thus farewell, most gallant Captain, farewell to my heart's content!
Count not *Spanish* Ladies wanton, tho' to thee my mind was bent:
Joy and true prosperity remain with thee."
"The like fall unto thy share, most fair Lady."

[Written, probably, by **Thomas Deloney**.]

[Black-letter, colophon cut away, apparently *Brooksby's*, but Bagford first copy was printed by and for *W. Onley*; the second, n.p.n., is in white-letter. Euing's printed for *F. Coles, T. V.*, and *W. G.*; Pepys for *Clarke*, *W. T.*, and *T. P.* One woodcut, on p. 110; second Roxb. has a poor copy of cut given on p. 27.]

*** Date of entry, to William White, in Stationers' Company Registers (= Arber's *Transcript*, iii. 237), 13 June, 1603. It was reprinted, among many of Thomas Deloney's other ballads, in *The Garland of Good-Will*, by *J. Wright*, William's son or grandson, whose shop was the sign of the Crown on Ludgate-Hill, 1678. There must have been numerous editions of the *Garland* previously issued, beside those known of 1631 and 1659. One came so late as 1709.

[Roxburghe Collection, III. 246.]

A Dialogue between an Englishman and a Spaniard.

A New Song. [Music in Egerton Leigh's *Ballads of Cheshire*, 1867, p. 17.]

A *Cheshire* man sail'd into *Spain*, there to trade for merchandise;
When he returned there again, a *Spaniard* by chance he espies.

He said, "You *English* rogue, look here! what fruits and spices fine
Our land produces twice a year: thou hast not the like in thine."

The *Cheshire* man ran to his hold, and thence fetch'd out a *Cheshire* cheese,
And said, "You *Spanish* rogue, look here! we can produce such fruits as these.

"Your fruits are ripe but twice a year, as you yourself did say;
But such as I present you here, our land produces twice a day."

"What signifies your *Cheshire* cheese, that you do boast so fine!
It don't my dainty palate please, so well as our country wine."

"Your wine makes drunken knaves and fools, likewise does [to] many ill,
And of mankind it maketh slaves; but mine doth the belly fill."

So to conclude and end my song, I would have them pay the gold,
Which they have robb'd us of so long, like knavish rogues and villains bold.

For while we here do rest at ease, the *Spaniards* take a mighty power,
To make our *Englishmen* their slaves, and use them basely every hour.

[White-letter. N.p.n. Two cuts: Turk's Head, and flagon. Date, *circâ* 1770.]

*** Since we are on the subject of English and Spanish people in friendly dispute, we give a later ditty, sometimes entitled "Cheshire Cheese." The two versions reprinted in *Ballads and Legends of Cheshire*, 1867, begin thus:—1st, "A *Cheshire* man set sail for *Spain*:" 2nd, "A *Cheshire* man went o'er to *Spain*."

[This woodcut serves to illustrate "The Spanish Lady's Love," of p. 555.]

Cupid's Revenge on King Cophetua.

"Her arms across her breast she laid; she was more fair than words can say:
Bare-footed came the beggar-maid before the King *Cophetua.*
In robe and crown the King stept down, to meet and greet her on her way;
'It is no wonder,' said the lords, 'She is more beautiful than day.'

"As shines the moon in clouded skies, she in her poor attire was seen;
One praised her ancles [! !], one her eyes, one her dark hair and lovesome mien.
So sweet a face, such angel grace, in all that land had never been:
Cophetua sware a royal oath: 'This beggar-maid shall be my Queen!'"

—*Alfred Tennyson*, 1842.

KING COPHETUA and the Beggar-maid was an early favourite, as may be plainly seen by the numerous allusions to the subject in the dramatic literature of Elizabethan and Jacobean times. Of the two versions extant the claim to priority must be given to Richard Johnson's *Crown Garland of Goulden Roses*, 1612 (for the most part a collected reprint of his scattered pieces), where it is entitled "A Song of a Beggar and a King," beginning, "I read that once in *Africa*" (see p. 659, where it is given complete), but that this was not the first of all ballads on the subject, or that there may have been a popular play founded on the Love-story, is tolerably clear. Shakespeare in his early *Love's Labour's Lost*, i. 2 (printed 1598, but probably written and acted several years before) makes the Euphuist Don Armado inquire of his page, Moth,

"Is there not a ballad, Boy, of the King and the Beggar?"

Whereto Moth answers: "The world was very guilty of such a ballad some three ages since, but, I think, now 'tis not to be found." The ballad, if lost, would have been anterior to Richard Johnson's. But in *Romeo and Juliet*, Act ii. sc. 1, Mercutio jests concerning

"Young *Adam Cupid*, he that shot so true, [misq. for '*trim*.'
When King *Cophetua* loved the beggar-maid."

Compare the second stanza of Richard Johnson's ballad, "The blinded Boy, that shootes so trim." In *Henry IV.*, Second Part, Act v. sc. 3, Falstaff, adopting Pistol's braggart style, demands,

"O base Assyrian Knight, what is thy news?
Let King *Cophetua* know the truth thereof."

Ben Jonson in *Every Man in his Humour*, 1598, Act iii. sc. 4, makes Oliver Cob say, "I have not the heart to devour you, an' I might be made as rich as King *Cophetua*." Somehow, neither painters nor poets have achieved great success with it, though Burne Jones made a winsome portraiture of the pallid maiden, daintily sweet in her slimness of figure and scantiness of sombre attire. Of Tennyson's heroine "yet the memory rankles" (says Browning in "Youth and Art"), with the irreverence of "she and her ancles!"

As to where King Cophetua originally reigned, the Johnsonian ballad rightly declares it to have been "in Africa;" a Coptic monarch, without his native bronze. There should be trace of him in Chaucer, had all his works survived, but the Italian and French story-tellers no doubt caught up the fable. Here is the *Crowne Garland* ballad, of date before 1612. It well deserves to be rescued from forgetfulness, *and contrasted with our broadside ballad.*

A Song of a King and a Beggar.

[We follow *verbatim* the Black-letter text, but run-on the lines, from '*The Crowne Garland of Golden Roses: Gathered out of England's Royall Garden.* Set forth in many pleasant *New Songs and Sonets,* with new additions never before imprinted. Divided into two Parts. By *Richard Johnson. London,* Printed for *John Wright,* and are to be sold at his Shop without *Newgate,* 1631.']

I Read that once in *Africa* a Prince that there did reigne,
Who had to name *Cophetua,* as Poets they did faine,
From Nature's lawes he did decline, for sure he was not of my minde,
He cared not for women-kinde, but did them all disdaine.
But marke what hapned on a day, as he out of his window lay,
He saw a Begger all in gray, which did increase his paine.

The blinded Boy, that shootes so trim, from heauen down did hie; [N.B.
He drew a dart and shot at him, in place where he did lye:
Which soone did pierce him to the quick, For when he felt the arrow pricke,
Which in his tender heart did sticke, he lookt as he would dye.
"What sudden chance is this?" (quoth he) That he to loue must subject be,
Which neuer thereto would agree, but still did it defie.

Then from the window he did come, and laid him on his bed,
A thousand heapes of cares did run within his troubled head:
For now he meanes to craue her loue, and now he seekes which way to proue,
How he his fancie might remoue, and not this Begger wed.
But *Cupid* had him so in snare, that this poore Begger must prepare
A salve to cure him of his care, or else he would be dead.

And as he musing thus did lye, he thought for to deuise
How he might haue her company, that so did maze his eyes.
"In thee," quoth he, "doth rest my life; for surely thou shalt be my wife,
Or else this hand, with bloody knife, the Gods should sure suffice."
Then from his bed soone he arose, and to his Palace gate he goes;
Full little then this Begger knowes, when she the King espies.

"The Gods preserue your Majestie!" the beggers all 'gaine crie;
"Vouchsafe to giue your charity, our children's food to buy!"
The King to them his purse did cast, and they to part it made great haste;
This silly woman was the last after them that did hye.
The King he cal'd her backe againe, and unto her he gaue his chaine,
And said, "With vs thou shall remaine till such time as we die.

"For surely thou shalt be my wife, and honoured like the Queene;
With thee I meane to lead my life, as shortly shall be seene;
Our wedding shall appointed be, and euery thing in it[s] degree;
Come on," quoth he, "and follow me, thou shalt goe shift thee cleane.
What is thy name? say on," quoth he. "*Penelophon,* O King!" quoth she;
With that she made a lowe courtsie, a trim one as I weene.

Thus hand in hand along they walke vnto the King's Palace;
The King with courteous comely talke this Begger doth embrace.
The Begger blushed scarlet red, and straight againe as pale as lead,
[But not a word at all she said,] she was in such a Maze. [Rec. from *al. text.*
At last she spake, with trembling voyce, and said, "O King, I doe rejoyce
That you will take me for your choyce, and my degree so base!"

And when the Wedding-day was come, the King commanded straight
The Noblemen both all and some upon the Queene to wait:
And she behau'd her selfe that day, as if she had neuer walkt that way;
She had forgot her gowne of gray, which she did weare of late.
The Prouerb old is come to passe, the Priest when he begins his Masse
Forgets that ever clarke he was: he knoweth not his estate.

Here you may reade *Cophetua*, through fancie long time fed,
Compelled by the blinded Boy the Beggar for to wed:
He that did louers' lookes disdaine, to doe the same was glad and faine,
Or else he would himselfe haue slaine, in stories as we reade.
Disdaine no whit, O Lady deare, but pitie now thy Seruant here,
Lest that it hap to thee this yeare, as to the King it did. 51

And thus they led a quiet life during their princely reigne,
And in a tombe were buried both, as writers show vs plaine.
The Lords they took it grievously, the Ladies took it heauily,
The Commons cryed pitiously, their death to them was paine.
Their fame did sound so passingly, that it did pierce the starry skye,
And thorowout all the world did flye to euery Prince's Realme.

By **Richard Johnson.**

Our Roxburghe Collection version is the one that appears in J. Roberts's *Collection of Old Ballads*, vol. i. p. 141, 1723, wherein the Editor or Compiler offers the suggestion that there may have been originally an intentional allusion to the marriage of Henry VI. of England to Margaret of Anjou: but assuredly with little plausibility. We believe that David Malloch, *alias* Mallet, had nothing to do with vol. i. (although he certainly handled vol. iii.), but it looks odd when the reader is referred "to Mr. Philips's tragedy *Humphry*, Duke of *Gloucester*," 1723, seeing that Ambrose Phillips is generally credited with writing the introductions to the *Old Ballads*.

The tune mentioned (but not in the very modern exemplar of our Roxburghe Collection, III. 278) is, *I often for my Jenny strove.* (See p. 148, where the original song is reprinted: the music is given in Pepys Coll., v. 253, of date *circâ* 1684, and in *Pills to Purge Melancholy*, iii. 261, 1719.) But '*Cophetua*,' being of far earlier date, must have had a different tune. The ballad was reprinted in Percy's *Reliques*, 1765; in R. H. Evans's *Old Ballads*, ii. 361, 1810.

The late Mortimer Collins (died 28 July, 1876) wrote "The King and the Beggar Maid, A New Reading" = "The young King stands by his palace-gate, O what a joy is the youth of a King!" With true lyric grace he ends thus:—

What the young King whispers none has heard,
Hey for the heath where the wild birds sing!
But the echo is caught of the Beggar's word:
"I love my love, and he is not a King."

We substitute two earlier appropriate cuts, for those mentioned on p. 662.

[Roxb. Coll., III. 278; Pepys, III. 42; Huth, I. 61; Douce, III. 18 *verso*.]

Cupid's Revenge;

Or,

An Account of a King, who slighted all Women, and at length was forced to marry a Beggar.

[To the Tune of, *I often for my Jenny strove*. See p. 660.]

A King once reign'd beyond the seas, as we in antient story find,
 Whom no [fair] Face could ever please, he cared not for
  Women-kind
He despis'd the fairest beauties, and the greatest fortunes too,
At length he marry'd to a Beggar! see what *Cupid's* darts can do!

The blinded Boy, that shoots so trim, did to his closet window steal,
Then drew a Dart, and shot at him, and made him soon his power feel,
He that ne'er car'd for woman-kind, but did females ever hate,
At length was smitten, wounded, swooned, for a Beggar at his gate.

But mark what happened on a day, as he look'd from Window high,
He spy'd a Beggar all in grey, with two more in her company.
She his fancy soon enflamed, and his heart was grieved sore;
"Must I have her, court her, crave her?—I that never loved before."

This noble Prince of high renown, did to his chamber straight repair,
And on his couch he laid him down, opprest with love-sick grief & care.
"Ne'er was Monarch so surprised, here I [lye] a captive slave;
But I'll to her, court her, wooe her, she must heal the wound she gave."

Then to his palace gate he goes, the beggars crav'd his charity;
A purse of gold to them he throws: with thankfulness away they fly.
But the King [he] call'd her to him, tho' she was but poor and mean:
His hand did hold her, while he told her, she should be his stately Queen.

At this she blushed scarlet red, and on this mighty King did gaze;
Then strait again as pale as lead, alas! she was in such a maze.
Hand in hand they walk'd together, and the King did kindly say,
He'd respect her. Strait they deck'd her, in most sumptuous rich array.

He did appoint the Wedding-day, and likewise them commanded strait,
That noble Lords and Ladies gay upon this gracious Queen should wait.
She appeared a splendid beauty, all the Court did her adore;
She in marriage shew'd a carriage, as if she'd been a Queen before.

Her fame thro' all the world did ring, altho' she came of parents poor;
She by her sov'reign Lord the King did bear one son and eke no more.
All the Nobles were well pleased, and the Ladies frank and free,
For her behaviour always gave her a title to her dignity.

At length the King and Queen were laid together in the silent tomb,
Their royal son the sceptre sway'd, who govern'd in his father's room.
Long in glory did he flourish, wealth and honour to increase,
Still possessing such a blessing, that he liv'd and reign'd in peace.

[No Colophon. In White-letter. Two woodcuts: 1st, a young man in a ruff, crowned; 2nd, a beggar girl standing at a palace gate. The Pepys exemplar was printed for *Philip Brooksby, J. Deacon, J. Blare,* and *J. Back.*]

Mucedorus and Amadine.

Theseus.— "I will hear that play;
For never anything can be amiss
When simpleness and duty tender it . . .
The kinder we, to give them thanks for nothing.
Our sport shall be to take what they *mistake*;
And what poor duty cannot do, noble respect
Takes it in 'might [have been],' not merit . . .
Love, therefore, and tongue-tied simplicity,
In least speaks most, to my capacity."

—*A Midsummer-Night's Dream,* Act V.

IN the year 1598 ('doubtless in existence before Shakespeare joined a theatrical company') was printed in 4to. *A most pleasant Comedy of Mucedorus, the King's Sonne of Valentia, and Amadine, the King's Daughter of Arragon, with the merry Conceits of Mouse.* Followed by many editions, it appears to have been frequently performed on the Stage, being resuscitated after the Restoration.

Moreover, it was included (with some additions) in the 1664 folio edition of Shakespeare's works, and is thus entitled to remembrance among the *Doubtful Plays* ascribed to the master-spirit. Charles Knight condemned it with severity, as "a rude, inartificial, unpoetical, and altogether effete performance." Knight, like other critics, was subject to cold fits of superfine exactingness, ready to 'die of a rose in aromatic pain,' and complain (after the manner of Hotspur's 'popinjay') against anybody bringing foul corpses 'betwixt the wind and his nobility.' With large-hearted tolerance Theseus (*see our motto*, p. 662) announces the true Catholic faith.

Henry Tyrrell, in 1851, accorded a more just estimate of *Mucedorus*, considering it to be "a pleasing and lively comedy, in which the interest never flags, or if so, but for a moment; and which frequently exhibits a warm and luxuriant vein of poetry. Throughout it there is the fresh sweet breath and glow of forest life; and the numerous adventures of the prince and princess are so far skilfully treated that we readily yield ourselves to a belief of them." With this we agree.

"*Mucedorus*" was reprinted in October, 1877, by John Payne Collier in his beautiful quarto edition, each work separate, of Shakespeare's Plays, Poems, and the Doubtful Dramas, almost his final labour; very precious to those among us who loved him and despise the base slanders of his calumniators, the self-conceited 'experts,' whose ignorance equalled their arrogance. He followed the edition of 1609, which contains the one scene esteemed by him as possibly the interpolated work by Shakespeare, perhaps for some performance before James I. He wrote, "On this account only we now reprint it; bearing in mind that, in its original state, the drama probably belongs to the beginning of the reign of Elizabeth." We suppose '*Mucedorus*' to have been written before the imperfect printed copy in 1598. Here is the specified scene, not found earlier than the 1609 edition:

[Scene IX.] *Sound Music. Enter the* KING OF VALENCIA, ANSELMO, RODERIGO, LORD BORACHIUS, *with others.*

King Valencia.—"Enough of music! it but adds to torment.
Delights to vexed spirits are as Dates
Set to a sickly man, which rather cloy than comfort.
Let me intreat you to repeat no more."
Roderigo.—"Let your strings sleep: have done there." [*Music ceases.*
King Valencia.—"Mirth to a soul disturb'd are embers turn'd,
Which sudden gleam with molestation,
But sooner lose their light for't. ["sight," 1610.
'Tis gold bestow'd upon a rioter
Which not relieves, but murders him:
'Tis a drug given to the healthful,
Which infects, not cures.
How can a father that hath lost his son,
A prince both wise, virtuous, and valiant,
Take pleasure in the idle acts of Time?
No, no! till *Mucedorus* I shall see again,
All joy is comfortless, all pleasure pain."
Anselm.—"Your son, my lord, is well."
King Valencia.—"I prithee speak that twice!" ["thrice," 1610.
Anselmo.—"The Prince, your son, is safe!" . . .
King Valencia.—"Thou not deceivest me? I ever thought thee,
What I now find thee, an upright loyal man . . .
Music, speak loudly! now the season's apt,
For former dolours are in pleasure wrapt."
[*Music. Exeunt Omnes.*

[Roxburghe Collection, II. 490; Pepys, III. 282; Jersey, I. 237.]

The Wandring Prince and Princess,

Or,

Musidorus and *Amadine*, both of Royal Progeny, who being unfortunately separated by means of their Parents disagreeing; as fortunately met in a Desert, while they both resolved never to cease from searching, till they had found out each other.

In shady Deserts where was none
But Beasts to hear these Lovers moan,
There these faithful Lovers met,
Their Marriage-day was quickly set.

—Tune, *Young Phaon.* (See p. 100.)

WHen *Musidorus* fell in love
With *Amadine* most fair,
Her Father cross to him did prove,
Which caus'd him to despair:
And for to ease his troubled mind,
He wandered in disguise,
Hoping he might soon comfort find,
Yet tears dropt from his eyes.

"Alas!" (quoth he) "what shall I do?
I am unfortunate,
And though my Love is firm and true,
I meet with Rigid fate;
For she who is my heart's delight,
Her Father is my foe,
Which causes me to take my flight,
Now to the woods I go.

"In woods and deserts I'll reside,
Since my poor *Amadine*,
Whom once I thought to make my bride,
She must not now be mine:
My father's Court I quite forsake,
Never again to see;
For love my heart will surely break,
My dear, I'le dye for thee."

Thus went this wandering Prince to seek
Throughout the deserts wide
Some secret place where he might keep
And secretly abide:

At last he did a Shepherd turn,
Still minding of his flocks;
Which caus'd his *Amadine* to mourn
And tear her golden Locks.

"Alas, alas!" this Princess cry'd,
"Has he forsaken me?
Who I did think could ne'r abide
Where I should absent be?
Some sudden change possest his brest,
That makes him prove unkind;
Whilst *Amadine* can take no rest
To ease her love-sick mind." [text, "heart."

Thus *Amadine*, whose troubled mind
Was sorely fill'd with grief,
For want of *Musidorus* pin'd,
And could find no Relief;
Then she a Resolution took,
What e're did her betide,
Her Prince so dear she would go look
Throughout the world so wide.

And privately away she went,
To all her friends unknown,
To give her troubled mind content
She wandred all alone,
Until she came into a place
Where savage beasts alone
Were known in numbers to increase,
And thus she made her moan.

"Ah! hapless wretch," quoth she, "I am
Of Lovers, yea, the worst;
While some delight to feel love's flame
I think myself accurst:
Yet will I never rest till I
Find out this Prince of mine,
Who strangely and so privately
Forsook his *Amadine*."

A shower of tears then trickled down
From her bright shining eyes,
Whose beauty did the deserts crown,
Whose sighs then fill'd the skies;
And *Musidorus* being near
Did chance to hear her voice,
Though first he was possest with fear,
At last he did rejoyce.

"Certain it is," quoth he, "the Tongue
Of my poor *Amadine*,
To whom I have done too much wrong,
Which grieves this soul of mine:
To her sad heart I will give ease,
Since she is in distress;
For love is such a strange disease
No tongue can well express."

To *Amadine* he then appear'd,
Who startled was to see
She was by any over-heard
And in a sound fell she: [swoon.]
But her dear Prince with kisses sweet
Brought her again to life;
That meeting was to them most sweet,
He made her soon his wife.

[In Black-letter. Publisher's name cut off from Roxburghe.]

[Pepys copy printed for *M.C.*, *T. Vere*, *J. Wright*, *J. Clarke*, *William Thackeray*, and *Thomas Passenger*. Four woodcuts: 1st, the Lady, of p. 157; 2nd, the long-haired Youth, p. 13; 3rd, a Shepherdess, and 4th, a Shepherd. Date uncertain, re-issued *circa* 1676. Reprinted in *Old Ballads*, i. 263, 1810.]

[*These woodcuts belong to our* p. 637.]

Fair Rosamund.

Rosamund (rising, after kneeling to Eleanor).—"I am a *Clifford*,
My son a Clifford and Plantagenet . . . .
And I will fly with my sweet boy to heaven,
And shriek to all the saints among the stars:
'Eleanor of Aquitaine, Eleanor of England!
Murder'd by that adulteress Eleanor,
Whose doings are a horror to the East,
A hissing to the West!' Have we not heard
Raymond of Poitou, thine own uncle—nay,
Geoffrey Plantagenet, thine own husband's father—
Nay, ev'n the accursed heathen Saladdeen—
Strike!
I challenge thee to meet me before God.
Answer me there."

—*Tennyson's* [*Thomas à*] *Becket*, act iv. sc. 2.

THOMAS DELONEY, "the balleting silk-weaver of Norwich," wrote, to his favonrite tune of *Flying Fame*, "The Death of the faire Lady Rosamond," the ballad beginning "When as King *Henry* ruled this land" (reprinted at the commencement of his GARLAND OF GOOD-WILL, to which we believe an entry refers, on 5 March, 159⅗, to Edw. White; the ballad is reprinted for the $m+n$th time, on our p. 673). He felt tolerably proud of having done so, as we may judge from the position he gave to it. He is supposed to have died A.D. 1600, and as most if not all of his writings were literally works of necessity, bread-winners, it is probable that the verses were originally issued some few years before the close of the sixteenth century. We know not the exact date of the first edition of the said *Garland* (one was in 1604, another was entered to Master Bird on 9 November, 1629, in "Three Partes"), but it appears to have been popular even to a proverb before 1633, at which time it is twice referred to by contemporary dramatists. Thus John Ford in his noble tragedy of *The Broken Heart*, Act iv. scene 2, after Gransis compliments, "Thou art the very Honeycomb of Honesty!" makes Phulas continue by saying, "*The Garland of Good Will.*" And in William Rowley's comedy, "*A Match at Midnight*," Act ii. scene 1, Bloodhound says, "These are out of ballads! she has all *The Garland of Good-Will* by heart."

Although this ballad is found in Thomas Deloney's (and some other writers') 'STRANGE HISTORIES, *or, Songes and Sonets of Kings, Princes, Dukes, Lordes, Ladyes, Knights, and Gentlemen*,' imprinted at London for W. Barley, etc., 1607, it is the Eleventh Canticle, while the *Table of Contents*, extending only to Cant. X., seems to mark the original bulk of the Collection. This affords a certainty that the date of the Rosamund ballad was, at the very latest, 1607.

Not improbably, it was added earlier, to immediately follow Deloney's other recognised works (before Nos. XII. and XIII., the latter of which, "Faire sweete, if you desire to know," is signed T.R., and XIV., "A Mayde's Letter," signed A.C.). The title here is "A Mournefull Dittie of the Death of Faire *Rosamond*, King *Henrie* the Second's Concubine." These words reappeared when it was inserted in the late editions of what originally, in 1612, had been Richard Johnson's Crown Garland of Golden Roses; the editions of 1659, 1692, etc.

On the historical foundation of the Rosamond legend, and the growth of the popular belief in the proffered poison cup or dagger, we cannot linger long. The existence of Rosamond Clifford (born *circâ* 1140, died *circâ* 1176, the daughter of Walter de Clifford of Herefordshire and Margaret his wife), the acknowledged mistress of Henry II., in and before 1174, is incontestably proved; also her having been hidden from Queen Eleanor at Woodstock in a chamber of 'Dædalian workmanship' (which popularly became styled a 'maze'), and afterwards buried at Godstow nunnery, whither she had possibly retired in her last days. The fact of a cup having been sculptured on her tombstone may have suggested the addition of the incident which caught the imagination of later poets and romancers, *viz.* the choice proffered by the jealous Queen between the dagger and the bowl. It appears in Samuel Daniel's impressive poem, "The Complaint of Rosamond" (4 February, 159½, such being most probably an enlarged re-issue), which thus begins:—

"Ovt from the horror of Infernall deepes,
My poore afflicted ghost comes heere to 'plaine it,
Attended with my shame that neuer sleepes,
The spot wher-with my kinde and youth did staine it.
My body found a graue where to containe it:
A sheete could hide my face, but not my sin,
For Fame findes neuer tombes to t' inclose it in.

"And which is worse, my soule is now denied
Her transport to the sweet *Elisian* rest,
The ioyfull blisse for ghostes repurified,
Th' euer-springing Gardens of the blest:
C[h]aron denies mee wattage with the rest,
And sayes my soule can neuer passe the Riuer,
Till Louers sighes on earth shall it deliuer." Etc.

Samuel Daniel has been far too long neglected. This "Complaint" alone, not to mention his "Civil Warres" and the Sonnets to "Delia," ought to ensure that loving reverence be paid to his memory. John Payne Collier was the earliest to do it justice, in his careful reprint, 1870, and the Rev. Dr. A. B. Grosart's scholarly edition of the "Complete Works in Prose and Verse," 4 vols. 1885, *et seq.*, has given to the world an authoritative and satisfactory text. The account of the poisoning deserves reproduction here.

"And this our stealth shee [*i.e.* Fame] could not long conceale,
From her whom such a forfeit most concerned:
The wronged Queene, who could so closely deale,
That she the whole of all our practise learned,
And watcht a time when least it was discerned,
In absence of the King, to wreak her wrong,
With such reuenge as shee desired long. 581

"The Laberinth shee entred by that Threed
That seru'd a conduct to my absent Lord,
Left there by chaunce, reseru'd for such a deed,
Where shee surpriz'd mee whom shee so abhor'd.
Enrag'd with madnesse, scarce shee speakes a word,
But flyes with eager furie to my face,
Offring mee most vnwomanly disgrace. 588

"Looke how a Tygresse that hath lost her whelpe
Runns fiercely ranging through the Woods astray:
And seeing her selfe depriu'd of hope or helpe,
Furiously assaults what's in her way,
To satisfie her wrath, (not for a pray,) [= prey.
So fell shee on mee in outragious wise
As could Disdaine and Iealousie deuise. 595

"And after all her vile reproches vsde,
Shee forc'd mee take the poyson she had brought
To end the lyfe that had her so abusde,
And free her feares, and ease her iealous thought.
No cruelty her wrath would leaue vnwrought,
No spightfull act that to Reuenge is common;
(No beast being fiercer than a iealous woman.) 602

"'Heere take (saith she) thou impudent vncleane,
Base graceles strumpet, take this next your hart;
Your loue-sicke hart, that ouer-charg'd hath beene
With pleasures surfeite, must be purg'd with arte.
This potion hath a power, that will conuart
To nought, those humors that oppresse you so.
And (Gerle) Ile see you take it ere I goe. 609

"'What, stand you now amaz'd, retire you backe?
Tremble you, (minion)? come, dispatch with speed;
There is no helpe, your Champion now you lack,
And all these teares you shed will nothing steed; [= stead.
Those dainty fingers needes must doe the deed.
Take it, or I will drench you else by force,
And trifle not, lest that I vse you worse.' 616

"Hauing this bloody doome from hellish breath,
My wofull eyes on euery side I cast:
Rigor about me, in my hand my death,
Presenting mee the horror of my last: [*query*, lust?
All hope of pitty and of comfort past.
No meanes, no power, no forces to contend,
My trembling hands must giue my selfe my end. 623

"Those hands, that beauties Ministers had been,
They must giue death, that me adorn'd of late,
That mouth, that newly gaue consent to sin,
Must nowe receiue destruction in thereat,
That body, which my lust did violate,
Must sacrifize it selfe t' appease the wrong.
(So short is pleasure, glory lasts not long.) 630

"And shee no sooner saw I had it taken,
But foorth shee rushes (proude with victorie)
And leaues m' alone, of all the world forsaken,
Except of Death, which shee had left with me.
(Death and my selfe alone together be:)
To whom shee did her full reuenge refer.
Oh, poore weake conquest, both for him and her." 637

Stow's *Chronicle of England*, 1580, mentions her as "*Rosamond*, the faire daughter of *Walter*, Lord *Clifford*." In the Hundred Rolls of Ed. I. (ii. 93, 94) the verdict of the jurors of Corfham runs, "Dicunt quod [Corfham erat in] antiquo dominico Regum, set *Henricus* Rex pater *Johannis Regis* dedit [*Waltero*] *de Clyfford* 'pro amore *Rosamundæ* filiæ suæ.'" Thus it is indisputable that so early as 1274 it was already accepted popularly on a Clifford Manor that Rosamond Clifford had been a mistress of Henry II. Some think that the connection began while he was still unmarried and uncrowned, but this is worse than doubtful. Giraldus Cambrensis tells that Henry II. after having imprisoned his wife Eleanor (whose previous character had been notoriously infamous), began to live in open adultery, and Rosamond is almost certainly indicated: "[Rex] qui adulter antea fuerat occultus effectus postea manifestus *non mundi quidem rosa* juxta falsam et frivolatissimam compositionem *sed immundi verius rosa* vocata palam et impudenter abutendo" (*De Principis Institutione*, pp. 21, 22). The date is fixed, as shortly after the suppression of the rebellion in September, 1174. John Brompton, Knyghton, and Higden (*circâ* 1350), following Giraldus, add details, all mentioning the Woodstock secret chamber, also that Rosamond died soon after the open acknowledgement by the King, and that she was buried in the Chapter House at Godstow; which latter fact is established by a charter (printed in the *Monasticon*, iv. 366, No. 13), the bestowal of a salt-pit at Wick on the Godstow Nunnery, by Osbert Fitz-Hugh (who is supposed to be Rosamond's brother-in-law), at the petition of her father Walter, for the salvation of her soul and that of his wife, "quarum corpora ibedem requiescant." Other charters prove that Walter endowed the nunnery at Godstow, "pro animabus uxoris meæ *Margaretæ Clifford* et nostræ filiæ *Rosamundæ*."

Fair Rosamond's tomb had in 1191 assumed almost the pomp and sanctity of a pilgrim shrine and sanctuary, for it was set in the middle of the church choir, in front of the altar, and was adorned with silken hangings, lighted lamps and waxen candles. The so-called St. Hugh, Bishop of Lincoln, found it thus distinguished, when on his visitation to Godstow, in that year, he gave command that her body should be taken up and buried outside the church. Episcopal mandates being eluded, she was re-interred in the Chapter-house, where her tomb bore the inscription :—

> Hic jacet in tumulo Rosa mundi non Rosa munda :
> Non redolet sed olet, quæ redolere solet.[1]

It remained undisturbed until the excesses of the Reformation, when it was partially destroyed (Leland, *Monasticon*, iv. 365).[2]

The commonly-received account of Fair Rosamond bearing two sons to Henry II., *viz.* Geoffrey, who became Archbishop of York, and William, known as William Longsword, Earl of Salisbury, was of late origin, and appears to be unworthy of credence, being refuted by the assigned dates. Geoffrey was born in 1151–52, and his mother's name was Ykenai, Aikenai, or 'Akeny.' 'The French Chronicle of London' tells of a Queen Eleanor's vengeance, but makes her the wife of Henry III., and she bleeds Rosamond to death in a hot bath at Woodstock. The silken clue first appears in Fabyan's *Chronicle* (Ellis's edition, pp. 276, 277) : "The comon fame tellyth that lastly the quene wane to her [= Rosamond] by a clewe of threde or sylke, and delte with her in such maner that she lyved not long after. Of the maner of her death speakyth not myne auctour."

In William Warner's *Albion's England*, Book II. 1586, the story of Fair Rosamond is 'ouer-passed.' It comes in cap. XLI., 1597 :—

> With that she dasht her on the Lippes, so dyed double red :
> Hard was the heart that gaue the blow, soft were those lips that bled. [p. 201.

Michael Drayton's *Heroical Epistles*, 1597, commence with one from Rosamond to King Henry, "If yet thine eyes (great Henry) may endure," and the Answer, from Henry to Rosamond, beginning "When first the post arrived at my tent."

Joseph Addison's opera of *Rosamond*, praised by Tickell, scarcely merits the briefest mention here : it was a musical mistake of 1707,

---

[1] The following paraphrastic translations of the inscription (reading "tumbo Rosa mundi") are given in the 1591 edition of *The Complaint of Rosamond* :—

> Heer lyes intoumbd w^th^in this compast stone,
> Fayre *Rosamond*, not nowe the world's fayre rose ;
> Who whilome sweetest smelt, follow'd by none,
> Doth nowe wth deadly staunch infest ye nose. F. L.

AND

> This marble stone doth here enclose the world's fayre not too sweet rose ;
> In whome too late the world's repose doth nowe wth stinch offend the nose.

[2] See T. A. Archer's excellent paper on Rosamond Clifford in *The Dictionary of National Biography*, xi. 75-77. To this we are greatly indebted for information.

(not wedded to the melodies of T. A. Arne till 1733,) adulatory of Queen Elinor, as though she were alive and likely to become his patroness. The poison-bowl is merely a sleeping draught, and when Rosamond retires to the nunnery, Henry becomes a good boy, *tout-à-fait*, and acknowledges the superior virtues of his Queen. Moral (drenchingly, *bis*):—

"Who to forbidden joys would rove
That knows the sweets of virtuous love?" [*Decree Nicey, Nisi!*

Another Roxburghe Ballad on the same subject follows, on our p. 676, "The Unfortunate Concubine; or, Rosamond's Overthrow," beginning, "Sweet, youthful, charming Ladies fair." It does not appear to be of much earlier date than its reappearance in J. Roberts's *Collection of Old Ballads*, 1723, where it begins volume first, p. 4. Ours is a late Aldermary Church-yard broadside, but little known. "Queen Eleanor's Confession" of our p. 680 is virtually a sequel to "Fair Rosamond:" the whirligig of Time brings about its revenges.

The present ballad was intentionally *mis*-quoted in Wm. Rowley's "Match at Midnight," 1633, Act iii. sc. 1, by the Welsh singing-man Randall,

"When high-king *Henry* rul'd this land, the couple of her name,
Besides hur queen was tearly lov'd a fair and princely —— widows."

In Act v. sc. 1, he perverts a verse from "The Spanish Lady's Love" (p. 655):

"Will you hear a noble *Pritain*, how her gull an English flag?" [= Ensign.]

So early as 1854, in his fascinating volume of *Poems by a Painter*, one of the Editor's friends, William Bell Scott, had adorned with pen and etching-needle the legend of Fair Rosamond. His "Woodstock Maze" ends thus:—

"'Hark! he comes! yet his footstep sounds
As it sounded never before!
Perhaps he thinks to steal on me,
But I'll hide behind the door.'
She ran, she stopped, stood still as stone—
It was Queen Eleanore,—
And at once she felt what sudden death
The hungering she-wolf bore.
*Oh the leaves, brown, yellow, and red, still fall,
Fall and fall over churchyard and hall.*

[Roxburghe copy has a modern cut of Queen Eleanor visiting Fair Rosamond in Woodstock Bower, probably copied from the copperplate illustration to the other Rosamond ballad (our p. 676), in J. Roberts's *Old Ballads*, vol. i. p. 1, 1723. Date of the present ballad, *circâ* 1598; but the *Bow Church-yard* copy nearly two centuries later. Pepys Black-letter copy was printed for *W. Thackeray* and *T. Passinger*, *circâ* 1670; Wood's for *F. Coles*, etc., perhaps a few years earlier: but the true date must have been before 1600. The Douce Coll., III. 25 *verso* (n.p.n.), like Ouvry Coll., II. 71 (*J. Pitts*), is entitled "A lamentable ballad of Fair *Rosamond*, Concubine to *Henry* 2nd, who was put to death by Queen *Eleanor*, in the famous Bower of *Woodstock*, near *Oxford*." The tune (unmarked in Roxb.) is *When Flying Fame*, see *Pop. Music*, p. 198.]

[Roxburghe Collection, III. 714; Pepys, I. 498; Wood, 401, fol. 7; etc.]

The Life and Death of Fair Rosamond, King Henry the Second's Concubine.

WHen as King *Henry* rul'd this land, the second of that name,
Beside the queen, he loved dear a fair and comely dame.
Most peerless was her beauty found, her favour and her face;
A sweeter creature in the world could never prince embrace.

Her crisped locks like threads of gold appear'd to each man's sight,
Her comely eyes like orient pearl, did cast a heavenly light.
The blood within her crystal cheeks did such a colour drive,
As tho' the lilly and the rose for mastership did strive.

Fair *Rosamond*, Fair *Rosamond*, her name was call'd so,
To whom dame *Eleanor* our Queen was known a deadly foe.
The king therefore, for her defence, against the furious queen,
At *Woodstock* builded such a bower, the like was never seen.

Most curiously that bower was built of stone and timber strong,
An hundred and fifty doors did to this bower belong:
And they so cunningly contriv'd, with turnings round about,
That none without a clue of thread could enter in and out.

Now for his love and lady's sake, who was both fair and bright,
The keeping of this bower he gave unto a valiant Knight.
But fortune, that doth often frown where it before did smile,
The king's delight, the lady's joy, full soon she did beguile.

For why, the king's ungracious son, whom he did high advance,
Against his father raised wars within the realms of *France*;
But yet before our gracious king the *English* land forsook,
Of *Rosamond*, his lady fair, his farewell thus he took:

"My *Rosamond*, my only Rose, who pleaseth best mine eye,
The fairest flower in all the world, to feed my phantasy,
The flower of my affected heart, whose sweetness doth excel,
My royal rose, an hundred times I bid you now farewell.

"For I must leave my fairest rose, my sweetest rose, a space,
And cross the Ocean into *France*, proud rebels to debase.
But still, my rose, be sure thou shalt my coming shortly see,
And in my heart, when hence I am, I'll bear my rose with me."

When *Rosamond*, the lady bright, did hear the king say so,
The sorrows of her grieved heart her outward looks did show.
And from her clear and crystal eyes the tears gush'd out apace,
Which like the silver pearly dew ran down her comely face.

Her lips like to the coral red, did wax both wan and pale.
And for the sorrow she conceiv'd, her vital spirits fail.
And falling down into a swoon before king *Henry's* face,
Full oft within his princely arms, her body [he] did embrace.

And twenty times with watery eyes he kiss'd her tender cheek,
Until he had reviv'd again, her spirit mild and meek.
"Why grieves my rose? my sweetest rose?" the king did often say.
"Because," quoth she, "to bloody wars my lord must pass away.

"But since your grace in foreign coasts, amongst your foes unkind,
Must go to hazard life and limb, why must I stay behind?
Nay, rather let me, like a page, thy sword and target bear,
That on my breast the blow may light that shall offend my dear.

"O let me in your royal tent prepare your bed at night,
And with sweet baths refreshen you, as you return from fight.
So I your presence may enjoy, no toil I will refuse:
But wanting you, my life is death, which doth true love abuse."

"Content thyself, my dearest love, thy rest at home shall be,
In *England's* sweet and pleasing court, for travels fit not thee.
Fair ladies brook not bloody wars, sweet peace their pleasure breeds,
The nourisher of heart's content, whose fancy first did feed.

"My rose shall rest in *Woodstock* bower, with music's sweet delight;
While I among the piercing pikes against my foes do fight:
My rose in robes of pearl and gold, with diamonds rich and bright,
Shall dance the galliards of my love, while I my foes do smight.

"And you, Sir *Thomas*, whom I trust, to be my love's defence,
Be careful of my gallant rose, when I am parted hence."
And herewithal he fetch'd a sigh, as tho' his heart would break:
And *Rosamond*, for very grief, not one plain word could speak.

And at their parting well they might in heart be grieved sore:
After that day, Fair *Rosamond* the king did see no more.
For when his grace passed the seas, and into *France* was gone,
Queen *Eleanor* with envious heart to *Woodstock* came anon.

And forth she calls the trusty Knight, who kept the curious bower,
And with a clew of twisted thread came from this famous flower.
And when that they had wounded him, the Queen this thread did get,
And went where lady *Rosamond* was like an angel set.

But when the queen, with stedfast eyes, beheld [t]his heavenly face,
She was amazed in her mind, at such exceeding grace. ["fine."
"Cast off," said she, "these [royal] robes, that rich and costly be,
And drink you up this deadly draught which I have brought to thee."

But presently upon her knees Fair *Rosamond* did fall,
And pardon of the queen she crav'd for her offences all.
"Take pity on my youthful years," Fair *Rosamond* did cry,
"And let me not with poison strong be forced for to die.

"I will renounce my sinful life, and in some cloister bide,
Or else be banish'd if you please, to range the world so wide.
And for the fault which I have done, tho' I was forc'd thereunto,
Preserve my life, and punish me, as you think fit to do."

And with these words her lilly hands she wrung full often there,
And down along her comely face proceeded many a tear.
But nothing could this furious queen herewith appeased be:
The cup of deadly poison strong, which she held on her knee,

She gave this comely dame to drink, who took it from her hand,
And from her bended knees arose, and on her feet did stand.
When casting up her eyes to heaven, she did for mercy call,
And drinking up the poison strong, she lost her life withal.

And when [that] death thro' every limb had done its greatest spite,
Her chiefest foes could but confess she was a glorious wight.
Her body then they did entomb, when life was fled away,
At *Woodstock*, near to *Oxford* town, as may be seen this day.

[Written by **Thomas Deloney**.

Printed and sold in *Bow-Church-Yard, London.* [White-letter. See p. 672.]

[Roxburghe Collection, III. 658; Douce, III. 98 *verso*; Euing, 238.]

The Unfortunate Concubine;

Or,

Rosamond's Overthrow. Occasioned by her Brother's praising her Beauty to two young Knights of Salisbury, as they rid along the Road.

[To the Tune of, *The Court Lady*.]

SWeet youthful charming ladies fair, fram'd of the purest mold,
With rosy cheeks and silken hair, which shine like threads of gold,
Soft tears of pity here bestow on the unhappy fate
Of *Rosamond*, who long ago prov'd most unfortunate.

When as the second *Henry* reign'd on the imperial throne,
How he this beautiful flower gain'd I will to you make known,
With all the circumstances too which did her life attend,
How first she into favour grew, and of her fatal end.

As three young Knights of *Salisbury* were riding on their way,
One boasted of a lady fair within her bower so gay:
"I have a sister," *Clifford* swears, "but few men do her know,
Upon her face the skin appears like drops of blood or snow.

My sister's locks of curled hair outshine the golden ore;
Her skin for whiteness may compare with the fine lilly flower.
Her breasts were lovely to behold, like to the driven snow;
I would not for her weight in gold King *Henry* should her know."

King *Henry* had a bower near, where they were riding by,
And he this *Clifford* over-hears. Thought he immediately,
"Tho' I her brother should offend; for that fair white and red,
For her I am resolv'd to send, to grace my royal bed."

The King, who was of high renown, would not his fancy pall;
For having wrote his pleasure down, he did young *Clifford* call:
"Come hither to me, out of hand, come hither unto me,
I am the King of *England*, my messenger thou shalt be.

"I to your sister here have writ three letters seal'd with gold,
No messenger I think so fit as you. Therefore, behold,
Convey them to her hand with speed, make not the least delay,
My will and pleasure let her read, and my commands obey."

Young *Clifford* then the letter took from *Henry's* royal hand,
Tho' with a melancholly look, and mounted out of hand.
Soft tears bedew'd his noble sight, his grieved heart was sad,
Altho' he was as brave a knight as ever *Henry* had.

With that this noble knight of fame rode on without delay,
Until he to the bower came, which was both rich and gay.
She said, when he knocked at the ring, "Who raps so fierce and bold?"
"Sister, I have brought from the King three letters seal'd with gold."

Then with her fingers long and small she broke the seals of gold:
And as she did to reading fall, at first you might behold
The smiles of pleasant sweet delight, as if well satisfied;
But e'er she had concluded quite, she wrung her hands and cry'd:

"Why did you go beyond your bounds, when *Oxford* you did see?
You might have talked of your hounds, and never brag'd of me.
When by the King I am defiled, my father's griefs begin,
He'll have no comfort of his child, nor come to my wedding.

"Go fetch me down my Planet book, straight from my private room,
For in the same I mean to look what is decreed my doom."
The Planet-book to her they brought, and laid it on her knee,
She found that all would come to nought, and poisoned she should be.

"I curse you brother!" then she cry'd, "who caus'd my destiny;
I might have been a Lord's fair bride, but you have ruin'd me."
With that she call'd her waiting-maid to bring her riding weed,
And to her groom she likewise said, "Saddle my milk-white steed."

Some rode before her to report her coming to the king,
As she approach'd the royal court, sweet peals of bells did ring.
A garland over her head they bore, to magnify her charms,
And as she came before the king, he clasp'd her in his arms.

With blushes then she did beseech the king on her bare knee,
These words she said, "I pray, my liege, what is your will with me?"
Said he, "I sent for you, my rose, to grace my royal bed"
Now as he did his mind disclose, she blush'd like scarlet red.

"Blush not, my fairest *Rosamond*, fear no disastrous fate;
For by my kindly power I can place thee in happy state.
No lady in this court of mine can purchase thy desert,
Thy pleasant looks and charms divine have won my royal heart."

The gifts and presents of a king did cause her to comply;
Thinking there was not anything like royal dignity.
But as her bright and golden scene in court began to shine,
The news was brought unto the queen of this new concubine.

At which she was enraged so, with malice in her breast,
That till she wrought her overthrow she could not be at rest.
She felt the fury of a queen, e'er she had flourished long,
And dy'd, just as she had foreseen, by force of poison strong.

The angry queen, with malice fraught, could not herself contain,
Till she had brought fair *Rosamond* to her sad dismal bane:
The said sweet and precious rose, King *Henry's* chief delight.
The queen she to the bower goes, and wrought her hateful spite.

But when she to the bower came, where Lady *Clifford* lay,
Enraged *Elranor* by name, she could not find the way,
Until the silken clue of thread became a fatal guide,
Unto the queen, who laid her dead, e'er she was satisfy'd.

Alas! it was no small surprise to *Rosamond* the fair;
When death appear'd before her eyes, no faithful friend was there,
Who could stand up in her defence, to put the poison by;
Thus by the hand of violence compelled she was to die.

"O most renown'd and gracious Queen, compassion take on me:
I wish that I had never seen this royal dignity.
Betray'd I was, and by degrees a sad consent I gave;
And now upon my bended knees your pardon I do crave."

"I will not pardon you, [she cry'd :] then take this fatal cup ;
And you may well be satisfy'd I'll see you drink it up."
Then with her fair and lilly hand the fatal cup she took ;
Which being drunk, she could not stand, but soon the world forsook.

Now when the king was well inform'd what *Eleanor* had done,
His breast he smote, in wrath he storm'd, as if he would have run
Besides his senses, and he swore, for this inhuman deed,
He never would bed with her more, his royal heart did bleed.

The king [then] stood not pausing long how to reward her spleen,
But straitway in a prison strong he cast this cruel queen.
Where she lay six-and-twenty years, a long captivity ;
Bathed in floods of weeping tears, 'till his death set her free.

Now when her son did [first] succeed his father, Great *Henry*,
His royal mother soon he freed from her captivity.
And she [was] set [once] more at large, who long for debt had lain ;
Her royal pity did discharge thousands in *Richard's* reign.

Printed and Sold at the Printing Office, in *Aldermary Church-Yard, Bow-Lane, London.*

[White-letter, one woodcut. An edition printed at *Tewkesbury*, about 1790, has B.M. press-mark 11621. e. 1. art. 52; another, n.p.n., has p.m. 1876. e. 1, fol. 22. Ening's broadside was printed for *W. Onley*, sold by the booksellers of *Pye Corner* and *London-bridge*. Date, *circâ* 1670-90.]

Queen Eleanor's Confession.

"'Alas! alas!' a low voice, full of care,
Murmur'd beside me : 'Turn and look on me :
I am that *Rosamond* whom men call fair,
If what I was I be.

"'Would I had been some maiden coarse and poor !
O me, that I should ever see the light !
Those dragon eyes of anger'd *Eleanor*
Do hunt me, day and night.'

"She ceased in tears, fallen from hope and trust :
To whom the Egyptian : 'O, you tamely died ;
You should have clung to *Fulvia's* waist, and thrust
The dagger thro' her side.'"

—Tennyson's *Dream of Fair Women.*

THE popular old ballad of "Queen Eleanor's Confession" is quite independent of historical reality, or originality of basis. It may possibly be true, as is asserted so persistently, that Queen Eleanor was not matrimonially unfaithful to her by-no-means-constant husband the young Count of Anjou, afterwards our King Henry II., who had married her in his nineteenth year, six weeks after her divorce But she had proved herself to be so incurably vicious in her former married state, while nominally the wife of Lewis VII., King of France, and indulging in forbidden pleasures with Saladin to an extent that scandalized the orthodox (who might have condoned her offences had they been shared with the faithful, and not extended to the Saracenic followers of Mahound), that we are free to give her the benefit of a doubt, the wrong way, and consider it to be unlikely she ever walked straight thereafter, although she may have gained by experience some skill in concealing her trespasses. If we admit her share in causing the death of Fair Rosamond (avowedly an open question), and in exciting the rebellion of her sons against their unhappy father, which is generally supposed to be incontrovertible, a few more crimes and misdemeanours can scarcely affect the verdict. She resembles the nigger who was so black that charcoal made a white mark on him.

We need not pursue the investigation into the early origin of such an incident as the surreptitiously obtaining a hearing of a guilty woman's confession by the husband going disguised as a priest to shrive and absolve her. Several of the old collections of nouvelles and fabliaux relate it. Among them are Boccaccio's *Decameron* (Giorn. vii. Nov. 5), Barbazan, *Du Chevalier qui fist sa fame [femme] confesse*, III. 229; Bandello's Novelli; those of Malespini; La Fontaine's *La Mari Confesseur*, which is copied from the admirable *Cent Nouvelles Nouvelles*, Nouvelle lxxviii. (Paris, 1887, ii. 174). Anyhow, it was a grave indefensible act of profanation and sacrilege, deserving of the heaviest condemnation and punishment that could possibly be inflicted. Still, the story is a good one, and told fairly well. Poetical justice was not carried out. Eleanor survived her husband Henry, who died in 1189, until the sixth year of her son John, in 1204. She had certainly been imprisoned in 1173, when she had endeavoured to escape in man's apparel and join her contumacious sons. It is satisfactory to learn that she had it not all her own way, "for she wor a bad un, wor she!" as Tennyson puts it, elsewhere. His 'Northern Farmer' had in 1864 a *Dream of some very Unfair Women.*

*** There are, as usual, garbled and fictitious traditional versions in the northern ballad-books. One in Kinloch's (p. 247) begins, "The queen fell sick, and very, very sick;" another had been given by Motherwell (*Minstrelsy*, 1829, p. 1), as "Earl Marshall," beginning the same as our Roxburghe; Buchan's *Gleanings of Scotch, English, and Irish Scarce Old Ballads*, 1825, p. 77, same title, begins, "The Queen's fa'en sick, and very very sick, sick and going to die."

Since there is an evident *lacuna* in Earl Martial's craving a boon, we interpolate four unauthorized long-lines, but keep them square-bracketted and in brevier italic type. Motherwell's '*traditionary*' stanza has no better claim to be authentic:—

"O no, O no, my liege, my king, Such things can never bee;
For if the Queene hears word of this, Hanged she'll cause me to bee."

[Roxburghe Collection, III. 634; Bagford, I. 33; II. 26; Jersey, II. 177; C. 22. e. 2. fol. 71; Euing, 291; Douce, III. 80.]

Queen Eleanor's Confession:

Shewing how King Henry, with the Earl Martial, in Friars Habits came to her, instead of two Friars from France, which she sent for.

To a pleasant new Tune. [See *Popular Music*, p. 174.]

QUEEN *Eleanor* was a sick woman, and afraid that she should die;
Then she sent for two Friars of *France*, for to speak with them speedily.
The King call'd down his Nobles all, by one, by two, and by three,
And sent away for Earl *Martial*, for to speak with them speedily.

When that he came before the King, he fell on his bended knee,
"A boon, a boon, our gracious King, that you sent so hastily.
[*You ask me to hear a sick Woman, who know not what she may say,*
And she may cause my overthrow, her words can a man betray.

"So I crave a boon from my liege Lord, to pawn his Faith and Crown,
That whatever Queen Eleanor says of me, no word the King writes down."]
"I'll pawn my living and my lands, my scepter and my crown,
That whatever Queen *Eleanor* says, I will not write it down.

"Do you put on a Friar's coat, and I'll put on another,
And we will to Queen *Eleanor* go, one Friar like another."
Thus both attired then they go, when they came to *Whitehall*,
The bells they did ring and the Quiristers sing, and the torches did light them all.

When they came before the Queen, they fell on their bended knee,
"A boon, a boon, our gracious Queen, that you sent so hastily."
"Are you two Friars of *France?*" she said, "which I suppose you be;
But if you are two *English* Friars, then hanged shall you be."

"We are two Friars of *France*," they said, "as you suppose we be,
We have not been at any Mass since we came from the Sea."
"The first vile thing that e'er I did, I will to you unfold,
Earl *Martial* had my maidenhead, underneath this cloth of gold."

"That is a great sin," then said the King, "God may forgive it thee."
"Amen, Amen!" quoth Earl *Martial*, with a heavy heart then spoke he.
"The next vile thing that e'er I did, to you I'll not deny,
I made a box of Poison strong, to poison King *Henry*."

"That is a vile sin," then said the King, "God may forgive it thee."
"Amen, Amen!" quoth Earl *Martial*, "and I wish it so may be."
"The next vile thing that e'er I did, to you I will discover,
I poisoned Fair *Rosamond*, all in fair *Woodstock* bower."

"That is a vile sin," then said the King, "God may forgive it thee."
"Amen, Amen!" quoth Earl *Martial*, "and I wish it so may be."
"Do you see yonder a little boy, a tossing of the ball?
That is Earl *Martial's* eldest son, and I love him the best of all.

"Do you see yonder a little boy, a catching of the ball?
That is King *Henry's* son," she said, "and I love him the worst of all.
His head is like unto a bull, his nose is like a boar."
"No matter for that," King *Henry* said, "I love him the better therefor."

The King pull'd off his Friar's coat, and appear[ed] all in red;
She shriek'd, she cry'd, she wrung her hands, and said she was betray'd.
The King look'd over his left shoulder, and a grim look looked he:
And said, "Earl *Martial*, but for my oath, then hanged should'st thou be."

Newcastle: Printed and sold by *Robert Marchbank*, in the *Custom-house* entry.

[White-letter, but Bagford's and Euing's are in Black-letter, both printed for *C. Bates*, in *Pye Corner*. One Woodcut: see *Notes*, pp. 672, 679.]

A Pattern of True-Love.

THIS now-forgotten ditty must once have been in great demand, there being at least seven copies extant, of three or more distinct editions or issues, one of which, for *John White*, at *Newcastle*, was the latest reprint. Something in it had touched the heart of the crowd, probably the trial of the lady's affection by the substituted head of "a hanged man" being shown to her, with the treacherous design of misleading her into a belief that her lover was slain, so that she need no longer be disobedient to her cruel father. Her love bears the strain; as did Imogine's, who had beheld the headless corpse of Cloten, disguised in the garments of Posthumous. The end of both stories is similar, the father yields, and the lovers are re-united. Certainly the husband of the noble Imogine deserved not to be so loved, and ultimately graced with her companionship. But the best women have squandered their affection on unworthy objects: like the sun "being a god, kissing carrion." This is an oft-told tale, generally a tragedy, renewed throughout the centuries.

The tune, *Daintie, come thou to me* (for which see *Popular Music*, p. 517), gained its name from the burden of "A new Northern Jigg" (printed in *Roxb. Bds.*, i. 629), beginning, "Wilt thou forsake me thus, and leave me in misery?" No other exemplar of it is known, beyond Roxb. Coll., I. 204. To the same tune was sung "*Ned Smith*" (*Ibid.*, ii. 465), "I am a prisoner poore, opprest with miserie." A variation of *Daintie, come thou to me* (J. P. Collier's *Old Manuscript Ballads and Songs*, 1869, p. 51, twelve stanzas), begins, "Wilt thou from me thus part, and leave me in miserie?"

[Roxburghe Collection, II. 579; III. 126; Bagford, II. 121; Douce, III. 68; Ouvry, I. 50; Rawlinson, 566, fol. 174; Wood's E. 25, fol. 35.]

[The Noble Lord's Cruelty;

Or, A Pattern of True Love.]

A Pattern of true Love to you I will recite, Between a Beautiful Lady and a Courtious Knight.

To the Tune of, *Dainty, come thou to me, etc.*

Licens'd and Entred according to Order.

"Dear Love, regard my grief, do not my suit disdain,
O yield me some relief, that am with sorrow slain:
These seven long years, and more, have I still loved thee;
Do thou my joys restore: *fair Lady, pity me.*

"Pity my grievous pain, long suffer'd for thy sake;
Do not my suit disdain, that no time Rest can take;
These seven long years, and more, have I still loved thee,
Do thou my joys restore: *fair Lady, pity me!"*

"How should I pity thee?" this Lady then reply'd,
"Thou art no match for me, thy suit must be deny'd:
I am of noble blood, you but of mean degree;
It stands not for my good, *fondly to match with thee."*

This Answer had he most, which cut his heart so deep,
That on his bed full oft would he lye down and weep:
With tears he did lament his froward destiny;
With sighs yet would he say, "*Fair Lady, pity me!*

"While I live, I must love, so Fancy urgeth me,
My [heart] cannot remove, such is my constancy: (text, "mind.")
My mind is nobly bent, though I [am] of low degree;
Sweet Lady, give consent *to love and pity me!"*

The Lady, hearing now the moan that he did make,
Did of his suit allow, and thus to him she spake,
"Sir Knight, mourn thou no more, my faith I plight to thee;
May this thy joys restore, thou hast thy wish of me."

"But first, sweet Love," (quoth she) "what shift then wilt thou make,
With speed to marry me, and thy delight to take?
It were a bargain bad to get a wanton Wife,
And lose with sorrow great thy sweet distressed life.

"If that my Father knew the Love I bear to thee,
We both the same should rue, therefore be rul'd by me:
When my Father is in bed, and all his waiting-men,
Through the window will I get, see that you meet me then."

"Content, Lady," (he said) "he's but a Coward Knight
Whom aught shall make afraid to win a Lady bright."
Thus then they went away, but by the Master-Cook—
Coming through the window wide—was this fair Lady took.

"O gentle Cook," (quoth she) "do not my deed bewray!
Some favour to me show, and let me pass away:
Love that doth conquer Kings forc'd me to do this deed;
Whilst others sits and sings, make not my heart to bleed."

"Not so, then," (said the Cook) "fair Lady, pardon me;
Who can this trespass brook, committed thus by thee?
My Lord, your Father, shall the matter understand;
For false I will not be, neither for house nor land."

Then from the Lady's face fell down the tears amain,
She was in wofull case and thus she made her moan:
"Alas! my own dear Love, little know'st thou my grief, [*al. l.* "Ah."
Great sorrows must we prove, hope yielding no relief."

Her Father, in a spleen, lock'd up his Daughter bright,
And sent forth armed men to take this worthy Knight:
Who then was judg'd to be quite banish'd from the land,
Never his Love to see, so strict was the command.

And at the Sessions next, after the Knight was gone,
To his Daughter, full of woe, they brought a hanged man,
Whose head was smitten off, the Maiden's truth to prove,
Quoth her Father, "Wanton Dame, now take thee here thy Love!"

Her tears fell down amain, when this sight she did see,
And sorely did complain of [her] Father's cruelty;
His body she did wash with tears that she did shed;
An hundred times she kist his body being dead.

"Alas! my Love," (she said) "dear hast thou paid for me;
Would God, in heaven's bliss, my soul were now with thee!
But whilst that I do live, a vow I here do make,
Seven years to live unwed, for my true Lover's sake."

Her Father hearing this, was grieved inwardly;
He pardon'd her amiss, and prais'd her constancy;
And to this courteous Knight, her Father did her wed:
God grant the like success: where perfect Love is bred.

Finis.

[Printer's or publisher's name cut off. In Black-letter. Three woodcuts: 1st and 2nd are small, a man and a woman, each in a peaked hat; 3rd is the Scaffold scene of Decapitation belonging to "The Lady Isabella's Tragedy," of our p. 653. 2nd Roxburghe is a *Newcastle-on-Tyne* reprint, for *Jn. White*. The Pepys exemplar was printed for *J. Clarke*, *William Thackeray*, and *Thomas Passenger*, with a title like our Roxburghe, II. 579, "A Pattern of True Love," unpreceded by the words "The Noble Lord's Cruelty; or, A Pattern of True Love," which John White probably copied from an early broadside. We square-bracket this, in larger black-letter, as heading. Date, before 1651.]

*** There are such strong resemblances of thought and treatment, ideas and language, connecting this ballad with "*The Lady Isabella's Tragedy*" of our p. 653, (both holding the same woodcut!) wherein another "Master Cook" figures more ignobly that this Master Cook Marplot, that *it appears probable the same author wrote both ballads.* Why was he so irate against the *Chef?* Had he ever been by him "personally conducted," at such an early time?

Jephtha, Judge of Israel.

Hamlet.—"O *Jephtha*, judge of *Israel*, what a treasure had'st thou!"
Polonius.—"What a treasure had he, my lord?"
Hamlet.—Why, 'One fair daughter and no more,
The which he loved passing well.'"
Polonius (Aside).—"Still on my daughter."
Hamlet.—"Am I not i' th' right, old *Jephtha*?"
Polonius.—"If you call me *Jephtha*, my lord, I have a daughter that I love passing well."
Hamlet.—"Nay, that follows not."
Polonius.—"What follows then, my lord?"
Hamlet.—"Why, 'As by lot, God wot,'
and then, you know,
'It came to pass as most like it was,'——
the first row of the pious chanson will show you more."—*Hamlet.*

TO have been thus quoted, even with burlesque intentions, in such a foremost work of the world's literature, one of its 'Hundred best Books,' is a sufficient plea to justify our reprint of this 'pious chanson,' although it be dull enough to suit the ballad-capacity of Polonius himself, or his prototype, Will Ceil, Lord Burleigh.

A strange tale is related by Dr. Thomas Percy (when printing an imperfect copy, said by him to have been "retrieved from utter oblivion by a lady, who wrote it down from memory as she had formerly heard it sung by her father: I am indebted for it to the friendship of Mr. Steevens"), to the effect that, having heard of the original ballad in black-letter being among Anthony à Wood's Collections in the Ashmolean Museum, "upon application lately made [1794], the volume which contained this Song was missing, so that it can only now be given as in the former Edition," *i.e.* of 1765.—*Reliques.* George Steevens was styled, by Isaac D'Israeli, "The Puck of Commentators!" Was the lady an apocryphal Mrs. Harris, and did *Puck* Steevens hide the volume after making an extract? Could a volume of Wood's ballads disappear bodily? Or is it some garbled episcopal bemuddlement, seeing that an Oxford broadside is extant in Rawlinson 566, fol. 123? Percy's version (six stanzas, two of them imperfect, instead of our eight) begins:—

"Have you not heard, these many years ago
Jeptha was judge of *Israel*?
He had one only daughter and no mo,
The which he loved passing well:
And as by lott,
God wott,
It so came to pass,
As God's will was,
That great wars there should be,
And none should be chosen chief but he."

On the close resemblance existing between the sacrifice of Jephtha's daughter (*Judges*, xi. 30–40) and the sacrifice of Iphigenia (with her *al. lect.* preservation, resembling that of Isaac), we need not linger.

[Roxburghe Collection, III. 201.]

A proper new ballad, intituled,

Jepha Judge of Israel.

I Read that many years agoe,
  when *Jepha* Judge of *Israel* [*sic*, for *Jephtha*, *passim*.
Had one fair Daughter and no more,
  whom he loved so passing well.
And as by lot, God wot,
It came to passe, most like it was,
Great warrs there should be,
  and who should be the chiefe, but he, but he.

When *Jepha* was appointed now chiefe Captain of the company,
To God the Lord he made a vow, if he might have the victory,
  At his return, to burn,
For his offering, the first quick thing should meet with him then,
  From his house when he came agen, agen.

It chanced so these warrs were done, and home he came with victory,
His Daughter out of doores did run to meet her Father speedily,
And all the way did play
To Taber and Pipe, and many a stripe, and notes full high,
For joy that he was so nigh, so nigh.

When *Jepha* did perceive and see his Daughter firm and formostly,
He rent his clothes and tore his haire, and shricked out most piteously.
"For thou art she" (quoth he),
"Hath brought me low, alas for woe! and troubled me so,
That I cannot tell what to do, to doe.

"For I have made a vow" (quoth he) "which must not be diminished,
A sacrifice to God on high, my promise must be finished."
"As you have spoke, provoke
No further care, but to prepare, your will to fulfill,
According to God's will, God's will.

"For sithence God hath given you might to overcome your Enemies,
Let me be offered up, as right, for to perform all promises.
And this let be!" quoth she,
"As thou hast said, be not afraid, although it be I.
Keep promise with God on high, on high.

"But, Father, do so much for me, as let me goe to [th'] Wildernesse,
There to bewail my virginity, three months to bemoan my heavinesse,
And let there go some moe,
Like Maids with me." "Content," quoth he, and sent her away,
To mourn, till her latter day, her day.

And when that time was come and gone that she should sacrificed be,
This Virgin sacrificed was, for to fulfill all pro[phecie], ["promises."]
As some say, for aye,
The Virgins there three times a year, like sorrow fulfill,
For the Daughter of *Jepha* still, still, still.

Printed for *F. Coles*, *T. Vere*, and *W. Gilbertson.*

[In Black-letter, with two rude woodcuts, one of an antique warrior with curved sword, as on p. 685; the other, a lady with half-opened fan (to represent Jephtha's daughter!) A MS. note on Rawlinson's copy gives the date of issue as 1675. But '*the godly ballet*' was of much earlier date, as shown in our Introduction, it being quoted, as already popular, in the 1603 edit. of *Hamlet.*]

*** Another version of the Jephtha ballad, preserved on a broadside in the Douce Collection, III. 46, *verso*, commences: "When Israel did first begin."

The Wandering Jew.

"Death have we hated, knowing not what it meant :
Life have we loved, through green leaf and through sere,
Though still the less we knew of its intent :
The Earth and Heaven through countless year on year,
Slow changing, were to us but curtains fair,
Hung round about a little room, where play
Weeping and laughter of man's empty day."
—*Epilogue* to Wm. Morris's *Earthly Paradise*, 1870.

THAT the idea of an indefinitely continued existence, testifying to the truth of the Incarnation and Atonement, was at first not regarded as punishment, but rather as a privilege, may be guessed rightly when we remember two passages of Holy Writ. The earlier of these belongs to a period before the Crucifixion; the second to that when the risen Saviour appeared on the shores of Lake Tiberias. When we read the words (*SS. Matth.* xvi. 28, *Mark,* ix. 1), "Verily, I say unto you, There be some standing here, which shall not taste of death till they see the Son of Man coming in his kingdom," our soul revolts against any poor and insufficient quibbling interpretation which assumes such a solemn declaration to apply merely to the not-far-distant time when Jerusalem should be destroyed. Such a comment is an insult to the understanding. But what here might seem to be a promise becomes a mysterious threat of doom in another passage (*S. Luke,* ix. 26, 27), "Whosoever shall be ashamed of Me, and of My words, of him shall the Son of Man be ashamed, when He shall come in His own glory, and in His Father's, and of the holy angels. But I tell you of a truth, there be some standing here, which shall not taste of death till they see the kingdom of God." If it be possible to exceed the solemnity and suggestiveness of such a declaration, we find this in the words spoken to S. Peter concerning S. John: "*If I will that he tarry till I come,* what is that to thee? Follow thou me!" In these words, decidedly not spoken as doom, but as implying a blessing on the beloved disciple, we have an explanation of what must always have been a haunting thought among those chosen men.

We who live in weariness and toil and sorrow, to a great extent, cannot welcome the possibility of an undying pilgrimage with anything like the joy wherewith such a prospect might have filled men of the earlier race. Yet perhaps the deep undertone of sadness among our present poets, the wailing and gloom, the perpetually reiterated complaint against Death closing the scene so early, and poisoning all enjoyment, is sufficient proof that the brevity of life is considered to be an evil, enough to outweigh or banish happiness.

Of old this myth of THE WANDERING JEW lent coherence to stray thoughts of an exemption from mortality. It was clearly recognised, in an age of faith, as being a heavy doom. And the committal of an atrocious crime was pre-supposed, in order to account for, that is, to justify, so awful a punishment.

It would not have been surprising if there had been a legend assigning to the traitor Judas the inability to die: the vain struggle to cease from feeling the agonies of remorse, which was unhallowed by contrition or repentance. One of our Roxburghe Collection Ballads (III. 737, sung to the tune of *Christ is my Love, He loves me*), beginning "Who that antique story reads, and ancient tales of old," tells in dreary verse, borrowing its horrors from the tale of Œdipus and Jocasta, of supposititious crimes and sins committed by the Betrayer, until there is "The Dream of Judas's Mother fulfilled." But even in this imbecile and harrowing broadsheet (reprinted in the *Appendix* to the present volume) there is no hint of Judas being reserved for such a doom as by legend was allotted to "the Shoemaker of Jerusalem," the Wandering Jew.

The ballad itself (of date 21 August, 1612) gives the narrative with commendable distinctness, and without straining after effect or adventitious ornament. We find it entered in the Stationers' Registers under the date of "21mo Augusti, 1612," to Edward Marchant, for his copy under "A ballad called *Wonderful strange newes out of Germanye of a Jewe that hathe lyued wandring euer since our Saviour CHRIST.*" Again (to John Marriott and John Grisman *alias* Grismond) "on 9° Octobris, 1620."

It is probable that we have an almost uncorrupted text, although none of the few broadsides still extant are of the 1612 or 1620 issue.

It is believed that the earliest known reference to the legend concerning the Wandering Jew was found in the book of the Chronicles of St. Alban's Abbey, transcribed and continued by Matthew Paris; since, for the year 1228, he mentions, "a certain Archbishop of Armenia major came on a pilgrimage to England to see the relics of the saints, and to visit the sacred places of the kingdom, as he had done in others; he also produced letters of recommendation from his Holiness the Pope," etc. At length it transpires that the Jew "*Joseph*, a man of whom there was much talk in the world, who, when our Lord suffered, was present and spoke to Him, and who is still alive, in evidence of the Christian faith," had eaten at the Archbishop's table in *Armenia*, and been conversed with. When asked what had passed, this Joseph had replied:—

"At the time of the sufferings of Jesus Christ, He was seized by the Jews, and led into the Hall of Judgement before *Pilate* the Governor, that He might be judged by him on the accusation of the Jews; and Pilate, finding no cause for adjudging Him to death, said to them, 'Take Him and judge Him according to your law;' the shouts of the Jews, however, increasing, he, at their request, released unto them *Barabbas*, and delivered Jesus to them to be crucified. When, therefore, the Jews were dragging Jesus forth, and had reached the door, *Cartaphilus*, a porter of the hall, in Pilate's service, as Jesus was going out of the door, impiously struck Him on the back with his hand, and said in mockery, 'Go quicker, Jesus, go quicker; why do you loiter?' and Jesus, looking back on him with a severe countenance, said to him, '*I am going, and you will wait till I return.*' And according as our Lord said, this *Cartaphilus* is still awaiting His return. At the time of our Lord's suffering he was thirty years old, and when he attains the age of a hundred years, he always returns to the same age as he was when our Lord suffered. After Christ's death, when the Catholic faith gained ground, this *Cartaphilus* was baptised by *Ananias* (who also baptised the Apostle *Paul*), and was called *Joseph*. He often dwells in both divisions of Armenia, and other Eastern countries, passing his time amidst the bishops and other prelates of the Church; he is a man of holy conversation, and religious; of few words, and circumspect in his behaviour; for he does not speak at all unless when questioned by the bishops and religious men; and then he tells of the events of old times, and of the events which occurred at the suffering and resurrection of our Lord, and of the witnesses of the resurrection, namely, those who rose with Christ and went into the holy city, and appeared unto men. He also tells of the creed of the Apostles, and of their separation and preaching. And all this he relates without smiling or levity of conversation, as one who is well practised in sorrow and the fear of God, always looking forward with fear to the coming of Jesus Christ, lest at the Last Judgement he should find Him in anger whom, when on His way to death, he had provoked to just vengeance. Numbers come to him from different parts of the world, enjoying his society and conversation; and to them, if they are men of authority, he explains all doubts on the matters on which he is questioned. He refuses all gifts that are offered to him, being content with slight food and clothing. He places his hope of salvation on the fact that he sinned through ignorance, for the Lord when suffering prayed for His enemies in these words, 'Father, forgive them, for they know not what they do!'"

Such, in its simplicity and solemn strength, is the legend of the Wandering Jew. Seeing that we have to do with the ballad solely, and are not writing any disquisition on the myth, or a sermon on the doctrine, or a bibliography of its literature, we leave students to follow up the subject in the able and interesting volume by the Rev. Sabine Baring-Gould, entitled *Curious Myths of the Middle Ages*, 1869, second edition: a work full of suggestive scholarship, worthy of him who more recently wrote the masterly novel, "Mehalah," and in a different style the grotesque "Court Royal." He traces many of the later accounts of the Wandering Jew; Philip Mouskes, afterwards Bishop of Tournay, his rhymed chronicle, 1242, his narrative drawn from the same Armenian prelate; the Bohemian story of 1505; the Arab capture of Elvan, with Fadhilah's interview with the Jew; the relation of Dr. Paul von Eitzen (1522-1598), Bishop of Schleswig, how in 1547 he had seen the Jew at Hamburg, "a tall man with his hair hanging over his shoulders, standing barefoot during the sermon, over against the pulpit," and how the man told, modestly, that he was a Jew by birth, a native of Jerusalem, by name *Ahasverus*, by trade a shoemaker, who had been present at the crucifixion of Christ, and had lived ever since, travelling through various lands and cities, etc., with exact details. Then follows the account given of the secretary Christopher Krause and Master Jacob von Holstein in 1575, legates to the Court of Spain; of a letter in December, 1599, from Brunswick to Strasburg; of Ahasverus being at Lubeck in 1601 or 1603; at Paris in 1604 (apud Rudolph Botoreus), and in 1721, 22nd of July, at Munich. Among the book-lists are noticeable, Grässe, *Die Sage vom Ewigen Juden*, 1844; M. Gustave Brunet's *Sur les Juifs-errants*, 1845; M. Mangin's *Causeries et Méditations historiques et littéraires*, 1843; the late esteemed Paul Lacroix ('Le Bibliophile Jacob'), Curator of the Imperial Library of the Arsenal, Paris, his *Légende du Juif Errant*, 1856, and his *Curiosités de l'Histoire des Croyances populaires*, 1859; also Moncure Daniel Conway's recent volume, entitled, *The Wandering Jew*, 1881. Of other treasures, the many admiring readers of Charles G. Leland cannot forget his rendering of "Ich bin der alte Ahasver!" beginning, "I am the old *Ahasuér*, I wander here, I wander there; my rest is gone, my heart is sair, I find it never, never mair." (See remainder in *Appendix*, p. 779.)

Of this justly-popular *Volks lied*, "*Ahasver*," the complete text is given on our p. 699.

In the Première Série (1843 edition) of *Chants et Chansons Populaires de la France*, published at Paris by Garnier Frères, Libraires-Editeurs (iii. 82), Le Bibliophile Jacob had declared that:

"La vieille légende du *Juif-Errant* est certainement une allégorie de la destinée du peuple juif, qui, depuis la mort de Jésus-Christ, se trouve dispersé parmi les autres peuples et promène de pays en pays son existence vagabonde, comme pour accomplir une grande expiation; car eux qui demandèrent que Jésus fût crucifié, disaient: 'Que son sang retombe sur nous et sur nos enfants!'

"Cette légende, dont nous ne rencontrons pas de traces avant le treizième siècle, était bien faite pour frapper vivement les esprits et pour s'y graver à l'aide d'une chant populaire; *l'ancien chant s'est perdu*, et la complainte, qui l'a remplacé et qui court encore dans les campagnes de France et de Belgique, ne remonte guère qu'au dix-septième siècle." (*Appendix*, p. 778.) The *Complainte du Juif Errant* is in twenty-four stanzas, beginning, "Est-il rien sur la terre" (on p. 691).

In the *STATIONERS' REGISTERS* we read, "11° *Augusti*, 1634, **Thomas Lambert.** The Wandering Jewes Chronicle . . . vj*d*." The tune (date Oct. 1623), *Our Prince is welcome out of Spain*, marks the abortive Spanish-marriage.

Of a later date than our present *Roxburghe Ballad* of the Wandering Jew, and wholly devoid of all romantic interest, though once popular among the rabble (as proved by there being three distinct editions exemplified in the same Vol. III. of the Roxburghe Collection), is another in the same collection, with a curious and dull list of English Sovereigns, *viz.* the never-recently reprinted "WANDERING JEW'S CHRONICLE" (see our p. 695). The writer, or writers, (for the original issue went not beyond Charles I. and his Queen Henrietta Maria, or "Mary") took no pains to preserve a semblance of the semi-Sacred character. Had it been Charles Dibdin's "Last Shilling" or Tom Dibdin's "Oak Table," the catalogue of events might have been given with far more vigour and brilliancy. Lead, not silver, is here, and it cannot ring clearly; nor does the sound echo from such elder-pith as it would have done from heart of oak. And so say all of us.

Goethe in 1774 projected and began an epic poem, *Der Ewige Jude.* There may be a connection or identity between T. Deloney's "*Repent, O England!*" (mentioned by Thomas Nash in 1596: see our p. 389) and our p. 693, '*The Wandering Jew.*'

Complainte du Juif-Errant.

Air de Chasse, 1774. (See p. 690.)

EST-il rien sur la terre qui soit plus surprenant,
Que la grande misère du pauvre Juif-errant ?
Que son sort malheureux parait triste et fâcheux !

Un jour, près de la ville de Bruxelles, en Brabant,
Des bourgeois fort dociles l'accostèrent en passant ; [*d'une façon civile l'accostent.*
Jamais ils n'avaient vu un homme si barbu.

Son habit, tout difforme et très mal arrangé,
Leur fit croire que cet homme était fort étranger,
Portant, comme ouvrier, devant lui, un Tablier.

On lui dit : " Bonjour, maître, de grâce accordez-nous
La satisfaction d'être un moment avec vous :
Ne nous refusez pas, tardez un peu vos pas."

" Messieurs, je vous proteste que j'ai bien du malheur,
Jamais je ne m'arrête, ni ici, ni ailleurs :
Par beau ou mauvais temps, je marche incessament."

" Entrez dans cette auberge, vénérable vieillard,
D'un pot de bière fraiche vous prendrez votre part :
Nous vous régalerons le mieux que nous pourrons."

" J'accepterais de boire deux coups avecque vous ;
Mais je ne puis m'asseoir ; je dois rester debout :
Je suis, en vérité, confus de vos bontés."

" De savoir votre âge nous serions curieux, [*a.l. connaître.*
A voir votre visage vous paraissez fort vieux :
Vous avez bien cent ans, vous montrez bien autant."

" La vieillesse me gêne ; j'ai bien dix-huit cents ans,
Chose sûre et certaine, je passe encore douze ans :
J'avais douze ans passés quand Jésus-Christ est né."

" N'êtes vous point cet homme de qui l'on parle tant,
Que l'écriture nomme *Isaac*, Juif-Errant ?
De grâce, dites-nous, si c'est sûrement vous ?"

" *Isaac Laquedem* pour nom me fut donné ;
Né à *Jérusalem*, ville bien renommée :
Oui, c'est moi, mes enfants, qui suis le Juif-errant.

" Juste ciel ! que ma ronde est pénible pour moi !
Je fais le tour du monde pour la cinquième fois :
Chacun meurt à son tour, et moi je vis toujours.

" Je traverse les mers, ler rivières, les ruisseaux,
Les forêts, les déserts, les montagnes, les côteaux,
Les plaines et les vallons, tous chemins me sont bons.

" J'ai vu dedans *l'Europe*, ainsi que dans *l'Asie*,
Des batailles et des chocs qui coûtaient bien des vies ;
Je les ai traversés sans y être blessé.

" J'ai vu dans *l'Amerique*, c'est une vérité,
Ainsi que dans *l'Afrique*, grande mortalité :
La mort ne me peut rien, je m'en apperçois bien.

"Je n'ai point de ressource en maison ni en bien ;
J'ai cinq sous dans ma bourse, voilà tout mon moyen ;
En tous lieux, en tous temps, j'en ai toujours autant."

"Nous pensions comme un songe le récit de vos maux ;
Nous traitions de mensonge tous vos plus grands travaux :
Aujourd'hui nous voyons que nous nous méprenions.

"Vous étiez donc coupable de quelque grand péché,
Pour que Dieu tout aimable vous eût tant affligé ?
Dites-nous l'occasion de cette punition !"

"*C'est ma cruelle audace qui causa mon malheur ;*
Si mon crime s'efface, j'aurai bien du bonheur ;
J'ai traité mon Sauveur avec trop de rigueur.

"Sur le mont du *Calvaire* Jésus portait sa croix :
Il me dit débonnaire, passant devant chez moi,
'Veux-tu bien, mon ami, que je repose ici ?'

"Moi, brutal et rebelle, je lui dis sans raison :
'Otes-toi, criminel, de devant ma maison,
Avance et marche donc, car tu me fais affront.'

"Jésus, la bonté même, me dit en soupirant :
'*Tu marcheras toi-même pendant plus de mille ans.*
Le dernier Jugement finira ton tourment.'

"De chez-moi, à l'heure même je sortis bien chagrin,
Avec douleur extrême, je me mis en chemin.
Dès ce jour-là je suis en marche jour et nuit.

"Messieurs, le temps me presse. Adieu la Compagnie ;
Grâce à vos politesses, je vous en remercie.
Je suis trop tourmenté quand je suis arrêté."

Finis.

[As it was to be long afterwards in Samuel Taylor Coleridge's 'Rime of the Ancient Marinere,' so had it been here in the legend and poem : brutal and inexcusable cruelty had to be punished by long probation and atonement, for the end could not come until the better nature revived. The wonderful series of designs by Gustave Doré, with the procession of the Cross recurring in each, shows the end of the pilgrimage when the World reaches the Judgement-Day.]

Another "Juif Errant, Complainte," of date 1805, to the air of a Vaudeville *Du Juif-Errant ; ou, Vite en route*, Anonymous, produced, successfully, at L'Ambigu-Comique, begins, "Voilà dix-huit cents ans et plus," with a refrain of

"*Marche ! marche ! paresseux, marche !*
Marche ! marche ! marche toujours !"

Yet another was written by Justin Cabassol, 1836, "Plaintes du Juif-Errant," beginning, "Depuis dix-huit cents ans, hélas !" to the tune of Béranger's *Le bonheur est là-bas.* William Wordsworth in 1800 wrote a "Song for the Wandering Jew," beginning "Though the torrents from their fountains roar down many a craggy steep." Here is the seventh and final stanza :—

"Day and night my toils redouble,
Never nearer to the goal ;
Night and day, I feel the trouble
Of the Wanderer in my soul."

[Roxburghe Collection, III. 718; Bagford, II. 8; Ouvry, II. 39; Pepys, I. 524; Wood, 401, 123.]

The Wandering Jew;

Or,

The Shoomaker of Jerusalem. Who lived when our Lord and Saviour Jesus Christ was Crucified, and by him [was] appointed to Live till his Coming again.

[Tune of, *The Lady's Fall*, etc. See pp. 650, 764.]

WHen as in fair *Jerusalem* our Saviour Christ did live,
And for the Sins of all the World his own dear Life did give;
The wicked Jews, with scoffs and scorns, did daily him molest,
That never, till he left this life, our Saviour could have rest.
Repent therefore, O England! *Repent while you have space;*
And do not (like the wicked Jews) despise God's proffered Grace.

When they had crown'd his head with thorns, and scourg'd him with disgrace;
In scornful sort they led him forth unto his dying place;
Where thousand thousands in the street did all him pass along;
Yet not one gentle heart was there that pity'd this his Wrong.
Repent [*therefore*, O England, *repent whilst you have space*], *etc.*

Both old and young reviled him, as thro' the streets he went;
And nothing found but churlish taunts, by every one's consent.
His own dear Cross he bore him self (a burden far too great!)
Which made him in the street to faint, with blood and water-sweat.

Being weary, thus, he sought for rest, to ease his burthen'd Soul,
Upon a stone; the which a Wretch did churlishly controul.
And said, "*Away, thou King of Jews, thou shalt not rest thee here;*
Pass on; thy Execution-place, thou seest, now draweth near." 21

And thereupon he thrust him thence, at which our Saviour said,
"*I sure will rest, but thou shalt Walk, and have no journey stayed.*"
With that this cursed Shoomaker, for offering Christ this wrong,
Left wife and children, house and all, and went from thence along.

Where after he had seen the Blood of Jesus Christ thus shed,
And to the Cross his Body nail'd, away with speed he fled,
Without returning back again unto his dwelling-place;
And wandereth up and down the world, a Runagate most base. [Renegade.

No resting could he find at all, no ease, or heart's content;
No house, nor home, nor dwelling-place, but wandering forth he went.
From town to town, in foreign lands, with grieved Conscience still,
Repenting for the hanious Guilt of his fore-passed Ill. 42

Thus, after some few Ages past, in wandering up and down,
He once again desired to see *Jerusalem's* fair town.
But finding it all quite destroy'd, he wander'd thence with woe;
Our Saviour's words which he had spoke to verify and show:

'*I'll rest,*' said he, '*but thou shalt walk!*' so doth this Wandering Jew
From place to place, but cannot stay for seeing countries new,
Declaring still the Power of Him, where'er he comes or goes;
And of all things done in the East, since Christ his death, he shows.

The World he still doth compass round, and see those nations strange,
That, hearing of the Name of Christ, their Idol Gods do change.
To whom he hath told wonderous things, of times fore-past and gone;
And to the Princes of the World declar'd his cause of moan.

Desiring still to be be dissolv'd, and yield his mortal breath;
But as the Lord had thus decreed, he shall not yet see Death.
For neither looks he Old [n]or Young, but as he did those times
When Christ did suffer on the Cross, for mortal sinners' crimes.

He passed many foreign lands, *Arabia*, *Egypt*, *Africa*,
Grecia, *Syria*, and Great *Thrace*, and through all *Hungaria*,
Where *Paul* and *Peter* preached Christ, those blest Apostles dear,
Where he hath told our Saviour's words, in countries far and near.

And lately in *Bohemia*, with many a German Town;
And now in *Flanders*, as 'tis thought, he wandereth up and down.
Where learned Men with him confer, of those his lingering days,
And wonder much to hear him tell his journeys and his ways.

If people give this Jew an alms, the most that he will take
Is not above a groat a time; which he for *Jesus'* sake
Doth kindly give unto the poor, and therefore makes no spare,
Affirming still that Jesus Christ of him hath daily care.

He was not seen to laugh or smile, but weep and make great moan,
Lamenting still his miseries, and days fore spent and gone.
If he hears any one Blaspheme, or take God's name in vain;
He tells them that they crucify Our Saviour Christ again.

"*If thou had'st seen grim Death,*" said he, "*as these mine eyes have done,
Ten thousand thousand times, would ye his Torments think upon;
And suffer for His sake all pains, all torments, and all woes.*"
These are his words, and this his Life, where'er he comes and goes.

[*Doubtful*, if originally by **Thomas Deloney.** *Cf.* p. 389.]

Printed and Sold at the Printing-Office in *Bow-Church-Yard, London.*

[There is an older edition, white-letter, of this ballad in the Bagford Collection, Vol. II. 8, "printed by and for *W. O*[*nley*], and sold by the Booksellers of *Pye-corner* and *London-bridge*. Licens'd and Enter'd according to Order." It has (*see next vol.*) a German woodcut of the Wandering Jew. We collate the Bagford text. Date of the original issue, 21 August, 1612; or 9 Oct., 1620.]

[Roxburghe Collection, III. 47, 732, 733; Pepys, I. 482; Wood's, 401, fol. 121; Douce, II. 240.]

The Wandering Jew's Chronicle;

Or,

The old Historian, his brief declaration,
Made in a mad fashion, of each Coronation,
That pass'd in this Nation, since *William's* Invasion,
For no great occasion, but meer Recreation,
To put off Vexation.

TO THE TUNE OF, *Our Prince is welcome out of Spain.*

(Woodcut portraits of the Kings, from William I. to Charles I. and Queen.)

WHen *William* Duke of *Normandy* with all his *Normans* gallantly
This Kingdom did subdue;
Full fifteen years of age I was, and what e're since hath come to pass,
I can repeat for true.

I can remember since he went from *London* for to conquer *Kent*,
Where, with a walking Wood,
The men of *Kent* compassed him, and he for aye confirm'd to them
King *Edward's* Laws for good. 8

Likewise I *William Rufus* knew, and saw the Arrow that him slew,
Hard by a Forrest side:
I well could tell [you] if I list, or better tell you if I wist,
Who next to him did ride. [Sir *Walter Tyrrel*?

First *Henry* I, and *Stephen* knew, who no man here but I did view,
I saw them Crown'd and dead;
I can remember well also the Second *Henry's* Royal show,
That day that he was wed. [flower,

I likewise was at *Woodstock* Bower, and saw that sweet and famous
Queen *Elenor* so did spight; [*Rosamond*, *cf.* p. 673.
I found the clew of thread again, after that worthy knight was slain,
'Twas green, blew, red and white. [Knt. = Sir *Thomas*.

I saw King *Richard*, in his shirt, pull out a furious Lyon's heart,
Whereby his strength was try'd;
I saw King *John*, when as the Monk gave him the Poison which he
And then forsooth he dy'd. [drunk,

I mark'd the Barons when they sent for the *French Doulphin*, with intent
To put Third *Henry* down: [*i.e.* the Dauphin.
I saw the Earl of *Leicester* stout (call'd *Simon Mun'ford*) with his Tent
Besiege fair *London* Town. ['Tent,' *qu.* rout?

And I have the First *Edward* seen, whose Legs I still thought to have [been
A yard and more in length:
With him I into *Scotland* went, and back again incontinent,
Which he subdu'd by strength.

I knew *Carnarron's* Minion dear, and saw the fall of *Mortimeer*,
With all the Barons' Wars.
And likely was to have been sent, at *Burton* Battel upon *Trent*,
Where I receiv'd these scars.

Third *Edward* and his valiant Son, by whom great feats of arms were [done,
I saw on *Cressy* Plain;
Which day, when bows and arrows keen, grew scant, with mighty [stones I ween,
Were many *French-men* slain.

I knew *Wat Tyler* and *Jack Straw*, and I the Mayor of *London* saw,
In *Smithfield*, which him slew:
I was at *Pomfret* Castle, when the Second *Richard* there was slain;
Whose death e're since I rue.

I saw when *Henry Bullingbrook* the crown and scepter on him took,
Which he became full well:
I saw when *Henry Hotspur*—he, and many Lords at *Shrewsbury*,
Were slain—in Battel fell.

I saw the brave victorious Prince (whose death I have bewailed e'er [since)
Henry the Fifth I mean:
And I can give you just report, how many *French* at *Agincourt*
Were in one Battel slain.

I saw the White and Red-Rose fight, and *Warwick* great in armour [bright,
In the Sixth *Henry's* Reign:
And present was that very hour, when *Henry* was, in *London* Tower,
By crook'd-back *Richard* slain.

I in a Gold-smith's shop have seen Fourth *Edward's* famous Concubine
Whose name was fair *Jane Shore*; [vol. i. p. 483.
I saw when *Richard's* cruelty did put her to great misery,
And I was griev'd therefore.

Also I was at *Bosworth* field, well armed there with spear and shield,
Meaning to try my force:
Where *Richard*, losing Life and Crown, was naked borne to *Leicester* [Town,
Upon a colliar's horse.

To the Seventh *Henry* then I was a servant, as it came to pass,
To serve him at his need:
And while I did in Court remain, I saw in the Eighth *Henry's* reign,
Full many great men bleed.

I, as a Souldier bold, with him o'er *Neptune's* curled breast did swim,
Unto the Realm of *France*:
I helpt to ransack *Bulloign* Town, and many places of renown,
Yet home I came by chance.

I knew Sixth *Edward* as a child, whose countenance was very mild,
A hopeful Prince he was.
I knew Queen *Mary*, in her reign, put Protestants to mickle pain,
And re-set up the Mass.

And (to my comfort), I have seen *Elizabeth*, that Maiden-Queen,
Queen *Mary's* only sister:
Though she reign'd four-and-forty years, her subjects show'd well by
That they too soon had miss't her. [their tears

I saw King *James* come from the North, like to a Star that shineth forth,
To glad the People's sight:
He brought a salve to cure our wounds, and made *Great Britain* safe
Through equity and right. [and sound,

He was in troth a Prince of peace, and made all former jars to cease,
'Twixt *English-men* and *Scots*.
The *English-men* sung merry Sonnets, the *Scots* they then threw up
For joy at their good lots. [their Bonnets,

In *Scotland* born, in *England* nurst, was Pious Princely *Charles* the
Who had to wife Queen *Mary*; [First,
But by the rage of Rebels' hate, Murthered and Martyr'd at his Gate,
This good King did miscarry.

King *Charles* the Second, that had spent many long years in Banishment,
And scap'd with life so nearly:
By Miracle and means unknown, sits in the brightness of his Throne,
Where he doth shine most clearly.

Queen *Katherine* his betrothed Wife, the Lady of his Love and Life,
Is likewise now come hither:
And may their bodies both encrease in Love and Children, joy, and
Long as they live together. [Peace,

Printed for *F. Coles*, *T. Vere*, *F. Wright* and *F. Clarke*.

[Three distinct issues are represented by the Roxburghe exemplars, the 1st copy ending as above, 1662 (early issue was 11 August, 1634), Black-letter with a double row of portraits of the Sovereigns, beginning with William the Conqueror, ending with Charles I. and his Queen "Mary," no space left for Charles II. The 2nd has *no cuts*, ends with George II., and was printed for *J. White, Newcastle-on-Tyne.* The 3rd, a *Bow Church-yard copy, has a different double-row of Monarchs, William I. to George II. and Queen Caroline.*]

*** This 3rd, Bow Church-yard *Continuation* follows on next page.

[Roxb. Coll., III. 732 33. *CONTINUATION, instead of the 25th Stanza.*]

I saw his Royal Brother *James*, who was led on to such Extreams,
Which made the Nation weep;
I saw his Coronation-day, and how he did the sceptre sway,
Which long he could not keep.

Lord Chancellor I saw likewise, when he did rule and tyrannize
By arbitrary power; [*i.e. George Jefferys.*
And I was in the Council-room, when *Peters* he was pleas'd to doom
The Bishops to the Tower.

I present was that very Morn, when the *Pretender* he was born,
Being the Tenth of *June*,
In Sixteen Hundred Eighty-Eight, but this day prov'd unfortunate,
It put all out of tune.

I saw King *William* cross the Seas, to give the Land and Nation ease,
With a most glorious Fleet;
I saw him cross to *Ireland*, with a right valiant armed Band,
Making his foes retreat.

I have his Royal Consort seen, *Mary*, our most religious Queen,
In all our Courtly Train;
I saw her Royal Funeral, and how the showers of tears did fall,
While Subjects did complain.

I saw the Duke of *Gloucester's* birth, the glory, triumph, joy and mirth,
That was on this great Day;
I saw his Royal Mother's tears, when in the blossom of his years
Death snatch'd him hence away.

I saw King *William*, when he dy'd, who was the Land and Nation's Guide,
A scourge to *France* and *Spain*.
I saw Queen *Ann* come to the throne, whose royal favours she made known,
During her glorious Reign.

I saw her Commons, Lords and Peers, who paid a tribute of sad tears,
Before her Royal Tomb;
I saw King *George* pass thro' the Town, all to possess the Royal Crown,
And govern in her room.

I saw King *George* the Second come, with loud Huzzas to *Britain's* Throne,
And glorious *Caroline*;
Like bright *Aurora*, sweet and gay, that chases all dim clouds away,
The joy of Woman-kind.

I saw their numerous progeny, the pledges of Prosperity
For many years to come;
I saw the King and Queen when crown'd, with men and angels compass'd round;
Long may they grace the Throne!

Printed and Sold in *Bow Church-yard*.

[Thus ends the extended version, evidently soon after the Coronation of King George II. and Queen Caroline, an event which took place on October 11, 1727.]

*** As giving a much later complaint of the Wanderer, and from that *Vaterland* which first (according to the Stationers' Registers of 1612) sent news of him, no mortal Editor could resist inserting this sublime Appendixial lied, p. 699: It is sung to the melody of Wilhelm Hauff's Volksweise 'Treue Liebe,' of 1821.

Ahasver.

Mel.—'Steh' ich in finst'rer Mitternacht.'

Ich bin der alte *Ahasver*, ich wandre hin, ich wandre her; meine Ruh' is hin, mein Herz ist schwer, ich find' sie nimmer und nimmermehr.

Es brüllt der Sturm, es rauscht das Wehr, nicht sterben können, o Malheur! mein Haupt ist müd', mein Herz ist leer, ich bin der alte *Ahasver*.

Es brummt der Ochs, es tanzt der Bär, ich find' sie nimmer und nimmermehr; ich bin der ewige *Hebrä'r*, meine Ruh' ist hin, ich streck s Gewehr.

Mich hetzt und jagt, ich weisz nicht wer, ich wandre hin, ich wandre her, zu schlafen hab' ich sehr Begehr, ich bin der alte *Ahasver*.

Ich komme wie von ohngefähr, meine Ruh' ist hin, mein Herz ist schwer, ich fahre über Land und Meer, ich wandre hin, ich wandre her.

Mein alter Magen knurret sehr, ich bin der alte *Ahasver*, ich wandre in die Kreuz und Quer, ich find' sie nimmer und nimmermehr.

Ich lehne an die Wand den Speer, ich habe keine Ruhe mehr, meine Ruh' ist hin, mein Herz ist schwer, ich schweite nach der Pendellehr'.

Schon lang' ist's dasz ich übel hör', Küraço ist ein fein Likör, einst war ich unterm Militär, ich finde keine Ruhe mehr.

Was hindert, dasz ich aufbegehr', meine Ruh' ist hin, mein Herz ist schwer, ich bin der alte *Ahasver*, jetzt aber weisz ich gar nichts mehr.

Finis.

[Perhaps in the old Johann-Fust days Ahasuerus had picked up part of his *refrain* from 'Gretchen, or she hers from him, at Leipzig. This is a curious question: resolvable when we know what name the son of Thetis bore (*Pyrrha*, says John Gay, 1733), before Deidameia found out his real one. Other discoveries have to be made: the sooner they are, the better, since the sands are falling swiftly.]

[These '*Doctor Faustus*' cuts belong to p. 705. The Conjurer, with Witches or Fairies, and the warm corner awaiting suggestively below, adorned the Bagford exemplar. The Buff-coated trooper is second cut in first Roxburghe. Bagford reads "to live in pleasure," line 24 of p. 704; Roxb. 'in peace.']

The Ballad of Dr. Faustus.

"When Goethe's death was told, we said—'Sunk then is Europe's sagest head:
Physician of the Iron Age, Goethe has done his pilgrimage.'
He took the suffering human race, he read each wound, each weakness clear—
And struck his finger on the place, and said *Thou ailest here, and here.*—
He look'd on Europe's dying hour of fitful dream and feverish power;
His eye plunged down the weltering strife, the turmoil of expiring life;
He said *The end is everywhere: Art still has truth, take refuge there.*
And he was happy, if to know causes of things, and far below
His feet to see the lurid flow of terror, and insane distress,
And headlong fate, be happiness."—*Matthew Arnold's Memorial Verses*, 1850.

THERE has grown up a maze of literature around the old myth, fable, or legend of Johann Faust or Fust, suspected of diabolical arts because he was able to print innumerable copies of what could not have been executed formerly without the careful handiwork of illuminators and transcribers. The true history offers us an example of the sadly-recurring mischance, the persecution and calumny attending on our benefactors, owing to the ignorance and malignity of those who were served in a generous spirit by leaders, "of whom the world is not worthy." In the poetic legend, we are fascinated by the revelation of a mere perishable mortal attaining superhuman powers of knowledge, and victory over the limitations of time and space: one who is admitted to view Nature's secret processes of creation and restorative changes, to whom the spiritual world is in a great measure unbarred, who flits through space and descends into the recesses of the earth: who has such access to wealth that he can afford to despise whatever is purchaseable by money, and whose supremacy in occult learning renders the past or future an open book for his study; who feels no sickness or age, but maintains unimpaired youthful vigour, intellectual supremacy, and the enjoyment of every faculty that takes tribute of pleasure and renown. All the dreams of philosophy, benevolence and poetry combine to shed some rays of glory on such an ideal embodiment; but, as of old, there is always heard a sad undertone of misery, that surely conquers the first triumphant notes of joy. The dark clouds gather round at the close, and he who has for a brief time soared above his fellow-sufferers, the toiling, the sordid, the oppressed and only half-emancipated, disappears at last with wailing and reproach, no longer envied but decried, scarcely lamented, only shuddered over by the pitying, abhorred by the bigotted and the cruel.

Elsewhere must readers turn for records of the legend in its dawn, closely associated as it is with the first glory of the printing-press. The puppet-plays, of the years following closely what we perhaps mistakenly call the Dark or Middle Ages, speedily familiarized the populace with the story of a compact between man and his arch enemy, whereby for great extension of powers, sensual, political, social, spiritual, and well-nigh universal, the Faustus of antiquity bartered his soul and hopes of salvation; soon to pay the forfeit, despairingly, after a brief and phrensied career devoid of happiness, because it was devoid of inward peace and religious trust. There were fantastic tricks and marvels, to amuse the populace, rude horse-play and sudden transformations or transmigrations, overturnings of thrones, mockery of tyrants, profuse indulgence in all luxurious excesses befitting the world, the flesh and the devil, in close alliance according to use and wont. Always came the remembrance of his impending doom, to intensify yet poisonously embitter each successive enjoyment. No wonder that the nobler minds delighted in meditating on this stupendous theme, while the common masses were content to be amused or terrified. Thus our own Marlowe, moulder of the "mighty line," threw into his magnificent tragedy, "Dr. Faustus," of 1588-93, so much of the loveliness, the gloom, the horror (if not also the buffoonery and the scholastic pedantry), which his soul recognised intensely, and flung together, as it were disdaining the auditory to whom it was submitted. So, nearly two centuries later, the last work of that most marvellous master-mind that our times have known, was to lend completion to the "Faust" on which he had laboured intermittingly more than thirty years (1774-1808, the first part; August, 1831, the end); which must for ever be, like "Hamlet," an embodiment of all that is highest, saddest, and most mysterious in human nature.

Byron's *Manfred*, Shelley's *Prometheus*, Bailey's *Festus*, and the late Dr. Edward Kenealy's *New Pantomime*, what are they all but reflected lights, caught from the one great legend: man's inordinate ambition, his soaring above mortality, his inevitable defeat?

To our Roxburghe Ballad of "The Judgement shewed upon one John Faustus, Doctor in Divinity," we need not look expectantly for anything sublime or rapturous in poetry. We believe it to have been issued *independently of*, if not *before* Marlowe's tragedy,

---

[1] Goethe's Faust, the first Part, was produced on the stage of the Brunswick *Hoftheater* on 19 January, 1829, at the desire of the young Duke Karl; the adaptation being made by August Klingemann, who had himself written and successfully introduced previously a dramatic version of the Faust legend, distinct from Goethe's. Later in the same year, on 27 August, 1829, Goethe's Faust was brought out at Dresden, under the management of Ludwig Tieck. The successful French adaptation in modern times, translated and transferred to the Princess's Theatre twenty-five years ago, 1854, during the management of Charles Kean (impersonator of a somewhat low-comedy Mephistopheles, with Carlotta Leclere as Gretchen, and the loveliest reproduction of Van Mücke's "Translation of St. Catharine" in the final scene), virtually prepared the way for the truly marvellous and effective "Faust" at the Lyceum, with the enchantment of scenic effects and dramatic completeness, including Henry Irving's unequalled triumph as Mephistopheles, such as can never be forgotten by any spectator. It transcends all possible praise. Yet there are idiots who rave against the Stage, and swell with envious venom against the dramatic profession. They also dislike Ballads!

(The foundation was P.F.'s translation of the Frankfort prose *Faustus*, 1587.) It attained enormous popularity among the common people. The number of extant early-copies is one sure token, solitary relics of distinct editions, frequently re-issued, and, pasted on walls of workshops, untimely destroyed.

In Stationers' Company Registers, Book B, f. 241*vo.*, f. 168*vo.*,

Nono die Maij [1580].
Henry Carre. *A ballat of the iudgement of GOD* . . . . . iiij*d.*
Ultimo die Februarij [158⅔].
Ric. Iones. Allowed vnto him for his Copie, *A ballad of the life and deathe of Doctor FAUSTUS the great Cunngerer* . . . . . . vj*d.*

This is sixteen years antecedent to the earliest known print of Christopher Marlowe's tragedy of '*Plaie of Doctor Faustus*,' which is entered in the Stationers' Registers on January 7, 1601; but was probably acted in 1589. Marlowe died June 1, 1593. To Henry Carre on xv. Aprilis, 1590, was entered "*A ballad wherein twoo lovers exclayme against fortune for the losse of their ladyes, with the ladies comfortable answere.*" This may be "*Fortune, my Foe,*" to which tune our *Dr. Faustus* was appointed to be sung: a tune again named on 15 July, 1592, in the Registers. Cuthbert Burbye was publishing *The second Reporte of Doctour JOHN FAUSTUS with the ende of WAGNER'S life* on xvi November, 1593. The "Doctor Faustus" ballad was transferred, with 127 others, on 14 Dec., 1624, to six publishers, Tho. Pavier, three Wrights (John, Cuthbert, and Edward), John Grismond and Henry Gosson.

[Roxburghe Coll., II. 235; III. 280; Euing, 145; Bagford, II. 55; Pepys, II. 142; Douce, III. 47; Wood, 401, 53; Jersey, II. 205; C. 22. e. 2, 132.]

The Judgment of God shewed upon one
John Faustus, Doctor in Divinity.

TUNE OF, *Fortune my Foe.* [See *Note* on p. 706.]

[This woodcut is from a copper-plate in the 1598 *Dr. Faustus*, ill copied in Roxb. Coll., III. 280. Other cuts are on pp. 699 and 702 (*Cf.* p. 705).]

ALl Christian men, give ear a while to me,
How I am plung'd in pain but cannot die;
I liv'd a life the like did none before,
Forsaking Christ, and I am damn'd therefore.

At *Wittenburge*, a town in *Germany*, [Born at *Rhodes*, *Weimar*.
There was I born and bred of good degree,
Of honest Stock, which afterwards I shamed,
Accurst therefore, for *Faustus* was I named.

In learning, loe! my Uncle brought up me, [*Cf.* P.F.'s *Faustus*.
And made me Doctor in Divinity:
And when he dy'd, he left me all his wealth,
Whose cursed gold did hinder my soul's health. 12

Then did I shun the Holy Bible book,
Nor on God's word would ever after look,
But studied accursed Conjuration,
Which was the cause of my utter Damnation.

The Devil in Fryar's weeds appeared to me,
And streight to my Request he did agree,
That I might have all things at my desire,
I gave him soul and body for his hire.

Twice did I make my tender flesh to bleed,
Twice with my blood I wrote the Devil's deed,
Twice wretchedly I soul and body sold,
To live in [pleasure], and do what things I would.

For four-and-twenty years this bond was made,
And at the length my soul was truly paid;
Time ran away, and yet I never thought
How dear my soul our Saviour Christ had bought.

Would I hed first been made a Beast by kind,
Then had not I so vainly set my mind;
Or would, when reason first began to bloom,
Some darksome Den had been my deadly tomb.

Woe to the day of my nativity,
Woe to the time that once did foster me,
And woe unto the hand that sealed the Bill,
Woe to myself, the cause of all my ill!

THe time I past away with much delight,
'Mongst princes, peers, and many a worthy knight;
I wrought such wonders by my Magick Skill,
That all the world may talk of *Faustus* still.

The Devil he carried me up into the Sky,
Where I did see how all the world did lie;
I went about the world in eight daies' space,
And then return'd unto my native place.

What pleasure I did wish to please my mind,
He did perform as bond and seal did bind,
The secrets of the Stars and Planets told,
Of earth and sea, with wonders manifold.

When *four-and-twenty years* was almost run,
I thought of all things that was past and done;
How that the Devil would soon claim his right,
And carry me to Everlasting Night.

Then all too late I curst my wicked Deed,
The dread whereof doth make my heart to bleed,
All daies and hours I mourned wondrous sore,
Repenting me of all things done before.

I then did wish both Sun and Moon to stay,
All times and seasons, never to decay;
Then had my time nere come to dated end,
Nor soul and body down to Hell descend.

At last, when I had but one hour to come,
I turn'd my glass for my last hour to run,
And call'd in learned men to comfort me,
But Faith was gone, and none could comfort me.

By twelve a clock my glass was almost out,
My grieved Conscience then began to doubt;
I wisht the Students stay in chamber by,
But as they staid they heard a dreadful cry.

Then presently they came into the Hall,
Whereas my brains was cast against the wall,
Both arms and legs in pieces torn they see,
My bowels gone: this was an end of me!

You Conjurors and damned Witches all,
Example take by my unhappy fall:
Give not your souls and bodies unto hell,
See that the smallest hair you do not sell.

But hope that Christ his Kingdom you may gain,
Where you shall never fear such mortal pain:
Forsake the Devil and all his crafty ways,
Embrace true faith that never more decays.

Printed by & for *A. M[ilbourne]* & sold by the Booksellers of *London*.

[In Black-letter. Three woodcuts: 1st, a rude early block, much worm-eaten, of a horned and tailed Devil appearing to Faustus in his study; 2nd, a single buff-coated figure; 3rd, the same as in iii. 107. But Roxb. Coll., III. 280, is in bold white-letter, n.p.n., with a single woodcut, a modern copy of the fine copper-plate frontispiece of the 1598 4to. of *Dr. Faustus*, (p. 703), a reprint from the broadside of 1628. Pepys copy p. for *W. Thackeray and T. Passinger*, *circâ* 1670. The Bagford II. 55 exemplar, in B.-letter, has our first-named cut and an additional small one, curious, of a Conjurationist standing in a circle (but looking like a boy trundling a hoop, as the circle is continued in front of him; see p. 702): London, printed by *W. O[nley]*, and sold by the Booksellers.]

[Roxburghe Collection, II. 531. Apparently Unique.]

Witchcraft discovered and punished.

Or,

The Tryals and Condemnation of three Notorious Witches, who were Tryed the last Assizes, holden at the Castle of Exeter, in the County of Devon: where they received Sentence for Death, for bewitching several Persons, destroying Ships at Sea, and Cattel by Land, etc.

To the Tune of, *Doctor Faustus*; or, *Fortune my Foe*. [See Note below.]

NOw listen to my song, good people all,
And I shall tell you what lately did befall
At *Exeter*, a place in *Devonshire*,
The like whereof of late you ne're did hear.

*** Since it is appointed to be sung to the same tune of *Dr. Faustus*, or *Fortune my Foe* (for which tune see *Popular Music*, p. 162; the words were given complete in our *Bagford Ballads*, 1878, p. 961), we here add the curious and probably unique ballad on the condemnation at Exeter in 1682 of three poor old women as witches. We would gladly exchange this Exeter witchcraft ballad for one (apparently lost) entered on 22 August, 1634, to Thomas Lambert, entitled 'The Witches Dance.' Visions of it arise, the Walpurgis-nacht Spiel!

At the last Assizes held at *Exeter*
Three Aged Women, that Imprisoned were
For Witches, and that many had destroy'd,
Were thither brought in order to be try'd,

For Witchcraft, that Old Wicked Sin,
Which they for long time had continued in:
And joyn'd with Satan, to destroy the good,
Hurt Innocents, and shed their harmless blood.

But now it most apparent does appear,
That they will now for such their deeds pay dear;
For *Satan*, having lull'd their Souls asleep,
Refuses Company with them to keep.

A known deceiver he long time has been,
To help poor Mortals into dangerous Sin;
Thereby to cut them off, that so they may
Be plung'd in Hell, and there be made his Prey.

So these Malicious Women, at the last,
Having done mischiefs, were by Justice cast:
For it appear'd they Children had destroy'd,
Lamed Cattel, and the Aged much annoy'd.

Having Familiars alway at their beck,
Their wicked rage on Mortals for to wreck:
It being prov'd they used wicked Charms
To murther men, and bring about sad harms;

And that they had about their bodies strange
And proper Tokens of their wicked change,
As pledges that, to have their cruel will,
Their Souls they gave unto the Prince of Hell.

The Country round where they did live came in,
And all at once their sad complaints begin:
One lost a Child, the other lost a Kine,
This his brave Horses, that his hopeful Swine.

One had his Wife bewitched, the other his Friend,
Because in some things they the Witch offend:
For which they labour under cruel pain,
In vain seek remedy, but none can gain,

But roar in cruel sort, and loudly cry,
"Destroy the Witch, and end our misery!"
Some used charms by *Mountabanks* set down,
Those cheating *Quacks*, that swarm in every Town.

But all's n vain, no rest at all they find,
For why all Witches to cruelty are enclin'd,
And do delight to hear sad dying groans,
And such laments as wou'd pierce Marble Stones.

But now the Hand of Heaven has found them out,
And they to Justice must pay lives, past doubt:
One of these wicked wretches did confess,
She four-score years of age was, and no less;

And that she had deserved long before
To be sent packing to the *Stigian* shore,
For the great mischiefs she so oft had done,
And wondered that her life so long had run.

She said the Devil came with her along,
Through crouds of people, and bid her be strong,
And she no [hurt] should have: but, like a Lyer, ["hand."
At the Prison-Door he fled, and ne're came nigh her.

The rest aloud crav'd Mercy for their Sins,
Or else the great deceiver her Soul gains;
For they had been Lewd Livers many a day,
And therefore did desire that all would pray

To God, to Pardon them, while thus they lie
Condemned for their Wicked Deeds to Die:
Which may each Christian do, that they may find
Rest for their Souls, though Wicked once inclin'd.

Finis.

[In Black-letter. Three woodcuts. 1st and 2nd are unimportant, two small fanciful figures in fluttering garments, crowned with feathers. The third is our Robin Goodfellow satyr, holding candle and broom, encircled by little black fairies and night-birds (1637), p. 706. No p.n. Date of ballad, 1682.]

*** A quarto tract is extant, entitled, *A true and impartial relation of the Informations against three Witches, who were indicted, arraigned, and convicted at* Exon., *August* 14, 1682, *with their several Confessions.* This refers to the same events and persons as our Roxburghe Ballad, and thus furnishes the date, usefully, since the colophon is lost from this unique broadside-ballad (J. Deacon's).

Another quarto tract, on the same subject, is extant: *The Tryal, Condemnation, and Execution of Three Witches*; viz. Temperance Floyd [*properly* Lloyd] Mary Floyd [*otherwise* Trembles], *and* Susanna Edwards, *who were arraigned at* Exeter *on the* 18*th of August*, 1682. *And being proved guilty of Witchcraft were condemned to be hanged which was accordingly Executed* [on 25 August] *in the view of many Spectators*, etc. Printed for *J. Deacon*, at the Sign of the *Rainbow*, a little beyond St. *Andrew's* Church, in *Holborn*, 1682.

One *Thomas Eastchurch* lived at *Bideford, Devon*, with his undeceased wife *Elizabeth's* maiden sister, *Grace Thomas*, whose nervous attacks were attributed to witchcraft. Suspicion fell on *Temperance Lloyd*, against whom informations were sworn at a Town-hall inquisition on Sunday, 3rd July. After arrest, she incriminated the two other women. She had been in similar trouble in 1670, about Wm. Herbert's death, but was acquitted. The new evidence was hearsay, but the harassed culprits believed themselves guilty. Lord Keeper North wrote a letter about it, still extant, from Exeter, dated 19 August, to Sir Leoline Jenkins.

King Lear and his Three Daughters.

" My grandsire, *Bladud* hight, that found the Bathes by skill, [*Bath, c.* 441 B.C.
A fethered king that practisde for to flye and soare;
Whereby he felt the fall, God wot, against his will,
And neuer went, rode, raign'd, nor spake, nor flew no more.
Who dead, his sonne my father *Leire* therefore
Was chosen King, by right apparent heyre,
Which after built the towne of *Leircestere.* [= *Leicester.*

" He had three daughters, first and oldest hight *Gonerell,*
Next after her, my sister *Ragan* was begote;
The third and last was I, the yongest, named *Cordell,* [*a.l. Cordila.*
And of vs all our father *Leire* in age did dote.
So minding her that lou'd him best to note,
Because he had no sonne t' enioye his lande,
He thought to giue, where fauour most he fande. [= found.

" What though I yongest were, yet men me iudg'd more wise
Then either *Gonerell* or *Ragan,* had more age;
And fayrer farre: wherefore my sisters did despise
My grace and gifts, and sought my praise t' swage.
But yet though vice gainst vertue die with rage,
It cannot keepe her vnderneath to drowne;
For still she flittes aboue, and reapes renowne.

" [My father] thought to wed vs vnto nobles three, or Peeres,
And vnto them and theirs diuide and part the lande:
For both my sisters first he call'd (as first their yeares
Requir'd), their minds and loue and fauour t' vnderstand.
(Quoth he) 'All doubts of dutie to aband,
I must assaye and eke your frendships proue:
Now tell me eche how much you do me loue?' "

—*A Mirour for Magistrates,* 1574 (fol. 48).

TO no reasonable person can there be difficulty in arriving at the conclusion that, if our present ballad of " King Leir and his Three Daughters " (of a date before 1620) were not founded on Shakespeare's tragedy of " King Lear," certainly the tragedy was not on the ballad. The external evidence supports this view, in addition to the fact that there was already a drama at the playhouse when Shakespeare's noble modification of it, amounting to a new creation, in December, 1606 (acted at Whitehall during the Christmas holidays, before James I.), gave us the completed work; two editions of which were printed in 1608, each bearing the name "M. William Shake-speare" at the top of their title-page. There being plenty of people in the world who are not wise, but otherwise, an auditory always awaits the irrational iconoclasts of the Donnelly order (*cf.* p. 720), maniacs of 'fads' and delusion , prone to 'believe a lie' or any absurdity sufficiently idiotic. To them may be left an opinion that the ballad-writer created the story. But whether he availed himself of Shakespeare's tragedy or of the two previous dramas on the subject (one of which may have been more closely followed by Shakespeare than the *Chronicle History*), or of Holinshed, Higgins, Warner, and Spenser, are different questions, less easily answered.

Our ballad-text is (virtually unchanged) the text of Richard Johnson's black-letter volume, *The Golden Garland of Princely Pleasures and delicate Delights*, the third time imprinted, 1620. No copy of the earlier editions is known, and even this one is nearly unique, an exemplar that belonged to Mr. Corser. The contents ensuring popularity, such a book would take few months to reach a third edition, and therefore we may feel certain that it could not possibly have appeared before 1616, the year of Shakespeare's death, when his tragedy had already been printed in quarto for eight years. Johnson gave this ballad the foremost place: it shows his own opinion of its attractiveness, and there had probably been a previous issue of it on a broadside, but the four years must amply cover this date of earliest publication.

The names of the daughters, in *The Golden Garland*, are Ragan, Gonorell, and Cordella (Shakespeare's Regan, Goneril, and Cordelia: names adopted in the modernized ballad-broadside). We follow the authentic black-letter text of the *Garland*, despite the variations or corruptions of R. Marshall's Aldermary Churchyard reprint, except the proper names. A second version is on our p. 717.

"*The moste famous Chronicle historye of LEIRE Kinge of England and his three Daughters*" was entered to Edward White on 14th of May, 1594, in the Stationers' Registers, B. fol. 307 (*cf. Transcript*, ii. 649), but no copy of earlier date than 1605 is now known. Shakespeare's tragedy is thus entered, "1607.—5 Regis. 26 *Novembris.* Nathanael Butter [and] John Busby. Entred for theer copie vnder t. handes of Sir George Buck, Knight, and th. Wardens, A book called Mr. William Shakespeare his '*historye of Kinge Lear*,' as yt was played before the kinges maiestie at Whitehall vppon Sainct Stephans night at Christmas Last by his maiesties servantes playinge vsually at the Globe on the Banksyde." (*Stationers' Registers.* C. 161 *verso* = *Transcript*, iii. 366: *cf.* J. O. Halliwell-Phillipps's *Outlines of the Life of Shakespeare*, sixth edition, 1886, i. 306). Steevens deduces (from the names of the fiends in "Lear" coinciding with those in Dr. Harsnet's *Discovery of Egregious Popish Impostures*) that the tragedy could not have been written as a whole before 1603: with which opinion we agree.

The subject of King Lear and his Daughters had long been familiar to the public. Geoffrey of Monmouth had told of it, and Holinshed had followed him. In that vast quarry of saddening monologues known as *A Mirour for Magistrates: being a true Chronicle Historie of the vntimely falles of such vnfortunate Princes and men of note*, etc., John Higgins's ninth portion (1575) tells "*How Queene Cordila in dispaire slew her selfe*, the yeare before Christ 800." Beginning thus, "If any wofull wight haue cause to waile her woe, Or griefes are past do pricke vs, Princes, tell our fall," Cordila the self-slain relates the story of her house. She wins the battle, with the aid of the French arms, and restores her father to his throne, so that he reigns for "three years in peace, after that he died." Her five years of untroubled rule is described.

"And I was Queene the kingdome after still to hold,
Till fiue yeares past I did this Island guyde;
I had the *Britaynes* at what becke and bay I wolde,
Till that my louing King, myne *Aganippus*, dyed.
But then my seat it faltered on each side. [*al. lect.*
My sisters sonnes began with me to iarre, ['Two churlish Imps.'
And for my crowne wag'd with me mortall warre."

One is Morgan, Prince of Albany; one Conidagus, King of Cornwall and Wales (ill omened, contentious place at all times). They prevail against the widowed queen and she is taken prisoner. Hopeless of redress or escape, after long suffering in her dungeon, she is tempted by Despair, and stabs herself. The next history tells of retribution, "*How King Morgan of Albany was Slaine at Glamorgan in Wales,* the year before Christ, 766," Morgan having quarrelled with his cousin Conidagus, son of Ragan; who is left in possession.

On 1st of December, 1589, Edmund Spenser published the early portions of his *Faerie Queene*; in Book II. canto x., "A Chronicle of Briton Kings, from *Brute* to *Uther's* rayne," lines 240 to 293 are devoted to "King Leyr and his daughters, Gonorill, Regan, and Cordelia." Six stanzas: we give the second and sixth:—

The eldest *Gonorill*, 'gan to protest 248
That she much more then her owne life him lou'd:
And *Regan* greater loue to him profest,
Then all the world, when euer it were proou'd; ['Then' = than: *passim.*
But *Cordeill* said she lou'd him, as behoou'd:
Whose simple answere, wanting colours fayre
To paint it forth, him to displeasance moou'd,
That in his crowne he counted her no hayre,
But twixt the other twain his kingdome whole did shayre.

So to his crowne she him restor'd againe, 285
In which he dyde, made ripe for death by eld,
And after wild, it should to her remaine;
Who peaceably the same long time did weld,
And all men's harts in dew obedience held;
Till that her sisters' children, woxen strong
Through proud ambition, against her rebel'd,
And ouercommen kept in prison long,
Till wearie of that wretched life, her selfe she hong.[1]

Note.—Not self-immolated, either with rope or dagger, was the later Cordelia "to be done to death," but by the hands of murderers at Edmund's bidding. Nor could Shakespeare tolerate the bathos of restoring the heart-stricken King Lear to the sovereignty which he had relinquished, and for which he knew himself to be no longer fitted. On this subject the final word was spoken in 1811 by Charles Lamb:—"A happy ending! as if the living martyrdom that Lear had gone through, the flaying of his feelings alive, did not make a fair dismissal from the stage of life the only decorous thing for him. If he is to live and be happy after, if he could sustain the world's burden after, why all this pudder and preparation? Why torment us with all this unnecessary sympathy? As if the childish pleasure of getting his gilt robes and sceptre again could tempt him to act over again his misused station; as if at his years, and with his experience, anything was left but to die."—(*Theatralia:* L. Hunt's *Reflector*, ii. 309).

Of King Leir and his Three Daughters.

(*From Warner's 'Albion's England,' Booke 3rd,* 1589.)

ABout a thirtie yeares and fiue did *Leir* rule this Land,
When, doting on his Daughters three, with them he fell in hand
To tell how much they loued him. The Eldest did esteeme
Her life inferior to her loue, so did the Second deeme:
The Yongest sayd her loue was such as did a childe behoue,
And that how much himselfe was worth, so much she him did loue.
The formost two did please him well, the yongest did not so:
Upon the Prince of *Albanie* the First he did bestoe:
The Middle on the *Cornish* Prince: their Dowrie was his Throne,
At his decease: *Cordella's* parte was very small or none
Yet for her forme, and vertuous life, a noble *Gallian* King
Did her, vn-dowed, for his Queene into his Countrie bring.

Her Sisters sicke of Fathers health, their Husbands by consent
Did ioyne in Armes: from *Leir* so by force the Scepter went:
Yet, for they promise pentions large, he rather was content.
In *Albanie* the quondam king at eldest Daughters Court
Was setled scarce, when she repynes and lessens still his Port,
His second Daughter then, he thought, would shewe her selfe more kinde,
To whom, he going, for a while did franke allowance finde.
Ere long, abridging almost all, she keepeth him so loe,
That of two badds, for betters choyse he backe agayne did goe.
But *Gonorill* at his returne, not only did attempt
Her father's death, but openly did hold him in contempt.

His aged eyes powre out their teares, when holding vp his hands,
He sayd: 'O God, who so thou art, that my good hap withstands,
Prolong not life, deferre not death, my selfe I ouer-liue,
When those that owe to me their liues, to me my death would giue.
Thou Towne, whose walles rose of my wealth, stand euermore to tell
Thy Founder's Fall, and warne that none do fall as *Leir* fell.
Bid none affie in Frends, for say, his Children wrought his wracke:
Yea, those, that were to him most deare, did lothe and let him lacke.
Cordella, well *Cordella* sayd, she loued as a Childe:
But sweeter words we seeke than sooth, and so are men begilde.
She only rests vntryed yet: but what may I expect
From her? to whom I nothing gaue, when these do me reiect.
Then dye, nay trye, the rule may fayle, and Nature may ascend:
Nor are they euer surest friends, on whom we most do spend.

He ships himselfe to *Gallia* then, but maketh knowne before
Unto *Cordella* his estate, who rueth him so poore,
And kept his there ariuall close, till she prouided had
To furnish him in euery want. Of him her King was glad,
And nobly intertayned him: the Queene, with teares among,
(Her ductie done) conferreth with her father of his wrong.
Such ductie, bountie, kindnes, and increasing loue, he found
In that his Daughter and her Lord, that sorrowes more abound
For his vnkindly vsing her, then for the others' crime.
And King-like thus in *Agamp's* Court did *Leir* dwell, till time
The noble King his Sonne-in-law transports an Armie greate,
Of forcie *Gaules*, possessing him of dispossessed Seate,
To whom *Cordella* did succeede, not raigning long in queate.

But how her Nephewes warre on her, and one of them slew th' other
Shall followe: but I will disclose a most tyrannous Mother. [*i.e.* Q. *Iden.*

[*Next 'Chapter' tells of Ferrex and Porrex: subject of Lord Brooke's tragedy.*]

Of all that is grandest and sweetest in the marvellous tragedy of "King Lear" our Shakespeare was the sole author. He made those dry bones live. According to his custom, as in *Othello* and *Macbeth*, he compresses time, and hurries on events, to accelerate the dramatic action. This trick (for in "Othello" it is indeed marvellous subtlety; as was demonstated in the *Dies Boreales* of 'Christopher North,') is such as others often used, among the dramatists. But none like Shakespeare could have lifted the self-indulgent doting king into his sublimity of outraged grandeur; claiming kindred with the heavens because they themselves are old; from the pitiful down-trodden supplicant for the cast-off scraps at his daughter's kitchen. Seldom, except by the cleansing and ennobling touch of Death's forefinger, do we see upraised, for a brief hour, an abject, contemned human castaway, crowned anew with the immortal radiance: such as Caroline Bowles had the grace and tenderness to show in her "Pauper's Death-Bed." But in Lear the transformation is even yet more wonderful, for it comes in this present life, and after the second childishness had begun. The man turns mad, phrenzied by his wrongs that outrage the laws divine and human; then at once the heavens take his part. In that wild scene of elemental storm upon the heath, mocked with the heartless assumption of 'Tom à Bedlam' craziness by Edgar, careful only of himself, the tearful half-witted affection and bewilderment of the poor Fool deepening the horror by his incongruous sarcasms, while loyalty is shown by Kent and by ill-starred Gloucester, soon to pay a heavy price for his fidelity, the gradual descent from reason to unreason of him who is, even in that terrific hour, "every inch a king"—one "more sinned against than sinning,"—is such as no other enchantment could have conceived or embodied. Far away, far above all suggestions of the prosaic chroniclers, ballad-mongers, and early weavers of dramatic tissue, to regions that are swept by the wings of none but Jove's noblest ministers—Æschylus, Sophocles and Dante, these his only peers—Shakespeare has lifted our thoughts, from the paltriness of human crime and folly, into contemplation of the eternal verities. We know once more, what amid the petty chicanery had been well nigh forgotten, that there is a God Who judges wrong-doing, and holds unerringly the balance.

No restoration to his shattered throne, no short-lived pampering with splendour or luxury, that in almost superhuman or prophetic insight he had awakened to understand and to scorn, was necessary for Lear, or was possible. Kent speaks the verdict of all true thinkers, when he pleads for his master the right to die in peace:

Kent.—"Vex not his ghost. O let him pass! He hates him
That would upon the rack of this tough world
Stretch him out longer."
Edgar.— "He is gone, indeed."

[Roxburghe Collection, III. 512. B. M., 1876, e. I. fol. 27 p.m.]

[A Lamentable Song of the Death of]
King Leare and his Three Daughters.

[To the Tune of *When Flying Fame.* See Note, p. 672.]

King *Leare* once ruled in this land, with princely [power] and peace:
And had all things with [heart's] content, that might his ioyes encrease.
Amongst those [gifts] that nature gaue, three daughters faire had he,
So princely seeming beautifull, as fayrer could not be.

So on a time it pleas'd the King, a question thus to mooue:
Which of his daughters to his grace could shew the dearest love:
"For to my age you bring content," quoth he, "then let me heare,
Which of you three in plighted troth the kindest will appeare?"

To [whom] the eldest [thus] began, "Deare father [mine]," (quoth she,) ["this . . . first . . mild."
"Before your face to doe you good my blood shall tend'red be:
And for your sake my bleeding heart shall heere be cut in twaine,
'Ere that I see your reuerend age the smallest griefe sustaine."

"And so will I," the second said, "Deare father, for your sake,
The worst of all extremities I'le [gently] undertake. ["for you."
And serue your highnesse night and day, with diligence and loue;
That sweet content and [quietnesse] discomforts may remoue."

"In doing so, you glad my soule," the aged [King] reply'd.
"But what say'st thou, my yongest Girle? How stands thy loue allyed?"
"My loue," quoth young *Cordelia*, then, "which to your grace I owe,
Shall be the duty of a childe, and that is all I'le [shew]."

"And wilt thou shew no more," (quoth he,) "than doth thy duty binde?
I well perceiue thy love is small, when as no more I finde.
Hence forth I banish thee my Court; thou art no child of mine:
Nor any part of this my Realme by fauour shall be thine."

Thy elder sisters' [loues are] more than well I can demand;
To whome I equally bestow my kingdome and my land,
My pomp[all] state and all my goods, that louingly I may
With these thy sisters be maintain'd, vntill my dying day."

Thus flattering speeches won renowne, by these two sisters here:
The third had causeless banishment, yet was her loue most deare:
For poor *Cordelia* patiently went wand'ring vp and downe,
Unhelp'd, vnpity'd, gentle maid, thro' many an English towne.

Untill at last, in famous *France*, she gentler fortunes found:
Though poore and bare, yet was she deem'd the fairest on the ground.
Where when the King her vertues heard, and this fair lady seene,
With full consent of all [his] Court he made her his wife and Queene.

Her father, old king *Leare*, this while with his two daughters stayed,
Forgetful of their promis'd loues, full soon the same denaide,
And liuing in Queen *Regan's* Court, the elder of the twaine,
She tooke from him his chiefest meanes, and most of all his traine,

[For] whereas twenty men were wont to waite with bended knee;
She gaue allowance but to ten, and after scarce to three.
Nay, one she thought too much for him, so tooke she all away:
In hope that in her Court, good King! he would no longer stay.

"Am I rewarded thus?" [quoth] he, "in giving all I haue
Unto [my] children? and to beg for what I want or crave?
I'le goe unto my *Gonoril*, my second child I know [a.l. lately gaue.
Will be more kinde and [pittifull] and will relieue my woe."

Full fast he hies unto her Court, where when she heard his moane,
Return'd him answer that she grieu'd that all his meanes were gone.
But no way could relieue his wants, yet, if that he would stay,
Within her kitchen, he should haue what Scullions gaue away.

When he had heard, with bitter teares, he made his answer then,
"In what I did, let me be made example to all men.
I will returne again," [quoth] he, "vnto my *Ragan's* Court;
She will not vse me thus, I hope, but in a kinder sort."

Where, when he came, she gaue command to driue him thence away;
When he was well within [her] Court, (she said) he could not stay;
Then backe againe to *Gonoril*, the wofull King did hie:
That in her kitchen he might haue what Scullion [boyes] set by.

But there of that he was denied, which she had promis'd late;
For once refusing he should not come after to her gate. [a.l. one.
Thus 'twixt his daughters, for reliefe, he wand'red vp and downe,
Being glad to feed on beggar's food, that lately wore a Crowne,

And calling to remembrance then his yongest daughter's words,
That said, 'the duty of a childe had all that loue affords.'
But doubting to repaire to her, whom he had banish'd so,
Grew franticke mad, [for] in his minde he bore the wounds of woe.

Which made him rend his milk white locks and tresses from his head;
And all with blood bestaine his cheekes, with age and honour spred:
To hills and woods, and wat'ry founts, he made his hourely moane;
Till hills and woods, and senceless things, did seem to sigh and groane.

Euen thus [possest] with discontents, he passed o're to *France*,
In hope from [faire] *Cordelia* there to find some gentler chance.
Most vertuous dame! where, when she heard of this her father's griefe,
As in duty bound, she quickly sent him comfort and reliefe.

And by a traine of noble Peeres, in braue and gallant sort,
She gaue in charge he should be brought to *Aganippus's* Court;
Her royall King, whose noble minde so freely gaue consent,
To muster up his knights at armes, to fame and courage bent.

And so to *England* came with speed, to repossesse King *Leare*,
And driue his daughters from their thrones by his *Cordelia* deare.
Where she, true-hearted noble Queene, was in the battell slaine;
Yet he, good King, in his old dayes, possess'd his crowne againe.

But when he heard *Cordelia* dead, who dy'd indeed for loue
Of her deare Father, in whose cause she did this battell moue;
He swounding fell vpon her breast, from whence he neuer parted,
But on her bosome left his life, that was so truely hearted. 88

The Lords and Nobles when they saw the end of these events,
The other Sisters vnto death they doomed by consents;
And being dead their crownes [were] left vnto the next of kin:
Thus haue you heard the fall of pride, and disobedient sinne.

[Written by **Richard Johnson**, printed before 1620.]

Printed and Sold by *R. Marshall, Aldermary Church-Yard, Bow-Lane, London.*

[White-letter broadside with one large woodcut of Cordelia going away weeping—Lear throned, in Georgian robes and crown, at centre, the other daughters sit on chairs at his right hand. In this late broadside the names are in accord with Shakespeare, *Cordelia*, *Gonevil*, and *Regan*; but in the 1620 *Garland* they had appeared as *Cordela*, *Gonorell*, and *Ragan*. There are some few corruptions of text in the broadside: *pride* for power, in 1st line; *things* for gifts, etc.]

*** The following additional version of "The tragical History of King *Leare* and his Three Daughters" belongs no less to our Roxburghe Collection. This broadside has not previously been reprinted. A modernized rescension of Richard Johnson's earlier black-letter ballad (*viz.* our pp. 714-716), it shows the continued popularity of the story. (Fifty years ago, in a melodrama, entitled "*The Lear of Private Life*," Dibdin Pitt held the *rôle* of the persecuted father.)

Name of printers or publishers, and of tune, left unmentioned on the two Roxburghe and Douce broadsides, modern, in White-letter, of the *Aldermary* and *Bow Church-yard* type, with a large central woodcut of a King and Queen in (Hanoverian) royal robes; a Cupid fluttering above each figure bearing a crown and palm-branch. Four small cuts surround this: one is the lady of our p. 13; another is a quaint cut (see J. P. Collier's *Black-letter Ballads*, p. 1, 1868).

[Roxburghe Collection, III. 275; Douce, III. 52.]

Tragical History of King Lear, and his three Daughters: *First*, Shewing how he gave the two Eldest the full and whole Possession of his Crown. *Second*, How he banish'd the Youngest his Court and Presence, who fled into *France*, and married the *French* King. *Third*, How his two eldest Daughters, in some time after, took away his Attendance, and turn'd him out of Court, when, being destitute, he travelled into *France*, where his youngest Daughter relieved him, raised an Army to restore him to the Possession of his Crown, in the Attempt of which she was kill'd in the Field of Battle, and her Father immediately died with Grief for the Loss of his Daughter.

Part I.

A Certain great King once did rule over this Land,
Who had all the pleasure a King could command,
And liv'd in great Splendour with Honour and Peace,
He reign'd many years not without great Increase.

He had three fine Daughters, of Beauty most bright,
In whom this same King he did take much delight;
For Virtue and Wisdom none could them come near,
Which caused their Father to love them most dear.

The King had a fancy to try all their Love,
Which pleased him well then this Question to move,
To see which of them then did love him the best,
So call'd them before him the Truth to protest.

"For unto my Joy and Comfort I see
Three beautiful Children do stand before me:
Now which of you three will do most for my Sake,
Suppose that my Life now should lie at the Stake?"

To which then the Elder did make this reply,
"The worst of all Deaths for thy sake I could die,
With the greatest of Tortures that Nature can name;
O this I will bear for your Majesty's Fame!"

The second made answer, "My Love is more dear
Than ever my Sister's, as it shall appear;
Although she expresses much fidelity,
My Love shall be seen unto your Majesty."

"Well spoke, my dear Daughters," the aged King said,
"My heart is enamour'd, and [nearly] betray'd; {'meerely'
But what says my youngest Girl? prithee tell me,
I want to hear thy Love amongst all the three."

"My Love," said the youngest, "that I to you owe,
Is the abundant duty a Child ought to show;
To honour my Father until that I die,
And ne'er in extremity from you will fly."

"Thy Love is but small," said the King, "I do find,
That you'll show no more than what Nature doth bind;
I thought you had Reason to be as sincere
As your eldest Sister, who loves me most dear.

"Henceforth I do banish you quite from my Court,
And charge you no more in my Presence resort;
I justly may say, thou art no Child of mine,
Because you in Love from the rest do decline.

"So I will make over my Scepter and Crown
To your eldest Sisters of fame and renown;
And they shall be Heirs to my whole Land,
For all that I have shall be at their command.

"My pompous Estate, nay, and my noble Train,
For those thy two Sisters shall be to maintain;
That peaceable now I may pass my Time away,
And live with my Daughters till my dying Day."

Part II.

The Youngest Daughter's Misfortune; of her travelling into France; *and how the King of* France *made her his Queen.*

THEIR flatt'ring speeches at length won his Heart,
But now mind at length how he had his Desert;
For his youngest Daughter's causeless Banishment,
The which he had Reason e'er long to repent.

For his poor young Daughter she wander'd up and down,
Through many a Village and brave *English* Town;
Because that her Father held her in Disdain,
She then did resolve for to cross o'er the Main.

At length to fair *France* then this fair Lady came,
The King then perceiving this beautiful Dame,
He quickly was wounded by young *Cupid's* Dart,
Which deeply did wound him to the very heart.

Likewise the King of her Virtues had heard,
His heart was more and more to her endear'd;
Said he, "That my love to her shall be seen,
Before my whole Court I will make her my Queen."

Her aged old Father is now all the while
With his eldest Daughters, who soon did beguile
Him of his whole Kingdom, nay, Scepter and Crown,
And quickly their aged old Father pull'd down.

The King for a while in his Court did remain,
But his eldest Daughter soon lessen'd his Train;
Then after so done, she did quickly contrive
Him of all his riches and means to deprive.

Whereas twenty Men he was wont for to have,
To wait and attend on his Majesty grave;
She lessen'd his Number, and brought him to ten,
And quickly reduc'd them to only three Men.

Nay, one she thought much for her Father to have,
She took him away, that her Father might leave
The Court and begone, and there no longer stay,
Which grieved the King, and made him thus say,

"Am I thus rewarded," the King then reply'd,
To be of my own at this rate so deny'd?
It grieveth my heart to think what I've done,
But now to my second Child I'll make my moan."

Part III.

How the King was dethron'd by his two eldest Daughters; and how his youngest Daughter restored him again.

"MY second dear Daughter with pity, I know,
Will quickly consider my sorrow and woe;
I'll go now unto her, and tell her my Grief,
I make no doubt but she'll afford me Relief."

The King he full fast to the Court then did go,
Desiring his sorrows for to let her know;
She made him this Answer, "That she was much griev'd
For all these repulses that he had receiv'd;

"But no ways could help him in this his Distress,
Nor yet in the least could afford him Redress;
But if he a while in the Kitchen would stay,
She'd order him such as the Scullions give away."

The King made this Answer to his Daughter then,
"Surely, I am served the worst of all men;
For doing as I did by my Daughter dear,
Which makes me lament, and shed many a tear.

"To my eldest Daughter again I'll return,
Perhaps she'll give ear to my pitiful moan."
Then straitway he went again to the Court,
In hopes to find her in a better sort.

And when he came there she straitway gave command,
For to have him sent away out of hand;
And order'd them quickly to drive him away,
Saying, "That in her Court he no longer should stay."

Then he to his second Child again did hie,
To eat of her scraps that her Scullion set by,
For such as for Charity ask'd at the door,
Which grieved the King to the heart more and more.

But there of her Promise he then was deny'd,
Which caused the King to be dissatisfy'd;
"For on his refusing her offer most kind,"
She said, "At her gate he small comfort should find."

Calling to remembrance his young Daughter's word,
It did to his grief new sorrow afford;
To think how he had this poor creature beguil'd
Of all her whole Fortune, and ruin'd the child.

Which made him be troubled, nay, to rave and tear,
And rending the locks of his silver hair,
Which was such an ornament to his old Age;
Yet nothing at all could his trouble asswage.

To rocks, and to rivers, and wat'ry founts,
To hills, and to woods, and the highest of mounts,
He made his Complaint, and his hourly moan,
Until at length all those things seem'd to [groan]. [text, "moan."

Then being thus possest with discontent,
Being fully resolv'd, he over Sea went,
And soon found his Daughter, being Queen of *France*,
Which made him amazed at her noble chance.

Most virtuous Lady! when this she did hear,
She sent for her Father, in duty most dear;
"Most welcome are you, my reverend Lord,
To what my whole Kingdom and Court doth afford."

Then her noble King, for to grace his Queen,
Shew'd him all the honour and love could be seen;
He for his whole Court then of Noblemen sent,
For [on] great acclamations of joy they were bent.

But as they in banqueting merrily were,
She said, "My dear Father, how goes your affairs?"
"Indeed, my dear Daughter, I quite am disown'd
By your eldest Sisters, who have me dethron'd."

Then she started up from the Table, and said,
"Of my cruel Sisters, who have me betray'd,
I will be revenged, and that instantly,
If that I am sure in the Battle to die."

The King and his Nobles did soon Answer make,
"My honoured Queen, for your dear Father's sake,
We'll venture our lives to see him on the Throne
In spight of all those that do him disown."

Then straight unto *England* they came in great haste,
But now comes the Tragedy here at the last;
The Fight was no sooner begun, to be plain,
But this noble Queen in the Battle was slain.

The Queen being dead, [w]hen her Father espy'd, ["then."
He laid himself by her, and instantly dy'd;
Then straightway seeing this sudden event,
They put the two Daughters to Death by consent.

The Crown was left vacant, for want of an Heir,
There being none equal the Crown for to wear;
The [Throne] was left useless, being without King; [" Crown."
So sad Disobedience is the wo[r]st of all Sin.

[Colophon cut off. White-letter, modern: See p. 716. Original date, *circâ* 1670.]

*** Since our p. 576 went to press, the be-trumpetted "*Great Cryptogram*" (prophesied to be fatal for ever to Shakespeare's fame), has whizzed and puffed, not as a rocket but as a squib, in the month of *un poisson d'Avril.* A faint odour of brimstone and a few inglorious sparks remain. *Sic non sequitur ad Astra.*

IGN. DONY.

PALTRY traducer of our Shakespeare's *name,*
Conceited egotist, spawn'd in the West,
Spitting thy venom, one sole chance of fame
Thy croaking notoriety as Pest;
'Mid Time's roll-call of follies, thou shalt claim
To have endorsed anew the silliest craze,
When men shall talk of Indignatius' *days,*
The mare's-nest Cryptogram, and Bacon's *shame.*
Thy petty malice hobbles blind and lame,
Mock'd by true scholars as a pointless jest,
Though quidnuncs echo while the Long-eared brays.

25 V. '88. J. W. E.

Lancelott du Lac.

. . . . . "Joyfully
Her cheek grew crimson, as the headlong speed
Of the roan charger drew all men to see,
The knight who came was Launcelot at good need."
—Wm. Morris's *Defence of Guenevere*, 1858.

THOMAS DELONEY is the accredited author of this ballad: in his *Garland of Good Will*. It is deludingly mis-named, for it tells nothing of the kingly acts of Arthur—but is merely a spirited episode (Sir Lancelot's combat with Tarquin), adapted from Sir Thomas Malory's *Morte d'Arthur*, Caxton, 1485: a work nobly reproduced by Dr. H. O. Sommer, 1889. (Arthur as the "blameless King" is shorn of his strength by Alfred Tennyson: "King Arthur as a modern gentleman.") Here is the concluding estimate of Sir Lancelot du Lac:—

"Then went Syr *Bors* vnto Syr *Ector*, and told hym how there laye hys brother Syr *Launcelot* dead. And then Syr *Ector* threw hys shielde, his swerd and hys helme from hym. And when hee beheld Syr *Launcelot's* visage, hee fell downe in a sowne. And when he awaked, it were harde for anie tongue to tell the dolefull complayntes, that he made for hys brother. 'Ah, Syr *Launcelotte*,' sayde hee, 'thou were head of all Chrystian Knyghtes, and now I dare saye,' sayde Syr *Bors*, 'that Syr *Launcel*, there thou lyest, thou were neuer matched of none earthlie Knyghtes handes. And thou were the curtiest Knyght that euer beare sheelde. And thou were the truest frende to thy louer that euer bestrood horse. And thou were the truest louer of a sinful man that euer loued woman. And thou were the kindest man that euer strooke wyth swerde. And thou were the goodlyest parson that euer came among presse of knyghtes. And thou were the meekest man and the gentlest that euer eat in Hall among Ladyes. And thou were the sterneste Knyght to thy mortall foe that euer put speere in the rest.' Then there was weepyng and dolour out of measure."—*Morte d'Arthur*, 1557 ed.

Although uttered in the *Sturm und Drang Zeit* of incongruous thoughts and commands, the opening line of our ensuing ballad having been warmly quoted by Sir John Falstaffe (*King Henry the Fourth*, Part II. Act ii. scene 4), is sufficient to renew the bill at interest for many succeeding generations:—

"When *Arthur* first in court . . . And was a worthy king!"

This identifies it, and Shakespeare knew the whole. What did he not know?

Malevole quotes the same line, "When *Arthur* first in Court began," in John Marston's *Malcontent*, Act ii. scene 2, 1604 (Arthur Bullen's edition, i. 240). Beaumont and Fletcher's *La Writ* (*The Little French Lawyer*, Act ii. scene 3, 1616) gives, "Was ever man for Lady's sake? *Down, down!*" and other scraps of our Lancelot ballad, the fourth being a free imitation of Deloney:—

"He strook so hard, the bason broke,
And *Tarquin* heard the sound."
"And then he struck his neck in two."

"Thou fierce man that like Sir *Lancelot* doth appear,
I need not tell thee what I am, nor eke what I make here."
"'Oh, ho,' quoth *Lancelot* though."

With his usual quick merry humour, Fletcher hits the blot, for in no other ballad is the rhyming eked out so frequently by the word "though" as it is here: in lines 25, 61, 82, 102, and 117. '*Oh, ho,*' *quoth* Lancelot *though*.

[Roxb. Coll., III. 25; Bagford, II. 14, 15; Pepys, II. 100; Wood, 401, fol. 62.]

The Noble Acts, newly found, Of Arthur of the Table Round.

To the Tune of, *Flying Fame* [See p. 672].

WHen *Arthur* first in Court began, and was approved King,
By force of arms great victories won, and conquest home did bring,
Then into *Brittain* straight he came, where fifty stout and able
Knights then repaired unto him which were of the round Table.

And many J[o]usts and Turnaments before him there were prest,
Wherein these knights did then excel, and far surmount the rest;
But one Sir *Lancelot du Lake*, who was approved well,
He in his fights and deeds of Arms all others did excel. 16

When he had rested him awhile, to play, and game, and sport,
He thought he would approve himself in some adventurous sort;
He armed rode in Forrest wide, and met a Damsel fair,
Who told him of adventures great, whereto he gave good ear.

"Why should I wot?" (quoth *Lancelot* tho') "for that cause came I hither!"
"Thou seem'st" (quo' she), "a knight right good, and I will bring thee thither
Whereas the mightiest knight doth dwell, that now is of great fame:
Wherefore tell me what knight thou art, and then what is thy name."

"My name is *Lancelot du Lake*." Quoth she, "It likes me then;
Here dwells a knight that never was o're matcht of any man;
Who hath in prison threescore knights, and some that he hath bound,
Knights of King *Arthur's* Court they be, and of the Table round."

She brought him to a river then, and also to a tree, 42
Whereas a copper bason hung, his fellows' shields to see;
He struck so hard the bason broke, when *Tarquin* heard the sound,
He drove a horse before him straight, whereon a knight was bound.

'*Mu*.. (then said Sir *Lancelot*) bring me that horse-load hither,
To hare .. *When men*..n and let him rest, we'l try our force together:
The mare's-ne..d, thou hast, as far as thou art able,
Thy petty mali..and shame unto the knights of the round Table."
Mock'd by true
Though quidnunc..ble round," quoth *Tarquin*, speedily, 58
25 V. '88. ..fellowship I utterly defie."
—th *Lancelot* tho', "defend thee by and by."
.. their steeds, and each at other flye;

They couch their spears, and horses run, as though they had been thunder,
And each struck then upon the shield, wherewith they break asunder;
Their horses' backs brake under them, the knights were both astoned,
To void their horses they made haste to light upon the ground. 72

They took them to their shields full fast, their swords they drew out then,
With mighty strokes most eagerly each one at other ran:
They wounded were, and bled full sore, for breath they both did stand,
And leaning on their swords awhile, quoth *Tarquin*, "Hold thy hand,

"And tell to me what I shall ask." "Say on," quoth *Lancelot*, tho.
"Thou art," quoth *Tarquin*, "the best knight that ever I did know;
And like a knight that I did hate, so that thou be not he,
I will deliver all the rest, and eke accord with thee." 88

"That is well said," quoth *Lancelot*, then, "but sith it so must be,
What is that knight thou hatest so, I pray thee shew to me?"
"His name is Sir *Lancelot du Lake*, he slew my brother dear;
Him I suspect of all the rest, I would I had him here."

"Thy wish thou hast, but now unknown, I am *Lancelot du Lake*,
Now knight of *Arthur's* Table round, king *Hands'* son of *Benwake*;
And I defie thee, do thy worst!" "Ha, ha," quoth *Tarquin* tho',
"One of us two shall end their lives, before that we do go. 104

"If thou be *Lancelot du Lake*, then welcome shalt thou be;
Wherefore see thou thyself defend, for now I thee defie."

They hurled then together fast, like two wild Boars so rashing,
And with their Swords and Shields they ran, at one another flashing:
The ground besprinkled was with blood, *Tarquin* began to faint,
For he had backt and bore his Shield so low he did repent; 116

That soon espyed Sir *Lancelot* tho, he leapt upon him then,
He pull'd him down upon his knee, and rushed off his Helm;
And then he struck his neck in two, and when he had done so,
From Prison threescore Knights and four *Lancelot* delivered tho.

[Written by **Thomas Deloney**.]

London, Printed for *F. Coles, T. Vere & J. Wright*.

[In Black-letter, no woodcut. Wood's exemplar also was printed for *F. Coles*, etc.; the Pepysian for *Alex. Milbourne*, in *Green Arbor Court*, in the *Little Old Baily*. Two columns of verse, undivided into stanzas. Date, before 1600. *Cf.* Malory's *Morte d'Arthur*, Bk. vi. cap. 7, 8, 9 (=106-108, 1634). On p. 760 we give one of the woodcuts from Bk. ii. 1557].

⁂ Algernon Charles Swinburne condemned Tennyson's suppression of Arthur's sin that led to the birth of Mordred, consequently leaving absent any retribution in his rebellion. This was enforced in S.'s "*Under the Microscope*," his conclusive answer to the base and cowardly pseud-anonymous poison-stabs against Dante Rossetti by *Truth's* 'not possible' R.B. (*nominis umbra*) 'Thomas Maitland,' 1871.

St. George for England, and the Dragon.

"When many hardy strokes he'd dealt, and could not pierce his hide,
He run his sword up to the hilt, in at the Dragon's side;
By which he did his life destroy, which cheer'd the drooping King,
This caus'd an universal joy, sweet peals of Bells did ring."
—Rich. Johnson's *Seven Champions of Christendom.*

IT is very sad for a true-born Englishman to have to confess it, in the face of bumptious (far from 'gallant') "little Wales"—where Taffy was proverbially what he has continued to be in modern days, noted for petty-larceny, of tithes-rent or other small matters since Rebecca's daughters broke toll-gates; and with the certainty that the meek Scot and the rational law-abiding Irish Leaguer (when found) may take a mean advantage of us for being candid; but it is really impossible to get up any enthusiasm for St. George, patron saint though he be chosen of our noble land, and glorified on our desirable golden coinage. We prefer the Dragon. Of the two he appears to be the more sincere character. Ugly whispers have long been heard of the Bacon-seller of Cappadocia, and how he made money—as people in the Commissariat department of other than the Roman army have generally contrived to do, down to the Crimean epoch and that of more lamentable Sedan. Alban Butler has not much to chronicle concerning so lucky a saint, except his birthplace, his mother's return to Palestine, and the "considerable estate which fell to her son George," before he became "a tribune *or* Colonel in the army," his promotion by Diocletian, and later abandonment of profitable posts when the Christians were next persecuted, so that he underwent imprisonment and decapitation. We must turn to the *Legenda Aurea* for the mythological narrative of the Princess Sabra being saved from the Dragon, whom she binds with her girdle after it has been taught good manners by sundry spear wounds; and how the king her father, with 15,000 men, and any convenient number of women and children, are all at once converted and baptized, so soon as ever the ill-used Dragon has had his head cut off. We offer no objection to the four carts, drawn by oxen, required to carry off the Dragon's body from that city of Lybia called Sylene near the stagnant lake. While we were about it we would have conceded a dozen carts, if demanded: "How a score of bullocks?" as Justice Shallow used to say. "*Sir Bevis of Hampton*" furnished the materials ready made. We may suspect that the Sir Bevis legend and the St. George legend were misremembered echoes of Perseus and Andromeda, perhaps also of St. Michael trampling on the Arch-enemy; with a nobly caparisoned steed thrown in, to add the spice of novelty as an angel on horseback. But if such a thing were mentioned what a grievous outcry might be made by the folklore maunderers, and how quickly they would all resolve it into a Sun-myth or Nature-apologue. Sabra then becomes a snow-ball and the Dragon a hard frost, St. George *alias* Sol riding his last horse, counteracting the chill, and 'making it hot' for the Dragon.

The other Champions of Christendom belong to Richard Johnson.

Ours was an old ballad when it was mentioned by Ben Jonson in his comedy of *Bartholomew Fair*, Act ii. scene 1, October, 1614, where Nightingale proffers his songs:—

> *Nightingale.*—"Ballads, ballads! fine new ballads!—
> Hear for your love, and buy for your money,
> A delicate ballad o' the ferret and the coney . . .
> Or *St. George that O! did break the Dragon's heart.*"

Percy printed the ballad in his *Reliques*, vol. iii. book 3rd (p. 306 of edit. 1767), from an old black-letter copy in the Pepys Collection, "imprinted at London, 1612." (This is Pepys Coll., I. 87, *given on our* p. 780, *viz.* "Why do you boast of *Arthur* and his Knights?")

A totally different ballad on St. George and the Dragon, beginning, "Of *Hector's* deeds did *Homer* sing, and of the sack of stately *Troy*," is in Roxburghe Collection, I. 128; III. 620; III. 819; and has been already reprinted in these *Roxburghe Ballads*, vol. i. p. 380. Also reprinted in *Merry Drollery*, 1661, ii. 122, and in the *Antidote against Melancholy* of the same year; in *Wit and Drollery* of 1682, p. 273; and in *Wit and Mirth*, 1684, p. 29.

That our present ditty was imitated, mocked, or parodied by the saucy and unexpurgated "New Ballad of King Edward IV. and Jane Shore" needs no formal demonstration. The imitation was 'written by D. D——,' and circulated *circâ* 1672. Its authorship was fraudulently assigned to Samuel Butler, in so-called *Posthumous Works* of 1719, iii. p. 72. A copy of this imitative ballad is in Roxb. Coll., III. 258, but it is unsuitable for our present Group. It begins (correcting "*Laius*" into *Lais*) thus,

> Why should we boast of *Lais* and her knights?
> Knowing such champions entrapt by whorish lights;
> Or why should we speak of *Thais'* curled locks?
> Or *Rhodope* that gave so many men [worse shocks]?
> Read old stories, and there you shall find
> How *Jane Shore, Jane Shore,* she pleas'd King *Edward's* mind.
> Jane Shore *she was for* England, *Queen* Fridegond *was for* France,
> *Sing Honi soit qui mal y pense!*

It is also in the *Pills to Purge Melancholy*, iv. 273, 1719 edition; in J. Roberts's *Old Ballads*, i. 153, 1723; and Evans's, i. 324.

Another burlesque ballad, belonging no less to the Roxburghe Collection (III. 626), and no less delayed for the present to the final volume vii. of *Roxburghe Ballads*, is that describing the victory won by Moore of Moore Hall over the Dragon of Wantley, beginning, "Old stories tell how *Hercules* a Dragon slew at *Lerna*." Pepys copy was printed for Randal Taylor, near Stationers' Hall, 1685.

Even the absurdity of the perpetual shifting of characters throughout our present "St. George and the Dragon" made it the greater favourite. It became a roll-call of chivalric tales, and helped to amuse those who remembered the goodly books which are now found unreadable; prized as specimens of early printers in black-letter or MSS. for the E.E.Text Society. The same principle of cataloguing names, but with an admixture of double entendre or direct grossness, was kept in view for the Edward IV. and Jane Shore ballad (of *Roxb. Ballads*, Vol. VII.).

Our "St. George for England" had a long *Second Part* attached to it by John Grubb (1645-1697); this, printed in 1688, "*The British Heroes*, A New Poem in honour of St. *George*, by Mr. John Grubb, School-master of Christ-Church, Oxon," not being in the Roxburghe broadsides, and already accessible in Percy's *Reliques*, vol. iii., and *Pills to Purge Melancholy*, p. 303 (1699), or iii. 315 (1719), need not burden our crowded pages. It is terrifically long-winded, being twelve irregular stanzas, a total of 402 lines as usually printed, but compressible into half the number. It begins thus:—

The story of King *Arthur* old is very memorable,
The number of his valiant knights, and roundness of his Table,
The Knights around his Table in a circle sate, d'ye see:
And all together made up one large hoop of chivalry.
He had a Sword, both broad and sharp, y-cleped *Caliburn*, [= *Excalibur.*
'T would cut a flint more easily than pen-knife cuts a corn;
As case-knife does a Capon carve, so would it carve a rock,
And split a man at single slash, from noddle down to nock.
As *Roman* Augur's steel of yore dissected *Tarquin's* riddle, [poppy-heads.
So this would cut both conjuror and whetstone through the middle.
He was the cream of *Brecknock*, and flower of all the *Welsh*;
But *George* he did the Dragon fell, and gave him a plaguy squelch. [= crush.
St. George *he was for* England; St. Dennis *was for* France,
Sing, Honi soit qui mal y pense!

With a pleasant humour it mentions the amazon Thalestris:—

She kept the chasteness of a nun, in armour as in cloyster:
But *George* undid the Dragon just as you'd undo an oyster.

A unique modernization of our St. George ballad, entitled "St. George for England, and St. Dennis for France," is in Wood's Collection, 401, fol. 117, subscribed "S. S." (probably Samuel Shepherd), printed *circâ* 1659 for Wm. Gilbertson, in Guilt-Spur Street (tune in *Popular Music*, p. 287). It begins thus:—

What need we brag or boast at all of *Arthur* and his Knights,
Knowing how many gallant men they have subdued in fights;
For bold Sir *Lancelot du Lake* was of the Table Round;
And fighting for a lady's sake, his sword with fame was crown'd;
Sir *Tarquin*, that great giant his vassal did remain: [*Cf.* p. 723.
But St. *George*, St. *George*, the Dragon he hath slain.
St. George *he was for* England, St. Dennis *was for* France,
O honi soit qui mal y pense!

[Roxburghe Collection, III. 716, 720; Bagford, II. 16; Jersey, II. 219; C. 22. c. 2. fol. 4; (Pepys I. 87;) Euing, 222; Douce, III. 89.]

An Excellent Ballad of
St. George and the Dragon.

[The Tune is, *When Flying Fame*.]

WHy should we boast of *Arthur* and his Knights,
 Knowing how many Men have performed Fights?
Or why should we speak of Sir *Lancelot du Lake*, [*Cf.* p. 726.
Or Sir *Tristram du Leon*, that fought for Ladies' sake?
Read but old Stories, and there you shall see
How St. *George*, St. *George*, he made the Dragon flee.
 St. George *he was for* England, *St.* Dennis *was for* France,
 Sing, *Honi soit qui mal y Pense!*

Note.—As mentioned on p. 672, this tune (given in Chappell's *Popular Music*, p. 287) takes its name from a lost ballad, beginning "*When Flying Fame*." Quite distinct from "*When Busy Fame*," of date 1684: see the words on p. 102.

To speak of [the] Monarchs it were too long to tell,
And likewise to[o] the *Romans*, how far they did excel.
Hannibal and *Scipio* in many a Field did Fight;
Orlando Furioso, he was a valiant Knight;
Romulus and *Rhemus* were those that *Rome* did build;
But St. *George*, St. *George*, the Dragon he hath kill'd,
St. George *he was for* England, *St.* Dennis *was for* France, etc.

Jepthah and *Gideon* they led their Men to fight, [See *Note* p. 729.
The *Gibbionites* and *Ammonites*, they put them all to Flight:
Herculus and his Labour was in the Vale of *Bass*;
And *Sampson* slew a Thousand with the Jaw-bone of an Ass;
And, when he was blind, pull'd the Temple to the ground:
But St. *George*, St. *George*, the Dragon did confound.
St. George *he was for* England, *St.* Dennis *was for* France, etc.

Valentine and *Orson*, they came of *Pepin's* Blood;
Alfred and *Aldricus*, they were brave Knights and good;
The four Sons of *Ammon*, that fought with *Charlemain*, [*i.e. Aymon.*
Sir *Hugh*[*on*] *de Bourdeaux*, and *Godfrey de Bulloign*,
These were all *French* Knights, the *Pagans* to convert;
But St. *George*, St. *George*, he pull'd out the Dragon's Heart.
St. George *he was for* England, etc.

King *Henry* the Fifth, he conquered all *France*; [*Cf.* p. 744.
He quartered their Arms his Honour to advance:
He rased their walls, and pull'd their Cities down, [text, "rais'd."
And he garnish'd his Head with a double-tripple-Crown:
He thumped the *French*, and after Home he came;
But St. *George*, St. *George*, he made the Dragon tame.
St. George *he was for* England, etc.

St. *David*, you know, lov'd Leeks and toasted Cheese;
And *Jason* was the Man brought home the Golden Fleece;
And *Patrick*, you know, he was St. *George's* Boy; [*Suggestive, very!*
Seven years he kept his Horse, then stole him away,
For which knavish Act a Slave he doth remain:
But St. *George*, St. *George*, he hath the Dragon slain.
St. George *he was for* England, etc.

Tamerlane, the Emperor in Iron Cage did Crown, [*Sultan Bajazet.*
With all his bloody Flags display'd before the Town;
Scanderberg, magnanimous, *Mahomet's* Bashaws did dread,
Whose victorious Bones were worn when he was dead;
His *Beglerbegs* he scorn'd like dregs, *George Castriot* was he call'd:
But St. *George*, St. *George*, the Dragon he hath maul'd.
St. George *he was for* England, etc.

Ottoman the *Tartar*, he came of *Persia*'s Race;
The great *Mogul* with 's chest so full of cloves and mace;
The *Grecian* Youth, *Bucephalous* he manfully did bestride: [*Alex.*
But these, with their Worthies Nine, St. *George* did them deride.
Gustavus Adolphus was *Swedeland*'s warlike King:
But St. *George*, St. *George*, he pull'd forth the Dragon's sting.
St. George *he was for* England, etc.

Pendragon and *Cadwallader*, of *British* Blood do boast;
Tho' *John* of *Gaunt* his Foes did daunt, St. *George* shall rule the Roast:
Agamemnon and *Clemedon*, and *Macedon* did Feats:
But compared to our Champion, they are but meer Cheats.
Brave *Malta* Knights in *Turkish* fights their brandish'd swords out-
drew: [text, "flights."
But St. *George* met the Dragon, and run him through and through.
St. George *he was for* England, etc.

Bidia the *Amazon*, *Poetus* overthrew, [*al. lect. Photius, Proteus, Porus.*
As fierce as either *Vandal*, *Goth*, *Saracen* or *Jew*:
The potent *Holofernes*, as he lay in his Bed,
In came Wise *Judith*, and subtiley stole his Head:
Brave *Cyclops* stout with *Jove* fought, tho' he shower'd down thunder:
But St. *George* kill'd the Dragon, and was not that a Wonder?
St. George *he was for* England, etc.

Mark Anthony, I'll warrant you, play'd feats with *Egypt*'s Queen;
Sir *Eglamore*, that valiant Knight, the like was never seen.
Grim *Gorgon*'s might was known in fight, Old *Bevis* most men frighted;
The *Myrmidons* and *Prester Johns*, why were not these men knighted?
Brave *Spinola* took in *Breda*, *Nassau* did it recover:
But St. *George*, St. *George*, turn'd the Dragon over and over,
St. George *he was for* England, [*St.* Denis *was for* France.
Sing Honi soit Qui mal y Pense].

[White-letter. 1st has no colophon, the 2nd and later was Printed and Sold in *Aldermary* Church-Yard, *Bow-Lane*, London. Each has one woodcut of St. George on horseback, slaying the Dragon: for which we substitute the cut from "Sir Eglamore," on p. 725. Euing copy was printed for *F. Coles*, *T. Vere*, and *J. Whitwood*. Others for *W. Onley*. Date before 1661.]

*** Of the numerous heroes mentioned, many were made the theme of separate ballads: Sir Lancelot du Lac, Sir Guy of Warwick, and Henry the Fifth, here preceding or immediately following. Jephtha, Samson, Alfred the Great, and Sir Eglamour, have been already reprinted, respectively in vi. 685; ii. 460; ii. 211; and iii. 607. *See the Appendix to present vol.*, p. 774 (Pepys' Version).

There are numerous variations in our St. George, from that given in the *Mysteries of Love and Eloquence*; *or*, *The Art of Wooing and Complimenting* [by Edward Phillips, Milton's nephew], 1658.

Not hitherto reprinted was the ballad mentioned by Pepys, as having been read by him, 6 March, 1667, "in praise of the Duke of Albemarle, to the tune of *St. George*—the tune being printed too" (see our p. 136, and the Luttrell Collection, I. 101), "made in August, 1666": it is given on our next page.

An Heroical Song on the Worthy and Valiant Exploits of our Noble Lord General,

George, Duke of Albemarle, etc.,

Both by Land and Sea.

Made in August, 1666. To the Tune of *St. George*. [See p. 727.]

KING *Arthur* and his Men they valiant were and bold,
The Table Round was high renown'd, twelve hardy knights did hold;
All, in the dayes of old, extoll'd for Chivalrie:
But they long since are dead, and under ground do lie.
To keep up *England's* Fame, our present Story tells
How Lord *George*, Lord *George*, in prowess now excells.
Lord George *was born in* England, *restor'd his Countrye's joy*;
Come, let us sing Vive le Roy! Vive le Roy!

The Monarchies, all four, were purchased with blood;
Carthage of old, and *Rome* as bold, each other long withstood;
And many lives were lost in every enterprize.
Orlando Furioso, he was more rash than wise:
But never heard before, so well contrived a thing,
How Lord *George*, Lord *George*, in Peace brought home our King.
Lord George *was born in* England, *restor'd his Countrye's Joy*, etc.

French Mounsieur complements, his cracks and cringes many;
The Spanish Don his Hat keeps on, and looks as big as any;
The *Irish Tory* fierce; *Venetians'* courage hot; [N.B.
The *Welshman* still high born; most subtle is the *Scot*:
But yet among them all, deny it now who can,
Still Lord *George*, Lord *George*, Renowned *Englishman*:
Lord George [*was born in* England], *&c.*

Darby and *Capel* both did Noble Martyrs die,
Their latest breath, unto the Death, pronouncing Loyaltie;
Good Subjects many more did suffer death most vile,
In *Scotland* brave *Montrose* was murder'd by *Argyle*:
For King and Countries sake, all these laid down their lives;
But Lord *George*, Lord *George*, to serve his Prince survives.
Lord George [*was born in* England], *&c.*

Brave famous Noblemen, and others here, did fight
For *Charles* his Cause, when 'gainst the Lawes detained was his Right,
In those unhappy Wars dy'd many Worthies good,
Did win Immortal Fame by losing loyal blood:
Yet maugre all their force, Usurpers got the Throne;
But Lord *George*, Lord *George*, he gave the King his own.
Lord George [*was born in* England], *&c.*

By many Battles fought, the *Turk's* a potent Lord;
King *Philip's* Son of *Macedon* got all the world by 's sword;
Great *William* 'gain'd this Land, and all the *Danes* drave out;
Fifth *Harry* Conquer'd *France*, by force and valour stout: [Vide p. 741.
Their greatness to encrease, these exercised their might;
But Lord *George*, Lord *George*, doth for his Master fight.
Lord George [*was born in* England], *&c.*

Jephtha and *Gideon* by Miracle did strike, [Vide p. 685.
The Son of *Nun* did stay the Sun, no Man did do the like;
Sampson was the strongest begot of humane race;
Jonathan and *David* kill'd *Philistin[e]s* apace:
All those did fight on Land, their foes when slaughter'd they;
But Lord *George*, Lord *George* rides Conquerour at Sea.
Lord George [*was born in* England], *&c.*

Of many brave Exploits do ancient Stories tell,
But Sea-fights such as ours with *Dutch*, yet none could parallel
Towards *Midsummer* the Moon works strongly on their brain,
If in the month of *June* they venture once again;
For thrice they had the worst at that time of the year,
And Lord *George*, Lord *George* still keeps them all in fear.
Lord George [*was born in* England], *&c.*

We often read of Knights, [who] wilde Beasts did overcome;
Our General, beyond them all, beats *Belgick Lyon* home;
A Beast of wondrous size, sometime did hold him play,
But he the Conquest gain'd upon St. *James's* day. [*i.e.* 25, 26 *June*, 1666.
The *Lyon* then was hurt, did lamentably rore,
But Lord *George*, Lord *George* since that did wound it more.
Lord George [*was born in* England], *&c.*

The Victory obtain'd, was further still made good,
Our *Englishmen*, unto their Den, the *Dutchmen* home pursu'd;
Their Fleet in Harbour fir'd, their Village sack'd and burn'd,
Made *Butterboxes* swear the *Monck* to Devil was turn'd; [= *Dutch*.
As flam'd the *Trojan* Walls, so did their Ships, or worse,
For Lord *George*, Lord *George* sent in the Wooden-horse.
Lord George [*was born in* England], *&c.*

If daring *French-men* now our Valour longs to try,
Soon as he will, we ready still, his mind to satisfie,
His Itch shall quickly Cure, when he shall feel our sword,
With *Dutch* not blunted yet, we'l t'other Bout afford;
And if he thinks it good, the *Dane* may likewise call,
For Lord *George*, Lord *George* doth hope to beat them all.
Lord George [*was born in* England], *&c.*

Success wait on his Arm, till Tryumph bring him home
To Native soil, enrich'd with spoil of Enemies o're-come:
Whilst they by *Weeping-Cross* are driven back again,
May he with joy return to his Dear Soveraign;
And in his proper Orb, with Honour still attend,
Till Lord *George*, Lord *George* 'mong Angels shall ascend.
Lord George *was born in* England, *Restor'd his Countrye's Joy,*
Come, let us end, Vive le Roy.

(*Licens'd* according to Order.)

London, Printed by *W. Godbid* for *John Playford* at his Shop in the *Temple*, 1667.

[In White-letter, with staves of music above, double columns, no woodcut.]

Sir Guy of Warwick.

Merrythought.—(*Sings.*) "Was never man for Lady's sake, *Down down,*
Tormented as I poor *Guy—De derry down.*
For *Lucy's* sake, that Lady bright—*Down, down,*
As ever man beheld with eye: *De derry down.*"
—*Knight of the Burning Pestle*, Act ii. sc. 7.

OUR ballad-hero, Sir Guy of Warwick, was so deservedly famous of old, thanks to romancers and minstrels who delighted to sing in praise of his valiant acts, and how 'he made a good end,' that to be named after him, and esteemed to resemble him in courage, faithfulness and purity, was high honour. *Nous avons changea tout cela!* To call any man 'a Guy,' or 'a regular Guy,' could scarcely be esteemed a compliment in modern days, when ignorant perversion of judgement has discredited the name of hapless Guido Fawkes, who had been willing to immolate his own life after the manner of Samson, to ensure the destruction of the enemies and persecutors of his faith and creed. There have been worse men, murderers and rebels against law, for whom party spite dares claim the title of martyrs, but few, except Charles Lamb and W. Harrison Ainsworth, tried to do justice to the man of forlorn hope, who died in 1605.

Registers of the Stationers' Company, B. fol. 283=*Transcript*, ii. 601, mark the original of our ballad:—

On Vᵗᵒ January 159½ to Richard Jones, was "entred vnto him for his copie under master *Watkins* hande, *A pleasante songe of the valiant actes of GUY of Warwicke*: to the tune of, 'Was euer man so lost [or tost] in love' . . . vj*d*."

This is indisputably our present Roxburghe Ballad, but of the earliest edition, and sung to its own tune. Bishop Percy tells that a French history of Sir Guy appeared in 1525, (and that it is alluded to in the old Spanish romance, *Tirante el Blanco*, written not long after 1430, according to the French translation thereof). Puttenham records that the antique English romance (an imperfect copy of which, printed for Wm. Copland, *circâ* 1560, is in Brit. Mus.), in verse, was 'sung to the harp at Christmas dinners and brideales.'—Puttenham's *Arte of English Poesie*, 1589. Richard Corbet (1582-1635) made an episcopal onslaught, by writing in his *Iter Boreale*:—

"May all the ballads be call'd in and dye,
Which sing the warrs of *Colebrand* and Sir *Guy*!"

Fletcher had launched a playful shaft of burlesque at it (motto above), in 1610; and Samuel Butler, in describing Talgol, sang,

'He many a boar and huge dun-cow
Did, like another *Guy*, o'erthrow;
But *Guy* with him in fight compar'd
Had like the boar or dun-cow far'd.'—
Hudibras, Part I. canto 2, l. 308.

The history of the various phases of the Guy of Warwick legend is interesting (see *Percy Folio Manuscript, Ballads and Romances*, 1868, ii. 509-526, Introduction to 'Guy and Colebrande' = "When meate and drinke is great plentye . . . the most I prayse Sir Guy of Warwicke, that noble knight"). We give here what remains of our ballad in the MS. The name of Guy's relinquished wife, now printed as Phillis, is by John Rous (appointed priest at the chapel of Guy's Cliff, erected by Richard Beauchamp in 1422, with a statue of Guy), given as Dame Felys; elsewhere, by Leland, as *Felice*. Guy flourished in the tenth century, in reign of Athelstan.

[Percy Folio Manuscript, Brit. Mus. Add. MS. 27879, fol. 125 = p. 254.]

[*Fragment of 'Guy and Phillis': beginning destroyed by Bp. Percy*, 1794.]

In Winsor Forest I did slay / a bore of passing might & strenght,
Whose like in England neu[er] was / for hugenesse, both for breadth & lenght;
Some of his bones in Warwicke yett / within the Castle there doth lye;
one of his sheeld bones to this day / doth hang in the Citye of Couentrye.
on Dunsmore heath I alsoe slewe / a mightye wyld & cruell beast
calld the Duncow of Dunsmore heath / wch many people had opprest.
Some of her bones in warwicke yett / there for a monument doth lye,
wch vnto euery lookers veue / as wonderous strange they may espye.
Another Dragon in this Land / in fight I also did destroye,
Who did bothe men & beasts oppresse / & all the countrye sore anoye:
& then to warwicke came againe / like Pilgrim poore, & was not knowen;
& there I liued a Hermitts liffe / a mile & more out of the towne.
Where wth my hands I hewed a house / out of a craggy rocke of stone,
& lined like a palmer poore / w^thin the caue my selfe alone.
& dayle came to begg my foode / of Phillis at my castle gate,
not knowing to my loued wiffe / who daylye moned for her mate. [known.
till att the last I fell soe sicke / yea, sicke soe sore t^hat I must dye.
I sent to her a ring of gold / by wch shee knew me presentlye:
then shee, repairing to the graue / befor t^hat I gaue vp the ghost,
Shee closed vp my dying eyes / my Phillis faire, whom I loued most.
thus dreadfull death did me arrest / to bring my corpes vnto the graue;
& like a palmer dyed I, wherby I sought my soule to saue,
tho now it be consumed to mold / my body t^hat endured this toyle, [*transp.*
my stature ingrauen in marble [c]old / this pre^sent time you may behold. [" Mold."

Fin[i]s.

[Oddly enough, such hiding away voluntarily from a beloved wife, yet contriving to see her daily, though unknown by her, meets us again in modern time, in Nathaniel Hawthorne's story of "Wakefield" (see *Twice-Told Tales*, 1851: compare his *Note-Books*, where the incident is recorded). Mentioning Guy, in *Hudibras*, Dr. Zachary Grey refers to *The Tatler*, No. 148; Heylin's *History of St. George*, Part I. cap. iv. sect. 8; Part II. c. i. s. 9; Nath. Salmon's *Hist. of Hertfordshire*, pp. 140, 141; Chr. Brooke's *Panegyric Verses upon T. Coryat and his Crudities*; and Dr. King's *Art of Cookery*, p. 27.]

The fragments of Humphrey Crouch's *History of Guy Earl of Warwick*, 1655, have been already mentioned on our p. 542 (read *prosaic*; not prose). Since they belong to the Roxb. Coll. (III. 218-219 *verso*), and are on the same subject, they are given on p. 737.

[Roxburghe Collection, III. 50; Bagford, II. 19; Pepys, I. 522; Douce, I. 92 verso; III. 83 verso; Wood, 401. 3; 402. 6.]

A pleasant song of the Valiant Deeds of Chivalry, atchieved by that Noble Knight, Sir *Guy* of *Warwick*, who for the love of fair *Phillis* became a Hermit, and dyed in a Cave of a Craggy Rock, a mile distant from *Warwick*.

To the Tune of *Was ever man, &c.*

WAs ever Knight for Ladie's sake so lost in love as I Sir *Guy*?
For *Phillis* fair, that Lady bright, as ever man beheld with eye;
She gave me leave myself to try the valiant Knights with shield and spear
Ere that her love she would grant me, which made me venture far and near.

The proud Sir *Guy*, a barron bold, in deeds of arms the Doubtful Knight, [*i.e.* the Redoubtable Knight.
That every day in *England* was, with sword and spear in field to fight:
An *English-man* I was by birth, in faith of Christ a Christian true;
The wicked Laws of Infidels I sought by power to subdue. 16

Two hundred twenty years and odd after our Saviour Christ his birth,
When King *Athelston* wore the Crown, I lived here upon the earth:
Sometimes I was of *Warwick* Earl, and as I said, in very truth,
A Ladie's love did me constrain to seek strange vertues in my youth.

To try my fame by feats of Arms, in strange and sundry heathen Lands,
Where I atchieved for her sake right dangerous conquests with my hands.
For first I sail'd to *Normandy*, and there I stoutly won in fight
The Emperor's daughter of *Almany* from many a valiant worthy Knight.

Then passed I the Seas of *Greece*, to help the Emperor to his right,
Against the mighty Soldan's Hoast, of puissant *Persians* foe to fight:
Where I did slay of *Sarazens* and heathen Pagans many a Man;
And slew the *Soldan's* Couzin dear, who had to name daughty *Calbron*.

Ezkeldred, that Famous Knight, to death likewise I did pursue,
And *Almain*, King of *Tyre*, also, most terrible too in fight to view.
I went into the *Soldan's* Hoast, being thither on ambassage sent,
And brought away his head with me, I having slain him in his Tent.

There was a Dragon in the Land, which also I myself did slay,
As he a Lyon did pursue, most fiercely met me by the way:
From thence I past the Seas of *Greece*, and came to *Pavy* land aright,
Where I the Duke of *Pavy* kill'd, his hainous treason to requite.

And after came into this Land, towards fair *Phillis*, Lady bright,
For love of whom I travelled far to try my manhood and my might:
But when I had espoused her, I staid with her but forty days,
But there I left this Lady fair, and then I went beyond the Seas.

All clad in gray in Pilgrim sort, my voyage from here I did take,
Unto that blessed Holy Land, for Jesus Christ my Saviour's sake:
Where I Earl *Jonas* did redeem, and all his Sons, which were fifteen,
Who with the cruel *Sarazens* in Prison for long time had been.

I slew the Gyant *Amarant* in battel fiercely hand to hand,
And Daughty *Barknard* killed I, the mighty Duke to that same Land:
Then I to *England* came again, and here with *Colbron* fell I fought,
An ugly Gyant, which the *Danes* had for their Champion thither brought.

[Otherwise, *Colebrand*, p. xxxi*.

I overcame him in the field, and slew him dead right valiantly;
Where I the Land did then redeem, from *Danish* tribute utterly:
And afterwards I offered up the use of weapons solemnly;
At *Winchester*, whereas I fought in sight many far and nigh.

In *Windsor* Forest I did slay a Boar of passing might and strength,
The like in *England* never was, for hugeness both in breadth and length;
Some of his bones in *Warwick* yet within the Castle there do lie;
One of his shield bones to this day hangs in the City of *Coventry*.

On *Dunsmore-heath* I also slew a monstrous wild and cruel beast,
Call'd the *Dun Cow* of *Dunsmore-heath*, which many people had opprest:
Some of her bones in *Warwick* yet still for a monument do lie;
Which unto every looker's view as wondrous strange they may espy.

Another Dragon in the Land I also did in fight destroy,
Which did both man and beasts oppress and all the Country sore annoy:
And then to *Warwick* came again, like *Pilgrim* poor, and was not known,[1]
And there I liv'd a Hermit's life, a mile and more out of the town.

Where with my hand I hew'd a house out of a craggy rock of stone,
And lived like a Palmer poor within that Cave my self alone:
And daily came to beg my food of *Phillis* at my Castle Gate,
Not known unto my loving Wife, who mourned daily for her mate.

Till at the last I fell sore sick, yea sick so sore that I must dye;
I sent to her a ring of gold, by which she knew me presently:
Then she repairing to the Cave, before that I gave up the Ghost;
Herself clos'd up my dying eyes, my *Phillis* fair, whom I lov'd most.

Thus dreadful death did me arrest, to bring my corps unto the Grave.
And like a Palmer dyed I, whereby I sought my life to save:
My body in *Warwick* yet doth lie, though now it be consum'd to mold,
My statue there was graven in stone, this present day you may behold.[2]

Finis.

Printed for *J. Coles*, *T. Vere*, *J. Wright*, and *J. Clarke*.

[Registered by Stationers' Comp., 5 January, 159½. Black-letter. Two cuts.]

[1] "Like Pilgrim poor, in place obscure," begins an early ballad. It is in *The Phœnix Nest*, 1593, and Harl. MS. No. 6910, etc.

[2] *Compare Note*, p. 781.

[Roxburghe Collection, III. 218, 219 *verso.*]

The Heroick History of Guy, Earle of Warwick.

London: Written by Hvmphery Crovch.

[*Fragments only . . . . .*]

Valiant *Guy* bestirs his hands, the Dragon back did shrink,
The Giant *Rumbo* quaking stands: and knew not what to think.
Guy gets the victory at last, which made great *Rumbo* glad:
He was full glad the fight was past, for he before was sad:
The greatfull Lion *Guy* did greet, when he to him did goe,
And thankfully did lick his feet.

Because

. . . . . .

And when my father heares the truth, take *Phelice* for thine owne.
Win honour by thy marshall hand, and by a war-like life,
When this I came to understand, take *Phelice* for thy wife."
"*Phelice*, I aske no more," said he, "call *Guy* a coward swain,
If he refuse to fight for thee, thy love for to obtaine."
O woe to him that counts that good, that doth procure his care,
Who wins a wife with losse of blood, doth buy his barga[i]n deare.
Yet whilst he hath a drop to bleed, *Guy* will not idle lye,
Performing many a worthy deed, and acts of Chivelry.
In France he prov'd himself a man, unhorst them one by one,
He there cast down both horse and man, and fame and honour won,
He then to England comes a maine, to see his Heart's delight,
But *Phelice* sends him forth againe, sence he so well could fight. [since.
To fight for her he would not grutch whom he esteemed deare,
Because he loved her so much, no danger did he feare,
No danger may he fear that strives to winn a Ladies love,
And howsoever the business thrives, obedient he must prove.

He

He takes his leave once more, and goes her pleasure to fulfill.
He longs to be a dealing blowes, to win more honour still.
And through a Forist as he rides, he meets a mighty Giant,
Two yards at every step, he strides, far stronger than a Lion,
"Friend," quoth the *Giant*, "hast thou heard
Of one they call him *Guy*, who all the power of *France* hath feard
With acts of Chivelrie.

And

. . . . . .

[Written by **Hvmphery Crovch.**]

London, Printed for *Jane Bell*, at the east end of *Christ Church*, 1655.

[With three large woodcuts. 1st, on title-page, Guy in full suit of armour, helmed and plumed, riding a plumed *Destrier* or war-steed, and holding aloft a Boar's-head, while the rescued lion trots beside him. 2nd, the combat between the lion and the dragon, which turns its head towards Guy, who is about to cut it down with his sword. 3rd, the duel between Colbrand the gigantic Dane and Guy of Warwick, both in armour. These four pages were printed on one side of the paper whereof *Richard Harper* afterwards used the blank *verso* for a ballad of "Mock-Beggars Hall" (reprinted on our p. 762), beginning, "In ancient times when as plain-dealing was most of all in fashion," with woodcut of a moated castle, a young knight and a lady, from Malory's *King Arthur*, book 2 (cut given, p. 766). W. Copland's edition, 1557.]

Chevy Chace.

"I neuer heard *the olde song of Percy and Duglas*, that I found not my heart mooued more then with a Trumpet."—Sidney's *Apologie for Poetrie*, 1595.

BE it knowen unto all men by these presents (and presents endear absents, as hath been emphasized with discretion), that we are requested to here reprint the Roxburghe ballad of "Chevy Chace."

A Meeting was held in the Elysian Fields *on the 31st of May, in this* Jubilee Year, 1888, *summoned and attended by the Shades of former Members of the* Ballad Society, *who had during their lifetime paid their subscription-money punctually to a well-beloved Secretary,* Arthur G. Snelgrove, Esq., *but they each had unfortunately omitted to instruct their own respective executors to continue such payments uninterruptedly, year by year, up to date.* Imprimis, Frederick Ouvry, *formerly President of the Society of Antiquaries, was unanimously called to the Chair,* then Thomas Babington Macaulay *was admitted by acclamation as an honorary member; he having requested this favour, since he deeply regretted that circumstances beyond his controul had summoned him away ten years before the foundation of the* Ballad Society: *moreover, he confessed that his utterly incompetent nephew,* G.O.T., *had* g.o.t. *none of his brains, his consistency, or his enthusiastic love of balleds; whatever else he might have unworthily inherited; and, after having been early known for self-conceit as a Competition Wallah, he would no doubt degenerate into a* 'Wobbler,' *and be too lazy for Lays.* John Payne Collier, *of the* Percy Society, *explained how he himself alone had been precluded from joining the* Ballad Society, *as he had long desired to have done. The report of the farther proceedings, in our Special* Ghostograph, *is deeply interesting, and it reminds the neutral world that a similar meeting of the living Subscribers has never yet been organized. Although now too late, it would put to the blush the conversational gatherings of the* Bacon-and-Beans Society, *the* Mutual-Admiration Log-Rolling Society, *with other Ego et non-Eggoists (some incubated, more addled). The chief business of the Meeting was,* 1st, *to enjoy reading the proof-sheets of Vol. VI. of the* Roxburghe Ballads; 2nd, *to congratulate one another on the near prospect of the* General Index *to the six volumes;* and, lastly, *to deprecate any omission of the long-winded but nationally popular* "Chevy Chace" *from the* 'Group of Legendary and Romantic Ballads,' *to which it indisputably belongs. It was accordingly moved that a memorial be presented, craving for the inclusion of the said* "Chevy Chace," *and forwarded to their faithful representative, the present* Editor, *at* Molash Priory, *before he rejoined their company (unlimited). Carried* nem. con., *and the Meeting dissolved (into thin air), hoping to re-coöperate with him speedily when convenient.*

By Authority. Long live the Queen and Empress *(at her* Windsor *Library), subscriber to the* Ballad Society!

While admitting ungrudgingly the version which has always been the most popular of the three principal sources, we feel utterly unable to spare the requisite number of pages to their elaborate exposition. Few ballads have been so exhaustively treated, and the books are by no means inaccessible to students or general readers (a lazy race, who never contribute one sixpence or an hour's labour, but who prefer the shallowest compilations and the flimsiest commentary, backed as they are by professional critics of the Press. "You know who the critics are: the men who have failed in literature and art," "with just enough of malice to misquote").

There is, *first*, the grand early version, taking the Scottish view of the events in Richard II.'s twelfth year, 1388,—the version mentioned by Hume of Godscroft: "The Scots song made of Otterbourne telleth the time—about Lammas; and also the occasion—to take preys out of England; also the dividing armies betwixt the Earls of Fife and Douglas, and their several journeys, almost as in the authentic history," and he quotes the first stanza, which is this:

> Yt felle abowght the *Lamasse* tyde,
>   Whan husbonds wynn ther haye,
> The dowghtye *Dowglass* bowynd hym to ryde,
>   In *Ynglond* to take a praye." [70 *stanzas in all.*

Of this "Battele of Otterburne" (from Cotton MS. Cleopatra, C. iv. fol. 64, *circâ* 1550, and Harl. MS. 293, fol. 52, etc.), a print is in Percy's *Reliques*, vol. i. book iii. p. 254, 1767.

Second.—"The more modern ballad of 'Chevy Chace'"—*here given* (pp. 740–743)—of many broadsides. By Henry Bold it was translated into Latin verse, at the bidding of Henry Compton, sometime Bishop of London (a translation printed in Dryden's *Miscellanies*, iii. 239, 1685, and in Bold's *Songs in Latine*, 1685). It begins,

> *Vivat Rex noster nobilis, Omnis in tuto sit, &c.*
> God prosper long our noble King, our lives and safetyes all. (See p. 740.)

The Percy Folio Manuscript held this ballad version (ii. p. 7, 1868). Also in Bagford Coll., I. 32, II. 37; Pepys, I. 92; Euing, 212, etc.

Thirdly.—"The Hunting of the Cheviot," from Hearne's Preface to the *History of Gulielmus Neubrigiensis*, p. lxxxii, 1719, taken from a MS. in the Ashmolean Collection at Oxford. It begins,

> The *Persè* owt off *Northomberlande*,
>   And a vowe to God mayd he,
> That he wold hunte in the mountayns
>   Off *Chyviat* within days thre,
> In the mauger of doughtè *Dowglas*,
>   And all that ever with him be. [24 *irregular stanzas.*

Also, *Fourth*, the *Minstrelsy of the Scottish Border* version:—

> It fell and about the *Lammas* time,
>   When husbandmen do win their hay,
> Earl *Douglas* is to the *English* woods,
>   And a' with him to fetch a prey. [14 *stanzas.*

[Roxburghe Collection, III. 66, 436, 438, 440; Ouvry, II. 47, 57; Wood, 401, 47; 402, 30; Douce, I. 27; III. 99, etc. *Cf.* p. 739.]

A Memorable Song on the unhappy hunting in *Chevy-Chase* between Earl *Piercy* of *England*, and Earl *Dowglas* of *Scotland*.

Tune of, *Flying Fame.* [See pp. 672, 750.]

GOD prosper long our noble King, our lives and safeties all,
A woful hunting once there did in *Chevy-Chase* befall:

To drive the Deer with hound and horn Earl *Piercy* took his way,
The child may rue, that is unborn, the Hunting of that day.

The stout Earl of *Northumberland* a vow to God did make,
His pleasure in the Scottish woods three summers days to take,

The chiefest harts in *Chevy Chase* to kill and bear away,
These tydings to Earl *Dowglas* came, in Scotland where he lay;

Who sent Earl *Piercy* present word, he would prevent his sport;
The English Earl, not fearing this, did to the woods resort,

With fifteen hundred Bowmen bold, all chosen men of might,
Who knew full well in time of need, to aim their shafts aright.

The gallant gray-hounds swiftly ran to chase the Fallow Deer,
On Munday they began to hunt, when day light did appear,

And long before high noon they had an hundred fat bucks slain,
Then, having din'd, the Drovers went to rouse them up again.

The Bow-men mustred on the hills, well able to endure,
Their backsides all with special care that day were guarded sure.

The hounds ran swiftly through the woods the nimble Deer to take,
And with their cries the hills and dails an Echo shrill did make.

Lord *Piercy* to the Quarry went, to view the tender Deer,
Quoth he, "Earl *Dowglas* promised this day to meet me here,

"But if I thought he would not come, no longer would I stay."
With that a brave young gentleman thus to the Earl did say,—

"Lo, yonder doth Earl *Dowglas* come, his men in armour bright,
Full twenty hundred *Scottish* spears, all marching in our sight;

All men of pleasant *Tivi[ot]dale*, fast by the River *Tweed*."
"Then cease your sport," Earl *Piercy* said, "and take your bows with speed.

"And now with me, my Countrymen, your courage forth advance,
For never was there champion yet, in *Scotland* or in *France*,

"That ever did on horse-back come, but if my hap it were,
I durst encounter man for man, with him to break a spear."

Earl *Dowglas* on a milk-white steed, most like a Baron bold,
Rode foremost of the company, whose armour shone like gold.

"Shew me" (he said) "whose men you be that hunt so boldly here,
That without my consent do chase and kill my fallow Deer."

The man that first did answer make was noble *Piercy*, he,
Who said, "We list not to declare, nor shew whose men we be:

"Yet will we spend our dearest blood, thy chiefest Harts to slay."
Then *Dowglas* swore a solemn oath, and thus in rage did say,—

"E're thus I will outbraved be, one of us two shall dye,
I know the[e] well, an Earl thou art, Lord *Piercy*, so am I.

"But trust me, *Piercy*, pitty it were, and great offence, to kill
Any of these our harmless men, for they have done no ill.

"Let thou and I the battel try, and set our men aside."
"Accurst be he," Lord *Piercy* said, "by whom this is deny'd."

Then stept a gallant Squire forth, *Witherington* was his name.
Who said he "would not have it told to *Henry* our King for shame,

"That e're my captain fought on foot, and I stood looking on.
"You be two Earls," said *Witherington*, "and I a Squire alone.

"I'll do the best that do I may, while I have power to stand,
While I have power to weild my sword, I'le fight with heart and hand."

The Second Part, TO THE SAME TUNE.

Our *English* archers bent their bows, their hearts were good and true,
At the first flight of Arrows sent, full threescore *Scots* they slew.

To drive the Deer with hound and horn Earl *Dowglas* had the bent;
A Captain mov'd with mickle pride, the Spears to shivers went.

They clos'd full fast on every side, no slackness there was found,
And many a gallant gentleman lay gasping on the ground.

O Christ! it was great grief to see, and likewise for to hear,
The cries of men lying in their gore, and scattered here and there.

At last these two stout Earls did meet, like Captains of great might,
Like lions mov'd, they laid on load, and made a cruel fight.

They fought, until they both did sweat, with swords of tempered steel,
Until the blood, like drops of rain, they trickling down did feel.

"Yield the[e], Lord *Piercy!*" *Dowglas* said, "in faith I will thee bring,
Where thou shalt high advanced be by *James* our *Scottish* King.

"Thy ransome I will freely give, and thus report of thee,
Thou art the most couragious Knight that ever I did see."

"No *Dowglas*," qd. Earl *Piercy* then, "thy proffer I do scorn;
I will not yield to any *Scot* that ever yet was born."

With that there came an arrow keen out of an *English* bow,
Which struck E[arl] *Dowglas* to y^e heart, a deep and deadly blow,—

Who never spoke more words than these, "Fight on, my merry men all,
For why, my life is at an end, Lord *Piercy* sees my fall." [=Because.

Then leaving life, Earl *Piercy* took the dead man by the hand,
And said, "Earl *Dowglas*, for thy life, would I had lost my Land.

"O Christ! my very heart doth bleed, with sorrow for thy sake,
For sure a more renowned Knight mischance did never take."

A Knight amongst the *Scots* there was, which saw Earl *Dowglas* dye,
Who straight in wrath did vow revenge upon the Earl *Piercy*.

Sir *Hugh Montgomery* was he cal'd, who with a spear most bright,
Well mounted on a gallant Steed, ran fiercely through the fight,

And past the *English* archers all, without [or] dread or fear, [text, "all."
And through Earl *Piercie's* body then he thrust his hateful spear,

With such a vehement force and might he did his body gore,
The spear went through ye other side, a large cloth yard and more.

So thus did both these nobles dye, whose courage none could stain;
An *English* archer then perceiv'd the noble Earl was slain.

He had a bow bent in his hand, made of a trusty tree,
An arrow of a cloath-yard long, unto the head drew he.

Against Sir *Hugh Montgomerie*, so right his shaft he set,
The grey-goose wing that was thereon in his heart blood was wet.

This fight did last from break of day till setting of the Sun;
For when they rung the evening bell, the battle scarce was done.

With ye Earl *Piercy* there was slain Sir *John* of *Ogerton*,
Sir *Robert Ratcliff*, and Sir *John*, Sir *James* that bold Baron.

And with Sir *George*, and good Sir *James*, both knights of good account,
Good Sir *Ralph Rabby* there was slain, whose prowess did surmount.

For *Witherington* needs must I wail, as one in doleful dumps,
For when his legs were smitten off, he fought upon his stumps.

And with E[arl] *Dowglas* there was slain Sir *Hugh Montgomery*,
Sir *Charles Carrel* that from the field one foot would never flye;

Sir *Charles Morrell* of *Ratcliff* too, his sister's son was he,
Sir *David Lamb*, so well esteem'd, yet saved could not be;

And the Lord *Markwell* in like wise did with Earl *Dowglas* dye;
Of twenty hundred *Scottish* spears, scarce fifty-five did flye.

Of fifteen hundred *English* men went home but fifty-three,
The rest were slain in *Chevy-Chase* under the Green-wood tree.

Next day did many Widdows come, their husbands to bewail;
They washt their wounds in brinish tears, but all would not prevail.

Their bodies bath'd in purple blood they bore with them away;
They kist them dead a thousand times, when they were clad in clay.

This news was brought to *Edenborg*, where *Scotland's* King did reign,
That brave Earl *Dowglas* suddenly was with an arrow slain.

"O heavy news!" King *James* did say, "*Scotland* can witness be,
I have not any Captain more of such account as he."

Like tydings to King *Henry* came, within as short a space,
That *Piercy* of *Northumberland* was slain in *Chevy-Chase*.

"Now God be with him!" said our King, "sith 'twill no better be,
I trust I have within my realm five hundred as good as he.

"Yet shall not *Scot* nor *Scotland* say but I will vengeance take,
And be revenged on them all, for brave Earl *Piercie's* sake."

This vow full well the K[ing] perform'd, after on *Humble Down*,
In one day fifty Knights were slain, with Lords of great renown;

And of the rest of small account did many hundreds dye,
Thus ended the hunting of *Chevy-Chase* made by the Earl *Piercie*.

God save the King, and bless the land, in plenty, joy, and peace,
And grant henceforth that foul debate 'twixt Noble men may cease!

Finis.

Printed for *F. Coles*, *T. Vere*, and *J. Wright*.

[Black-letter. No woodcut. For date, see Introduction, but *circâ* 1580.]

The other Roxburghe copies are modern, white-letter, n.p.n. One of the many parodies on Chevy Chace, 1747, sung to the same tune, is a political squib given on p. 777, entitled "The Lord's Lamentation; or, The *Whittington* Defeat:"

> God prosper long our noble King, our lives and safeties all,
> A woeful Horse-race late there did at *Whittington* befall,
> Great *B[edfor]d's* Duke, a mighty Prince, a solemn vow did make,
> His pleasure in fair *Staffordshire* three summer days to take.

King Henry the Fifth's Conquest.

> "*Agencourt, Agencourt!* know ye not *Agencourt?*
> Where the English slew and hurt
> All the French foemen:
> With our guns and bills brown,
> O the *French* were beaten downe,
> Morris-pikes and bowmen."
> —T. Heywood's *King Edward IV.*, Part I. iii. 2, 1599.

WE have neither space nor inclination to enter on the subject of Henry V. and his French Wars. "There would have been a time for such a word," but not now, near the close of our Group.

"*Agincourt*" was a favourite subject. Far beyond "A Council grave our King did hold" (tune of *When Flying Fame*), in *The Crowne Garland of Goulden Roses*, the noblest praise of Henry V.'s Conquests is Michael Drayton's poem to the Cambro-Britons, beginning, "Fair set the wind for *France*." (It inspired Tennyson to celebrate, in precisely similar rhythm, the glorious Balaclava *Charge of the Light Brigade*: the 'noble Six Hundred!'

They now to fight are gone, [*Drayton's* 8th stanza.
Armour on armour shone,
Drum now to drum did groan,
To hear, was wonder;
That with the cries they make
The very earth did shake,
Trumpet to trumpet,
Thunder to thunder.)

[Roxburghe Collection, III., 358; Coll. Bibl. Lindesiana; Chet. Manchester.]

King Henry V. his Conquest of France.

In Revenge for the Affront offered by the French King; in sending Him (instead of the Tribute) a Ton of Tennis Balls.

[For Tune, see *Note*, on p. 745.]

AS our King lay musing on his bed,
He bethought himself upon a time
Of a tribute that was due from *France*,
Had not been paid for so long a time.
Fal, lal, [de ral de ra, fal lal, fa la la] etc.

He called for his lovely page, [O, then, . . . trusty.
His lovely page then called he;
Saying, "You must go to the King of *France*,
To the King of *France*, Sir, ride speedily."

O then went away this lovely page,
This lovely page then away went he;
When he came to the King of *France*,
And low fell down on his bended knee.

"My master greets you, worthy Sir,
Ten ton of Gold that is due to he,
That you will send him his tribute home,
Or in French land you soon will him see." *Fal, etc.*

"Your master's young and of tender years,
Not fit to come into my degree;
And I will send him three Tennis Balls,
That with them he may learn to play."

O then returned this lovely page. [read trusty, *passim.*
This lovely page then returned he;
And when he came to our gracious King,
Low he fell down on his bended knee.

"What news, what news, my trusty page? [*Line cut off.*
"What is the news you have brought to me?"
"I have brought such news from the King of *France*,
That he and you will ne'er agree.

"He says you're young and of tender years,
Not fit to come into his degree;
And he will send you three Tennis Balls,
That with them you may learn to play."

"Recruit me *Cheshire* and *Lancashire*, [See *Note*.
And *Derby* Hills that are so free!
No marry'd man, or widow's son,
For no widow's curse shall go with me!"

They recruited *Cheshire* and *Lancashire*,
And *Derby* Hills that are so free;
No marry'd man, nor no widow's son,
Yet there was a jovial bold company.

O then we marched into the *French* land, [*del.* 'the.'
With drums and trumpets so merrily;
And then bespoke the King of *France*,
"Lo yonder comes proud King *Henry*."

The first shot that the *Frenchmen* gave,
They killed our *Englishmen* so free.
We kill'd ten thousand of the *French*,
And the rest of them they run away.

And then we march'd to *Paris* gates,
With drums and trumpets so merrily;
O then bespoke the King of *France*,
"The Lord have mercy on my men and me!

"O I will send his tribute home,
Ten ton of Gold that is due to he;
And the finest flower that is in all *France*, [*i.e.* *Kate*.
To the Rose of *England* I will give free."

Printed and sold in *Aldermary Church Yard, Bow Lane, London.*

⁂ The present Editor learnt the ballad and its traditional tune from his father, Joseph Ebsworth (who died on June 22nd, 1868, aged 80); he having heard it sung by his own grandmother, a South-Berwick woman, nearly a centenarian. Thus discrepancies and corruptions of the broadside version could be corrected. James Henry Dixon was the earliest to reprint it, partly from the singing of a man named King, known in Yorkshire as the 'Skipton Minstrel,' and it was published in 1846 for the Percy Society.

Among other corruptions in the printed version, the recurring substitution of the word *lordly* ("after the scole of Stratford-atte-Bowe," whether English or Prioress' French) should be rectified by the Molash Prior's *genuine text* reading "Trusty Page." Fortunately, the manly cadence of the ninth stanza is virtually uninjured. The Editor remembers it flowing thus, in the traditional version:—

'*No married man, no widow's son:*
No widow's curse shall go with me!'

Such a verse embalms the ballad. No ancient exemplar of it is known.

The quotations are so twisted in Martin Parker's "Excellent new Medley, to the tune of *Tarleton's Medley*," beginning "In Summer time when folkes make Hay, all is not true which people say," that one dare not lay stress on the thirty-third line, "When the fifth *Henry* sail'd for France." It was reprinted in vol. i. p. 52 of these *Roxburghe Ballads*, 1869, edited by Mr. Wm. Chappell. But the Roxburghe two copies of Martin Parker's *Medley* are not the only copies that are extant. Another is in Pepys Coll., IV. 342; a fourth is Euing, No. 86; and the fifth belonged to the late J. P. Collier, afterwards Frederick Ouvry's.

King John and the Abbot of Canterbury.

"Not with blinded eye-sight poring over miserable books!"
—Tennyson's *Locksley Hall.*

TO be inconstant in their moods, so as at times to decry the pursuit of knowledge which had earlier won their heart, is the common fate of students; such it was caused Faustus to listen to Mephistopheles, when regretting his past relinquishment of enjoyment: such also may have suggested the popular ballad of "The King and the Abbot of Canterbury."

Spiteful Puritans of later times (see p. 750, *quotat.*) exultantly seized the chance of depreciating book-learned Churchmen, by contrasting the superior sense of the illiterate laity, to which themselves belonged. Modern realistic novelists might similarly demonstrate a monopoly of virtues and intellect in the laborious poor; whether it be to level them up, or more probably to level down the episcopate to '*Les Misérables*'—'*Les Travailleurs de la Terre,*' or Zola's '*La Terre,*' itself.

Attempts have been made to trace to their origin the employment of such presumably insoluble questions as those in our text, questions admitting of simple and conclusive answers, such as would disappoint the propounder's greediness for gain of an expected forfeiture. The search leads through the literature of many nations and to remote ages.

It is not only to the *Gesta Romanorum*, to Sacchetti's *Novelli*, No. 4; to the *Contes à Rire*; or to the translation from Alain Chartier, 1511 and 1566: *Delectable Demaundes and Pleasant Questions*; but to the disputations or wit-combats of the Middle Ages, such as the so-called Anglo-Saxon of *Salomon and Saturn*. The opposition of a clownish buffoon, such as Marcolf, enhanced the solemnity of the other disputation. (We trace this contrast throughout the bantering between Olivia and Feste the Jester, in *Twelfth Night.*) Reference is made elsewhere to Jewish tradition; to the questions interchanged by King Solomon and Hiram of Tyre, or with the Queen of Sheba. Of such disquisition we pass not the threshold. As in Browning's *Solomon and Balkis*—

"She proves him with hard questions: before she has reached the middle
He smiling supplies the end, straight solves them, riddle by riddle."

The story is ancient, exemplifying that 'Riddle-me-Ree' Puzzlewit suitable for minstrels of interminable verbosity, at winter firesides in rural mansions. The earliest and most complete version extant is in the Percy Folio MS. (p. 184), as "Kinge John and Bishopp," beginning "Of an ancient story I'le tell you anon, of a notable Prince t[hat] was called *K. John*:" (printed direct from the MS., our own collation, in Miss De Vaynes's *Kentish Garland*, pp. 461-465). It is in length 166 lines, and was afterwards condensed *temp. Jac. I.*, into its present form. Other versions begin respectively, "An ancient story," "I will tell you a story," etc. Bürger translated it into German, as *Der Kaiser und der Abt*, beginning, "Ich will euch erzahlen ein Märchen, gar shnurrig." The tune (known later as *Death and the Cobler*, and from Richard Leveridge's song, '*A Cobler there was*'), with its burden of *Derry down*, is in *Popular Music*, p. 350. Other copies are in Bagford Coll., II. 27; Pepys, II. 128; Euing, 223; Ouvry, I. 60. Compare the two following ballads on the same theme, on our pp. 751-754.

[Roxburgh Collection, III. 494, 883; Jersey, II. 124. *Cf.* p. 746.]

A New Ballad of King John and the Abbot of Canterbury.

To the Tune of *The King and the Lord Abbot.*

With Allowance. **Ro. L'Estrange.**

ILe tell you a Story, a Story anon,
Of a noble Prince, and his Name was King *John*,
For he was a Prince, and a Prince of great might,
He held up great Wrongs, he put down great Right.
Derry down, down, hey derry down.

Ile tell you a Story, a Story so merry,
Concerning the Abbot of *Canterbury*,
And of his House-keeping and high Renown,
Which made him resort to fair *London* Town.
Derry down, [down, hey derry down.]

" How now, Brother Abbot? 'tis told unto me
That thou keepest a far better House than I:
And for thy House-keeping and High Renown,
I fear thou hast Treason against my Crown."
Derry down, [down, hey derry down.]

" I hope, my Liege, that you owe me no grudge,
For spending of my true-gotten goods."
" If thou dost not answer me questions three,
Thy head shall be taken from thy Body. *Derry down.*

" When I am set on my steed so high, [As in l. 51.
With my Crown of Gold upon my head,
Amongst all my Nobility with joy and much mirth,
Thou must tell me to one penny what I am worth. *Derry d.*

" And the next Question you must not flout,
How long I shall be riding the World about:
And the third Question thou must not shrink; [*al. lect.* 'And from.'
But tell to me truly what I do think." *Derry down.*

" O these are hard Questions for my shallow wit,
For I cannot answer your Grace as yet;
But if you will give me but three days' space,
I'le do my endeavour to answer your Grace."
Derry down, down, hey derry down.

" O three days' space I will thee give,
For that is the longest day thou hast to live;
And if thou dost not answer these questions right,
Thy head shall be taken from thy body quite." *Derry d.*

And as the Shepherd was going to his fold,
He spy'd the old Abbot come riding along,
"How now, Master Abbot? you'r Welcome Home,
What News have you brought from good King *John*?" *Derry.*

"Sad news, sad news, I have thee to give,
For I have but three days' space for to live;
If I do not answer him questions three,
My head shall be taken from my body. *Derry down.*

"When he is sat so high on his Steed, [transp. in III. 883.
With his Crown of Gold upon his head,
Amongst all his Nobility with joy and much mirth,
I must tell him to one penny what he is worth. *Derry down.*

"And the next Question I must not flout,
How long he shall be riding the World about;
And the third Question thou must not shrink. [*a.l.* And from.
But tell to him truly what he does think." *Derry down.*

"O Master, did you never hear it yet,
That a Fool may learn a Wise man wit; ['learn' = teach.
Lend me but your Horse and your apparel,
Ile ride to fair *London*, and answer the Quarrel." *Derry down.*

"Now I am set so high on my steed, [*The King asks.*
With my Crown of Gold upon my head,
Amongst all my Nobility with joy and much mirth,
Now tell me to one penny what I am worth." *Derry down.*

"For thirty pence our Saviour was sold,
Amongst the false Jews, as you have been told;
And nine-and-twenty's the worth of thee,
For I think thou art one penny worser than he." *Derry down.*

"And the next question thou mayest not flout,
How long I shall be riding the World about?"
"You must rise with the Sun, and ride with the same,
Until the next morning he rises again; *Derry down.*

"And then I am sure, you will make no doubt,
But in twenty-four hours you'l ride it about."
"And the third question you must not shrink, [*i.e.* shirk.
But tell to me truly what I do think." *Derry down.*

"Well that I can do, and 'twill make you merry,
For you think I'm the Abbot of *Canterbury*;
But I'm his poor Shepherd, as you may see,
And am come to beg pardon for him and for me." [*a.l.* 'he and me.'
Derry down.

The King he turn'd him about, and did smile,
Saying, "Thou shalt be the Abbot the other while."
"O no, my Grace, there is no such need, [*a.l.* "my Liege."
For I can neither Write nor Read." *Derry down.*

"Then four pounds a week will I give unto thee,
For this merry true jest thou hast told unto me;
And tell the old Abbot when thou comest home,
Thou hast brought him a pardon from good King *John.*"
Derry down, down, hey derry down.

Finis.

Printed for *P. Brooksby* at the *Golden Ball* in *Pye-Corner.*

[Roxb. Coll., III. 883, is in Black-letter, of not later date than August, 1685, licensed by Roger L'Estrange: two woodcuts, a king and the man of p. 50. Roxb. Coll. (III. 491) is in White-letter, with two woodcuts, one on p. 217: colophon, "*Newcastle-upon-Tyne.* Printed and sold by *John White*" (*circâ* 1777), reprinted from an earlier edition than Philip Brooksby's, which has, twice, misprint "sat on his steed so high," spoiling the rhyme, instead of "sat so high on his steed;" also, "for he and for me," line 89.]

The King and the Bishop.

"Ah! que vous savez mal vous défendre pour un homme de cour."—*Molière.*

THIS is No. 22 in *Thackeray's List*, April, 1685. (*Bagford Ballads*, p. lxi.) So long ago as 1882, in a foot-note to the second volume, p. 469, of Miss Julia H. L. De Vaynes' *Kentish Garland* (printed by Messrs. Stephen Austin and Sons, Hertford, a book already 'rare' and prized), the present Editor recorded a definite promise to reprint "The King and the Bishop;" also "The old Abbot and King Olfrey." This promise is now fulfilled, on our pp. 751, 753. Every promise may be kept in due time, if the Wandering J.W.E. be allowed a long lease, like the other Wandering JEW, *vide ante* pp. 688-700). The reprint comes fitly into the "Group of Legendary and Romantic Ballads," dedicated to the same faithful friend, in whose *Kentish Garland* the promise was made.

There are inconveniences in having acquired a good character. Persons who enjoy the possession of an utterly bad one place us at a terrible disadvantage. If they ever, by accident or design, perpetrate a generous and meritorious action, their good deed so shines in a naughty world, and brings upon people the sense of surprise from being wholly unexpected and unprecedented, that praise and pudding become their instantaneous payment. Few men feel truly grateful to an habitual benefactor? (see Margaret Veley's '*Damocles*'). A benefactress who has devoted her life to sweetness and generous gifts can seldom in this world meet her due reward. Ingratitude to a woman is "No new thing," as W. E. Norris has shown, and Thackeray, with unwonted sweetness, foreshadowed it, when thus describing Lady Castlewood:—

"It was this lady's disposition to think kindnesses, and devise silent bounties, and to scheme benevolence, for those about her. We take such goodness, for the most part, as if it was our due; the Marys who bring ointment for our feet get but little thanks. Some of us never feel this devotion at all, or are moved by it to gratitude or acknowledgement; others only recall it years after, when the days are past in which those sweet kindnesses were spent on us, and we offer back our return for the debt by a poor tardy payment of tears. Then forgotten tones of love recur to us, and kind glances shine out of the past—O so bright and clear! O so longed after!—because they are out of reach; as holiday music from withinside a prison-wall—or sunshine seen through the bars; more prized because unattainable—more bright because of the contrast of present darkness and solitude, whence there is no escape."—*Esmond*, Book I. chapter ix.

Bishop Percy's words are these (*Reliques*, 1767 edition, ii. 306):—

"The common popular ballad of '*King John and the Abbot*' seems to have been abridged and modernized about the time of James I. from one much older, entitled '*King John and the Bishop of Canterbury*.' The Editor's folio MS. contains a copy of this last, but in too corrupt a state to be reprinted; it however afforded many lines worth reviving. The archness of the following questions and answers hath been much admired by our old ballad-makers: for besides the two copies above mentioned, *there is extant another ballad on the same subject* (but of no great antiquity or merit), *entitled KING OLFREY AND THE ABBOT.**

"Lastly, about the time of the civil wars, when the cry ran against the Bishops, *some Puritan worked up the same story into a very doleful ditty, to a solemn tune, concerning* '*King Henry and a Bishop*,' *with this stinging moral*:

'*Unlearned men hard matters out can find,*
When learned bishops princes' eyes do blind.'"

* *Percy's Note.*—"See the *Collection of Hist. Ballads*, 3 vols. 1727. Mr. Wise supposes *Olfrey* to be a corruption of *Alfred*, in his pamphlet concerning the *White Horse* in Berkshire, p. 15."

[The pamphlet here indicated by Dr. Percy is *A Letter to Dr. Mead, concerning some Antiquities in Berkshire*: By Francis Wise, B.D., Oxford, 1738. He declares that King Alfred "is the person meant by King Olfrey in the original ballad, tho' more modern bards have transferred the story to King John;" and he cites J. Roberts's *Collection of Old Ballads*, 1723, vol. ii. p. 50. Wise's erroneous allegations were controverted by a Mr. Bumpstead, who under the pseudonym of *Philalethes Rusticus* in 1740 wrote a shilling quarto, entitled, *The Impertinence and Imposture of Modern Antiquaries Displayed; or, a Refutation of the Rev. Mr. Wise's Letter to Dr. Mead*, etc. This, in 1741, was followed by *An Answer to the scandalous Libel, entituled* '*The Impertinence and Imposture*.']

Probably for the first time, these three distinct versions are now brought together (the Percy Folio MS. earlier version is reprinted in *The Kentish Garland*). The unwise attempt to connect good King Alfred's name with such a transaction is absurd and libellous. Thomas Hill's ballad, "Can you Dance *The Shaking of the Sheets?*" 1589, has been reprinted in vol. iii. p. 184 of *Roxburghe Ballads*, by Mr. Wm. Chappell, who gave the tune in his *Popular Music*, p. 85; and on his pp. 198, 199 the two tunes for *Chevy Chace*, one being *In peas-cod time*, the other, alternatively, *When flying Fame.*

[Roxburghe Collection, III. 170; Douce (*dupli.*), I. 109 *verso*; Pepys, I. 472.]

The King and the Bishop;
Or,
Unlearned Men hard matters out can find, When Learned Bishops [miss the mark, and] Princes eyes do blind.

To the Tune of, *Chery Chase.* [See pp. 672, 740, 750.]

IN Popish time, when Bishops proud in *England* did bear sway,
Their Lordships did like Princes live, and kept all at obey;
Their Palaces with arrace hang'd, their houses shin'd with gold: [arras.
Their train of gallant Gentlemen, most stately to behold.

A King then in this land did raign, (some say 'twas old *Henry*)
One day he for a Bishop sent, his scholarship to try;
Then straightway to the Court he went, in all his pomp and state,
And took it for a favour great, upon the King to wait.

And when [he] came unto the King, he did both bow and bend,
His Grace's pleasure he did crave, why he for him did send.
"Bishop" (quoth he), "I sent for thee, to put thee to a task,
And I resolved true will be of three things I will ask.

"And three weeks' time I will thee give on it to meditate,
And then if you not tell me true, I vow to have thy pate."
"If that it like your Majesty" (the Bishop then did say),
"I'le try the utmost of my skill your will for to obey."

"The first thing now" (then said the King) "is this that I would know,
Unto a very hour the time a traveller may go
About the vast and spacious world, and then return again
Unto the place he did set forth, and this I know would fain.

"The second thing that tell you must, even to one poor half-crown,
What I am worth, that am a King;" (this made the Bishop frown)
"The third thing it is this" (he said) "the which you must explain,
To tell to me what I do think, when you come here again.

"And so, good Bishop, you do know what things I do desire,
And for to be resolv'd therefore of you I do require.
Tell me the truth and keep your time, or else your head shall flye
From off your shoulders when you come: your wits you now must try."

"These are hard things to be resolv'd," unto the King he said;
"No man on earth can tell the same, I greatly am afraid:
Yet I will try the greatest skill," and so he took his leave—
The task and sentence both were hard, which made his Lordship grieve.

The Second Part, to the same tune.

WHen he came home to study hard the Bishop then did go,
His brains did hammer in his head, his heart was fill'd with woe:
But yet for all his learning great, these things he could not find.
The time began for to expire, which did torment his mind.

The heavy sentence of the King did touch him to the quick;
With grief and overstudying he presently fell sick.
The Bishop he a brother had, a man that hard did fare,
A Shepherd by profession, for whom he did not care.

This Shepherd when that he did hear his brother sick did lye,
To visit him he did think best before that he should dye.
With much ado, at length he got admittance him to see;
It griev'd the poor man to the heart at this his misery.

Saluting his Lord brother then, asked him how he did do;
He answered him with heavy heart, "O full of grief and woe;
You cannot help my misery, no man my life can save,
The task's too hard for me to do, the King my head will have."

"Dear brother" (then the Shepherd said) "to me your grief explain,
And if that I can save your life, I'le venture to be slain."
The Bishop told him every thing 'cause he ado did make.
"If this be all," the Shepherd said, "the same I'le undertake.

"You know that we are very like in person, speech and face,
Let me put on your Robes of State, I'le execute the place.
Your trains of gallants to the Court must bear me company,
And if I do not tell these things, instead of you I'le dye."

The time being come, next day he went to see his Majesty,
Who presently was entertain'd with courtlike courtesie.
"Now, welcome, Bishop," (quoth the King) "can you resolve me true?
And if you cannot," he did say, "I know what I must do."

"Unto your Grace's question, the first, I answer make:
Let any man ascend the sky, and the Sun's chariot take,
In twenty and four hours' time, about the world may ride,
The which is but one day and night, this journey to abide."

"Thou sayest true" (then said the King), "unto the second then."
"Now unto that" (the Shepherd said), "I answer thus agen;
The King of Kings, our Saviour Christ, for thirty pence was sold,
I under-value you by far, for all your Crown of gold."

Then said the King, "Bishop, 'tis right, what thou hast said before;
Now tell me truly what I think, and I will ask no more."
"You think that I the Bishop am," the Shepherd then did say:
"Why so I think," then quoth the King, "in spight of all says nay."

"You have confest I told your thought, an't like your Majesty,
Although I w[e]are the Bishop's robe, a Shepherd poor am I:
One father and one mother both we had, and brethren are,
And for to please your Royal Grace my brother had a care.

"He now lies sick neer unto death, and hither did me send,
Who bid me tell you all these things, for fear he should offend."
"Commend me to him" (quoth the King) "and thank him heartily,
He now hath satisfied my mind, and pleased well am I."

A hundred pound the King bestowed upon the Shepherd then,
And taking leave away he went with all his Gentlemen.
When to the Bishop he did come, all things he did relate,
He thank'd his brother, and was glad of this his happy fate.

Upon him he bestow'd a Farm, of forty pounds a year,
As well he might for he did find of him a brother dear.
And thus unlearned men sometimes, hard matters out can find,
When learned Bishops miss the mark, and Princes' eyes do blind.

London, Printed for *F. Coles*, *T. Vere*, and *J. Wright.*

[Black-letter, two cuts: 1st, a King (on p. 661), 2nd, a Bishop (*Williams*). Pepys p. for *J. Wright*, *J. Clarke*, *W. Thackeray*, *T. Passinger*. Written, 1612.]

[Pepys Collection, II. 127; Douce, II. 169.]

The Old Abbot and King Olfrey.

To the Tune of, *The Shaking of the Sheets.* [See p. 750.]

IN old times past there was a King, we read, was bountiful in each degree,
That gave rewards to each Subject's need, so orderly as it might be;
And kept his Princely Pallaty, in every kingly quality,
Maintaining Hospitality.

Then the King was given to understand, there liv'd an Abbot in those days,
That kept a noble House, and such a band of comely Men at all assays:
That made the King to marvel much, the Abbot's living should be such,
And how he came to be so rich.

Then the King sent for the Abbot strait, to come to Court he might him see,
To number the Men on him did wait, the multitude as it might be;
And thither went the Lord Abbot then, and after him Five Hundred Men,
To guard him out and home again.

Then the noble King he did demand, of his House-keeping and all his Train,
"How chance you keep so many men?" quoth he, "Or how come you by all your Gain?" [*Sic. qu.* 'Quoth he' *redundant?*
"Unto your Grace I'll make it known, I hope my cause is quickly shown,
For I spend no more than is my own."

"Thou art too wealthy," said the King, "and it is time to cut off your Head:
For I do suppose in every thing how daintily you must be fed;
Unless you can resolve to me, within one year these Questions three,
Your Head shall be off, I'll warrant ye.

"First of all, you must declare to me, to the uttermost what I am worth;
See that you have a ready care," quoth he, "for to study, and to bring it forth.
And Secondly, the Truth to know, How I about the World must go;
This is the Second Riddle, you know.

"The last o[illegible]l, To tell me what I Think; and then you shall your Pardon have,
Readily set down with pen and ink, your Lands and Livings all to save.
If you your Livings mean to hold, with all your Gallants in their Gold,
See these Riddles you readily unfold."

And then the Abbot he sought out to the cunningest Man that there might be,
How his Purpose then he might bring about, and for to set his Livings free:
But yet by no good men could he these Riddles expound in any degree,
Nor yet by University.

Then the old Abbot he a Brother had, a silly Man that kept his Sheep;
Who musing how his Brother came so sad, and how he came in Dump so deep;
Saying, "Dear Brother, tell to me how chance you look so heavily,
That none of your Friends can remend ye."

Then the Lord Abbot told his Brother all the Questions three, which made him sad;
He said, "Dear Brother, shall I be so bold to answer them, and make you glad?
Let me put on your Abbot's Weed, and I'll go to Court like in your stead,
And see, dear Brother, how I shall speed."

"If you these Questions readily can put out, and answer them to my Discharge;
Half of my Living that I have, no doubt, shall be thy own, to live at large."
And thither went the Shepherd then, and after him five hundred Men,
To guard him out and home again.

"Now you be very welcome!" said the King. "Indeed your Day is just come forth;
I make no doubt but to me you bring to the uttermost what I am worth."
"Yea, I'll assure your Grace," quoth he, "Worth Nine and Twenty Pence you be,
Not a Peny more, I'll warrant ye.

"For *Jesus Christ*, who was the King of Kings, was sold but for one Peny more,
When *Judas* sold him to the *Jewish* Things, the Scripture bringeth forth theretore.
Then I do trust your Grace will say, You are worth no more, no manner of way,
But a Peny lesser than they did pay.

"Then touching how to go the World about: In twice twelve Hours, as you may see,
The Sun doth take its speedy Course about, so speed[il]y as it may be;
If you about the World would go, in twice Twelve Hours you may do so:
And this is the Second Riddle, you know.

"Then last of all, to tell you what you Think; I am sure you think that it is I
Am the Lord Abbot which to you did bring these Questions so readily;
No, I am but his Brother, God wot, in field which after his sheep do trot,
For Lands and Livings I have not."

When as the Noble King had heard, his Questions he had answer'd so,
He hearing that the Shepherd had need, a Living on him did bestow:
And his Brother likewise he did yield Half of the Livings which then he held;
Thus was he promoted from the Field.

[Pepys', in Black-letter, with two woodcuts: printed for *J. Wright*, *J. Clarke*, *W. Thackeray*, and *T. Passinger*; Douce's, for *A. Milbourne*. Date, *circâ* 1682.]

The Old and New Courtier.

Steward.—"The case is altered since we lived i' the Country;
We do not now invite the poor o' the parish
To dinner, keep a table for the tenants;
Our kitchen does not smell of beef; the cellar
Defies the price of malt and hops; the footmen
And coach-drivers may be drunk like gentlemen,
With wine; nor will three Fiddlers upon holidays
With aid of bag-pipes, that called in the country
To dance and plough the hall up with their hob-nails,
Now make my Lady merry. We do feed
Like Princes, and feast nothing else but princes."

—James Shirley's *Lady of Pleasure*, Act ii. sc. 1. 1635.

HE who reads the rich store of Plays belonging to the reigns of James I. and his son Charles I., the choicest Comedies of Ben Jonson, Massinger, Fletcher, and Shirley, will find luxurious revellings, profuse expenditure, proud wantonness and arrogant folly enough to satisfy the most inordinate craving for satirical and social records. What our ensuing ballad tells of the degeneracy into riot and effeminacy of The King's Young Courtier is amply borne out by contemporary description. Professional historians never enjoyed the humour of the playwright. They show only the dullness and formality of law and politics, State-craft and foreign warfare, rivalries of Court favourites, and envious plotting or rebellion of mock patriots; they preach dreary sermons about the vanity of this world, and the price paid for glories. It is from the ballad-singers, the poets of the bye-ways, the lively chroniclers of passing follies, passing sorrows, that we receive best instruction, concerning the daily life of rich and poor, the soundness or the rottenness of our citizens and countrymen: before the modern novel, that mirrors common life, had found a few of its earliest students.

Regarding the decay of Hospitality, here alleged, we may not be tempted into any lectures on political economy, most exasperating and pretentious of nuisances. The older style of wastefulness had worked evil in increasing pauperism and idleness. (But see p. 762.)

Although we have no certain record in print of this ballad before Tom Underhill's political parody in 1642, it had circulated freely before Charles the First sat on his tottering throne. Nevertheless, it seems to have been a novelty to Samuel Pepys, when he heard it sung on the 16th of June, 1668 (Tuesday), at Newbury, where he had dinner—"and musick: a song of the old Courtier of Queen Elizabeth's, and how he was changed upon the coming in of the King, did please me mightily, and I did cause W. Hewer to write it out."—*Diary*, v. 309-310, 1877 (Mynors Bright's edition).

There are many variations. One version, modernised, "With an Old Song," is in Ritson's *English Songs*, ii. 140, 1783 (music in vol. iii.). Also with music, the old song had been given in *Pills to Purge Melancholy*, iii. 280, 1719. When reprinted in *the Convivial Songster*, 1782, p. 210, with music, a foot-note told that "Some people, instead of the above burden of the *Old and New Courtier*, sing—'*Moderation, moderation, this was ancient moderation!*' and, at the change of the burden—'*Alteration, alteration, this is modern alteration!*' Edwin the actor (as Gregory, in J.S.'s "Battle of Hexham," act iii. sc. 2) sang the following imitation, or parody, at the Theatre Royal, Crowe Street, London, in 1789:—

Moderation and Alteration.

IN a quiet old parish, on a brown healthy old moor,
Stands my master's old gate, whose threshold is wore,
With many old friends who for liquor wou'd roar,
And I uncork'd the sherry that I tasted before.
Moderation!

Then I had my quiet pantry, of the servants was head,
Kept the key of the old cellar, old plate, and chipp'd the brown bread;
If an odd old barrel was missing, it was easily said,
That the very old beer was one morning found dead.
Moderation!

But we had a good old custom, when the week did begin,
To shew by my account I had not wasted a pin:
For my lord, tho' he was bountiful, thought waste was a sin,
And never wou'd lay out much, but when my lady lay-in.
Moderation!

Good lack, good lack, dame Fortune on me did frown,
And I left my old quiet pantry, to trudge from town to town,
Worn off my old legs, in search of bobs, thumps, and cracks of the crown,
I was fairly knock'd up, and almost foully knock'd down.
Alteration!

—Written by **George Colman**, the Younger.

Old Courtier.

[Our earliest printed copy follows '*Le Prince d'Amour*,' printed for *William Leake*, at the Crown in Fleet Street, betwixt the two Temple Gates, June, 1660.]

AN old song made by an old aged Pate,
Of an old worshipful gentleman, had a wealthy estate,
That kept an old house at a bountiful rate,
And an old Porter to relieve poor people at his gate,
Like an old Courtier of [the] Queen's, [*i.e.* of Q. *Elizabeth*.
And the Queen's old Courtier.

With an old Lady whose anger one word asswageth,
Who every Quarter paid his old Servants their wages,
Who never knew what belonged to Coachman, Footmen, nor Pages,
But kept two and fifty men in Blew caps and badges.
Like an old Courtier [of the Queen's], &c.

With an old Study, stuft full of old learned books,
And an old Parson, you may know him by his looks;
And an old Butt'ry-hatch worn quite off the old hooks,
And an old Kitchin that maintain'd half a dozen old Cooks.
Like an old [Courtier of the Queen's], &c.

With an old Hall hung with Pikes, Guns, and Bows,
And old blades and Bucklers, had borne many shrowd blows,
With an old Freezadoe coat to cover his trunck hose,
With an old cup of Sherry to comfort his old nose.
Like an old [Courtier of the Queen's], &c.

With an old fashion, when Christmas was come,
To call in all his old neighbors with a Bagpipe or a Drum,
And good cheer enough to furnish out every old room,
And Beer and Ale would make a cat to speak, and a wise man dumb.
Like an old [Courtier of the Queen's], &c.

With an old Faulkner, a Huntsman, and a Kennel of Hounds,
That never Hauked nor hunted but in his grand-father's old grounds,
Who like a wise man kept himself in his own old bounds [*misp.* "pounds."
And when he died gave each child a thousand old pounds.
Like an old [Courtier of the Queen's], &c.

But to his son and heir his lands he assign'd,
With an old will to charge him to keep the same bountiful minde,
To be good to his old Tenants, and to his old neighbours kinde,
But in the next ditty you shall hear how he was inclin'de.
Like a new Courtier of the King's, [*i.e.* of James I.
And the King's new Courtier.

[The Second Part, To THE SAME TUNE, of the *Queen's Courtier.*]

New Courtier.

WITH a new flourishing Gallant, [who] is newly come to his land,
Who keeps a brace of painted Creatures at his own command,
And can take up readily a thousand pounds on his new Bond,
And drink in a new Tavern, till he can neither go nor stand,
Like a new Courtier [of the King's, and the King's new Courtier].

With a new Lady whose face is beautiful and fair,
Who never knew what belong'd to House-keeping nor care,
But purchas'd seven colour'd Fans to play with the wanton ayr,
And seventeen new Dressings of other women's hair,
Like a new [Courtier of the King's], &c.

With a new study full of Pamphlets and playes,
With a new Chaplain, that drinks oftener than he prays,
With a new Butt'ry-hatch opens once in five or six days,
With a new *French* Cook to devise Kickshaws and toys, [quelques-choses.
For the new [Courtier of the King's], &c.

With a new Hall builded where an old Hall stood,
Hung round with new pictures, does the poore little good,
With a new Shouel-board whereon never stood food,
With 22 fair Chimnies never burnt coals nor wood.
For the new [Courtier of the King's], &c.

With a new fashion when *Christmas* was drawing on,
Upon a new journey they must all to *London* be gon,
And leave none to keep house in the Country, but their new man *John*,
Who relieves all his Neighbors with a great thump on the back with a cold stone,
Like a new [Courtier of the King's], &c.

With a new Gentleman-Usher whose carriage is compleat,
With a new Coachman, and two footmen to carry up the meat,
With a new waiting Gentlewoman whose dressing is very neat,
Who when her Lady hath dined gives her fellows very little meat,
Like a new [Courtier of the King's], &c.

With new titles of honor bought with his Grand-father's old gold,
For which most of his father's Mannors were all sold,
And that's one cause housekeeping is grown so cold,
Yet this is the new course most of our new Gallants hold.
Like new Courtiers of the King's, and the King's new Courtiers.

Thus have you heard of the old Courtiers and the new,
And for the last I could wish never a word were true,
With these rude lines which I dedicate to you,
And these rude verses I present to your view,
By the poor Courtier of the King's, and the King's poor Courtier.

[Roxburghe Collection, III. 72; Pepys, II. 211; Douce, II. 172 *verso.*]

An Old Song of the Old Courtier of the King's, [prop. *Queen's.* with a New Song of a new Courtier of the King's.

THE TUNE IS, *The Queen's Old Courtier.*

Old.

AN old song made, of an Old aged pate,
Of an old Gentleman who had a wealthy estate,
Who kept an old House at a bountiful rate,
[And an old Porter to relieve the old poor at his gate], [*caret.*
Like an old Courtier of the King's, [*sic.* mis-printed for "*Queen's*"
And the King's old Courtier.

New.

A new flourishing Gallant, newly come to his Land,
And can take up a thousand pound on his own new Band, [bond.
Who keeps two painted creatures at his own command,
[And gets drunk in a Tavern, till he can neither go nor stand:] [*caret.*
Like a young Courtier of the King's, and the King's new Courtier.

Old.

An old Lady, whose anger one word asswages,
And every quarter pays her old Servants their wages;
Who never knew what belongs to Coach, Footmen, nor Pages,
But keeps fifty-two stout fellows in blew Coats and badges;
Like an old Courtier [of the Queen's], &c.

New.

A new Lady, whose face is beautiful and fair,
And never knew what belong['d] to house-keeping nor care,
But buyes a new Fan to play with the wanton air,
And several new dressings of other women's hair;
Like a young Courtier [of the King's], &c.

Old.

An old Hall, hung round with Pikes, Bills, and Bows,
Swords, blades, and bucklers, that have endured stout blows,
And an old Frizadow Coat, to cover his worship's Trunck-hose,
And an old cup of Sherry to burnish up his honourable Nose.
Like an old [Courtier of the Queen's], &c.

Note.—Our copy (Roxb. Coll. III. 72) "printed for *F. Coles*, in *Wine-Street*, on *Saffron-Hill*, neer *Hatton Garden*," early in the reign of Charles II., is declared to have been "Written by T. Howard, Gent." Evidently this means that he wrote the said broadside version. It is improbable, therefore, that he wrote the (p. 756) *Prince d'Amour* version. No one who possessed the skill there displayed could have been idiot enough to mutilate and disintegrate the complete ballad by interweaving the two Parts, alternating each stanza of the "Old Courtier" with one of "The New Courtier," moreover making them both "Courtiers of the *King's*" (*sic*). T. Howard is to be held merely as the cobbler or patcher-up of a garbled version. Nevertheless (as it belongs to the Roxburghe Collection, and is a rarity in this broadside reconstruction), it is reproduced here. The *original* was of 1611-14, when the newly-made £1080 baronets and £40 knights were drugs in the market: compare p. 757, lines 79 to 84 (omitted from T. Howard's version).

The Second Part, to the same Tune.

New.

A New Hall, built where the Old Hall stood,
Hung round with pictures, that does the poor but little good,
And a new Chimney that never burnt cole nor wood,
And a new Shufle-board-table whereon meat never stood.
Like a new Courtier [of the King's], and the King's new Courtier. 36

Old.

And an old Study, stuft full of old learned books,
And an old reverend Chaplain, you might know him by his looks;
And an old Kitching that maintains half a dozen old Cooks,
And an old butt'ry-hatch [that is] worn off the old hooks,
Like an old Courtier [of the Queen's], &c.

New.

A new Study, stuft full of Pamphlets and plays,
And a new drunken Chaplain, [who] swears faster than he prays,
And a new buttery-hatch opens once in four or five days,
[And a new *French* Cook, to devise fine *kick-shaws* and Toys.] [*caret.*
Like a new Courtier [of the King's], &c. 48

Old.

An old Faulkner, a Huntsman, and a kennel of hounds,
And his worship did never hawk nor hunt but in his Grand-father's grounds,
And when he dyed left every child a thousand of old pounds,
Like an old [Courtier of the Queen's], &c.

New.

A new fashion when Christmas was drawing on,
This new Knight and his Lady to *London* must be gone,
And left none at home, but the new Porter *John*,
To relieve poor people with a thump on the back with a cold stone.
Like a new Courtier [of the King's], &c. 60

Old.

An old fashion when *Christmasse* was drawing on,
Calls all his neighbours and tenants together with bag-pipe and drum,
And meat enough to furnish every old room,
And beer that will make a [Cat] speak, and a wise man dumb. [text, 'Car.'
Like an old [Courtier of the Queen's], &c.

New.

And when he dyed to his Son and heir he assign'd
To be good to his Neighbors, and to his Tennants kind,
And to keep still the same bountiful mind,
Like an old Courtier [of the Queen's], &c. 72

New.

A new Gentleman Usher whose carriage is compleat,
And the Coachman, Grooms, and Foot-men to carry up the meat,
And when they din'd left them little to eat.
Like a new Courtier of the King's,
And the king's new Courtier.

Written by **T. Howard**, Gent.

London, Printed for *F. Coles*, in *Wine-Street*, on *Saffron-Hill*, neer *Hatton-Garden.*

[In Black-letter. Two woodcuts, given already. 1st, is of Prince Henry (?), on p. 66, Left; 2nd, the man making obeisance, p. 478. Date of this issue (same as Pepys') probably *circâ* 1661-74; *bis-cocta* by T. Howard. See *Note*, p. 758.]

Here Ends the Group of Legendary and Romantic Ballads.

Editorial Epilogue.

HERE *ends our* " Group of Ballads choice,
  Romantic Legendary lore ; "
Whereto the Minstrel tuned his voice
And twanging harp in days of yore.

The grim old Baron bent his ear,
Miladi, still the wanderer's friend,
Gave largesse, and perchance a tear,
When sadder story near'd the end.

Gather'd around them, glad to trace
The varying fortunes of the tale,
The sturdy henchmen, bronzed of face,
With young handmaidens, flush'd or pale.

Then heard they of Adventures brave,
Of Love that could nor faint nor fail,
Of Faith triumphant o'er the grave,
Of Dames oppress'd, and Infant's wail ;

How Kings must yield to Cupid's *dart :*
How Traitors are unmask'd by Time ;
How loyal Service plays its part,
To punish arrogance or crime.

Behind th' enraptur'd fire-lit throng,
Contented, happy, warm and fed—
From bleak grey moorland, boding wrong,
Lurk'd spectral Shadows of the Dead.

Thus, while you scan these Ballads rare,
COMRADE, *of many a bygone year,*
We raise anew some Visions fair,
Gleaming from background dark and drear.

17. vii. '88. J. W. EBSWORTH.

Appendix.

> "Let us alone. Time driveth onward fast,
> And in a little while our lips are dumb.
> Let us alone. What is it that will last?
> All things are taken from us, and become
> Portions and parcels of the dreadful Past."
>
> —Tennyson's *Lotus-Eaters*, 1832.

A FEW light taps of the drum, and "the tune of our catch played by the picture of Nobody," ought to suffice to call around the *Appendix* Maypole those who have not yet grown weary of Roxburghe Ballads. The Sixth Volume is nearly ended, but it seems hard to leave outside, shivering in the cold, three 'strays' for which no shelter had been afforded within the "Group of Legendary and Romantic Ballads." One is the doleful ditty sang or screeched by a ballad singer amid the crowd gathered at the window of "The Distressed Musician," as painted and engraved by Hogarth in 1740: that "*Lady's Fall,*" the tune of which had been already cited on pp. 650, 651, 693, and elsewhere. A second is "The Fair Maid of Dunsmore's Lamentation, occasioned by Lord Wigmore, once Governor of Warwick Castle." Neither of these won admittance to the group, for substantial and patent reasons. The third (now placed before them on p. 762), entitled "Mock-Beggar's Hall," holds sufficiently close connection with "The Old and Young Courtier" of our pp. 754, 759, to justify it being here brought into contrast without delay. It moreover resembles "The Map of Mock-Beggar's Hall," already reprinted in *Roxburghe Ballads*, vol. ii. pp. 132-136, 659.

"Mock-Beggar's Hall" was a conventional title for a showy outside, cheerless within; a palatial structure devoid of hospitality. This is well described in the penultimate stanza of the ensuing ballad, the pretentious mansions having been built sumptuously to extol the repute of their owners, and not to harbour strangers: they are hypocritical whited-sepulchres of evil guise.

> Let any Poor to such a door
> Come, they expecting plenty,
> They there may ask till their throats are sore,
> *For Mock-Beggar Hall stands empty.*

Charles I. attempted to stem the influx of town-seeking country gentry, which had caused much discontent in rural districts. In modern times also complaints have been frequent against *Absenteeism*; but this always meant absent-dinnerism.

[Roxburghe Collection, III. 218.]

Mock-Begger's Hall,

With its situation in the spacious Country called Anywhere.

To the Tune of, *It is not your Northern Nancy*; or, *Sweet is the Lass that loves me*. (See p. 763.)

IN ancient times, when as plain dealing was most of all in fashion,
  There was not then half so much stealing, nor men so given to passion;
But now-a-days Truth so decays, and false knaves there are plenty,
So Pride exceeds all worthy deeds, *while Mock-begger Hall stands empty.*

The Hangman now the fashion keeps, and swaggers like our Gallants;
While Love and Charity sits and weeps, to see them waste their Talents;
Spend all their store, untill no more, such Prodigals there are plenty,
Thus brave it out, while men them flout, *and Mock-begger Hall stands empty.*

Ned Swash hath fetched his cloth[e]s from pawn, with dropping of the barrell;
Joan Dust hath bought a smock of Lawn, and now begins to quarrell:
She thinks her selfe, poor silly Elfe, to be the best of twenty,
And yet, the whore is wondrous poor, *while Mock-begger Hall stands empty.*

I read in ancient times of yore, that men of worthy calling, [*N.B.*
Built Alms-houses and Spittles' store, which now are all down falling;
And few men seek them to repair, nor now is there one among twenty,
That for good deeds will take any care, *while Mock-begger Hall stands empty.*

[With this, our *fourth* stanza (which is the *first* in the other, Roxb. Coll., I. 252), the two versions coalesce, for nine stanzas (see *Roxburghe Ballads*, vol. ii. pp. 131-136); the tenth of the other being substituted for our thirteenth of Roxb. Coll., III. 218; the next-following stanza being common to both.]

Farm-houses, which their fathers built, and Land well kept by tillage,
Their prodigal sons have sold for gilt, in every town and village. [*i.e.* cash.
To the City and Court they do resort, with gold and silver plenty;
And there they spend their time in sport, *while Mock-begger Hall stands empty.*

Young Landlords, when to age they come, their rents they would be racking;
The Tenant must give a golden sum, or else he is turn'd packing:
Great fines, and double rent beside, or else they'll not contented be:
It is for to maintain their monstrous pride, *while Mock-begger Hall stands empty.*

Their fathers went in homely freez, and wore good plain cloth breeches; [*frieze.*
Their stockings with the same agrees, sowed on with good strong stitches;
They were not then call'd Gentle-men, though they had wealth great plenty,
Now every Gull's grown worshipfull, *while Mock-begger Hall stands empty.*

No gold or silver parchment Lace was worn, but by our Nobles; [*2nd Part: same tune.*
Nor would the honest harmless face wear Cuffs with so many doubles;
Their bands were to their shirts sown then, yet cloth was full as plenty;
Now one band hath more cloth than ten, *while Mock-begger Hall stands empty.*

Now we are Apes in imitation, the more indeed's the pity;
The City followes the Stranger's fashion, the Country follows the City:
And ere one fashion is known throughout, another they will invent yee;
'Tis all your Gallants study about, *while Mock-begger Hall stands empty.*

Me thinks it is a great reproach, to those that are nobly descended,
Wh[o] for their pleasure cannot have a Coach, wherewith they might be attended,
But every beggerly *Jack* and *Gill*, that eat scant a good meal in twenty,
Must through the streets be jaunted still, *while Mock-begger Hall stands empty.*

There's some are rattled thorow the streets; *Probatum est*, I tell it,
Whose names are wrapt in parchment sheets; it grieves their hearts to spell it:
They are not able two men to keep, with a Coach-man they must contented be,
Which at Goldsmiths-hall door in's box lies asleep, *while Mock-begger Hall stands empty.*

Our Gentle-women, whose means is nothing, to that which they make shew of,
Must use all the fashions in their cloathing, which they can hear or know of;
They take such care themselves to deck, that Money is oft so scanty,
The belly is forc'd to complain to the back, *while Mock-begger Hall stands empty.*

There is a crue, and a very mad crue, that about the Town doth swagger,
That seems like Knights to the people's view, and wear both sword and dagger;
That sweetens their clothes once a week; Hunger with them is so plenty,
The Broker will not have them to seek, *while Mock-begger Hall stands empty.*

[For the above, our thirteenth stanza, the "*Map of Mock-Begger Hall*" version gives an equivalent, tenth stanza, as already told, *viz.*:—

It may well be that some will muse, Wherefore, in this relation,
The name of Mocke-begger *I doe use, without any explanation;*
To cleare which doubt before I end, because they shall all content be,
To shew the meaning I doe intend, of Mock-begger Hall stands empty.

The next stanza coincides in both broadsides, beginning, "Some Gentlemen."]

Some Gentlemen and Citizens have, in divers eminent places,
Erected Houses fine and brave, which stood for the Owners' graces.
Let any poor to such a door come, they expecting plenty,
They there may ask till their throats are sore, *for Mock-begger Hall stands empty.*

[Next follows a final stanza, in each, differing so far that we add in *Italic type* the other version for comparison in a footnote below. This is our exemplar's:—]

Thus plainly I to you declare how strangely times are changed;
What Humours in the people are, how virtue is estranged:
How every *Jackanapes* can strut, such Coxcombs there are plenty;
But at the last in [the] Prison shut, *so Mock-begger Hall stands empty.*

Finis.

Printed at *London* for *Richard Harper*, at the *Bible and Harp, Smithfield.*

[In Black-letter, with a woodcut, *Malory's*, used for "Love's Lunacie," now reproduced on p. 766. Date, *circâ* 1636-42, not later, and probably earlier.]

Note.—Here is the final stanza, twelfth, of "*The Map of Mock-Begger Hall,*" "printed neere to the *Hospitall-gate* in *Smithfield*, for *Richard Harper.*"

Thus in these times we can perceive small Charity, comfort yielding,
For Pride doth men of Grace bereave, not only in Cloathes, but in Building;
Man makes the senselesse stones and bricke, which by Heaven's goodnesse lent be,
Expresse his pride by these vaine trickes; thus Mock-begger Hall stands empty.

*** Of the two names to the tune, mentioned for this ballad, the first is *Northern Nancy*, or '*It is not your Northern Nancy*' (probably the first line of the lost ballad). See Wm. Chappell's *Popular Music*, p. 355. The other tune-name, *So sweet is the Lass that loves me*, is of Martin Parker's ballad, "Love's Solace" (reprinted in *Roxburghe Ballads*, vol. i. p. 623), to a new Court tune called *The Damask Rose*, believed to be *Omnia vincit Amor* of the Skene MS., "O! that I were with my true Love."

[Roxburghe Collection, III. 148, 164, 570; Pepys, I. 510; Euing, 196; Douce, III. 62 *verso*; Jersey, II. 317.]

A Lamentable Ballad of the Ladie's Fall.

Declaring how a Gentlewoman through her too much trust came to her end, and how her Lover slew himself.

The Tune is, *In Pescod time.* [See p. 650.]

MArk well my heavy doleful tale, you Loyal Lovers all,
And heedfully bear in your brest a gallant Ladie's fall:
Long was she woo'd e're she was won to lead a wedded life,
But folly wrought her overthrow before she was a wife.

Too soon, alas! she gave consent to yield unto his will,
Though he protested to be true, and faithful to her still:
She felt her body altered quite, her bright hue waxed pale,
Her fair red cheeks turn'd colour white, her strength began to fail.

So that with many a sorrowful sigh this beauteous Maiden mild, [Lady.
With grievous heart perceiv'd her self to be conceiv'd with child:
She kept [it] from her father's sight, as close as close might be,
And so put on her silken gown none might her swelling see.

Unto her lover secretly she did her self bewray, [a.l. her grief she.
And walking with him hand in hand, these words to him did say:
"Behold," said she, "a Maid's distress, my love, brought to thy bow,
Behold I go with child by thee, but none thereof doth know.

"The little babe springs in my womb to hear the father's voice;
Let it not be a bastard call'd, sith I made thee my choice:
Come, come, my love, perform thy vow, and wed me out of hand;
O leave me not in this extream, in grief alwayes to stand!

"Think on thy former promise made, thy vows and oaths each one;
Remember with what bitter tears to me thou mad'st thy moan:
Convey me to some secret place, and marry me with speed,
Or with thy rapier end my life, ere further shame proceed."

"Alas! my dearest Love," quoth he, "my greatest joy on earth,
Which way can I convey thee hence, without a sudden death?
Thy friends they be of high degree, and I of mean estate,
Full hard it is to get thee forth out of thy father's gate."

"Dread not thy [life] to save my fame, and if thou taken be,
My self will step between the swords, and take the harm on me;
So shall I scape Dishonour quite, if so I should be slain,
What could they say? but that true love did work a Ladie's bane.

"And do not fear any further harm, my self will so devise,
That I will go away with thee unseen of mortal eyes; [a.l. ride.
Disguised like some pretty Page, I'le meet thee in the dark;
And all alone I'le come to thee hard by my father's park."

And then, quoth he, "I'le meet my love, if God do lend me life,
And this day moneth without all fail, I will make thee my wife."
Then with a sweet and loving kiss, they parted presently,
And at their parting brinish tears stood in each other's eye.

At length the wished-day was come, where[in] this lovely Maid, [‘as.’
With lo[nging] eyes and strange attire for her true lover staid;
When any person she espy'd come riding o're the plain,
She thought it was her own true love, but all her hopes were vain.

Then did she weep, and sore bewail her most unhappy state,
Then did she speak these woful words, when succourless she sat.
“O false, forsworn, and faithless wretch, disloyal to thy love, [*a.l.* man.
Hast thou forgot thy promise made, and wilt thou perjur'd prove?

“And hast thou now forsaken me, in this my great distress,
To end my days in open shame, which thou might'st well redress?
Wo worth the time I did believe that flattering tongue of thine,
Would God that I had never seen the tears of thy false eyne!”

And thus, with many a sorrowful sigh, homewards she went again;
No rest came in her wat'ry eyes, she felt such bitter pain.
In travel strong she fell that night, with many a bitter throw,
What woful pangs she felt that night doth each good woman know.

She called up her waiting-maid, that lay at her bed's-feet,
Who musing at her Mistress woe, did strait begin to weep.
“Weep not,” said she, “but shut the door and windows round about,
Let none bew[ray] my wretched case, but keep all persons out.” [‘bewail.’

“O Mistress, call your mother dear, of women you have need,
And of some skilful mid-wives' help, the better you may speed.
“Call not my mother, for thy life, nor call no women here;
The mid-wives' help comes now too late, my death I do not fear.”

With that the babe sprang in her womb, no creature being nigh,
And with a sigh that broke her heart, this gallant dame did dye:
This living little infant young, the mother being dead, [*a.l.* little lovely.
Resign'd his new-received breath to Him that had him made.

Next morning came her Lover true, affrighted at this news, [*a.* own true l.
And he for sorrow slew himself, whom each one did accuse:
The mother with the new-born babe, were both laid in one grave,
Their Parents overcome with woe, no joy of them could have. [over worn.

Take heed, you dainty damsels all, of flattering words beware;
And of the honour of your name have you a special care!
Too true, alas! this story is, as many one can tell,
By others' harms learn to be wise, and thou shalt do full well.

Printed for *F. Coles, T. Vere, J. Wright*, and *J. Clarke*.

[In Black-letter. Four woodcuts. 1st and 2nd on p. 163, *ante*; 3rd, new, a woman in bed, another woman standing near; 4th, adjoined, the man killing himself, as on p. 794. This ballad of the “*Lady's Fall*” was entered to William White on 11th June, 1603, in the Stationers' Registers, book C., fol. 97 (=Arber's *Transcript*, iii. 237), along with other ballads (*cf.* pp. 571, 653, 656). It is in the *Reliques*, and Ritson's *English Songs*, ii. 209. Lines 19, 20, and last couplet *carent* in *Percy Folio MS.*, pp. 268–270, whence corrections are won. Roxb. Coll., III. 570, is modern, n.p.n.]

*** Another tragic ballad, of heartless seduction and misery, is the account of Fair Isabel of Dunsmore Heath, Warwickshire, and Lord Wigmore of Warwick Castle. We give two versions. *Dunsmore-Heath* had previously produced the *Dun Cow*, which was slain by *Guy of Warwick* (pp. 729, 733, 736, 781), before it gave nurture to the apocryphal maiden, *Isabel*, of next page.

Lord Wigmore and Fair Isabel of Dunsmore.

"There lately was a Maiden fair, . . that lived on *Dunsmore-Heath*, Sir."
—*Dunsmore Kate*, 1698. (*Cf.* p. 772.)

ANOTHER version of the story of Lord Wigmore and Isabel of Dunsmore Heath, differing in diction but not in the incidents from our pp. 767-770, and issued by the same publishers, is preserved in *Cupid's Garland, set round about with Guilded Roses: containing many pleasant Songs and Sonnets, newly written*. The motto is, '*Omnia amatore Debuerat fortis implicuisse comas.*' Printed for *John Clarke*, *William Thackeray*, and *Thomas Passinger*. The contents in part coincide with Richard Johnson's *Crowne Garland of Goulden Roses*, of much earlier date, *viz*. 1612, including this very piece; named in *Cupid's Garland* as 'A song of the Lord *Wigmore* and the Fair Maid of *Dunsmore* in *Warwickshire*, which may be a warning to all maids to shun the alurements of wanton Gallants.' Tune of, *The Earl of Essex's last good night* [for mention of which see our p. 623]. It begins, like ours on p. 771 (in which we accept *The Crowne Garland* version). "In *Warwickshire* there stands a down." It is followed immediately by its second part, "The sad Complaint of fair *Isabel*, for the loss of her maiden honour; at the end whereof, like *Roman Lucrece*, she slew her self. To the same Tune." It begins differently from ours, "Lord *Whigmore*, pitty take on me!" five stanzas of eight lines each, and the burden of '*Lord Whigmore, this is long of thee*:' fourteenth line of "The Complaint." Richard Johnson's *Crowne Garland of Golden Roses* was entered to John Wrighte (Stationers' Registers, C. 216 *verso*), 18 Feb., 16$\frac{11}{12}$.

[Woodcut (from *Morte d'Arthur*, Book 2nd), belongs to pp. 710 and 762.]

[Roxburghe Collection, II. 170; III. 893; Bagford, II. 28; Jersey, II. 187; Euing, 117: Wood, E. 25. 71.]

The Fair
Maid of Dunsmore's Lamentation.

Occasioned by Lord Wigmore, once Governour of Warwick-Castle.

Being a full and true Relation, how Lord Wigmore enticed the fair Isabel of Dunsmore, in Warwick-shire, a Shepherd's daughter, to his Bed; she afterwards perceiving her self to be with child by him, rather than she would undergo the vulgar disgrace amongst her Friends, did stab her self, and dyed immediately.

TUNE OF [*When*] *Troy Town.* [See p. 548.] **With allowance.**

ALl you that ever heard the name
Of *Wigmore*, that renowned Lord,
Who once had gain'd a glorious fame,
But lost it of his own accord,
A lustful love did cause her woe,
Which did his Honour overthrow.

The King had made him Governour
Of *Warwick-Castle*, where he dwelt
Not long, but quickly heard of her,
Whose name to name my heart doth melt:
A lustful love [*did cause her woe*], etc.

Fair *Isabel* they did her call,
A Shepheard's Daughter fair and bright,
Which caus'd this man of might to fall
In love with her at the first sight:
A lustful love [*did cause her woe*], etc.

Lord *Wigmore* on a Summer's day,
With his own Servant walkt the field,
By a small river they took their way,
Whose murmuring current did pleasure yield,
But a lustful love [*did cause her woe*], etc.

They had not walked very far,
But easily they might espye
Fair *Isabel's* body to appear,
A-washing of herself just by:
A lustful love [*did cause her woe*], etc.

She in the silver stream alone
Was washing of her milk white skin;
But had she her misfortunes known,
She would not in that place have been:
A lustful love [did cause her woe], etc.

The more he lookt, the more he lov'd,
Till looking did for action call;
With flames of lust his heart was mov'd
To work her ruin and his fall.
A lustful love [did cause her woe], etc.

Thus viewing her with burning pain,
He could no longer there abide,
But to his castle returns again,
And there would fain his passion hide.
But lustful love [did cause her woe], etc.

But all in vain, the more he strove
From love-sick fancies to retire,
The more he burnt in lustful love,
And *Isabel* must quench the fire:
A lustful love [did cause her woe], etc.

A trusty servant forth he sends,
To bring her to him without delay,
Resolving for to have his ends,
And quickly too, he could not stay,
A lustful love [did cause her woe], etc.

The servant goes at his command,
And vows he will not be deny'd,
There did he spy fair *Isabel* stand,
Just dressed by the river side,
A lustful love [did cause her woe], etc.

The servant told her courteously,
His Lord desired her for to come,
For he must speak with her instantly;
She grants, and went into his room.
A lustful love [did cause her woe], etc.

Lord *Wigmore* fell upon his knees,
And beg'd to him she would be kind,
Crying, "*Isabel*, my dear, none sees,
Blush not, my sweetest, love is blind."
A lustful love [did cause her woe], etc.

Her innocence was overcome,
Oh pitty 'twas, she was beguil'd,
She afterwards returned home,
And from that time conceiv'd with child.
A lustful love did cause her woe[, etc.].

Fair Isabel's Mournful Recantation.

AT *Dunsmore* the fair *Isabel*
  Near unto *Warwick*, that brave town,
There 'twas she mournfully did dwell,
  Repenting what was yet unknown.
    With sighs she cryes, "Heaven pity me,
    Lord Wigmore, *this is 'long of thee!"*

Quoth she, "Alas! what shall I do,
  Or unto whom shall I make my moan?
Each day and hour increase my woe,
  And yet I dare not make it known."
    With sighs [*she cryes, "Heaven pity me!"*] etc. 96

"Oh, that I had ne'r been born,
  [Or] being born, had dyed just then! [Text "and."
Each Virgin will hold me in scorn,
  And shall be scoff'd by all young men."
    With sighs [*she cryes, "Heaven pity me!"*] etc.

At six months' end she could perceive
  Her belly swelled and big did grow,
The Babe within her womb did strive,
  And friends began the cause to know.
    With sighs [*she cryes, "Heaven pity me!"*] etc. 108

Poor *Isabel*, distrest with grief,
  Laments her folly, but too late;
Instead of giving her relief,
  Her friends do prosecute their hate.
    With sighs [*she cryes, "Heaven pity me!"*] etc.

But she, not able to endure
  Their anger and her own disgrace,
Resolves to find a speedy cure,
  In some convenient private place.
    With sighs [*she cryes, "Heaven pity me!"*] etc. 120

With this sad resolution bent,
  She takes a dagger in her hand;
'Twill make a heart of stone relent
  The truth of this to understand,
    With sighs [*she cryes, "Heaven pity me!"*] etc.

She prays that heaven would her forgive,
  Then to her heart her dagger sent,
And down she dropt; let those that live
  Take care betimes, and all Repent.
    At last she cry'd, [*"Heaven pity me!"*] etc. 132

Lord *Wigmore* hearing of this [deed],
He never more had quiet rest,
His guilty heart did in him bleed,
And privately his sins confest,
"*Fair* Isabel, *forgive, and I*
Will pine with sorrow till I dye.

"I must confess I did thee wrong,
And openly will it proclaim;
Let all young men that hear this song
Take care they ne'r commit the same.
Fair Isabel, [*forgive, and I*], etc. 111

"And when I am dead, and blood is cold,
To shew my dear I lov'd thee well,
One Tomb shall both our bodies hold,
Such is my love for *Isabel.*
Fair Saint, forgive my crime, and I
Will pine with sorrow till I dye." **Finis.**

Printed for *J. Wright, J. Clarke, W. Thackeray*, and *T. Passinger.*

[Black-letter. Three woodcuts. 1st and 2nd (originally conjoint) are on p. 47. 3rd, the girl stabbing herself, p. 794, *left*. Substituted cut is given below.]

[Crowne-Garland of Goulden Roses, 1612, 1659; Cupid's Garland, c. 1638.]

The Lamentable Song of the Lord Wigmoore, Governor of Warwicke Castle, and the Fayre Maid of Dunsmoore: as a Warning to all Maids to have care how they yeeld to the wanton Delights of young Gallants.

To the Tune of, *Diana* [*and her Darlings deare.* See vol. ii. p. 520].

IN *Warwick*-shire there stands a downe, and *Dunsmoore-Heath* it hath to name,
 Adjoyning to a country toune, made famous by a maiden's fame:
Faire *Isabel*, she called was, a Shepheard's daughter, as some say;
To *Wigmoore's* eare her fame did passe, as he in *Warwicke*-Castle lay.

Poore Love-sick Lord immediately upon her fame set his delight;
And thought much pleasure sure did lie, possessing of so sweet a wight.
Therefore to *Dunsmoore* did repair, to recreate his sickly mind;
Where in a Summer's evening faire his chance was *Isabell* to find.

She sat amidst a meddow greene, most richly spred with smelling flowers,
And by a river she was seene to spend away some evening howers,
There sat this maiden all alone, washing her self in secret wise,
Which Virgin faire to look upon did much delight his longing eyes.

She, thinking not to be espied, had lay'd from her her countrey 'tire;
The tresses of her Haire untied hung glist'ring like the golden wire;
And, as the flakes of winter snow, that lie unmelted on the plaines,
So white her body was in show: like silver springs did run her veines.

He, ravisht with this pleasant sight, stood as a man amazed still;
Suff'ring his eyes to take delight, that never thought they had their fill.
She blinded his affection so, that Reason's rules were led awry;
And Love the coales of lust did blow, which to a fire soone flamed hye;

And, though he knew the sinne was greate, yet burned so within his brest,
With such a vehement scorching heat, that none but she could lend him rest.
Lord *Wigmoore* being thus drown'd in lust, by liking of this dainty dame,
He call'd a Servant of great trust, inquiring straight what was her name.

"She is," quoth he, "no married Wife, but a Shepheard's daughter, as you see,
And with her father leads her life, whose dwellings by these pastures bee:
Her name is *Isabel* the faire." "Then stay" (quoth he), "and speak no more,
But to my Castle straight her beare, her sight hath wounded me full sore."

Thus to Lord *Wigmoore* she was brought; who with delight his fancies fed,
And through his sute such meanes he wrought, that he entic'd her to his bed.
This being done, incontinent, she did return from whence she came,
And every day she did invent to cover her received shame.

But ere three months were fully past, her crime committed plaine appeares:
Unto Lord *Wigmoore* then, in haste, she long complain'd with weeping teares.

[*Second Part.*]

The Complaint of Fair Isabell for the Losse of her Honour; at the end whereof she slew her selfe.

"LOrd *Wigmoore!* thus I have defil'd and spotted my pure Virgin's bed;
 Behold I am conceiv'd with childe, to which vile folly you me led.

"For now this deed that I have wrought throughout this country well is knowne,
And to my woful parents brought, who now for me do make great mone. [" whom "]
How shall I looke them in the face, when they my shamelesse selfe shall see?"
Then sed [she]: "*Eve!* I feele thy case, when thou had'st tasted of the tree;

"Thou hid'st thy selfe, and so must I, but GOD thy trespasse quickly found;
The dark may hide me from man's eye, but leave my shame still to abound.
Wide open are mine eyes to look upon my sad and heavy sinne;
And quite unclasped is the Booke where my accounts are written in.

"This sin of mine deserveth death: be judge, Lord *Wigmoore*, I am shee,
For I have tread a strumpet's path, and for the same I needs must die!
Be-spotted with reproachfull shame to ages following shall I bee,
And in records be writ my blame: Lord *Wigmoore*, this is 'long of thee!

"Lord *Wigmoore*, prostrate at thy feete, I crave my just deserved doom,
That death may cut off from the roote this Body, blossom, branch and bloome!
Let Modesty accurse this crime! let Love, and Law, and Nature speak!
Was ever any wretch yet seene that in one instant all did breake?

"Then, *Wigmoore*, justice on me show, that thus consented to this act,
Give me my death: for death is due to such as sinne in such a fact:
O that the wombe had beene my grave, or I had perisht in my birth!
O that same day may darknesse have, wherein I first drew vitall breath!

"Let GOD regard it not at all! Let not the sunne upon it shine!
Let misty darknesse on it fall, for to make knowne this sinne of mine!
The night wherein I was conceiv'd, let be accurst with mournefull eyes!
Let twinckling starres from skyes be reav'd, and clouds of darknesse thereon rise!

"Because they shut not up the powers that gave the passage to my life.
Come Sorrow, finish up mine howers, and let my time here end with greefe!"
And having made this wofull moane, a knife she snatched from her side,
Where *Lucresse'* part was rightly showne, for with the same, fayre *Isabell* dyed.

Whereat Lord *Wigmoore* grieved sore, in heart repenting his amisse,
And after would attempt no more to crop the flowers of maidens' blisse:
But lived long in woefull wise, till Death did finish up his dayes,
And now in *Isobel's* grave he lyes, till Judgement comes them both to raise.

[Written by **Richard Johnson**.]

At *London*. Printed by *G. Eld* for *John Wright*, and are to be sold at his Shop at *Christ Church Gate*, [*February*] 1612.

[*Various readings* in the Edition of 1659. Line 40, "O cursed *Eve*, I feel thy case," etc. Line 42, "*No* dark may hide me from *God's* eye," etc. Line 46 (which we adopt instead of *tread*, as in 1612 edition), "For I have *trod*," etc., and line 49 (also here adopted), "*Just* deserved doom," but 1612 edition is misprinted "*first*." Line 51 has "Let Modesty *accurse* this crime!" (preferable to "*accuse*" of 1612). Lines 55-60 are paraphrased from *Job*, chapter iii. 3, et seq. "*Let the day perish wherein I was born*, and *the night* in which it was said, There is a man child *conceived*. *Let that day be darkness; let not God regard it* from above; neither let the light shine upon it. Let darkness and the shadow of death stain it . . . Let the stars of the twilight thereof be dark . . . Why died I not from the womb?"]

Dunsmore-Kate (p. 766) begins thus (in *Dancing-Master*, 1698; *Pills*, iv. 210:

"There lately was a Maiden fair, with ruddy cheeks and nut-brown hair,
Who up to Town did trudge, Sir;
This pretty Maid, whose name was *Kate*, met here a hard unlucky fate,
As you anon shall judge, Sir . . .

"Quoth she, 'If these be *London* tricks, God send me down among my *Dicks*,
That live on *Dunsmore* Heath, Sir;
If ever I come here again, or e'er believe one man in ten,
May the De'll come stop my breath, Sir.'" [*Finis.*

The Roxburghe Collection unique copy of "A New Northern Jigge" is in *Roxburghe Ballads*, vol. i. p. 629; with it compare the following, from J. P. Collier's MS., *Twenty-Five Old Ballads*:—

Daintie, come thou to me.

[*He begins*:—]

WIlt thou from me thus part, and leave me in miserie,
When I gave thee haud and hart, onely with thee to live and dye?
Cast from thy hart all care, from thee I nere will flee,
Let them say what they will [*dare*], *Daintie, come thou to mee!*

Were my state or good or ill, rich or else in povertie,
Yet would I ever love thee still; prove thou me, and thou shalt see.
Cast from thy hart, etc., Daintie, come thou to me!

Were you rich, or were you poore, it sholde be the same to mee,
I would beg from doore to doore, if neede were, to maintaine thee.
Cast from thy hart, etc. [*sic. passim.*]

Were I a Lord, were I a Knight, or came I of a hie degree,
All my landes should be thy right, prove thou me, and thou shalt see.

If the *Indian* golde were mine, and all the countless welth of *Spain*,
That, and more, it shold be thine: prove me, Love, yet once againe.

Thy beauty doth the world excell, above all worldes I love but thee;
With thee I faine would ever dwell: prove me, Love, and thou shalt see.

I promise truely for thy sake, all other[s] I will constant flee,
And to thee only will I take: prove me, Love, and thou shalt see.

Let me, then, thy love obtaine, or my death thou 'rt sure to bee;
Return to me now once againe: Sweete, I love, and onelie thee.

If thy frendes doe frowne and fret, and thy parentes angrie bee,
That, I pray thee, be no lett [=hindrance]: I will love but onelie thee.

[THE SECOND PART, TO THE SAME TUNE. *She replies.*]

"HEre is my hand, and here my hart, faith and troth I plight to thee,
From thy side I nere will part, prove thou me and thou shalt see.

"Friendes and parentes I forsake, with thee I vow my life to spend,
And refuse no paine to take, untill my life doe come to ende."

[*He sings*:]—Fare thee well, thou trustie Love, of me thou never shalt complaine;
I will ever constant prove, and full soone we meete againe.

(*He and She.*)—*Cast from thy hart all care,*
From thee I never will flee,
Let them say what they will [*dare*],
Daintie, come thou to me!

Finis.

[In the Roxburghe Collection printed version the burden runs,

Cast no care to thy heart, from thee I will not flee,
Let them say what they will: Dainty, come thou to me!

It does not bring clearly the Lady's reply, dialogue-wise, or the combination of the two voices at the end, like the manuscript. *Quantum valeat. Cf.* pp. 250, 681.]

"Love in a Calm" is mentioned, at foot of p. 570. The song, when extended into the Douce ballad, was called "Love's Tide; or, A Farewell to Folly."

Love in a Calme.

To the Tune of, *Wert thou much fairer than thou art*, or, *Lusty Bacchus.*

HOw cool and temperate am I grown,
Since I could call my heart my own!
Beauty and I now calmly play,
Whilst others burn and melt away.
Not all those wanton hours I have spent
Can rob me of this new content. 6

Love's mists are scatter'd from my sight,
Which flatter'd me with new delight,
And now I see 'tis but a face
That stole my heart out of it's place.
Then Love forgive me, I'le no more
Thine Altars or thy Shrine adore. 12

Farewell to all heart-breaking eyes,
Farewell each look that can surprize,
Farewell those curls and amorous spells,
Farewell each place where beauty dwells.
And farewell each bewitching smile,
I must enjoy my self a while. (1659. Music by Hy. Lawes.)

Diaphantus and Charidora.

EIGHT poems are declared to have been "writ by Sir *Robert Aytoun*, Secretary to *Anne* [of *Denmark*] and [*Henrietta*] *Mary*, Queens of *Great Britain*," and were published in the Third Part of the often-cited and rare compilation (not in the British Museum) entitled *A Choice Collection of Comic and Serious Scots Poems, both Ancient and Modern. By several hands. Edinburgh, Printed by James Watson, and sold at his Shop next door to the Red-Lyon, opposite to the Lucken-booths*, 1711." Of "Diaphantus and Charidora," the first of these eight poems, no earlier edition is known to us; but it may have been printed separately during the lifetime of its accredited author. (He was born at Kinaldie in 1570; died at Whitehall, 1638; and buried in Westminster Abbey.) But William Drummond of Hawthornden, in a list of his own English books, mentions one called "*Diaphantus*, price 6d." This occurs in his diary, A.D. 1611, a hundred years before James Watson reprinted the poem. Aytoun in a Latin panegyric addressed to James I. in 1603 alludes to *Diaphantus* by name:—

Culpa quidem ingenii permultum deterit, at nos [copied *litm.*
Non adeo agresti carmen tenuamus avenâ,
Ut tibi non olim patrio vernacula versu
Riserit, occultos dum suspiraret amores,
Et *Charidoreo Diophantus* ferveret æstu
Forsit et haec, quamvis grandi fastosa boatu
Non fremat at tenui tantum spiramine musset,
Oceani transvecta domos et cærula regna,
Augustas grata novitate morabitur aures. [*Delitiæ Poet. Scot.*

We have (on pp. 584-586) reprinted the poems '*Diaphantas and Charidora*' (or '*Caridora*'). There is no evidence adduced of these being so early in date as *circâ* 1603; and they probably were later. But the date is uncertain, like the authorship. Possibly they were written by Sir Robert Aytoun. We suspend judgement, but add the longer poem, to our reprinted *Roxburghe Ballads.*

On Diaphantus and Charidora.

(*By Sir Robert Aytoun, before* 1603.)

WHen *Diaphantus* knew the Destinies decreet,
How he was forced to forgoe his dear and only Sweet,
O'ervaulted with the vail of beam-rebeating trees,
And ghastly gazing on the ground, even Death-stroke in his eyes:
Oft pressed he to speak, but whyll he did assay,
The agonizing dreads of Death his wrestling voice did stay.
At last, as one that strives against both woe and shame,
"Dear *Charidora*, ah!" he cryes, "my high adored Dame;
First I attest thy name, and then the Gods above,
But chief of those, the Boy that bears the stately style of *Love*.
Let those record with me what was my constant part,
And if I did not honour thee with a well-hallowed Heart:
I sacrificed to thee my secret chaste Desires,
Upon thy Beautie's Altar burnt, with never-quenching fires.
Thou was that Idol still whose image I adored,
The Saint to whom I made my vows, whose pitties I implored:
The Star that saved my ship from tempest of Despair,
When the Horizon of my Hope o'er-clouded was with care:
Thou was the sovereign Balm, that sweet *Catholicon*, [= *Panacea*
Which cured me of all my cares, when I did grieve and groan;
Tho' now, such strange events are interveen'd since syne,
As I dare not avow to say, or think that thou art mine;
Which makes me thus insert, in those my sorrowing Songs,
The History of my Mishap, my Miseries and Wrongs:
Not that I can accuse my *Charidora*, no!
I only execrate the Fates, chief workers of my Woe.
"Should She whom I have lov'd, so many loathsome years,
For whom my dew-distilling eyes have shed such streams of tears—
Should She, I say, be made a prey to such an one,
Who for her sake yet never gave not one untymely groan?
No, surely, surely no; the Fates may do me wrong,
And make her, by their bad Decreet, to whom they please belong.
Yet I dare boldly say, and peradventure vaunt,
That she is mine by Lot of Love, tho' Luck in Love I want.
And tho' my Horoscope envy my worldly things,
Yet unto Love it gave me leave for to compair with Kings,
And if I knew the Vyer, under the starry sky, [*Vyer* = Rival.
That durst avow to love my Dame more faithfully than I,
I should tear out this heart, that entertains my breath,
And cast it down before her feet, to dye a shameful death.
"But since both Time and She have try'd me to be true,
And found such faithfulness in me as shall be found in few;
I rest secure in this, and care not who pretend,
The mo'e pursues, the more my part proves perfect to the End.
And others' faithless Faiths in ballance weigh'd with mine,
Shall make my Faith for to triumph, and as the Sun to shine.
There shall no change of things, of time, of soyl, nor air,
Inforce me to forgoe the Vows made to my fairest Fair,
Which here I do renew in solemn form again,
To witness, as I did begin, so shall I still remain.
"I swear by those two Eyes, my only dearest Dear,
And by the *Stygian* stanks of Hell, whereby the Gods did swear,

That thou art only she whose Countenance I crave, [=she alone.
And shall be both in life and death thy best affected Slave;
That there shall no deceits of lovely laughing Eyen,
No sugar'd sound of *Syren* songs, with far-fetch'd sighs between,
Deface out of my mind what Love did so ingrave,
Thy words, thy looks, and such things else, as none but Angels have.
And this which here I swear, and solemnly protest,
Those Trees which only present are shall witness and attest.
But Chiefly, above all, this holy Shade and Green,
On which the Cyphers of our Names character'd shall be seen.
"O happy, happy Tree, into whose tender rynd
The trophies of our Love shall live eternally inshryn'd;
Which shall have force to make thy memory remain,
Sequestrate from the bastard sort of Trees which are prophane.
And when with careless looks the rest ov'rpast shall be,
Then thou shall be ador'd and kist for *Charidora's* Tree.
And peradventure too, for *Diaphantus'* sake,
Some civil person that comes by shall Homage to thee make.
Thus blest shall thou remain, while I unhappy prove,
And doubtful where I shall be blest, when I shall leave my Love.
"Indeed, all is in doubt; but thus I must depart, ["but this." MS.
The Body must a Pilgrim be, and she retain the Heart.
The thoughts of which Exile and dolorous Divorce
Works sorrow; Sorrow doth from me those sad Complaints inforce:
For while I was resolv'd to smoother up my Grief,
Because it might but move in men more marvel than belief:
The never-ceasing frowns of mal-encountrous Fates
Extorted those abortive births of importune Regrets,
To witness to the world that my Mishaps are such,
As tho' I mourn like one half mad, I cannot mourn too much.
For if of all Mishaps this be the First of all,
To have been highly happy once, and from that height to fall,
I'm sure I may well say that *Diaphantus'* name
Is the Synonyme of Mishaps, or else exceed the same.
Or if there be no Hell but out of Heaven to be,
Consider what her Want should work, whose Sight was such to me."
I think all these that speak of Sorrow, should think shame,
When *Diaphantus* shall be heard, or *Charidora's* name;
Her Worth was without spot, his Truth was unreprov'd:
The one deserv'd at least to live, the other to be lov'd.
Yet hath the dev'lish Doom of Destinies ordain'd
That he should lose both Life and Love, and she a faithful Friend.
Wherefore all you that hears those am'rous tragick Plays,
Bestow on him a World of Plaints, on her a World of Praise.

The Whittington Defeat.

THE race-course on Whittington Heath, near Lichfield, was the scene of this "Banging Bout," August 1747 (*Cf.* p. 743). "Mr. Heston Humphrey, a country attorney, horsewhipped [John] the [fourth] Duke [of Bedford], with equal justice, severity and perseverance on the course at Lichfield. Rigby and Lord Trentham were also cudgelled in a most exemplary manner."—*Letters of Junius*, Letter xxiii., by H. S. Woodfall. Trentham was son of John, first Earl Gower, "The Staffordshire Jacobite," father-in-law of Bedford. 'The Three-Legged Mare' and *Triple-stump* refer to the adjacent gallows. Line 24: "All who did joke the *Royal Oak*, were well rubb'd by its towels." So may it ever be, we hope!

[Roxburghe Collection, III. 440.]

The Lord's Lamentation;

Or, The Whittington Defeat.

"[*Tum vero*] *immensas surgens ferit aurea clamor*
Sydera; —— . . . .
Sævit atrox Volscens."—*Virg*[*ilii*] *Æn*[*eidos*, Lib. xi. 832-4].

[To the Tune of *Chevy Chase* (*vide ante*, p. 743).]

GOd prosper long our noble King! our Lifes and Safeties all: [*sic.*
A woeful Horse-race late there did at *Whittington* befall.

Great *B*[*edfor*]*d's* Duke, a mighty Prince! a solemn vow did make;
His pleasure in fair *Staffordshire* three Summer's days to take.

At once to grace his Father's race, and to confound his Foes;
But ah! (with grief, my Muse does speak) a luckless time he chose.

For some rude *Clowns*, who long had felt the weight of Tax and Levy,
Explain'd their case unto his G[rac]e, by arguments full heavy.

"No *G*[*o*]*w'r*," they cry'd! "No tool of pow'r!" At that the E[ar]l turn'd pale:
"No *G*[*o*]*w'r*, *G*[*o*]*w'r*, no tool of pow'r!" re-echo'd from each dale.

Then *B*[*edfor*]*d's* mighty breast took fire, who thus inrag'd did cry,
"To horse, my *Lords*, my *Knights*, my '*Squires*; we'll be reveng'd or die."

They mounted straight all Men of Birth, Captains of land and sea;
No Prince or Potentate on earth had such a troop as he.

Great Lords, and Lordlings close conjoin'd, a shining squadron stood:
But, to their cost, the *Yeomen* host did prove the better blood.

"A *G*[*o*]*w'r*, a *G*[*o*]*w'r*! ye son o' th' whore, vile spawn of *Babylon*!"
This said, his Grace did mend his pace, and came full fiercely on.

Three times he smote a sturdy foe, who undismay'd reply'd,
"Or be thou *Devil*, or be thou *D*[*uk*]*e*, thy courage shall be try'd."

The Charge began; but on one side some slackness there was found;
The smart *Cockade* in dust was laid, and trampled on the ground. [*white c.*

Some felt sore thwacks upon their backs, some, pains within their bowels;
All who did joke the Royal Oak were well rubb'd with its towels.

Then terror seiz'd the plumed troop, who turn'd themselves to flight;
Foul rout and fear, brought up the rear, Oh! 'twas a piteous sight!——

Each warrior urg'd his nimble steed; but none durst look behind;
Th' insulting foe, they well did know, had got 'em in the wind:

Who ne'er lost scent, untill they came, unto the gallow-tree:
"Now," said their foes, "We'ill not oppose your certain destiny.

"No farther help of our ye lack, gra'-mercy with your doom!
Trust to the care o' th' Three Legg'd-Mare, she'll bring ye *all* safe home."

Then wheel'd about, with this old shout, "Confusion to the *R——p*,"
Leaving each Knight to mourn his plight, beneath the triple-*stamp*.——

Now Heaven preserve such hearts as these from secret treachery!
Who hate a *Knave*, and scorn a *Slave*, may such be ever *free*!

Finis.

[White-letter. Re-printed in *The Foundling Hospital for Wit*, under the title of "The Whittington Defeat." Date, Sept. 1747.]

It is better to swell the bulk of the present volume than to make a wholesale "Slaughter of the Innocents," as in Parliament at the close of a protracted Session. *Our* Innocents are more valuable. Who ensures to us the completion of another volume, containing all that should fitly be given to regale the worthiest Lovers of Ballads?

Since we have given one French version of *The Complaint of the Wandering Jew* (on p. 690) and a German *Volks-Lied* of 'Ahasverus,' we add a specimen of an earlier *Chanson*, and Leland's translation from the German *Ahaser*.

Connected with p. 690, Paul Lacroix's words are memorable:—

"Le passage du *Juif-Errant* en France, dans le cours de 1604, fut signalé par la publication de diverses brochures, entre lesquelles on distingue le *Discours véritable d'un Juif-Errant* . . . ., imprimé, in-8, à Bordeaux, en 1608, et par la composition d'une *Complainte en forme et manière de Chanson* sur l'air des *Dames d'Honneur*. Cette complainte, qui a servi de texte à celle que les *porteurs de rogatons* et les rhapsodes de villages ont refaite sur un autre air à la fin du dix-septième-siècle, renferme presque les mêmes particularités, souvent exprimées de même:—

Le Juif-Errant.

LE bruit courait çà et là par la *France* depuis six mois, qu'on avait espérance
Bientôt de voir un *Juif* qui est errant parmi le monde, pleurant et soupirant.

Comme de fait, en la rase campagne, deux gentilshommes au pays de *Champagne*,
Le rencontrèrent tout seulet cheminant, non pas vêtu comme on est maintenant.

De grandes chausses il porte à la marine, et une juppe comme à la *Florentine*,
Un manteau long jusqu'à terre trainant: comme un autre homme il est au demeurant. 6

Ce que voyant, lors ils l'interrogèrent d'où il venait, et ils lui demandèrent
Sa nation, le métier qu'il avait: mais cependant toujours il cheminait.

"Je suis," dit-il, "juif de ma naissance, et l'un de ceux qui par leur arrogance
Crucifièrent le Sauveur des humains, lorsque *Pilate* en lava ses deux mains." . . .

De son métier, cordonnier il dit être, et à le voir, il semble tout champêtre:
Il boit et mange avec sobriété, et est honnête selon sa pauvreté. 12

Lacroix adds that the Wandering Jew returned more than once to France:—

——"ne fût-ce que pour avoir le plaisir d'entendre chanter sa complainte; mais on n'a pas gardé malheureusement les dates de ses apparitions, excepté celle de son arrivée à Bruxelles, le 22 Avril, 1774: cette date à jamais célèbre accompagne son portrait, dessiné sans doute d'après nature par les bourgeois de la ville qui eurent l'avantage de le voir 'si barbu.' Ce portrait, gravé en tailles de bois par les imagiers d'Epinal et de Troyes, illustre la complainte nouvelle qui a des échos dans toutes les foires et tous les marchés où la langue française n'est pas absolument inconnue. Ce portrait figure dans toutes les chaumières, appendu à côté du portrait de l'Empereur."—*Chants et Chansons Populaires de la France*, 1843 (=Tom. 3, No. 82: of undated edition, *Paris, Garnier Frères, circâ* 1868).

Here, by Charles George Leland (author of *Hans Breitmann*, etc., Trübner, 1872), is his own *Gaudeamus* translation of '*Ich bin der alte Ahaser*': compare our pp. 690 and 699. We run each of the eight-line stanzas into two lines:—

Ahasuerus: The Song of the Wandering Jew.

"I Am the old *Ahasuér*; I wander here, I wander there.
My rest is gone, my heart is sair; I find it never, never mair.

Loud roars the storm, the mill-dams tear; I cannot perish, O Malheur!
My heart is void, my head is bare: I am the old *Ahasuér*.

Belloweth Ox, and danceth Bear; I find them never, never mair.
I'm the old *Hebrew*, on a tear [*Amériqué*=rampage]: I order arms, my heart is sair.

I'm goaded round, I know not where; I wander here, I wander there.
I'd like to sleep, but must forbear; I am the old *Ahasuér*.

I meet folks alway unaware; my rest is gone, I'm in despair.
I cross all lands, the sea I dare: I travel here, I wander there.

I feel such pain, I sometimes swear; I am the old *Ahasuér*.
Criss-cross I ramble anywhere: I find it never, never mair.

Against the wall I lean my spear; I find no quiet, I declare.
My peace is lost, I'm in despair; I swing like pen-dulum in air.

I'm hard of hearing, you're aware. *Caraçoa* is a fine *liqueur*.
I listed once *en militaire*. I find no comfort anywhere.

But what's to stop it? Pray declare! My peace is gone, my heart is sair.
I am the old *Ahasuér*. Now I know nothing, nothing mair."

[Perhaps this is "playing it low" on the old man, who is well nigh a Bible character, but Jehu is a proverbial charioteer, for driving furiously, "the piper that played before Moses" was cited by Patlanders while they had any fun in them, and it is our national habit to laugh at the most solemn beliefs or subjects.]

Our *Appendix* would be incomplete, were we not to give here the following adjuncts to preceding ballads:—

1st.—(Instead of keeping them for the '*Second Group of Naval Ballads*' in the final Vol. VII.) the intertwined 'Nell and Harry' Series, mentioned in our "Group of One Hundred Love Ballads," p. 283. (*These we now give on pp.* 789-792.)

2nd.—The Pepysian version of 'The Birds' Harmony,' belonging to our p. 307. (*This is now on p.* 782.)

3rd.—The Bodleian version of "The Seaman's Song of Captain Ward," mentioned on pp. 423, 425. (*Now reprinted on our p.* 781.)

4th.—The identification, never before made, of the supposed-to-be-lost ballad (cited as name of tune by Martin Parker in his "Inns of Court" ballad of 1635, and by Laurence Price in his "Honour of Bristol," p. 428), *viz. Our noble King in his Progress*: see for this our p. 786. Not improbably by Martin Parker, or Price.

5th.—Martin Parker's original "Saylors for my Money," (on p. 797,) to be compared with the later popular adaptation of it, beginning "You Gentlemen of England," as indicated on p. 431.

6th.—After having given the Roxburghe Collection version of "St. *George* [for *England*] and the Dragon," on p. 727, we add, on p. 780, the variations belonging to an earlier version, of 1612.

[Pepys Collection, I. 87, apparently unique. *Cf. ante* p. 726.]

(*The Earlier Version of* "*St. George for England and the Dragon*," 1612.)

Saint George's Commendation to all Souldiers;

Or,

S. George's Alarum to all that professe Martial discipline, with a memoriall of the Worthies, who have been borne so high on the winges of Fame, for their brave adventures, as they cannot be buried in the pit of Oblivion.

To A *pleasant new Tune.*

1.—Why doe you boast of *Arthur* and his Knightes? etc. [p. 727.
. . . endured fightes?
For besides King *Arthur*, *Lancelot du Lake*,
. . . Dragon made to flee, etc.
Or Sir *Tristram de Lionel* . . old Histories. Etc.

2.—Mark our father *Abraham*, when first he resckued *Lot*,
Onely with his household, what conquest there he got:
David was elected a Prophet and a King,
He slew the great *Golia*[*t*]*h*, with a stone within a sling:
Yet these were not Knightes of the Table round;
Nor St. *George*, St. *George*, who the Dragon did confound.
St. George *he was for* England, *St.* Dennis *was for* France;
Sing, Honi soit qui mal y pense.

3.—*Jephtha* and *Gideon* did lead their men to fight, etc. [p. 728.

4.—The warres of ancient monarches it were too long to tell, etc. [*Ibid.*

5.—The noble *Alphonso*, that was the *Spanish* king,
The Order of the Red scarffs and Bandrolles in did bring; [*Note.*
For he had a troope of mighty Knightes, when first he did begin,
Which sought adventures farre and neare, that conquest they might win:
The rankes of the *Pagans* he often put to flight,
But St. *George*, St. *George* did with the Dragon fight.
St. George *he was for* England, *St.* Dennis *was for* France;
Sing, *Honi soit qui mal y pense.*

6.—Many [Knights] have fought with proud *Tamberlaine;*
Cutlax the Dane, great warres he did maintaine:
Rowland of *Beame*, and good [Sir] *Olivere*,
In the Forest of *Acon* slew both Woolfe and Beare;
Besides that noble *Hollander* [Sir] *Goward* with the Bill:
But St. *George*, St. *George* the Dragon's blood did spill.
St. George *he was for* England, *St.* Dennis *was for* France:
Sing, *Honi soit qui mal y pense.*

7.—*Valentine* and *Orson* were of King *Pepin's* blood, etc.
These were all *French* Knightes that lived in that age,
But St. *George*, St. *George* the Dragon did assuage, etc. [v. p. 728.

Note.—Line 62 refers to *The Order of the Band*, v. *Ames*, Typ., 327.

*** The variations are so numerous in the Roxburghe Collection broadside, or others, from this valuable and much earlier exemplar, that we have here given the original for comparison, not reprinting the lines which are identical in both.]

8.—*Bevis* conquered *Ascupart*, and after slew the Boare,
And then he crost beyond the Seas to combat with the Moore;
Sir *Isenbras* and *Eglamore* they were Knightes most bold;
And good Sir *John Mandeville* of travel much hath told:
There were many *English* Knights that *Pagans* did convert,
But St. *George*, St. *George* pluckt out the Dragon's heart.
St. George *he was for* England, *St.* Dennis *was for* France:
Sing, *Honi soit qui mal y pense.*

9.—The noble Earl of *Warwick*, that was call'd Sir *Guy*,
The Infidels and Pagans stoutly did defie; [*vide Note, and* p. 732.
He slew the Giant *Brandimore*, and after was the death
Of that most g[h]astly Dun Cowe, the divell of *Dunsmore* Heath;
Besides his noble deeds all done beyond the seas:
But St. *George*, St. *George* the Dragon did appease.
St. George *he was for* England, *St.* Dennis *was for* France;
Sing, *Honi soit qui mal y pense.*

10.—*Richard Cœur-de-Leon*, erst King of this Land,
He the Lion gored with his naked hand;
The false Duke of *Austria* nothing did he feare,
But his son [*Richard*] killed with a boxe on the eare;
Besides his famous actes done in the Holy Lande:
But St. *George*, St. *George* the Dragon did withstande.
St. George *he was for* England, *St.* Dennis *was for* France;
Sing, *Honi soit qui mal y pense.*

11.—*Henry* the Fifth he conquered all *France*,
And quartered their Arms, etc. [*Cf.* p. 728.
He their Cities razed, and threw their Castles down,
And his head he honoured with a double Crowne;
He thumped the *French*-men, etc.

12.—St. *David* of *Wales* the *Welsh*-men did advance,
St. *Jaques* of *Spain*, that never yet broke lance;
St. *Patricke* of *Ireland*, which was St. *George's* boy.
Seven years he kept his Horse, and then stole him away:
For which knavish act, as Slaves they doe remaine. [*Cf.* p. 728.
But St. *George*, St. *George* he hath the Dragon slaine.
St. George *he was for* England; *St.* Dennis *was for* France;
Sing, *Honi soit qui mal y pense.*

Imprinted at London by *W. W*[*right*, or *White*], 1612.

[In Black-letter, with one woodcut. Probably unique exemplar.]

Note, l. 121.—The Rev. Samuel Pegge, M.A., read to the Society of Antiquaries (May 7, 1767), a *Memoir of the Story of Guy, Earl of Warwick* (printed in *Bibl. Topogr. Britan.* No. xvii., with copper p. eng. of the neglected remains of Guy in the chapel at Guy's Cliff, from sketch, 30 July, 1782, by S. Carter. Felicia (whose son was named *Reynburn*=*Reinbrun*, *vide* Auchinleck MS.) was the only daughter of Rohand, Earl of Warwick, who flourished in the reigns of Alfred and Edward the Elder. Guy, son of Siward, baron of Wallingford, married her, and became in her right Earl of Warwick. —*Dugdale*, p. 299. Guy died A.D. 929, aged 70. (*Cf.* p. xxxi*.)

[Pepys Collection, IV. 268; Douce, I. 13 *verso*.]

The Birds' Harmony. [*Cf.* pp. 307, 779.]

The Silvan woods seem'd to complain
  Of gross inconstancy, the Birds in vain
Did warble forth their griefs to ease their minds,
  And all did Sympathize, though ease none finds.

Tune, *The delights of the Bottle*, &c. [1675: for music, see vol. iv. p. 43.]

As I was walking in the shade
  Which Summer's heat with leaves had made,
The Birds did seem for to lament,
  And did complain of grief and discontent;
But as they fled from Tree to Tree,
  They made such moan as sorely troubled me.

Then came the *Cookooe*, bold and stout,
  Flying the country round about,
While other birds her young ones feed,
  And they for help of others stand in need,
The Syre unkind no care doth take,
  But leaves the young ones some strange shift to make.

Then said the *Black-bird* as he fled, [text, "she."
  "I had a Love, but now she's dead;
And now my love I dearly lack,
  Which is the cause that I do go in black;
And by my self I sadly mourn,
  Like one forsaken, helpless, and forlorn."

Then said the pretty *Nightingale*,
  "Attend, and hear my mournful tale,
Whilst other Birds do sleep, I mourn,
  Leaning my brest against some prickly thorn;
And in the silent darksome night
  To send forth mournful Notes I take delight."

Then said the *Sparrow* from her Nest,
  "I had a Love, but 'twas in jest,
And ever since, for that same thing,
  I made a promise I would never sing;
Which I intend, for my love's sake,
  That I will keep, and will by no means break."

Then said the *Lark* upon the grass,
  "Once I did love a pretty Lass,
But she'd not hear her true Love sing,
  Although he had a voice would please a King; [*text*, 'she.'
And since, on high, into the Air
  I fly, that none my warbling voice may hear."

Then next poor *Robin* she exprest
  What chang'd the colour of her brest,
Because her love he would not yield,
  She would desert the grove and flow'ry field:
And near the Houses there complain
  In Winter Morn, how she did love in vain."

The *Swallow*, with the wings so long,
  Complain'd that she received wrong,
And being past all kind of hopes
  Of love, complain'd in strange confused Notes:
No one can understand her tale,
  In such disorder she doth brawl and raile.

The *Thrush* also did make her moan,
  And sayes that kindness she found none,
But loves to be in silent holes,
  Where none may hear how she her Case condoules:
Far from the Houses in the Wood
  She chants her Notes, so little understood.

The little [*W*]*renn*, whose love unkind
  Did cause those griefs to [seize] her mind, [misp. "cease."
Which hindred her to grow or thrive,
  Because her love no longer could survive;
This was the cause she was so small,
  Her love being dead she could not thrive at all.

Thus may you see how little Birds
  Do grieve for love in mournful words,
Let men and women then be true
  And constant to each other, so that you ["others."
In peace may live, and when you die,
  You then may boast of Truth and Loyalty.

Let not your minds be discompos'd
  When your poor eyes must needs be clos'd,
But rather let your faithful mind
  Be such as you from thence may comfort find:
Be kind, be true, that so you may
  Find peace on Earth, comfort another day.

Who so proves faithful, firm and true,
  Shall have no reason for to rue,
But Triumph over grim-fac'd Death,
  When he shall come to stop his latest breath:
Young people all, let this you move,
  For to be true and loyal in your love.

[*London*,] Printed for *M. Coles*, *T. Vere*, *J. Wright*, *J. Clark*, *W. Thacker*[*a*]*y*, and *T. Passenger*.

[Black-letter. Three cuts. Date, *circá* 1676.]

[Wood's Collection, 401, fol. 79; 402, fol. 39; Douce, II. 199; Euing, 327.]

The Seaman's Song of Captain Ward, the famous Pyrate of the World, and an English-man Born.

TUNE, *The King's going to Bulloign.* [See pp. 422, *et seq.*]

GAllants, you must understand,
Captain *Ward* of *England*,
A Pyrate and a Rover on the Sea,
Of late a simple Fisherman
In the merry town of *Feversham*,
Grows famous in the world now every day.

From the Bay of *Plimouth*
Sayled he towards the South,
With many more of courage and of might,
Christian Princes have but few
Such Seamen, if that he and we were true,
And would but for his King and Country fight.

Lusty *Ward* adventurously
In the Straights of *Barbary*
Did make the Turkish Gallyes for to shake.
Bouncing cannons fiery hot
Spared not the *Turks* one jot,
But of their lives great slaughter he did make.

The Islanders of *Malta*,
With Argosies upon the Sea,
Most proudly braved *Ward* unto his face,
But soon their pride was overthrown,
And their treasures made his own,
And all their men brought to a wofull case.

The wealthy ships of *Venice*
Afforded him great riches;
Both gold and silver won he with his sword.
Stately *Spain* and *Portugal*
Against him dare not bare up sail,
But gave him all the title of a Lord.

Golden seated *Candy*,
Famous *France* and *Italy*,
With all the countries of the Eastern parts,
If once their Ships his pride with-stood,
They surely all were cloath'd in blood,
Such cruelty was plac'd within their hearts.

The riches he hath gain'd,
And by blood-shed obtained,
Well may suffice for to maintain a King;
His fellows all were valiant Wights,
Fit to be made Prince's Knights,
But that their lives do base dishonors bring.

Note.—Virtually the genuine text of the original "*Seaman's Song of Captain Ward,*" entered on the Stationers' Company Registers, 3 July, 1609; written before news of Ward's death arrived. "*Captain Ward's fight with the Rainbow*" (p. 426) popularly displaced the present ballad, *which we are the first to reprint.*

This wicked-gotten treasure
Doth him but little pleasure,
The land consumes what they have got by sea,
In drunkenness and letchery,
Filthy sins of sodomy,
These evil-gotten goods do wast[e] away.

Such as live by thieving
Have seldome-times good ending,
As by the deeds of Captain *Ward* is shown :
Being drunk amongst his Drabs,
His nearest friends he sometimes stabs :
Such wickednesse within his heart is grown.

When stormy tempest riseth,
The Causer he despiseth,
Still denies to pray unto the Lord.
He feareth neither God nor Devil,
His deeds are bad, his thoughts are evil,
His onley trust is still upon his Sword.

Men of his own Country
He still abuseth vilely,
Some back to back are cast into the waves ; [N.B., cf. p. 797.
Some are hewn in pieces small,
Some are shot against a wall ;
A slender number of their lives he saves.

Of truth it is reported,
That he is strongly guarded
By *Turks* that are not of a good belief ;
Wit and reason tells them
He trusteth not his country-men,
But shews the right condition of a thief.

At *Tunis* in *Barbary*
Now he buildeth stately
A gallant Palace and a Royal Place,
Decked with delights most trim,
Fitter for a Prince than him,
The which at last will prove to his disgrace.

To make the world to wonder,
This Captain is Commander
Of four-and-twenty mighty Ships of sayl,
To bring in treasure from the sea
Into the markets every day :
The which the *Turks* do buy up without fail.

His name and state so mounteth,
These countrey-men accounteth
Him equal to the Nobles of that Land ;
But these his honours we shall find
Shortly blown up with the wind,
Or prove like letters written in the sand.

Finis.

London : Printed for *F. Coles*, *T. Vere*, and *William Gilbertson*.

[In Black-letter. Three cuts. Date of first issue, 3 July, 1609 ; see p. 422.]

A Pleasant Ditty of

The King and the Souldier.

TO A NEW TUNE. [*See* p. 779.]

OUr noble King in his progress, as he went to the South,
Upon a goodly plain, a plain, which men do call a down a down,
So merrily he walked towards the Town of *Portsmouth*,
Always by a bankside, not passing half a mile, a mile,
a mile from *Guil*[*d*]*ford* Town,
There met he with a Souldier, was full of great lamentation,
O sick and faint he was, and ready for to dye,
Saying, "Wo[e] be unto Death, and Fortune variable!"

Upon a goodly Gelding this Souldier did ride, did ride,
His arms they were unfolded, his shield hung by his side,
The one foot in the stirrop, the other hung beside;
His saddle was ungirt, his bridle was unti'd:
This Souldier kept not path, but wandered here and there,
Sighing and sorrowing, great ruth it was to hear;
Most like a doleful man, he rent and tore his hair;
Saying, "Woe be unto Death, and Fortune variable!"

It was not onely I alone, but thousands as well as I, as I,
That did behold the forlorn man that ready was to dye.
A Captain of Leagure, a very bold souldier,
Sometimes a Martial-man to our noble King *Henry*.
At all manner of pastimes he was our Sovereign's minion;
A gamester with our noble king, men called him *Labinion*.
Just he was in judgment, it was this man's opinion;
Saying, "Woe be unto Death, and Fortune variable!"

[*Possibly by* **Martin Parker** or **Laurence Price**.]

*** In giving back to the world this long-lost (supposed-to-be-irrecoverable) old "Ditty," we venture to transpose several of the lines in the final division, restoring what we believe to be the original construction, which had become corruptly disorganized; but we make no other change beside this transposition. Our disorderly exemplar reads "Sovereign's minion, Saying, Woe be unto death, and fortune variable. Just he was in judgment, it was this man's opinion; A Gamester with our noble King, men called him *Labinion*. A Captain of Leagure, a very bold Souldier, Sometimes a Martial man to our noble King *Henry*." *Thus it ends.* We think the re-arrangement simply restorative: ***the finale must have been identical with the end of the preceding stanzas.*** And the regulation of the rhymes in the *second* stanza guide our choice of them in the third. It bears token of an earlier hand than Martin Parker's. Is not *Labinion* a ***Huguenot!***

We now give an elegy (Luttrell Coll., II. 16.), hitherto unreprinted, on the Colonel Thomas Blood, who stole the Crown Jewels on May 9, 1671.

An Elegie on Colonel [Thomas] Blood,

Notorious for Stealing the Crown, etc.

(Who dyed [on] the *Twenty-sixth* of *August*, 1680.)

THanks, ye kind Fates, for your last Favour shown
Of stealing *BLOOD*, who lately stole the Crown; [*Cf.* iv. p. 688.
We'l not exclaim so much against you since;
As well as *BEDLOE*, you have fetcht him hence,
He who hath been a Plague to all Mankind,
And never was to any one a Friend:
Nay to himself such torment was at last,
He wisht his Life had long ago been past.
For who can bear a discontented minde,
Or any Peace with an ill Conscience finde,
Thro' his whole Life he practis'd Villany,
And lov'd it, tho' he nothing got thereby;
At first uneasy at the King's return,
With secret Malice his bold heart did burn
Against his Sovereign, and on pretence
He had much wrong'd his feigned Innocence,
To *IRELAND* went, and several ways did try, }
Rather than he would unrevenged dye, }
To vent his Malice on his MAJESTY. }
But finding there all his attempts prove vain
To *ENGLAND* forthwith he returns again,
And after some small time he had liv'd here,
The first great thing in which he did appear
Was rescuing from Justice CAPTAIN *MASON*,
Whom all the World doth know t' have been a base one.
The next ill thing he boldly undertook
Was barbarously seizing of a DUKE, [*James Butler.*
Whom, as he since confess'd, he did intend
To hang for injuries he did pretend
The DUKE had done him: though the World does know
His Grace was ne'er to a Good Man a Foe:
Having through all his many well-spent days
Served his King and Country several ways,
And patiently his troubles underwent
Finding a sweetness ev'n in Banishment,
And Death he patiently won'd have endur'd,
The King's Restoring cou'd he have secured:
A DUKE who, being by Providence preserv'd [*i.e.* of *Ormond.*
Hath begot sons who valiantly have serv'd
His Majesty, and great Renown obtain'd
In many battles by your valour gain'd:
Great *OSSERY*, who by his conduct wise
Did oft by Stratagems his Foes surprize
And hath as often beat them with his Sword,
Was the Eldest Son of this most noble Lord.
But I my HEROE almost had forgot,
And th' next thing he engag'd in was a PLOT
To seize the CROWN, and without doubt he who
So great a piece of villany would do,
When he saw time wou'd have attempted too
His MAJESTY; but failing of the prize,

About the Town he undiscover'd lies
Harbour'd by some of 's fellow-Rogues, yet see
How few can 'scape concern'd in Villany.
In a short time he apprehended was,
And brav'd his MAJESTY ev'n to his face:
Yet when one wou'd have thought he shou'd have had
Reward for 's Villany, and have been made
Example to all Ages, our good King
Gave him his Life (who long has strove to bring
Destruction on him,) and did him restore
To liberty, thinking he ne'er wou'd more
Do any thing unjust again, when loe,
His stirring Spirit was not contented so,
For he engages in th' Conspiracy
To ruine th' honour, life and liberty
Of a deserving noble honest Peer, [*i.e. D. of Buckingham.*
And had him brought unto Destruction near,
But Divine Providence, for ever blest,
Prevented this, as well as all the rest,
By th' coming in of some that were concern'd
Which all your PLOT into confusion turn'd.
  At last our famous Heroe, Colonel *BLOOD*,
Seeing his prospects all will do no good,
And that Success was to him still deny'd,
Fell sick with Grief, broke his great Heart and dy'd.

The Epitaph.

HERE Lies the Man, who boldly hath run through
  More villanies than ever ENGLAND knew;
And nere to any Friend he had was true.
Here let him then by all unpittied lye,
And let's rejoyce his time was come to Dye.

Finis.

London, Printed by *J.S.*, [*i.e. J. Shorter*], in the year 1680. [White-letter.]

*** A manuscript note of it having been purchased by Narcissus Luttrell, 30th of August, 1680, is on this rare broadside, possibly unique. It is here reprinted for substantial reasons, the final '*Epitaph*' having been quoted, by the Editor of *Roxburghe Ballads*, in Messrs. Smith and Elder's *Dictionary of National Biography*, vol. v. p. 235; where he has given a full account of the Colonel's eventful life and daring adventures. He was mentioned in *Roxb. Bds.* vol. v. pp. 688, 689, and (probably) his son, in connection with Monmouth's imprisonment.

"The Batchelor's Triumph" of *Roxburghe Ballads*, vol. ii. pp. 427-429, is defective in the endings of several lines (supplied *by guess*, *Ibid.* p. 682). Here are the authoritative corrections, in *Italic*.

Line 57.—Of what they possess there's nou*ght that's deny'd.*
,, 60.—When Love's sweet accents so plen*tifully flow:*
,, 63.—And can abridge them when wear*y we grow.*
,, 66.—Frownings and poutings from wi*ves when displeas'd;*
,, 69.—Which on their Gallants so kindly *bestowes:*
,, 72.—Whilst the lov'd silver procures *us fine cloaths.*
,, 75.—And by the cradle a rocking he *sits.*
,, 78.—But we'r resolv'd to court sing*le delight:*
,, 81.—Slaves for his wife both by day *and by night.*

[*Neptune's Fair Garland.* Licensed by Richard Pocock, 1686.]

A New Song of Nelly's sorrow at the parting with her well-beloved Henry, that was just ready to set Sail to Sea.

The Tune is, *My dearest dear and I must part*; Or, *In Summer time.*

FAir *Nelly* and her dearest dear, their love the world could never stain,
But yet at last it did appear, that he must cross the Ocean Main.

Alas! he was compell'd to go, with her he could no longer stay;
Tears from fair *Nelly's* eyes did flow, when he to her these words did say:

"My Love, I come to take my leave, now we are hoisting up our sail,
Take here a kiss and do not grieve; pray we may have a pleasant gale.

"Love, set thy heart and mind at rest, fear not but *Neptune* will be kind:
When I have cross'd his throbbing breast, thou shalt by letters know my mind.

"Thy praises I will dayly sing, though we shall now divided be:
My dearest, here take thou my Ring, and keep it as a pledge for me."

Then with a sigh she did reply, "Alas! is there no remedy?
Sweet Death, come ease my misery, 'tis thou alone can'st set me free."

Thus bitterly she did bewail, her heart was fill'd with grief and woe:
Her sweet complexion waxed pale, and tears in multitudes did flow

From her fair eyes, which did declare the perfect message of her mind,
She almost drowned in despair, but he was most exceeding kind.

Said he, "My Love, do not lament, let not thy sorrows much abound;
If thou wilt labour for content, then joy and comfort will be found.

"My dear, be not possest with fears! why should my absence thee surprize?
Why should those soft distilled tears flow from the fountains of thine eyes?

"Sweet *Nelly*, prythee, tell me why thou should'st in sorrow thus complain?
There's many more as well as I, with me must sail the Ocean Main.

"Love, I must bid thee now adieu, for why I can no longer stay,
Our Noble Captain and his crew, they'll hoist up Sail and will away."

"Well, Love," said she, "since thou must go, the Heavens be thy careful guide;
Unto my dear some pitty show, when thou art on the Ocean wide.

"To guard my Love from frightful fears, and then the less will be my care."
With many solid sighs and tears, these Loyal Lovers parted were.

[*The Sequel* here follows, from the same *Garland.*]

A New Song of Henry setting forth to Sea; with an account of their unhappy Voyage, wherein their Ship was cast away, and most of their Men drowned; but Henry escaping with some few more, through many difficulties is returned to fair Nelly his love, where their joys was at length compleated.

To the Tune of, *The First Part.* [See *Note.*]

THeir Sails were spread, and Anchor weigh'd, they had a pleasant Gale of wind,
Their Flag and streamers they display'd, the Seas were calm, and *Neptune* kind.

Their hearts was fill'd with sweet content, when they their Voyage first did take,
Then to the Seas away they went, with all the Sail that they could make.

Their joys was quickly turn'd to woe, their sails were rent, their ship did roul;
The rain did beat, the wind did blow, the Seas was most exceeding foul.

The Clouds was dark'ned in the Skyes, the Billows then began to roar,
A Storm and Tempest did arise, when they were many leagues from Shore.

They had not sailed past a week, before this Storm their joys deprives;
Their Ship began to spring a Leak, they pumpt and labour'd for their lives.

But yet, alas! 'twas all in vain, for why, the leak could not be found;
Their Ship was sinking in the Main, and they in sorrow compast round.

They handed forth the Long Boat then, but yet behold their woful case,
Their Ship, with many of their Men, was swallow'd up before their face.

But they continued still in Prayer, that Heaven would preserve their Boat,
Alas, alas! their lives to spare; while they about the Seas did float.

Each Wave did make them sigh and grieve, no sign of help approached nigh,
Yet we have cause for to believe their Prayers was heard to Heaven high.

For in the midst of all their grief, while they was in this doleful plight,
The Heavens did afford relief, a Ship came sailing in their sight.

The sight of which did them revive, now in their sad extremity;
Eleven went aboard alive, that had been floating in the Sea.

The ship was bound to *Yarmouth* then, where they in safety did arrive,
And there these poor distressed men rejoyced that they were alive.

Fair *Nelly's* Love was one of those that Providence had brought on shore,
And then away to her he goes, which he ne'r thought to have seen more.

To her he freely did unfold the sorrows which they had gone through:
As sad a thing as e'er was told, and yet no more than what is true.

"My dear," said she, "thou shalt not roam, nor run the hazzards of the Sea,
Thou shalt in safety stay at home, I'm glad thou art alive with me."

Her friends and his were all agreed, and he himself did give consent,
That they should marry'd be with speed, and live at home in sweet content.

Printed by *J.M.* [*John Millet*] for *J*[*onah*] *Deacon*, at the *Angel*,
in *Guilt-spur-street*, without *Newgate*, 1686.

*** We have not yet found the ballad which gives name to the tune of these ditties, it either began with the words "*My dearest Dear and I must part,*" or held them as its burden. The alternative tune (*cf.* p. 274) is *In Summer time*, which had long been a favourite, belonging to three of the twelve Robin Hood ballads reserved for our final volume. They begin thus, "In Summer-time, when leaves grow green." 1.—*Robin Hood* and the Curtal Friar; 2.—*Robin Hood* and the Jovial Tinker; 3.—The Noble Fisherman; or, *Robin Hood's* Preferment.

We refuse to believe the faithful *Henry* of the *Neptune's Fair Garland*, 1686, to be the same person as the un-named "Unkind Lover" of the next-following song, "*Nelly's* Constancy," and its Answer. Two different Nellies, perhaps, but either one deserving a toast as the Lass that loves a Sailor.

"Some sweet-heart or wife, that he loved as his life,
Each drank, while he wish'd he could hail her;
But the standing toast, that pleased the most,
Was, 'The wind that blows, the ship that goes,
And the Lass that loves a Sailor!'"

[Pepys Collection, V. 217. Apparently unique.]

An excellent New Song, call'd Nelly's Constancy;
Or,
Her Unkind Lover. Who, after Contract of Marriage, leaves his first Mistress, for the sake of a better fortune.

To a pleasant New Tune; or, *Languishing Swain.* [See pp. 27, 283.]

Licensed according to Order.

I Lov'd you dearly, I lov'd you well,
I lov'd you dearly, no Tongue can tell.
You love another, you love not me,
You care not for my company.

You love another, I'll tell you why,
Because she has more means than I,
But *Means* will waste, Love, and *Means* will fly;
In time thou may'st have no more than I.

If I had gold, Love, you should have part,
But as I've none, Love, thou hast my Heart:
Thou hast my Heart, Love, and free good will,
And in good truth I love thee still.

How often has your tongue this told,
You lov'd [me] not for silver nor gold:
And this to me you did impart,
All you desired was my Heart.

Your tongue did so inchant my Mind,
Till I for ever must be kind,
Though you prove false, yet I am true,
And own I am undone by you.

What makes young Men be thus unkind,
To gain Maids' loves, then change their mind?
As here I find it to my grief,
He's stole my Heart, *Stop Thief! Stop Thief!*

My Heart you have, go where you will,
And though you leave me I love you still;
But had I sums of gold in store,
You'd court me as you did before.

'Tis Money is your chiefest aim,
All Women else would be the same.
Oh! what a world is't we live in,
No true love can be found in Men!

Although you do another take,
And leave your first Love's Heart to break,
It pleases me to dye for Love,
And do a faithful Virgin prove.

Then my advice is to each Maid,
Be careful lest your Heart's betray'd:
Believe not all young Men do say,
They'll vow they'll Love, yet go their way.

Like my dear Love that courted me,
Who's wed another, and gone to Sea,
Yet I a Sailor Boy love still,
And none but such shall gain my will.

Then call a Boat, boys, unto the ferry,
For we are come, Boys, to be merry;
It sha'll nere be said, Boys, when we are dead,
But the Jolly Sailors are rarely bred.

Printed and Sold by *Charles Barnet*. [In White-letter. Date, *c.* 1686.]

[Earl of Jersey's Osterley Park Collection, III. 42.]

The Seaman's Answer to his Unkind Lover.

Tune of, *I lov'd you dearly*, etc., or, *Languishing Swain* [see pp. 27, 283].

Licensed according to Order.

FAir Maid, you say you lov'd me well; I do believe it, honest *Nell*,
And likewise tell you what is true, Once there was none I *lov'd* like you.

'Twas not for Money that I wed, I never ask'd her what she had,
You said you would not married be, Till I return['d] again from Sea.

That was the reason, pritty Dove, which made me seek for another Love,
I thought when I to Sea was gone, You'd wed before I cou'd return.

As for thy kindness still to me, A thousand thanks I return to thee.
And I am glad you do impart *A Seaman still shall have thy Heart.*

I have a Brother with me here, who's younger than I by one year,
He is a Seaman truly bred, My dearest *Nell*, let him thee wed.

You cry *Stop Thief*, your Heart I have, My Brother he the same do[es] crave,
And begs that I would write to you, to give thy free consent thereto.

If you but saw us both together, you could not tell one from the other;
Then prithee, *Nell*, do not deny, though I am wed, let him *enjoy*.

I hear thou'rt ranging o'er the Sea, with full intent to come to me;
May Heavens keep thee from all harms, and bring thee safely to my arms.

We're both in the *Britannia* bold, i' th' *Straights* where strangers much behold,
For there was never seen before So great a ship near the *Turkish shoar*. [*Cf.* p. 79..

Then come, my fair One, come away! My Brother longs to see the day
That you will be his happy Bride, Then waft her hither, wind and tide!

If thou wert come, then we'd be merry, in Bowls of Punch and good Canary,
And thou wilt find he'll love thee well, Though I did leave my honest *Nell*.

I prithee, *Nell*, do not deny, thou'lt find him kinder far than I.
Although you prove not to be my Wife, yet my dear Sister all my life.

Printed and Sold by *T. Staples*.

[In White-letter. Without woodcut, or music. Date, *circâ* 1686.]

[(Roxburghe Collection, III. 441;) Pepys, V. 361; Jersey, III. 67.]

The Faithful Marriner;
Or,
A Copy of Verses, writ by a Seaman on Board the *Britannia*, in the Streights, and directed to Fair *Isabel* his loyal Love, in the City of *London*.

Tune of, *The False-hearted Young Man; or, The Languishing Swain.* [See *Note*.]

FAir *Isabel*, of Beauty bright,
To thee in Love these lines I write
Hoping thou art alive and well
As I am now, as I am now, Fair *Isabel*.

On Board the brave *Britannia* bold, [*Roxb.* text misp. "*Beauty*."
I have the fortune to behold
The sweet delightsome banks of *Spain*,
While in the *Straits*, while in the *Straits*, we do remain.

The *Spanish* Lords of high renown,
And gentry come swarming down,
To see the *Brittish* Royal Fleet,
With swelling sails, with swelling sails, and streamers sweet.

While we appear'd in all our Pride,
The Seas were ne're so beautifi'd,
With able Men of War before,
Along the Straits, along the *Straits*, of *Spanish* shore.

We have no storms, or weather foul,
To make the Roaring Billows roll,
But pleasant breathing gentle-gales,
Enough to fill, enough to fill, our swelling sails.

Along the Coast of *Barberie*
The *Algerines* they flock'd to see
Our Royal Fleet of noble fame, [*Jersey* reads "warlike fleet"
And stood amaz'd, and stood amaz'd, to see the same.

The longer they the Fleet beheld
The more they were with wonder fill'd
As knowing we were *Britains* bold,
And that the *French*, and that the *French*, false Tales had told.

Note.—This ballad has been already mentioned on p. 410, and should have been specified previously on pp. 27 and 28 (under sections *a* and *c*), as being allotted to the tune which is indifferently named *The Languishing Swain* and *The False-hearted Young Man*. We have shown this tune to coincide with *I loved thee dearly, I loved thee well* (*cf.* p. 283: we print the title-ballad words on p. 791), and *All happy times when free from Love*, and *Charon make haste* (words given on our p. 24). Despite the difference of sweethearts' names, *Nellie* and *Isabel* (like the change from 'Britannia' to 'Beauty' as name of the seaman's ship, in successive issues of this *Isabel* ballad), there may be closer connection between these two ballads of "*The Straights* [*of Gibraltar*]" than merely the tune. (Compare p. 792.) Therefore, they are better brought together at once, and in the same vol. as "The Frighted French" antecedent ballad of p. 446.

For *Turrye* made the *Turk* believe [*scilicet Tourville*, p. 446.
That they no damage could receive;
For of a Truth he did declare,
That Masters of, that Masters of, the Seas they were.

This will for Truth no longer go,
For *Turrye* fears great *Russel* so,
That from *Toulon* he steard away, [*Roxb.* "they stear'd."
He ha'n't forgot, he ha'n't forgot, the mouth of *May*.

With *Russel* he is loath to deal,
For fear a second warlike Real
Should shake their whole foundation so [*Roxb.* "the," omits "so."
That it might prove, that it might prove, their overthrow.

Once more, my Dear and tender Dove,
Fair *Isabel*, my Loyal Love,
Accept of these few lines I send, [*misp.* "Except of."
Who will remain, who will remain, your Faithful Friend.

Tho' we are separated now,
I'll not forget that Solemn Vow
Made, when I left my Native Land,
I'll go on board, I'll go on board, under command.

My Dearest, do not grieve or mourn, [*Jersey*, "Then dearest, do."
With Patience wait my safe return,
And then we'l' both united be,
In lasting Bonds, in lasting Bonds, of Loyalty.

The Figure of a Heart I send,
And round the same these lines are pen'd,
'*The Chain of Love has link'd it fast,*
So long as Life, so long as Life and breath shall last.'

Finis.

London: Printed for *J. Blare*, on *London-Bridge*.

[In White-letter. Colophon and text followed from Pepys and Jersey earlier copies, better than the corrupt modern Roxburghe. Date, probably, 1692-3.]

[These cuts belong to p. 770.]

[Roxburghe Collection, II. 550; Jersey Coll., I. 123.]

The Unchangeable Lovers.

No stormy winds can fright the Seaman bold,
Nor can his mind be easily controul'd,
His love is seeled, ne'r to change his mind
Whilst *Amarillis* voweth to be kind.

Tune [or, *Ah!*] *Cloris, awake.* [See p. 128.]

DEar, comfort I must, though it grieves me to go,
To leave thee behind me breeds sorrow and woe,
But the greatest of Storms shall ne'r cause me to fear,
For I'le cheer up my heart *with the thoughts of my dear.*

When the winds they do blow, and the Billows do roar,
If I call but to mind my dear Love on the Shore,
My heart will rejoyce, and I'le banish all fear,
In hopes to return *to my love and my dear.*

Then be but as Loyal as I'le be to thee,
And nothing but death shall e're part thee and me,
If women like Angels to me should appear,
Yet still I'le be true *to my Love and my dear.*

'Tis true that we Sailers strange wonders do see,
And strangers oft kind to the *English* will be,
But the beauties of *Venice* can never come near
Thy feature, my Darling, *my Love and my dear.*

Believe what I say, my heart's chiefest delight,
That think on thee still both by day and by night.
For at home and abroad it shall alwaies appear,
That I will be true *to my Love and my dear.*

The Maiden's Answer.

I Hear, my true-love, this most sorrowful news,
Which makes me lament, alas! how can I choose?
The Seas, I do fear, will my comforts destroy,
And rob me at last *of my comfort and joy.*

Oh! when thou art absent, what joy can I find;
Or what can give ease to my troubled mind?
E'ry wind that doth blow will my pleasures destroy,
For fear I should lose *my delight and my joy.*

Go thou but to *Venice*, thou never shalt find
A lover so true, or so faithful and kind.
Though at first I did seem to be childish and coy,
Thou now art my comfort, *my love and my joy.*

Then never forsake me, for profit or gain;
Nor leave thy true love, for the wealth of the main;
A Jewel to Love, is an absolute Toy;
Then never forsake me, *my love and my joy.*

But if thou wilt go to the Seas that do rage,
Give me but thy promise, and firmly ingage,
Then I'le wait thy return, nothing shall me annoy,
But I constant will prove *to my comfort and joy.*

Such Loyalty never by any was shown
As I'le show to thee, for I love thee alone;
When we once are fast ty'd, I'le applaud the Blind Boy,
That taught me to love thee, *my comfort and joy.*

Printed for *J. Conyers*, at the *Black Raven*, in *Duck Lane.*

[In Black-letter. Two woodcuts, one on p. 278. Date, *circâ* 1680.]

*** The other woodcut (new) represents a Gentleman and Lady walking beside a river (Thames, opposite St. Mary Overy), looking at the numerous wherries. The burden or *refrain* of the Second Part identifies the tune of this ballad with another tune-name than *Ah, Chloris, awake!* viz., *Comfort and Joy.*

Saylors for my Money.

ALTHOUGH unable to give in the present volume an already carefully-prepared "*Second Group of Early Naval Ballads*" (as to which see our *Preface*, p. xiii*), it is much that we who had for the first time mentioned and reprinted the excellent ballad of "The Jovial Mariner; or, The Seaman's Renown," by J. P., (on p. 369), now add Martin Parker's original "Saylors for my Money" (on p. 797); both ditties being written to the same tune, used for Laurence Price's ballads, "*I am a jovial Batchelor,*" and "*I am a Jovial Cobbler, Sir,*" printed for W. Thackeray and T. Passinger. It was in Black-letter, with a single woodcut.

There seems to have been a friendly competition between Parker and Price, for they frequently chose the same theme and the same melody (two instances being cited, *viz.* one on p. 779, the other here). Martin Parker remains known of the rival balladists; but Laurence Price had in his own day enjoyed nearly equal popularity. He was a voluminous writer, as we have shown on p. 64, many of whose ephemeral pamphlets have perished or escaped observation.

We have here no available space for redeeming half-promises made on pp. 268, 528, 688, etc., concerning 'London's Tryumph,' 'The Dream of Judas's Mother Fulfilled;' 'A worthy Example of a Virtuous Wife' (p. 541 = 'In Rome, I read, a noble man'); 'A Young Man put to his Shifts' ('Of late did I hear'); and a continuation of the *Naval Ballads*. For the present we appropriately close with the far-back original of Tom Campbell's "Ye Mariners of England."

Modern warfare has so far changed the situation, introducing such explosive-ammunition, long-ranges, armour-plating, and steam-power for swift cruisers, that it is by no means certain "Britannia needs no bulwark, no towers along the steep." But her seamen have not degenerated, and will do their best for their country. "Her march is o'er the mountain-waves, her home is on the deep."

"Where *Blake* and mighty *Nelson* fell
Your manly hearts shall glow,
As ye sweep through the deep,
While the stormy tempests blow."

Saylors for my Money.

A new Ditty composed in the praise of Saylors and Sea affaires, breifly shewing the nature of so worthy a calling, and effects of their industry.

To the Tune of, *The Iovial Cobbler* [*cf.* pp. 368, 431, 796].

COuntrie men of *England*, who live at home with ease,
And little thinke what dangers are incident o' th' Seas:
Give eare unto the Saylor who unto you will shew
His case, his case: *How ere the winde doth blow.*

He that is a Saylor must have a valiant heart,
For, when he is upon the sea, he is not like to start;
But must, with noble courage, all dangers undergoe:
Resolve, resolve: *How e're the wind doth blow.*

Our calling is laborious, and subject to much [care]; [text, "woe."
But we must still contented be, with what falls to our share.
We must not be faint-hearted, come tempest, raine or snow,
Nor shrinke: nor shrinke: *How e're the winde doth blowe.*

Sometimes on *Neptune's* bosome our ship is tost with waves,
And every minute we expect the sea must be our graves. ['minite.'
Sometimes on high she mou̅teth, then falls againe as low:
With waves: with waves: *When stormie winds do blow.*

Then with unfained prayers, as Christian duty bindes,
Wée turne unto ye Lord of hosts, with all our hearts and minds;
To Him we flie for succour, for He, we surely know,
Can save: can save, *How ere the wind doth blow.*

Then He who breaks the rage, the rough and blustrous seas,
When His disciples were afraid, will straight ye stormes apease.
And give us cause to thanke, on bended knees full low:
Who saves: who saves, *How ere the wind doth blow.*

Our enemies approaching, when wée on sea espie,
Wée must resolve incontinent to fight, although we die,
With noble resolution we must oppose our foe,
In fight, in fight: *How ere the wind do[e]s blow.*

And when by God's assistance, our foes are put to th' foile
To animate our courages, wee all have share o' th' spoile.
Our foes into the ocean we back to back do throw, [See *Note*.
To sinke, or swimme, *How ere the wind doth blow.*

Note.—Judging from line 31, the piratical ways of Captain Ward (*cf.* p. 785, line 63) were imitated in our British navy. Clemency to a conquered foe was not learnt early. In later days popular sympathy is reserved for imprisoned criminals malingering. The 56th line in original is misprinted "*th'eile roare o' th' shore.*"

The Second Part, TO THE SAME TUNE.

Thus wée gallant Sea-men, in midst of greatest dangers,
Doe alwaies prove our valour, wée never are no changers:
But what soe ere betide us, wée stoutly undergoe,
Resolv'd, resolv'd, *How ere the wind doth blow.*

If fortune doe befriend us, in what we take in hand,
Wée prove our selves still generous whē ere we come to land,
Ther's few y^t shall out brave us, though neere so great in show,
Wée spend, and lend, *How ere the wind doth blow.*

We travell to the *Indies*, from them we bring som spice,
Here we buy rich Merchandise at very little price. ["prize."
And many wealthy prizes, we conquer from the foe: ["prices."
In fight: in fight, *How ere the wind doth blow.*

Into our native Country, with wealth we doe returne:
And cheere our wives and childrē, who for our absence mourne.
Then doe we bravely flourish, and where so ere we goe,
We roare: we roare: *How ere the wind doth blow.*

For when we have received our wages for our paynes,
The Vintners and the Tapsters by us have golden gaines.
We call for liquor roundly, and pay before we goe:
And sing: and drink, *How ere the wind doth blow.*

Wée bravely are respected, when we walke up and downe,
For if wee méete good company, wee care not for a crowne,
Ther's none more free than saylors, where ere he come or goe,
Tho' he'll roare o' th' shore, *How ere the winde doth blow.*

Then who would live in *England* and no[u]rish vice with ease,
When hée that is in povertie may riches get o' th' seas?
Let's saile unto the *Indies*, where golden grass doth grow:
To sea, to sea, *How ere the wind doth blow.*

Finis. M[artin] P[arker].

Printed at *London* for C[*uthbert*] *Wright*.

Accredited Authors

of Roxburghe Ballads, given complete in this Volume.

Armstrong (*sus. per col.*), T., 600.
Aytoun, Sir Robert (probably), 585, 586, 775.
Behn, Afra, Aphara, or Aphra, 7, (47?), 123, 136, 178, 181, 241.
Bowne, Tobias, 157, 158.
Bradley, A., 463.
Brereton, John Le Gay, 362.
Breton, Nicholas, 580.
Brome, Richard, 575.
Buckingham (George Villiers), Duke of, 39.
Burn ('Violer'), Nicol, 607, 608.
Burnand, Francis Cowley, 318.
Burns, Robert, 193, 445.
Canning, Geo. (attributed), 221.
Cleland, William (eight st.), 453.
Cokain, Sir Aston, 61.
Colman (younger), George, 755.
Crouch, Humphrey, 543, (probably 552, 563, 565); 560, 737.
Davenant, Charles, 100.
Deloney, Thomas, 384, 387, 390, 402, 655, 673; (?) 693; 722.
Dick, Lady (attributed), 201.
Dorset, (Charles Sackville), Earl of, 133.
Dryden, John, 21 (?), 37, 40, 152.
D'Urfey, Thomas, 43, 55, 58, 59, 152, 195, 276, 617.
Editorial, in *Preface*, vii*, xxiii*, *Introductory Notes*, xxxi, 310, 448, 449, 464, 518, 539, 720, 760, 800.
Essex (Robert Devereux), Earl of, 404.
Etherege, Sir George, 115, 252.
H., C. (probably not=H.C., *i.e.* Humphrey Crouch, *q.v.*), 324.
Hinton, John, 364.
Howard, T. (adapter), 759.
J., T. (Perhaps T. Jones), 393.
Johnson, Richard, 659, 714, 771.
Jordan, Thomas, *Introductory Notes*, xxvii, (probably) 490.
Kirkham, John, 399.
L., F., 671.
Lanfiere, Thomas, 340, 343, 415.
Lang, Andrew, 541.
Lee, Nathaniel, 289.
Leland, Charles George, 779.
Lyly, John, 467.
Montrose (James Graham), The Marquis of, 581.
O'Keefe, John, 383.
P., J. (probably John Playford), 110, 137, 369.
Parker, Martin (altered from), 432; 786? (his original), 797.
Person of Quality, A, 31.
Philips, Ambrose (Namby), 97.
Pope, Dr. Walter, 507.
Porter, Thomas (dramatist), 109.
Price, Laurence, (*Add. List*, 64), 67, 73, 105, 429, 567, 786?
R., T. (Thomas Robins?), 604.
Raleigh, Sir W. (attributed), 166.
Rochester (John Wilmot), Earl of, 88, 134.
S., Sir C. (Scrope, or Sedley), 101.
S., J., 378.
S., T. (Tho. Stride?), *Int.* xxv.
Scott (of Biggar), R., 232.
Scrope, Sir Car (probably), 101.
Sedley, Sir Charles 101; 130.
Shadwell, Thomas, 79.
Sidney, Sir Philip, *Introd.*, xxii.
Tennyson, Alfred, 658.
Wade, John, 332, 337, 346, 470, 475.
Walcot, Dr. John, 609.
Warner, William, 712.
Wedderburn, J. (imperfect), 201.
Wild, Dr. Robert, 456.

Editorial Finale to Vol. VI.

"What shadows we are, and what shadows we pursue!"—*Burke.*

To A. M. Adam, of Boston.

IT *seems unto me, whose thoughts flit free,*
(Not in grooves, like Parson-professionals',)
That this world of ours, with its brambles and flowers,
Is a race-course for crazed processionals.
Whence they all flow, or whither they go,
None know, or can show in Historia?
Living-dead, dead-alive, they junket and strive,
A ghastly Phantasmagoria.

Hans Holbein, *of old, in quaint emblems told*
What he thought of Life's Masque precarious;
To their latest breath, in such Dance of Death,
Mortals frolic, like Saint Macarius:
In a phrensied whirl, they twist, and twirl,
Shout Hélas! *or* Juch he! *or* Gloria!
Neither daring to pause, nor consider the cause
They are only Phantasmagoria.

Ballad Book-men choose quiet, apart from mad riot,
But can little boast, in comparison:
Unless we shut out each beleaguering Doubt,
We find mutiny cripples the garrison.
Laugh we or weep, or grim silence keep,
Servile drudge, and luxurious Doria,
We too fade away, from our own brief day,
Like the giddy Phantasmagoria.

We mingle betimes, with sermons and rhymes,
Love and war, wealth and poverty pitiful;
Whether Hermit *recluse, or* Roué *profuse,*
Heeding all diverse lives, a whole city-full:
Half-angel, half-brute, clad in Motley suit,
'Vae Victis!' *we gasp; not* 'Victoria!'
Having seen quite enough, of smooth and rough,
In our share of Phantasmagoria.

J. Woodfall Ebsworth.

The Priory, Molash, 1888.

[This cut belongs to pp. 147, 247.]

Index

Of First Lines, Burdens, Titles and Tunes.

Prefatory Note.—This list includes "First Lines," *burdens*, titles and sub-titles (*i.e.* secondary titles), and tunes. It distinguishes the ballads that are merely alluded to in passing, as 'mentioned,' from those whereof the opening stanza or other portion is given, as 'quoted': while the absence of either sign shows those that are given complete. "First Lines" are indicated by being within double quotational commas. Tunes are named as tunes. *Burdens, refrains, or choruses* are so entitled, in *Italic* type. Most ballads of old were printed without being dated; but we have endeavoured throughout vols. iv., v., and vi. to supply this deficiency within square brackets, after careful study of external and internal evidence. Every clue of publisher or printer's name or initials, tune, burden, or allusion to contemporary events, becomes valuable in these investigations (and we recover from other collections what was mutilated by the binders of the Roxburghe), since we generally re-arrange our material chronologically or in 'groups' when practicable.—J. W. Ebsworth.

PAGE

"A CERTAIN great King once did rule over this land" 717
"A Cheshire man sail'd into Spain" (='set sail'='went o'er to') 657
"A company of gossips that love good bub" .... quoted, 482
A contented mind it is most rare, etc. ..... burden, 351, 356
"A council grave our King did hold" .... mentioned, 713
"A country life is sweet" .... mentioned, 520
"A country that draws fifty feet of water" .... quoted, 434
"A curse on the zealous and ignorant crew" 56
"A dainty spruce young Gallant" 200, 205
"A damsel, I'm told, of delicate mould" .... mentioned, 528
"A female Quaker in Cheapside" .... mentioned, 6
"A gallant damosel in Bristol City." (See "An amorous") ..... tune, 161
A good wife is a portion every day .... burden and title, 331, 332
"A King once reign'd beyond the Seas" ..... 254, 264; given, 661
A lustful love did cause her woe, etc. .... burden, 767

PAGE
A man he may work all the days of his life, etc. ..... burden, 482
"A merchant's son of worthy fame." (See 'Garland, Bristol') mentioned, 428
"A merry jest I shall declare" (='A pretty') ..... mentioned, 315, given, 515
"A merry Milkmaid on a time" .... mentioned, 177, 199
"A Miller lived near Overton" .... mentioned, 27
A Mock to "Begone! that fatal fiery fever" ..... title, mentioned, 564
A penny well saved is as good as one earned ..... burden, 348, 349
"A pretty jest I shall declare" .... mentioned, 315, given, 515
A Pudding (compare *With a fading*) burden and tune mentioned, 515
"A Queen beyond seas did command" .... mentioned, 148
A Seaman hath a valiant heart, etc...... .... burden, 369
"A Seaman loved a maiden pretty" .... mentioned, 364, 365
"A thousand times my love commend" ..... and tune, quoted, 105, 259
"A virgin famed for her virtue and beauty" .... mentioned, 28
"A wealthy man, a farmer, who had of corn great store" 535
"A wealthy Yeoman's Son" .... mentioned, 639
"A week before Easter, the day's long and clear" 229, 230, 233
"A weel's me!" etc. (See "Ah, woe's me!") .... mentioned, 183
"A youthful Serving-man of late" .... mentioned, 148
Abbot and King Olfrey, The Old .... title, 750, 753
Abbot of Canterbury, King John and the .... title, 746, 747
"About a thirty years and five did Leir rule this land" 712
Accession of King George I., Song on the ..... title, quoted, 618
Account of a King who slighted all Women, An ..... sub-title, 661
Account of the many Evils, etc. .... sub-title, 16
Address to Charon, The Despairing Lover's .... title, 24, 28
Adieu, The Seaman's .... title, mentioned, 368
"Adieu to grief and discontent" .... mentioned, 445
Adieu to his Mistress, A noble Seaman's .....sub-title, mentioned, 43, 438
Admirer of Beauty, The True .... sub-title, 124
Admonition, A Father's Wholesome..... .... title, 215, 217
Admonition, The True Lover's .... title, 217, 219
Adventures, The Faithful Maid's .... title, mentioned, 64
Advice, The Merry Toper's .... sub-title, 502
Advice, The Subtle Damosel's .... title, mentioned, 177, 199
Advice to the Beaus .... title, quoted, 15
Advice to the Ladies of London .... title, mentioned, 15
Advice to the Maids of London, The Virgin's ..... title, mentioned, 336
Advice, Too Late .... title, 101
Æneas, the Wandering Prince of Troy .... title, 547
Age of Despair, The (H. D. Traill's *Recaptured Rhymes*) ..... quoted, 474
"Agencourt, Agencourt! know ye not Agencourt?" ..... quoted, 743
Agincourt .... tune, 650
Agincourt ('Fair stood the wind for France') .... quoted, 743
Agreement of William and Susan, The Happy ..... sub-title, mentioned, 28
Ah! ah! my love's dead..... .... burden, mentioned, 39
"Ah! Chloris, awake!" .... and tune, 123, 128, 410. 417. 795, 796
"Ah! Chloris, that I now could sit 130, 133, 194, 199
"Ah! Chloris, 'tis time to disarm your bright eyes" 133
"Ah! Cupid, thou provest unkind and too cruel" 120
Ah! how pleasant 'tis to love .... tune, mentioned, 307
"Ah! Jenny, gin your eyes do kill" and tune, 156, 170, 176, 178, 180, 181, 184, 186, 189, 190, 199, 259
"Ah! my cruel Shepherd" .... mentioned, 130
"*Ah! Nanny," quoth he, "be not cruel," etc.* .... burden, 174
Ah! ope, Lord Gregory, thy door" (Dr. Walcot's) 609

PAGE
Ah! woe is me! poor harmless maid!" ..... mentioned, 177, 183, 184
Ahasuer ..... title, mentioned, 690, 778; given, 699; translation, 779
Aim not too high, at things beyond thy reach ..... tune, mentioned, 331
Air de Chasse .... tune, 691
Alack! for my love I must die .... burden and tune, 204, 205
Alarum to all that profess martial discipline, St. George's ..... sub-title, 780
" Alas! my dearest love is gone" .... mentioned (*bis*), 27
" Alas! my love, you do me wrong" (=Greensleeves) quoted, 397, 398
" Alas! my youthful Coridon" .... mentioned, 133
Alas! poor Scholar, whither wilt thou go? ..... burden and title, 455, 456
Ale that is so brown, The .... burden, 342, 351
Algiers Slave's Releasement, The .... title, 410; given, 447
" All Christian men give ear a while to me" 703
" All company-keepers come hear what I say" 483
" All hail to the days, that merit more praise" .... mentioned, 481
" All happy times when free from love" mentioned, and tune, 26, 27, 793
" All in the West of England fair" 113
" All jolly blades that inhabit the Town" .... mentioned, 15
" All jolly rake-hells that sup at the Rose" .... quoted, 15
" All joy I bid adieu" .... mentioned, 639
" All the Flatteries of Fate, and the glories of State" and tune, 292, 293
" All the woes Prodigious Fate" .... mentioned (guessed), 145
All Trades .... tune, mentioned, 276
" All you brave damsels come, lend your attention" ..... mentioned, 108
" All you that are brave Sailors" .... mentioned, 428
" All you that are freemen of Ale-Drapers' Hall" 315, 486
" All you that cry 'O hone! O hone!'" .... mentioned, 623
" All you that do in love delight" 177, 191, 199
" All you that ever heard the name of Wigmore," etc. 767
" All you that lay claim to a Good-fellow's name" ..... quoted, 256
" All you that list to look and see" 387
Alteration, alteration, this is modern alteration .... burden, 755
Alteration, Time's .... title, mentioned, 276
Amarillis and Colin .... title, 109
" Amarillis I did woo, and I courted Phillis too" 108
" Amarillis tear thy hair!" 109
" Amarillis told her swain" .... and tune, 109, 110, 113
" Amarillis, you express in your looks such happiness" ..... mentioned, 109
Amendment, The Bad Husband's .... sub-title, 340
Amintas on the new-made hay (*cf.* 'Phillis') ..... tune, 108, 115, 116
" Amongst the Foresters of old" 615
Amoret and Phillis (prop. 'As Amoret with') title and tune, 100, 101, 133, 134
Amoret's advice to Phillis .... title, 101
Amorous damsel of Bristol City, An .... tune, 159, 166
" An amorous damsel of Bristol City" .... mentioned, 428
" An ancient story I'll tell you anon" ..... variation, mentioned, 746
" An old song made by an old ancient pate" 756
" An old song made of an old ancient pate" (T. Howard's re-cast) 758
An Orange .... burden and tune, mentioned, 515
And all was for want of money ..... burden (*bis*), quoted, 342; given, 499
And alongst the coast of Barbary .... second burden, 409
And I like my humour well .... burden, quoted, 336
And I never will play the Bad Husband no more ..... burden, 343
And I wish in heaven his soul may dwell, etc. .... burden, 470
And I wish that his heirs may never lack Sack, etc. ..... burden, 466
And I'll be thy True Love until I die ..... second burden, 74

PAGE
"And I'll go to my Love." (See "I will go to my Love") 36, 39, 65
And keep my money in store .... burden, 339, 340
And never be drunk again (bis) .... tune and burden, 276, 317
And never married be .... burden varies, 238, 246
And sing, '*Go from the window, Love, go!* ..... burden, 200, 205
And we ran and they ran, etc. .... burden, quoted, 617
Andrew Barton, Life and Death of Sir ..... title, mentioned, 367
Angel Gabriel (of Bristol) ..... part title and burden, 428, 429
Annie of Lochroyan, Fair .... title, quoted, 212, 611
Answer, The Faithful Young Man's..... .... title, 295
Answer, The Young Farmer's .... title, mentioned, 237
Answer, The Young Man's .... title, 564, 565
Answer to Cupid's Trapan .... title, mentioned, 528
Answer to his Unkind Lover, The Seaman's .... title, 792
Answer to 'O what a plague is Love!' .... title, 463
Answer to Parthenia's Complaint .... title, 30
Answer to Love's Lamentable Tragedy, The Young Man's ..... sub-title, 79, 81 to 83
Answer to the Covetous-minded Parents ..... title, mentioned, 639
Answer to the Injured Maiden (not 'Mistress,' misprint) title, ment., 26, 27
Answer to the Lady's Tragedy .... title, mentioned, 639
Answer to the Lover's Enquiry .... title, mentioned, 32
Answer to the Love-sick Maiden .... title, mentioned, 148
Answer to the Love-sick Serving-Man, An ..... title, mentioned, 148
Answer to the Scotch Haymakers .... title, mentioned, 237
Answer to the Shepherd's Song, Fair Flora's .... title, 106
Answer to the Unfortunate Lady (No. 5*) ..... omitted from mention, 27
Antidote of Rare Physic, An .... title, 354, 356
Apology, The Pensive Prisoner's .... title, mentioned, 557
Après Février vient le Juin .... *Edit. Envoi* title, 448
"Are the Fates so unkind?" 226
"Argyle and Mar are gone to war" 620
Argyle and the Earl of Mar, Dialogue between .... title, 620
"Arise from thy bed, my turtle, my dove!" .... mentioned, 66
Armada (Deloney's contemporary ballads), The Spanish ..... 382 to 392
Armada (Macaulay's ballad), The .... quoted, 371
Armada, The Spanish (John O'Keefe's) 383
Armstrong (the original) John ..... title, quoted, 603; tune, 635
Armstrong's Good Night (Thomas) .... title, 600
Armstrong's Last Good Night, Johnnie ..... title, 427, 594, 600, 604
Arthur of the Table Round, the Noble Acts of King ..... title, 722
"As Amoret with Phillis sate" .... and tune, 101, 133, 134
"As at noon Dulcina rested" 166
"As Chloris, full of harmless thoughts" 133, 134, 199
"As he lay in the plain, his arm under his head" 31
"As I came down the Highland town" .... quoted, 618
"As I did travel in the night" 622
"As I lay on my lonely bed" .... mentioned, 148
"As I once walk'd in a May morning" 307
"As I of late was walking" (= Rare News) .... mentioned, 237
"As I sate in a pleasant shade" .... mentioned, 296
"As I through Sandwich town passed along" .... mentioned, 367
"As I walk'd forth to take the air" (Desp. M.R.) ..... mentioned, 177
"As I walk'd forth to take the air" (New b. M.) mentioned, 177, 199
"As I walk'd forth to take the air" (T. Love Rew.) tune, 115, 259, 260
"As I walk'd forth to view the plain" .... mentioned, 681

PAGE
" As I was walking forth of late, I heard a man" .... mentioned, 237
" As I was walking forth of late (" in the prime," etc.) ..... mentioned, 237
" As I was walking forth of late (within the meadows)" 237, 238
" As I was walking in the Shade" (Birds' Harmony) 782
" As I went forth one evening tide" .... mentioned, 318
" As I went forth to view the Spring" ..... mentioned, 170, 228
" As it befell upon one time" 595
" As it fell one holyday, *hay downe*" 631
" As it fell out on a high holyday, as many," etc..... ..... 633, 631
" As it fell out upon a day" 641
" As it fell upon a day" (Richard Barnfield's) ..... mentioned, 136, 309
" As Jenny Crack and I" .... mentioned, 183
" As lately I travell'd towards Gravesend" ..... mentioned, 66, 368
" As one that for a weary space has lain" 541
" As our King lay musing upon his bed" 744
" As Roger and Mary were toiling" .... mentioned, 170
As she lay sleeping in her bed .... tune, mentioned, 148
As she sailed on the Low-lands low .... burden, 419
" As Thurot in his cabin lay" .... mentioned, 446
" As Tourville in his cabin lay" (incorrect version) ..... mentioned, 446
Ashford, The Kentish Yeoman and Susan of ..... title, mentioned, 639
" Assist me, you Muses, to make my sad moan" .... mentioned, 32
Astrea (= Aphra Behn), D'Urfey's Song to .... title, 43
" At Dunsmore the fair Isabel" 769
Attempt on the town of Cales (= Cadiz) .... title, 420
" Attend all ye who list to hear" .... quoted, 371
" Attend you and give ear a while" 429
" Attend, you loyal Lovers all" .... mentioned, 27
" Attend, young lasses all, of Edinburgh town" .... mentioned, 237
Aughrim, The Lass of. (See 'Ocram') ..... title, mentioned, 612
Austinian Bird-Catcher's Delight, The .... *Edit. title*, 310
Awake, Chloris (see, properly, 'Ah! Chloris, awake!') ..... tune, 123
Awake, O my Chloris (= Ah! Chloris, awake) .... tune, 410, 447
" Away, you fool! wilt thou love less?" .... mentioned, 564
" Away, you grievous things call'd Mistresses!" .... mentioned, 564
Aye, marry, and thank you too! .... burden, indicated, 241

BACCHUS overcome .... title of variation, 505
Bachelor, The Bashful .... title, mentioned, 639
Bachelor's Ballad, The .... title, mentioned, 57
Bachelor's Forecast, The .... title, mentioned, 528
Bachelor's Triumph (lost end-lines recovered), The ..... title, 788
Bacon and Beans ..... (not yet found, except title and tune), 279
Bad Company did me undo, but I'll do so no more ..... burden, 493
Bad Husband (= Unthrifty: see 'Husband') 315, 468, 477, 483, 493
Bailiff's Daughter of Islington, The..... ..... sub-title, 241, 243
Ballads, Sundry Groups of (see 'Group') 7, 313, 361, 465, 536
Ballads on King Lear (and Warner's poem), Two 714, 717
Ballads on Lord Thomas and Fair Eleanor, Two 643, 645, 647
Ballads on Mar's Insurrection, Three .... 617, 620 to 622
Ballard and Babbington, A Proper new Ballad on title, mentioned, 388
Balloo, ballow, ballowe, and *baloo* or *balow* .... 574 to 580
" *Ballow, ballow* burden ('Peace, wayward bairn'), and tune 575 to 577
" Ballowe, my babe, lie still and sleep" (*tr*) .... mentioned, 576
" Baloo, my boy, lie still and sleep" .... mentioned, 576

PAGE
" Balow, my babe, frown not on me" .... mentioned, 576
" *Balow, my babe, weep not for me*" .... and burden, 576, 577
Balow, The New .... title and tune, 575 to 579, 601
Bar up the door ! (See '*Come away !*') .... tune, 212, 213
Barnaby doubts me ! .... burden, 463
Barnard and the Little Musgrave, Lord .... title, 629, 649
Barnard, The old ballad of Little Musgrave and the Lady ..... title, 631
Barton, Life and Death of Sir Andrew ..... title, mentioned, 367
Bashful Bachelor, The .... title, mentioned, 639
Bateman, Young .... sub-title, mentioned, 650
Battle at Sea, The .... sub-title, mentioned, 368
Battle of Killiecrankie, The memorable ..... title and tune, 615, 616
Battle of the Baltic, The .... title, mentioned, 431
" Be gone ! thou fatal fiery fever " 559, 563
" Be your liquor small, or as thick as mud " 466
Beauty, The Tyrannical..... .... title, 145
Beccles (in Suffolk), Lamentation of ..... title, mentioned, 388
Bedlam Schoolmen .... title, 452
Beggar Maid (Tennyson's), The .... title, 658
Behold the man with a glass in his hand ..... tune, mentioned, 368
" Behold the touchstone of true Love ! " .... quoted, 428
" Behold ! what noise is this I hear ? " .... mentioned, 509
Belgic Boar, The .... title, mentioned, 650
Bellamira, Song to .... title, 289
Berkshire Damsel, The Beautiful .... title, mentioned, 27
" Betrayed me ! how can this be ? " 590
Betty, A merry song in Praise of .... sub-title, 159
Betty's Compassionate Love extended, etc. .... sub-title, 202
Betty's Reply to the Gallant Seaman 416
Billy and Joany (=" I often for my Joany strove ") ..... title, 148
Billy and Molly. (See ' Willy and Molly ') .... tune, 218, 228
Billy's Invitation to his sweetheart Joany ..... sub-title, mentioned, 148
Biographers Interviewed (at Richmond), The title, mentioned, *Preface*, xvii
Bird-Catcher's Delight, The .... tune, 136, 299 to 301, 307
Bird-Catcher's Delight, The Austinian ..... *Intermezzo title*, 310
Birds' Harmony, Part Second of the (=" Down as ") ..... title, 308
Birds' Harmony, The (=' As I was ' : Pepysian) title, 307, 779, 782
Birds' Harmony, The (=Woody Choristers) ..... sub-title, 268, 301, 303
Birds' Lamentation, The (=' Oh ! says the Cuckoo ') title, 300, 304, 305, 307
Birds' Notes on May-day last, The .... title, quoted, 307, 309, 323
Black Jack, The bonny .... burden and title, 466, 469
" Blame not your Armida, nor call her your grief " 36, 37
" Blame not your Calista, nor call her your grief " 41
Blantyre, Lennox's Love to .... sub-title, 304
Bleeding Lover's Lamentation, The..... ..... title, mentioned, 639
" Blink over the burn, sweet Betty ! " Scotch version, fragment, 204
Bliss, The True Lover's..... .... sub-title, 113
Blood, An Elegy on Colonel (Thomas) .... title, 786, 787
Bloody Jack of Shrewsbury ..... *Ingoldsby Legend*, mentioned, 358
Bloody News from Germany .... title, mentioned, 650
" Blush not redder than the morning " ..... and tune, 289, 290
Boatswain, The Unchangeable .... sub-title, 419 ; given, 447
Boatswain's Call, The .... title, mentioned, 639
Bonny Bessie Lee (=" Oh ! bonny Bessie Lee ") ..... quoted, 653
Bonny black Bess .... burden and tune, 127, 346
Bonny bonny Bird .... tune, 528

PAGE
Bonny bonny Broom, The .... tune, 474
Bonny Katharine Ogie .... title mentioned, and tune, 618, 622
Bonny Sweet Robin (is all my joy) .... tune, mentioned, 66
Born too early! .... (heavy) burden, *Prologue*, vii*
Bottel-Maker's Delight The .... tune, 469, 470
Boxall to Margaret Mills, last dying words of Robert title, mentioned, 43
Brave boys! .... burden and tune, 526 to 528
Breaking up of the Camp, An excellent song of the title, mentioned, 381
Bride, The Seaman's Sorrowful .... title, 177, 350, 351, 441
Bridegroom, The Bristol .... title, mentioned, 428
Bride's Burial, The .... title, mentioned, 40, 650, 653
Bristol Bridegroom, The (=' You loyal lovers all ') title, mentioned, 428
Bristol Garland (' A merchant's son of worthy fame ') mentioned, 428
Bristol, The fair and loyal Maid of (*cf.* 444) .... title, 408, 443
Bristol, The Honour of .... title, 368, 428, 429, 779
Bristol, The Loyal Maid of .... sub-title, 441, 442
Bristol, The Ship-Carpenter's love to the Merchant's daughter of, title, m., 428
Bristol Tragedy, The .... title, mentioned, 27
British Heroes, The .... title, quoted, 726
" Britons, now let joys increase " .... quoted, 618
Broken Contract, The .... title, mentioned, 27
Broom, broom on hill, broom .... and burden, mentioned, 586
Broom, The bonny bonny .... tune, 583, 585, 586
Broom, The New .... title, quoted, 586
Burn (the Violer), The Words of .... title, 608
Busy Fame (properly, ' When busy Fame ') .... tune, 102, 103
But I'll be loyal to thee, my Love .... second burden, 30
But now I may with sorrow sadly say, etc. ..... burden, quoted, 474
" But when the bottles rowl and glasses " ..... second movement, 58
By and bye .... burden, varies, 449
" By shallow rivers," etc. (See " Come live with me ") ..... mentioned, 556
" By the side of a murmuring stream " 221

CALAMITY, The Duchess of Suffolk's ..... title, mentioned, 547
Calculation, The Countryman's ..... sub-title, mentioned, 5
Cales Ballads (*i.e.* Cadiz) 398, 401, 402, 411, 420
Cales, The Earl of Essex going to .... title, mentioned, 398
Cales, The Winning of .... title, 401, 402, 411
Calino (=Calen o custore me) .... tune, 284
Calista, The Lover's Farewell to .... sub-title, 36, 40
" Call not your Clarinda your life and your soul "..... 439
Call to Charon, A ....alternative title, 23, 25, 66
Camarades Deux .... title, *Preface*, xviii*
" Can love be controul'd by advice ? "..... .... mentioned, 221
" Can you dance the Shaking of the Sheets ? " ..... mentioned, 750, 753
Candlemas (probably title of ballad)..... .... mentioned, 389
Canterbury, King John and the Abbot of .... title, 746
Canterbury Tales (Chaucer's, from Ellesmere MS.) ..... quoted, 522
Captain Jennings his song .... title, mentioned, 408
Captain Ward, his Fight with the Rainbow title and tune, 422, 426, 427, 784
Captain Ward, The Seaman's Song of title, 422, 425, 779 ; given, 784
Captive, The Reprieved .... title, mentioned, 152
Caridora. (See Charidora.) 583, 585, 586, 774, 775
Carouse to the Emperor, A .... title, mentioned, 284
Carrack, Seaman's Carol for taking of the great..... title, mentioned, 398

PAGE

Cast from thy heart all care, etc. .... burden, 773
Cast no care to thy heart (etc.), Dainty come thou to me! ..... burden, 280
Catalogue of Contented Cuckolds, A..... ..... title, mentioned, 32
Catch, A (Amarillis and Colin) .... title, 109
Catch by Tom D'Urfey, A .... title, 55
Catholic Ballad, The (="Since Popery of late") title, mentioned, 506
Cavalier, The Discontented .... title, mentioned, 328
Cavallily Man, The .... tune, 2
Caveat for all Spendthrifts, A .... part title, 343
Caveat, The Conscionable .... tune, 542, 543
"Cease rude Boreas, blust'ring railer" (Roxb. Coll. III. 401.) quoted, 365
Celia and Phaon .... title, mentioned, 32
Celia Optained, Fair .... sub-title, 155
"Celia, that I once was blest" ....mentioned, 127; given, 152
Celia's Complaint for the Loss of her Virginity ..... sub-title, 47, 52
Celia's Eyes, Song on .... title, 152
Celia's Joy .... sub-title, mentioned, 156
Celia's sweet Reply to her Faithful Friend .... title, 66, 68
Centurion of London, Wonderful Victory achieved by the title, mentioned, 398
Chambermaid, The Loving .... title, mentioned, 218
Champion, Queen Elizabeth's .... title, 405
Champions of Christendom (Rich. Johnson's), Seven title, quoted, 724
Character of Sundry Callings, A .... sub-title, 532
Charge of the Light Brigade (Tennyson's) .... mentioned, 743
Charidora, Diaphantus and various titles, 198, 583, 585, 586, 774, 775
Charidora's Reply to the forlorn Lover Diaphantas ..... title, 586
"Charon, make haste, and ferry me over" ..... and tune, 24 to 26, 28, 793
Charon, The Despairing Lover's Address to .... title, 24
"Chaunt, birds, in every bush!" 309
"Cheer up, my mates, the wind does fairly blow" ..... quoted, 399
Cheese-monger, The Jolly .... title, mentioned, 237
Cheshire Cheese, The .... alternative title, 657
Cheviot, The Hunting of the .... title, quoted, 739
Chevy Chace (or Chase), modern ballad of, and tune, 643, 645, 738 to 743, 750, 751, 777
"Chloe, your pride abate (='your scorn abate')..... and tune, 58, 59
"Chloe, your unrelenting scorn" (inadvertently repeated) 26, 60
Chloris awake. (See, properly, "Ah! Chloris, awake!")..... tune, 130
Chloris, The Lamentation of .... title, 130, 131
Choice, The Fair Maid's .... title, mentioned, 367, 414
Choice, The Knight's Happy .... sub-title, 96, 97
Choristers, The Woody .... title, 136, 268, 299, 307; given, 301
Christ is my love, He loves me .... tune, mentioned, 688
Chronicle, The Wandering Jew's .... title, 690, 695
City of Dreadful Night (James Thomson's), The ..... mentioned, 88
Clans' Lamentation against Mar, and their own folly, The ..... title, 618, 622
"Clavers and his Highland men" 616
Clerk's Two Sons of Owsenford, The ..... title, mentioned, 600
Cleveland, Constance of..... .... title, 571, 572, 635, 653
Clorinda, The kind Return of his .... sub-title, mentioned, 26
Cloris. (See 'Chloris,' *passim*) .... 130, 133, etc.
Clothworker caught in a Trap, The .... title, mentioned, 66
Cobler, Death and the (="A Cobler there was") ..... tune, 746
Cobler, The Jovial ..... title and tune, mentioned, 368, 431, 796, 797
Cobler, The Queen and the .... sub-title, mentioned, 148
Cock, The Grey ....occasional title, quoted, 304

PAGE
Coffee, A Satire on .... (vol. v. p. 184) title, mentioned, 6
Colin and Amarillis (*alias* Amarillis and Colin) .... tune, 115
Colin's Complaint .... title, mentioned, 221
" Come all loyal Lovers, so courteous and free " 66, 70, 115
" Come, all my kind neighbours, and listen a while " 6
" Come, all you bachelors so brave " .... mentioned, 356
" Come all you jolly Ploughmen " .... mentioned, 520
" Come all you maidens fair " .... mentioned, 428 ; given, 411
" Come, all you old Bakers, attend and give ear ".... .... mentioned, 32
" Come all you very merry London girls " .... mentioned, 318
" Come and help me to complain ! " 284
Come away, pretty Betty, and open the door ! .... burden, 212, 213
Come away to my chamber, and bar up the door ! burden and tune, 212
" Come, for they call you, Shepherd quoted, 87, 150 ; mentioned, 155
" Come gallants, and listen unto me a while " .... mentioned, 292
" Come hear a song, and a very fine song " .... mentioned, 300
" Come, hearken to me, whilst the truth I do write " .... mentioned, 5
" Come hither, good fellows, and hear what I say " 480
" Come hither, my dutiful Son " 217
" Come hither, my own sweet Duck " and tune, quoted, 489, 491, 493
" Come hither, sweet Husband " .... mentioned, 66
" Come hither, sweet Nancy, and sit down by me " mentioned, 64, 66
Come let us sing, ' Vive le Roy ! Vive le Roy !' .... burden, 730
" Come, listen all unto my Song " .... mentioned, 236
" Come, listen all you that to mirth are inclined " .... mentioned, 5
" Come, listen to me, my true Love ".... .... mentioned, 115, 116, 263
" Come listen, young Gallants of Shrewsbury's fair town " 359, 414
" Come, little Babe ; come, silly soul ! " 580
" Come, live with me, and be my love " .... mentioned, 556
" Come, mournful Muse, assist my quill " 558
" Come, my hearts of gold, let us be merry and wise ! " .... mentioned, 318
" Come on, thou fatal messenger from her that's gone " 565
" Come, open the door, sweet Betty ! " 202
" Come, pity a damsel distressed " (omitted to be ment. as 2*) 170, 251
" Come, sound up your trumpets, and beat up your drums " 405
" Come, turn thy rosy face " 153
" Come, turn to me, thou pretty little one " 273, 276, 277
" Come, you lusty lovers " .... mentioned, 237
" Come, young men and listen to what I'll you show " 332
Comfort and Joy .... burden and tune, 795, 796
Commendation of Sir Martin Frobisher (John Kirkham's) .... title, 399
Commendation to all Soldiers, St. George's .... title, 780
Company of Horsemen, etc., Ballad showing the title, mentioned, 382
Compass, The Seaman's (=" As lately I travell'd ") title, mentioned, 64, 368
Complaint against a Young Man's Unkindness, The Kind Virgin's title, 253
Complaint, Colin's .... title, mentioned, 221
Complainte du Juif Errant (*bis*) .... title, 690, 692 ; given, 691
Complaint for his Unkind Mistress at Wapping, The Seaman's title, m., 27
Complaint for the death of her Willy, Peggy's .... title, mentioned, 382
Complaint for the loss of her Virginity, Celia's .... sub-title, 47, 52
Complaint of Fair Isabel for the loss of her Honour, The title, 771
Complaint of Rosamond (Samuel Daniel's), The.... .... title, 668
Complaint of the unkindness of Strephon, The Nymph's title, mentioned, 127
Complaint, Parthenia's. (See also 'Answer.') .... title, 30, 46, 47
Complaint, The Country Lover's .... sub-title, 461
Complaint, The Despairing Lover's .... title, mentioned, 27

PAGE
Complaint, The Dying Lover's .... title, mentioned, 127, 190
Complaint, The Good-Fellow's .... sub-title, 315, 486
Complaint, The Old Man's .... title, mentioned, 276
Complaint, The Shepherd's .... title, mentioned, 170
Complaint, The West-Country Damosel's .... title, 635
Concubine, The Unfortunate .... title, 672, 676
Confession, Queen Eleanor's .... title, 672, 678, 680
Congratulation, The Valiant Seaman's ..... title, quoted, 431
Conquest, Love's (=" Young Phaon strove ") .... title, 100
Conquest, Love's Glorious (=" Adieu to grief ") title, quoted, 445
Conquest of France, King Henry the Fifth's .... title, 743, 744
Conquest over the French, Adm. Killigrew's glorious sub-title, ment., 368
Conscience and Fair-Dealing .... title, mentioned, 75
Conscionable Caveat, The .... tune, 542, 543
Conscionable Couple, A .... title, mentioned, 542
Consideration, The Good-Fellow's .... title, mentioned, 338
Conspirators, Joy made in London at the taking of the title, mentioned, 389
Constable, Master ..... burden and sub-title, 315, 468, 509, 515
Constance of Cleveland .... title, 571, 572, 635, 653
Constancy Lamented .... title, mentioned, 27
Constancy, Love and .... title, 65, 70
Constancy, Loyal .... title, mentioned, 177, 199
Constancy, Nelly's .... title, mentioned, 27, 283, 791
Constancy, The True Pattern of .... title, 43, 44
Constant Lovers, The (=" I often for ") ..... title, mentioned, 148
Constant Lovers, The Two .... title, mentioned, 115, 263
Constant Maid's Resolution, The .... title, mentioned, 161
Constant Penelope .... sub-title, 552, 553
Continuation of the Wandering Jew's Chronicle..... ..... title, 698
Contract, The Broken .... title, mentioned, 27
Cook Maid's Tragedy, The .... mentioned, 33
Cook, The Master (his Lamentation) 652, 683
Cope, Ballad-squib against Sir John .... mentioned, 625
Cophetua, King. (See 'Cupid's Revenge,' and 'Song of a Beggar') 659, 661
Coranto, The Jew's .... tune, 489, 490
Cordelia's Lamentation for the absence of her Gerhard ..... sub-title, 563
Coridon and Parthenia .... title, quoted, 102
Coridon and Phillis .... title, 133, 134
Corn-hoarders, A Warning to all .... title, mentioned, 534
" Could man his wish obtain " .... and tune, 61, 62
Counsel, A Groat's-worth of Good .... title, 468, 479, 480
Counsel, A Pennyworth of Good .... title, mentioned, 482
Counsel to her Daughter, A Mother's .... sub-title, 349
Counted no man .... burden, varies, 346
Country Dance, A new .... tune, 489, 492
Country Farmer, The .... tune, 531, 532
Country Lover's Complaint, The .... sub-title, 461
Country Lovers, Faithful Wooings of Two (=' As I was ') title, 237, 250
Country Maid, The Constant .... title, 272
Country Man's Calculation, The .... sub-title, mentioned, 5
" Country-men of England, who live at home with ease " 431 ; given, 797
Country People's Felicity, The .... title, mentioned, 237
Couple, A Conscionable .... title, mentioned, 542
Couple, The Crost .... tune and title, 495, 496
Couple, The Unequal-match'd .... sub-title, mentioned, 276
Courage, Royal .... title, mentioned, 225

PAGE
Courageous Cornel, The .... title, mentioned, 639
Couragious Soldiers of the North, The .... title, mentioned, 606
Court Lady, The .... (undiscovered) tune, 676
Court of Equity, Cupid's .... title, mentioned, 91
Courtier of the King's, A New ....title, 757 to 759
Courtier, The Modish .... sub-title, 56
Courtier, The Old and Young ....title, 754 to 759
Courtier, The Queen's Old .... tune, 757, 758
Courtship, Crafty Jockey's .... sub-title, mentioned, 236
Courtship of the King of France's Daughter .... part title, mentioned, 571
Covetous-minded Parents, Answer to the .... title, mentioned, 639
Coy Celia's Cruelty .... title, mentioned, 127 ; given, 152
Coy Shepherd and Kind Shepherdess, The .... sub-title, 128
Crafty Jockey's Courtship .... sub-title, mentioned, 236
Crafty Miss, The .... title, mentioned, 170
Crimson Velvet .... tune, 571, 572
Crost Couple, The .... tune and title, 495, 496
Cruel Black, Blackamoor, The .... title, mentioned, 650
Cruel Landlord, The .... title, mentioned, 33
Cruelty, Another Song on Chloe's (repeated by misadventure) title, 26, 60
Cruelty, Coy Celia's .... title, 127 ; given, 152
Cruelty, Cupid's .... sub-title, mentioned, 122
Cruelty, Gallius's treacherous .... sub-title, 21
Cruelty, The False Man's .... title, mentioned, 177, 199
Cruelty, The Forsaken Damsel's Lamentation for sub-title, mentioned, 43
Cruelty, The Noble Lord's .... title, 682, 683
Cruelty, The Parents' .... sub-title, mentioned, 28
Cruelty, The Step-Mother's .... sub-title, 651
Crumbs of Comfort for the Youngest Sister .... title, 248
Cryptogram, Epigram on the so-called Great (Mare's-nest) 576, 720
Cuckolds, A Catalogue of Contented.... .... title, mentioned, 32
" Cuckoo then on every tree mocks married men," etc. .... indicated, 307
Cuckoo's Song, The .... title, 307
Culloden Moor, The Duke of Cumberland's Victory at title, 623, 624, 626
Cumberland, The Exploit of the Earl of .... title, mentioned, 382
Cumberland, Two Songs in laudation of William, Duke of 624, 626
Cunning Young Man Fitted, The .... sub-title, mentioned, 318
" Cupid, go and hang thy self ! " 119
" Cupid once when weary grown " 289
Cupid Unblest .... sub-title, mentioned, 528
Cupid's Courtesy (= 'Thro' the cool shady woods') tune, 252, 253, 255
Cupid's Courtesy in the Wooing of Sabina ('As on a day') title, ment., 252
Cupid's Cruelty .... sub-title, mentioned, 122
Cupid's Revenge (= " A King once reign'd ") title, 148, 251, 658, 661
Cupid's Revenge (= " Now, now, you blind boy ") title, mentioned, 254
Cupid's Vision .... sub-title, mentioned, 118
Cupid's Trappan .... tune, 525, 526, 528, 529
Cupid's Trappan, Answer to .... title, mentioned, 528
Cure, Love's only .... title of song, 26
Curragh of Kildare, The .... alternative title and burden, 240
Curtal Friar, Robin Hood and the .... title, mentioned, 570

DAINTY, come thou to me ! burden, title, and tune, 280, 681, 682, 773
Dainty Damsel's Dream, The .... title, mentioned, 148
Dal dera rara, del dara, etc. .... burden, 513

PAGE

Damask Rose, The .... tune, 763
" Dame Flora in her rich array" 113
Dames d'Honneur, Les .... tune, 778
Damon and Strephon, The Loves of .... title, 152, 153
Damon comforted in Distress .... sub-title, 89, 152
" Damon in the Shades was walking " 89
Damon's Triumph .... title, mentioned, 156
Damosel's Tragedy, The .... title, mentioned, 28
Damsel, The Beautiful Berkshire .... title, mentioned, 27
Damsel, The Forlorn .... title (omitted entry as 2*), 170, 251
Dancing on Primrose Hill, The .... title, mentioned, 254
Daniel Cooper .... tune, 6
Dansekar the Dutchman, The Seaman's Song of.... .... title, 423
Daughter, The Northamptonshire Knight's .... title, mentioned, 27
" Day was spent, and night approached " .... (*Second Part*), 167
" Dear, comfort I must " .... mentioned, 448; given, 795
" Dear Lord, what sad and sorrowful times" .... mentioned, 64
" Dear Love, regard my grief" 682
Dearest, cast care away, etc. .... second burden, 282
Death and the Cobler (= *Derry Down* = ' A Cobler there was ') tune, 746
Death and the Lady .... (woodcut in common), 80
Dedication of the Group of Legendary and Romantic Ballads 538, 539
Death's Dance .... tune, mentioned, 557
Deeds of Chivalry achieved by Guy of Warwick .... title, 734
Deeds of McCabe an Irishman, The Valiant .... title, mentioned, 382
Deep in love. (See ' I am so deep in love.') .... tune, 252, 253
Defeat, The Whittington .... sub-title, 743, 777
Delia, Samuel Daniel's Sonnets to .... mentioned. 668
Delight, The Bird-Catcher's .... tune, 136, 299 to 301, 307
Delight, The Maiden's .... title, quoted, 368
Delight, The Shepherd's .... title, mentioned, 66
Delights of the Bottle, The .... tune, 782
Delights of the Spring, The various.... .... sub-title, mentioned, 307
" Depuis dix-huit cent ans, hélas ! " .... mentioned, 692
Derry down, down, down derry down .... burden and tune, 746, 747
Description of Pleasure, A brief .... sub-title, mentioned, 237
" Despairing beside a clear stream" .... mentioned, 221
Despairing Maid Revived, The .... title, mentioned, 199, 259
Devonshire Nymph, The .... title, 92, 96, 97
Dialogue, A pleasant (=" Now would I give ") title, mentioned, 136
Dialogue, A dainty new (= Maiden's Delight) .... sub-title, quoted, 368
Diaphantas' words, etc., upon a Disaster (see ' Charidora ') .... title, 585
Dido and Æneas, The Sonnet of .... title, 552
Dido, Queen .... tune, 547, 548, 553
" Dido was a Carthage Queen " 552
Difficulty, The Irish (Reserved Forces) .... title, ment., *Preface*, xvii
Digby = Captain Digby's Farewell : Mr. Digby's. (See *Digby's*) 30, 39, 65
Digby's Farewell tune, 36, 40, 65, 70, 114, 115, 331, 346, 480 to 482
Digby's Farewell (=' Farewell, my Armida') 36, 39, 40, 65
Digby's Farewell (=" I'll go to my Love," in vol. iv. p. 393) 36, 39, 65
Digby's Farewell (=' Oh ! pity, Arminda ') 38, 65, 70
Disconsolate Lover, The .... title, mentioned, 43
Discontented Lover overcome with grief, The .... altern. sub-title, 25
Discontented Young Man and the Loving Maid, The title, mentioned, 43
Discourse between two Lovers, Serious .... title, mentioned, 254
Distress which the Spanish Navy sustained, The late wonderful title, m., 382

PAGE
Distressed Virgin, The — title, mentioned, 105
Distracted Young Man, The (="I loved one") — title, mentioned, 115, 296
Ditty of Encouragement to Englishmen — title, mentioned, 381
Ditty of the Death of Fair Rosamond, A mournful — title, 668
Don', Ign. (See Cryptogram.) — 576, 720
Don Juan (Byron's) — quoted, 87, 629
Donkin Dargason — tune, mentioned, 180
Doting Old Dad, The — title, mentioned, 151
Doubting Virgin, The — tune and title, 152, 155 to 157
"Down as I lay, one morning in May" — (Part second) 308
"Down by the side of a fair crystal fountain" — 28, 29
"Down in a meadow, the river running clear" and tune, mentioned, 237, 323
Downfall, Love's — title, 114
Downfall of the Brown Girl, The — sub-title, 647
Downfall, Sir Hugh in the Grime's — title, 598
Dragon of Wantley, Moor of Moor Hall, and the — title, mentioned, 725
Dragon, St. George and the — title of two ballads, 725; one given, 727
Drake, A Song on Sir Francis — title, 376, 377
Drake, The Fame of Sir Francis — title, 376
Drake's Ship, Cowley's Ode written in a Chair made out of title, quoted, 399
"Draw near, young maidens, every one" — 265
Dream of Fair Women (Tennyson's); and of Unfair — quoted, 643, 678
Dream of Judas's Mother Fulfilled (in vol. vii.) — title, mentioned, 688, 796
Dream on his Wedding Night, Sweet William's — sub-title, 641
Dream, The Dainty Damsel's ('As I lay on my lonely') title, mentioned, 148
Dream, The Damsel's ('I once lay sleeping') — title, mentioned, 148
Dream, Thurot's — title, mentioned, 446
Drinker, The Reformed — title, 276, 317
Drinking and Bad Company — burden, 475
Drinking, Five Reasons for — title, 318
Drive the cold Winter away — burden and tune, mentioned, 256
Drummer, The Famous Woman (*cf. Kentish Garland*, p. 628) — ment., 318
Dub a dub — tune, 401, 402, 403
Duchess of Suffolk's Calamity, The — title, mentioned, 517
Duke of Monmouth's Jig — title, mentioned, 565
Duke William's Triumph over the Rebels, etc. — title, 626
Dulcina, The Shepherd's Wooing of Fair — title and tune, 163 to 166, 482
Dumblane, The Bob (*anglicé*, Fight) of — mentioned, 617, 619
Dunsmore, Kate of — title, quoted, 765, 772
Dunsmore, Lamentation of the Maid of — title, 767 to 772
Dutch Fleet, The Royal Victory over the — title, 435
Dying Lover's Complaint, The — title, mentioned, 127

EARL of Essex, The — tune, 623, 624
Earl of Essex's Fight at Sea — 405
Earthly Paradise (William Morris's) — quoted, 687
Eck iddle dee, and the Low-lands low — burden, 419
Edward IV. and Jane Shore, King — title, quoted, 725, 726
Edward IV. and the Tanner of Tamworth — title, mentioned, 570
"E'er since I saw Clorinda's eyes" — mentioned, 26
Eglamour, Sir — tune, 495
Eleanor, Lord Thomas and Fair (Two ballads on) — 613, 645, 647
Eleanor's Confession, Queen — title, 672, 678, 680
Eleanor's Tragedy, Fair — sub-title, 645
Elegy in a country Churchyard (Gray's) — title, stanza quoted, 521

PAGE

Elegy on Colonel Thomas Blood .... title, 786, 787
Elegy on Madame Blaise (='Good people all') .... quoted, 342
Elegy on the Earl of Essex .... title, quoted, 400
Elegy sacred to the Memory of Sir E. B. Godfrey title, mentioned, 542
Elizabeth (her Entrance into London), Queen ..... title, mentioned, 382
Elizabeth, Queen of England ! .... burden varies, 393
Elizabeth's Champion, Queen .... title, 405
Encounter, The Night .... title, mentioned, 557
Encouragement to Englishmen, A Ditty of ..... title, mentioned, 381
Encouragement to English Soldiers, A Ballad of title, mentioned, 381
England's Glory .... title, 625, 626
England's joy and delight, A new ballad of ..... title, mentioned, 382
England's joy in the merry month of May ..... title, mentioned, 307
England's Resolution to beat back the Spaniards title, mentioned, 398
English Seaman's Resolution, The .... title, mentioned, 276
Englishman and a Spaniard, A Dialogue between an ..... title, 657
Enquiry, The Young Man's .... title, mentioned, 31
Entertainment of the Frenchmen .... title, mentioned, 397
Entrance of Queen Elizabeth, The Royal ..... title, mentioned, 382
Epilogue .... title, *Editorial*, 760
Epistle from Fair Rosamond to Henry II. and his Answer title, ment., 668
Epistles (Michael Drayton's) Heroical ..... title, mentioned, 668
Esquire's Tragedy, The .... title, mentioned, 27
Essex, A Passion of my Lord of .... title, quoted, 404
Essex Ballad, The ("In Essex long renown'd") title, mentioned, 516
Essex, Elegy on the Earl of .... title, quoted, 400
Essex going to Cales (Cadiz), The Earl of ..... title, mentioned, 398
Essex, The Earl of .... tune, 623, 624
Essex, The noble departing of the Earl of ..... title, mentioned, 398
Essex, Verses made in his trouble by the Earl of ..... title, 404
Essex. Verses upon the Death of the Lord of ..... title, mentioned, 376
Essex's Lamentation .... tune, mentioned, 623
Essex's Last Good Night .... tune, 623, 624
Essex's Last Voyage to the Haven of Happiness..... title, quoted, 407
"Est-il rien sur la terre" 690, 691
Eve of St. John, The ('The Baron of Smay'holm') title, mentioned, 587
Every man to his mind, Shrewsbury for me ! .... burden, 359
Example of a Virtuous Wife, A Worthy ..... title, mentioned, 541, 796
Execration, The 88

FAERIE QUEENE (Spenser's) .... quoted, 711
"Fair Angel of England, thy beauty most bright" mentioned, 65 to 67
Fair Annie of Lochroyan .... title, quoted, 611
"Fair Isabel of beauty bright" ....410; given, 793
"Fair Isabel of Rock Royal, she dreamed where she lay" mentioned, 612
Fair Lady of the West, The .... title, 161
Fair Lucina conquered by prevailing Cupid .... title, 177, 189
Fair Maid of Dunsmore's Lamentation, The ....title, 767 to 772
Fair Maid of London, Princely Wooing of the ..... title, mentioned, 65
"Fair Maid, you say you loved me well" (omitted mention, 27), 283, 791, 792
Fair Maid's Choice, The .... title, mentioned, 367, 414
Fair Margaret and Sweet William .... title and tune, 640, 641
Fair Nelly and her dearest dear 789
Fair one let me in, The burden and tune, 177, 188, 189, 191, 195, 199, 259, 350 to 352
"Fair set the wind for France" (Drayton) .... quoted, 743

PAGE
" Fairest of fair ones, if thou should'st prove cruel" ..... mentioned, 119
Fairing for Maids, A .... title, mentioned, 108
Faithful Damon .... title, 152, 155
Faithful Friend, The .... tune, mentioned, 512
Faithful Inflamed Lover, The .... title, 123, 124, 151
Faithful Lover's Last Farewell, The .... sub-title, 635
Faithful Mariner, The .... title, 26; given, 793
Faithful Lovers of the West, The .... title, quoted, 18, 257
Faithful Lovers, The Two .... title, 159, 217
Faithful Lovers well met, The .... sub-title, 284
Fall of Folly, The .... sub-title, 284
Fall, The Lady's title and tune, 650, 651, 653, 761, 763; given, 764
False-hearted Knight, The .... sub-title, mentioned, 292
False-hearted Young Man, The .....title and tune, mentioned, 26 to 28, 793
False Young Man and the Constant Maid ..... sub-title, mentioned, 105
Fame of Sir Francis Drake, The .... title, 376
Fancy in the Bud .... sub-title, 110
Fancy's Favourite .... title, mentioned, 356
Fancy's Freedom .... title, 112, 113, 263
Fancy's Phœnix .... tune, 354, 356
" Farewell, dear Armeda," etc. (See 'Farewell, fair Armida') 36
" Farewell, dear Revechia, my joy and my grief!" 36, 38
Farewell, Digby's ('*Digby*') title and tune 30 to 38, 65, 70, 115, 331, 346
480 to 482
" Farewell, fair Armida" (or 'my Almeda,' 'my Arminda') 36, 37, 42 to 44, 65
" Farewell, false-hearted Love!" .... mentioned, 43
" Farewell, farewell, my heart's delight!" .... mentioned, 199
Farewell, Flora's. (See 'Flora's Farewell') ..... title and tune, 105, etc.
" Farewell, my Calista, my joy and my grief!" ..... and tune, 36, 40, 65, 138
" Farewell, my Clarinda, my life and my soul" 438
" Farewell, my dear Johnny, whom I loved so" .... mentioned, 43
" Farewell, my dear Peggy, whom I loved so" .... mentioned, 43
" Farewell, my dear Puggy, my pullet, my low bell!" ..... mentioned, 42
" Farewell, my dearest Love!" mentioned (reserved for vol. vii.), 119
Farewell, my Lord Sandwich's .... tune, 38
Farewell, Tarleton's .... title, mentioned, 382
Farewell, The Faithful Lover's Last .... sub-title, 635
Farewell, The Seaman's doleful .... title, mentioned, 119
" Farewell, the world and mortal cares!" 136
" Farewell, thou Flower of false deceit!" 43, 44
Farewell to Calista, The Lover's .... sub-title, 36, 40
Farewell to Folly, A .... sub-title, mentioned, 570, 774
Farewell to his fickle Mistress, The Forsaken Lover's title, mentioned, 583
" Farewell, ungrateful Traitor!" 20, 21
Fare-you-well, Gilnock-hall! .... tune, 601, 606
Farmer's Answer, The Young .... title, mentioned, 237
Farmer, The Northern (Tennyson's) ..... title, quoted, 679
Farmer's Ruin, The Rich ....title, 534 to 536
Farmer's Son, The Fortunate .... sub-title, 161
Farmer's Song, The .... title, mentioned, 520
Father's Wholesome Admonition, A .... title, 215, 217
Faust (Goethe's) .... title, mentioned, 701
Faustus (Christopher Marlowe's) .... title, mentioned, 701, 705
Faustus, Doctor of Divinity, The Judgement showed upon title, 701 to 706
Favourite, Fancy's .... title, mentioned, 356
Feast at Brougham Castle, The .... title, quoted, 427

PAGE
Felicity, The Country People's .... title, mentioned, 237
Festus (Philip James Bailey's, 1839) ..... title, mentioned, 701
"Fie, Shepherd, fie! thou art to blame" 106
Fight at Malaga, The Famous. (See 'Five Sail.') ..... title, 411, 412
Fight at Sea in the Straights (of Gibraltar) Report of a ..... mentioned, 411
Fight at Sea, The Earl of Essex's .... part title, 405
Fight upon the Seas between the George and the Bonaventura ment., 408
Figure of Two, The .... burden and title, 324
"Five Sail of Frigates, bound for Malago" ..... and tune, 376, 411, 412
Flatteries of Fate (properly 'All the Flatteries of Fate') ..... tune, 292, 293
"Flora, farewell! I needs must go" .... and tune, 7, 43, 65, 105
Flora happily Revived .... title, mentioned, 99
Flora's Answer to the Shepherd's Song, Fair .... title, 106
Flora's Departure .... title, 99, 100; given, 103
Flora's Farewell title and tune, 7, 65, 99, 105 to 107, 259, 260, 265, 268, 269, 567, 570
"Flora's in her grove she lied" 98, 99
Flora's Lamentable Passion .... title, 98, 99
Flower of all the Nation..... .... burden, 284
Flower of Serving-men, The Famous .... title, 567
Flying Fame (properly, When flying fame) tune, 183, 667, 672, 714, 722, 727, 740, 743, 750
For I do come to woo thee .... burden varies, 250
For I will go with my Love to the world's end .... burden, 293
For it must and shall be so .... second burden, 149
For Love is dead and buried, etc. .... burden, 8
For now I will lay up my money, good store, etc..... ..... burden, 343
"For this same night" (Fragment, beginning lost from MS.)..... 629
For thou art the man that my husband shall be .... burden, 416
Forecast, The Good Wife's .... title, 348, 349
Forester, The Unfortunate .... title, 640, 643 to 645
"Forgive me, if your looks I thought" (*ter*) ..... mentioned, 27, 28
Forgo me now, come to me soon! .... burden, 166, 169
Forlorn Damsel, The (see 'Come pity') (t. omit. f. *List*, as No. 2*), 170, 251
Forlorn Lover, The ('A Week before Easter') ..... title, 229, 232 to 234
Forlorn Lover, The (D'Urfey's "O yes!") ..... title, mentioned, 28
Forlorn Lover's Lament, The .... title, 586
Forsaken Maid, The .... title, mentioned, 576
Fortune my Foe .... tune, mentioned, 331, 702, 703, 706
"Four-and-twenty handsome youths" .... mentioned, 630
"Four-and-twenty Ladies fair" .... mentioned, 630
Fragments of Humphrey Crouch's 'Guy of Warwick' ..... given, 737
Fragments of the ballad of Little Musgrave (Percy Folio MS.) given, 629
French, The Frighted .... title, 368, 445, 793; given, 446
French Tricotees .... tune, 489, 492
Friar in the Well, The .... tune, 495
Friars'-Carse Hermitage, Burns's Lines written at ..... quoted, 506
Frighted French, The .... title, 368, 445, 793; given, 446
Frobisher, A Sorrowful Song on Sir Martin ..... title, mentioned, 398
Frobisher, John Kirkham's Commendation of Sir Martin ..... title, 399
Frolic Ended, How the .... Editorial Sequel, title, 518
Frolic, The Good Fellow's .... title, 339, 350; given, 351
Frolic, Mark Noble's .... title, 468, 509, 510, 514
Frolic, The Jolly Gentleman's .... title, 509, 513
"From Fairy-land, I hear, it is reported" 8
"From merciless Invaders, from wicked men's device" 378

PAGE
" From the lawless dominion of Mitre and Crown " 2
From the Priory to the Abbey .... *Editorial title*, 464
" Full fifty winters have I seen " 327
" Full forty years the Royal Crown." (See *The King enjoys*, etc.) quoted, 323
" Full ten honest tradesmen did happen to meet " (*Roxb. B.* iii. 481) ment. 32

GALEAZZO (Galleazzo), Of the happy obtaining of the Great t. 381, 384
Gallant Grahams of Scotland, The ..... title, 587, 590, 601
Gallant Grahams, The (*bis*) .... title, 587, 588, 590, 601
" Gallants [all come mourn with me] .... first line, unmentioned, 398
" Gallants, come list a while " 281, 283
Gallants, Lusty tune mentioned (distinct from both Captain Ward's), 427
" Gallants, you must understand " mentioned, 422, 423, 425; given, 784
Gallius's Treacherous Cruelty (to Olympia) .... sub-title, 21
Garland, The Bristol (=" A merchant's son of worthy fame ") title, m. 428
Gather-Gold and Scatter-Gold ..... (lost title) mentioned, 327, 335
" General George, that valiant wight " .... mentioned, 136
General Monk hath advanced himself, etc. ..... tune, mentioned, 136
General Monk sail'd through the Gun Fleet ..... tune, mentioned, 136
" General Monk was a noble man " .... mentioned, 136
Geneva Ballad, The (=" Of all the factions," etc.) title, mentioned, 506
Gentleman in Thracia, A .... part-title, mentioned, 650
Gentleman's Frolic, The Jolly .... title, 509, 513
Gentlemen of England. (Properly, " Ye Gentlemen ") mentioned, 431, 796
George Aloe and the Swiftstake, The 408, 409
George, Duke of Albemarle, Worthy Exploits of, title, 136, 729; given, 730
Gerhard's Mistress (Cordelia) ..... tune-title, 559, 560, 564, 566
Germany, Bloody News from .... title, mentioned, 650
Ghost, The True-Lover's .... title, 23, 79; given, 85
Gilderoy (was a bonny boy) .... tune, mentioned, 130
" Give ear a while unto my song " .... mentioned, 177, 199
" Give ear to a frolicsome ditty " .... 315, 509; given, 513
Glass of Christian Reformation, A Chrystal ..... title, mentioned, 364
Glen's Unhappy Voyage to New Barbary, Captain title, mentioned, 410
Glory, England's .... title, 625, 626
Glory, Great Britain's .... sub-title, 405
Go from my window, Love, go! .... burden, 200, 201, 207
" Go from the window, go ! " .... mentioned, 381
" God above that made all things " .... 315; given, 470
" God above who rules all things " .... mentioned, 469
" God bless the King, God bless the State's defender ! " 618
" God prosper long our noble King " (Chevy Chase) title and tune, 739, 740
" God prosper long our noble King " (Whittington Defeat) 743; given, 777
" God Speed the Plough " .... title, 520, 521, 523
Golden Age, The .... tune, mentioned, 276
Golden Vanity, The .... title, 419
" Good Englishmen, whose valiant hearts " 393
Good Fellow, The (A Catch) .... title, 315
Good Fellow, The (A new Song) .... title, 245
" Good Fellows all, both great and small " 319
" Good Fellows all, come lend an ear " 340
Good-Fellow's Complaint for want of full measure, The sub-title, 315, 486
Good-Fellow's Consideration, The .... title, mentioned, 339
Good-Fellow's Counsel, The .... title, quoted, 342
Good-Fellow's Frolic, The .... title, 339, 342; given, 351

PAGE
Good-Fellow's Folly, The ..... sub-title, 346
Good-Fellow's Observation, The sub-title, quoted, 256
Good-Fellow's Resolution, The ..... title, 339, 342, 343
Good-Fellows, The King of .... title, 315, 501, 502
Good-Fellow's Vindication to all his Companions, The ..... sub-title, 327
" Good God! what will at length become of us?" ..... mentioned, 376
" Good Lord John is a hunting gone" .... mentioned, 598
Good Night, and joy be wi' you a! .... burden, 600
Good Night (Earl of) Essex's Last .... tune, 623, 766
Good Night, Johnny Armstrong's Last ..... title, 594, 600, 604, 606
Good Night, Thomas Armstrong's 600
" Good people all, I pray you understand" (Tipping's) ..... mentioned, 331
" Good people all, pray lend an ear" (Ingelbrod) .... mentioned, 534
" Good people, I married a turbulent wife" .... mentioned, 32
" Good people, I pray now attend to my moan" .... mentioned, 32
" Good people, I'll tell you now of a fine jest" .... mentioned, 66
Good Saint Anthony and his Temptations .... quoted, 87
Good Wife's Forecast, The .... title, 348, 349
Gossip's Vindication, The Merry .... title, quoted, 482
" Gracious Princess, where Princes are in place" .... mentioned, 376
Graeme (see *Grahams*, *Grime*, and *Hugh*), Sir Hugh ..... 594, 597, etc.
Grahams of Scotland, The .... title, 587, 590, 601
Grahams, The Gallant (*bis*) .... title, 587, 588, 590, 601
Great Britain's Glory .... sub-title, 405
" Great Charles, your valiant Seamen" .... quoted, 431
Greeks' and Trojans' Wars, The .... title, 512, 543, 559
Green-sleeves, A Reprehension (Elderton's) against title, mentioned, 397
Green-sleeves (= Alas, my Love!"), A Sonnet of the Lady quoted, 397, 398
Green-sleeves and Countenance, etc. .... title, mentioned, 397
Green-sleeves' Answer to Donkyn her friend, Lady title, mentioned, 391
Green-sleeves is all my joy, etc. .... burden and tune, 397, 398
Green-sleeves is worn away, etc. .... title, mentioned, 397
Green-sleeves moralized by the Scripture ..... title, mentioned, 397
Gregory, Lord (or Love Gregory) .... titles, mentioned, 610, 612
Grenville, The Tragedy of Sir Richard ..... title, mentioned, 376
Grief crown'd with Comfort, The Squire's .... title, 226
Grief crown'd with Comforts, The Damsel's .... sub-title, 297
" Grim King of the Ghosts, make haste!" and tune, 216, 221, 224; given, 222
Grime (Graeme), Sir Hugh of the ..... title, 594, 595, 598
Groat's worth of Good Counsel for a Penny, A title, 468, 479; given, 480
Group of Early Naval Ballads .... 361 to 448
Group of Good-Fellows (First and Second) ..... 313 to 352; 465 to 519
Group of Legendary and Romantic Ballads .... 537 to 760
Group of True-Love Ballads .... 7 to 312
" Gude Lord Scroop's to the hunting gane" .... mentioned, 597
Guenevere (William Morris's) Defence of ..... title, quoted, 721
Guide of Directions for Penitent Sinners, A Godly title, mentioned, 331
Gun-Fleet The. (See 'General Monk' and 'Gun-Fleet') ..... tune, 136
Guy and Colebrande (woodcut, *circá* 1560, in vol. i. p. 500) title, ment., 733
Guy and Phillis (Fragment of) .... title, 733
Guy, Earl of Warwick, Heroic History of ..... title, 559, 736, 737
Guy of Warwick, Valiant Deeds of .... title, 542, 559, 732, 734

HAD-LAND'S Advice, John .... title, mentioned, 474
Had-Land's Lamentation, Jack title, 315, 468, 469, 474; given, 475

PAGE
" Hail to the myrtle shades!" .... tune, 152, 153
Hallo! my Fancy, whither wilt thou go! title, tune, and burden, 450 to 455
Hang Pinching; or, The Good-Fellow's Observation title, quoted, 256
Happiness, The True-Lover's .... title, 108, 115, 116
Happiness, The Virgin's .... alternative title, 289
" Happy's the man that's free from Love!" .... 26; given, 224
" Happy's the swain that's free from Love!" .... mentioned, 28
" Hark! hark! my masters, and be still" .... given, 379
" Hark! hark! my masters, and give ear" .... mentioned, 379
" Hark! how sweet the birds do sing" .... mentioned, 307
Hark! I hear the cannons roar .... tune, 284
Harmony of true Content, The .... sub-title, quoted, 445
Harmony, The Birds' ('As I was walking in') ..... title, 307, 779, 782
Harmony, The Birds' ('Down as I lay') .... title, 308
Harmony, The Birds' ('Oh, says the Cuckoo') ..... sub-title, 268, 301, 303
" Harpagus, hast thou salt enough?"..... .... quoted, 650
Hart-Merchant's Rant, The (query, misp. Hare-merchant?) tune, 619, 620
Have at thy coat, old woman! ..... burden and tune, quoted, 252
" Have you not heard these many years ago" .... quoted, 684
Haymakers, The .... tune, 236, 238
Haymakers, The Scotch (='Twas within a furlong') title and tune, 236, 237
Haymarket's Mask, The .... tune, mentioned, 237
He pays me with disdain .... burden varies, 191
" He that first said it" (*i.e.* 'Nulla manere diu,' etc.) ..... quoted, 539
He that hath the most money .... tune, mentioned, 108
" Heard you not lately of a man" .... mentioned, 542
Heavy Heart and Light Purse, The..... .... title, 336, 337
Heigh-ho, holiday! .... tune, mentioned, 398
Helen of Greece and Paris .... alternative title, 546
Henry and Elizabeth .... title, mentioned, 66
Henry setting forth to Sea, A new Song of .... title, 789
Henry [the Eighth] and a Bishop, King .... title, 750
Henry the Fifth, his Conquest of France, King..... ..... title, 743, 744
Henry the Second's Concubine .... part of sub-title, 668, 673
Henry's going to Bulloign, The King .... tune, 423
" Her arms across her breast she laid" 658
" Here ends our 'Group of Ballads' rare" .... *Epilogue*, 760
" Here I will give you a perfect relation" .... mentioned, 236
" Here is a crew of jovial blades" 351
" Here lies entomb'd within this compast stone" 671
" Here must I tell the praise of worthy Whittington" ..... mentioned, 280
" Here's a Lamentation"..... .... mentioned, 237
" Here's a pleasant ditty" .... mentioned, 237
Here's to the Figure of Two, etc. .... burden, 324
" Here's joyful news come late from Sea" .... mentioned, 368
Hero and Leander, An old Ballad .... title, mentioned, 557
Hero and Leander, The Loves of (H. Crouch's)..... title, 542, 559, 560
Hero and Leander, The Tragedy of .... title, 556, 558
Heroes, The British .... title, quoted, 726
Heroic History of Guy Earl of Warwick, The .... title, 559, 737
Heroical Song on Lord General George Duke of Albemarle title, 729, 730
Hey, boys, up go we! .... tune, 199, 339, 340, 350, 351
Hey ding a ding! .... burden and tune, mentioned, 276
Hey down, down .... burden, 627, 631
" Hey, Johnny Cope! are ye wauking yet?" .... mentioned, 625
Ho derry derry down! .... burden, 598

PAGE
Hohenlinden (=' On Linden, when the sun was low ') .... title, mentioned, 41
Holidays, The True Lovers' .... title, 65; given, 73
" Holland, that scarce deserves the name of land " .... quoted, 434
" Honest Shepherd, since you're poor " 119
Honour made known, The Plough-man's .... tune, 343, 345
Honour of Bristol, The .... title, 348, 428, 429, 779
Honour of the Inns of Court Gentlemen, The .... title, mentioned, 428
" How bright art thou, whose starry eyes " .... and tune, 76
" How can I conceal my passion ? " 82, 83
" How cool and temperate am I grown ! " 570, 774
How e'er the wind doth blow .... burden, 797
" How fares my fair Leander ? " .... 542; given, 560
" How happy could I be with either " tune (earlier known as the Rant), 509
" How long, Elisa, shall I mourn ? " .... mentioned, 177
How many crowns and pounds have I spent .... tune, mentioned, 300
" How short is the pleasure that follows the pain " 170
How the Frollic Ended .... *Editorial title*, 518
" How wretched is the slave to Love " 79
Hudibras (Butler's) .... title, quoted, 732, 733
Hugh in the Grime's Downfall, Sir .... title, 598
Hugh of the Grime, Life and Death of Sir .... title, 594, 595, 601
Hughie Græme (or Graham) .... title, mentioned, 597
Hughie the Græme .... title, mentioned, 597
Hunting of the Cheviot (=" The Persè owt of Northum.") quoted, 739
Hunt's Up, A .... title, 627
Husband, The Male and Female .... title, mentioned, 236
Husband turn'd Thrifty, the Bad .... sub-title, 479, 483
Husbandman and a Serving-man (Dialogue between) .... title, 523
Husband's Amendment, The Bad .... sub-title, 340
Husband's Folly, the Bad .... title, 315, 468, 477, 493
Husband's Recantation, The Bad .... sub-title, 342, 499
Husband's Repentance, the Bad .... sub-title, 480
Husband's Return from his Folly, The .... sub-title, 343
Hyde Park Frollic, The .... alternative title, and tune, 315, 495

" I AM a Bachelor bold and brave " .... mentioned, 64
" I am a jovial Bachelor " .... and tune, quoted, 368, 369, 796
" I am a jovial Cobler, Sir " .... mentioned, 368, 796, 797
" I am a jovial Mariner, our calling is well known " 369, 796
" I am a Lass of beauty bright " .... mentioned, 27
" I am a lusty lively lad " 328, 329
I am a Maid, and a very good Maid burden and tune, mentioned, 218
" I am a poor and harmless Maid " .... and tune, mentioned, 274
" I am a poor man, God knows " .... mentioned, 276, 532
" I am a prisoner poor, oppress'd with misery " .... mentioned, 260, 681
" I am a stout Sea-man, newly come on shore " 415
" I am a young man that do follow the plough " 526
" I am a young wife that has cause to complain " .... mentioned, 33
" I am a young woman, 'tis very well known " .... mentioned, 33
" I am an undaunted Seaman .... mentioned, 276
" I am quite undone, my cruel one " .... mentioned (for next vol.), 27
" I am so deep in love, I cannot hide it " .... 252 to 254
" I am so sick for love, as like was never no man " .... quoted, 252
" I am so sick of love " .... mentioned, 252
I am the Duke of Norfolk .... tune, 520, 523
" I am the faithful damsel " .... mentioned, 64

PAGE
" I am the King and Prince of Drunkards" 315, 502
" I am the old Ahasuer, I wander here," etc. ....690; given, 779
" I built my Love a gallant ship" 613
" I do not sing of triumph, no!" .... mentioned, 27
" I had no more wit, but was trod under feet" 499
" I have a good old Father at home".... .... 236, 245, 248
" I have a good old Mother at home" and tune, 236, 243, 245, 246
" I have a good old Wife at home" .... tune, mentioned, 245
" I have a good old Woman at home" ..... tune, mentioned, 245
" I have a Ship in the North Countrie" 419
" I have a Tower in Dalisberie" .... mentioned, 630
" I have been a Bad Husband this full fifteen year" 339, 343
" I have been a traveller long" 324
" I have got a certain habit" .... quoted (*Introd. Notes*) xix
" I have heard talk of Robin Hood .... mentioned, 64
" I kill'd a man, and he was dead" .... quoted, 505
' *I know you not!*' .... burden, quoted, 254
" I love thee dear, but dare not show it" ..... tune, mentioned. 161
" I loved a Lass, a fair one" .... mentioned 773
" I loved thee dearly, I loved thee well and tune, 26, 27, 791 to 793
" I loved thee once, I'll love no more" ..... and tune mentioned, 296
" I loved you both beautiful and bright" .... mentioned, 115
" I loved you dearly, I loved you well" (=I loved thee), and tune, 27, 283, 791, 792
I maun away, and I will not stay (or, tarry) .... tune 587, 590
" I often for my Jeany (=Joany) strove" and tune, 26, 148, 149, 254, 660, 661
" I once lay sleeping on my bed" .... mentioned, 148
I pray now attend to this ditty (*Bagford Ballads*, p. 205) ..... mentioned, 509
I prithee, Love, turn to me! (=" Come turn")..... tune mentioned, 276
" I read that many years ago" 685
" I read that once in Africa" 658, 659
" I saw the Lass whom dear I loved 220
I should not now be poor .... burden varies, 478
I still will be constant and true to my friend, etc. ..... burden, 293
" I tell ye all, both great and small" .... quoted, 380
" I told young Jenny, I told her true" .... mentioned, 183
" I was a modest maid of Kent" .... mentioned, 27
I will away, and I will not tarry .... tune, 587, 590
I will be constant to thee till I die .... burden, 126
" I will go to my Love, where he lies in the deep" mentioned, 36, 39, 65
I will live a maiden still..... .... burden, 155
I will never love thee more burden, title, and tune, 556, 558, 581 to 583, 585
" I will tell you a story, a story anon" (Roxb. Coll. III. 494), variation, 746
I wish that his heirs may never lack Sack, etc. .... burden, 466
" I wish I was those gloves, dear heart!" ....557; given, 584
I wish in heaven his soul may dwell, etc. .... burden, 470
I would give ten thousand pounds thou wert in Shrewsbury! burden, 280, 281, 283
" Ich bin der alte Ahasver!" ..... mentioned, 690, 778; given, 699
" Ich will euch erzählen ein Märchen," etc. .... mentioned, 746
" If all the world my mind did know" ..... 276, 315; given, 478
" If any woful wight have cause to wail her woe" ..... quoted, 710
" If I could but attain my wish" .... quoted, 505
" If I live to be old, for I find I go down" (see " If . . . to grow") var. of, 507
" If I live to be old, which I never will own" .... mentioned, 507
" If I live to grow old, for I find I go down" 507

PAGE
" If Love does give pleasure, why does it torment ?" mentioned, 32, 33
" If Love's a sweet passion, why does it torment ?" and tune, 31, 33, 34
" If on this theme I rightly think" 318
" If she be as kind as fair, but peevish and unhandy" 252
" If the heart of a man is oppress'd with cares" (*Beggar's Opera*) 55
" If the Whigs shall get up, and the Tories go down" ..... mentioned, 505
If thou can'st fancy me .... burden varies, 238
" If when I lay me down to sleep" (= In the Garden) *Introd. Notes*, xviii, 304
" If Wine be a cordial, why does it torment ?" ..... mentioned, 32, 33
" If yet thy eyes, great Harry, may endure" .... mentioned, 671
Ign. Don. (*in re* the great sham Cryptogram) .... title, 720
I'll ever love thee more (used for *I'll ne'er = I will never*) ..... tune, 584
I'll fix my fancy on thee .... burden and tune, 19
I'll ne'er be drunk again ! .... burden, 276, 317
I'll never love thee more burden and tune, 556, 558, 581, 583, 584
" I'll never trust Good-Fellow more" .... mentioned, 328
" I'll sing a song, and a dainty fine song" .... quoted, 300
" I'll tell you a story, a story anon" 747
I'll warrant thee, boy, she'll take it 219
I'm here at thy gate, Lord Thomas" .... mentioned, 644
" Immortal Lovers smile, and run your happy race" 276
" In a humour I was of late" .... mentioned, 276
" In a May morning, as I was walking 159
" In a quiet old Parish, on a brown heathy (? healthy) old moor" 755
" In ancient times, when as Plain-dealing" 762
" In Blackman street there dwelt" .... mentioned, 237
" In Dorsetshire lived a a Young Miller by trade" ..... mentioned, 33
" In 'Eighty-eight, ere I was born" 378
" In Essex, long renown'd for calves" .... mentioned, 515
" In January last, on Monanday at noon .... mentioned, 183
" In London lived a Squire, where," etc. .... mentioned, 27
" In London there lived a beautiful maid" .... mentioned, 33
" In May fifteen hundred and eighty and eight 383
In my freedom is all my joy .... burden mentioned, 273, 274
" In old time past there was a King, we read" 753
" In pescod time, when hound to horn," etc. ..... tune, 650, 750, 764
" In Popish time, when bishops proud" 751
" In Rome, I read, a noble man" (= Roman Wife) mentioned, 541, 796
In Summer time (usually or " In summer leaves grow green") tune, 789, etc.
" In Summer time when folks make hay" (M. Parker's Medley) ment., 745
" In Summer time when leaves are green" 274, 283
" In Summer time when leaves are green" (*ter.*) and tune, 567, 570, 789, 790
" In Summer time when Phœbus' rays" 284
" In swords, pikes, and bullets, 'tis safer to be" 39
" In the days of old, when fair France did flourish" ..... mentioned, 571
In the Garden (= 'If when I lay') title, quoted (*Intro. Notes*), xviii, 304
" In the merry month of May" .... quoted, 307, 309, 323
" In the pleasant month of May" .... mentioned, 254
" In the West, in Devonshire" (= True Love Exalted) 93
" In the West of Devonshire" (= Devonshire Nymph) 96
" In Warwickshire there stands a Down" 336, 371
" In Windsor Forest I did slay a bore" (boar) .... fragment, 733
" Indeed, this world is so unjust" 354
Indies, The Gallant Seaman's Return from the .... title, 414, 415
Industrious Smith, the .... title, mentioned, 485, 542
Injured Maiden (not 'Mistress'), The sub-title, mentioned (*bis*), 26

PAGE

Innocent Love at length rewarded .... sub-title, 272
Inn of Court Gentlemen, The Honour of the ..... title, mentioned, 779
Insatiate Lover, The .... title, quoted, 489
Instructions to a Painter (concerning the Dutch War) title, mentioned, 137
Intelligence, Rosebery's ..... (*Trowbesh* MS.), Title, *Preface*, 170
Invincible Love .... mentioned, 170
Irish Difficulty, The (=" We could do well without thee ") title, *Preface*, xvii
" Is she gone? let her go! " .... mentioned, 27
" Is there never a man in all Scotland " 604
Isabel of Dunsmore Heath (Maid of Dunsmore) part-title, 765 to 767
Isabel of Roch-Royal, Fair .... title, mentioned, 612
Isabel, The Complaint of Fair .... title, 771
Isabel, The stout and loving Seaman's heart-token to ..... title, 26, 793
Isabel, Verses writ by a Seaman on the Britannia to Fair ..... title, 789
Isabella's Tragedy, The Lady .... title, 650, 651, 683
Isabel's mournful Lamentation, Fair title to second part, 765, 767, 769
Isabel's mournful Recantation, Fair..... .... title, 7.9
I'se for ever should be, could be, would be, etc. .... burden, 118
I'se often for my Jenny strove (see " I often ") .... tune, 148, 149
Islington, The Bailiff's Daughter of..... ..... sub-title, 241, 243
" It fell about the Lammas tide " (=" Yt fell ... tyde ") ..... mentioned, 739
" It fell and about the Lammas time "..... .... quoted, 739
" It fell on a Wednesday " .... mentioned, 612
" It fell upon a Martinmas time " .... mentioned, 630
" It is good to be merry and wise " .... quoted motto), 1
It is not your Northern Nancy .... tune, 213, 762, 763
It is Old Ale hath undone me burden and tune, quoted, 326, 465, 469, 471, 475
" It seems unto me, whose thoughts flit free " ..... *Edit. Finale*, 800
" It was a bold keeper that chased the deer " 230
" It was a rich Merchant man " (Merch. and Fiddler's Wife) ..... mentioned, 370
" It was a youthful Knight, loved a gallant Lady " 572
It was in the prime of cucumber time identified, 300, 310
Iter Boreale (Bishop Corbet's) ..... title, quoted, 732
" It's four and-twenty bonny boys " .... mentioned, 630
" ' It's gold shall be your hire,' she says " ..... mentioned, 630
" It's true thou justly may complain "..... mentioned 26 to 28
I've left the world as the world found me ..... tune, 528

JACOBITE SONG of " Let mournful Britons " ..... title, 623
Jamaica .... tune, 328, 329
Jamaica, the Seaman's Return from..... ..... sub-title, mentioned, 64
Jane Shore she was for England, etc. ..... burden, quoted, 725
Janet, Lady .... title, mentioned, 612
Jealous Father beguiled, The .... sub-title, 200, 205
Jealous Nanny .... title, mentioned, 170
Jealousy, Jockey's .... tune, 218, 220, 228
Jealousy, Moggie's (A new Song of)..... title and tune, 170, 171, 228
Jeering Lovers, the Two .... title, mentioned, 64, 69
Jeering Young Man, The ..... (ballad not found) tune, 458, 459
Jennings his song, Captain .... title, mentioned, 408
Jenny gin (abbreviation for " Ah! Jenny, gin ") tune, 443 to 445, etc.
Jenny, Jenny .... title and tune, 292 to 295
Jenny my handmaid .... (*not yet found*) title mentioned, 279
Jenny yields at last .... sub-title, 181
Jenny's Lamentation for the loss of her Jemmy..... title, 177, 181, 196
Jenny's Prudent Resolution ..... alternative title, mentioned, 236

PAGE

Jephtha Judge of Israel, A proper new ballad on ..... title, 684, 685
Jerusalem, The Shoemaker of .... sub-title, 693
Jest, A .... title, 315, 468, 509, 514; given, 515
Jew (Wordsworth's) Song for the Wandering ..... title, quoted, 692
Jew, the Wandering .... title, 687, 690, ; given, 693
Jew's Chronicle, the Wandering .... title, 690, 695
Jew's Coranta .... tune, 489, 490
Jig, A new Northern .... title mentioned, 280
Jig, The Duke of Monmouth's ....title mentioned, 56, 57, 170
Jockey and Jenny, The Loves of .... title, 176, 178
Jockey's Jealousy .... tune, 218, 220, 228
Jockey's Lamentation turn'd to Joy..... .... title, 181
Jockey's Vindication .... sub-title, 170, 171
John for the King (Deloney's Jig) .... title, mentioned, 389
John True and Susan Mease .... title, mentioned, 650
John's Earnest Request and Betty's Compassion .... title, 200, 202
Johnny Armstrong's Last Good Night title and tune, 427, 594, 600, 604, 635
Jolly Gentleman's Frollic, The .... title, 509, 513
Jovial Bachelor, The .... title and tune, 368, 369, 796
Jovial Cobler, The ..... title and tune, mentioned, 368, 431, 796, 797
Jovial Mariner, The .... title, 199, 363, 369, 796
Joy after Sorrow, being the Seaman's Return from Jamaica title, ment., 64
Joy, the Maiden's .... sub-title, mentioned, 69
Joy, the Sailor's ..... title mentioned, and tune, 398, 408, 409
Joys Completed, The True Lover's .... sub-title, 44
Juan, Don (Byron's) .... quoted, 87, 629
Judas's Mother, The Dream fulfilled of (*postponed*), title, ment., 688
Jude, Der Ewige (Goethe's) .... title, mentioned, 690
Judge of Israel, A proper new ballad on Jephtha ..... title, 684, 685
Judgement of God shewed upon John Faustus, The title, 701 to 706
Judgements of God, The Strange .... title, mentioned, 389
Juif Errant, Complainte du (*bis*) .... title, 690, 692; given, 691

KAISER und der Abt, Der .... title, mentioned, 746
Kate, Dunsmore..... .... title, quoted, 765, 766, 772
Kate the Queen .... title mentioned, 43, 114
Katharine Loggy (Bonny) title and burden, quoted. 618; tune, 622
Katharine Ogie (or *Ogee*, or Ogle) .... burden, 618; tune, 622
Keeper, The Bold .... title, 229, 230
Kent-street Club, The .... sub-title, 339, 342; given, 351
Kentish Yeoman and Susan of Ashford, The ..... title, mentioned, 639
Kind Lady, The .... title, 177, 188, 195, 200
Kind Lady, The Comfortable Returns of the ..... sub-title, mentioned, 148
"Kind Sir, for your courtesy" .... mentioned, 292
Killkenny for me! (cf. Shrewsbury for me!) ..... burden, mentioned, 360
Kilkenny, The Boys of. (Attributed to Tom Moore.) title, mentioned, 360
Killiecrankie, The memorable Battle fought at title and tune, 615, 616
Killigrew's glorious Conquest over the French Admiral title, mentioned, 368
King and the Beggar Maid, The .... title, quoted, 660
King and the Bishop, The .... title, 749
King and the Lord Abbot, The .... tune, 747
King and the Soldier, The .... title, 786
"King Arthur and his men they valiant were and bold" 136; given, 730
King Edward Fourth and Jane Shore, A new ballad of title, mentioned, 725
King Edward the Fourth and the Tanner of Tamworth title, mentioned, 570
King Henry the Fifth's Conquest of France .... title, 743, 744

PAGE
King Henry's going to Bulloign (=The King's going) ..... tune, 422, 784
King John and the Abbot of Canterbury .... title, 746, 747
King John and the Bishop (Percy Folio MS.) title, mentioned, 746, 750
King Lear and his Three Daughters, O (William Warner's)..... 712
King Lear and his Three Daughters, A Lam. Song of the Death of title, 711
King Lear and his Three Daughters, Tragical History of ..... title, 717
"King Lear once ruled in this Land" 714
King Olfrey, The Old Abbot and .... title, 750, 753
King of France's Daughter, Courtship of The ..... part title, mentioned, 571
King of Good-Fellows, The .... title, 315, 501, 502
King William's Happy Success in Ireland ..... sub-title, mentioned, 226
King William is come to the Throne .... mentioned, 82
King's going to Bulloign, The (see 'Henry's) ..... tune, 422, 423, 784
Kingston Church .... tune, and conventional title, 58
Kinmont Willie .... (Scott's ballad title), mentioned, 603
Knight, Constance of Cleveland's disloyal ..... sub-title, 572, 653
"Know then, my brethren, heaven is clear" .... mentioned, 339

LABOUR LOST, The Young Man's .... title, 458
Ladies, A Looking-glass for .... title, 517, 552, 553
"Ladies all behold and wonder" 85
Ladies of London .... tune, 15, 16
Lady Isabella's Tragedy, The .... title, mentioned, 612
Lady Janet .... title, mentioned, 612
Lady, The Comfortable, Returns of the Kind, ... sub-title, mentioned, 118
Lady, The Kind, ... title, 177, 188, 195, 200
Lady, The Somersetshire .... title, mentioned, 33
Lady, The Unfortunate (*cf.* "What dismal") ..... title, mentioned, 27
Lady, The Wronged .... title, mentioned, 33
Lady who fell in love with a Horse Rider, song of a young alt. title, 237
Lady's Fall, The ..... title and tune, 650, 651, 653, 761, 764, 765
Lady's Lamentation, The .... title, mentioned, 27
Lady's Tragedy, The .... title, mentioned, 639
Lament for his Rebellion, Mar's .... title, 617, 621
Lament, The Forlorn Lover's .... title, mentioned, 19
Lamentable Song of the Lord Wigmore, etc , The ..... title, 771
Lamentation, Essex's .... tune, mentioned, 623
Lamentation for Cruelty, The Forsaken Damsel's part of sub-title, ment. 43
Lamentation for her Gerhard, Cordelia's .... sub-title, 568
Lamentation for the late Treasons, etc., England's title, mentioned, 389
Lamentation for the Loss of her Jemmy, Jenny's title, 177, 184, 196
Lamentation for the Loss of her Sweetheart, A Wench's sub-title, 577
Lamentation for the Unkindness of Sylvia, The Fond Lover's sub-title, 24
Lamentation for want of a Husband, The Younger Sister's sub-title, 236, 246
Lamentation, Jack Hadland's ..... title, 315, 468, 469, 471; given, 475
Lamentation of Beccles, a Town in Suffolk ..... title, mentioned, 388
Lamentation of Chloris, The .... title, 91, 130, 131
Lamentation of Edward Smith, The Woful (Ned Smith tune) title, ment., 280
Lamentation of the Languishing Squire, The Last ..... title, 170, 228
Lamentation of the Master Cook and the Step-mother ..... title, 652
Lamentation of Thomas the Coachman, The ..... title, mentioned, 32
Lamentation of Two Loyal Lovers, The Languishing title, mentioned, 115
Lamentation occasioned by Lord Wigmore, The Maid of Dunsmore's title, 767
Lamentation, The Birds..... .... title, 300, 304, 307
Lamentation, The Bleeding Lovers'..... ..... title, mentioned, 639
Lamentation, The Clans' .... title, 618, 622

PAGE

Lamentation, The Deluded Lass's .... title, mentioned, 27
Lamentation, The Lady's .... title, mentioned, 27
Lamentation, The Languishing Lovers sub-title, mentioned, 127
Lamentation, The Lord's .... title, 743; given, 777
Lamentation, The Love-Sick Sail-man's .... sub-title, 34
Lamentation, The Seaman's .... title, mentioned, 177
Lamentation, The Young Damsel's .... title, mentioned, 237
Lamentation, The Young Man's .... title, mentioned, 252
Lamentation turn'd to joy, Jockey's .... title, 181
Lamenting for his fair Cordelia's death .... sub-title, 565
Lamenting Shepherdess, The .... title, mentioned, 130
Lancashire Gentleman, The Unfortunate Love of a title, quoted, 204
Lancelot du Lac (see "When Arthur first") .... sub-title, 721
Lancelot du Lac, his combat with Tarquin 722
Landlord, The Cruel .... title, mentioned, 33
Languishing Lover's Lamentation, The .... title, mentioned, 26, 28
Languishing Squire, The First Complaint of the title, mentioned, 224
Languishing Squire, The Last Lamentation of the title, 170, 224, 228
Languishing Swain made happy, The .... title, 26 to 29, 224
Languishing Swain, The (= "Down by the side") title and tune, 26 to 29, 793; given, 29
Languishing Swain, The ("Happy's the man") title, 26; given, 224
Languishing Young Man, The .... title, 33, 34
Lass of Lochroyan, The Bonny .... title, quoted, 212, 610, 611
Lass of Ochram (*query* = Aughrim?), The .... title, 609, 613
Last Good Night (see Armstrong, Essex, and Night) titles, 600, 604, 623, 766
Last Lamentation of the Languishing Squire, The title, 170, 224; given, 228
Last Shilling, The (Charles Dibdin's, "As pensive," 1799) title, ment., 690
"Lately in a shady bower Celia with her love conversed" 155
"Le bonheur est là-bas" .... tune, mentioned, 672
Le bruit courait ça et là par la France" .... quoted, 777
Leader Haughs and Yarrow .... title and burden, 607, 608
"Leander on the Bay of Hellespont" (2nd stanza = Scotch 1st) 557, 558
Leander, The Tragedy of Hero and (see 'Hero') title, given, 558
Leander, The Unfortunate Loves of Hero and (see 'Hero') title, given, 560
Leander's Love for Loyal Hero .... title, mentioned, 557
Leather Bottél, The .... tune and title, 466, 468: given, 470
Legacy, The unhappy Shepherd's last .... sub-title, mentioned, 130
Leicester Tragedy, The .... sub-title, mentioned, 27
Lennox's Love to Blantyre .... sub-title, given, 304
Lenten Entertainment (*From the Trowbesh MSS.*) title in *Preface*, xvi*
Let all, I say, be warned by me, from Drinking and bad company burden, 475
"Let England and Ireland and Scotland rejoice" 435
Let Mary live long! .... tune, 224, 225
"Let mournful Britons now deplore" 623
"Let Rufus weep, rejoice, stand, sit, or walk" 97
"Let the grave folks go preach that our lives are but short" 315
Let the soldiers rejoice .... (query, Hy. Purcell's) tune, 227
"Let's call, and drink the cellar up!" ....315; given, 490
"Let's drink and droll, and dance and sing" .... mentioned, 328
Letter, A Maid's .... title, mentioned, 668
Letter, Joan's loving .... title, mentioned, 33
Libera nos, Domine! .... burden, 2
Libertatis Amator .... title, 2
Libertine, The Rejoiced .... sub-title, 59
Life and Death of Fair Rosamond, The .... title, 667, 672, 673

PAGE
Life and Death of Sir Hugh of the Grime, The .... title, 594, 595, 601
Life is not all Beer and Skittles! .... burden, *Preface*, xvi*
Life of Love, The .... title, mentioned, 177, 199; given, 191
Light o' Love .... tune, mentioned, 408
Like an old Courtier of the King's .... burden, 757 to 759
Like an old Courtier of the Queen's .... burden, 756 to 759
" Like pilgrim poor" .... and tune, mentioned, 736
" Like quires of Angels we'll loyally sing" 314
Lily and the Rose, The (see 'The Damask Rose') .... tune, 218
Litany of 1681, A .... sub-title, 2
Little fools will drink too much, and big fools not at all! (C.M.) quoted, 316
" Little I knew of what troubles you" 362
Little Musgrave and Lady Barnard .... title, 601, 606, 631 to 634, 649
" Little Musgrave is to the church gone" .... mentioned, 630
Lochroyan (or Loch-ryan), Fair Annie of .... title, quoted, 611
Logan Water .... tune, 509
" Long had the proud Spaniards advaunted to conquer us" 402
Long-nosed Lass, The .... title, mentioned, 208
" Long Sporting on the Flowery Plain" .... mentioned, 130
" Look, you faithful Lovers!" .... quoted, 204
Looking-Glass for Ladies, A .... title, 547, 552, 553
Looking-Glass, The Lady's .... title mentioned, 148
" Lord Barnard's awa'" .... mentioned, 630
Lord George was born in England, etc. .... burden, 730
Lord Gregory (or Love Gregory) ....title, 610 to 612
Lord Lovel and the Lady Nancie Bell .... title, mentioned, 640
" Lord Thomas and Fair Annet sat a' day on a hill" .... quoted, 614
" Lord Thomas he was a bold Forester" .... and tune, 647
Lord Wigmore, once Governor of Warwick Castle, and Fair Isabel of Dunsmore Heath title, 761, 767, 771
Lord Wigmore, this is 'long of thee! .... burden, 766, 769
" Lord Wigmore, thus I have defil'd and spotted my pure Virgin's bed." 771
Lord's Lamentation, The .... title, 743; given, 777
Lotus Eaters, The (Tennyson's) .... title, quoted, 761
Love, A Pattern of .... title, 286
Love, A Pattern of True ....title or sub-title, 681 to 683
Love, A Trial of True .... title, 292 293
Love and Constancy .... title, 65, 70
Love and Gallantry .... title, mentioned, 43
Love and Honesty .... title, 56, 592
Love and Honour .... title, 37, 40, 65
Love and Loyalty rewarded with Cruelty .... sub-title, mentioned, 252
Love and Loyalty well met .... title, mentioned, 119
Love at length rewarded, Innocent .... sub-title, 272
Love Exalted, True .... title, 93
Love Gregor (or, Gregory) ....title, 610 to 612
Love in a Calm .... title mentioned, 570; given, 774
Love in a Tub .... title, mentioned, 6
" Love in fantastic triumph sat" 7
Love in joy my heart, The .... title or first line, (*Not yet found*) 279
Love in the Blossom .... title, *Introd. Notes*, xxi; 108 to 110
Love in Triumph .... alternate sub-title, 289
Love Invincible .... title, mentioned, 170
Love is better than Gold; or, Money's An Ass .... title, 13
Love is Dead (by Sir Philip Sidney) .... title, *Introd. Notes*, xxii
Love is the Cause of my Mourning (*bis.*) burden and title, 229, 232, 235

PAGE
Love me little and love me long, etc. .... and title, 249, 250
Love, no Life. No .... title, 88, 89, 91
Love of Sir Thomas and Fair Eleanor, The Unfortunate ..... title, 647
Love overcometh all things .... sub-title, 218
Love Overthrown .... title, mentioned, 27
Love Passion Song, The Shepherd's..... .... sub-title, 105
Love Requited, True .... title, 243
Love rewarded with Loyalty, True title and tune 257, 259, 260, 265, 268, 269, 272, 274
Love Song, A favourite..... .... title, 207
Love Song between a Young Man and a Maid, A true ..... sub-title, 583
Love, The Life of .... title, 170, 190, 191, 199
Love Songs, The Master-piece of .... title, 230
Love, The Spanish Lady's ..... title, 653, 655, 657, 672, 683
Love to the Merchant's Daughter, The Ship-Carpenter's title, ment., 428
Love will find out the way! ..... burden, title, and tune, quoted, 123
Love with loyalty ought to be paid, True ..... sub-title, mentioned, 43
Love without Blemish .... title, mentioned, 199
Love without Deceit, True .... title, 123, 126, 127, 199
Lovel and the Lady Nancie Bell, Lord ..... title, mentioned, 640
Lovely Peggy .... title, quoted, 232
Lover Catcht, The Stubborn .... title, mentioned, 133
Lover, Charidora's Reply to (Diaphantus) the Forlorn ..... title, 586
Lover Defeated, The Scotch .... sub-title, mentioned, 292
Lover overcome with Grief, The Discontented ..... alternative sub-title, 25
Lover, The Despairing .... sub-title, 235
Lover, The Faithful Inflamed .... title, 123, 124
Lover, The False-hearted .... title, mentioned, 115
Lover, The Forlorn (" A week before Easter ")..... .....229, 232 to 234
Lover, The Forlorn (Oh Yes! Oh Yes!") ..... title, mentioned, 28
Lover, The Passionate (=" As I sate in ") ..... title, mentioned, 296
Lover, The Passionate (=" Sighs and groans ")..... title, 296; given, 297
Lover, The Pining .... sub-title, mentioned, 276
Lover, The Resolved .... title, mentioned, 217
Lover, The Ruined .... title, mentioned, 236
Lover, The Seaman's Answer to his Unkind .... title, 792
Lover, The Secret .... title, mentioned, 200, 205
Lover, The Successful .... title, mentioned, 218, 220
Lovers, A pleasant Song of two Country ..... title, mentioned, 237, 250
Lover's Address to Charon, The Despairing .... title, 24, 28
Lovers Bliss, The True .... sub-title, 113
Lover's Complaint, The Despairing (see 'Complaint') title, mentioned, 27
Lover's Farewell to his fickle Mistress, The Forsaken title, mentioned, 583
Lover's Ghost, The True .... title, 23, 79; given, 85
Lover's Happiness, The True .... title, 108, 115, 116
Lover's Joys completed, The True .... sub-title, 44
Lovers Lamentation for Cruelty, The Forsaken Damsel's sub-title, ment., 43
Lovers last Farewell, The Faithful .... sub-title, 635
Lovers of the West, The Faithful .... title, 18, 257
Lover's Overthrow, The True .... title, 120
Lovers, The faithful Wooing of two Country alternative title, ment, 237, 250
Lovers, The happy Meeting of two faithful .... sub-title, 415
Lovers, The Languishing Lamentation of two Loyal .....title, ment., 115
Lovers, The Loyal .... (under divers titles) and tune, 115, 116
Lovers, The Northamptonshire .... title, 273, 274
Lovers, The Overthrow of two Loyal sub-title, mentioned, 115, 119, 296

PAGE
Lovers, The Pleasant Wooings of Two Country..... ..... title, 250
Lovers, The Two Constant ..... title, mentioned, 115, 116, 263
Lovers, The Two Country .... alternative title, 249, 250
Lovers, The Two Faithful .... title, 147, 152, 159, 247
Lovers, The Two Jeering .... title, mentioned, 64, 69
Lovers, The Two Unfortunate ..... sub-title, 558; title, 33, 559, 560
Lovers, The Two Unhappy .... title, mentioned, 33
Lovers, The Unchangeable ..... title, mentioned, 418; given, 795
Lovers, The Unfortunate Voyage of Two ..... sub-title, ment., 364, 368
Lover's Tragedy, The .... title, mentioned, 28
Lover's Welcome home from France, The True.... ..... sub-title, 65
Love's Downfall ..... title, 114, 148, 263, 264, 274; given, 265
Love's Dying Passion .... sub-title, 109
Love's fierce desire and hopes of Recovery .... title, 66, 67
Love's lamentable Tragedy (and sequels to it) ..... title, 82, 83, 85, 87
Love's Moods (By Ælian Prince, *pseudonym*) .... quoted, 11
Loves of Damon and Strephon, The..... .... title, 152, 153
Loves of Hero and Leander, The Unfortunate .... title, 559, 560
Loves of Jockey and Jenny, The .... title, 176, 178
Loves of Stella and Adonis .... sub-title, mentioned, 188
Loves of Tommy and Nanny, The .... sub-title, 174
Love's only Cure .... (original) title, 26
Love's Power .... title, mentioned, 170
Love's Return .... title, mentioned, 66, 69
Love's Solace .... title, quoted, 218
Love's Tide .... tune and title, 567, 570, 774
Love's Triumph over Bashfulness .... title, mentioned, 127
Love's Tyrannic Conquest .... title, 289, 290
Love's Unlimited Power .... title, mentioned, 122
Love's Unspeakable Passion .... title, mentioned, 83
Love's Victory Obtained..... .... title, mentioned, 283
Love-sick Maid quickly Revived, The .... title, 236, 238
Love-sick Maid, The (Gerhard's Mistress, Cordelia) ..... title, 563
Love-sick Serving-man, The .... title, mentioned, 26
Loving Lad and Coy Lass, The .... tune mentioned, 300
Lowlands of Holland, The ..... title and burden, mentioned, 412
Loyal Damosel's Resolution, The .... sub-title, 293
"Loyal Lovers, far and near" .... mentioned, 115
"Loyal Lovers, listen well!" .... and tune, 115, 116
Loyal Lovers, The .... tune (or divers tunes), 115, 116
Loyal Song of 1683, A .... title, 314
Loyal Subject's Wish, The .... title, mentioned, 224
Loyalty rewarded with Cruelty, Love and ..... sub-title, mentioned, 252
Loyalty, The true Pattern of .... title, mentioned, 28
Loyalty, True Love rewarded with (see 'Love rewarded') title and tune, 260
Lucina conquered by prevailing Cupid, Fair ..... title, 177, 188, 189
"Lucina, sitting in her bower" .... 177; given, 189
Luck at Last, Good .... title, mentioned, 177
Lucky Minute, The (=Corydon and Cloris) ..... original title, 133, 135
Lullabie, A Sweet .... title, 575, 576, 580
Lusty Bacchus .... tune, 570, 774
Lusty Gallants ..... tune mentioned (distinct from Captain Ward), 427

MACCABE, or M'Cabe, The valiant deeds of..... title, mentioned, 382
Mad Man's Morris, The .... title, mentioned, 512
Mad Marriage, The .... title, mentioned, 170

PAGE
Magistrates, A Mirror for .... title, quoted, 709, 711
Maid of Bristol, The Loyal .... sub-title, 441
Maid of Bristowe (=Bristol), the Fair and Loyal title, 408; given, 443
Maid of London, Princely Wooing of the Fair ..... title, mentioned, 65
Maid of Portsmouth, The Love-sick..... .... title, 177, 186
Maid of the West, the Witty .... title, mentioned, 161
Maid of Wapping, the Love-sick .... title, mentioned, 177, 199
Maid quickly revived, the Love-sick..... .... title, 236, 238
Maid revived, The Despairing (see properly 'Maiden') title, ment., 177, 199
Maid, The Constant Country .... title, 272
Maid, The Forsaken .... title, mentioned, 576
Maid, the Love-sick (*i.e.* Cordelia = Gerhard's Mistress) ..... title, 563
Maid, The Love-sick (=The Curragh of Kildare) ..... title, 237, 240
Maid, The Pensive .... title, mentioned, 251
Maid, The Slighted .... title, mentioned, 276
Maiden Revived by the Returning of her dearest Love title, ment., 177, 199
Maiden, The Injured (not 'Mistress') ..... sub-title, mentioned, 26, 27
Maiden, The Kentish .... title, mentioned, 27
Maidenhead, The Young Man's hard shift for a..... ..... title, 213
Maidenhead. Vindication of a departed ..... sub-title, mentioned, 218
Maidens, A Warning to .... title, mentioned, 650
Maiden's Delight, The .... title, quoted, 368
Maiden's Joy, The .... sub-title, mentioned, 69
Maiden's Resolution, The Constant .... title, mentioned, 161, 428
Maiden's New Wish, The .... title, mentioned, 27
Maiden's Vow, A pleasant ditty of a..... ..... title, mentioned, 557
Maid's Choice, The Fair (*Bagford Ballads*, 289), title, ment., 367, 414
Maid's Letter, A .... title, mentioned, 668
Maids Look about You, This is call'd ..... title, mentioned, 318
Maids of London, The Virgin's Advice to the ..... title, mentioned, 326
Maid's Resolution, The Constant .... title, mentioned, 161
Maid's Resolution, The Virtuous .... title, mentioned, 274
Maid's Twitcher, The .... tune, 528
Make much of a penny as near as you can, etc. .... burden, 346
Make use of time while time serves .... sub-title, quoted, 445
Malaga, The Famous Fight at .... title, 411, 412
Male and Female Husband, The .... title, mentioned, 236
Maltster's Daughter of Marlborough, The ..... part-title, mentioned, 237
Manfred (Byron's, written 1816-17)..... ..... title, mentioned, 701
Map of Mock-Beggar's Hall, A .... title, quoted, 761, 763
Mar, A Dialogue between Argyle and .... title, 620
"Marche! marche! paresseux, marche!" etc. ..... burden, quoted, 692
Margaret and Sweet William, Fair .... title and tune, 640, 641
Margaret's Ghost .... colloquial title, 640
Margaret's Misfortune, Fair .... title, 640, 641
Maria's Kind Answer (to the Languishing Young Man) 35
Marigold, The new-blossomed .... title, mentioned, 177
Mariner, The Faithful .... title, 26, 789; given, 793
Mariner, The Jovial .... title, 199, 368, 369, 796
Mariner (Coleridge's) Rime of the Ancient ..... title, mentioned, 692
Mariner's Misfortune, The .... title, mentioned, 364, 368
Mark Noble's Frollic .... title, 315, 468, 509, 510, 514
"Mark well my heavy doleful tale" 764
Marlborough, The Maltster's Daughter of ..... part-title, mentioned, 237
Marmion (Tercentenary Edition of) .... quoted, 331
Marriage, A Mad .... title, mentioned, 170

PAGE
Married-Women, A Mirror for .... sub-title, 553
Married-Women, A Warning for .... title, mentioned, 650
Marry, and thank you too .... burden, indicated, 241
Mar's Lament for his Rebellion .... title, 617, 621
Mary (a Minister's Daughter in Dorsetshire), Beautiful ..... sub-title, 638
" Mary doth complain : Ladies, be you moved " .... mentioned, 571
Mask, The Haymarket's .... tune. mentioned, 237
Master Constable ..... burden and sub-title, 315, 468, 509, 515
Master-piece of Love-Songs, The .... title, 229, 230
Match, The Unequal .... title, mentioned, 33
Match to go a-Maying .... sub-title, 218
May I govern my passions with an absolute sway, etc. ..... burden, 507
Medley, A (" Let's call, and drink ") .... title, 489
Medley, Martin Parker's excellent new ..... title, mentioned, 241, 745
Medley, Tarleton's .... tune, mentioned, 745
Meeting of two Faithful Lovers, The happy .... sub-title, 415
" Melpomene, now assist a meek Lover ! " 225
Memorial Verses (by Matthew Arnold) ..... title, quoted, 700
Memoriam, In (*i.e.* Matthew Arnold) ..... *Prefatory Addenda*, xxxii*
Men are not so false as women be .... burden, 50
Men of Old, The .... title of motto, quoted, 537
Merchant and the Fidler's Wife, The ..... title, mentioned, 370
Merchant's Daughter of Bristol, The Ship-Carpenter's love to the t. m., 428
Mermaid, A New Song called the .... title, mentioned, 428
Merry and Wise .... title, 215, 217
Merry Gossips Vindication, The .... title, quoted, 482
" Merry Knaves are we three-a " 467
Merry Man's Resolution, The .... title, mentioned, 64
Merry Toper's Advice, The .... sub-title, 502
Methinks the poor Town has been troubled too long " ..... quoted, 127
" Miladi Clara Vere de Vere " (Trowbesh MS.) .... *Preface*, xv*
Milkmaid, the Merry Ploughman and The ..... title, mentioned, 177
Milkmaid's Morning Song, The .... title, mentioned, 177, 179
Milkmaid's Resolution, The .... title, 525, 529
Miller and the King's Daughter, The ..... title, mentioned, 601
Miller, The Hampshire .... title, mentioned, 27
Mills, Dying Words of Robert Boxall to Margaret title, mentioned, 43
Minute, the Lucky .... title, 133
Mirror for Magistrates, A .... title, quoted, 709, 711
Mirror for Married Women, A .... sub-title, 553
Mirror of the Times, The .... sub-title, mentioned, 356
Mirth and Joy after Sorrow and Sadness .... sub-title, 260
Miser Slighted, The Old .... title, mentioned, 148
Miser, The Old (" What ails thee, Old Fool ? ") ..... title, mentioned, 506
Misery one suffers by being too kind, Relation of the ..... sub-title, 478
Misfortune, Fair Margaret's .... title, 640, 641
Misfortune, the Mariner's .... title, mentioned, 364, 368
Miss, The Crafty .... title, mentioned, 170
Mistress, A Noble Seaman's Address to his sub-title, mentioned, 43, 438
Mistress, (Ballad composed by a Lover) in Praise of his ..... title, 19
Mistress Mitchel and Borlan .... title, 200, 201
Mistress of Phil'arete, The (by George Wither) ..... title, quoted, 108
Mock-Beggar's Hall .... title, 737, 761 ; given, 762
Mock Song (*id est*, Parody), A .... title, mentioned, 33
Mock to " Be gone ; thou fatal fiery fever," A ..... title, mentioned, 564
Moderation and *Alteration* ..... title and alternate burdens, 755

PAGE

Moderation, moderation, this was ancient moderation burden, ment., 755
Modish Courtier, The .... sub-title, 56
Moggie's Jealousy, A new song of .... title and tune, 170, 171, 228, 251
Money is an Ass .... sub-title, 13
Money, The Wonderful Praise of .... title, 15, 16
Monk (see "General George," also "General Monk") 136
Monk hath confounded (= My L. M.'s March to London ?) .... tune, 136, 137
Monmouth's Jig, The Duke of .... tune, 56, 57, 170
Monstrous Shape, A .... title, mentioned, 64, 208
Montrose's Lines; or, A proper new Ballad ....title, 581 to 583
Moods, Love's (see 'Love's Moods') .... title, quoted, 11
Moore of Moor Hall and the Dragon of Wantley title mentioned, 725
More News from from the Fleet .... title mentioned, 217, 725
More Strange News from the Narrow Seas .... sub-title, mentioned, 428
Mother-in-law, My (Trowbesh MS.) title and burden, quoted, 339
"Mother, let me marry" .... mentioned, 237
Mother's Counsel to her Daughter after Marriage, The .... sub-title, 349
Mountebank of York, The .... tune, mentioned, 368
Mounseur's Almaigne (*sic*) .... tune, 384
Mournful Bride, The Seaman's (properly, Sorrowful Bride) .... title, 444
Mournful Shepherd, The .... title, 61, 63
Mucedorus (= Musidorus) and Amadine .... sub-title, 662, 664
"Much they prized his lightest word" (private issue, *cf.* p. xxxii*) xiv*
Musgrave and the Lady Barnard, The old Ballad of Little .... title, 631
Musgrave, Lord Barnard and the Little .... title, 629, 649
Musgrove and Lady Barnet, Lamentable Ballad of the Little title, 633
"Musing on the roaring ocean" (by Burns) .... title, 445
My bleeding heart with grief and care .... tune, mentioned, 108
"My daughter dear, now since you are become a bride" 349
"My dear and only love, I pray" .... mentioned, 555, 581; given, 581
"My dear and only love, take heed" ....556, 581 to 583
"My dearest baby, prithee sleep" .... mentioned, 576
"My dearest, come hither to me" .... mentioned, 170
"My dearest dear and I must part" .... tune, 789, 790
"My dearest dear, could I relate" .... mentioned, 156
"My dearest Katy, prithee be but constant now".... .... mentioned, 170
My dearest Love and I must part .... tune, 283, 789
"My fairest and rarest" .... mentioned, 292
"My fairest, my dearest, I've heard what thou'st told" 292, 295
My father was born before me! .... burden, 329
"My friend and I, we drank whole pint pots" .... misquoted, 505
"My friend, whose thirst for ballad-lore" .... *Dedication*, 539
My heart is fill'd with woes, etc. .... burden, 474
"My husband builded me a bower" (see 'Sweet Willie') .... mentioned, 570
My kind heart hath undone me .... burden, 337
My Lord Monk's march to London (Monk hath confounded?) tune 326, 327
"My Love has built a bonny Ship" .... mentioned, 442
My Love he is safely returned from France .... burden, 70
"My Love, I come to take my leave" .... mentioned, 148
"My Love is on the brackish Sea" .... 177, 350, 477, 445; given, 444
My Maidenhead is such a load .... burden, quoted, 251
My Maidenhead will undo me! .... burden varies, 250
"My Mother duns me every day" .... mentioned, 148
My Mother-in-law! .... (to most men an intolerable) burden, 339
"My noble friends, give ear" 523
"My noble Muse, assist me!" .... mentioned, 428

PAGE
" My own dear Nanny, my fair one" .... mentioned, 170
" My pretty little Rogue" .... mentioned, 254
" My pretty Turtle Dove, my Love," etc. 208, 213
" My Shepherd's unkind, alas! what shall I do?"..... ..... 91; given, 131
" My son, if you reckon to wed" 216
" My sweetest, my fairest, my rarest, my dearest" 73
My Wife will be my Master .... title, mentioned, 237
" My youthful charming Fair!" .... mentioned, 639

NANCY at her last Prayer .... title, mentioned, 33
Nanny, Jealous .... title, mentioned, 170
Nanny, The Loves of Tommy and .... sub-title, 174
" Near a fair fountain a damsel sat weeping" .... mentioned, 236
" Near to a fountain all alone" .... mentioned, 27
" Near unto Dover lived of late" .... mentioned, 27
Necessitated Virgin, The .... title, mentioned, 236
Nectar preferred before scornful Cynthia .... sub-title, 226
Ned Smith (see Smith, Wofull Lam. of Edward) tune, 280, 281, 681
Nell and Harry (= Nelly's Constancy) title, mentioned, 283, 789 to 792
Nelly's Constancy .... title, 27, 283; given, 789, 791
Nelly's Sorrow at parting with Henry ..... title, 283; given, 789, 795
Neptune's raging Fury .... title, 431, 432
Never was Woman more false than you ..... burden varies, 29
New Stave to an old Tune, A .... title, 449
News for Young Men and Maids .... title, 8
News from Hyde Park .... title, 315, 495
News from the Fleet, More .... title, mentioned, 217, 725
News from the Narrow Seas, More Strange ..... sub-title, mentioned, 428
News of the Worthy and Valiant Exploits, etc. .... mentioned, 375
News out of Germany of a Jew, Wonderful strange ..... title, 688
Nick and Froth, ... title, 315, 485; given, 486
Night Encounter, The .... title, mentioned, 557
Nimble-pated Youngster's Forgeries, The ..... sub-title, mentioned, 212
No body else shall enjoy thee but I! .... burden, 73
No body else shall plunder but I .... tune, 73
No charm's above her, Oh! how I love her, etc. .... burden, 149
No love like a Contented mind .... tune, 354
No Love, no Life! .... title, 88, 89, 91
" No more, silly Cupid, will I sigh or complain" .... mentioned, 57
No Wealth can compare unto True Love .... sub-title, 274
Noble Acts of King Arthur, The .... title, 722
" Noble Argyle, when he went on" 621
Noble Lord's Cruelty, The .... title, 682, 683
Noble Prodigal, The .... title, 489, 490
Noble's Frollic, Mark .... title, 315, 468, 509, 510, 514
" None can endure the Flames of Love" .... mentioned, 177
North Country Lass, The .... tune, mentioned, 307
Northamptonshire Knight's Daughter, The ..... title, mentioned, 27
Northamptonshire Lovers, The .... title, 273, 274
Northern Ditty of the Lady Green-sleeves, a New title, mentioned, 397
Northern Jig, A New .... tune, 280, 681, 773
Northern Lass's Ballow, The (R. Brome's) .... given, 575
Northern Tune, A new .... tune, 495
" Not a drum was heard, nor a funeral note" .... mentioned, 193
Nothing Venture, nothing Have .... sub-title, 115, 116
" Now comes on the glorious year" (properly, " Now, now") and tune, 617, 621

PAGE
" Now fare thee weel, sweet Ennerdale " 588, 589
" Now fare thee well, my dearest dear " ..... mentioned, 115
" Now farewell to St. Giles's " (given in *Amanda Group*) ..... mentioned, 64
" Now God above," *vel* " Now God alone " .... variations, 469
" Now I am in a merry vein " 269
" Now listen, and be not mistaken " .... mentioned, 170
" Now listen to my song, good people all " 706
" Now my dearest sweet jewel " 124
Now, now the Fight's done! .... tune, mentioned, 254
" Now, now the Tories all shall stoop " .... mentioned, 339
" Now, now you blind Boy! you clearly deny " .... mentioned, 254
Now or never .... sub-title, 58, 140
" Now that bright Phœbus his rays doth display " 108, 137
" Now the Tyrant hath stolen my dearest away " ..... tune, 64 to 70, 115
" Now thou knowest I love more " .... mentioned, 564
" Now Trading is dead, I resolve to contrive " 532
Now we have our Freedom .... tune, 336, 337
" Now would I give my life to see " .... mentioned, 136
Nymph, The Devonshire .... title, 92, 95, 97
Nymph, The West Country .... title, 428; given, 441

O! and Oh! (*indexed together, as though identical, being often interchanged.*)
" O Chloris! awake! " (properly, " Ah! Chloris ") tune, 123, 127, 131
" O Cupid! thou now art too cruel " .... mentioned, 170
" O! did you not hear of a rumour of late?" .... mentioned, 208
O! do not, do not kill me yet, for I am not prepared to die ..... burden, 557
" O! England, England, 'tis high time to repent " (Roxb. Coll., III. 236), 440
" O, England! now lament in tears! " .... quoted, 400
" Oh! English-men with Romish hearts " .... quoted, 389
" O, hark! my Love " .... tune, 259, 260
" Oh, Love! that stronger art than Wine " 241
O! man in desperation .... tune, mentioned, 389
" Oh, my dearest! come away " 116
O no, no, no! not yet .... tune, 557, 583
" O noble England, fall down upon thy knee " 384
" O open the door, Lord Gregory! " (Scotch fragment) 212
" O open the door, Love Gregory! " (Ditto.) .... qnoted, 612
" O open the door, some pitty to show! " 193
" O! pity a Lover who lies, I declare " .... mentioned, 33
" O pity, Arminda, those passions I bear! " 38, 65
" O saw ye my father, and saw ye my mother?" .... quoted, 304
" 'O!' says the cuckoo, loud and stout " (*bis*) 301, 305
O, such a fellow's True-Blue! .... burden, quoted, 256
O such a Rogue would be hang'd! .... burden, mentioned, 276
" O! that I were with my true-love! " .... mentioned, 217
O! that I were young for you .... tune, mentioned, 336
" O! the Boys of Kilkenny are all roving blades " ..... quoted, 360
" O treacherous Lovers, what do you intend?" .... mentioned, 33
" O wanton King Edward! " .... mentioned, 66
" O welcome, my dearest! welcome to the shore! " ..... second part, 416
" O wert thou in the cauld blast " .... mentioned, 204
" O! wha is that at my chamber door?" .... quoted, 201
" O wha will shoe my bonny feet?" (*bis*) .... quoted, 610
" O! what a pitiful passion! " .... mentioned, 276
" Oh! what a madness 'tis to borrow or lend! " 346
" O! who 'll comb my yellow locks?" .... mentioned, 612

PAGE
" O who would fix his eyes" 328
" O why does my True-Love so sadly disdain?" .... 33; given, 34
" O ye powers be kind unto me!" 81
" O yes! O yes! I cry" .... mentioned, 28
Oak Table, The (Tom Dibdin's, 'I had knock'd out the dust') title, ment., 690
Observation, The Good-Fellow's .... sub-title, quoted, 256
" Obstinate as mule, we know him" ..... (*Trowbesh MS.*) *Preface*, xv*
Obtaining of the Great Galleazzo, The .... title, 381
Ocram (*vel* Aughrim?), The Lass of .... title, 609, 613
" Of a constant young Seaman a story I'll tell" 410, 447
" Of a maiden that was deep in love" .... mentioned, 318
Of all sorts of tradesmen, a Sailor for me! ..... burden, mentioned, 414
" Of all the brave birds that ever I see" 299
" Of an ancient story I'll tell you anon" (*Percy Fol. MS.*) ..... mentioned, 746
" Of English acts I intend to write" .... mentioned, 217
" Of Greece and Troy I shall you tell" 544
" Of Hector's deeds did Homer sing"..... .... mentioned, 725
" Of horned Vulcan I have heard" .... mentioned, 64, 208
" Of late did I hear a young damsel complain" ..... quoted, 525, 528
" Of late I did hear a young man domineer" 529
" Of Nelson and the North sing the glorious days renown'd"..... mentioned, 431
Offender, A Harden'd (*Trowbesh MS.*) ..... title (*Preface*), xv*
" Oft have I heard the wives complain" .... mentioned, 326
Ogle, The Lady Catharine .... tune, mentioned, 618
Old and Young Courtier, The .... title, 754 to 759, 761
Old Man's Complaint, The .... title, mentioned, 276
Old Man's Wish, The ....title, 505 to 507
Old Shepherd on his Pipe, The .... title, 318
Old Sir Simon the King..... .... tune, 276, 317, 323
" Old stories tell how Hercules a Dragon slew at Lerna" ..... mentioned, 725
" Old Time and I set out together" .... *Editorial Preface*, xix*
Old Woman's Wish, The .... title (*bis*) mentioned, 506
Olfrey, The Old Abbot and King .... title, 750, 753
Oliver, Little (Wm. S. Gilbert's *Bab Ballad*) .... quoted, 263
Olympia's Unfortunate Love .... title, 21
Omnia vincit Amor ..... burden and tune mentioned, 218, 228, 763
" On Friday morning as we set sail" .... mentioned, 428
" On Hellespont, guilty of true-love's blood" .... quoted, 556
" On the banks of a river, close under the shade"..... ..... mentioned, 127
" Once did I love a bonny bonny bird" ..... quoted, 525, 528
" Once did I love and a very pretty girl" .... mentioned, 528
" One evening, a little before it was dark" 315, 496
" One night as I lay on my bed" 207
" One night at a very late hour" 315, 510
" One Saturday night we sate late at the Rose" .... mentioned, 15
" One summer evening, fresh and fair" 110
Open me the window, my Love, do! .... burden varies, 207
Opportunity Lost .... title, mentioned, 292
Orange, An..... .... burden, mentioned, and tune, 515
Otterbourne, The Scots Song made of ..... title, quoted, 739
Our Lady of Pain (A. C. Swinburne's "Dolores") burden, quoted, 467
" Our Lords are to the mountains gane" .... mentioned, 597
Our noble King in his progress ..... and tune, 428, 429; given, 786
Our Prince is welcome out of Spain..... .... tune, 695
" Ours came to Cales, three thousand cannon shot" 420
" Out from the horror of infernal deeps" quoted, 668

PAGE
" Over hills and high mountains" ..... and tune, 123, 124, 126
" Over the mountains, and under the waves" ..... quoted, 123
Overthrow, Beauty's .... title, 58, 59
Overthrow, Fair Rosamond's .... sub-title, 676
Overthrow, The True Lover's .... title, 120
Oxfordshire Betty .... title, quoted, 300
Oxfordshire Tragedy, The ..... title, mentioned, 28

P. R., In Defence of the ..... *Trowbesh MSS.* (*Preface*), xvi*
Packington's Pound ..... tune, 331, 332, 346, 435, 480, 483
Painted in Full Canonicals (*Trowbesh MS.*, partially repressed) *Preface*, xiv*
" Paltry traducer of our Shakespeare's name" *Editorial responsibility*, 720
Panegyric Verses upon Coryat and his 'Crudities' title, mentioned, 733
Pantomime, A New (Edward Kenealey's 'Goethe') title, mentioned, 701
Paradise and the Peri (Tommy Moore's) ..... title, quoted, 1
Paragon of the Times, The Peerless..... ..... sub-title, mentioned, 356
Parents, A Warning to .... sub-title, mentioned, 27
Part my love and me (*cf.* p. 789) .... burden varies, 444
" Parthenia unto Chloe cried" (*cf.* "Sitting beyond") ..... tune, 47, 52
Partheniades (by George Puttenham) ..... title, mentioned, 376
Parthenia's Complaint (see also Answer to it, p. 50) title, 30, 46, 47
Passage to the Elizium [*sic*] Shades, Address to Charon for a title, 24
Passage crown'd with joy, etc., Flora's lamentable ..... title, 98
Passion, Love's Dying .... title, 109
Passion, Love's Unspeakable .... title, 83
Passion of my Lord of Essex, A .... title, quoted, 404
Passionate Lover, The (= "As I sate") ..... title, mentioned, 296
Passionate Lover, The (= "Sighs and groans") ..... title, 296, 297
Pattern of Constancy, The True .... title, 43, 44
Pattern of Love, A .... title, 284
Pattern of Loyalty, The True .... title, mentioned, 28
Pattern of True Love, A sometimes title, sometimes sub-title, 681 to 683
Pauper's Death-Bed (= "Tread softly, bow the head") title, mentioned, 713
" Peace, wayward bairn!" 575
Peerless Paragon of the Times, The..... ..... sub-title, mentioned, 356
Peggy, Lovely .... quoted, 232
Peggy's Complaint for the Death of her Willy ..... title, mentioned, 382
Penelope, Constant .... sub-title, 552, 553
Penny-worth of Good Counsel for Bad-Husbands, A lumping title, 216, 482
Penny-worth of Wit for a Penny, Two ..... title, 479, 482, 483
Pensive Maid, The .... title, mentioned, 254
Pensive Prisoner's Apology, The .... title, mentioned, 557
Petition to beautiful Phillis, The loving Shepherd's humble sub-title, 143
Phaon, Young (= " Young Phaon sate") ..... and tune, 7, 100, 101
Phaon, Young (= " Young Phaon strove") ..... and tune, 7, 100, 101, 130
Phaon's humble petition to beautiful Phillis .... title, 101, 143
Phil'arete, Fair Virtue the Mistress of .....title (Wither's), quoted, 108
Phillida flouts me! .... burden and title, 460, 461, 473
Phillida, my Phillida, is all the world to me! (Dobson's) burden, quoted, 460
Philip and Mary (= " To every faithful Lover") title, mentioned, 431
Phillis and Amintas .... sub-title, mentioned, 108
" Phillis, be gentler, I advise" 88
Phillis on the new-made hay ..... tune, 108, 109, 113, 115, 116
Phœnix, Fancy's .... tune and title, 354, 356
Physic, An Antidote of rare .... title, 354, 356
Pilgrims, The Three .... tune, 515

PAGE
Pin for the Spaniards, A ..... registered title, mentioned, 398
Pining Lover, The .... sub-title, mentioned, 276
Pipe, The old Shepherd on his .... title, 318
Plaintes du Juif-Errant..... .... title, mentioned, 692
Planter's Song, The .... title, mentioned, 328
Playhouse tune .... (various) tunes, 573, etc.
Plough ! God speed the..... .... title, 520, 521, 523
Plough, The Painful .... title, mentioned, 520
Plough, The Useful .... title, mentioned, 520
Plough-man and Milk-Maid, The Merry ..... title, mentioned, 177
Ploughman, True Blue the ..... title, mentioned, 520, 531, 532
Ploughman's Art of Wooing, The .... title, 526
Ploughman's Honour made known .... tune, 343, 345
Ploughman's Prophecy, The .... title, mentioned, 5
Politic Girl, The .... title, mentioned, 170
Politic Young Man, The .... title, mentioned, 212
"Poor Coridon did sometimes sit" .... quoted, 586
Poor Robin's Maggot .... tune, 55
"Poor Tom the Tailor, don't lament" .... quoted, 300
Portsmouth, The Love-sick Maid of..... .... title, 177, 186
Posie for pretty Maidens, A pretty .... sub-title, 137
Power, Love's .... title, mentioned, 170
Power, Love's Unlimited .... title, mentioned, 122
Praise of his Mistress, Ballad by a Lover in .... title, 19
Praise of Money, The Wonderful .... title, 15, 16
Praise of Sailors here set forth, The title, mentioned, 431, 796; given, 797
Praise of the Black-Jack, In .... title (*bis*), 466, 469
Praise of the Leathern Bottél, A Song in .... title, 470
Prayer and Progress, A new Song of ..... title, mentioned, 381
Prayer, Nancy at her last .... title, mentioned, 33
Prelude, Editorial .... *Introductory Notes*, xxxi
'Prentice obtained his Master's Daughter, The sub-title, mentioned, 115, 263
Presbyter's Wish, Jack .... title, mentioned, 505
"Pretty Betty, now come to me" 157
Pride abated, Summer's .... sub-title, 103
Prince and Princess, The Wandering ..... title, 101; given, 661
Prince of England's Courtship, etc. .... title, mentioned, 571
Princely Wooing of the Fair Maid of London ..... title, mentioned, 65
Princess Royal, The .... tune, 489, 491
Prisoner's Apology, The Pensive .... title, mentioned, 557
Prisoners in Dublin, A copy of Verses on the ..... part-title, mentioned, 148
Prodigal, The Noble .... title, 489, 490
Prodigious Fate .... tune, 145
Prologue, Editorial .... *Preface* vii*
Prometheus Unbound (Shelley's) .... title, mentioned, 701
Proper new Ballad, A .... title, 581
Prophecy, The Ploughman's .... title, mentioned, 5
Prophecy, The Protestant's .... title, mentioned, 5
Prophecy, The Quaker's .... title, 5; given, 6
Protestant's Prophecy, The .... title, mentioned, 5
Protestants, The noble and imprisoned ..... part-title, mentioned, 148
Pudding, With a .... burden and tune, 515

QUAKER'S Prophecy, The .... title, 5, 6
Queen and the Cobler .... sub-title, mentioned 148
Queen at Tilbury, The (Ballad by Deloney on the) title, mentioned, 381, 390

PAGE

Queen Dido .... tune, 547, 548, 553
"Queen Eleanor was a sick woman" 680
Queen Eleanor's Confession ..... title, 672, 678, 680
Queen, Kate the (Browning's *Pippa Passes*) title, mentioned, 114
Queene, The Faërie (Spenser's) ..... title, quoted, 711
Queen's Old Courtier, The .... tune, 757, 758
Question to Cupid, The Bachelor's .... sub-title, mentioned, 31
"Quicquid agit Rufus, nihil est, nisi naevia Rufo" 97
"Quho is at my windo, quho, quho?" .... quoted, 201

RACE of the Sheriffmuir, The .... title, quoted, 617
Raderer tu, tandara te, etc. .... burden, 404, 405
Ragged and torn and true ..... burden and tune, 276, 323, 324, 532
Rainbow, Captain Ward's Fight with the .... title, 375
Raleigh sailing to the Low-lands, Sir Walter .... title, 417
Ramble, The City .... sub-title, 509, 513
Ramble through the City, The ranting Gallant's sub-title, mentioned, 509
Rambler, The Ranting .... title, 514, 518
"Ranging the silent shades" .... mentioned, 639
Rant, The Hart (*query* Hare?) Merchant's .... tune, 619, 620
Rant, The New .... tune, 509, 510, 518
Ranting Rambler, The .... title, 514, 518
Rare News for the Female Sex .... title, mentioned, 237
Readiness of the Shires, etc., A Joyful Sonnet of the title, mentioned, 381
Reasons for Drinking, Five .... title, 318
Rebellion, Mar's Lament for his .... title, 621
Recantation, Fair Isabel's mournful..... .... title, 769
Recantation, The Bad-Husband's ....second title, 499
Receiving of the Queen's Majesty into her Camp at Tilbury..... title, 381, 393
Reformation, Wade's (*Bagford Ballad*) title, quoted, 336, 465, 469
Reformed Drinker, The .... title, 276, 317
Regret of a true Lover for his Mistress's Unkindness sub-title, 557, 584
"Rejoice, England" .... mentioned, 382
"Rejoice in heart, good people all" .... mentioned, 388
Relation of the great Floods, A true. (By J. White, "O England,") m., 440
Relation of the Life and Death of Sir Andrew Barton title, mentioned, 367
Relation of the misery one suffers by being too kind ..... sub-title, 478
Releasement, The Algiers Slave's .... title, 410, 447
Remonstrance, A Cavalier's (*Trouhesh MS.*) ..... title (*Preface*), xiv*
Renown, The Seaman's (=The Fair Maid's) sub-title, mentioned, 367, 414
Renown, The Seaman's (=The Jovial Mariner) ..... sub-title, 367 to 369
Renown, The Seaman's (="There was a bold S.") (res. for vol. vii.) t. m., 229
"*Repent, England, Repent!*" first line, or burden, or title (*cf.* 693), 389
Repent therefore, O England, repent while you have space! ..... burden, 693
Repentance, A Soldier's (see "Song made") .... title, 283, 284
Repentance, The Bad-Husband's .... sub-title, 480
Repentance Too Late .... title, 47, 50, 51; given, 52
Report of a Fight at Sea in the Straits, etc. ..... title, mentioned, 411
Reprehension against Green-Sleeves (Elderton's) title, mentioned, 397
Reprieved Captive, The .... title, mentioned, 152
Repulsive (*i.e.* Repellant) Maid, The ..... title, 200, 208, 209
Requited, True Love .... title, 243
Resolution, Jenny's Prudent (="'Twas within") title, mentioned, 236
Resolution, The Constant Maiden's .... title, mentioned, 161, 428
Resolution, The English Seaman's .... title, mentioned, 276
Resolution, The Good-Fellow's ..... title, 339, 342, 343

PAGE
Resolution, The Loyal Damosel's .... sub-title, 293
Resolution, The Merry Man's .... title, mentioned, 61
Resolution, The Milk-maid's .... title, 525, 529
Resolution, The Ranting Young Man's ..... sub-title, mentioned, 525
Resolution, The Sea-man's Wife's ranting ..... title, quoted, 445
Resolution, The Virtuous Maid's .... title, mentioned, 274
Resolution to beat back the Spaniards, England's title, mentioned, 398
Resolved Lover, The .... title, mentioned, 217
Resurrection, A Glorious .... title, mentioned, 381
Return from the Indies, The Gallant Seaman's .... title, 414, 415
Return, Love's .... title, mentioned, 66, 69
Return of his Loyal Love, The Happy .... sub-title, 29
Return of the Figure of Two .... title, 323, 324
Return, The Seaman's Joyful .... title, mentioned, 119
Return, The Soldier's .... title, mentioned, 99
Return, The Valiant Seaman's happy ..... title, mentioned, 254
Returns of the Kind Lady, The Comfortable ..... sub-title, mentioned, 148
Revechia, A Song to .... title, 38
Revenge, Cupid's (= "A King once reign'd") ..... title, 254, 659, 661
Revenge, Cupid's (= "Now, now, you blind Boy") title, mentioned, 254
Review of the Times (Thomas Jordan's) ..... title, mentioned, 328
Rich Farmer's Ruin ....title, 534 to 536
Rich Widow's Wooing, A merry new song of a ..... title, quoted, 252
Ring of Gold, The (original ballad not found) .... tune, 638, 639
"Rise, Chloris, charming maid!" 123
Robin Hood and the Curtal Friar .... title, mentioned, 570
Robin Hood's Golden Prize .... title, mentioned, 61
Robin the Devil .... tune, mentioned, 252
Robin's Maggot, Poor .... tune, 55
Rock Royal, Fair Isabel of .... title, mentioned, 612
Roger and Mary .... title, mentioned, 170
Room for a Ballad .... title, mentioned, 506
Roman Charity (= The Roman Wife) title, mentioned (*vide* vol. vii.), 541, 796
Rome, A Ballad for .... sub-title, mentioned, 506
Rosamond, A mournful ditty of the Death of Fair ..... title, 668
Rosamond (Michael Drayton's) Heroical Epistle from Fair title, ment., 668
Rosamond (Samuel Daniel's), The Complaint of title, quoted, 668
Rosamond, The Life and Death of Fair ..... title, 667, 672, 673
Rosamond's Overthrow .... sub-title, 676
Rosebery's Intelligence (*Trowbesh MS.*) .... *Preface*, xv*
Round about our coal fire .... tune, mentioned, 276
Royal Triumph, The .... title, mentioned, 367
Royal Victory, The .... title, 368; given, 435
Rucklaw-Hill, The bonny Lass of .... title, mentioned, 612
Ruin, The Rich Farmer's ....title, 534 to 536
Ruined Lover, The .... title, mentioned, 236
"Russell on the Ocean, minding Tourville's motion" 446
Russell scouring the French Fleet, Admiral ..... title, mentioned, 368
Russell scouring the Seas sub-title, mentioned, 368, 415; given, 446
Russell's Farewell .... tune, mentioned, 190
Russell's Triumph .... tune, mentioned, 156

SACK for my Money .... title, 318, 319
"Sad as death, at dead of night" and tune, 50, 52
Sailing in the Lowlands, The ..... burden and tune, 421
Sail-man's Lamentation, The love-sick ..... sub-title, 34

PAGE
Sailor Song. (By the late Dr. J. Le Guy Brereton) .... title (motto), 362
Sailors and Sea-Affairs, The Praise of .... title, 431 : given, 797
Sailors for my Money .... title, 779, 796, 797
Sailor's Joy, The .... title and tune mentioned, 398, 408, 409
Sailors new Tantara, The .... title, mentioned, 402
Saint George and the Dragon (=" Of Hector's deeds ") .... mentioned, 725
Saint George and the Dragon (=" Why should we boast ") title, 726 ; g. 727
Saint George for England, and Saint Dennis for France (S.S.'s) title, q. 726
St. George for England, William Grubb's second Part of title, quoted, 726
Saint George he was for England, etc. and tune, 136, 726, 727, 729, 730, 780
Salisbury Ballad, The (=" Oh ! Salsbury people, give ear ") title, m. 506
Sally in our Alley (Henry Carey's) .... title, mentioned, 473
Salutation on Primrose Hill, The Sweet .... title, quoted, 254
Sandwich's Farewell, My Lord .... tune, 38
Sappho, Song of .... title, 100
Satire on Coffee, A .... title, mentioned, 6
Satisfaction, The Subject's .... title, mentioned, 82
" Says Billy to Molly " .... mentioned, 218
Schoolmen, Bedlam .... title, 452
Scholar Gipsy (Matthew Arnold's, *cf. Preface*, xxxii*) title, q., 87, 450, 455
Scorner Scorned, The .... sub-title, mentioned, 528
Scotch Haymakers, The.... .... title and tune, 236, 237
Scotch Lover Defeated, The .... sub-title, mentioned, 292
Scotch Wedding, Second Part of the .... title, mentioned, 183
Scotch Wedding, The .... sub-title, 178
Scots Song made of Otterbourne .... title, quoted, 739
Scottish Versions of Legendary Ballads, various 612
Sea-Fight between Captain Ward and the Rainbow, The .... title, 422, etc.
Seaman and his Love, pleasant new Song of a title, mentioned, 367
Seaman, Betty's Reply to the Gallant .... title, 416
Seaman, The Undaunted .... title, mentioned, 148
Seaman's Adieu, The (=" Sweet William ") .... title, mentioned, 368
Seaman's Answer to his Unkind Lover, The .... title, 792
Seaman's Carol for taking of the great Carrack .... title, mentioned, 398
Seaman's Compass, The.... .... title, mentioned, 64, 368
Seaman's doleful Farewell, The .... title, mentioned, 119
Seaman's happy Return, The Valiant .... title, mentioned, 254
Seaman's Jovial Return, The .... title, mentioned, 119
Seaman's Lamentation, The .... title, mentioned, 177
Seaman's last Adieu to his Mistress, A Noble .... title, 43 ; given, 438
Seaman's Renown, The (see " Renown ") three titles, 229, 367 to 369, 414
Seaman's Resolution, The English .... title, mentioned, 276
Seaman's Return from the Indies, The Gallant .... title, 414, 415
Seaman's Song of Captain Ward, The title, 422, 425, 779 ; given, 784
Seaman's Song of Danseker the Dutchman, The .... title, 422, 423
Seaman's Sorrowful Bride (*al. lect.*, mournful), The title, 177, 350, 351, 444
Seaman's Sufferings, The Gallant .... sub-title, 431, 432
Seaman's Tantara rara .... tune, 401 to 403
Seaman's Victory, The .... title, mentioned, 368
Seaman's Wife's Ranting Resolution, The .... title, quoted, 445
Sea-men and Land-soldiers, Song of the .... title, quoted, 399
Season, A Word in .... title, 58, 140
Second Part of the Scotch Wedding.... .... title, mentioned, 183
Secret Lover, The .... title, mentioned, 200, 205
Sequels to " I loved you dearly " and other ballads 27, 28, 789, 791
Sequels to Love's Lamentable Tragedy various titles, 82, 83, 85, 87

PAGE
Serving-Man, The Lady turn'd .... sub-title, 567
Serving-Man, The Love-sick .... title, 26, 148, 149, 263
Serving-Man's Good Fortune, William the sub-title, mentioned, 263
Serving-Men, The Famous Flower of .... title, 567
Sex, Rare News for the Female .... title, mentioned, 237
Shackley Hay .... tune, mentioned, 557
Shaking of the Sheets, The (= "Can you dance," etc.) ..... tune, 750, 753
" Shall I, shall I? No, no, no!" .... title, 152, 156, 157
" Shall I wasting in despair." (By George Wither.) ..... mentioned, 296
Shall we go dance the Round, around? etc. .... burden, 364
Shape, A Monstrous .... title, mentioned, 64, 208
Shapeless Monster, A .... sub-title, mentioned, 64, 208
She raise and loot me in .... burden and title, 197
She rose and let me in .... burden and tune, 188, 197, 203
" She sailed west, she sailed east" (fragmentary) .... mentioned, 612
Sheets, The Shaking of the (see "Shaking") .... tune, 750, 753
Shepherd and Kind Shepherdess, The Coy .... sub-title, 128
Shepherd crown'd with good Success, The .... sub-title, 153
Shepherd made happy, The Languishing ..... sub-title, quoted, 102
Shepherd on his Pipe, The Old .... title, 318
Shepherd Phaon's Petition to beautiful Phillis, The loving ..... title, 101, 143
Shepherd, The Faithful..... .... title, 170, 174
Shepherd, The Loving .... title, 142, 143
Shepherd, The Mournful .... title, 61, 62
Shepherd, The Unkind .... sub-title, mentioned, 130
Shepherd Tom, The Old Ballet of .... title, mentioned, 601
Shepherdess, The Coy .... title, mentioned, 108
Shepherdess, The Dying .... title, mentioned, 133
Shepherdess, The Forsaken .... sub-title, 47
Shepherdess, The Hard-hearted .... sub-title, 224
Shepherdess, The Lamenting .... title, mentioned, 130
Shepherdess, The Surprised .... title, mentioned, 170
Shepherdess, The Wanton .... sub-title, 131
Shepherd's Complaint, The .... title, 170, 232
Shepherd's Delight, The .... title, mentioned, 66
Shepherd's Glory, The .... title, 268; given, 269
Shepherd's Last Legacy, The Unhappy ..... sub-title, mentioned, 130
Shepherd's Love-Passion Song, The .... sub-title, 105
Shepherd's Slumber, The .... title, quoted, 650
Shepherd's Vindication, The Wronged .... sub-title, 50
Shepherd's Wooing of Fair Dulcina, The .... title, 164, 166
Sheriff-muir, The Race of the .... title, quoted, 617
Shiftless Student, The .... alternative title, 450, 455; given, 456
Shilling, The Last (Charles Dibdin's) ..... title, mentioned, 690
" Shining stars are Celia's eyes" 152
Ship-Carpenter's love to the Merchant's Daughter of Bristol title, m., 428
Shoe-maker of Jerusalem, The (see "Wandering Jew") ..... title, 688, 693
Shoe-maker Outwitted, The .... title, mentioned, 32
Shooting of the Gun at Court, The Dangerous ..... title, mentioned, 389
" Should you be passing through the Weald of Kent" ..... *Prelude*, vii*
Shrewsbury for me! burden, title, and tune, 280, 359, 588, 359, 414
Shrewsbury (I would give a thousand pounds thou wert in) burden, 280, 281
" Shut the door after me, pull off the boule!" .... quoted, 218
Sick, [sick], and very sick .... tune, mentioned, 389
" Sick, sick, in grave I would I were!" ..... title, mentioned, 389
" Sighs and groans, and melancholy moans" ..... and tune, 115, 296, 297

PAGE
"Since her beauty's grown a snare" 145
"Since 'It was in the prime of Cucumber-time'" *Editorial Intermezzo*, 310
Sing *Honi soit qui mal y pense* .... burden, 726, 727
"Sing we seamen now and then" .... mentioned, 422; given, 423
"Sir, do not think these words have flowed" 19
"Sir Drake, whom well the world's end knew" 376
Sir Eglamour .... title and tune, mentioned, 136, 495
"Sir Francis, Sir Francis, Sir Francis is come" 377
Sir Guy of Warwick (see 'Guy') .... ballads on, 732 to 737
Sir Martin Frobisher (see 'Frobisher') ..... ballads and poems on, 398
"Sir Walter Raleigh has built a ship, *in the Netherland*" 421
"Sitting beyond (= by yonder) a river side" ..... and tune, 46, 47
"Six long years have I served of my time" 245
Slave's Releasement, The Algiers .... title, 110, 447
Slee willy Ste'nson, and *pretty Peggy Benson* ..... burdens, mentioned, 292
Slighted Maid, The .... title, mentioned, 276
Slighted Virgin, The .... title, mentioned, 237
Slumber, The Shepherd's .... title, quoted, 650
Smith, Ned (see 'Smith, The wofull,' etc.) ..... tune, 280, 281, 681
Smith, The Industrious .... title, mentioned, 485, 542
Smith, The wofull Lamentation of Edward ..... title, mentioned, 280
So I am resolved, as long as I live to be a Good-Fellow still ..... burden, 245
So little value that false creature Man ..... burden, varies, 47
So sweet is the Lass that loves me burden, sub-title, and tune, 217, 762, 763
Solace, Love's .... title, quoted, 218
Soldier his Repentance, The .... part title, 283, 284, 307
Soldier, The King and the .... title, 786
Soldier, The Valiant .... tune, 387
Soldiers, Ballad of Encouragement to English ..... title, mentioned, 381
Soldiers of the North, The Courageous ..... title, mentioned, 606
Soldier's Return, The .... title, mentioned, 99
Solomon and Balkis (Queen of Sheba), Browning's title, quoted, 746
"Some thirty, or forty, or fifty at least" 55
"Some years of late, in 'Eighty-eight" 379
Somersetshire Lady, The .... title, mentioned, 33
Something like a Martyr .... title of *Prelude*, vii*
Song, A New .... title, 624, 625
Song by a Person of Honour .... title, 31
Song by Tom D'Urfey, A .... title, 617
Song for the Wandering Jew (Wordsworth's) ..... title, quoted, 692
Song in John Lyly's "Sappho and Phao," A Three-part ..... given, 467
Song in Praise of the Leather Bottél .... title, 470
Song in Sir Charles Sedley's Comedy, "The Mulberry-Garden" 130
Song made by a Soldier whose bringing up had been dainty ..... title, 284
Song of a Beggar and a King, A .... title, 658, 659
Song of Captain Ward, The Seaman's title, 422, 425, 779; given, 784
Song of Dansekar the Dutchman, The Seaman's ..... title, 423
Song of Prayer and Progress, A new ..... title, mentioned, 381
Song of the Sea-men and Land-soldiers ..... title, quoted, 399
Song of the Wandering Jew .... title, 779
Song on Sir Martin Frobisher, A sorrowful ..... title, mentioned, 398
Song on the Lady G—— by Tom D'Urfey 152
Song to a Beautiful but very proud Lady (D'Urfey's) ..... title, 58, 59
Sorrow at Parting with Henry, A new Song of Nelly's ..... title, 283, 789
Sorrowful Song on Sir Martin Frobisher, A ..... title, mentioned, 398
Sound the trumpets, beat the drums, etc. ..... burden varies, 446

PAGE

Spaniard, Dialogue between an Englishman and a ..... title, 657
Spaniards, A Pin for the .... registered title, mentioned, 398
Spaniards, Victory obtained over the ..... title, mentioned, 384
Spanish Armada, The (from "The Siege of Curzola") ..... title, 383
Spanish Lady's Love, The ..... title, 653, 655, 657, 672, 683
Spanish Navy, The late distress sustained by the ..... title, 382
Spanish Tragedy, A new .... title, mentioned, 428
Spanish Tragedy, The .... title, mentioned, 547
Spendthrifts, A Caveat for all .... part-title, 343
Spittle-fields, Strange and Wonderful News from ..... sub-title, 6
Spring's Glory, The .... *Introd. Notes*, xxi, 108, 136, 137
Squire, The Faithful .... title, mentioned, 28
Squire, The Frantic .... title, 225
Squire, The Last Lamentations of the Languishing title, 170, 221; given, 228
Squire's Grief crowned with Comfort, The .... title, 226
Stable Groom (see "Draw near, young maidens") book-trade title, 263
Stand thy ground, Old Harry! .... tune, mentioned, 252
Standing Toast, The (="The moon on the Ocean," C.D.'s) title, quoted, 790
"State and Ambition, alas! will deceive you" ment., and tune, 119, 120, 122
Steh' ich in finst 'rer Mitternacht .... tune, 699
Stella and Adonis, The Loves of .... sub-title, mentioned, 188
Step-mother's Cruelty, The .... sub-title, 651
Still she answered, "No, no, no!" .... burden, 157
Stormy winds do blow (When the) burden and tune, 428, 431, 432, 797
"Stout Seamen, come away!" .... mentioned, 639
Strange Alterations .... sub-titles, 456
Strange and Cruel Whips, etc, The..... part of title, 382; given, 387
Strange and Wonderful News from Spittlefields..... ..... sub-title, 6
Strange News from the Narrow Seas, More ..... sub-title, mentioned, 428
Strange News out of Germany, etc., Wonderful..... ..... title, 688
"Strange News to England lately came" .... mentioned, 108
Street Musician (Wordsworth's "An Orpheus") ..... quoted, 522
Strephon and Chloris .... title, 123, 127, 128
Strephon, The Loves of Damon and..... .... title, 152, 153
Strephon, Unfortunate .... title, mentioned, 130
"Strephon vowed and swore to be" .... mentioned, 127
Strephon's Answer to Flora's Complaint .... title, 99
"Strike up, you lusty Gallants!" 426
Stubborn Lover Catch'd, The .... title, mentioned, 133
Student, The Shiftless ..... alternative title, ment., 450, 455; given, 456
Subject's Satisfaction, The .... title, mentioned, 82
Subject's Wish, The Loyal .... title, mentioned, 224
Subtle Damosel's Advice, The .... title, mentioned, 177, 199
Successful Lover, The .... title, mentioned, 218, 220
Sufferings, The gallant Seaman's .... sub-title, 431, 432
"Sum speike of lords, sum spekis of lairds" .... quoted, 603
Summer time (properly, 'In Summer time,' *q.v.*) tune, 567, 570, 789
Summer's Pride abated .... sub-title, 103
"Susan, my heart's delight!" .... mentioned, 639
Susan of Ashford, The Kentish Yeoman and ..... title, mentioned, 639
Sussex Tragedy, The (="Young men and maidens") title, mentioned, 27
Swain made happy, The Languishing title, mentioned, 26 to 29, 224, 793
Swain, The Languishing ..... title and tune, 26 to 29, 224, 793
Swearers, The Thunderbolt against .... title, mentioned, 389
"Sweet England's Prize is gone! *Well-a-day!*"..... ..... mentioned, 623
"Sweet, if thou wilt be, as I am to thee" 277

PAGE

Sweet is the Lass that loves me (=" So sweet") ..... tune, 762, 763
" Sweet Nelly, my heart's delight" .... mentioned, 520
" Sweet, open the door, and let me come in !" 209
" *Sweet Phillida, be kind !* .... burden, 76
" Sweet, use your time, abuse your time" ..... and tune, 58, 140
" Sweet Virgin, hath disdain moved you to passion ?" 255
" Sweet William and Pretty Betty" .... mentioned, 368
Sweet William's Dream on his Wedding-night .... sub-title, 611
" Sweet Willie and fair Annie sat a' day on a hill" ..... mentioned, 644
Sweet Willie (=" My husband builded me a bower") title, mentioned, 570
" Sweet, youthful, charming Ladies fair" 672, 676
Swimming Lady, The (*Bagford Ballad*) .... title, 557
Sylvia, The fond Lover's Lamentation for the Unkindness of sub-title, 24

TABLE ROUND, The noble acts of Arthur of the ..... title, 722
Table, The Oak (Tom Dibdin's "I had knock'd out the dust") t. m. 690
Tailor, The Trapann'd .... title, quoted, 300
Tailor, Tom (see "Tom") .... various titles, 520
Tailor's Wanton Wife of Wapping, The ..... title, mentioned, 236
Take her in the Humour ! .... sub-title, 100
Tam O'Shanter (Burns's) .... title, quoted, 212
Tantara rara, tantiree .... burden and tune, 495, 496, 499
Tantara rara (modernised form of *Tandara te* : see '*Raderer tu*'), 404, 405
Tantara rara, The Seaman's .... tune, 401 to 403
Tantiree (see "*Tantara rara, tantiree*") b. and tune, 495, 496, 499, 501, 505
Tarleton's Farewell .... title, mentioned, 382
Tarleton's Medley .... tune, mentioned, 745
" Tender hearts of London City" and tune, 7, 79, 80, 83, 85, 89, 92, 93, 96, 98, 99
" Thanksgiving unto God for His mercy, A Ballad of" title, mentioned, 384
That God above .... variation, mentioned, 469
That no body else shall enjoy thee but I .... burden, 73
" That time of year when the enamour'd Sun" .... mentioned, 376
" That Tyrant Girl ! that Tyrant Girl !" (probably by F. C. Burnand) q. 88
The Angel Gabriel .... burden and tune, 428, 429
" The bonniest Lass in all the Land" .... mentioned, 397
The bonny Broom, the well-favour'd Broom, etc. ..... burden, 586
The cannons roar (see "Hark ! I hear the cannons roar") ..... tune, 284
The Clans are coming .... tune, 623
The clean contrary way .... burden and tune, mentioned, 339
" The damask Rose, nor Lily fair" .... and tune, quoted, 218
The Fair One let me in tu. and b., 177, 188, 189, 191, 195, 199, 249, 350 to 352
The flower of all the Nation .... burden, 284
" The four and twenty day of June" .... mentioned, 557
" The gallant Esquire named before" .... mentioned, 27
" The George-Aloe and the Sweep-stake too" 409
" The George Alow came from the South" 408
" The Gordian Knot which true lovers knit" (Second Part), mentioned, 123
The Humour of dal derra rara, etc. .... burden, 513
The Hunt is up .... tune, 627, 650
" The Hunt is up, the Hunt is up !" (as quoted by the Wedderburns), 627
The Invincible Spanish Armada .... burden, 383
" The Lady of Northamptonshire" .... mentioned, 27
" The Lord of Hosts hath blest our land" .... mentioned, 643
The Love in Joy my heart (*not yet found*) perhaps a first line, mentioned, 280
" The Love that I had chosen" .... mentioned, 442
The Maid is best that lies alone .... burden and tune, 474

PAGE
The Maid is the best that lies alone (bis) .... burden, mentioned, 326
"The Man in the Moon drinks claret" .... quoted, 317
"The night her blackest sable wore" 177, 195
"The night her silent sable wore" 197
"The night is my departing night" 600
"The passions of Love are too great and too cruel" .... mentioned, 122
"The Perse owt of Northomberlande" .... quoted, 739
The purest wine so brisk and fine, etc. .... burden, 320
"The Queen fell sick, and very very sick" (and "The Queen's fa'en") m., 679
The Rant, dal derra rara, etc. burden and tune, 509, 513, 514, 516, 519
"The Robin cam' to the Wren's nest, an' keekit in, an keekit in" 204
"The Spheres are dull, and do not make" 61
"The story of King Arthur old is very memorable" .... quoted, 726
"The sweetest Saint incensed may be" .... 19; given, 585
The want of my dear (Betty) is worse than a grave burden, varies, 447
"The ways on Earth have paths and turnings known" 404
The Wayzgoose of Hertfordshire .... burden intermittent, 310
"The week before Easter, the day being fair" .... and tune, 229, 230, 235
"The winter it is past, and the Summer come at last" 240
"The Wren she lies in Care's [Carey's] bed" 304
"The young King stands by his palace gate" .... quoted, 660
"Their sails were spread, and anchor weigh'd" 789
Then come and go with thy Love all the world over .... burden, 295
Then Covetousness out of England will run .... and tune, 5, 6
Then Presbyter Jack out of England will run .... burden, 6
"There is a lad in our town" 177, 186
"There lately was a maiden fair" .... quoted, 766, 772
"There lived in Bristol city fair" ....mentioned, 428; given, 441
"There was a bold Seaman, a ship he could steer" .... mentioned, 229
"There was a brisk Lass" .... mentioned, 531
"There was a damsel young and fair" .... mentioned, 27
"There was a gallant ship, and a gallant ship was she" .... quoted, 419
"There was a Lass in our town" (*bis*) .... mentioned, 292, 294
"There was a Lord of worthy fame" 651
"There was a maid, as I heard tell" .... mentioned, 64
"There was a maiden fair and clear" .... mentioned, 27
"There was a poor man lived in Somersetshire" .... mentioned, 33
"There was a youth, and a well-beloved youth" 243
"There was an a bonny young Lad" .... and tune, 171, 174
"There was an a bonny young Lass" .... mentioned, 170
"There was an Exciseman so fine" .... mentioned, 170
"There was, I tell you, a faithful young Squire" .... mentioned, 28
"There were four and twenty gentlemen" .... mentioned, 630
"There's some say that we won" .... quoted, 617
These things must be, if we sell Ale .... burden, quoted, 485
"They err who say, 'Those years are fled.'" .... *Editorial motto*, *
This is call'd, "Maids, look about you!" .... title, mentioned, 318
"This wilderness is a place full of bliss" .... mentioned, 328
Thomas and Fair Annie, Lord .... title, quoted, 644
Thomas and Fair Eleanor, Lord (Two ballads on) .... title 640 to 647
Thomas, Lord (from "The Cigar") .... title, mentioned, 644; tune, 647
"Thomas, why come you not hither to see me?" .... mentioned, 639
Thomasine and Fair Ellinor, Lord .... garbled title, quoted, 649
"*Thou shalt married be!*" .... burden, 218
"Thou that loved'st once, now lovest no more" .... mentioned, 296
Though Father angry be .... alternative tune, mentioned, 254

PAGE
"Though the torrents from their fountains" .... mentioned, 692
"Though the Tyrant hath ravish'd," etc. (see also, "Now the Tyrant") 69
Thracia, A Gentleman in .... title, mentioned, 650
Three Daughters, King Lear and his (see "Lear") ..... title, 714, 717
Three notorious Witches (see Witchcraft) .... sub-title, 706
Three-part Song, in John Lyly's "Sapho and Phao" ..... given, 467
Three Pilgrims, The .... tune, 515
Three Slips for a Tester' (*i.e.* testern) semi-title, mentioned, 232, 233
"Through the cool shady woods" = Cupid's Courtesy mentioned, 252, 253, 255
Throgmarton, the late Treasons conspired by Francis title, mentioned, 389
Thunderbolt against Swearers, The .... title, mentioned, 389
Thuret's Dream .... title, mentioned, 446
"Thursday in the morn, the Ides of May" .... mentioned, 368
Tide, Love's..... .... tune and title, 567, 570, 774
Tilbury, A Joyful Song of Receiving the Queen into ..... title, 381, 393
Tilbury, The Queen's visiting of the Camp at .... title, 381, 390
"Till from Leghorn I do return" .... mentioned, 177, 199
Times, A Review of the (Thomas Jordan's) ..... title, mentioned, 328
Time's Alteration .... title, mentioned, 276
Times, The Mirror of the .... sub-title, mentioned, 356
Times, The Peerless Paragon .... sub-title, mentioned, 356
"'Tis a pitiful thing that now-a-days, Sir" .... quoted, 469
'*'Tis for the love of thee I die, Jenny, Jenny!*' ..... burden, quoted, 294
"*'Tis good to be merry and wise*" .... burden varies, 1, 216, 217
'Tis Money that makes a Man .... title, 346
Titus and Gisippus .... title, mentioned, 571
"To all Good-Fellows I'll declare" .... 315; given, 475
"To all Good-Fellows now I mean to sing a song" ..... given, 493
"To all Good-Fellows now I'll plainly shew" ..... mentioned, 315, 474
"To every faithful Lover" (= The Valiant Virgin) 1st line, not mentioned, 431
"To God alone let us all Glory give" (Title lost)..... ..... mentioned, 445
"To thee, loving Roger, this letter I write" .... mentioned, 33
Toast the Standing (in C. Dibdin's "Round Robin," 1811) quoted, 790
Tom Taylor and his wife Joan .... sub-title, mentioned, 520
Tom Tell-Troth .... title, 501
"Tom the Tailor near the Strand" .... mentioned, 520
Tom, the old ballet of Shepherd .... title, mentioned, 601
Tom Thumb, The History of .... ballad title, mentioned, 542
"Too long have I been a drunken sot" twice quoted (inadvertently), 336, 465
Toper's Advice, The Merry .... sub-title, 502
Torment of Loving and not being loved again, The ..... sub-title, 62
Touch and Go .... title, mentioned, 328
Tragedy, A new Spanish .... title, mentioned, 428
Tragedy, Fair Eleanor's..... .... sub-title, 645
Tragedy, Love's Lamentable (and the Young Man's Answer) titles, 79 to 83
Tragedy of Hero and Leander, The .... title, 556, 558
Tragedy of Sir Richard Grenville, the most Hon. title, mentioned, 376
Tragedy, The Bristol .... title, mentioned, 27
Tragedy, The Cook-maid's .... title, mentioned, 33
Tragedy, The Damosel's .... title, mentioned, 28
Tragedy, The Esquire's..... .... title, mentioned, 27
Tragedy, The Lady Isabella's .... title, 650, 651, 683
Tragedy, The Lady's (and Answer to it) ..... title, mentioned, 639
Tragedy, The Leicestershire .... title, mentioned, 27
Tragedy, The Lover's .... title, mentioned, 28
Tragedy, The Oxfordshire ..... title, mentioned, 28

PAGE

Tragedy, The Spanish .... title, mentioned, 547
Tragedy, The Sussex .... title, mentioned, 27
Tragedy, The Virgin's .... title, mentioned, 177
Tragedy, The Young Lady's .... title, mentioned, 236
Tragical History of King Lear and his Three Daughters title, 709, 712, 717
Trappan, Cupid's .... tune, 525, 526, 528, 529
Trapann'd Tailor, The .... title, quoted, 300
Treachery of the Wicked. A Song wherein is cont. the title, mentioned, 384
Treasons conspired by Francis Throgmorton, The late title, mentioned, 389
Treue Liebe (Volksweise) .... tune, 698
Trial of True-Love, A .... title, 292, 293
Trials and Condemnation of Three Notorious Witches, The sub-title, 706
Tricatees French (*bis*) .... tune, 489, 492
Triumph and Joy .... tune, 393, 397, 398
Triumph at an End, The .... title, 75, 76
Triumph, Love in .... alternative sub-title, 289
"Triumph, O England! and rejoice" .... mentioned, 375
Triumph over Bashfulness, Love's .... title, mentioned, 127
Triumph, Russell's .... tune, mentioned, 156
Triumph showed before the Queen and French Embassadors title, ment., 397
Triumph, The Bachelor's (*recovered ends* of lines) .... title, 788
Triumph, The Royal .... title, mentioned, 367
Troy, The Wandering Prince of .... title, 539, 547, 548
Troy Town (see properly "When Troy town") .... tune, 547, 552, 553, 767
True Blue the Plough-man .... title, 520, 531, 532
True Love (see "Love" *passim*).
True Love, A Pattern of .... title and sub-title, 681 to 683
True Love, A Trial of .... title, 292, 293
True Love Exalted .... title, 93
True Love Requited .... title, 243
True Love rewarded with Loyalty (see "Love rewarded") title, given, 260
True Love without deceit .... title, 123, 126, 127, 199
True Lover's Admonition .... title, 217, 219
"True Love's a sweet passion" .... mentioned, 33
Truth's Integrity .... title, quoted, 123
Turn Love, I prithee Love, turn to me! ....burden and tune, 276 to 278
Turtle Dove, The .... title, mentioned, 307
"'Twas a youthful knight" (see "It was a youthful") .... given, 57
"'Twas within a furlong of Edinburgh town" .... mentioned, 236
"'Twas within a mile of Edinburgh town" (original) .... mentioned, 236
Twitcher, The Maid's .... tune, 528
Two Lovers (various: see "Lovers") titles, 237, 250, 296, 364, 559
"Two Lovers by chance they did meet" .... mentioned, 170
Two-penny-worth of Wit for a Penny .... title, 479, 482; given, 483
Two to One is Odds .... sub-title, 101
Two Unfortunate Lovers, The .... sub-title, 558; title, 559, 560
Tyranness Defeated, The .... sub-title, 76
Tyrannical Beauty, The.... .... title, 145
Tyrant, The (see "Now the Tyrant" and "Tho' the Tyrant") tune, 64 to 70

UNCHANGEABLE Boatswain, The .... sub-title, 447
Unchangeable Lovers, The .... title, 418; given, 795
Undaunted Seaman, The (reserved for vol. vii.) title, mentioned, 148
"Under a pleasant Willow shade" 50
Unequal Match, The .... title, mentioned, 33
Unequal Match'd Couple, The .... sub-title, mentioned, 276

PAGE

Unfortunate Concubine, The .... title, 672, 676
Unfortunate Forester, The .... title, 640, 643 to 645
Unfortunate Lady, Answer to the .... mention, omitted from 72
Unfortunate Lady, The (*cf.* "What dismal") .... title, mentioned, 27
Unfortunate Love of Lord Thomas and Fair Eleanor .... title, 647
Unfortunate Lovers, The Two .... sub-title, 558; title, 559, 560
Unfortunate Loves of Hero and Leander, The .... title, 559, 560
Unfortunate Strephon .... title, mentioned, 130
"Unfortunate Strephon, well may'st thou complain!" 126, 127
Unfortunate Voyage of Two Lovers, The sub-title, mentioned, 364, 368
Unkindness of Strephon, The Forsaken Nymph's Complaint of the t. m., 127
Unlearned men hard matters out can find, etc. .... sub-title, 750, 751
Up the green forest .... tune, 525, 528
Usurpation of Cupid's throne, On the .... title, 119

VALIANT Commander and his Resolute Lady, The .... title, 279, 283
"Valiant Protestant Boys!" .... mentioned, 367
Valiant Seaman's Congratulation, The .... title, quoted, 431
"Valiant Sir Guy bestirs his hands" (fragments).... 737
Valiant Soldier, The .... tune, 387
Valiant Virgin, The ("To every faithful Lover") title, mentioned, 431
Vanity, The Golden .... title, 419
Verses made by the Earl of Essex in his trouble .... title, 404
Verses of a Baker and a Meal-man .... title, mentioned, 237
Victoria's Song (in Sir Charles Sedley's 'Mulberry-Garden') given, 130
Victory obtain'd against the Dutch Fleet, The Royal title, 368; given, 435
Victory obtained, Love's.... .... title, mentioned, 283
Victory obtain'd by the Centurion of London registered title, ment., 398
Victory obtain'd by the young Earl of Essex, A.... .... sub-title, 405
Victory, The Seaman's (*Bagford Ballad*) .... title, mentioned, 368
Vienna (*i.e.* the Siege of Vienna, 1683) .... tune, 286
Vindication against the Virgin's Complaint, The Young Man's title, 252, 255
Vindication, Jockey's .... sub-title, 170, 171
Vindication of a departed Maidenhead .... sub-title, mentioned, 218
Vindication of Top-Knots, The London Lady's .... title, mentioned, 35
Vindication, The Merry-Gossip's .... title, quoted, 482
Vindication, The Wronged Shepherd's .... sub-title, 50
Virgin, The Distressed .... title, mentioned, 105
Virgin, The Doubting .... tune and title, 152, 155 to 157
Virgin, The Necessitated .... title, mentioned, 236
Virgin, The Slighted .... title, mentioned, 237
Virgin, The Valiant (="To every faithful Lover") title, ment., quoted, 431
Virginity grown Troublesome .... title, 236, 246
Virgin's Complaint, The Young-man's Vindication against the title, 252, 255
Virgin's Tragedy, The .... title, mentioned, 177
Virtuous Maid's Resolution, The .... title, mentioned, 274
Vision, Cupid's .... sub-title, mentioned, 148
"Vivat Rex noster nobilis" (=Chevy Chase) .... mentioned, 739
"Voilà dix-huit cents ans et plus" .... mentioned, 692
Vow, A pleasant ditty of a Maiden's.... .... title, mentioned, 557
Voyage of Two Lovers, The Unfortunate sub-title, mentioned, 364, 368
Voyage to New Barbary, Captain Glen's Unhappy (vol. vii.) title, m., 410

WADE'S REFORMATION (*Bagford Ballad*) title, quoted, 336, 465, 469
Waddle, Will (G. Colman's 'Who hath e'er been to London') m. 224
Wager, The Frollicsome .... title, mentioned, 509

PAGE
"Walking in a pleasant Garden" .... mentioned, 283
Walter Raleigh (see "Raleigh," and "Sir Walter") 417, 421
Wandering Jew, A Song for the (Wordsworth's) title, mentioned, 692
Wandering Jew, Complaint of the (French original) title, 690, 692; g., 691
Wandering Jew (Leland's translation of the German) .... title, 779
Wandering Jew, The (original German Ahasver) 690, 778; given, 699
Wandering Jew (News from Germany of the) title, 650, 687, 690; g. 693
Wandering Jew's Chronicle, The .... title, 690, 695; continuation, 698
Wandering Prince and Princess, The .... title, 101, 664
Wandering Prince of Troy (Æneas), The .... title, 539, 547, 548, 551
Wandering Prince, The (1564-65) .... title, mentioned, 551
Wantley, Moor of Moor Hall and the Dragon of title, mentioned, 725
Wanton Shepherdess, The .... sub-title, 134
Wanton Willie .... tune, mentioned, 300
Wapping, The Love-Sick Maid of .... title, mentioned, 177, 199
Wapping, The Seaman's Complaint for his Unkind Mistress at title, m., 27
Wapping, The Tailor's Wanton Wife of .... title, mentioned, 236
Ward, Captain .... tune (not "Lusty Gallants"), 426, 427
Ward, The Seaman's Song of Captain title, 422, 425, 779; given, 784
Ward's Fight with the Rainbow, Captain title, 375, 422, 426, 427, 784
Warning for Married Women, A .... title, mentioned, 650
Warning to all Corn-hoarders, A .... title, mentioned, 534
Warning to all false Traitors by example of Fourteen title, mentioned, 398
Warning to all Tailors to beware how they marry, A sub-title, quoted, 300
Warning to Maidens, A.... .... title, mentioned, 650
Warning to Parents, A .... sub-title, mentioned, 27
Wars (Drayton's), The Civil .... title, mentioned, 668
Wars, The Greeks' and Trojans' .... title, 542, 543, 559
Warwick Castle, Lord Wigmore sometime the Governor of part-title, 761, 767
Warwick, pleasant Song of the acts of Guy of .... title, 732
Warwick, Sir Guy of (see Guy) .... title, 542, 559, 734
"Was ever Maiden so scorn'd?" .... mentioned, 276
Was ever man (for Lady's sake) .... tune, 734
"Was ever man so tost in love?" .... and tune, 732
"Was ever young noble so tortured as I?" .... mentioned, 33
"'Was this fair face the cause,' quoth she" 545
"We be three poor Mariners, newly come from the seas" 364
"We that are bonny country-girls" .... mentioned, 199
"We that do lead a country life" .... mentioned, 177
"We Seamen are the bonny boys!" 399
Weaver, The West-country .... title, mentioned, 32
Wedding, The Scotch (and Answer to it) .... sub-title, 178, 183
Wedding, The West-Country ("Come all you") title, mentioned, 32
Wedding, The West-Country ("Now listen") .... title, mentioned, 170
Weep, weep.... .... tune, mentioned, 388, 389
"Weep, weep, still I weep," etc. .... quoted, 389
Welcome home from France, The True Lover's .... sub-title, 65
"Welcome, my dearest, with joy now I see thee" .... mentioned, 119
Welcome, sweet Death! the kindest friend I have" .... quoted, 407
Well-a-day! .... tune, 623
We'll drink this old Ale no more, no more .... burden and tune, 485, 486
"Well met, my Susan sweet, whom I do adore" .... mentioned, 28
Well met, neighbour! .... title, mentioned, 276
"Wert thou much fairer than thou art" .... tune, 470, 774
West-country Damosel's Complaint, The .... title, 635
West-country Nymph, The .... title, mentioned, 428; given, 441

PAGE
West-country tune, A pleasant new .... tune, 246, etc.
West-country Weaver, The .... title, mentioned, 32
West-country Wedding, The (=" Come all you old Bakers ") title, m., 32
West-country Wedding (=" Now listen, and be not mistaken ") title, m., 170
West-country Wonder, The .... title, mentioned, 263
West, Sir William of the .... title, 638, 639
West, The Faithful Lovers of the .... title, 18; given, 257
West, The Witty Maid of the .... title, mentioned, 161
Wet and Weary .... tune, 318, 319
" What an innocent loving life" .... mentioned, 66
" What! Ash-Wednesday, and not come to Church?" (*Trowbesh*) *Preface*, xvi*
" What dismal tidings do I hear?" (omitted to be mentioned as No. 5*) 27
" What if a day, or a month, or a year" first line and tune, mentioned, 623
" What need we brag or boast at all of Arthur and his Knights?" quoted, 726
" What Protestant can now forbear" .... mentioned, 148
" What shall I do, in this deep distress?" .... mentioned, 236
What shall I do, shall I die a maid? .... burden, 236, 238
What shall I do, shall I die for love? burden and tune, 236, 238, 245, 246
What shall I do, to show how much I love her? tune, mentioned, 236
" What shall my viol silent be?" 608
" What strange affections" .... mentioned, 505
" What's this, my dearest Nanny?" .... mentioned, 237
" When Arthur first in Court began".... .... 720, 721
" When as in fair Jerusalem" 693
" When as King Henry ruled this land" 672, 673
When busy Fame o'er all the plain tu., 102, 103, 177, 183, 184, 177, 191, 199
" When Cupid's fierce and powerful dart" .... mentioned, 177, 199
" When daisies pied, and violets blue" .... mentioned, 307
" When Diaphantus knew the Destinies decreet" 775
" When Dido found that Æneas would not come" 547
" When first Amintas charm'd my heart" 115
" When first on my Phillis I cast my eye" 143
" When first the gracious God of heaven" .... mentioned, 388
" When first the post arrived at my tent" .... mentioned, 671
" When first thy feature and thy face" 19
" When Flora she had deck'd" .... mentioned, 307
" When Flora with her fragrant flowers" .... mentioned, 367
When Flying Fame tune, 183, 667, 672, 714, 722, 727, 743, 750
" When God had taken for our sins" .... mentioned, 547
" When Greeks and Romans fell at strife" (*delete* comma) 553
" When I do travel in the night" .... quoted, 336
When I have no want of money .... second burden, 499
" When I smoke, I sees in my Pipe".... 318
" When I survey the world around" .... variation, mentioned, 469
" When I went early in the Spring" .... mentioned, 27
" When Israel did first begin" .... mentioned, 686
" When I've a saxpence under my thumb" .... quoted, 342
When Love with unconfined wings .... tune, mentioned, 557
" When meat and drink is great plenty" .... mentioned, 733
" When Musidorus fell in love" 664
" When my hairs they grow hoary" .... mentioned, 507
" When Phœbus addrest (=had dress'd) his course" .... quoted, 557
" When Phœbus bright the azure skies" (line 8, read " *Ceres*' sel'") 607
" When Phœbus with his glittering beams" .... mentioned, 99, 199
When Popery out of this nation shall run .... burden, mentioned, 5
" When Sol could cast no light" .... mentioned, 367

PAGE
" When the British warrior Queen " .... quoted, 388
" When the heart of Hope is dry and crush'd within us " *Editorial Envoi*, 448
When the King enjoys his own again .... burden, quoted, 323
When this old cap was new .... tune, mentioned, 276
" When Tommy became first a Lover " .... mentioned, 170, 174
" When Troy town for ten years' wars " and tune, 547, 548, 552, 553, 767
" When we all grow so rigidly moral " .... *Editorial Intermezzo*, 449
" When will you marry me, William ? " 635
" When William, Duke of Normandy " 695
Whigmore, Lord (see, also, Wigmore) .... part-title, 761, 767, 771
While I have ears and you a tongue, etc. .... burden, 61
While Mock-Beggar Hall stands empty .... burden, 218, 763
Whim-wham (=" Our gardens you find ") .... *Edit. Cave-Canem*, viii*
Whips, etc., The Strange and Cruel (Spanish Armada) part-title, 382, 387
" Whither away, good neighbour ? " .... mentioned, 276
Whittington Defeat, The sub-title, mentioned, 713, 774; given, 777
" Who is at my window, who, who ? " (see " Quho is at my windo ? ") q., 201
Whittington's Advancement, Sir Richard .... title, mentioned, 280
Who list to lead a Soldier's life .... tune, mentioned, 613
" Who that antique story reads " .... mentioned, 688
" Who will may foot it here with me " .... *Editorial Prelude*, xxxi
" Who's here so ingenious, mis-spending his time ? " 170
" Who's that at my chamber-door ? " 201
" Why are my eyes still flowing ? " .... tune, 319, 535, 536
" Why do we boast of Arthur and his Knights ? " 725, 780
" Why do you boast of Arthur and his Knights ? " 725, 780
" Why is my Love unkind ? " .... mentioned, 639
" Why should friends and kindred gravely make thee " 13
" Why should I not complain of thee ? " .... mentioned, 27, 28
" Why should I thus complain of thee ? " .... mentioned, 18
" Why should not I complain on thee ? " .... mentioned, 26, 257
" Why should we boast of Arthur and his Knights ? " 727
" Why should we boast of Lais and her Knights ? " .... quoted, 725
Widow's Wooing, A merry new Song of a rich .... title, quoted, 252
Wife, The Roman (=Roman Charity) alternative title, mentioned, 541, 796
Wigmore, Lord (begins, " All you that ever heard) part title, 547, 766, 767
Wigmore, Lord (begins, " In Warwickshire ") .... part-title, 766, 771
Wilde or Wile (see *Wilson's* and *Wolsey's*) .... tunes, 388, 390
Will Waddle (=Lodging for single gentlemen) .... mentioned, 221
" Will you hear a noble Britain " (parody or mocking) .... mentioned, 672
" Will you hear a Spanish Lady, how she loved an English-man ? " 655
" Will you know why the old Misers adore " 16
William and Margaret (=William's Dream) .... colloquial title, 641
William and Susan, The Happy Agreement of .... sub-title, mentioned, 28
" William and Susan, They happily meeting " .... mentioned, 28
William of the West, Sir ....title, 637 to 639
William the Serving-man's Good-fortune .... sub-title, mentioned, 263
" William the Weaver, that lives in the West " .... mentioned, 161
William's Dream on his Wedding-night, Sweet .... sub-title, 641
Willow turned into Carnation, The .... second sub-title, mentioned, 528
Willie, Sweet (=" My husband builded me a bower ") title, mentioned, 570
Willy and Molly .... title and tune, 218
Wilson's Delight .... tune, mentioned, 388
Wilson's new Tune .... tune, mentioned, 380
Wilson's Wilde, or Wile .... tune, 388, 390
Wilt thou be wilful still, my jo ? .... tune, 170, 171

PAGE
" Wilt thou forsake me thus, and leave me in misery ? " quoted, 280, 681
" Wilt thou from me thus part ? " 681, 773
" Winds now may whistle, and waves may dance to 'em " 411
Winning of Cales, The .... title, 401, 402, 411
Wish, A Young Man's (" If I could but attain ") title, mentioned, 505
Wish, A Young Man's (" What strange affections ") title, mentioned, 505
Wish, Jack Presbyter's .... title, mentioned, 505
Wish, The Loyal Subject's .... title, mentioned, 224
Wish, The Maiden's New .... title, mentioned, 27
Wish, The Old Man's .... title, 505 to 507
Wish, The Old Woman's (" If I live " and " When my hairs ") titles, m., 506
Wit bought at a dear rate ..... title, 276, 315, 468 ; given, 478
Wit for a Penny, Two-pennyworth of ..... title, 479, 482 ; given, 483
Witchcraft Discovered and Punished .... title, 706
Witches' Dance, The .... title, mentioned, 706
Witches, Trial and Condemnation of Three ..... title, mentioned, 706
With a fading (cf. A pudding !) .... burden and tune, 328, 515
With a fal lal la ! .... burden, mentioned, 136
With a hah, hah, hah ! you will undo me burden, mentioned, identified, 283
" With a new flourishing Gallant, newly come to his land " 757
With a Pudding ! .... burden mentioned, and tune, 515
" With brinish tears, with sobbing sighs " .... mentioned, 389
With hey ho, my honey, my heart shall never rue, etc. burden, 489, 491
With hey, with hoe, for and a nony no .... burden, 409
" With sobbing sighs and trickling tears " .... mentioned, 388
" Within a solitary grove despairing Sappho sat " 100
" Within the year of Christ our Lord a thousand," etc. 390
Witty Maid of the West, The .... title, mentioned, 161
Woe be unto Death, and Fortune variable ! .... burden, 786
Wolsey's Wild .... tune, mentioned, 358
Woman Drummer, The Famous (*vide The Kentish Garland*) title, ment., 318
Woman rent by a Devil, Strange News of a ..... title, mentioned, 64
Woman's Wish, The Old (see *Wish*) ..... title, mentioned, 506
Wonder, The West-Country : *bis* .... title, mentioned, 263
Wonder, The World's .... title, mentioned, 108
Wonderful Strange News out of Germany of a Jew ..... title, 688
Woodstock Maze (By William Bell Scott) ..... title, quoted, 672
Woody Choristers, The .... title, 136, 268, 299, 307 ; given, 301
Wooing, A merry new song of a rich Widow's ..... title, quoted, 252
Wooing of fair Dulcina, The Shepherd's .... title, 164, 166
Wooing of the fair Maid of London, Princely ..... title, mentioned, 65
Wooing, The Ploughman's Art of .... title, 526
Wooing, Winning, and Wedding of a fair Damosel, The (Soldier) s.-title, 73
Wooings of Two Country Lovers, The faithful alternative title, ment., 237, 250
Wooings of Two Country Lovers, The pleasant .... title, 250
Word in Season, A .... title, 58, 140
Words of Burn the Violer, The .... title, 608
World's Wonder, The .... title, mentioned, 108
" Would ye have a young Virgin of fifteen years ? " ..... mentioned, 55
Wren, The .... title, 304
Writer of Ballads, What some said of a ....*Cancel-leaf*, xiii*
Wronged Lady, The .... title, mentioned, 33
Wronged Shepherd's Vindication, The .... sub-title, 50

YAROW (=Yarrow), Leader Haughs and .... title, 607
" Ye mariners of England, that guard our native seas " quoted, 431, 796

PAGE
Yeoman and Susan of Ashford, The Kentish ..... title, mentioned, 639
"Yes, perhaps, our tastes are brutal".... (*Trowbesh MS.*) *Preface*, xvii*
York, The Mountebank of .... tune, mentioned, 368
"You are no love for me, Margaret" .... (fragment), 640, 641
"You beauteous Ladies, great and small" 567
"You country damsels, fine and gay"..... 272
"You Gentle-men of England, that live at home at ease" 431, 432, 779, 797
"You have heard of the trolliesome Wager" ..... *Editorial Sequel*, 518
You Ladies of London (properly see 'Ladies of London') tune, ment., 161
"You Lasses of London, attend me" .... mentioned, 170
You London lads, be merry! .... tune, 170, 171
You loyal lovers all ..... tunes (four distinct ballads), mentioned, 115
"You loyal lovers all draw near" (see Bridegroom, Bristol) ..... mentioned, 428
"You loyal lovers attend to my ditty" .... mentioned, 28
"You loyal lovers, far and near" (see Ship-Carpenter) ..... mentioned, 428
"You loyal young damsels, whose lovers are bent" 292, 293
"You maidens" (Open the door!) .... mentioned, 215
"You Muses, guide my quivering quill" .... quoted, 399
"You pretty young men all, come listen to my ditty" 219
"You say I am false, and I freely confess" 43
"You shall enjoy your heart's delight" ..... mentioned, 177, 199
"You subjects of Britton" (=Britain) 621
"You that enjoy your heart's delight" ..... mentioned, 177, 199
"You that have lost your former joys" .... mentioned, 547
"You traitors all that do devise to hurt our Queen," etc. ..... quoted, 398
"You young maids that would live chary" .... mentioned, 326
Young Bateman .... sub-title, mentioned, 650
"Young Coridon, whose stubborn heart" .... mentioned, 133
Young Damsel's Lamentation, The .... title, mentioned, 237
"Young Gallants all, and Ladies fair" .... mentioned, 177
Young Jamie (was a lad) .... tune, 441
Young Lady's Tragedy, The .... title, mentioned, 236
"Young Lovers most discreet and wise" .... mentioned, 27
Young man fitted, The cunning .... sub-title, mentioned, 318
Young man put to his shifts, The ..... title, mentioned, 525, 528, 796
"Young man, remember, delights are but vain!" ..... mentioned, 542
Young man, The Distracted .... title, mentioned, 115
Young man, The Languishing (and Maria's Answer) title, 33; given, 34
Young man's Answer (lamenting Cordelia's death), The ..... title, 564, 565
Young Man's hard shift, The 208, 212, 213
Young man's Labour lost, The .... title, 458
Young man's Lamentation, The .... title, mentioned, 252
Young man's Unkindness, Kind Virgin's Complaint against the title, 253 to 255
Young man's Wish (*bis*: see 'Wish'), The ..... titles, mentioned, 505
"Young married Women, pray attend" .... mentioned, 27
"Young men and maidens, pray draw near" .... mentioned, 27
"Young Phaon sate upon the brink" .... and tune, 7, 100, 101
"Young Phaon strove the bliss to taste" and tune, 7, 100, 101, 130, 661
"Young Strephon fain the bliss," (properly "Young Phaon strove") tune, 130
"Young William met his love" 638, 639
Younger Sister's Lamentation for want of a Husband, The sub-title, 246
Youngest Sister, Crumbs of Comfort for the .... title, 248
Youth and Art (="It once might have been, once only") title, quoted, 658
"You've all heard tell of one Captain Wattle" .... mentioned, 315
"Yt fell abowght the Lamasse tyd" .... mentioned, 739

Finis.

(P.S.)

A Mugwump speaks the Verdict.

"THINK not, because I laugh and jest,
Quaffing at banquets with the best,
I cannot see, or seeing feel,
The woes of those who lack a meal.
My revels are unsought and rare:
Of Banian-days I took my share.

"Think not, because I rave not loud
With all the factions' vicious crowd,
Who preach for Plunder levelling creeds,
I heed no wrongs where victim bleeds.
Too well I know the hateful gang,
Misleaders, who leave dupes to hang.

"Think not that I, with narrow'd mind
Keeping aloof, grow deaf or blind
To gross defects in Church and State,
That crush the Poor, maintain the Great:
But while gaunt Evils thus increase,
I till my little rood in peace.

"Do thine own work! in patience wait,
And leave the Demagogues to prate;
Toil in the Present, none may know
What Future dawns on us below.
Be just and fear not, though thou be
Mis-judged: no hurt can come to thee!"

J. W. EBSWORTH.

Important Notice.

In the twenty years of its existence (founded in 1868, but the *Roxburghe Ballads*, Part 1, not issued until 1869), the Ballad Society has had necessarily to sustain annually a heavy loss in the death of Subscribers; additional to the "dropping away" of payments, by the lukewarmness, fickleness, or abatement of interest in heedless members. From the date when the present Editor first joined the Society (it then being already most wofully weakened, and restricted in funds), he has done his best to carry on the thankless work, keeping it at least to not less than its former rate of progression, but, he hopes, with still more completeness, despite the totally-inadequate support by the Society's funds, required wholly for the expenditure on print and paper. His experience has been enough to damp the courage, and disgust the liking, of any other Editor. Nevertheless, we have here reached successfully the end of the Sixth Volume. *One more volume is needed* to contain the still-remaining ballads (nearly three hundred, unreprinted), and thus *complete befittingly the celebrated ROXBURGHE COLLECTION.*

The Editor (as the sole remaining means of advance in printing) most urgently calls on the diminished number of Subscribers to the Ballad-Society, to enable him (by prompt payment of their subscriptions to the Treasurer, Mr. W. A. Dalziel), to speedily issue Part XX. and other parts of the *final Volume*, with the *General Index* to the whole work; and thus render "The Roxburghe Ballads" a completed work, of eminent historical interest. "The Civil War Ballads" cannot be proceeded with until this, "The Roxburghe Collection" is finished; but there is no encouragement of hope for a fresh undertaking.

His personal friends have nearly all died and left us. The few subscribers who remain might well take the warnings, after so many have been given, and avoid the risk of the *Roxburghe Ballads* being left incomplete, in case the health or life of the Editor should be prematurely ended. Death must come to him as to the others. To no one could he willingly or hopefully transfer his duties; for now that J. P. Collier, William Chappell, and J. O. Halliwell-Phillipps, have passed away (compare *Preface* to this Sixth Volume), there is absolutely no man known to him in England, and certainly not in America, possessing the qualifications to adequately carry on the work, in case death deprived the Members of the willingly-rendered services of their ill-supported friend,

J. Woodfall Ebsworth.

PUBLICATIONS OF THE BALLAD SOCIETY.

These can be had only by the Subscribers.

Annual Subscription of One Guinea, due on the 1st January, each year.

Ballads from Manuscripts. Two Volumes. Edited by F. J. Furnivall, M.A., and W. R. Morfill, M.A. 1868-1873. (Nos. 1, 2, 3, and 10.)

Captain Cox, his Ballads and Books. Re-edited by F. J. Furnivall, M.A., with a separate issue of '**Love-Poems and Humourous Ones**,' by the same. 1871-73. (Nos. 7 and 11.)

The Roxburghe Ballads. First Series, in Three Volumes. Edited by (the late) William Chappell, F.S.A. 1869-1880. (Nos. 4, 5, 6, 8, 9, 12, 13, 18, and 19.) *With copies of the original Woodcuts.* Ready for binding.

The Bagford Ballads. Two volumes, complete. Edited by the Rev. J. W. Ebsworth, M.A. 1876-1878. *With General Index, and copies of the original Woodcuts.* (Nos. 14, 15, 16, and 17.) Ready for binding.

The Amanda Group of Bagford Poems on London Apprentices and Doll-Tearsheets. Edited by J. W. Ebsworth, M.A. 1880. *Illustrated with his Woodcut copies*, and with full Indexes. (No. 20.) Ready for binding.

The Roxburghe Ballads. Second Series. Three Volumes. Ready for Binding. Containing, in addition to the miscellaneous Ballads, large groups, chronologically arranged, of Anti-Papal Ballads, The Struggle for the Succession between the Dukes of York and Monmouth, One Hundred True-Love Ballads, Early Naval Ballads, Two Groups of Good-Fellows' Ballads, and the Early Legendary and Romantic Ballads. Edited and illustrated by Joseph Woodfall Ebsworth, M.A., F.S.A., Vicar of Molash by Ashford, Kent. 1881-1889. *With his copies of the original Woodcuts.* (Nos. 21 to 30, inclusive.) With Ballad-Index to each of the three volumes.

*** Also, *Ready to go into the Printer's hands.*

The concluding volume of Roxburghe Ballads (concerning which see pp. xii*, xiii*, and 855 of this present volume). Thanks to one generous friend (*A. T.*, Esq.) this volume will be proceeded with, immediately.

HERTFORD, PRINTED BY STEPHEN AUSTIN AND SONS.

www.ingramcontent.com/pod-product-compliance
Lightning Source LLC
Chambersburg PA
CBHW032312280326
41932CB00009B/789

* 9 7 8 3 7 4 4 7 7 5 0 0 7 *